1964

University of St. Francis
GEN 956 S747
Spencer

SO-AYG-959
3 0301 00041866 1

POLITICAL EVOLUTION IN THE Middle East

THE LIPPINCOTT COLLEGE SERIES IN POLITICAL SCIENCE

UNDER THE EDITORSHIP OF

Professor John Perry Horlacher

UNIVERSITY OF PENNSYLVANIA

POLITICAL
EVOLUTION
IN THE
Middle East

WILLIAM SPENCER

GEORGE WASHINGTON UNIVERSITY

J. B. LIPPINCOTT COMPANY : PHILADELPHIA AND NEW YORK

LIBRARY
College of St. Francis
JOLIET, ILL.

Copyright © 1962 by J. B. Lippincott Company
Library of Congress Catalog Card Number: 63–7028
Printed in the United States of America

956
S 747
c. 2

TO MOTHER AND THE SKIPPER

Change is the keynote of Middle Eastern politics in the twentieth century. Territorially, the region is a checkerboard of states, chiefly the result of twentieth-century political action. With one or two exceptions, however, these states have not evolved to any mature political status. Most Western observers regarded the Hashimite monarchy of Iraq and its Premier Nuri al-Sa'id as well-entrenched; yet that same government was swept away in the dawn hours of a single day, July 14, 1958. Syria seceded from the United Arab Republic in just five days. Since it was divided into pieces cut from the hulk of the defunct Ottoman Empire in 1919, the Middle East has been a parade ground of hostile factions, in a state of chronic (or endemic) political instability.

In terms of history, the Middle East's political evolution is far more consistent. But the true history of the area does not begin with the Peace Settlement after World War I, or the completion of the Suez Canal, or the Turkish capture of Constantinople, or even the Hegira of Muhammad and the start of the Islamic calendar. The Middle East has a continuous political history, interwoven of many strands, that goes back more than 5,000 years. Less than two centuries have been crammed into the development of the United States from colony to republic, while in forty centuries the Middle East has endured all types of rulership, from the frankest autocracy to the supreme individualism of the Greeks.

For twenty centuries of recorded history, the Middle East set the pace for political, cultural, and historical development in the civilized world. (This is not to minimize the very real achievements of the Chinese—but by acting as a conduit for Far Eastern trade and civilization, the ancient Middle East educated the Western world while building its own sophisticated and cultured world.) Due to its unique geographical position at the junction of Europe, Asia, and Africa, it was exposed to an enormous variety of human contacts. The slow-moving caravan that carried Ayesha's camels north from Mecca, carried Muhammad with the seed of a new religion. The Macedonian warriors of Alexander, pushing across High Asia, left islets of Greek thought and culture that mingled with Eastern thought to produce the rationale of Hellenism. Even the bitter struggles of the Crusades, at the hinge-point of Palestine, let loose a flood of interchanges beyond the military contact itself.

The area stretching from Egypt's western border to Afghanistan's boundary with Pakistan and northwest to southeast from the Bosporus to Aden is the Middle East of this study. Excluded are North Africa, Ethiopia ("a Christian island in a Muslim sea"), Greece, the Balkans, Sudan, and Pakistan, all occasionally included. Admittedly these limits are arbitrarily imposed. The term "Middle East" is equally arbitrary; "Near East," "Arab East," "Southwest Asia" or any of various other geographic labels would do quite as well. However, a stand must be taken somewhere. Inasmuch as my purpose is to delineate modern twentieth-century political history in the Middle East in the light of its gradual evolution, this particular "Middle East" has considerable homogeneity. In antiquity the Nile Valley and Mesopotamian civilizations enjoyed extensive interchange over North Arabian-Syrian trade routes. The civilizing process gradually expanded to embrace Asia Minor, the Iranian Plateau, the African Red Sea coast, and The Levant. Although inner Arabia remained culturally isolated, the outer Arabian rimlands were included in this widening circle.

This is a huge area, larger than the continental United States, about 5 million square miles, with a population of roughly 86 million. The population is thus roughly half that of this nation. The fantastic diversity of this population has already been referred to. Diversity is also important in physical terms. A little less than 5 per cent of the total land area is cultivable, and agricultural expansion is limited by the available water. Rainfall varies from fairly abundant in some narrow coastal areas (35 inches per year in Beirut, for example) to almost none in Cairo; in many places in the deserts, rain may not fall for twenty years or more. The seas —the Red, the Mediterranean, the Black, and the Indian Ocean—hem in the region, while medium-sized but rugged mountain ranges fling claws across it. The result is a sort of stippled pattern, green spots of fertility on a vast gray canvas.

There are five broad epochs in the total span of Middle East political history, covering roughly 5,000 years. The first of these is pre-Islamic. Of the four oldest identifiable nations in the world, two, Egypt and Persia, are Middle Eastern, and a third, India, was probably civilized first in the borderland Indus valley around Mohenjodaro. The various cultures that succeeded one another in the Tigris-Euphrates Valley constitute another unit of the Middle East. The pre-Islamic epoch, then, begins at the beginning of recorded civilization and extends through the periods of Pharaonic and Assyrian domination, the Persian Empire, Alexander's fusion of East and West, Rome, Parthia, and early Byzantium, ending with the disintegration of political authority in the region in the sixth century A.D. due to the mutually exhaustive wars of the Byzantines and the Sassanid rulers of Persia and the eruption of Islam. The second epoch is Muslim. Inspired by the world's newest religion, Arab monotheists broke out of the confines of Arabia to eliminate the Byzantine and Sassanid powers and establish a Muslim empire built from within. The extraordinary civilization of the Muslim Caliphate centered around Baghdad is well-known; it was the "Silver Age of Islam." But as Voltaire once observed, "God created Man in His own image, and Man has returned the compliment." The Mongol and Turkish invasions of the thirteenth and fourteenth centuries were like scourges, senselessly destroying this civilization. They ushered in a third epoch, one of renewed external intervention substituting Ottoman Empire for Islamic Caliphate. In the nineteenth century, as this Empire weakened, European nations began to interfere in the Middle East, causing a fourth epoch which ended in the dissolution of the Ottoman Empire after World War I. These four epochs have, of course, ended; but the fifth epoch, that of independent states in the Middle East, is haltingly getting underway. All that can be said with safety is that these new states, the products of a tremendously long history, must now work out their destinies in the atomic age, somehow free of both East and West. If this does not happen, the Middle East will again vanish under foreign domination.

As was mentioned earlier, change is the keynote of the twentieth-century Middle East. It is dynamic; almost daily, as the call for Arab unity echoes in minaret, radio, coffeehouse, new leaders are thrown up by the masses. A scant hundred years or so ago the keynote was isolation or lack of change. As had happened so often during the Middle East's development, a form of unity had been imposed by external forces; this time it is the major powers of Europe imposing the unity. Within the greater part of the region the nominal authority was Ottoman, originally foreign itself. The degeneration of Ottoman authority bred a corresponding revival of political diversity, as the Arabs slowly became aware that their *Millet,* or nation, was worth defending.

Political diversity merely echoed the existing diversity of the Middle East, however. Its forty centuries of evolution have produced a diversity which is racial, linguistic, cultural, social, religious, even psychological. The negroid riverain peoples of southern Sudan can, by broad definition, be called Middle Eastern; so can the highland mountaineers of Afghanistan. The mark of Crusader passage may be seen in the occasional blond, blue-eyed Turkish child in remote Anatolian villages. The *fellah* of Egypt, conversely, could have stepped direct from a wall-painting in some Pharaoh's tomb. Arabs, Turks, and Iranians all live within the confines of the Middle East, as do Afghans, Kurds, Armenians, Greeks, and a host of others. Linguistically, there is still the Babel of tongues described in the Bible, except that the twentieth century speaks in Arabic, Turkish, Persian, Hebrew, Pashto, plus assorted dialects and all the imported languages of the West. Three of the world's great religions have their origins and draw their traditions from the soil of the Middle East; and the area's long history of foreign assault has produced a multitude of cults, as groups withdrew from invasion to some secure bastion. Perhaps the psychological diversity is more extensive and surprising than the political, cultural, and racial. The Arab element is an important one, yet the period since 1946 displays the evolution to leadership of two separate states, Egypt and Iraq, each claiming to be *primus inter pares* in Arab affairs. The intensity with which the radio "voices" of the various Arab states attack each other is matched only by the suddenness with which they seem to resume their friendships.

From the Treaty of Carlowitz in 1683 until World War II, the decline of Middle-East political power was matched by a large-scale decay of self-respect. The Ottoman Empire and its subject peoples sank into lethargy, secure in their belief in the superiority of Islam. The realization that Europe was more powerful eluded the masses, while their leaders lacked vision and real statecraft. No statesman of stature defended Middle-Eastern interests before the councils of the world; political decisions concerning these were made in London, Paris, or St. Petersburg. Thus the Treaty of Paris (1856) *imposed* territorial integrity on the Ottoman Empire. European officialdom did not support the nascent reform movements within the Empire; Muhammad Ali's try at rebuilding Middle-Eastern prestige and self-respect was summarily blocked by an order from the "Big Three" to cease and desist. The very existence of the Empire prohibited normal contact between the peoples of the West and the Middle East from the Crusades to the twentieth century; trade routes turned elsewhere, out to sea. Earlier periods of balance between East and West as to relative strength (i. e., Byzantium and Persia, Rome and Parthia) were ultimately destructive, based on armed conflict. The signal achievement of the twentieth century as regards the Middle East is the resumption of full-scale contact in many fields of human activity—political, economic, educational, strategic—with the West brought about by the modern East-West conflict, in which the Middle East has reverted to its rightful pivotal role, thereby regaining its self-respect.

ACKNOWLEDGMENTS

The task of preparing an introduction to the politics of the Middle East at once comprehensive, accurate, and impartial, has been facilitated by the generous cooperation of many colleagues and other persons who took time from their busy lives to assist me. Dr. Elie Salem of The Johns Hopkins University, Dr. Kerim Key of The American University, and William Sands, Editor of the *Middle East Journal,* read individual chapters and made valuable suggestions for improving the text. Dr. Wendell Cleland of The American University rendered especially valuable assistance to me in the supervision of doctoral research papers, portions of which are included in the present text by permission. Special thanks are due other former associates in The Middle East Institute, Majid Khadduri and Marschal Rothe, Jr., for inspiration and advice, and to Philip K. Hitti and Cuyler Young of Princeton University, for unfailing encouragement to seek the truth in Middle-Eastern complexities.

Space forbids mention of those many colleagues whose special knowledge has given me new insights into the Middle East. A collective debt of gratitude is due also to the hundreds of George Washington University students who served as guinea pigs for the development of a text suited to their needs.

Finally, I wish to thank the J. B. Lippincott Company for editorial assistance, Dr. John Perry Horlacher for valuable editorial supervision, the Carnegie Fund for a generous grant-in-aid, Vicki Powers and Marie Worsham for typing the manuscript, Douglas and Dorothy Brown for constant encouragement, and my wife and children for assistance with the index and for their extraordinary patience.

Transliteration of Middle Eastern names is difficult, among other reasons because of the many variant spellings. In my spelling of Turkish names I have used the modern phonetic alphabet, although I have not dotted the *u* in *Ataturk* since the name appears so frequently. In the spelling of Arabic names I have followed the standard transliterations— e.g., *Muhammad, 'Abd al-Nasir*. My approach to Persian has been more of a scatter-shot technique because of its internal inconsistencies. Whatever other errors and shortcomings the book possesses are, of course, my own.

WILLIAM SPENCER

GARRETT PARK
MARCH 1962

CONTENTS

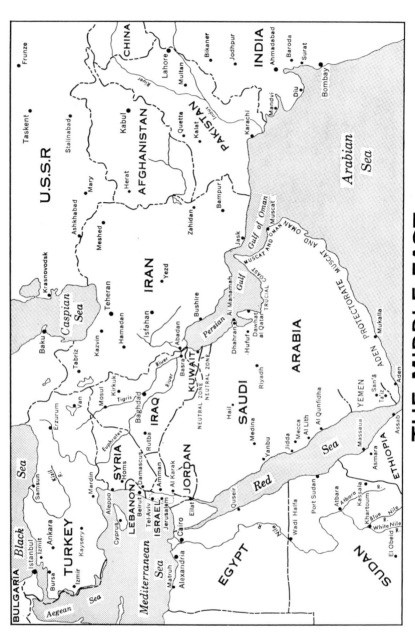

THE MIDDLE EAST

CHAPTER 1

ISLAM: THE SUBSTRUCTURE

"la ilaha illa-l-Lah: Muhammadun rasulu-l-Lah."
(There is no god but Allah; Muhammad is the messenger of Allah.)

These are the first words to strike the uncomprehending ear of the newborn child in Muslim lands; these are the last spoken at the grave.[1] In between are thousands of reiterations as the Muslim takes his place within the framework of a religion that is also a social, juridical, even political system. Many and complex are the influences that have come to bear on the Middle East throughout its history, but none with the significance of Islam. The cleavages between Middle Eastern states in the present century are all too apparent, but with one exception all subscribe to the bond of a common religion—and that one exception contains a sizeable minority of subscribers. The Arab nation, *al-Umma al-Arabiya*, envisaged by President Gamal abd al-Nasir of the United Arab Republic and other Arab leaders, is unlikely to occur; but if it does, the success will be found in large part in the magnetic attractions of language and religion.

Perhaps the most substantial event in the Middle East's evolution, then, occurred thirteen centuries ago. Prior to that time, the Near East had spawned great civilizations, even a sort of world-empire out of Persia. But years of conflict between the Roman, later the Byzantine, and the

[1] Cf. Hitti, Philip, *History of the Arabs,* 6th edition, New York: St. Martin's Press, Inc., 1956, pp. 130 *et seq.*

Sassanian powers had largely disrupted the ancestral civilized patterns. The Christian peoples of Syria, Palestine, and Egypt were oppressed more by their co-religionist Byzantine rulers than by the Persians, who periodically over-ran the Near East. The region was even less of a definable political entity than it is today; Roman proconsuls sent to manage these unruly lands (such as one Pontius Pilate, Procurator of Judea) considered the assignment as a sort of frontier exile. Then in the sixth century, and in a place even more remote by world standards than the Syria-Palestine-Mesopotamia complex, a small flame flickered, caught, then spread across the known world. With this spreading, the Middle East was given a *raison d'etre,* a motivation, that continues to uphold its people to this day.

ARABIA THE REMOTE

In the seventh century A.D. the Near East, and the broader Middle East as we know it today, were divided between two great but declining powers—Byzantium and Persia. A century earlier Byzantium under Justinian very nearly recouped the shattered fortunes of Imperial Rome; Italy, Sicily, and North Africa were recovered to the Gates of Hercules. Justinian made a dignified peace with his Persian rival. Their successors, unable to resist the temptation, fell upon each other with army after army in a hundred places. Too evenly matched for the *coup de grace,* Byzantine and Sassanid could merely hack at each other. Under the Emperor Heraclius, Byzantium stood near defeat as the Persians closed in on Constantinople; then with a sudden bold stroke Heraclius routed them, drove them all the way back to their capital, Ctesiphon, burnt it, and brought back the True Cross which he reinstalled in Jerusalem in 629.

Arabia proper played a slight role in this internecine struggle. In the northern borderlands were petty kingdoms, such as the Ghassanids and their rivals, the Lakhmids, subsidized by Byzantium and Persia respectively. The Ghassanid ruler al-Harith (ca. 529–569) dominated Arab politics at this time; he was sufficiently respected by Justinian to obtain for his friend Jacob Baradaeus the appointment of Monophysite Bishop of the Syrian Christian Arabs. This bishop's tremendous work in winning converts for his church was so successful that the Syrian Monophysite Church became known as the Jacobite, after him.[2]

---

[2] Cf. Hitti, pp. 79–80.

The Ghassanids moved north from their South Arabian homeland sometime between 542 and 570 A.D., when the great dam at Ma'rib, in what is now Yemen, collapsed, either from natural causes or (as the Arab chroniclers tell us) because a rat turned over a stone that fifty men could not budge! South Arabia had been the center of a number of polished, cultured kingdoms in the pre-Christian and early Christian eras.[3] The roads built by the Sabaeans, in fact, are better than the present roads of Yemen. The breaking of the Ma'rib dam seems to have been one of a number of events that overwhelmed these kingdoms; first Ethiopia and then Persia secured control of them.

The remainder of Arabia, excluding the deserts, was relatively free of foreign influences and not involved in the power struggle. The chief role of the towns of inner Arabia was as an entrepot for trade and communications centers. And the chief of these towns, the most successful, was Mecca in the Hejaz. Mecca lies on the important spice route passing through Arabia from south to north. The name comes from Makuraba, a Sabaean word meaning sanctuary, indicating that from very early times it must have had a religious association of some kind. Mecca was both religious and commercial in outlook. The city was ruled by an oligarchy of wealthy merchants and landowners, all members of a large multibranched family, the Quraysh. Twice a year huge caravans, laden with the spices and perfumes of Araby, brought northward to the middlemen of Mecca by traders, set off from the town for the markets of the Mediterranean. While the caravans of the Quraysh thus went out of Mecca, people from all over Arabia, unlettered tribesmen as well as townspeople, came to Mecca, which had acquired a reputation as a tourist attraction. As a tourist attraction, even for seventh century bedouin, it had its drawbacks; it lay in a hot, damp, unhealthy area called the Tihama of southern Hejaz, about fifty miles from the Red Sea, surrounded by barren flinty mountains. The valley of Mecca is described in the Koran as "unfit for cultivation."[4] But this unprepossessing place had objects of veneration intimately bound up with the legendary chronicles of the Arab race.

The most important of these objects was the Black Stone, which was believed to have fallen from the moon and was, therefore, sacred to the moon god Hubal. The stone was kept in a small unroofed temple, the Ka'ba (lit. Cube); and at the time of the new moon following the

[3] See Chapter 8.
[4] Sura 14, Verse 40.

summer solstice, pilgrims came, stripped off their clothing in humility, kissed the stone, and walked seven times around the Ka'ba. Nor was this all. The pilgrims drank next from the unpalatable waters of Zam Zam, a holy well regarded by Arab chroniclers as the place where Hagar found water for her son Ishamael. (The Ka'ba was traditionally built by Adam and rebuilt by Abraham and Ishmael after the Deluge.) Then followed the pilgrimmage walk to the holy mountain of 'Arafat and the sacrifice of animals at Mina, a bleak plain near Mecca. All of these actions have been absorbed into Islamic religious ritual—the difference is that only one of the many gods of early Arabia, called Allah (the principal deity of the Meccan pantheon), survives.

THE PROPHET MUHAMMAD

In about 570–571 A.D. a male child was born into a collateral family branch of the Quraysh. His name was Muhammad, "the praised one." His great-grandfather was Hashim.[5] His grandfather, Abd-al-Muttalib, had earlier found a treasure at the bottom of Zam Zam well while digging for water, and later he was appointed keeper of the Ka'ba.

The boy Muhammad had two strikes against him from the start. Despite the respect accorded his grandfather, the family of Hashim was a minor branch of the Quraysh and had little prestige, social or financial. He was orphaned at an early age; his father, Abdullah, died before he was born, and his mother, Amina, was sickly and unable to care for her son. When he was two, he was sent to Taif, a town in the highlands south of Mecca, where the air was healthier; he was raised there by shepherds.[6] Four years later his mother died; and, in the Eastern fashion, he was taken in by Abd al-Muttalib. When he died, an uncle, Abu Talib, assumed the duty of caring for the helpless child. Seldom has the leader of a community in the stratified Middle East reached power from such mean beginnings.

Abu Talib hired Muhammad out to camel caravans to earn his keep; and from the age of ten onwards, he traveled with various caravans on plodding journeys to Syria and the markets of the north. He also tended his uncle's herds. On one of these caravan journeys he met a Nestorian Christian monk, Bahira, who is supposed to have been the first to name

---

[5] This explains why his descendants in the direct line (through Fatima) are called Hashimites.

[6] Cf. Payne, Robert, *The Holy Sword,* New York: Harper & Brothers, 1959. Hitti, *op. cit.,* p. 102, also refers to the paradise of Taif, "a bit of Syrian earth," which must have influenced the Prophet in his designation of an Islamic paradise.

him as God's messenger and to have found between his shoulders the seal of prophetic office.[7] Hundreds of such legends have grown up around the early life of Muhammad, but in fact he could hardly be distinguished from other Arab boys of his age and must have little expected the events that happened to him.

When he was twenty-five, he caught the eye of Khadija, a widow of forty with considerable wealth inherited from two husbands she had outlived. She hired Muhammad to manage her estates and direct her caravans; then she married him. Islam is often known as the polygamous religion; but in Khadija's lifetime, Muhammad had but one wife, although he did acquire eight others in his later years, most of them for political and charitable reasons.

Marriage to Khadija freed him from the economic burdens of life; his days became a placid round of business affairs and time with his family, six children by the age of thirty-five. In those years a great restlessness grew in Muhammad. He was much influenced by *hanifs,* devout Arabs who railed against the iconoclasm of the day and who sought an unclear monotheism as a means of elevating society. He held long, abstract discussions with his wife's cousin, Waraqa, a Hanif who seems to have given Muhammad (since he could not read) that curiously distorted knowledge of the Christian Bible and the sacred Jewish books which appears in his later pronouncements. Like the Hanifs, he used to go into the desert and meditate, sometimes for days at a time. As he himself revealed, during one of these meditations, he received the first heavenly visitation. Wrapped in a cloak against the cold desert air, he was dozing in a little cave outside of Mecca called *Hira.* A voice cried out: "Read!" He answered: "I cannot read." The command was repeated; he answered: "I do not know how to read." A third time, the voice thundered:

"Recite then in the name of the lord who
created man from clots of blood. . . ."

and, according to Muhammad's own statement, "I awoke from my sleep, and it was as if they had written a message in my heart. I went out of the cave, and . . . I heard a voice saying: 'O Muhammad, thou art Allah's apostle, and I am Gabriel.' "[8] He saw the figure of an Angel in the sky; and wherever he turned to evade the brightness, the Angel

[7] Andrae, Tor, *Mohammed: The Man and His Faith,* translated by Theophil Menzel, New York: Barnes and Noble, Inc., 1935, pp. 36–38.

[8] *Ibid.,* p. 44.

appeared before him. In this mystical visionary manner came the birth of the latest of the universal religions.

For several years after the visitation Muhammad made little effort to preach in public the new faith he had acquired; his only converts were his wife, Waraqa, and a handful of others. Then he went out in the streets of Mecca and spoke openly, denouncing the idol-worship at the Ka'ba, declaring the might and power of the One God, predicting the terrible day of judgment unless the world rediscovered the ways of God. There was much hellfire and brimstone in his early preachings, but the directness and simplicity of the message attracted converts in increasing numbers.

He also attracted the hostility of the Quraysh leaders. At first they laughed at this obscure cousin, crying the praises of Allah over all the other gods they worshipped. Then the ridicule turned to anger. When Muhammad denounced the idols of the Ka'ba, they realized that he meant to eliminate an important source of income (and prestige) from Mecca. They began to persecute his followers; they drove him to take refuge in Abu Talib's castle and excommunicated the entire clan. Muhammad's reaction was a stiffening of his religious principles. Certainly the misfortunes of these early years added the militant missionary aspect —conversion or death—to Islam.

The hostility he faced in Mecca—though the converts were increasing in number, including such notables as 'Umar—forced Muhammad to consider a new base of operations. When a deputation from Yathrib, a town some three hundred miles northeast of Mecca, suggested that he come there to arbitrate between two factions, he decided to accept. Thus in 622 A.D. occurred the famous Hegira (Ar. *Hijrah*) which marks the start of the Muslim calendar and the beginning of "official" recognition of the new religion.[9] Muhammad and his followers eluded the Quraysh and reached Yathrib, which was re-named al-Madinah ("The Town"), as an organized community. The people of Yathrib received the name *Ansar* (helpers) in return for their aid. Muhammad resolved the disputes of the two chief tribes of Medina and concluded an agreement with the Jews, the bulk of the population. He even adopted a number of features of Judaism, such as Friday Holy Day and circumcision.

[9] There is a tradition that sometime before the Hegira, Muhammad was transported to Heaven on a winged horse with a woman's face and peacock's tail. He was embraced by God, and spoke with Moses and Jesus and Abraham. The place where he ascended and came down was the site of the Temple in Jerusalem.

But Medina was a temporary capital; Muhammad had enough political sagacity to realize that Islam could not advance unless it were based in the richest, most strategically located, religiously-dominant city of Arabia. At Medina Muhammad established the *Umma,* the nation-community, to replace the pre-Islamic tribal socio-political structure. The tribes kept their ancient social habits but accepted Muhammad as the final arbiter in disputes. In this way the Prophet could move against the Quraysh with a following that accepted his leadership, yet were inspired with fraternal zeal for the religion.

At the battle of Badr the Muslims defeated a much larger force of Quraysh; and Muhammad acquired a double-pointed sword, rather like a meat cleaver, which became his good luck charm and sign of ultimate victory. There were many defeats, or Pyrrhic victories; [10] but, at last, after six years of exile, Muhammad returned to Mecca and the Quraysh accepted (or submitted to) Islam.

Eight years had elapsed between the Hegira and the day in January, 630 A.D. when Muhammad entered the Ka'ba and smashed the three hundred sixty-odd idols mounted along the walls. "Truth hath come, and falsehood hath vanished!" he said. Seven times on foot he made the circumference of the building, and he declared it *haram* (forbidden) to nonbelievers.[11] Two years of ministry were left to him. In those two years he led his followers in many campaigns against pagan tribes in Arabia, sent letters to the Byzantine Emperor and the Great Persian King, Chosroes (which were not answered), preached sermons; and in 632 he died in the arms of his favorite wife, Ayesha. The cause of his death was probably malaria.

Muhammad's great contribution to civilization was not only a unique monotheistic religion spattered with traces of Christianity and Judaism but also one which is unlike them in significant ways. Islam focused the attention of the Arabs upon themselves. They discovered that community of religion meant community of spirit. The ancient tribal bond, or the blood relationship, was replaced by the *Umma.* For the first time in its history Arabia was organized socially under a theocracy whose final governor was God. Furthermore, within this theocratic state all were brethren. As Muhammad said in his final sermon on Mount 'Arafat:

[10] During this period Muhammad broke with the Jews, particularly a Jewish tribe which had made contact with the enemy, for which he massacred all of them.

[11] The injunction still applies to the Holy Cities as well, and only a handful of Westerners (in disguise) have seen Mecca or Medina.

"Know ye that every Muslim is a brother unto every
other Muslim, and that ye are now one brotherhood. . . ." [12]
With one bold stroke of his cleaver, Dhu'l Faqar, Muhammad split
the age-old loyalties that had kept Arabia in anarchy and made it possible for Islam to leap beyond Arabia while maintaining the heartland
there.

ISLAM AND ITS BELIEVERS

The religion which the Prophet propounded was given the name
Islam from the Arabic verb *aslama*, "to submit"; hence it is submission
or surrender to the will of Allah. Because it had to appeal to a simple,
unlettered people, Islam had to be simple, stern, uncompromising. It
was born in conflict and in a time of relative laxity in morals as well
as behavior. Opposition made Muhammad harsh, and Islam developed
in an atmosphere of bitter warfare. It was not necessarily more militant
than, let us say, medieval Christianity; but the Christian tenderness,
the meekness of Jesus, and even the concepts of suffering and morti-
fication of the flesh were lacking from the very start. A much more
extensive social order developed along with, was in fact part of, the
religious order based on the patriarchal, familial structure extant in
Arabia. Yet the elaborate social structure was at variance with the
simplicity of the actual faith. There was to be no priesthood, no Vatican
City, no hagiography. The person designated to lead the believers in
prayer after Muhammad's death, called the *imam*, could be anyone,
rich or poor, high or low, who had certain qualifications. God was single, personal, and all-powerful.

The lighthouse of Islam is founded upon three rock bases: the Koran
(Ar. *Qur'an*, "recitation") with the *hadiths* (sayings and actions) of
Muhammad; the oneness of God; and the pillars, collectively, of faith.
Everything else is accretion, alien to Muhammad and the Muslims,
added by more sophisticated peoples.

Perhaps symbolically, the appellation "Muhammadans" ascribed to
them by the Crusaders enraged the Muslims of the Near East more than
any other since it implied worship of the Prophet himself.[13] Elevation
of the Meccan god, Allah, to the position of Supreme Being required
little effort, metaphysical or intellectual. The Koran was put together

---

[12] Quoted in Hitti, p. 120.
[13] Cf. Landau, Rom, *Islam and The Arabs*, New York: The Macmillan Co.,
1959, p. 29 *et seq.*

after Muhammad's death in order to preserve his revelations for later, less-inspired generations. 'Uthman, one of Muhammad's companions who became the third Caliph or head of the Islamic state, was probably the Muslim who ordered that every revelation of Muhammad's should be collected "whether inscribed on palm-leaves, shreds of leather, shoulder-blades, white stone tablets, or from the breasts of men." [14] Previously all such revelations had been taken down orally by professional memorizers (*huffaz*) who were dying out. The Koran itself is divided into 6,236 verses and 114 *suras* (chapters) which vary greatly both in length and quality. The cement binding this inchoate, diverse mass together is the oneness of God, which is constantly reiterated. Along with God's unity—a distinct rejection of the Christian Trinitarian doctrine—His power is stressed. So powerful is He that submission alone makes man worthy of Him; and in that submission Muhammad found peace, believing Him merciful and just to the faithful. The Christian love of God is also absent from the Koran. This would seem to derive from the barren desert milieu in which Islam was nurtured.

The Koran also provides the believer with concepts of angels and of *jinni* (spirits), with a guide to Paradise, a description of Hell, and a listing of the various attributes of God—ninety-nine in all. [15] The angels are winged; they are God's messengers, carrying His words through seventy curtains of fire to the believer. *Jinni*, survivals of the animism and fetishism of pagan Arabia, also found a place in Islam as low-level spirits able to climb to the lowest of the seven Muslim heavens but no higher, hence a little lower than man.

The third basic element of Islam is the practice of its ritual, known familiarly as the Five Pillars. These five religious duties (*ibadat*) consist of: the profession of faith (*shahada*), prayer (*salat*), the almsgiving (*zakat*), the fast during Ramadan, and the pilgrimmage (*hajj*). The profession of faith is a double formula taken from the Koran: *La ilaha illa-l-Lah. Muhammadun rasul-l-Lah.* (There is no God but Allah, Muhammad is the messenger of Allah.) Prayer is to be engaged in five times daily according to a prescribed formula and with the worshipper's face turned toward Mecca. Prayer is both physical—a series of prostrations with final submission when the believer's toes,

[14] Hitti, *op. cit.,* p. 123. Payne, *op. cit.,* p. 68.
[15] There is a hundredth attribute, but man has forgotten it; and only the camel remembers it, according to the Arabs. The Muslim rosary has ninety-nine beads.

knees, hands, and forehead are touching the ground—and spiritual—commencing with the *fatiha* (first sura) and various short suras memorized from the Koran. The *zakat* is in one sense a tax levied for humanitarian purposes and, in another, a social leveller since those who can are expected to give more out of conscience toward the support of the less fortunate or the upkeep of the mosques, etc. Fasting is obligatory for the devout during the Arabic month of Ramadan.[16] During this period, from sunrise until sunset when a white thread can (or cannot) be distinguished from a black one, the believer must abstain from food, drink, perfumes, tobacco, and sexual intercourse; must hear or recite the entire Koran; and is enjoined to spend as much time as possible in the mosque.

The last pillar, the pilgrimage, is not obligatory but is highly desired. At least once in his lifetime the Muslim hopes to go to Mecca wearing the seamless clothing of a pilgrim to circle the Ka'ba seven times, to kiss the black stone, and to carry out the various other lesser ceremonies connected with the *hajj*. Having made the pilgrimage gives a Muslim a place of respect among his co-religionists; he may be called *hajji* and is allowed to wear a green turban.

The equalizing and unifying qualities of Islam, therefore, lay in its very principles; with all men equally obeisant to a mighty God, there quickly arose a close-knit community of true believers. Muhammad also had proclaimed the doctrine (at one time considered a sixth pillar) of *jihad,* or holy war against the enemies of the faith.[17] The emphasis on allegiance to Allah, the common postures of prayer, the *zakat* had cut across the tribal loyalties; the *umma,* or community, was substituted for the narrower family kinships in Arabia. The Koran, after it had been codified, was another lubricant for the universal society envisioned by the Prophet. The Arabic in which it is written has become the literary standard for the Muslim, providing speakers of diverse Arabic dialects (as well as those of non-Arab Muslims) with a common bond of communication. Finally, insistence on the *hajj* brought pilgrims together from the corners of the globe, returning them refreshed to their own lands to propagate Islam. Of all world religions, Islam seems to have

---

[16] This varies each year according to the lunar calendar. It was originally picked because the victory of Badr was won in this month by the Muslims.

[17] So considered by the Kharijites, formerly a puritanical sect, and carried on sporadically by their descendants, the Ibadites.

attained the largest measure of success in demolishing the barriers of race, color, and nationality.[18]

ESTABLISHMENT OF THE CALIPHATE

All this was to grow in succeeding centuries; but meanwhile the world was divided into two parts, a large and hostile *dar al-harb* (abode of war) and a weak, infant *dar al-Islam* (abode of Islam). The balance must be redressed. But how could this be accomplished now that Muhammad was dead? He had left no son, no instructions for a successor. He was the last of God's messengers, and no one could replace him. The words of the Koran itself—"Muhammad is no more than a messenger; all messengers before him have passed away. If he dieth or is slain, will ye turn back on your heels? He who turneth back will do no harm to God, but God rewards those who are grateful." [19] —were crumbs of comfort to the puzzled Muslims.

As it happened, the succession was decided in the customary elective manner of tribal Arabia. The successor to the Prophet was designated *Khalifah* (*caliph,* deputy or temporal leader). The first to be named and recognized by the Muslim community as a whole was Abu Bakr (632–634), Muhammad's father-in-law and closest friend, an old man, and, therefore, able to command respect. He was followed by the redoubtable 'Umar (634–644); the patriarch 'Uthman (644–656), compiler of the Koran; and finally by Ali, Muhammad's son-in-law and first cousin. At the death of Ali, the elective caliphate came to an end, to be replaced by the more authoritarian caliphate of the Umayyads, the dominant branch of the Quraysh.

So began that astonishing burst of energy which carried the green banner of Islam east to the Indus, west to the Atlantic shores of Morocco. Then the factionalism and the vigorous individualism which are so basic to the Arab character were resumed. The Muslim kingdom became an empire, yet an empire which commanded no real allegiance except to the religion itself. Always the difficulty of Islam has been to reconcile the absence of an identifiable supreme temporal leader (as Jesus has become in literal Christianity) with the presence of God. Moving in short sudden streaks, the Muslim leaders fashioned a universe, then drifted into quarreling while it collapsed around them.

[18] Hitti, *op. cit.,* p. 136.
[19] Quoted in Payne, *op. cit.,* p. 88.

It is not within the scope of this study to detail the tortuous history of the Islamic state from Abu Bakr's assumption of leadership to the time, just under a thousand years later, when a non-Arab, alien, Ottoman Turk became Caliph and the spiritual capital of Islam was moved to Constantinople. But a number of factors are worth noting. The Muslims were able to accomplish much by the inspiraton of their faith, by the quick-striking force of their armies, and by the skill of their generals. But they benefited greatly also from the general state of the world. The Byzantine and Persian Empires had bled each other white with continual conflict. Arabia, as was mentioned earlier, was totally disunited. The eastern provinces of Byzantium, although Christian, suffered greatly from the exactions of the Byzantine tax-gatherers and from Byzantium's insistence that it alone could represent orthodox Christianity. The moderate behavior of the Muslims contrasted favorably with Byzantine excesses. Khalid ibn-al-Walid, when he issued terms for the capitulation of Damascus, told the city's Christians that "so long as they pay the poll tax, nothing but good shall come to them." [20] Either from an instinctive realization of their numbers and political inexperience or from the indifference to completion of projects, which, again, is part of the Arab character, the Muslims changed little of the political and social structure of the conquered territories. Thus, the Caliph Muawiya who ruled from Damascus appointed the Christian Sarjunids, the family of St. John of Damascus, to manage the treasury.

The early wars of the Muslims in Arabia were called *ridda,* or wars of reconversion. They were concerned with the forced reconversion of tribes which had accepted Islam and lapsed into idolatry after Muhammad's death. Under the four orthodox Caliphs, Islam's power was expanded to embrace Syria and Egypt, Iraq was conquered, and the Persian power crushed. After the murder of Ali (661), spiritual and temporal power passed to the Umayyad family of the Quraysh, the same ones who had opposed Muhammad so bitterly. Muawiya, who said of himself, "I am the first of the kings," sent his generals in three directions: northward against Byzantium, eastward toward India, and west across Africa. The religiously-inspired levies of the early Caliphs gave way to conscripted standing armies with cavalry and armor and siege weapons, all on the Byzantine model. Muawiya and his Umayyad successors were fortunate in their leaders. The viceroy of Iraq, al-Hajjaj, restored order there and in Yemen. Qutaybah, another military leader,

[20] Hitti, Philip, *History of Syria,* New York: The Macmillan Co., 1951, p. 415.

islamized Khurasan (the eastern province of Iran, now Afghanistan), Central Asia, and what is now West Pakistan.[21] Twice Constantinople was besieged by the Arabs and narrowly escaped. In the west, Uqbah ibn-Nafi, nephew of Amr ibn al-ʻAs, the conqueror of Egypt, led an Arab army all the way to the Atlantic where, by tradition, he denounced the sea for having blocked him from going into still remoter regions to spread the glory of God's name. His success was temporary; but another Muslim leader, Hassan, used naval power to drive Byzantines from Carthage (i.e. Tunisia) and Libya. Musa ibn-Nusayr, appointed by and directly under the Caliph at Damascus, governed North Africa as a separate province, extending Islam to Morocco and Algeria and converting the intractable Berbers. One of them, a freedman named Tariq, crossed the narrow strait between Africa and Spain, gave his name to the Rock of Gibraltar (Jabal al-Tariq, "Mountain of Tariq"), and conquered Spain for Islam except for a small mountainous section in the far north where the last Christian Visigoths had an impenetrable refuge. One hundred years after Muhammad's death, the green banner fluttered over an empire ruled—at least, formally—by the word of God, transmitted by His Messenger, inscribed in the Koran, and executed by the Caliph in Damascus and stretching from the Pyrenees to China.[22]

The Umayyad dynasty contained in itself the seeds of its own destruction; Muawiya had reached the Caliphate through Ali's acceptance of arbitration and his subsequent murder by a Kharijite. Both the Kharijites and the Shiʻite partisans of Ali were hostile.[23] Other Muslims resented the Umayyad disregard of the elective principle in appointing Caliphs. Another branch of the family of Muhammad, the Abbasids (claiming descent from his uncle al-Abbas), also pressed its rightful claim to the Caliphate. But the *force majeure* that overturned the Umayyads was a socio-economic one. Muslims from non-Arab lands, after their conversion, were called *mawali* (clients). They had expected full partnership in the Islamic empire but instead were placed under a number of restrictions, including a capitation tax. Significantly, these restrictions were most resented in Iran and Khurasan, centers of an ancient and honor-

[21] Cf. Hitti, *op. cit.*, Chapter XIX for a full account.

[22] In the same year a minor battle occurred near Tours in southern France between the Franks under the Governor of the Palace, Charles Martel, and an Arab raiding force. This was the farthest penetration into Western Europe of Islam. Provence was controlled by Muslim Spain for a short time, however.

[23] The murder of Ali's son, Husayn by Muawiya's partisans was another black mark, particularly as Husayn had been recognized as Caliph in Mecca and Medina.

able civilization higher than the Arabian. The Shi'as made common cause with the *mawali,* and in 747 an obscure Persian freedman named Abu Muslim, acting as agent for the Abbasid clan in Mecca, raised the black flag of revolt in Merv. Three years later the army of the Abbasids entered Damascus wearing the black robes of martyrdom.

Although the Abbasid Caliphate endured several centuries longer than its Umayyad predecessor—it could be said that Abbasid Caliphs remained as symbols of organized Islam until the time of the Ottoman Sultan Selim I in the 16th century—and called together a brilliant civilization while Europe floundered in darkness, it bore small resemblance to the world of believers envisioned by Muhammad. The pious 'Umar, receiving the spoils of the Persian conquest, said, "I fear all this wealth and luxury will, in the end, ruin my people." [24] Not only wealth and luxury, not only religious sectarianism, but also the influence of Persia, and indirectly of classical Greece, increasingly dominated the Muslim empire. Pristine Arabness was secondary; the role of the Holy Cities of Arabia reverted to the purely spiritual as they would be henceforth. The Abbasid capital was moved to Baghdad, which was built up from an obscure village to a vast, opulent walled city in less than four years under the Caliph Al-Mansur. Baghdad under Harun al-Rashid (786–809) and his son, Al-Mam'un (813–833), was a world capital unequalled for artistic and intellectual accomplishments. In the translations of Greek thought into Arabic, the philosophers of the Abbasid court rendered yeoman service, ultimately, to the Western world. Unfortunately, the almost total lack of political stability, even under the early Caliphs, distinguished the Caliphate. The last twenty-four Caliphs were controlled by their "Pretorian Guard" of Turkish slaves. The irregularity of the hereditary principle of succession, with some Caliphs designating their sons and others their brothers, encouraged palace revolts. Other rebellions, usually stirred up by some mystic, like the Veiled Prophet of Khurasan, or over a piece of doctrine were continually breaking out on the fringes. After the tenth century, the Caliph of Baghdad was not even sure of his stature in the Muslim World. His authority was disputed by the Umayyad Emir in Cordova, where the last Umayyad, Abd al-Rahman, had established a Spanish Moorish kingdom; by the Fatimids in Egypt who began in Tunisia in 909 as a deliberate Shi'ite challenge to the Abbasids and who spread over North Africa to found Cairo; and by

[24] Hitti, *History of Syria,* p. 104.

fanatical dissident movements like the Qarmatians.[25] In 1253 a Mongol general, Hulagu, grandson of Genghis Khan, entered Khorasan with an army intent on ending the Caliphate. By 1256 the strongholds of the "Assassins," another fanatic sect, smokers of hashish, defenders of the empire's borders, had been reduced. In 1258 Hulagu captured Baghdad, murdered the Caliph and most of the population, and destroyed the thousand-year-old irrigation system. The Abbasid Caliphate was at an end.[26]

THE INNER CONFLICTS OF ISLAM

As far as political history is concerned, the last seven hundred years of Islam are interesting only in their decline into total desuetude. The evangelical enthusiasm of the early *muwahhidun* (missionaries), who ranged even farther than the Muslim military forces, was distorted into sectarianism. Though missionary activity continued in the days of decline, as far as Southeast Asia, this sectarianism, feeding upon itself, produced a cancer at the heart of the Islamic body politic.

The major schism in Islam developed around Ali and his place in the succession. The *Sunni,* often called the orthodox believers, constituting the majority in Islam, accepted the succession of Caliphs from Abu Bakr as satisfactory to Muhammad and pleasing to Allah. The *Shi'a,* the largest single minority (about 15 per cent), even a majority in Iran where Shi'ism is officially recognized by the state constitution, differ from the Sunni in the caliphal hierarchy and in certain concepts which reflect the Persian cast of mind. Shi'ism really came into existence on the 10th of the month Muharram (October 10, 680) when Muhammad's grandson Husayn was decapitated near Karbala, Iraq, by troops of the Umayyad Caliph Yazid.[27] They maintain that Ali was actually designated by Muhammad as his successor and was thus displaced by Abu

---

[25] Hitti, *op. cit.,* pp. 444–445. They were a group of Iran and Iraq with communistic tendencies (common property, including wives), ceremonial rites, and guild organization. They believed it was all right to shed the blood of any of their enemies, even Muslims. They established a base of operations at Bahrayn on the Persian Gulf, raided and destroyed nearby territories, and even sacked Mecca and carried off the Black Stone.

[26] The Fatimids kept a line of pseudo-Abbasid Caliphs going until the sixteenth century when Sultan Selim conquered Egypt and assumed the title.

[27] Shi'ites traditionally observe the first ten days of Muharram as a period of mourning, followed by a passion play depicting Husayn's suffering and death. In some places, notably Bahrein, the players flagellate and mutilate themselves with whips and iron nails or cut themselves with swords without drawing blood.

Bakr (although they revere no less the humble, stooped merchant of cloth from Mecca, the first Muslim, for his "usurpation.") The rightful line of Caliphs, they maintain, began with Ali and descended in the blood line from Muhammad. But the Shi'a added a third article of faith, an intermediary between the Muslim and Allah; they called it the *imamate*, to be limited to lineal descendants of Muhammad through his daughter Fatima and her husband Ali. In the Shi'a view, neither the Umayyad nor the Abbasid Caliphates have existed except in a temporal sense. They believe the *imam* is the sole legitimate leader of the Muslim community, not divine but possessed of a mysterious divine power and enjoying infallibility (*Ismah*).[28] The first imam was Ali; followed by Hasan, whose hundred-odd marriages have set some sort of record and who died in bed; and then Husayn, who was less fortunate. Obviously few of their descendants became imams, but in the Muslim world they bear such titles of respect as *Sharif* (noble) and *Sayyid* (lord) and often hold political power.[29]

The Shi'a themselves differ on the number of imams since Ali. The *ithna 'Ashariya* (Twelvers) accept a line of twelve imams, the last nine of them descendants of Husayn. One of them, the Imam Ali Rida, reached a high position under the Abbasids and was named heir apparent by the Caliph al-Mam'un (818). Martyred (according to legend by a bunch of poisoned grapes given to him by the Caliph himself), he was buried in a magnificent shrine in Meshed, Iran, which is the holiest city after Karbala of Shi'a Islam. A second Shi'a sect, the Ismailis, accepted only the first six imams and supported Ismail, brother of the designated seventh, as the rightful imam.[30] The modern Ismailis, a compact and influential community, owe allegiance to the Aga Khan, at least until the coming of the Mahdi.

The doctrine of Mahdism, an outgrowth of the imamate, further distinguishes the Shi'a from the Sunni. In 878 the twelfth designated imam, a boy of seven, disappeared down a flight of steps leading to the cellar of his house inside the Great Mosque of Samarra, Iraq, and was never seen again. The Shi'a believe that he is merely in hiding, in a tem-

[28] The Shi'a creed adds: "I believe that the imam especially chosen by Allah as the bearer of a part of the divine being is the leader to salvation." Hitti, *op. cit.*, p. 248.
[29] Cf. *Sharifs of Mecca*, Chapter II *passim*. The present king of Morocco heads the Sharifian Dynasty. The Imams of Yemen also trace descent from Ali (cf. Chapter VIII).
[30] Ismail was first named Imam by his father Ja'far, but on learning of his son's drunkenness, Ja'far changed his mind.

THE RELATIONSHIP OF THE TWELVE IMAMS

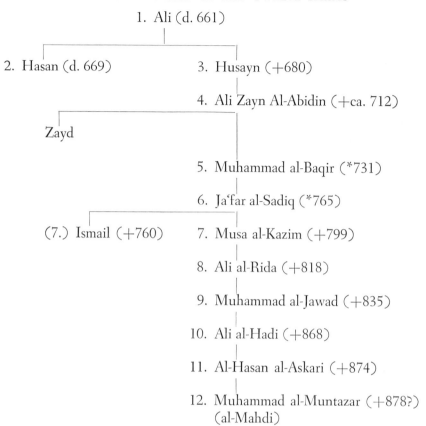

1. Ali (d. 661)

2. Hasan (d. 669)

3. Husayn (+680)

4. Ali Zayn Al-Abidin (+ca. 712)

Zayd

5. Muhammad al-Baqir (*731)

6. Ja'far al-Sadiq (*765)

(7.) Ismail (+760)

7. Musa al-Kazim (+799)

8. Ali al-Rida (+818)

9. Muhammad al-Jawad (+835)

10. Ali al-Hadi (+868)

11. Al-Hasan al-Askari (+874)

12. Muhammad al-Muntazar (+878?)
(al-Mahdi)

porary state of occultation, somewhere on the outer fringes of the world
and will return before the Day of Judgment as *al-Mahdi*, "the awaited
one" to prepare the Muslims for the final dissolution of mankind. From
time to time, inspired men have appeared to announce themselves as
al-Mahdi. The most notable one was the Mahdist movement of Muhammad Ahmad in the Sudan in the 1880's.

Aside from these major divisions, Islam, like Christianity, is sprinkled
with sects; some highly organized; some, as the Druzes of the Levant, so
infused with esoteric ritual as not to be Muslim although founded by a
Fatimite Caliph. Throughout Islam's history, men (and women too)
have appeared whose desire for mystical communion with God has not
been assuaged by the unadorned ceremonies of Muhammad's faith.
Deeply religious and richly philosophical, these people wandered about

the Muslim world, preaching a sort of mystical gospel, living almost without material possessions. Called *Sufis,* probably from their long robes of wool (*suf*) which they wore upon entering their mystical careers, they taught the gnostic creed of the inner light by which the human soul would come to know God and be united with Him in this world. Various syncretic elements from Greek philosophy and Eastern Christianity were absorbed into Sufism as the devotees wandered. It was through Hellenism that its present aspect of true knowledge attainable through religious ecstasy was shaped. Colonies of sufis also began to live together, usually in Iraq, Turkey, and Persia where the movement was strongest, after the twelfth century. This communal practice of Sufism was called the *dervish* order (Arabic *darvish,* from Persian "poor" or "a mendicant"). Several of these orders (*tariqa*) became numerous and, ironically, wealthy. The Mevlevi ("Whirling") Dervishes, under the patronage of the Seljuk sultans, had a famous center of learning in Konya in Central Asia Minor. Their founder, the brilliant poet-mystic, Jalal al-din Rumi (Mevlana), introduced music and dancing into Sufi ceremonies. Another *tariqa,* the Sanusi, was responsible for the unifying of Libyan resistance to the Italians and eventually for the establishment of the modern kingdom of Libya, whose ruler, Idris II, is also the present head of the Sanusi.

REFORMS AND MODERNISM

When the companions of Muhammad elected a caliph to succeed him, they entered Islam in the lists of world politics. Once religious zeal, rather than Alexandrian love of power, Roman orderliness, Russian protectionism, or any of the other various motives that have prompted world conquest, had brought the bulk of the known world under the green banner, Islam had no choice but to enter political history. Working in the full light of history, the Muslims suffered its penalties: loss of faith, sectarianism, external attacks, the enervation of moral fiber. The moral purity of the Arabian warriors could not flourish unaltered in luxurious, sophisticated surroundings.

Thus Islamic civilization languished and was almost forgotten until the nineteenth century. Then came many reformers, men who aspired, like Wahhab in central Arabia, to restore the vigor, austerity, and crystal logic of the Prophet's time. Perhaps the greatest of these was Jamal al-din al-Afghani (1839–1897). "Supremely comprehensive, the complete Muslim of his time," Afghani saw the malady of the Islamic world as a universal loss of values, emphasized by the tentacles of foreign (Western) control. He tried to reconcile Sunnis and Shi'as. He favored local nationalisms and broader groupings whether they contradicted each other or not. His grand goal was pan-Islam. He was an active leader in the Muslim fight against European imperialism and intrigued so much against the Ottoman Sultan and the Persian Shah, thinking them in league with the Europeans, that the two rulers handed him back and forth like a hot potato. Both the assassination of the Shah in 1896 and the Arabi revolt in Egypt in 1882 were inspired by him. Afghani's creed, taken from the Koran—"God does not change the condition of a people until they change their own condition"—contained the basic appeal under which Arab nationalism has developed. It was Afghani, too, who made fashionable the present glorification of Umayyad-Abbasid civilization which is part of the canon of Arab unity. None of the other Muslim reformers, not even Muhammad 'Abduh, who reformed Al-Azhar University along Western scientific lines and became Grand Mufti—highest interpreter of Koranic law in Egypt—had such broad prestige or cumulative effect.

Because 'Abduh had sat at the feet of Afghani, he too became converted to the policy of a restoration of values for Islam; and because he had lived in the West, he realized that Islam no longer fulfilled the needs of Muslim society. 'Abduh observed the Western acceptance of Christianity as a part of life, without surrendering to orthodoxy, and compared this with the rigidity of tradition-bound Islam in the East. To him, as to Afghani the *dar al-Islam* could prosper only if it offered its citizens something beside sterile custom. But a specifically and purely Islamic way of life, renewing the flexibility of the early days, could be strong enough to withstand the temptations and pressures of the Christian European way of life.[31] Muhammad 'Abduh is responsible for the more personal, as opposed to ritualistic, attitude toward Islam taken by Egyptian intellectual and educated classes. His work at Al-Azhar, also, while it did not fully succeed in making the university over into the fountainhead of Arab nationalism in the nineteenth century, made possible its secularization in the twentieth century. President Nasir, whose observance of the forms of Islam is less important to him than his inner faith,[32] has

[31] Lichtenstadter, Ilse, *Islam and The Modern Age,* New York: Bookman Associates, Inc., 1958, pp. 158–160.
[32] Robert St. John, in *The Boss,* New York: McGraw-Hill Book Co., Inc., 1960, p. 229, says that Nasir disclaims belief in the outward forms of religion, but "I do believe in something deep in my heart."

seen to it that the curriculum will include, henceforth, history, politics, economics and sociology as well as theology, and as of 1961, women are permitted to enroll at the 1200-year-old institution.

Out of the efforts of Afghani, of 'Abduh, of political writers with religious convictions such as 'Abd al-Rahman Kawakibi of Aleppo, developed Islamic modernism, which in the nineteenth century became one aspect of the developing Arab nationalist movement which will be examined in more detail in the next chapter. While the Arabic language was merely an incidental means of fusion and Arab race meant far more to the desert bedouin than the urban peoples of the Levant, Islam was an element which could be understood and accepted by all those who professed it. Islamic modernism reminded the faithful that in past centuries they had chosen their ruler, who obeyed their wishes and worked for the general good—and had not Islam been successful in those days? Here was a concept which appealed equally to the camel-driver, the Syrian merchant, the farmer of Palestine, the Transjordan sheepherder, reminding them of their blood brotherhood. Slowly the idea of Arabism took root, of unity based on "a common desert ancestry strengthened by a common language, a common religion and a common aspiration toward freedom." [33]

Islamic modernism offered long-term solutions for the problems of the Arabs, but it was unable to restore the sense of special identity which they had lost at some point in their transfer from a cohesive clan to an international political force. In the nineteenth century, the liberal tendencies which young Arabs (who came almost entirely from those regions of the Ottoman Empire most exposed to foreign influences anyway) imbibed in the West, were seen in terms of what could be done to seek Arab autonomy within the Empire. There seemed to be little connection between what the nations of Europe had made of themselves and the system under which they functioned. Furthermore the more articulate members of the young Arab group were Christians. To them the attraction of Western liberalism lay in some vague alignment with Christianity against the infidel Ottomans. In the nineteenth century, also, the intricate power relationships existing between Europe and the Empire, rendered any restoration of a genuinely Islamic power unlikely, just as in the twentieth century a nation like Pakistan, carved out of India by Muslims as an *Islamic* republic, has found the going so rough as to be

[33] Marlowe, John, *Arab Nationalism and British Imperialism*, New York: Frederick A. Praeger, Inc., 1961, p. 15.

forced to switch to a military dictatorship, with national education directed toward "guided democracy" in political units scaled upward from village council to central administration.

RECOMMENDED READINGS

1. Andrae, Tor, *Muhammad: The Man and His Faith*, New York: Barnes & Noble, Inc., 1935.
2. Arberry, A. J., *Classical Persian Literatures*, New York; the Macmillan Co., 1958.
3. ———, *Revelation and Reason in Islam*, London: Allen & Unwin, 1957.
4. ———, *Sufism*, London: Allen & Unwin, 1956.
5. Atiyah, Edward, *The Arabs*, London: Penguin Books, 1955.
6. Brockelmann, Carl, *History of the Islamic Peoples*, London: Routledge & Kegan Paul, 1949.
7. Ellis, Harry B., *The Heritage of the Desert*, New York: The Ronald Press Company, 1956.
8. Fernau, F. W., *Moslems on the March*, New York: Alfred A. Knopf, Inc., 1954.
9. Frye, R. N., ed., *Islam and The West*, The Hague: Mouton, 1957.
10. Gibb, H. A. R., *Mohammedanism*, 2nd ed., London: Oxford, 1954.
11. ———, ed., *Shorter Encyclopedia of Islam*, Leiden: E. J. Brill, 1953.
12. Guillaume, Alfred, *The Life of Muhammad*, London: Oxford University Press, 1955.
13. Hitti, Philip, *History of the Arabs*, 6th ed., New York: St Martin's Press, Inc., 1956.
14. Izzeddin, Nejla, *The Arab World: Past, Present, Future*, Chicago: Henry Regnery Co., 1953.
15. Jurji, Edward, *The Middle East: Its Religion and Culture*, Philadelphia: The Westminster Press, 1956.
16. Lewis, Bernard, *The Arabs in History*, 3rd ed., London: Hutchinson's University Library, 1956.
17. Payne, Robert, *The Holy Sword*, New York: Harper & Brothers, 1959.
18. Pickthall, M. M., *The Meaning of The Glorious Koran*, New York: New American Library of World Literature, Inc., 1953.
19. Smith, W. C. *Islam in Modern History*, Princeton: Princeton University Press, 1957.
20. Von Grunebaum, G. E., ed. *Unity and Variety in Muslim Civilization*, Chicago: University of Chicago Press, 1955.
21. Watt, W. Montgomery, *Muhammad at Mecca*, Oxford: Clarendon Press, 1953.
22. ——— *Muhammad at Medina*, Oxford: Clarendon Press, 1956.

CHAPTER 2

THE OTTOMAN EMPIRE AND
WESTERN POLICY TO 1939

Islam as an aggressive international force was largely spent after the
twelfth century A.D. but Western Europe, which then became in a sense
the aggressor, inaugurated a series of vitally significant contacts with the
Middle East. The clergy of Christendom, for a variety of reasons ranging from pious religiosity to barefaced ambitions for power, invoked the
aid of Western military knighthood to rescue Palestine from infidel domination. The series of rescue operations which we call the Crusades are
outside the scope of this study, but several facts of importance to modern
Middle Eastern politics are worthy of note. The First Crusade was the
only one to "succeed," in the sense of capturing the goal, the Holy City
of Jerusalem. On July 15, 1099, Godfrey de Bouillon and his knights
entered the city, and began an indiscriminate massacre of its inhabitants
regardless of age, sex, religion, or nationality.[1] This ruthless brutality
was an unfortunate contrast to the Muslim capture four hundred years
earlier and to the entire experience of the people of Palestine under a
more tolerant Muslim rule. From the First Crusade stemmed the general hostility of Muslims for Christians (and vice versa) which has
given the affairs of the Holy Land such a dreadful complexity and, when
given a third dimension by Jewish nationalism, puts Christian nations
in a difficult situation.

The establishment of Latin principalities furnished a model for the
modern disunity of the area, also. Whether the Allies consciously

[1] According to both Christian and Muslim sources, between sixty-five and
seventy thousand were slaughtered at the Aqsa Mosque. Godfrey de Bouillon rode
his horse waist-deep in blood to reach the Dome of the Rock.

22

thought of their crusading predecessors as they cut up the Middle East into mandates after World War I is debatable but the process was essentially the same. The principalities created Christian islands in an Islamic ocean, intensified communal strife, and produced little of value. The entire crusading period may rightly be viewed as another manifestation of the long history of the interaction of East and West, from the Persian Wars to the Cold War.[2]

THE OTTOMAN EMPIRE

The modern political history of the Middle East and the regenerative forces of Arab nationalism were set in motion under the long period of Ottoman Turkish administration, nearly five centuries in span. Under an alien power which nevertheless became thoroughly indigenous, adopting elements of language, culture, religion, and even social attitudes which were not its own into a thorough fusion, unmistakably Ottoman, the Middle East was unified. The Arabs, who had been the active agents in the transmission of Islam, passed the work of administration over to the disciplined, organized Turks. The Turks, after a similar burst of successful energy, gradually fell into the same spirit of apathy. Meanwhile the energy galvanizing Western Europe into scientific, exploratory, and political expansionist interests revived European interest in the Ottoman lands as sources of commercial productivity. The three sets of factors—Turco-Arab stagnation, Ottoman military weakness, and Western commercial expansionism—all coalesced in the nineteenth century. There developed an aspect of East-West relations which (in European terms at least) was called "The Eastern Question." It was a combination of European promises, of mutual as well as opposing commitments; and in time it produced a political disintegration which completed the cycle, return to the disunity of Crusader times, with the grim added component of technological militarism.

The Ottoman Turks in Perspective. During the span of their empire, the Ottoman Turks set a record of sorts in international relations. Their government remained in the hands of a single ruling family, the House of Osman. They introduced and developed a set of political innovations which permitted the continuation of a reasonably harmonious comity of nationalities. Despite the degeneration of imperial administration which affected their empire in the latter half of its existence, they provided a high degree of stability for the western half of the Middle

[2] Cf. Hitti, *op. cit.,* pp. 635 *et seq.*

East, and shielded it from foreign pressures other than the purely economic. The palace struggles of the successive sultans and the interweaving of Turkish-Western policies affected the mute villagers of Anatolia very little except for the periodic conscriptions, and the rural folk
of Lebanon, Palestine, and Egypt even less. Out in the deserts of Arabia,
the bedouin followed an ancestral way of life, free and unaltered since
Muhammad's time.

The Ottoman state originated as a fief of the Selcuk Turks, who had
seized much of Anatolia from Byzantium after their defeat of the Emperor Romanus Diogenes at Manzikert (Malazgirt) in 1071. The Selcuks were crude nomadic clansmen who had been converted to Islam by
missionaries and taken service under the Caliph. They were the first to
be styled Ghazis (Defenders of the Faith), and their success enabled
them to dictate more often to the Caliph than he to them. Their sultanate in Anatolia, with its capital at Konya, was a glittering beacon of
civilization in uncertain, Mongol-threatened times. The Selcuks were
eclectic; absorbing Armenian, Byzantine, Persian and Arabic influences,
they created an unusual fusion of architecture, with a unique decorative
style. The Selcuks also kept the peace. They built a chain of watch-
towers across their territory, developed mobile cavalry columns to deal
with emergencies, and garrisoned *hans* (inns) along the roads for travelers. Encouraged by the security of the Selcuk realm in the thirteenth
century, poets and philosophers flocked to the court at Konya. The most
famous visitant was Jalal al-din Rumi, called *Mevlana* ("Our Lord") by
his disciples, who founded there a mystical order, the *Mevlevi* (Whirling) Dervishes.[3] Rumi's teachings stress the mystical, Sufi approach to
God, and Konya remains a monument to his thought as well as to the
achievements of the Selcuks. Unfortunately their political skill did not
equal their artistic and intellectual gifts, and it was the Selcuk failure to
administer cohesively their scattered territories that led to their replacement by the Ottomans.

The canon of classical Turkish literature contains three legends which
offer considerable insight into Ottoman character and motivation. The
first is the grey wolf. There are different versions, but the most attractive (and the least believable) traces the origin of the Turks to a Central
Asian princess who was rescued by a gigantic wolf from a band of rob-

---

[3] There are many references to Rumi. One of the most thorough is Afzal Iqbal,
The Life and Thought of Rumi. Lahore, Pakistan: 1955. See also Chapter 1 for
cross references.

bers. She married the highly intelligent wolf out of gratitude, and their descendants became the Turks, gifted beyond all men for their combination of human and wolf-like characteristics. The second legend pictures the Turks as an army of horsemen, riding silently, with perfect discipline, out of nowhere into the sunset. These two legends suggest an explanation of the rise of the Ottomans from obscurity to domination of an area nearly as large as the Roman Empire; they possessed in full measure many of the necessary qualities—discipline, efficiency, military spirit, ruthlessness, firm unity of purpose, and versatility.

A third story from the canon tells of a band of Turanian tribesmen who were riding westward across Anatolia in search of new grazing lands. They came upon a battle in which one side was clearly having the worst of it. Some of the more ignoble spirits in the band felt they should help the winners, but their leader, one Ertoghrul ("the Right-Hearted") insisted that the tribal code of honor required them to aid the losers. His counsel prevailed, and the entry of the Turanians reversed the balance of the conflict. The former losing side proved to be a party of Selcuks led by the Sultan himself. In gratitude he gave Ertoghrul a tract of land for his clan on the Sea of Marmara, a border area southwest of Constantinople. The location was to prove highly useful to Ottoman expansionism.

Ertoghrul's son and successor, Osman (1281–1324) was converted to Islam and took all his clansmen with him. This explains why he, and not his father, bears the credit for the founding of the Empire, and is the eponymous ancestor of the Ottomans. In two centuries of steady expansion at the expense of the Selcuks and the Byzantines, the Ottomans gained the dominant position in the entire Middle East from Persia westward, coastal North Africa as far as Morocco, the Balkans, and Central Europe to the gates of Vienna (see map on page 26). In 1453 Sultan Mehmet II entered Constantinople; the last Byzantine Emperor, Constantine XII Palaelogus, died defending the imperial city. The Greeks took their Megali ideal, or Greater Greece, west with them; Greece itself became a part of the Ottomans' domains. In 1517 Sultan Selim I Yavuz ("Inflexible") added Syria and Egypt, but more important, he succeeded to the title and functions of the Caliph, ending the last pale shadow of the Abbasids. In terms of later political history, the reigns of Selim and his son and successor Sulayman I, "The Magnificent" and the "Lawgiver" (*Kanuni*) had a wider impact than the capture of Constantinople. The Caliphate passed into the hands of a non-Arab people, the Turks. The

LIBRARY
College of St. Francis
JOLIET, ILL.

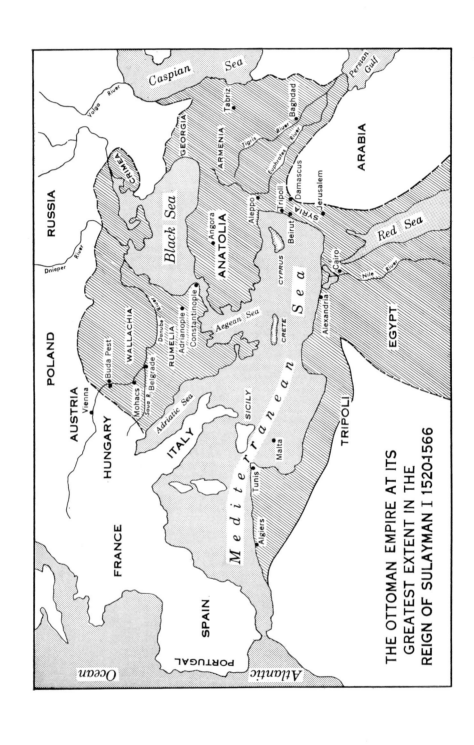

THE OTTOMAN EMPIRE AT ITS
GREATEST EXTENT IN THE
REIGN OF SULAYMAN I 1520-1566

decline in Arab fortunes was all the more melancholy because the Ottoman conversion had been so recent.[4] The center of Islam passed from the
Arab World; the great cities of the Islamic past, Baghdad, Damascus,
Cairo, became provincial cities; Jerusalem's walls were rebuilt and Christians and Jews were even encouraged to settle there.[5] The Holy Cities of
Arabia were forgotten except in men's devotions and the *Hajj*. The Ottomans, skilled and disciplined administrators (which the Arabs were not)
welded an empire of diverse peoples and religion together through a
unique arrangement of political institutions. Although they scorned Europeans as inferiors,[6] the Ottomans mixed freely with the Byzantines in
the period before the Conquest; Sultans and princes even contracted
matrimonial alliances with noble Christian ladies. Bayezid's favorite wife
was a Serbian princess, the Despina, for example. To an increasing extent, the Ottoman Empire was an open doorway between East and West,
a role played by their descendants with equal zest.

The major political institutions of the Empire evolved largely in the
fifteenth and sixteenth centuries; although not original with the Ottomans, they were amplified and utilized with typical thoroughness by
them to place the stamp of unity on their heterogeneous possessions.
The first was the Caliphate, with its "field command," the *'Ulema*—for
while Islam strictly speaking has no priesthood in the Western-Catholic
Christian sense, very early in the Muslim community there were those
who proved they could pray better and interpret better than the majority. The clansmen of Osman were simple, literal folk; they swallowed
shari'a whole and accepted its interpreters with equal fervor.[7] The first
codification of Ottoman law for the Empire was made by Sulayman I,
and was called the *kanun-name;* parts of it were drawn from concensus
(*ijma'*) or learned interpretations, and some elements even from Western law, but the core was *shari'a*. Theoretically, after the assumption of
the Caliphal office by Selim, the Sultans were the final arbiters, but in
practice the hierarchy of *'ulema*, composed of *cadis* (judges) and muftis
(learned jurists) whose head was the Grand Mufti of Constantinople
(Shaykh al-Islam), interpreted or justified the Sultan's decrees according

[4] Osman I supposedly became friendly with a pious Muslim, and one night
read the Koran all the way through, *standing up*.
[5] Polk, W., Stamler, D., Asfour, E. Y., *Backdrop to Tragedy: The Struggle
for Palestine,* Boston: Beacon Press, 1957, pp. 28–30.
[6] Cf. Sultan Murad's famous letter to the Emperor Nicephorus, "thou dog of a
Roman."
[7] The Selcuk letters patent to Osman confirming the Ottoman fief stated that
shari'a would be the law there.

to shari'a law. So long as the ruling Sultan was strong, this system worked effectively, but quite obviously it posed a threat to stability, whenever weak Sultans ruled.

The ethnic and religious diversity within the Empire prompted the Ottomans to devise a system whereby non-Muslims—mainly Christian and Jewish subjects—could be controlled without becoming subject to Islamic law, which could not apply to them. Under the Caliphate they had generally been left alone except for payment of a poll-tax and various minor restrictions. This had not ensured their loyalty, however. The Ottomans formalized it into their own arrangement, the *millet* (nation) system. Each religious community was given autonomy in internal affairs under its own ecclesiastical authority. Immediately after the capture of Constantinople, Mehmet II formally invested a Greek ecclesiastic, George Scholarios, as Gennadios III, to be Patriarch of the Orthodox community, with full authority to represent that community in dealings with the conquering Turks, for example. Other Christian communities such as the Armenians received similar treatment. These reserved powers were given rather freely, partly because the Sultans were sagacious enough to realize the importance of maintaining Byzantium's former position as a trade entrepot and partly due to implicit Ottoman faith in their automatic superiority over other races.

A second Ottoman institution was the *Capitulations*. These were special rights and privileges conferred on foreigners trading with the Empire. They were first granted to the merchants of Venice and Genoa; Mehmet realized that the economic health of his new capital depended on the continuation of good relations with the European powers who had carried on the bulk of its trade. Capitulations of a sort were a traditional feature of Mediterranean economic life, but the Ottomans brought them into the sphere of foreign relations. In 1535 A.D. Sulayman signed a treaty of friendship and commerce with Francis I which extended the system directly to France. The privileges were called *Capitulations* because the treaty was prepared in *chapters* (Latin *capitula*). From the Ottoman viewpoint, they surrendered nothing and gained much. They encouraged European nations to continue trading with the Empire, and freed the Turks from the burden of conducting commerce, for which they had little stomach and less skill. Also they suited the Ottoman mentality; they were favors graciously granted by an all-powerful Muslim Sultan to infinitely inferior Christian rulers, presenting no danger whatever.

The 1535 treaty gave France freedom of trade and navigation in Ottoman ports, reduced the ad valorem duty to 5 per cent for French merchants, exempted French citizens from Ottoman jurisdiction, and placed them under their own consuls. It also accepted French rights of custody over the holy places of Christendom in Palestine. The French capitulations became a model for later ones granted to other European nations.

The administration of the Empire was summed up by the term "Sublime Porte" (a term derived from the "High Gate," or Bab-i-Ali, through which envoys passed when they entered the palace of the Sultan on official business). The Sublime Porte included the Sultan himself, the vast imperial harem, the civil service, and by extension the Janissary order. The early sultans were men of extreme simplicity and vigor, but their successors became as corrupted by the venality of Constantinople as their Byzantine predecessors had been. The Ottomans adopted many features of Byzantine court life, features which were in fact contradictions of their Turkish social codes brought from Central Asia. They began to seclude their women, they kept slaves and concubines in vast numbers; veiling became standard practice. Parallel to the imperial household was the "Ruling Institution," a bureaucratic civil service which was recruited from both Muslims and non-Muslims. However, so long as the sultans were able men, the service was administered effectively, filled on the basis of merit, and operated effectively over an unwieldy empire.

The best-known political institution developed by the Ottomans was the Janissary order. The Janissaries (*Yeni Tcheri,* "new troops," in Turkish) evolved from the custom of reserving one-fourth of the booty and captives from victories for the sultan himself. The royal fourth usually included healthy boys who were formed into an elite guard of mercenaries for the royal protection. When the Ottoman armies began to fight battles against infidel armies on European soil, the Grand Mufti sanctioned the use of Christian boys for the guard, a prudent move since the supply of Muslim captives had dropped alarmingly. The system was further refined by the *Devshirme,* a method of recruitment. Recruiting teams made yearly visits to Christian villages, mostly in the Balkans, to take back to Constantinople a percentage of the best physical specimens among the young male population. Some were trained to be pages, others entered the civil service. All were converted to Islam, and the healthiest were assigned to the Janissaries. Completely severed from their families, forbidden to marry (at first), rigorously trained, and fanatically loyal, the Janissaries became the best military corps in the Western world.[8] They were closely allied with the equally fanatical Bektashi dervishes, whose chief was a Janissary colonel.

The Decay of the Ottoman State. From its peak during the reign of Sulayman I, the Ottoman Empire entered a long period of decline, gradual at first but accelerating rapidly in the eighteenth and nineteenth centuries. That the polyglot, unwieldy empire took so long to disintegrate, may be attributed to three major factors: the vitality of its basic institutions, its resources of manpower, and the ingrained respect of its Muslim citizens, Turks as well as Arabs, for the forms of Islam. The mute peasantry, which fought, died, and bore the crushing burden of Ottoman taxation, knew little of the world except that the Sultan was Caliph, the Deputy of the Messenger of God. This was sufficient.

Decline in the integrity of the system of government and intrenchment of privileged groups at the expense of the general welfare characterized the Empire's dessication. To begin with, Sulayman's successors were lesser men. Increasingly they operated from within the harem; the court intrigues of the imperial household too often resulted in advancement to high position on the basis of favoritism. The absence of a Salic Law or clear-cut design for the succession led to fratricidal quarrels between the sons of a Sultan on his death. When this proved uneconomical, the ruling class resorted to the *Kafes* ("Cage"), a sort of sterilized inner harem where male princes of the royal family were confined. Their physical wants were cared for, but they received no intellectual stimulation. Occasionally a prince emerged from the Kafes degenerate in mind and body to become Sultan and to sire degenerate sons who became Sultans in their turn.[9]

Elsewhere the Ottoman system displayed a parallel degeneration. The Janissaries acquired vast privileges and in turn dictated to their weak rulers. They were permitted to marry in the seventeenth century, and their officers were exempted from taxation. In conjunction with the Bektashis, they would demand dismissals of ministers or viziers who tried to curtail their powers and even depose Sultans who displeased them. The

---

[8] One of their ablest commanders was George Castriot, son of an Epirote chieftain, who became known as Scanderbeg (Lord Alexander). Scanderbeg broke with the Janissaries during a campaign, reverted to his Christian faith, and returned to his native Albania where he used Janissary tactics so effectively that he maintained Albania's independence from the Ottoman Empire's entire weight for twenty-two years (1445–1467).

[9] Alderson, A. R., *Structure of the Ottoman Dynasty,* London: Oxford University Press, 1956, Chapter V, "The Kafes," pp. 32–37.

overturning of the cooking-kettles in the Janissary barracks was a periodic warning of trouble.

The millet system and the Capitulations also became instruments of abuse which contributed to the inner decay of the Empire. Rather than insuring loyalty to the Ottoman State, the millet system was the means of subverting imperial authority, notably by Christians. The successful rebellions of the Greeks, Serbs, and others were possible (at least initially) because of the growth of national, ethnic consciousness under the millet. The Capitulations attracted legitimate business and certainly benefited the Empire at the start, but the increasing weakness of the Ottoman government meant that foreign nationals became totally immune to its laws. As a result all types of dishonest speculators converged on the major parts of the Empire, secure from arrest behind their consuls. An Ottoman citizen could be arrested on the slightest provocation, while a foreign entrepreneur could defraud the Ottoman government of thousands of pounds without encountering punitive action.

The rigidity of the Ottoman system also contributed heavily to its weakening. A feudal system of military grants for service and the assignment of governorships to public officials who paid for them under the table and were tacitly expected to recoup their fortunes through taxation permitted the grosser forms of maladministration to flourish throughout the empire. The 'ulema, holding the power of religious sanction as interpreters of Islamic law, were able to block decrees which would have curbed them in order to prepare for a more efficient legal system. The influence of the 'ulema was felt most painfully in military matters, ironically. Thus Sultan Selim III's attempt to bring in European officers to modernize and train the Ottoman army was denounced by them on grounds that infidels could not command, let alone train, the forces of the true faith. Even Western-style uniforms were frowned upon, and the Ottomans went into battle in a variety of colorful but inefficient costumes.

In summary, the internal state of the Empire was like a decomposing head loosely fitted by a few tendons to a great shapeless body.[10] The Ottoman sovereign and his court lived a remote life from the mass of the peasantry. The connection between the two was limited to the mention of the Sultan-Caliph in prayers, the tax-gatherer, and the conscription officers. The language of the Sublime Porte was Osmanli, a flowery mixture of Old Turkish, Persian, and Arabic, incomprehensible to the

---

[10] Cf. the Turkish proverb, "The fish begins to stink at the head."

peasantry. The very word "Turk" was a term of contempt, applied to the common people by their rulers, who called themselves Osmanlis.

In the nineteenth century several Sultans made a sincere effort to promote reforms. They made no effort to reform society, however, but imported alien ideas, usually European, which they imposed by fiat. Selim III set up technical schools and a military force as a counterweight to the Janissaries, who had developed the practice of setting fire to parts of Constantinople if an imperial order displeased them. The 'ulema, the landowners, and the Janissaries opposed him, and the last named rebelled in 1807. Mahmud II (1808–1839), who succeeded his uncle, won the 'ulema to his side aided by the successes of the Egyptian governor Muhammad Ali against the imperial armies. In 1826 the Janissaries mutinied again, but Mahmud surrounded them in their barracks and destroyed the order. Mahmud's success paved the way for the Tanzimat ("Reforms") Period (1839–1876) when two reform-minded Sultans, Abdul Majid (1839–1861) and Abdul Aziz (1861–1876) with the cooperation of a Turkish reform group of officials under Reshid Pasha and the great statesman, Midhat Pasha, seriously undertook to modernize the Empire.

In 1839 Abdul Majid issued the Charter of Liberties (Hatti-Sharif of Gul-Hane). It was an attempt to unify the polyglot empire and regularize the various bodies of legislation applying to its races. All Ottoman subjects were declared equal regardless of religion or race. The Charter contained a bill of rights, a common taxation system, an equitable conscription system, and civil and penal codes borrowed from the West which were still subject to Islamic law in the final analysis. In 1856 the Hatti Humayun was issued; while reaffirming the equality of Ottoman subjects, it defined the rights of minorities, indicating the altered attitude of France and Britain toward Turkey as the result of the Crimean War. Between 1869 and 1876 a serious effort was made to codify differing Muslim civil laws within the Empire. Called the *Mecelle,* it was again based on Islamic law but defined civil relationships in many areas between Ottoman subjects and foreigners. Finally, Midhat Pasha, who had risen from provincial governor in neglected Baghdad to Grand Vizier, pressured the incoming Sultan, Abdul Hamid II, to grant a constitution in 1876 because of the threat of foreign invasion. When this threat receded the Sultan suspended it, closing the door on lasting reforms in the Turkish state until it was forced open by Kemal Ataturk. Abdul Hamid's act placed the final judgment on Ottoman reform movements in the nineteenth century. The reformers were frustrated by many factors: unwillingness of the Sultans to surrender their own powers and privileges, resistance of the ʻulema, inability to industrialize, inability of a pastoral, agrarian society to be able to absorb modern political institutions, and, not the least, the expansionist interests of Europe.

THE GREAT POWERS IN THE MIDDLE EAST

When the Ottoman Turks crossed the Dardanelles and captured Adrianople, making it their capital in 1366, they were *in* Europe; but they were not *of* Europe. Not until six centuries later, perhaps symbolized by republican Turkey's admission to the North Atlantic Treaty Organization, were the Turks accepted as a European power. The first period of Ottoman-European interrelationships was carried on chiefly by the Hapsburg Empire, with France cast in an ambiguous role by her capitulatory, most-favored-nation arrangement. Hapsburg policy was to contain the usually successful Ottomans, who had imperialistic aims of their own. After the second siege of Vienna (1683) when a relieving force of Poles under Jan Sobieski utterly routed the Ottomans, the Treaty of Carlowitz (1699) put them on the defensive. Thereafter the declining health of the Empire [11] brought on what became known as the "Eastern Question." This "question," shared by England, France, Austria, Russia, and (after 1871) Germany, concerned: how to maintain the integrity of the Ottoman state, since it was the only stabilizing factor in a political vacuum, while establishing equitable distribution of its territories *if this* should become necessary.[12]

The major extension of Ottoman Turkey's foreign relationships was with Russia. Under Peter the Great and his successors, Russian land-power was consolidated, and the Czars looked even more hungrily at the warm-water outlets to the south, all of them in Turkish hands. In the period of two-hundred-odd years, the two powers fought thirteen major wars, most of them won by the Russians. Final victory was never possible, however, since the gentleman's agreement under which the game of international power politics was waged, formed an integral part of the Eastern Question. The treaty landmarks in this long, tortured series of conflicts, which have given the Turks a deep-rooted suspicion of *"Moskov"* which endures today, were:

[11] Czar Nicholas II of Russia coined the phrase, "Sick Man of Europe," when he observed, "Gentlemen, we have on our hands a very, very, sick man."
[12] The Eastern Question in a different sense, applied to Persia, was the exclusive concern of England and Russia in their contest over Central Asia. See Chapter 4.

(1) The Treaty of Kuchuk Kainardji (1774)—This gave Russia access to the Black Sea, control over the mouths of the Bug and Dnieper Rivers, the Don River outlet, and the Straits of Kerch, the right to establish consulates in Constantinople and other cities, free trade privileges, protectorate status over the Christians of Moldavia and Wallachia and the Greek Orthodox minority within the Empire.

(2) The Treaty of Unkiar Iskelessi (1833)—This resulted in an alliance for joint defense by the two states of the Straits, with secret clauses that gave Russia freedom of passage in the Straits in the event of war while closing them to ships of other nations.

(3) The Treaty of Paris (1856)—This concluded the ill-organized Crimean War, undertaken partly out of fear that Czar Nicholas was planning to eliminate the "Sick Man." The treaty had four major provisions—demilitarization of the Black Sea, free navigation on the Danube, the end of the Russian protectorate over Moldavia-Wallachia, and cession of southern Bessarabia to Turkey.

(4) The Treaty of Berlin (1878)—This replaced the Treaty of San Stefano (which was more favorable to Russia) and provided for the independence of Serbia, Rumania, and Montenegro; the cession of Bessarabia, Kars, and Ardahan in eastern Anatolia, and Batum to Russia; Austrian occupation of Bosnia-Herzegovina; and British occupation of Cyprus.

This was as close as the powers could come to a solution of the Eastern Question before World War I. Italy revealed ambitions toward Libya, which was annexed in 1911–12, and the offshore Aegean Islands; and France imposed a protectorate over Tunisia. Germany alone sought no territorial advantages; after 1880 the Germans gradually replaced Britain in the favorite's role with the Ottomans, largely due to British support for the new Balkan states but also because of the favorable economic terms offered by the Germans.

Russia was the European power most closely involved in Ottoman affairs from territorial and military standpoints. Great Britain, conversely, took the lead in dealing with the Eastern Question on moral and legalistic bases. Stratford Canning, when he arrived in Constantinople for the second time as Ambassador, carried instructions "to impart stability to the Sultan's government by promoting judicious and well-considered reforms." [13] This was the general attitude of British statesmen

[13] Quoted in Kedourie, Elie, *England and the Middle East,* London: Bowes & Bowes, 1956, p. 11.

—Canning and Palmerston—who saw in the Empire something rotten at its core, yet a rottenness which could be purged by reform, in the old-fashioned English Liberal manner. There were men in British public life who disagreed; Lord Clarendon said in 1865, "The only way to improve them is to improve them off the face of the earth." [14] But by and large British policy toward the Empire was to help a sickly animal to recover, British duty was to see the cure handled in a proper manner. This gave Britain a rather unsoiled appearance in Turkish eyes, until Germany's propulsion into the Eastern Question simultaneously with her arrival as a force in international affairs shifted the delicate balance of a century.

THE YOUNG TURKS (1865–1914)

The *rapprochement* with Germany which led to Turkey's final dismemberment as an imperial state was aided immeasurably by the reform group which terminated Abdul Hamid's despotic rule and which came to be called the "Young Turks." [15] In 1865 the Turkish patriotic poet Namık Kemal founded the New Ottoman Society with a number of other young intellectuals as a protest movement against the slowness of reforms and the inadequacy of Tanzimat. Namık Kemal believed in Pan-Ottomanism, which meant uniting the disparate elements in the empire through a constitution, an end to foreign intervention, and patriotic appeals to Islam. [16] Namık Kemal's movement dissolved at his death; but his poetry, particularly his "Ode to Freedom" which denounced the Sultan for violating the fundamental principles of Islam were the inspiration for the Young Turk Movement of the next generation. [17]

The Young Ottomans wanted a constitutional monarchy; their successor groups, which met in secrecy after 1876, wanted Abdul Hamid to restore the Constitution which had been granted in that year. In 1889 the Ottoman Union and Progress Committee (*Osmanli Ittihat ve Terakki Cemiyeti*) was founded in Istanbul; in 1902 it held its first Congress in Paris. This group, which had advocated a policy of nonviolent inter-

[14] Gooch, G. P., Temperey, H. V., eds., *England and the Near East,* London: HMSO, 1936, p. 165. (1898–1914), Vol. X, British Documents on the Origins of the War.

[15] See Ransaur, Ernest, *The Young Turks and the Revolution of 1908,* Princeton: Princeton University Press, 1957, for a documented account.

[16] Davison, R. H., "Turkish Attitudes Concerning Christian-Muslim Equality in the Nineteenth Century," *American Historical Review,* July, 1954, p. 863.

[17] See Halide Edib (Adivar), *Conflict of East and West in Turkey,* Lahore: Ashraf, 1935, pp. 198 ff.

nal revolution, split into two groups, and one of these merged in 1906 with the Ottoman Freedom Association established in Salonika by army officers and minor officials.[18] The Committee of Union and Progress, as the combined movement was called, acquired strong support from Muslims and even disaffected Christians in the Balkans, the latter sensing an opportunity to break the Ottoman shackles. Young army officers formed the core; they were ardently nationalistic and had the military acumen to carry out their nationalist ideas. In 1908 the pressures of the Western Powers on Abdul Hamid for economic concessions in the Balkans set off an alarm that they were about to dismember the Empire and frightened the C.U.P. into action. It sent an ultimatum, backed both by force and the popular will, to Abdul Hamid. The "Red Sultan" yielded; the constitution of 1876 was reinstated; and three C.U.P. leaders, Enver, Talaat, and Djemal, became a junta ruling the affairs of Turkey although Muhammad V, an elder member of the House of Osman, was named Sultan in 1909 after Abdul Hamid had been legally deposed.[19]

The Young Turk revolution encouraged feelings of unity between the various ethnic groups of the Empire at first; there was much fraternization, even between Muslim Turks and Christian Armenians. Constitutional government was the national purpose and Pan-Ottomanism the creed. It quickly became apparent, however, that the Young Turk leaders had other ideas. Pan-Turkism with its complement Pan-Turanism, the uniting of all those of Turkish blood under one government, were their goals. Enver and his colleagues wished to purify the Turkish language and to impose it on all nationalities. The Arab Nationalist movement, although directed against foreign intervention in the Empire and limited to demand for local autonomy, was roughly handled and forced to go underground. After 1913, authority rested in the hands of Enver alone, and Enver's infatuation with German methods drew Turkey steadily into an alignment with Germany.

WORLD WAR I AND THE MIDDLE EAST

The Middle East was a minor theatre of war during 1914–1918 measured against the massive trench conflict in Western Europe. But in terms of the Middle East's political evolution, particularly the claims and attitudes of today's Middle Easterner, the "Great War" was crucial.

[18] Ramsaur, *op. cit.*, pp. 95 ff.
[19] The Grand Mufti was moved to issue a *fetva* (decree having the force of law), saying that under *Shari'a* law it was legal to depose him. See Yale, William, *The Near East*, Ann Arbor: University of Michigan Press, 1959, p. 170.

Far more significant than the military maneuvers were the political gambits, the pledges to this or that people, the secret agreements. The Ottoman Empire, despite its many faults, had provided a safe, respectable, solid cushion of dependability for its peoples for nearly five centuries; when this was swept away, the Middle Easterner lost his anchor and even today can find neither peace nor a safe haven.

The lineup of the war was itself a reversal of traditional foreign relations. Britain, the traditional ally and friend of the Turks, was allied with Russia, the hereditary enemy. So was France, whose language and culture had molded a generation of educated Osmanlis. German nationalism rather than German liberal traditions appealed to the army officers who dominated the C.U.P.; and in 1913 General Liman von Sanders went to Turkey with a military mission to train the Turkish army for modern warfare. This suited Enver perfectly since his program had three phases, all contingent on revived nationalism. They were Pan-Turkism (the reunification of the Empire, limiting it to Turkish and related peoples); Pan-Turanism (expansion to embrace the Turkic peoples of Central Asia, who were then as they are now under Russian control); and Pan-Islam (the restoration of a powerful Caliphate under Ottoman leadership).

Not all the members of the Ottoman Government leaned toward Germany. One of the ruling triumvirate, Djemal Pasha, leaned toward Britain politically and France culturally, while Enver and Talaat were militantly pro-German.[20]

The Archduke Ferdinand of Austria was assassinated at Sarajevo in June 1914, and tension grew rapidly among the European powers. Turkey professed neutrality. Three years earlier the Ottoman Government had purchased two battleships in England—the *Reschadiye* and the *Sultan Osman.* They were to be reconditioned and delivered in 1914–1915; but the British, apparently fearful of Turkey's position in the developing conflict, confiscated them. The action ranged popular support in the Empire on the side of the pro-German party. On August 1, 1914, war broke out; the next day, Turkey and Germany signed a secret military alliance. Article 2 committed the Turks to enter the war to aid Germany in the event of a Russian attack. The next move was the *"Goeben-Breslau* incident." Two German warships, the *Goeben* and the

---

[20] Djemal Pasha, Ahmed, *Memoirs of a Turkish Statesman,* New York: Hutchinson, 1922. Djemal stated that he preferred an alliance with Germany to complete isolation.

Breslau, were cruising in the Mediterranean when the war broke out. Although the Straits were officially closed to all warships by Turkey's mobilization (and the Constantinople Agreement), the *Goeben* and the *Breslau* headed for them, pursued by a British naval force. The Turks gave asylum to the two ships and then (prodded by the German diplomats who had been pouring into Constantinople) announced that the Germans had sold them to Turkey. The *Goeben* and *Breslau* were never seen again; but two warships, the *Yavuz Sultan Selim* and the *Midilli,* identical in appearance and flying the Ottoman flag, steamed into the Black Sea under German crews to attack the Russian fleet shortly thereafter.

As the war progressed, the Ottoman armies gave ground here and there but maintained their long frontiers with stubborn resistance. They even won some notable victories; an entire British task force of thirteen thousand under General Townsend was captured in southern Mesopotamia; the Russians were held on the hideous Caucasus front; and a Pyrrhic victory was won at Gallipoli.[21] In the latter a young Turkish officer named Mustafa Kemal distinguished himself so much that he earned a hero's welcome on his return to Constantinople. The Turks had to contend not only with invading armies but also with hostile ethnic groups in the rear. The Armenians were the most prominent of these. In 1914 the Armenian *Catholicos,* or head bishop, living at Etchmiadzin across the border in Russian Armenia, declared that the Czar was the protector of all Armenians. The Ottoman Government in 1915, doubtful of the loyalty of its Armenians, began a systematic deportation of them from Eastern Anatolia to the west or to the south into Syria. Although Ottoman motives were at least understandable in terms of military necessity, the deportations were accompanied by totally unnecessary brutalities and destruction of property. Even German pressure did not deter Talaat Pasha, who was acting as Minister of the Interior, from carrying out his policy. The "Armenian massacres" permanently destroyed the reasonable harmony which existed between the two groups and cannot really be justified on any grounds.[22]

[21] See Moorehead, Alan, *Gallipoli,* New York: Harper & Brothers, 1956, for the best recent account of this ill-starred campaign.
[22] The writer spoke recently with persons who survived the deportations; now in their sixties, they still cannot find a good word to say about the Turks. Djemal Pasha, even in 1922, could write, "We Young Turks unquestionably prefer the Armenians, and particularly the Armenian revolutionaries, to the Greeks and Bulgarians." *Op. cit.,* p. 241.

ARAB NATIONALISM AND THE REVOLT

From the thirteenth century onwards the Arabs had ceased to be a political factor in the Middle East. In fact, since the reign of Sultan Selim I, they had lost their special identity, being merely a large minority group in the Ottoman state. It is a peculiar cultural characteristic of the Arabs to show great bursts of creative energy, followed by long lapses into inactivity; [23] and Arab behavior adhered rather faithfully to this pattern. The arrival of Napoleon in the area had broken it. Napoleon's military victories (and defeats) left no indelible impression on the Arabs, but the cultural emissaries of France which followed him—educators, archaeologists, doctors, scientists, and others—did. The Jesuits and other orders opened schools in the Levant, awakening an awareness of the need for education among the Arabs. Their impact was narrow, but it helped to create a small class exposed to French culture, French language, and liberal Western thought. American missionaries followed. They founded schools also, notably the Syrian Protestant College (1866), later renamed the American University of Beirut, and Robert College in Constantinople, which trained a large number of the young men who later became leaders of the new Republican Turkey. American missionaries also translated the Bible into Arabic and introduced a printing press which placed textbooks and educational materials in Arabic into the schools. This helped mold Arab consciousness of nationality and revised the almost forgotten heritage of the Caliphate.

The success of the Young Turk Movement encouraged the Arabs to seek a higher, more legitimate national status than the Pan-Turk policies of Enver Pasha allowed. There was no particular desire among the Arab intellectuals in the van of nationalism to break with the Ottomans and to attain independence. The Sultan-Caliph was their legitimate ruler, and they had no desire to seek aid from infidel powers against him. The extent of their ambitions was autonomy within a decentralized federal Ottoman state.[24] In 1908 Arab leaders in Constantinople organized the Ottoman-Arab Brotherhood for this purpose; it had the blessing of the C.U.P. But the honeymoon was brief. Intensifying Committee control of the state and the Pan-Turkish policy of Enver made cooperation difficult. In 1909 the Ottoman-Arab Brotherhood was officially pro-

[23] Cf. Hamady, Sania, *The Temperament and Character of the Arabs*, New York: Twayne Publishers Inc., 1960.
[24] See Hassan Saab, *The Arab Federalists of the Ottoman Empire*, The Hague: Djambatan, 1956.

scribed. The Arabs reacted by forming a "Literary Club" which appeared innocuous to the C.U.P. but which became a facade for various secret societies dedicated to more drastic forms of nationalism. The two most important of these were *Al-Qahtaniya,* whose aim was a dual Turko-Arab monarchy with equality for the Arabs, and *Al-Fatat* (The Young Arab Society), Pan-Arabist and devoted to the cause of full Arab sovereignty for their "heartland" in Western Asia. *Al-Fatat* encouraged the Arabs in Syria and Lebanon, culturally the most advanced in the Arab world, to support the cause of sovereignty through a series of congresses, mass meetings, and public pronouncements in the name of the Beirut Committee of Reform. More covertly, the members initiated contacts with Arab leaders who had never evidenced disloyalty to the Turks but were highly respected by all Muslims because of their lineage or position. Chief of these was the family of Husayn ibn Ali, the Grand Sharif of Mecca and a descendant of the Prophet.

The C.U.P. reacted in a Hamidian manner by pretending to accept the conditions for Arab autonomy of the Beirut Committee (known as the Paris Agreement because it was drafted by an Arab Congress held in Paris in 1913 on the initiative of *Al-Fatat*). Their "acceptance" however, was drafted in typically misleading Ottoman rhetoric; in fact, a careful reading convinced the Arab nationalists that there was no intention on the Ottoman side of carrying out its terms. A number of Arab officers serving in the Ottoman armies then formed a third secret society, *Al-Ahd* (The Covenant), and swore in blood to lead an Arab military revolution against the Sultan.

The outbreak of World War I gave the Arab nationalists an opportunity to put their revolutionary plans into effect. It also multiplied their problems and deepened the gulf between Turk and Arab to a nearly unbridgeable point due largely to the normal measures taken by a nation at war and not to any nonexistent cultural or racial hostility. Djemal Pasha, third member of the C.U.P. triumvirate ruling Turkey, went to Damascus to take command of the Fourth Army which was later to be mauled by the Anglo-Arab forces of Allenby. Djemal learned from incriminating documents seized at the French consulate of the extent of the Arab conspiracy against the Empire but did not move against the nationalists at first, believing that long habit and the call for a jihad would win them over. When this did not happen, his policy changed abruptly. Arab regiments serving in the Ottoman army were broken up. Many Arab leaders were arrested; and a number were hanged, after courts-martial held in secrecy, including the Mufti of Gaza.[25] Djemal's espionage system was nearly as effective as Abdul Hamid's. The normal dislocations of war—the Allied sea blockade, financial chaos caused by speculation, widespread epidemics, and confiscation of crops and property by starving Turkish forces—added to Arab bitterness.

The major figures in the drama were Sharif Husayn of Mecca and his second and third sons, Abdullah and Faísal, on the Arab side; Sir Henry MacMahon, who replaced Kitchener as High Commissioner of Egypt in 1914, T. E. Lawrence, later Mark Sykes, and David Balfour on the British side; the French diplomat Georges Picot; and Chaim Weizmann, spokesman for the Jewish Zionist movement. The lesser figures ranged in the hundreds. From the interweaving of three major strands—Anglo-French interests, Arab ambitions, and Zionist dreams—emerged the shape of the modern Middle East, less territorially than politically and socially.

It was a shape which really satisfied none of the participants; it contributed materially to forty years of unnecessary strife, setting in motion a conflict which is still unresolved. This drama of Anglo-Arab-Jewish affairs was the greatest triumph of self-interest over enlightened statesmanship of modern times. In this light, Djemal Pasha's observation from the opposite corner—"I told him (Faisal) . . . that on the day when the Arabs severed their connection with the Turks they would fall under the yoke of the English and French and be wholly deprived of the protection of the Khalif of Islam" [26]—becomes deeply prophetic.

The flush of war, the resentment of the Arabs towards the Turks, and Western blandishments far outweighed prudence in the minds of the Hashimites and their co-conspirators, however. Statements of support even from Arab deputies in the Ottoman Parliament further convinced the rather naive Husayn that he was the rightful leader of Islam.[27] Under Abdul Hamid he had spent considerable time with his family as a "guest" in Constantinople and had succeeded to the position of Grand Sharif of

[25] Storr, Ronald, *Orientations*, London: Reader's Union, 1939, p. 351. The best account of these tangled years is still George Antonius, *The Arab Awakening*, London: Hamish Hamilton, 1938, 1945.

[26] Djemal Pasha, *op. cit.*, p. 233.

[27] In 1911 after a violent scene in Parliament, thirty-five deputies sent such a letter to Husayn. The key phrases were "We are ready to rise with you, if you wish to shake off the yoke which weighs on the Arabs . . . Those of our deputies who are sufficiently courageous to defend their nation . . . recognize you as Caliph, alone responsible for the interests of all the Arab lands." Barbour, Nevil, *Nisi Dominus*, London: Harrap, 1946, pp. 81–82.

Mecca through the Sultan's intercession. But resentment rather than gratitude was his reaction.

Husayn began a correspondence with MacMahon in 1915, and the series of guarded letters which they exchanged have become known as the Husayn-MacMahon Correspondence. They are the basis of the Arab claim that self-determination of the Arab lands of the Ottoman Empire was pledged as a precondition of the Arab entry into the war on the side of the Allies. The first letter, from Husayn, requested British acknowledgment of Arab independence within the area bounded by Mersin and Adana in the north, up to latitude 37°, to the Persian border, south to the Gulf of Basra, including all of Arabia except Aden, and west to the Red Sea. MacMahon's reply reiterated earlier British "desires" for Arab independence but said that any discussion of specific boundaries would be premature "in the heat of war." Husayn pressed the Commissioner for a more definite delineation. MacMahon's reply, after he had conferred with Whitehall, was to exclude "Mersina and Alexandretta and portions of Syria lying to the west of the districts of Damascus, Homs, Hama, and Aleppo" which "cannot be said to be purely Arab." [28] The British also reserved an interest in the vilayets of Baghdad and Basra. No specific reference was made to Palestine in the commitment, so that the Arab state envisaged by Husayn already had several holes in its fabric. The Sharif was sufficiently trustful of British integrity, however, to accept MacMahon's terms, and on this incomplete foundation proclaimed the Arab Revolt in June, 1916. The proclamation contained eleven points of accusation against the C.U.P. These ranged from the arbitrary execution of Arab leaders, confiscation of their property, etc., to misgovernment and even fundamental changes in Islamic law without proper authority.[29] Arab volunteers flocked to Faisal, whom Djemal had allowed to go to Medina from Damascus with the somewhat vague hope that his Muslim sense of duty would outweigh his Hashimite ambitions. Two Arab armies were formed—one under Husayn's eldest son, Ali; the other under Faisal. Both were advised—perhaps even led—by British officers, among them Col. T. E. Lawrence. They operated against the Turks in the Hejaz, forcing the surrender of their garrisons in Mecca and other towns except Medina. Then Faisal's army joined the main British Middle East force under General Allenby. It captured a number of towns, forcing the Turks

[28] *Hussein-MacMahon Correspondence,* Government of Great Britain, Command Papers 5957, pp. 3–8, *passim.*
[29] The full text is in Djemal Pasha, *op. cit.,* pp. 226–227.

to retreat as tribal desertions from their cause increased rapidly. On October 1, 1918, Faisal and the British jointly entered Damascus, the former leading a mounted Arab escort and dressed as an Arab desert chieftain. The remainder of Syria (including Palestine) was liberated up to Aleppo where Mustafa Kemal, transferred from Gallipoli, organized a successful Turkish rearguard action which was terminated by the signing of an Anglo-Turkish armistice at Mudros.[30]

While this rather successful military collaboration was going on, the British were active on other fronts. The India Office, independent of the Foreign Office, negotiated with Ibn Sa'ud for a pledge of either neutrality or active support; it promised him leadership of an Arab state essentially the same as the one proposed to Husayn. Secondly, the Allies (including the Russians) began to put into practice the often-discussed "final alternative" for the Ottoman Empire. This meant the assumption that it would be defeated and the subsequent division of its territory into spheres of influence. These negotiations were conducted in extreme secrecy and led to the conclusion of secret agreements for the partition of the Empire. There were four major ones. The first was the Constantinople Agreement (1915), concluded by Russia, Great Britain, and France through an exchange of notes. Russia was to annex Constantinople—a departure from previous British policy regarding Ottoman territorial integrity—to control the Straits, and to be given southern Thrace, the islands of Imbros and Tenedos, and a large section of Turkey's Black Sea coast. In return for annexation of Constantinople, the Russians were to make it a free port with freedom of navigation in the Straits. Arabia and the Holy Cities were to be placed under an independent Muslim protectorate. Persia was divided into "spheres of influence" —Russian in the north, British in the south; the Russians were granted full freedom of action in their zone. The French were to annex Syria and Cilicia.

In the same year, Britain, France, Russia, and Italy signed the Treaty of London which made concessions to Italy as her price for entering the war on the Allied side. Libya was formally transferred to Italy from the Sultan; the Dodecanese Islands off the Turkish coast, occupied by the Italians since 1912, were recognized as Italian possessions; and the Italian interest in the eastern Mediterranean was to be confirmed after the

[30] Details of these campaigns are in: Lawrence, T. E., *Revolt in the Desert* and *Seven Pillars of Wisdom;* Edmund Dane, *British Campaigns in the Nearer East,* 1914–1918; and others.

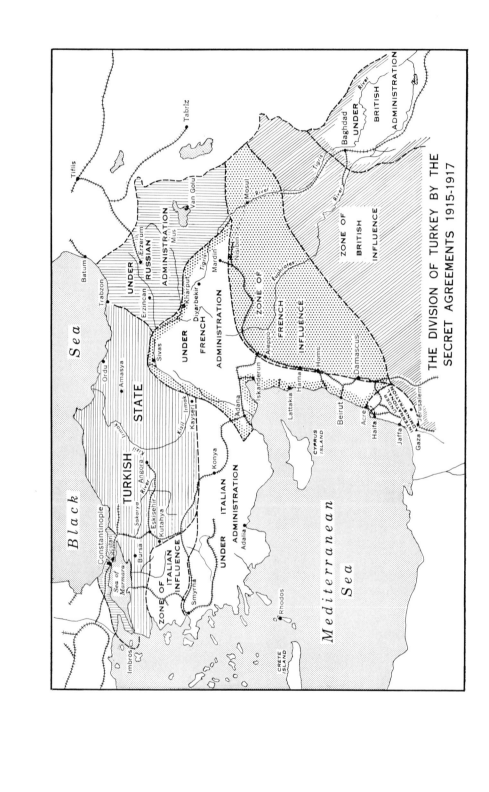

THE DIVISION OF TURKEY BY THE
SECRET AGREEMENTS 1915-1917

war by a zone of influence along the southern coast in the Antalya area.

The most famous (or notorious) of the secret agreements was the Sykes-Picot (1916). These two names, when coupled, still cause Arab nationalists to foam at the mouth; and indeed, few more blatant examples of arbitrary action exist in the annals of international relations. Britain and France setttled their claims to Ottoman territory (or would have) with Russia adhering later in a companion settlement called the Sazonov-Palaelogue Agreement (Sazonov was Foreign Minister of Russia and Palaelogue French Ambassador there at the time.) It contained the following provisions:

(1) To Russia—the vilayets of Erzerum, Trebizond, Van, Bitlis, and northern Kurdistan, all in eastern Turkey.

(2) To France—coastal Syria; Adana vilayet; Cilicia, along the Mediterranean Coast; and a large section of inner Anatolia from Ala Dag' northward to Kayseri and southeastward to Kharput–Aintab–Mardin.

(3) To Great Britain—southern Mesopotamia with Baghdad, plus Haifa and Acre in Palestine.

(4) To the Arabs—an independent state or confederation between assigned French and British territories with the reservation that inland Syria and Mosul were to be a French sphere of influence and the territory between Palestine and the Persian border a British sphere of influence.

(5) Palestine was to be placed under an international administration and Alexandretta made a free port.

The St. Jean de Maurienne Agreement, concluded in 1917, clarified the Italian right to control Antalya.

Had these four agreements been carried out, the Ottoman Empire, after its assumed defeat, would have shrunk to a small territory in north-central Anatolia, about the size and in the same location as the Hittite kingdom of 1500 B.C. The collapse of the Czarist government in 1917 negated these agreements. Not only did the Soviet government reject them, but it published their texts with all the Czarist Foreign Office archives in 1917. This is one reason why the Arabs have never fully associated Soviet Russia with imperialist policies.[31]

---

[31] Texts of the various agreements are in: Temperley, H. W. V., *A History of the Paris Peace Conference,* London: Oxford, 1920–1924; see also Howard, Harry N., *The Partition of Turkey, 1913–1923,* Norman: University of Oklahoma Press, 1931; Antonius, *op. cit.;* and others.

The third of the interlocking circles of interest working to effect a Middle Eastern settlement was Zionism. Zionism, which in its early stages was primarily a movement for the resettlement of devout Jews in colonies in Palestine, the fountainhead of Judaism. During the nineteenth century a number of these religious colonies were established there. Sir Moses Montefiore, London agent for the Rothschilds and one of twelve Jews allowed to trade on the London Exchange, was the leader of a movement to help these colonies among English Jews.[32] By 1893, in part due to these efforts but largely to the pogroms of the 1880's in Russia, about one hundred thousand Jews were living in Palestine. The Basle Conference and the work of Theodor Herzl shifted the emphasis from religion to politics.[33] Herzl laid the groundwork by holding semiofficial discussions with officials in England, Germany, and Turkey about setting up a Jewish state in Palestine. When the war broke out, Britain did not at first consider Zionist principles as worthy of recognition. The Arabs seemed a more useful ally to cultivate.

The capture of Jerusalem in 1917 had a profound effect on the British public with its long Judaeo-Christian heritage. Allenby's entry into the city was the first by a Christian conqueror since the expulsion of the Crusaders. Allenby himself was profoundly moved by the city which was so consecrated to three religions. He entered Jerusalem bareheaded, unarmed, on foot—the Caliph 'Umar had done the same as conqueror in his time, wearing sackcloth and carrying a begging bowl. British sympathy was exploited by influential Jews in England in 1915–1917 to enlist the concrete support of the British Government. The Zionist leader, Dr. Chaim Weizmann, had rendered Britain important services during the war as a chemist and had made friends in high places. Mark Sykes, secretary of the war cabinet for Middle Eastern affairs, was one of his converts. Two others were C. P. Scott, the editor of the *Manchester Guardian,* and his chief editorial writer, Herbert Sidebotham. Another was Lord Arthur J. Balfour, the Foreign Secretary. These men, although not Jews, were oriented toward the Zionist cause on grounds of idealism. Their Christian, English-school education had also taught them a sense of fair play and sympathy for the underdog. It seemed to them only right that the Jews should have their homeland back after nineteen centuries of exile.

The zenith of Zionist achievement in the field of political diplomacy

[32] Polk, Stamler, Asfour, *op. cit.,* p. 50.
[33] See Chapter 7.

was reached on November 2, 1917, with the publication of the Balfour Declaration.[34] Until the creation of Israel settled the matter, the Declaration was as vital to the Zionist cause as the Husayn-MacMahon Correspondence was to the Arabs. For each it meant support for the cause from the great power most concerned. For each it was also justification of the goal, the final rallying point in the struggle to displace the other and the British in Palestine.[35] Ironically, the Declaration is as ambiguous as the commitments which were made to Husayn.

A number of factors contributed to British willingness to make a Zionist commitment while negotiating with the Arabs. Britain preferred a Western-oriented Jewish population in the Palestine sector, part of the Suez-India lifeline complex, to the undisciplined Arabs. The financial and moral aid of world Jewry was needed in order to push the United States into the war. There was also an element of time involved; the British were afraid that Germany would beat them to the draw with a proclamation supporting a Jewish national home in Palestine. After much soul-searching, the Cabinet devised an innocuous definition which appeared to provide moral support for Zionist aspiration but which was not to be taken literally. In the Middle East, in fact, it was not even read publicly until 1919.

The Declaration, in the form of a letter to Lord Rothschild, read as follows:

> His Majesty's Government view with favor the establishment in Palestine of a National Home for the Jewish People, and will use their best endeavors to facilitate the achievement of this object, it being clearly understood that nothing shall be done which may prejudice the civil and religious rights of existing non-Jewish communities in Palestine, or the rights and political status enjoyed by Jews in any other country.[36]

The Balfour Declaration won general Zionist support for the Allies; a subsequent move by Germany and Turkey to offer Zionists in Germany a chartered Palestine settlement company failed. The other Allies approved; and just before the Armistice of Mudros, President Wilson gave America's blessing in a letter to Rabbi Stephen Wise. It was far less than Weizmann had sought. At first he wanted a British state in Palestine with home rule and unrestricted immigration. Later he reduced his goals to:

[34] In 1957, official Arab publications called attention to the fortieth anniversary of the Declaration as a black day in their history.

[35] Polk, *et al., op. cit.,* p. 61.

[36] Cmd 5479, Palestine Royal Commission, *Report,* 1937.

(1) Separate Jewish nationality in Palestine; (2) Jewish participation in local government; (3) Minority rights safeguarded; (4) Jewish autonomy in religion, education, communal organization; (5) Legal recognition of Jewish colonies; (6) A Jewish-chartered company to direct the rightful resettlement of Palestine by Jews.

It should be noted that the Balfour Declaration cancelled General Allenby's announcement to the population of Palestine after the capture of Jerusalem upholding the Arabs' right to independence and full control over Palestine, as well as the Sykes-Picot clause internationalizing Palestine. A large and influential section of British Jewry also opposed Zionism very strongly on the grounds of the designation of Palestine as *the* national Jewish homeland. Against the organized efficiency of Weizmann's group and the moral support of Cabinet Ministers, including Lloyd George himself, anti-Zionist Jews could make little headway.

The armistice of Mudros ended the independence of the Ottoman Empire. Defeated, along with Germany, the Turks could only wait for their conquerors to decide what to do with them. The Allies were in an awkward position, however, and this was largely due to Britain's three-way commitments. These were: an independent Arab state embracing all of the Arab portions of the Empire with certain strategic exceptions; a Jewish national home in Palestine; and an agreement with France (and Italy) to carve the Empire up into mandates and spheres of influence. Various other peoples, inspired by the brilliantly-enunciated Fourteen Points of President Wilson, made their way to the peace table and wangled other commitments. The most concrete of these was an independent Armenia. The Allies behaved like sleepwalkers throughout the Peace Conference. The desire of the Arab nationalists for independence quickly coalesced in the Arab kingdom of Syria under Amir Faisal but which lasted only for a few months in 1920 before the French overthrew it. Previously the sending of the American King-Crane Commission to the Middle East to determine the feelings of the people, had revealed the depth of anti-imperialist sentiment in the area. If the Arabs could not have their own monarchy, the King-Crane Report revealed, they would prefer a mandate under the United States, with a British mandate a second choice, and a French mandate not at all. Moving blithely ahead at San Remo in 1920, the Allies set up a Class A mandates for Syria, Lebanon, Palestine, and Iraq; ignored the King-Crane report; and divided up the Ottoman Empire in a fashion which was to bring them unending headaches in the ensuing forty years.

Having been the focal point of early Arab nationalism, Syrian leaders hoped, and even assumed, that the promised independent Arab state would be essentially theirs, with other noncontiguous Arab regions free to join. The Syrian Congress of 1920 in Damascus called for a constitutional monarchy under Amir Faisal. Yet Faisal, who was the symbol of Syrian national aspirations, realized the unworkability of an independent Arab state as long as Britain and France evinced a determination to maintain trusteeship over the Arab portions of the Ottoman Empire. He concluded an agreement with Clemenceau early in 1920 which seemed to strike a balance between French and Arab nationalist claims. France guaranteed Syrian independence; Faisal agreed to accept French assistance. Arabic and French were recognized as joint official languages. The Lebanese, who had already expressed their desire for sovereignty outside of the Syrian state, were so recognized by both parties. The Druze were to be autonomous within Syria. With this in hand, Faisal returned to Damascus, at least reasonably confident of French reliability. On March 7 he was proclaimed King of Syria, and the Syrian Congress declared the country an independent constitutional monarchy. Lebanon refused to accept Faisal, largely due to the fears of Lebanese Christians of submersion in a holy Sharifian Muslim state. Instead, leaders of the various religious communities declared Lebanon's independence with tacit French approval.[37] Henceforth the two Levantine states were to pursue parallel but divergent courses of political development.

Faisal's moderate course between the reefs of French ambition and the shoals of nationalist truculence solved nothing. The die was already cast. At the Conference of San Remo, April 26, 1920, the Allied Powers approved British mandates over Palestine and Iraq and French mandates over Syria and Lebanon. Britain moved more cautiously, and perhaps moderately, to establish her mandates although the later uprising of the Iraqi nationalists was to be handled ruthlessly; and because they form part of the unified political development of Iraq and Palestine, these mandates are considered elsewhere in this text. But France had other plans.

French General Gouraud, commanding the forces in Beirut, moved first to abolish the Council governing Lebanon, which had opted for full independence following Faisal's investiture. He then sent an ultimatum to Faisal demanding that Syria accept the mandate, disband the army,

[37] General Gouraud in 1920 announced the independence of "Greater Lebanon," comprising the districts of the Biqa', Tyre, Sidon, and Tripoli.

and scrap the elements of government built up over a painful period of months. French troops easily defeated a hastily-assembled militia near Damascus. Faisal telegraphed European leaders asking them to intervene, but he received no support from that quarter. His own subjects, notably the Congress, felt that he had sold them out, and there were ugly demonstrations. Irony pursued Faisal to the end of his Syrian days. The telegram he sent Gouraud accepting the French demands was not received in time to prevent French troops from shedding unnecessary blood. At the end of July, Faisal left Syria for Iraq, where he found a new kingdom under British supervision waiting for him. What Syria's future would have been under Faisal, as a constitutional monarchy, belongs in the sphere of chimerical speculation, but the brief span of the Syrian Kingdom suggests that without outside interference Faisal and his ministers would have succeeded. The Arab administration operating from a base of strong political conviction bolstered by patriotism, stabilized the government, set up the nucleus of an army, and even wrote a constitution.[38]

THE FRENCH MANDATES

The postwar political insecurity (almost a phobia) of Syria and the religious imbroglios of Lebanon can be attributed almost exclusively to French policy under the mandates. The formal internationalized terms of the mandatory agreements were harmless enough. Organic laws were to be prepared for both mandates within three years. Local autonomy was encouraged and the interests of minority groups protected with due reference to the majority. French and Arabic were designated twin official languages. The Capitulations were ended although traces of them continued up to World War II. The mandatory power reserved to itself control of foreign relations and the right to keep military forces in both states, for defense, but agreed to train the Syrians and the Lebanese for self-government, in accordance with Article 22 of the Covenant of the League of Nations. It was the French interpretation of the *spirit* of the mandate which led the Levant into uncertainty instead of toward the sure ground of political education. In Lebanon, French policy reinforced the religious divisions transferring them into national politics; in Syria, France built up separate administrative enclaves, with the adage *divide et impera* very much in mind.

[38] See Longrigg, S., *Syria and Lebanon under French Mandate,* London: Oxford University Press, 1958, pp. 102–105, for a complete discussion of the short-lived Syrian kingdom of Damascus.

The Mandate Over Lebanon. Lebanon enjoyed better luck as a mandate than Syria by a narrow margin. The irony of their situation was not lost on the Lebanese. With one hand, Gouraud decreed the independence of Greater Lebanon; and with the other, he placed it under French protection. The old Christian districts were combined with Muslim ones. Four *sanjaqs* were created—North Lebanon, Mount Lebanon, South Lebanon, and the Biqa'—with the cities of Beirut and Tripoli given independent status. The whole was governed by a French official and an Advisory Council nominated by the High Commissioner. The Maronites were pro-French, but they were merely the largest single Christian group. Tripoli, predominantly Muslim, had little in common with Beirut, where Christians encircle the Muslim *Basta* (quarter). In the Biqa', Druze, Sunni, and Mutawalli villagers were twice the number of Christians. In Tyre and Sidon, Christians numbered two-fifths of the population. The old Ottoman sanjaq of Mount Lebanon had been a solid Christian bloc; the new Lebanon was hopelessly mixed, with a basic Christian-Muslim antipathy which had burgeoned as the Muslims developed political awareness. The Muslims were apathetic but developed increasing antipathy to France after the expulsion of Faisal in 1920 and particularly from the crushing of the 1925 Syrian revolt. The close-knit nature of Lebanese families and the large loyal followings of various tribal and village *shaykhs* were responsible for the expansion of personal feuds into national, and eventually international, Lebanese politics. The Ottoman period, when the villages were shut off by themselves and were unconcerned with urban problems, began to seem halcyon indeed.

Lebanon became a republic in 1926; and a French-sponsored constitution set up a Western parliamentary structure with a president, a cabinet, and a single-chamber parliament. (It was a two-chamber legislature at first.)[39] Article 30 stated specifically Lebanon's dependent relationship with France under the mandate. Lebanon's foreign relations were in French hands until after World War II. In fact, France reserved to itself control of military and defense matters and internal security as well, leaving a minimum of self-government in Lebanese hands. The Lebanese constitution (drawn up by a French commission) emphasized religion in internal politics by stating (Article 95) that representation in parliament and the cabinet should be based on religious confession. Considerable authority was given to the Lebanese President, subject always to the final decision of the French High Commissioner. The Constitu-

[39] Lenczowski, George, *The Middle East in World Affairs,* 2nd ed., Ithaca: Cornell University Press, 1956, p. 268.

tion was twice amended, notably in 1929 to give the President a six-year term and authority to dissolve Parliament if the Cabinet agreed.

In 1932, after three years of increasing political anarchy as government after government failed to embark on an effective administrative program, it was suspended by High Commissioner Ponsot. The "temporary regime" that followed made a start toward solving the political and economic problems of the state. Three serious strikes, part economic and part political in motivation, took place in 1935. Although they did not participate in the strikes, Lebanon's young men of the 1930's were groping toward some form of political action which would express their feelings about the mandate and the *beni-oui-oui's* [40] that ran it for the French. Several political organizations were founded, the first being the Syrian National Party, a secret society until 1935 but after that a genuine political organization with branches in Syria, Palestine, and Egypt. The Syrian National Party and its founder, Anton Sa'ada, a Christian, stood for a unified *Syrian* nation. It would abolish the confessional system, establish a unified Arab state centered around Syria with local autonomy (including Lebanese) excluded, and expel all traces of foreign influence. When it appeared publicly it had 8,000 members and was organized along Nazi standards, from the top downwards. The members even wore brown shirts in parades.

The Phalanges Libanaises, which grew out of the Party of Lebanese Unity, were paramilitary in nature, dominated by Maronites, and led by Pierre Jumayyil, a member of an important Lebanese family. Their interest was in conserving Lebanese unity. In the largely Muslim cities and in the Basta, the Phalanges were rivaled by the Najjada, an all-Muslim, politico-military organization dedicated even in the late 1930's to Arab nationalism.

A new Lebanese constitution was drawn up by the High Commissioner, Count de Martel, in 1934, in response to these varying pressures. It permitted parliamentary representation to the professions (which helped equalize, though it did not solve, the imbalance of feudal landlords and family leaders). The executive was strengthened, in line with French interest in developing a corporate state rather than republican institutions. Freedom of worship was not mentioned, so in practice the Turkish millet system was retained. Between 1937 and 1939, the High Commissioner dissolved the paramilitary organizations. They had been

[40] A term coined by Muslims in Algeria to describe their co-religionists who cooperated with, and served under, the French. Lit. "yes-yes-men."

permitted by the decree accompanying the 1934 constitution to function as athletic clubs; but like the German groups they were modeled upon, they had developed an increasingly anti-French militaristic appearance. The Popular Front Government of Leon Blum, through the High Commissioner, negotiated in 1936 a treaty with Lebanon which established a bargaining ground for future independence, although it closed the door on any reunification with Syria. The treaty was not ratified by the French National Assembly, as the government changed and France became seriously alarmed over resurgent German militarism. In 1937, the original constitution of 1926 was reinstated, and a new electoral law permitted parliamentary elections on the basis of two-thirds religious sectarianism and one-third direct nomination. With little change in its confused factionalist internal politics, Lebanon drifted toward World War II and eventual independence.

The Syrian Mandate. Syria fared less happily during the twenty years of the mandate. The more or less unified kingdom of Faisal disintegrated under French intransigence, and the nationalist movement lost much of its enthusiasm as San Remo's terms were translated into occupation. General Gouraud, who mistakenly viewed himself as another Lyautey,[41] divided Syria into four separate administrative units. Counting Lebanon, they were Aleppo, Damascus, and Lattakia. This cheerful fragmentation, as time proved, "ignored the basic facts of Syrian ethnography and culture and the strength and convictions of the majority community."[42] The Jabal Druze, the mountainous territory of the Druze sect, was formed into a separate unit in 1922 under a local governor elected from the influential al-Atrash family, and the Druze were permitted local autonomy as well as their traditional right of carrying arms. The 'Alawis (Nusayris), a distinct Muslim sect dominant around the tobacco port of Lattakia, were also organized separately and detached from Syria under their own statute with a governor responsible to the High Commissioner only. Like the Druze, the 'Alawi had their secret, esoteric rites and a feudal structure which their separate status merely intensified. Finally, the sanjaq of Alexandretta in the north, with a 40 per cent Turkish minority, was reconstituted in 1924 as an autonomous enclave within Aleppo.

[41] Marshal Lyautey, administrator of Morocco under the French Protectorate from 1912 to 1920, is the prototype of the "enlightened" French administrator, in that he recognized the right to existence of a native culture without arbitrarily trying to remake it into a French culture.

[42] Longrigg, *op. cit.,* p. 117.

In 1925, General Weygand, Gouraud's successor, was himself succeeded as High Commissioner by General Sarrail, who proceeded to antagonize nearly every faction in Syria. The four "submandates" were replaced by the unified vilayet of Aleppo-Damascus (Syria), while the 'Alawis and the Druze continued in their isolation. But the Druze, innately suspicious of all governmental rule, resented French appointment of governors. The Druze leaders also objected to well-meaning efforts to improve their lot by road-building, new schools (under Catholic teachers), a revised land-tenure system, all tending to reduce feudalism.[43] When a delegation of Druze chiefs waited on Sarrail to ask for less centralization, it was summarily arrested. The angry Druze rebelled and quite unexpectedly defeated a strong French column. Although this success did not provoke a general uprising, resistance developed in scattered parts of Syria. French forces bombarded Damascus, exiled a number of Druze families to Transjordan, and dealt ruthlessly with villages identified with rebel activity. Even so, order was not restored fully for two years. Sarrail's tactless actions (he had refused to attend the traditional recognition of him by the Maronite community in Beirut as the Protector of Christians in the Levant) and dictatorial impatience sparked the uprising; but the general nature of French policy—centralized control, division of the mandates, rejection of the mandate theory—was the main cause. The results were negative. No Syrian national consciousness sufficiently strong to force France to acknowledge it emerged, and the French, on their side, became more unpopular than ever.

In 1930 the new High Commissioner, Ponsot, announced by decree a Syrian constitution, which gave Syria control over its internal but not external affairs. Elections held in 1932 resulted in a majority for the "moderates," with the National Bloc winning one-quarter of the seats. Haqqi al-'Azm was named Prime Minister. In 1936, France signed a treaty with Syria similar to the one made with Lebanon and modeled on the Anglo-Iraqi Treaty of 1930. A "close alliance" officially replaced the mandate, to run for twenty-five years after Syria's admission to the League. Military and defense prerogatives for France were maintained. Economic aid and technical assistance from France would continue. The Jabal Druze and 'Alawi region were both exempted in the treaty from inclusion in the Syrian state, under their own special regimes.

The Sanjaq of Alexandretta was not specifically exempted from possible inclusion in an independent Syria, nor was it even mentioned in the

[43] For the first time in the sect's history, taxes were collected in full. See Bouron, *Les Druzes,* Paris, 1930, for a general summary of conditions in the Jabal Druze.

1936 treaty. This caused some alarm in Ankara, where the feeling was that negotiations with independent Syria over the status of the Sanjaq's Turks was quite another thing from the protection afforded them by the French mandate. The deteriorating world situation made France doubtful of the treaty principle of transition to independence; also a Turkish ally seemed preferable to an Arab contingent which had already bitten the hand that fed it and which would probably do so again if given its way. The evidence of short-term thinking on the part of French leaders is inescapable. But as is so often true of political problems in the Middle East, there was no simple solution. Ethnically mixed, neatly balanced between Arab and Turk, an area strategically vital since Alexandretta is the only choice port on the eastern Mediterranean, the Sanjaq represented the international pressures that determine action in the Middle East all too often. Like Cyprus in 1960, the Sanjaq's people were divided down the middle; again like Cyprus, the major powers concerned began with a grant of separate political status with internal autonomy. The Cyprus of 1962 has become an independent republic, limited only by the presence of Greek, Turkish, and British troops as a protective measure. The Sanjaq received a constitution as a separate demilitarized territory in 1937. Special safeguards were included in the Statute of the Sanjaq for the Turkish population, which alarmed the Arabs, and communal strife became general during 1937–1938. The 1938 elections, supervised by France and Turkey, produced a government that was dominated by the Turks. The Turkish Government, for the first time since the War of Independence, pressed irredentist claims. The elected Assembly changed the name to the Republic of the Hatay and swiftly Turkicized its administration; Turkish legal, fiscal, and legislative procedures were adopted. The last act in the drama was played out in mid-1939. France and Turkey signed a pact of mutual assistance which contained a section ceding the Hatay to Turkey. Unrecognized by Syria even today,[44] the Hatay became a Turkish vilayet—the price of a wartime ally.

RECOMMENDED READINGS

1. Alderson, A. D., *Structure of the Ottoman Dynasty*, London: Oxford, 1956.

[44] See Avedis Sanjian, "The Sanjak of Alexandretta, 1939–1956," *Middle East Journal*, Autumn, 1956, for a fairly recent appraisal. Not long after the merger of Egypt and Syria into The United Arab Republic, Syrian leaders called for the return of the Sanjak, and received the same stony-faced answer as before from the Turks.

2. Antonius, George, *The Arab Awakening*, London: Hamish Hamilton, 1938.
3. Baker, Robert L., *Blood, Oil and Sand*, New York: Appleton-Century, Inc., 1942.
4. Bonne, Alfred, ed., *State and Economics in the Middle East*, London: Routledge, 1955.
5. Bullard, Sir Reader, *Britain and the Middle East*, New York: Longmans, Green & Co., Inc., 1951.
6. Cooke, Hedley V., *Challenge and Response in the Middle East*, New York: Harper & Brothers, 1952.
7. Emin, Ahmed (Yalman), *Turkey in The World War*, New Haven: Yale University Press, 1930.
8. Fisher, Sydney, ed., *Social Forces in the Middle East*, Ithaca: Cornell U. Press, 1955.
9. ——— *The Middle East: A History*, New York: Alfred A. Knopf, Inc., 1959.
10. Gibb, H. A. R., & Bowen, R., *Islamic Society and The West*, Vol. I, Part I, London: Oxford, 1950.
11. Howard, Harry N., *The Partition of Turkey, 1913–23*, Norman: University of Oklahoma Press, 1931.
12. Kedourie, Elie, *England and The Middle East*, London: Bowes & Bowes, 1956.
13. Kirk, George, *A Short History of the Middle East*, rev. ed., New York: Frederick A. Praeger, Inc., 1955.
14. Kohn, Hans, *Nationalism and Imperialism in the Near East*, London: Routledge, 1932.
15. Lawrence, T. E., *Seven Pillars of Wisdom*, London: J. Cape, 1935.
16. Lenczowski, George, *The Middle East in World Affairs*, 2nd ed., Ithaca: Cornell University Press, 1956.
17. Moorehead, Alan, *Gallipoli*, New York: Harper & Brothers, 1956.
18. Marriott, J. A. R., *The Eastern Question*, Oxford: Clarendon Press, 1917.
19. Ramsaur, E. E., *The Young Turks and the Revolution of 1908*, Princeton: Princeton University Press, 1957.
20. Spector, Ivar, *The Soviet Union and The Muslim World, 1917–56*. Seattle: University of Washington Press, 1938.
21. Storrs, Sir Ronald, *Orientations*, London: Nicholson and Watson, 1937.
22. Temperley, H. V., *A History of the Paris Peace Conference*, London: Oxford, 1920–24.
23. Toynbee, A. J., *The Western Question in Greece and Turkey*, London: Constable, 1922.
24. Webster, Sir Charles, *The Foreign Policy of Palmerston, 1830–41*, London: G. Bell, 1951.

CHAPTER 3

THE REPUBLIC OF TURKEY

$\mathcal{T}$ $\hslash\varepsilon$ demise of the Ottoman Empire was made certain by World War I. The Turkish field commanders stated their views firmly to their government: peace on the best possible terms, since total defeat was at hand. The Sultan, Mehmed VI Vahdettin (1910–1922), bowing to the military will, sent representatives to treat with the British. On October 30th, 1918, the Turks signed the Armistice of Mudros, by a twist of irony on H.M.S. Agamemnon, in Mudros harbor. The unlucky Young Turk chiefs fled in several directions, Talaat to assassination later in Berlin, Djemal to write his memoirs from a discreet distance, and the evil genius Enver to meet his death fighting the Bolsheviks near Bukhara in a characteristically mad Pan-Turkish venture. The Young Turk legacy was mainly one of disaster and destruction, yet it presented more realistic Turkish Nationalists with an unexpected opportunity to build again on a *tabula rasa*.[1]

In the early period of its rule, the C.U.P. introduced, albeit timidly and temporarily, the principles of multi-party democracy.[2] After 1913 they returned to autocracy. As a result the handful of young officers who basically sought no less than a Turkish national revival were helpless. The peace settlement with the humiliating terms of the Treaty of Sèvres, was a second example of good fortune derived from bad; it "forcibly homogenized the Turkish nation, and thus permitted a sense

---

[1] See Frey, F. W., "Arms and the Men in Turkish Politics," *Land Reborn* (American Christian Palestine Committee), August, 1960, a good article on the subject.
[2] Karpat, Kemal, *Turkey's Politics,* Princeton: Princeton University Press, 1959, pp. 30 ff.

of national identity to spread through the people." [3] Allied behavior toward the defeated Ottomans was not calculated to win friends or influence Anatolia but it did not need to. First British and then French troops debarked at Constantinople in a thinly disguised "occupation." The French commander, Franchet d'Esperey, rode a white horse into the capital in imitation of Mehmed II. But worse was to follow. The Greek Prime Minister, Venizelos, presented Greece's claim to territory in western Turkey, based on Lloyd George's wartime commitments, to the peace conference sitting at Paris. The Allies accepted, and in 1919 Greek troops landed in Smyrna (Izmir). With British, French, and Italian forces jockeying for position in Anatolia, the truncated Ottoman heartland had no further excuse to exist as a state, although Sultan Vahdettin still governed in meaningless ostentation in Constantinople. The Greek landings, and the subsequent Greek advance eastward to occupy more of Anatolia in the "interest of preserving order," fused the smoldering resentment of the Turks towards their conquerors. Foreign occupation of the inviolate homeland was bad enough, but occupation by the Greeks, their former subjects, was unendurable. Protest meetings, bitter but still nonviolent, were held in the cities, while bands of ex-soldiers took to the hills to oppose the Greeks as guerrillas. But the resentment was unorganized and ill-directed. The Allies continued to deal with the Sultan and in 1920 compelled the Porte to sign the Treaty of Sèvres. Few treaties have imposed such harsh terms on a defeated nation. The Straits were to be neutralized and managed by a permanent Allied commission. Eastern Anatolia was divided between independent Kurdistan and an independent Armenia. Smyrna and its hinterland almost to the Sakarya River and Thrace passed to Greece. Southwestern Anatolia around the bay of Antalya was ceded to Italy, while France received Cilicia. Britain, having been given a free hand in Mesopotamia, Palestine, and Transjordan, made no direct claims to Anatolia, but insisted on insertion of a clause requiring the Turks to surrender Constantinople if they were adjudged guilty of bad behavior toward their remaining minorities. The once-proud Ottomans were reduced to Constantinople and northern Anatolia, a territory little larger than Osman's fief.[4]

The combination of Greek aggrandizement and the terms of Sèvres

[3] Frey, *ibid.*
[4] Lewis, Geoffrey, *Turkey*, New York: Frederick A. Praeger, Inc., 1955, p. 63. The full text of the treaty is in Hurewitz, J. C., *Diplomacy in the Near and Middle East*, Vol. II, Princeton: D. Van Nostrand Co., Inc., 1956, pp. 81–89.

aroused the Turkish nationalists. Political activity became intense; meetings of patriotic societies formed to defend Turkish interests and became as common as they were secret. One of the first, the Ottoman Defence Committee of Thrace had as its main goal to keep Thrace Turkish, but it and other groups were shortly inspired by a Turkish patriot whose aims were much higher than mere regional protectionism.

THE TURKISH REVOLUTION

The Turkish patriot who gave direction and leadership to the Nationalist cause was Mustafa Kemal. Few men have been so badly misjudged initially by their opponents, especially the British, who had observed his military skill at Gallipoli.[5] Yet the British leaders who dealt with the developing situation in Turkey showed no more political acumen toward Mustafa Kemal than those Arabists who preferred Sharif Husayn over Ibn Saʿud. They continued to work with the Sultan as the sole personage who could revive the defeated Turks; and Vahdettin trusted nobody. In 1919 the Sultan ordered Mustafa Kemal to Samsun as Inspector General of the Third Army there; his responsibility was to maintain order. The Sultan regarded him as a too-popular malcontent, although untainted by political affiliations; it was always possible that the war hero might capitalize on his popularity to seize power. It seemed

[5] *The London Times*, May 22, 1920, commented, "Mustapha Kemal is no Hotspur, and his rabble lacks cohesion."

Mustafa Kemal speaking to villagers. (Courtesy Turkish Press Attache)

safer to post him to remoter places. The maneuver recoiled on the Sultan, however. Mustafa Kemal made contact with patriotic groups soon after reaching Samsun. He found in Anatolia a downtrodden peasant population with reserves of fortitude and even self-respect unsuspected by anyone. The Allies assumed that the meek plasticity of the Sultan represented the entire Turkish people. Mustafa Kemal showed them their error. The various Associations for the Defense of Rights (*Müdafaa-i Hukuk Cemiyetleri*) merged under his leadership into two groups dedicated to "self-defense against foreign occupation, opposition to territorial succession, and preservation of individual rights,"[6] one in Thrace, the other in the Eastern provinces, and then into one Nationalist group. Word of Kemal's activities reached Constantinople early in 1919; the Sultan's War Ministry sent a telegram ordering him to desist, which was ignored, and another ordering him home, which he countered by resigning. From that time until the Nationalist Congress gave him a new commission he remained in mufti.

Two nationalist conventions in the same year, at Erzurum and Sivas, set the tone for the Turkish liberation. A number of concepts were expressed in the form of a national pact (*Milli Misak*). The pact, which was accepted by the House of Deputies convened in 1920 under the authority of the anti-imperialist faction, declared that Turkey was a sovereign, indissoluble state. It rejected all foreign mandates and such privileges as the Capitulations. It insisted on Turkish supervision of the Straits.[7] The Sultan meanwhile had fallen under the Allied thumb, even to concluding a secret agreement accepting a British mandate over Turkey. Mustafa Kemal was denounced as a rebel; the deportation of a number of nationalist deputies and intellectuals to Malta aroused barely a ripple[8] in the capital. The elderly Mehmed VI Vahdettin occupied his last years on the Ottoman throne in a furious attempt to marry the eighteen-year-old daughter of a palace gardener, and add her to his harem. His last two "actions" were to condemn Kemal to death, and sign the Treaty of Sèvres. The nationalists, operating by then from the inland citadel of Angora (Ankara) had no intention of accepting the terms of Sèvres. The Grand National Assembly declared that all treaties and agreements made by the Sublime Porte after 1920 were

[6] Karpat, *op. cit.*, p. 35 n.
[7] The text is in Hurewitz, *op. cit.*, pp. 74–75; *see also* Lewis, *op. cit.*, pp. 58–59.
[8] See Yalman, Ahmed Emin, *Turkey in My Time,* Norman: University of Oklahoma Press, 1956, Chapter 9.

null and void. Thus there were two governments operating in Turkey. The odds at first favored the duly recognized imperial government. Imperial troops fought pitched battles with Kemal's nationalists. But Kemal had certain advantages in the contest to determine who would speak for Turkey. He had in inner Anatolia reserves of manpower, the same human fodder which had carried uncomplainingly the burden of imperial militarism for many centuries. He had a vast area to maneuver in and interior lines of communication. He had a well-organized supply system —munitions and weapons stolen from Allied dumps in Constantinople were concealed in Black Sea fishing boats, carried up to Samsun, disassembled, and carried over the Pontic Mountains piece by piece on human backs to Angora. The nationalists were further blessed by Allied disunity, and by the active cooperation of the Russian Soviets in their rear. Finally, they were fighting with the determination born of despair. Wilson's Fourteen Points had been seized on as a gospel by many subject peoples: the Turks, overlords for so many years, but shamed by their backwardness, seized on Wilsonian slogans with a passion. The Nationalists under Kemal and his commanders had to battle on several fronts in addition to their abbreviated contest with the Sultan's forces. In the first phase of their struggle guerrilla leaders like Osman Aga, a feudal chief from Giresun on the Black Sea who had been permitted to keep his private army by the last two Sultans in return for allegiance,[9] carried the burden of warfare against the Greeks. As the Nationalist Army grew stronger through its well-organized supply system, its leadership, and its morale, guerrilla tactics were replaced by regular warfare. Some of the guerrilla units were absorbed, but Çerkes Ethem, the most effective guerrilla leader, refused to put his "mobile forces" under Ismet (Inönü), Mustafa Kemal's chief of staff. The regulars had to fight Ethem in addition to the foreign occupation forces and the Sultan's army; when the guerrilla leader's forces were defeated he joined the Greeks. The Greek army then advanced, believing the Turks too disorganized to make a stand, but Ismet defeated them at Inönü near Eskişehir, thereby driving them back, while earning a brigadiership and a name which was to suit him when the Turks all were required to take last names.

The progress of the war of liberation was attended by many heroic episodes which are effectively described in the books of eyewitnesses

---

[9] See Yalman, *op. cit.*, pp. 118–119, who tells an amusing story of the Aga's methods in dealing with the Greeks.

as well as participants.[10] Aintab, in southeastern Anatolia, was besieged by 12,000 French troops for ten months before lack of food and water forced its inhabitants to yield. The Grand National Assembly renamed the whole town Gaziantep (Defender of the faith of Aintab), and Gaziantep holds a position in Turkish mythology comparable to Lidice and Malta in other cultures. The Soviets were the first to enter into agreements with Kemal's government as the lawful authority in Turkey; the French followed. Material from Soviet Russia helped bolster the Nationalists against the Greeks. Not bothering to read the British papers (which had accepted at face value such Greek reports as "the Nationalists have everywhere been repudiated by the Muslim population";[11] Ismet's forces retreated slowly beyond the Sakarya River, then turned, and in a great three-day battle routed the Greeks. Mustafa Kemal, appointed Commander in Chief by a reluctant assembly, inspired the Turks with a famous "no further inch of Turkish ground is to be given up.". . . (Order of the Day.) A year later the Nationalists advanced again, refusing to accept any Allied mediation until the hated Greeks had been driven from Anatolia. This time the Greek army broke and fled; the survivors reached safety aboard Greek ships in Smyrna harbor a little ahead of the Turks. The city was thoroughly pillaged, and a fire of undetermined origin gutted most of it. The victors then moved toward Thrace to deal with a Greek army there. Between them and Thrace was a neutral zone held by British forces under General Harington. Slowly the Turks advanced, but before any more war could develop, an armistice was hastily signed at Mudanya between the Allies and the Nationalists (October 11, 1922). The armistice represented de facto recognition of the Nationalists and the National Pact and negated the terms of Sèvres.

Mustafa Kemal's military victories were now brought before the conference table for translation into political success. The Lausanne Conference was called in November, 1922, and the Allies sent invitations to both his and the Sultan's government. The nightmare of diplomats,

[10] See Halide Edib, *Turkey's Ordeal*, N. Y., 1928; Ann Bridge, *The Dark Moment* (A fictional account); Halide Edib, *Memoirs*, 1926; Cebesoy, Ali Fuad, *Milli Mucadele Hatiralari* (Recollections of the Liberation War), Istanbul, 1953, 1956; Karabekir, Kazim, *Isiklal Harbimizir Esaslari* (Foundation of our War of Liberation), Istanbul, 1951; Toynbee, *The Western Question in Greece and Turkey*, N. Y., 1922, all *passim*.
[11] Lewis, *op. cit.*, p. 63.

negotiations with two duly recognized governments, did not occur. Instead, the Grand National Assembly in Ankara unilaterally abolished the Sultanate as an usurpation of the sovereign rights of the Turkish nation. Mehmed VI Vahdettin left Turkey on a British warship; a new Caliph (but not Sultan), Abdulmecid, replaced him. The negotiations at Lausanne were carried on between equal sovereign states, Turkey on one side, Britain, France, Italy, Japan, Greece, Romania, and Yugoslavia on the other. They were characterized by the stubborn resistance of Ismet, now Turkey's Foreign Minister. He argued any concession which seemed to threaten Turkey's newly won self-respect. Finally, on July 24th, 1923, the Treaty of Lausanne was signed. It upheld all of Turkey's demands. Turkey's boundary with Greece was the Maritza River (except for a small enclave to the west of the river as reparations). The Greek and Turkish populations of Turkey and Greece respectively, were to be exchanged, except for the Greek minority in Constantinople and the Turks of western Thrace.[12]

The Straits were demilitarized—navigation conditions were to be settled in a later convention. The Capitulations were abolished. Foreign troops were to be withdrawn from Turkish soil. Except for the Iraq frontier, which was delimited later in an agreement with Great Britain, and the Hatay, the Turkish state was reconstituted in its present compact form. A number of reasons accounted for the Nationalist success in resuscitating a beaten nation. Certainly the leadership of Kemal was of vital importance; the military hero made enemies and even detractors when he stepped into parliamentary debate, but his singleness of purpose and forceful personality reconciled diverse elements into a smoothly functioning movement. The foreign occupations, notably the Greek, and the humiliation of Sèvres stirred up nearly all Turks. But in the final analysis it was the strict limits placed on Turkish goals that facilitated the Nationalist success. Unity of a homogeneous Turkish population, without territorial ambitions, was their aim. In forty years of republican rule Turkey has never really abandoned that standard.

[12] This exchange was conducted smoothly on the whole, but in view of the deep-rooted attachment (of generations) of the two peoples to their foster-land, their arrival among their compatriots was as refugees in a hostile land. They could hardly understand their native tongue, for example. See Elias Venezis, *Beyond the Aegean*, New York: The Viking Press, Inc., 1956, a fictionalized study of Greek families in Anatolia. The standard reference is Stephen P. Ladas, *The Exchange of Minorities; Bulgaria, Greece, and Turkey,* New York: The Macmillan Co., 1932.

THE REFORMS OF ATATURK

The infant Turkish republic which Mustafa Kemal had delivered by rough surgery was largely a political revolutionary innovation, at least for the Turks. The clan of Ertoghrul and Osman was a compact, disciplined unit of population when it settled in Anatolia, but there were other Turkish clans too, Sélcuk, Karamanli, Oghuz, to name a few. During the imperial period the Ottomans were the "elite," specialized "upper crust"; the very word "Turk" was a term of contempt, applied to boors, commoners, and the Anatolian peasants. The large Greek, Armenian, and Kurdish minorities presented an initial obstacle to ethnic religious homogeneity which was solved largely by mass exchanges; the Armenians were mostly gone after 1916 and the Greeks after 1922. But the national revolution, in Kemal's view, required not only the end of foreign control and a homogeneous Turkish population, but a total break with outmoded social institutions, to succeed. To this end he bent the entire vigor of his personality.

The Grand National Assembly was convened in 1923, during the negotiations at Lausanne, and the League for the Defence of Rights in Anatolia, the modus operandi of the nationalist movement which included a majority of deputies, transformed itself into the Peoples Republican Party (Cumhuriyet Halk Firkasi).[13] There was a split in views between Kemal's group, which favored modernization, and the conservatives, who supported Turkish progress but felt this should properly be done under the Caliph as leader since the Caliphate and the government were inseparable. In order to undertake political reforms, Mustafa Kemal "encouraged" the Assembly to dissolve itself after the two groups had reached a procedural deadlock. Then he proposed that it be reconstituted as the Assembly of a Republic, headed by a President to be elected by the Deputies, with a constitutional amendment to that effect. This was accepted and he was elected as Turkey's first Republican President by a vote of 158–0 (the rest of the 287 delegates abstained).[14] He then named Ismet Inönü as prime minister. The G.N.A. then voted to transfer the capital from Istanbul (Constantinople) to Angora (Ankara). This symbolized the determination of the Nationalists to start afresh; the Assembly also realized that the remaining anti-Nationalist

[13] A political party with a nine-point platform prepared by Mustafa Kemal.
[14] See Lewis, *op. cit.*, pp. 74–78; Webster, Donald, *The Turkey of Ataturk,* Philadelphia: American Academy of Political and Social Science. 1939, pp. 103 ff.

Turkish groups were concentrated in the old capital. Another irritation present there was the person of the Caliph. Abdulmecid took his new job seriously; he even made noises in the direction of acquiring real power. Furthermore, many ordinary people who did not care beans whether they were ruled by a sultan or a president so long as he was a Turk, cared very much about the Caliph of Islam. Mustafa Kemal attacked the Caliphate, in speech after speech, not in terms of its meaning for Turks, but as something grafted onto Islam from outside, and possessing no present value. He claimed that the flower of Anatolia had been cut down fighting foolish wars of religion in far-off lands. Even these strong arguments might not have swayed the assembly, but fortunately for Kemal, the Aga Khan, leader of the Ismaili sect, who resided in India, intervened. He wrote to Ismet Inönü, urging the necessity of invigorating the Caliphate as a pillar of the Turkish state. Since the Aga was not an Orthodox Muslim in the eyes of the Turks, but the head of a heretical body, his argument had the opposite effect intended, and antagonized the Deputies as an infringement on Turkish privileges. On March 3, 1924, the Assembly agreed with Kemal to abolish the Caliphate and expel Abdulmecid. The Law of Unification of Instruction brought all educational establishments, secular and theological, under direct government control. A *Dijanet Isleri* (Directorate of Religious Affairs) superseded the Ottoman Ministry of *şeriat* and *Evkafs*, likewise centralizing administration of shari'a and of the Pious and Charitable Foundations (*Evkafs-'Wakfs'*, in Turkish). With the swiftness which was to characterize most of his reforms, Mustafa Kemal swept away an institution which had occupied the central position in Islam, for all but the first decades of its existence, some 1300 years.[15] Within six months Turkey moved from a theocratic state to a quasi-republican status, albeit on one man's initiative and under his terms.

The Assembly next adopted a new constitution which, with amendments, remained on force until suspended by the military coup d'etat of May, 1960. The constitution specified that Turkey would be a Republic. Although sovereignty belonged "unconditionally" to the nation, it was exercised by the Grand National Assembly. The G.N.A. reserved both executive and legislative power to itself. The deputies were to select one of their number as president; the president then would appoint a prime

[15] Yalman, *op. cit.*, pp. 140–41, reports that Mustafa Kemal convinced a group of leading newspaper editors that the Caliphate had to go, and then arranged for them to attack the government for not realizing its obsolescence or its danger to achievement of the revolution's full goals.

minister, and the prime minister a cabinet. This process, coupled with the popularity of Kemal, seemed to many influential Turks as steps towards totalitarianism, and a number of his colleagues in the nationalist revolution now broke with him.

The path towards secularism and modernization along western lines taken by Mustafa Kemal was a bold departure from Ottoman precedent, but his ideas as well as the nature of the evolving Turkish state owed much to Ziya Gökalp (1875–1924). Gökalp, "the most original and influential among the Turkish writers of the twentieth century"[16] introduced the subject of sociology into the Turkish educational system, and organized the first systematic analysis of the Turks *as a people* distinct from the polyglot Ottoman Empire, with which they had become identified. His life spans the period which began with the absolutism of Abdul Hamid II, and ended with the Caliphate. Although he never participated formally in politics, he was active as a writer and lecturer, notably in Salonika, where he went as a young man and became associated with the fiery nationalists of the early Committee of Union and Progress. He took a pen name, *Gökalp* (lit. "hero from the sky") which identified him in romantic terms at least with the heroic, uncorrupted ancient days of the Turkish race. Born in Diyarbakir, a provincial town in southern Anatolia with strong Kurdish elements,[17] he was not exposed in his formative years to European culture or cosmopolitan life in Istanbul, and it was easier for him to blaze a path as a true Turkish nationalist. Though mesmerized for periods by such pre-revolutionary liberals as Namīk Kemal, the Pan-Ottomanist poet (1840–1888) Tevfik Fikret, a humanist in the Western intellectual tradition and to the end of his life bemused by Sufism, Ziya's hardheaded Anatolian realism remained dominant in his thinking. It enabled him to speak to the nationalists in their own tongue and to assume a role in their movement similar to that of the mürshid, the spiritual teacher and guide familiar in the Orient, above politics, yet gifted with charismatic leadership.

Gökalp built his Turkist rationale around the concept of the *millet*, which he broadened from a narrowly religious base to embrace an exclusively (and proudly) Turkish nationhood. In the years immediately before World War I, he stimulated the production of the publication

[16] Ziya Gökalp, *Turkish Nationalism and Western Civilization*, edited and translated by Niyazi Berkes, New York: Columbia University Press, 1959. Translator's introduction. See also Heyd, Uriel, *Foundation of Turkish Nationalism*, London: Harvill Press, 1950.
[17] Cf. his essay, *My Nationality*, in Berkes, *op. cit.*, pp. 43–45.

Türk Yurdu (Turkish Homeland) and helped organize the *Türk Ocaklari* (Turkish Hearths), which promoted nationalism for the Turks within the empire.[18] He wrote, in words seemingly tailored to Mustafa Kemal's personality: "The idea of a state or homeland supposedly common to diverse nationalities, is nothing but a mere concept. . . . A land that is not the home of a nation is like a public kitchen where everyone merely feeds himself." [19] He stressed the cultural affinity of all Turks, and their glorious historical past. He was deeply concerned about language, ". . . the basis of social life, the texture of morality, the substratum of culture and civilization," and taught that the Turkish language should be purified of all foreign accretions, with Istanbul vernacular the accepted standard. Noting that the official leaders of the Turks, (i.e., the Osmanlis) forgot national tradition for the sake of their court life," he added that fortunately the folk elite preserved their oral tradition and saved the nation from total extinction.[20] He veered from an early Pan-Ottomanism to Turkism, yet insisted on collective action, bringing collective security—the individual is only important as he serves the community or group. He believed that a natural oligarchy of talent—the intelligentsia—would rise to power in a nation and would provide a leadership of the elite. Within the elite, a strong leader (Gazi) [21] would automatically accede to command; while this was necessary at first in order to educate the populace, in time this leader in concert with the intelligentsia would guide them in concert toward democracy.

Though he became a member of Mustafa Kemal's *Society for the Defense of Rights* in Ankara, and after his return from deportation in Malta he made lecture tours in 1920–22 in rural areas and bestowed lavish praise on Kemal, Gökalp does not appear to have been particularly close to Turkey's first president. Furthermore, Kemal's secularization program far exceeded anything Gökalp ever expressed, and Gökalp's death (1924) preceded the period of most energetic reformism. Some downgrading of his writings occurred as Kemal's anti-religious views pressed Turkey into a rationalist, sharply secular mold. Yet the

[18] The Halk Evleri functioned from 1932–1951, when they were abolished by Menderes. In May 1960 they were revived as *Türk Kultur Dernegi* (Turkish Cultural Associations).
[19] Berkes, *op. cit.*, p. 81.
[20] *Ibid.*, pp. 89–90.
[21] Gazi (Ar. *Ghazi*), lit. ("Hero") was bestowed by the caliphs on warriors who had triumphed or led successful wars of *jihad* against the enemies of Islam. See *Encyclopaedia of Islam.*

principles of "Kemalism" as enunciated in the Constitution, which Gökalp helped to draft, are rooted in Gökalp's philosophy.

Six general principles guided the Turkey of Mustafa Kemal on the road to republican government and modernization. They are symbolized in The Peoples Republican Party flag of six arrows, representing nationalism, secularism, populism, statism (*etatism*), republicanism, and revolutionism. Five of them are specifically, and populism generally, enunciated in the constitution.[22] The arrows of "Kemalism" are in effect guidelines for the future course of the Turkish Republic; he who endangers them or follows a divergent path is at best a dissenter, at the worst an enemy of the state.[23] *Nationalism* meant the replacement of all previous political ideologies in the Ottoman Empire by a concentrated Turkish unity; this was the basis of the Ataturk regime. The spirit of national consciousness was instilled in the individual Turk by every sort of public and private pronouncement. Neither Pan-Turanism nor Pan-Islam had proved valuable in reviving the Turks. The abolition of the Caliphate aroused a good deal of antagonism in some quarters, notably among the Kurds. In 1925 the first Kurdish revolt broke out in the eastern provinces, led by Shaikh Said.[24] The Kurds sought to restore the Caliphate and coincidentally establish an independent Kurdistan. This Kurdish reaction was typically anti-Turkish but also anti-government; the Kurds had come to realize that Mustafa Kemal's purpose was a unitary Turkish rather than multi-national state. Extreme measures such as martial law and revolutionary tribunals were required to subdue the Kurds, and insurrections broke out later, even as late as 1936–1937, in protest against the Turkicization process of the Republic. Henceforth, the Kurds of Turkey were to be referred to officially as "Mountain Turks."

Secularism may be considered the right arm of nationalism in Turkey since it redirected attitudes away from the slavish obedience to organized religion which characterized the latter years of the empire. Secularization extended into many fields not normally affected by religion because of the weblike inclusiveness of Islam. As noted earlier, the requirement that the Ottoman Sultans follow the guidance of the 'ulema even in secular matters permitted the growth of another privileged hierarchy;

[22] Article 2. cf. Lewis, *op. cit.,* pp. 197–208.
[23] Cf., Fernau, F. W., *Moslems on the March,* New York: Alfred A. Knopf, Inc., 1954, Chapter VIII, pp. 226–30.
[24] The Shaykh was head of the Nakhshabandi order of dervishes, one of the conservative orders that became a major target of Kemal's secularism program.

the Grand Mufti's *fetvas* thus had the force of law. The disenfranchisement and later deposition of the last Caliph even required a *fetva*. Mustafa Kemal's most spectacular reforms concerned matters of secularism. The most fanatical enemies of reform were the dervish orders. The complicity of the Nakhshabandis in the Kurdish revolt, and the antagonism of the Bektashis and Mevlevis, two other prominent orders, to Kemal's famous head-dress reform, settled their fate. Their *tekkes* (lodges) were closed; exaggerated veneration of the *türbes* (tombs) of revered dervish leaders and holy men was discouraged; finally the *tarikat* (lit. "way") or structure of the orders themselves were proscribed.[25] Considerable rioting ensued, notably in Mevlana's city of Konya, where today a central artificial hill crowned by a public park and a pink sandstone shaft commemorate the martyrs killed in this internal "holy war."

Suppression of the tarikats and passage of the *Takriri Sükün* (Law of the Maintenance of Public Order) which enabled the government to deal from a position of strength with all disaffection marked a new phase in the reform program. Mustafa Kemal assumed the role of *hoca*. The strong didactic streak in his character was given free rein as he traveled throughout the provinces "to sell" his secularization program. In traditional Turkish society, clothes were more important to the wearer than they are to the modern, mid-twentieth century Turks, encased in rather nondescript western style suits, usually grey or brown, and seldom well-fitted. Even the baggy trousers and the long embroidered shirt of the peasant served to mark him off from Christians and from other nationalities. The fez, the little red brimless cap with a tassel, worn over a skull cap was the special hallmark of the good Muslim. Mustafa Kemal sensed that secularism required a shift in costume as well as attitudes. Ignoring the implication of apostasy,[26] he led a group of government officials to Kastamonu, a north central town noted for its conservatism, where the group exchanged their fezzes publicly for Panama hats. Kemal's arguments were nationalistic ("the fez is not of Turkish but of Christian-Byzantine origin"), realistic ("the fez requires more material than a hat"), and generally irrefutable. Like a teacher who preps his prize students for a stiff examination he pushed his Turks into adoption of hats, European suits, and dresses for women. The veil and çarşaf [27]

[25] See Chapter 4 for Reza Shah's methods of dealing with the dervishes in Iran.

[26] *Şapka giymek* ("put on a hat") in the vernacular meant to become an apostate from Islam.

[27] A long, black, shapeless cloak worn as an outer garment in public.

were discouraged, although not wearing these was never fully enforced in rural areas owing to the resistance of the husbands.

Perhaps the most interesting of the reforms were various miscellaneous edicts which seemed to have no direct bearing on the transformation of the state but were designed rather to evolve a new social order. For example, three dating systems were still in use—the lunar Islamic calendar, the Mali (Financial) calendar, actually the Julian calendar reckoned from A.H. 1167 (1789 A.D.), and the Gregorian Calendar. On January 1st, 1926, the Gregorian calendar replaced all three. A second innovation was the use of surnames. Under the Ottoman Empire the Muslim Turks, like the Arabs, were known by their first names. Since there was a limited supply of these, qualifying adjectives of diminutives were added to separate the innumerable Alis, Mehmeds, Mustafas, etc. This was not wholly satisfactory in terms of identity, mail, communications and other appurtenances of a modern state. It made little difference to a tax gatherer whether the taxes from Mehmed of Sivas were paid by Mehmed the son of Ali from Sivas, so long as they were paid. To Mustafa Kemal, who had received his first name from his mother and "Kemal" from his mathematics teacher, this was an intolerable continuation of the dead hand of Islam. In 1935 a law required that all Turks must take a surname. He himself was accorded the honorific "Ataturk" (Father of the Turks) by the Assembly. There was much scurrying about by Turks forced in this curious way to create a pedigree and inevitably many Turkish adjectives cropped up to perpetuate duplication, this time in surname. But at least the mails went through.[28]

In 1928 the Arabic script which had been adopted for written Turkish under the Ottomans was replaced by the Latin alphabet. All newspapers suddenly appeared in the "New Turkish," and courses in Arabic and Persian were dropped from the school curriculum.

The *medreses* (religious schools usually attached to mosques) had been closed, so the national schools (*millet mektepleri*) set up under the ministry began to promote the use of Turkish words for their Arabic equivalents (e.g., *oğretmen*, "teacher," for *hoca; baba*, "father," for *abu*). Ataturk himself went with blackboard and chalk to provincial towns to give lessons in modern Turkish. This return to cultural origins produced one major problem—the language of the Turkish horsemen did not include terms to fit most twentieth-century concepts. The *Türk*

[28] The writer once received in error a letter addressed to Mustafa, the Baker, Çankaya, Ankara, Turkey.

Dil Kurumu (Turkish Language Institute) grappled with this problem and came up with the solution of phoneticizing these concepts into the language from their European equivalents, hence *trençkot* (trench-coat), *felsefe* (philosophy), *vagonli* (wagons-lits), and *skrudrayt* (screw-driver). For this reason Turkey's billboards are probably the easiest to read in the Middle East. In 1936 part of the rewriting of Turkish national history, which declared that the Turks were descended from heroic Central Asian clans and more remotely in time from the ancient Hittites who had held equal power-status with Pharaonic Egypt from their Anatolian highland base some 5,000 years earlier, was the Sun-Language Theory, which held that the Turks and their language were descended from the sun (i.e., because of descent from the Hittites), hence all words in all languages had ultimately a Turkish origin. All these various maneuvers had a common purpose of reviving a sense of national pride in the Turks and of re-emphasizing the total break with Ottomanism.

Populism (*halkçilik*) was the justification for the dictatorship imposed by Ataturk. Since the constitution clearly vested sovereignty in the nation, with the G.N.A. designated as the agent of the Turkish people, nearly all measures of reform or repression could be ascribed to the popular will. Populism aimed at social economic and political progress within the existing social framework. It did not envisage a class struggle, and on this point Ataturk parted company with the Soviet Communists who had helped him so mightily in the revolution. But the fundamentally independent, conservatively democratic character of the Turks would have worked effectively against communism even if it had not been stained by Russian fingers.

Two-Party Experiment and Repression

By 1928 Ataturk's sweeping experiments in modernization had aroused considerable resentment.[29] The policy of *etatism* intensified this. *Etatism*, perhaps the weakest of the republican principles, had been intended as artificial respiration applied to the suffocating national

---

[29] In 1924 a group of Kemal's early colleagues, including two distinguished soldiers, Kazim Karabekir and Ali Fuad (Cebesoy), Adnan Adivar, Halide Edib, and others broke with him on personal grounds, and formed the Progressive Republican Party. They were opposed to the abolition of the Caliphate and Kemal's dictatorial leadership. The Party was suspected, not without cause, of complicity in the 1925 Kurdish Revolt and was suppressed. This first experiment in two party systems fell afoul of Kemal's feeling that he knew the best course for Turkey.

economy. Initially the government went into the banking business. In 1924 Celal Bayar and others formed the İş Bank to provide capital for local industries. In 1925 the Industrial and Mineral Bank (now known as the Sümerbank) was set up to provide capital for heavy industries. Other etatist measures followed. Railroads and shipping lines were nationalized. Nationalism was actually the bonding element in etatism. The Turks were not only determined to catch up with the rest of Europe, but to prove that they were a European nation rather than a land of Asiatic peasants. But a series of bad harvests brought severe hardship to many parts of the country. Also the protectionist element in etatism discouraged foreign capital. The influence of the public sector of the expansion of industry denigrated agricultural improvements, which were equally necessary. By a twist of fate, the Menderes government reversed this policy during the early years of its decade in power and it too, got into trouble. Some instances of personal aggrandizement and nepotism by government officials, while not connected with Ataturk himself, added to the general public dissatisfaction. Many conservatives still resented the secularist trend of the reform program, while a small influential group of liberals, Francophile in their thinking, felt that Ataturk was moving away from the liberal goals of the revolution. These various pressures contributed to the forming of the Free Party of the Republic (*Cumhuriyet Serbest Firkasi*) in 1930; Ataturk himself suggested it to Fethi Bey (Okyar), then ambassador to Paris, who had served briefly as first Prime Minister before the political crisis which precipitated the Republic.[30] Fethi published the Party's new program in the newspaper *Yarin*. He promised to work for freedom of thought and the press, reduction of taxes, lessening of etatism, and various other liberalizing principles. The party was presented to the public as a spontaneous opposition movement. Ataturk hoped it would serve as a safety valve for popular discontent, but the reaction was stronger than he had anticipated. Fethi's speeches in Izmir and other cities were received with loud enthusiasm, whenever he criticized the economic problem and the conduct of Republican Party leaders (but not Ataturk). There were even hostile riots in Izmir and religious feelings rose to the surface. A particularly unpleasant illustration of the threat which still

[30] Ataturk wrote to Fethi: . . . "I consider it one of the bases of the Republic to have a new party in the Assembly, which based on similar principles (anti-clerical) will debate freely the affairs of the nation." *Cumhuriyet*, August 12, 1930, quoted in Karpat, *op. cit.*, p. 65 n.

existed to Ataturk's dream of a truly modern sectarian republic occurred near Izmir where a crowd was demonstrating against the "impious Republic." A young officer ordered them to disperse. The leader of the crowd, one Mehmed the Dervish, then shot and decapitated him, and the officer's severed head was paraded through the streets. Earlier the municipal elections held as a test of the viability of the young two-party system had failed abysmally. Fethi accused the government of rigging them; realizing that he was about to become identified with the anti-Kemalist group, he then dissolved the Free Party of the Republic. Two other minor parties formed in the same year, the Populist Republicans (*Ahali Cumhuriyet Firkasi*) and the Workers and Peasants Party, were suppressed for the same reasons. For the next fifteen years Turkey remained subject to a one-party, one-man rule, with etatism dominant in economic and secularism-nationalism in political matters.[31]

The reforms of the 1930's emphasized *revolutionism* (*Inkilapçilik*), an implicit doctrine in Kemalism which was adopted by the Republicans as a formal principle. Revolutionism stressed willingness to make changes, however drastic, in the social and political fabric of the Turkish nation, in order to achieve the desired goals of secular modernization. Polygamy was officially proscribed. Women, often described as the real strength of the Kemalist revolt, were allowed to vote in municipal elections in 1930; in 1934 they gained the full franchise and were given the right to run for the G.N.A. as well. The weekly holiday was changed from Friday to Sunday to conform with European practice. Foreigners writing to Turkish city addresses were politely reminded by the Turkish Post Office, that letters to Ankara, Izmir, Istanbul, were acceptable; those to Angora, Smyrna, Constantinople (their Anglicized equivalents) were not, and would probably not be delivered. Important legal reforms had been accomplished earlier; the *Mecelle,* the Ottoman code which was itself the first organized attempt to codify *shari'a* as well as customary law under the Empire, was junked in favor of various western codes: the Swiss Civil Code, with almost no changes, the Italian Penal Code, with almost no changes, and the German Commercial Code in 1926. These eliminated vestiges of special treatment accorded to Jews and Armenians, and made all Turkish citizens subject to the same laws.

[31] The bitter rivalry between Celal Bayar and Ismet Inönü which dominated the 1950–1960 period of Democratic government and provoked the severe repressive measures of the Menderes regime began with their difference on economic policies. Bayar placed economic above political development, for example.

Revolutionism, republicanism, and nationalism were to a large extent fused in the *Halk Evis* (Peoples Houses) which replaced the existing *Türk Ocaklari*, inspired by Gökalp, after 1932. They were to function "in a sincere spirit of brotherhood, embracing all citizens of a nationalist outlook and loyal to the Revolution."[32] As community centers, they sponsored free public lectures, concerts, sports clubs, literacy and Turkish culture classes, welfare programs, and a variety of other activities all designed to spread the Kemalist gospel throughout the provinces. Their crusading work was supplemented by *Halk Odalari* (Peoples Rooms) and after 1939 by the Village Institutes (*Koy Enstitüsü*), designed specifically to end the illiteracy and backwardness of the Turkish villager. Their system was to recruit promising boys and girls from villages, give them five-year training courses at state expense and return them to their villages where they would teach children (and adults) better agricultural methods, better hygiene, and better education. The Institutes had certain drawbacks: the training period was rather short; the graduates tended to assume elite status in their villages, and were sometimes resented by their elders; and sometimes their own readjustment did not work.[33] But generally speaking the Institute shared in the inspiring, dynamic spirit of Ataturk and represented the best in the Turkish modernization movement. When the Grand National Assembly convened in November 1938, the opening address was read by Celal Bayar, the Prime Minister, on behalf of the President of the Republic. It was the first such occasion which Mustafa Kemal Ataturk had missed in the history of the G.N.A. On November 10th he died, occasioning a mass display of grief for the normally unemotional, disciplined Turkish people.[34] Ataturk was fortunate to have two decades of peace in which to develop his ambitions for Turkey, but otherwise, luck had little to do with his success. Rather it was due to planning, staff method, willingness to experiment boldly, and force of personality. Ataturk was not easy to get along with. He was an intellectual, but his sure practical grasp of affairs, his sharp wit, and his pedagogical skill often outmaneuvered his better-educated colleagues. A number of these broke with him for

[32] Webster, Donald, *op. cit.*, pp. 186 ff.
[33] Mahmut Makal, in *Bizim Köy* (Our Village), translated by Sir Wyndham Deedes, London, 1950, describes in diary form the experience of one such teacher in a backward section of Anatolia.
[34] The same display but on a more limited scale took place in 1954 at the first exhibition of a film showing scenes of the funeral procession through Istanbul sixteen years earlier. (Personal communication).

this very reason. He was ruthless toward political enemies. His vices were common knowledge (though subsequent biographies have inflated them beyond the bounds of reason or taste [35]) while the Turks had placed a halo around him. The strengths and weaknesses of Ataturk were those of a very human figure, a man possessed of a dream for his country, who answered "Yes, there is!" for the question of the Turkish poet, "Is there nobody to resurrect this country from its ruins?" The main support for Ataturk's policies came from three population groups— the teachers, the army (which saw him as the national war hero even in mufti), and the women. In the more remote villages there was some conservative opposition through the bulk of the Ataturk period, but gen- erally speaking, his picture hung on every coffeehouse wall. It might have been expected that his death would see a scramble for power, but this did not happen. Indeed his plan for Turkey's future, expressed on hundreds of statues and in countless speeches, continued to inspire those around him. Once he said, "I will lead my people by the hand until they can learn to walk alone. Then my journey will be done." So far (unless Gamal Abd-al Nasir of Egypt proves otherwise) he is the only political reformer in the Muslim World who has left behind him a national political doctrine independent of his person, a concrete ideal.[36] The Turkish state continued without a hitch, in the name of Atatürk and the principles of Kemalism. By unanimous vote, the G.N.A. chose Ismet Inönü as President.

EXTERNAL RELATIONS BETWEEN THE WARS

A cardinal point in the Lausanne Treaty, on the Turkish side, was the surrender of Ottoman territorial ambitions. This coincided with the Republican Party's nationalist principle; Turkey was to become a com- pact homogeneous state purged of extraneous elements. In the interwar period Turkey pursued a consistent pattern in rejecting foreign or ir- redentist territorial claims, with two exceptions. The first of these was the Mosul Question, which was settled against Turkey but with adequate compensation.[37] The Armistice between Turkey and the Allies had oc- curred before northern Mesopotamia had been brought under control. Consequently the Turks took the position that the Peace Settle-

[35] Cf. Brock, Ray, *Ghost on Horseback*, New York: Duell, Sloan, and Pearce, 1955, an incredibly offensive piece of lurid journalism. There is yet to be a good biography of Ataturk.
[36] Fernau, F. W., *op. cit.*, p. 230.
[37] See Chapter 7.

ment should have included Mosul in the truncated Turkish state. The nationalists went further and insisted that it was an ethnic part of Turkey since the predominantly Kurdish population was kin to the Kurds (Mountain Turks) of Eastern Anatolia. The adverse decision turned the Turks in the direction of a Russian *rapprochement,* in 1925 they signed a nonaggression pact with the Soviets. This followed a 1921 treaty returning Kars and Ardahan to Turkey, and ceding Batum to Russia. But the historical antipathy of the Turks for the Russians in time translated itself into communist terms; Ataturk even secretly encouraged a group of his associates, including Celal Bayar, to set up a communist-type party in order to keep communism under surveillance and control. Between 1925 and 1935 Turkish-Soviet relations were as nearly harmonious as could be possible in the light of history. The other Turkish irredentist claim was to the subprovince (Sanjak) of Alexandretta, called the Hatay, about half of which lies outside Anatolia proper, along the extreme eastern end of the Mediterranean. The population was 40 per cent Turkish, 40 per cent Arab, with the remainder belonging to various minority sects. The Turks had recognized French authority over Syria-Lebanon, including the Sanjak, in the 1921 Agreement which pulled France out of opposition to the Kemalist revolution. After 1937 Italy's increasing boldness in Mediterranean affairs and Turkey's growing strength gave France second thoughts about the Sanjak, particularly in view of the sizable Turkish elements. France had consistently treated the area as a sort of special prefecture, and it was not too difficult to reach agreement on a condominium arrangement. In local elections in 1938, the Turks in the Sanjak won 22 of 40 seats, and promptly declared a Republic of Hatay. The next year in June, the Assembly of the transitory republic voted for union with Turkey. In October the French received their lagniappe, a mutual aid pact with Turkey (and Britain).[38]

In 1936 the other unsettled question left by the treaty of Lausanne, namely the control of the Dardanelles, was adjusted. The Lausanne Conference had provided for an International Commission to supervise freedom of passage through the Straits, which were partly demilitarized. Turkey was a member of the Commission, but this did not give her the right to control a waterway which in effect ran through her territory. In a convention signed at Montreux (June, 1936), the Commission

---

[38] See Chapter 6 for the Syrian viewpoint.

was abolished and its functions returned to Turkey. The significant clauses in the Montreux Convention were as follows:

(1) The demilitarization clauses of Lausanne were abrogated.
(2) Merchant shipping was guaranteed passage in time of peace and in wartime, if Turkey was neutral.
(3) In peacetime small warships of all nations were allowed freedom of passage upon proper notification to the Turkish government; Black Sea powers could send ships of over 15,000 tons in single passage.
(4) In wartime, if Turkey were neutral, no ships of belligerent nations could transit the Straits except under special conditions. If Turkey herself were neutral or believed herself threatened by war, she could ban all transit by warships, and limit merchant shipping to daytime passage.

In 1937, Turkey [39] signed the Saadabad Pact with Iran, Iraq, and Afghanistan, aimed less at Soviet imperialism than at avoiding the recurrence of old border disputes between neighbors whose only common bond was Islam. The pact bound the signatories to consult in matters of common interest and to respect their common frontiers, but not to mutual assistance against aggression. When World War II broke out, the members went their separate ways, Turkey withdrawing into a shell of neutrality as laid down in the policy of Ataturk.

The war years were difficult ones for Turkey. The pact with Britain and France was broken, and a nonaggression treaty with Germany negotiated in 1941. Turkey sat out the war and equivocated until 1944, when it became apparent that Germany had lost and the hopes for annihilation of the Russian army would not take place. In February, 1945, Turkey declared war on Germany and Japan as of March 1st, thus sliding under the wire for the right to join the United Nations as a founding member.

A domestic situation which caused much hardship but conversely helped usher in the two-party system, was the *Varlik Vergisi* (Capital Levy). Maintaining a defensive army of a million men put a severe drain on the economy. In 1942 a law passed the G.N.A. levying a tax on income and capital accumulated by means which were not usually taxable, such as brokerage commissions, speculative profits, and the like. While the purpose was justifiable, the collection methods, imposed by a committee of officials and businessmen, fell heaviest on the minorities,

[39] In 1934, The Balkan Pact, first effort at negotiated rapprochement with Turkey's former subjects was signed between the Turks, Greeks, Bulgarians, and Romanians.

there being lists of Muslims and non-Muslims in each locality.[40] The tax had to be paid in fifteen days after imposition, and the penalty for nonpayment was confinement at hard labor. The reaction among businessmen was bitter; many firms increased the prices of their products in order to recoup their losses. Criticism from abroad was equally strong. A year after it was passed, the *Varlik Vergisi* was put in abeyance, though never formally abrogated. Those who had been compelled to pay the levy received no compensation; the rest, whom the taxation committees had not caught up with were more fortunate and lost nothing. The sputtering fuse of political opposition to government policies was fully ignited. As a result of it, latent, disorganized opposition to the continuing one-party dictatorship finally became organized.

THE DEVELOPMENT OF OPPOSITION PARTIES, 1946–1950

Of major significance to Turkish political development was the opposition movement which got underway toward the end of the war. Dictatorship, or at least one-party rule, had been the norm throughout the republican period; for six centuries earlier power had been wielded automatically by the Ottoman Sultans. No parliamentary tradition existed among the Turks beyond the rudimentary council meetings of the Central Asian clans. This absence of source models, the tight discipline and obedience to authority of the Turkish people, and the great reliance upon Ataturk makes the Turkish achievement in multiple-party democracy, however shaky its underpinnings, brilliant indeed.

World War II brought Turkey into increasingly close relations with Western European powers, although neutrality was observed until late in the war. U.N. membership and contacts with Western Europe and the United States, made many Turks sensitive to the shortcomings of their democracy. Ismet Inönü, who had continued as President throughout the war, to his credit encouraged multiparty growth and recognized the value of political opposition. In November, 1945, he addressed the G.N.A., speaking of the democratization of public life as its new objective.[41] Earlier he had declared: "As the conditions imposed by war disappear, democratic principles will gradually acquire a larger place in the political and cultural life of the country." [42] Significantly, five years

[40] The *Dönme* (Islamic Jews) were taxed twice as much as ethnic Turks, as were the Greeks.
[41] Fernau, *op. cit.*, p. 235.
[42] Jashchke, G., *Die Turkei im den Jahren,* 1942–1951, Wiesbaden, 1955, p. 45.

later, the second greatest leader of the Turkish Republic was to be found in the opposition back-benches he himself helped to create! Taking Inönü's promise literally, four deputies, Celal Bayar, Adnan Menderes, Refik Koraltan, and Fuad Köprülü, now submitted the *Dortlu Takrir* (Proposal of the Four) to the Assembly. The essential elements of their position were: (1) return to the individuals of their constitutional rights; (2) termination of wartime restrictions; (3) restoration of parliamentary and legislative powers to the G.N.A.; (4) multiparty political activity; and (5) reinvigoration of Turkey's basic democracy.

The Republican Party rejected the proposal. Meanwhile two opposition parties had formed. The first, *Milli Kalkinma* (National Resurgence) had no concrete program other than the general ideas of the founder, Nuri Demirağ, a wealthy industrialist. Its establishment, however, proved that the government would keep its promise. Far more important was the founding of the *Demokrat Partisi*, January 7, 1946, under the leadership of Bayar and his fellow-authors of the *Dortlu Takrir*. It expanded fairly rapidly, helped by a benevolent attitude on the part of the Republicans, (who felt that its efforts would supply window-dressing for Turkish democracy without endangering seriously the authority they had held for nearly a quarter of a century). The increasing spread of the new party [43] after a slow start alarmed the RPP, however. It was decided to call elections a year ahead of schedule. These were held in July, 1946; 85 per cent of the electorate participated. The over-all results returned a handsome Republican Party majority to the G.N.A., 395–64, with 6 independents. But at least the Democrats got on the board. Several liberalizing measures were passed in the months prior to the elections. The Press Union was dissolved, and various credit and licensing checks on publication were eliminated. The right to form associations was restated in accordance with the Turkish Civil Code. The elections themselves were held in an atmosphere of relative liberty. For the first time in Turkey's Republican history, the people took an active part in the campaign—Republican candidates even had to stump those districts where they were faced with Democratic rivalry. Most of them won, but Democratic strength showed up surprisingly well, notably in concentrated areas like Istanbul.

The results of the election were bitterly criticized for fraud and falsification. Even Inönü's speech opening the G.N.A. was not well received.

[43] Groups of citizens in nearly all towns and many villages formed branches in mid-1946. cf., *Tanin*, July 8, 1947, quoted in *Karpat, op. cit.*, p. 153.

The Democratic minority called long and loud for a revision in the electoral laws. Early in 1950, ahead of the elections scheduled for that year, a new electoral bill finally passed the Assembly by 341–10; it provided what the Democrats considered adequate guarantees. Between 1946 and 1950 the Democrats literally took their case to the people. İnönü had been re-elected President of the Republic by a large majority over Marshal Fevzi Çakmak, an old war hero and friend of Atatürk's who had decided without actually joining the Democrats to run with them. Recep Peker, a strong leader, and rather conservative adherent of one-party rule, became Prime Minister. But neither the popularity of "Ataturk's shadow" İnönü,[44] nor a return to repressive tactics slowed the Democratic drive. They profited tremendously by the general dissatisfaction over economic matters and by the general willingness to blame the Republicans for all Turkey's post-war problems. The Democratic organizers fanned out into the remote interior of Anatolia, as well as the cities. Wherever they went, and most unexpectedly in the villages, they found an alert and even well-informed citizenry. Their pre-election tours took the appearance of bayrams,[45] so enthusiastic were the crowds. The Declaration of President İnönü, July 12, 1947, while it went beyond the desires of his party, was an impartial call for multiparty cooperation. The Republican Peasant National Party was formed in 1948 (in 1954 it was renamed Republican National Party) from dissidents and expellees from the Democratic Party, as Turkey's third major party. Its first leader was Marshal Çakmak, but his death in 1950 robbed it of its best drawing card.

THE FIRST TURKISH REPUBLIC

On May 14, 1950, Turkey's voters again went to the polls. 89.3 per cent of the electorate cast their ballots. The Democrats had hammered away at the "time for a change" theme; their candidates had stressed the importance of bringing a sense of democratic participation back to the nation. They said that Turkey's economic troubles were caused by a defective organization; if elected they were going to amend the constitution so as to reorganize and separate governmental powers. The National Party campaigned on the basis of populism alone. To their

[44] According to some authorities İnönü was never more than a good staff officer whose "blinkered vision" kept him from greatness. See Lewis, *op. cit.*, for İnönü's career.
[45] *Bayram* is the Turkish word for festival or holiday.

Tabulating the ballots after elections in Turkey. (Courtesy Turkish Press Attache)

surprise, the Democrats not only won the popular vote, but they received a two-thirds majority. Their margin was 4,242,831 votes to 3,165,-096 for the Republicans, 240,209 for the National Party, and 258,698 for the Independents. Under the majority system the seats in the G.N.A. were divided as follows: Democrats 396, Republicans 68, Independents

7, and National Party 1.[46] Celal Bayar was chosen President by the deputies, Adnan Menderes, Prime Minister, Refik Koraltan, Head of the Assembly, and Fuad Köprülü later became Menderes' Foreign Minister. Ismet Inönü, deputy for Malatya, took his seat as chief of the opposition, after twelve years as President. The accession of the Democrats ushered in a ten-year period which began as a multiparty, or at least two-party, honeymoon, which was terminated May 27, 1960, by intervention of the nonpolitical Turkish Army. Between these two Mays the forward progress of Turkish democracy was arrested and very nearly jolted into reverse. Between 1950 and 1954 the Democrats instituted a number of reforms aimed at continuing the liberation begun by Inönü's regime. The *azan* (call to prayer) was allowed to be made in the original Arabic. The authorities looked the other way as such ancient social practices of Islam as the wearing of the çarsaf and village weddings performed by imams were revived openly. Freer opportunity was afforded to Turks to travel abroad, as students or even as tourists. Turkey was added to the European Recovery Program with $100 million in funds earmarked for her economic advancement.[47] Foreign policy, never a particular cause for disagreement among parties became firmly rooted in the West through alliances. The Law on Foreign Capital encouraged investment from abroad. Modest beginnings were made in an oil refining industry based on production in the Ramandağ field; both the government and private investors, mostly banks, invested capital in heavy industry—power plants, sugar, and textile factories, and large-scale mechanized farming. A vast program of road-building was also undertaken with large doses of American aid. The Turkish farmers, who had perhaps the most to gain from a change in government were given the full treatment in accordance with Democratic election pledges. Etatism was shifted to agriculture. Farm loans at low interest rates were made easily available to farmers, major crops like wheat and cotton were subsidized at better than world prices. While industrial workers and salaried personnel were taxed heavily to support the expanding industrial plans and adjunct public services, agriculturalists had their taxes remitted. A series of excellent harvests, notably in 1953, further aided the Turkish farmer. In general an economic boom occurred in 1951–53.

[46] The 1951 by-elections increased this to 411 Democrats, 61 Republicans, 12 Independents, 1 National Party, and 2 vacant.
[47] H.A.R.P., "Turkey Under the Democratic Party," *World Today*, September, 1953, p. 385.

Even then there were danger signals, however. As one of the members of the International Bank Mission to Turkey wrote later, "Turkey has tended to follow—first in industry, now in agriculture—what I would call the 'showcase' type of economic development. That is at the expense of the population at large, some small groups of producers are heavily protected subsidized and otherwise favorably treated to become a symbol of progress in which few of their fellow-citizens can share. A few islands of privilege in a sea of poverty nonetheless are a poor indicator of economic development."[48] Private enterprise was encouraged—the Republican Peoples Party in their 1953 Annual Congress adopted a platform urging private enterprise as the basis of the economy (a far cry from the Etatism of the 1930's).[49] The Menderes government was spurred by ambition into taking the major role in economic development. The lack of a sense of social responsibility among the capitalists or entrepreneurial classes, a holdover from Ottoman days, reinforced government's role. Democrat successes in the economic sphere were the basis of their campaign program in the 1954 elections.

The Democrats approached these first elections since attaining power, without the magic name (or association) of Ataturk, but with a number of advantages helping their case. Economic progress has already been mentioned; the impact on the rockbound peasantry of Anatolia was extraordinary. Thousands of traditionally mute Mehmets had begun to enjoy many of the pleasures of their city cousins—radios, bicycles, roads to connect them with the outside world, electricity, even plumbing and a reliable water supply. In some villages status symbols crowned nearly every rooftop.[50] The impact of this was not lost on the shrewd peasant. As one observer wrote: "He has quickly sensed his pivotal role, the vital importance of HIS vote. . . . Mehmet is artful. He is demanding service in return for his vote."[51] Although the Democrats as well as the Republicans were required to court the village vote, the Democrats were associated with its liberation. One villager, when asked how he in-

[48] Nicholls, W. H., "Investment in Agriculture in Underdeveloped Countries," *American Economic Review*, May 1955, p. 71.
[49] In 1933 Ataturk launched a five-year plan of state-supported industrialization which ground to a halt in 1940 under the impact of World War II. See Robert W. Kerwin, "Private Enterprise in Turkish Industrial Development," *Middle East Journal*, winter, 1951, pp. 21–38.
[50] Cf. Daniel Lerner, *The Passing of Traditional Society*, Glencoe: Free Press, 1958, Chapter II, "Balgat."
[51] Reed, Howard A., "A New Force at Work in Democratic Turkey," *Middle East Journal*, winter, 1953, p. 35.

tended to vote, indicated a preference for the Democrats. He was asked why. In answer he crossed his index fingers and said: "The Republicans have always meant two things, the landlord and the gendarme."[52]

Modest steps in the direction of reviving Islam encouraged certain conservative groups to look favourably upon the Democrats. Hundreds of new mosques were built after 1950 and thousands more repaired and refurbished, usually by legally chartered mosque-building societies. Religious teaching was inserted into the regular school curriculum. The opposition—Nation Party—emphasized the balance of religious tradition and rationalism in the social order. Extremism won the upper hand in its ranks—one member, a publisher, declared in a headline of his newspaper that "It is not at all true that the nation is indebted to the Ataturk revolution"[53]—and in 1953 the government suppressed it on grounds with infringing on secularism (it was re-established in 1954 as the Republican National Party and took part in the elections). The *hajj* was permitted, and in 1954, 10,086 pilgrims traveled to Mecca. With express government permission, the 681st anniversary of the death of Mevlana was celebrated in Konya with a revival of the *Mevlevi* (whirling) dervish dance. Without surrendering to religious dictation (the leaders of the Ticani dervishes were sentenced to long prison terms in 1952 for smashing statues of Ataturk),[54] the Democrats managed to instill a general feeling in the population that religion privately practiced was an asset to the state.

That dedication to autocratic administration which became the mark of the Menderes regime, as it had Ataturk's, began to sharpen in 1953–54 with two measures designed to curb criticism. The first was a retroactive law requiring the surrender of such "unlawful" acquisitions of the R.P.P. as funds, movable property, newspaper establishments, and real estate. The second was the March, 1954, amendment to the Press Law providing stiff penalties for publishing material harmful to the national interest, insulting the honor or invading the privacy of public officials. The amendments caused less stir at the time than they were to later, in fact, the editor of *Vatan*, Ahmed Emin Yalman, defended

[52] H.A.R.P., "Turkey Under the Democratic Party," *World Today*, Sept., 1953, p. 383.
[53] Rustow, Dankwart, "Politics and Islam in Turkey, 1920–1955," in *Islam and the West*, ed., R. N. Frye, The Hague: Mouton, 1957, p. 101.
[54] Reed, H. A., "Religious Life of Modern Turkish Muslims," Frye, ed., *op. cit.*, p. 138.

Turks do not take voting rights lightly. (Courtesy Turkish Press Attache)

them in a letter to the *New York Times,* (Feb. 23, 1954) as necessary to curb abuse of freedom of the press by irresponsible elements in the press.

Turkey went to the polls in a holiday mood in 1954, and retained the Democrats in power by a whopping majority. Although their popular vote was 5,313,000 against 3,193,000 for the R.P.P., they won 503 of the 541 seats in the Assembly or 93 per cent. The discrepancy between the popular vote and the G.N.A. representation resulted from the provincial unit system of representation, under which (with two exceptions) all Turkish provinces returned candidates from the same party.

With this enormous vote of confidence behind him and operating under the Turkish constitutional structure, which concentrates all power in the Grand National Assembly, Adnan Menderes stood on a nearly equal footing with Ataturk as a Turkish power-leader in 1954. His colleague Celal Bayar continued as President—due to personal prestige, position as an elder statesman of the party, and the power of suspensive veto, he has had great influence in intraparty matters—and Fuad Köprülü remained Foreign Minister.[55] But Menderes became identified as the architect of Democratic policy. Writing in 1953, one author noted that "under the guidance of such men, Turkey's recent experiments in liberal procedures have revealed a political maturity that her friends hardly suspected." [56]

The period 1955–1960 was a very trying one for Turkey, economically as well as practically. Menderes pressed ahead on all fronts with a huge construction program, largely on a credit basis. The stress was on capital investment, in hydroelectric projects, heavy industry, agricultural mechanization, etc. Undeniably, there was progress, but also much waste and unnecessary uneconomic practices. Newly-rich land-owners concentrated their wealth in luxury items; taxation practically bypassed the farmer, so that the civil servant or middle-class wage-earner carried the burden of taxation for public finance. Essential consumer goods were in short supply; even Turkish coffee ("the national beverage") [57] had to be replaced by tea. The government's foreign exchange reserves shrank visibly; the Turkish lira, pegged to the United States dollar at 2.8, dropped 43 per cent on world markets. Foreign governments showed increasing hesitancy to extend additional credits; on several occasions oil companies exporting to Turkey shut off oil and gasoline supplies until the Turks paid an instalment on their debt.

The Democrats went ahead, however, with a combination of bland confidence that their Western partners would bail them out, and stubborn refusal to take any advice from these same partners which might help them set their economic house in order. Indeed the finance minister went to Washington in 1956 to request a $300 million loan, and was surprised and hurt when this was not granted. This did not deter "Adnan the Builder" as the stocky Prime Minister had become known, from plunging ahead on various pet projects—notably a new boulevard cut through the houses of Istanbul's Golden Horn waterfront. New hotels shot up as fast as the masons could buy plaster, although there were no plans for training hotelkeepers to run them.[58] Significantly,

[55] He resigned in 1956 in opposition to Menderes policies and joined the opposition.
[56] H.A.R.P., *op. cit.*
[57] Turkish coffee is not produced domestically but imported from abroad, much of it from Yemen; shortage of foreign exchange during this period caused the suspension of coffee imports.
[58] Freya Stark, in *Riding to the Tigris*, London; John Murray, 1960, notes that "the Turks have the most splendid country to visit in Europe, but the most abominable accommodations."

the wheat harvest in Central Anatolia failed in 1954, a warning to the government that its ambitious schemes required the cooperation of nature and the prudence of man to succeed. Foreign criticism of the development program was largely brushed aside by the regime. But dissatisfaction at home could not be so easily discounted. The government reacted in the manner of authoritarian regimes everywhere when threatened with loss of popular support, or more specifically, of power. The repressive measures became commonplace. The press received particularly rough treatment. Turkish journalists spent so much of their time bouncing in and out of jail [59] that an apt cartoon in the newspaper *Cumhuriyet* depicted their wardrobe as a set of tails, hanging beside a striped convict's uniform. The secretary of the R.P.P., Kasim Gülek, was constantly harassed in his political tours, as was İnönü, by government restrictions. For example, it was possible for the action of two men shaking hands on the street, to be interpreted as a political meeting, bringing jail terms and/or fines. The government's long arm reached into the faculties of Istanbul and Ankara Universities. In 1958 a number of professors on the political science faculty at the University of Ankara resigned after they were told to desist criticizing the regime in their classes.

The mounting unrest prompted Menderes to advance the elections to October 1957. The results kept the Democrats in power, but by a sharply reduced margin, 424 seats in the Assembly to 186 for the combined opposition. They trailed in the popular vote by 351,000 votes, but the majority system and the amended election law prohibiting the opposition from presenting a united slate of candidates, assured them of re-election.[60]

THE REVOLUTION OF MAY, 1960

Early in 1960 the infusion of new foreign money provided by the O.E.E.C. debt stabilization agreement for Turkey, of April 1958, and a modest austerity program at home along with strict price controls, improved the economic situation enough so that Menderes seriously considered calling for new elections. The campaigns of press intimidation and vilifying the opposition had not achieved 100 per cent efficiency, however, and the Prime Minister set out to ensure an absolute Demo-

[59] Eight hundred and eleven sentences by government account between 1950 and 1958.
[60] Karpat, *op. cit.,* pp. 428–429.

cratic dominance over political life in the Ataturk manner, but without the Ataturk "grand design." The Democratic deputies in the Assembly, except for a few leaders above suspicion, such as Köprülü, who had bolted the party, were held in line by full dossiers on their private speculations.[61] In April Menderes formed a parliamentary investigative commission to look into the affairs of the R.P.P. All political activity was banned for three months, and the commission received dictatorial powers. An official statement even accused Republican leaders of trying to undermine national security.

This sort of imputation on the character of Inönü, whose devotion to the ideals of Ataturk had been as unquestioned as his loyalty to his old chief, crystallized widespread but unorganized resentment. The days of 1908 were repeated. A new generation of "Young Turks"—students in the universities—took to the streets, beginning April 28. Shouting "Hürriyet!" "Hürriyet!" (Freedom! Freedom!) they paraded in the major cities. The police, loyal to the government, handled the students roughly. A number were injured, and some were reported killed. Groups of lawyers joined the student demonstrators, and were themselves joined by the cadets of the Turkish Army War College. The Turkish Army, however, continued its traditional neutrality in domestic policies although obeying government orders to break up the demonstrations. In the absence of Army support and a general popular reaction, the student opposition seemed as futile as the South Korean student riots against Syngman Rhee had at the beginning.

The resentment of the Army, particularly among the younger officers, ran deeper than the regime had suspected, however. An attempt to prevent Inönü from traveling to Kayseri to address a political rally backfired when the soldiers sent to detain the old hero opened their ranks to let him pass. General Cemal Gursel, the commander of land forces, denounced this attempt to interfere with personal freedom and criticized the use of troops to put down student parades and the "shedding of innocent Turkish blood." [62] Army leaders asked moderate members of the Democratic party to urge Menderes to abolish his parliamentary investi-

---

[61] Lewis, Geoffrey, "Turkey: The End of the First Republic," *World Today,* September 16, 1960, p. 337. Mr. Lewis, who was in Turkey through the revolution, maintains that the general corruption of the Democrats was a reversion to the Ottoman code of conduct of public officials, which had become rare during the first two and one half decades of the Republic.

[62] The General said; "I will not obey any orders, signed, sealed, or delivered, to shoot my own people." *Washington Star,* May 28, 1960.

gating commission. A petition by ninety deputies to Menderes to do this was rejected; the prime minister would concede only that its work was complete. There were clear-cut indications that the cabinet planned to execute some opposition leaders, massacre all the War College Cadets, and even turn over Kars and Ardahan to the Russians in return for hard cash and military intervention. The army moved quickly, 24 hours ahead of schedule. In the early hours of May 27th, a group of young officers carried out a coup d'etat with the speed and thoroughness (and blood-lessness) of the Egyptians in 1952. President Bayar, Menderes, Foreign Minister Zorlu, and leading Democrats were rounded up and then interned in Yassiada Island near Istanbul. The leaders of the coup formed a "committee of national unity" with General Gursel as President and Prime Minister.[63] The Committee broadcast that its aim was "to organize free and fair elections for the formation of constitutional and democratic government. The administration then will be handed over to the winning side whichever political party it may be." [64]

The new government received generally wide support apparently even in rural Anatolia, where Democratic strength had been greatest. An amnesty was declared for jailed political opponents of Menderes, continuation of Turkey's foreign commitments was reaffirmed, while a committee of jurists and university professors began drafting a new constitution. Gursel announced that the Army had acted to avoid "bloody fratricide"; he disavowed any wish to become a dictator, emphasizing his belief that the military should avoid political conflicts.

A full-scale reassessment of the direction being taken by the new Turkish state would be premature. The Committee of National Unity has undertaken various measures in support of its avowed purpose of re-establishing the "path to democracy" blazed by Ataturk.[65] The draft constitution, as published June 14, 1960, and submitted to the pro tempore Constituent Assembly in May, 1961, for ratification, merely confirmed the *de facto* arrangement in effect since the coup. According to Article I, "the Committee of National Unity shall exercise sovereign

[63] Col. Turkeş, a fiery Nationalist who in 1944 had advocated a Turkish alliance with Germany to recover Soviet Central Asia in fulfillment of Pan-Turanianism, and General Madanoglu were among the leaders of the coup. Gursel, like Cincinnatus of ancient Rome, was found weeding his strawberry patch by the conspirators, and elevated to leadership in the same manner.
[64] *Washington Post*, May 28, 1960.
[65] Lewis, in "Turkey," writes that Ataturk is enjoying a new vogue, in pictures and conversation, since the coup. The revolution was carried out in the name of Ataturk.

authority in the name of the Turkish nation until . . . it transfers the administration to the Grand National Assembly that is to be formed anew by way of the general elections. . . ." At that time (Art. 8) the Committee will automatically dissolve. Separation of power is not indicated; the committee exercises legislative power directly, and executive power through the Council of Ministers appointed by the President with the Committee's approval (Art. 3). Judicial power is exercised by impartial and independent courts operating within the provisions of the law and in the name of the nation (Art. 5).[66] A second committee was formed to draft a new electoral law, which, according to General Gursel would reorganize the election system on the basis of proportional rather than majority representation. A target date of May 27, 1961, was set for elections; this was subsequently deferred to October. As to other reforms urgently needed to broaden the base of political activity and reduce the danger of single-party domination, there was no official decision on them. Such formal changes as a bicameral, truly national Assembly, a checks and balances system, the introduction of a national supreme court, expansion of the powers of the President to counterbalance those of the Prime Minister, must wait until after the elections.

While the Turkish revolution clearly has general support from most social groups, there is mounting evidence that (to paraphrase a Turkish proverb), having thrown Menderes and Co. off their tiger, the Committee of National Unity is having some difficulty in staying glued to its back. This is natural when regimes change and expression replaces repression; the danger is that the new leaders will refuse to listen to voices other than their own. General Gursel has declared that the press is free, but the ten-day suspension in 1961 of *Havadis,* the Democratic Party newspaper, for divisive, provocative, and anti-revolutionary activity, suggests that there continue to be degrees of freedom in Turkish journalism.[67] A High Council of Inquiry, similar in form to the tribunal of independence formed by Ataturk in the 1920's, was created to try officials of the deposed regime and Democratic deputies of the Assembly, for high treason. Minister of the Interior, Namik Gedik, the man behind the police killings of students and an obvious Public Enemy No. 1, committed suicide in jail; ex-President Bayar, who had pulled a gun on the

---

[66] Provisional law number 1 (June 14, 1960), *Official Gazette,* Republic of Turkey, issue No. 10, 525, reprinted by the Turkish Information Office, New York City, July 5, 1960.
[67] *The New York Times,* July 29, 1960.

New Constituent Assembly session, 1961, in the Grand National Assembly Building, Ankara. (Courtesy Turkish Press Attache)

officers who came to arrest him, tried suicide but failed.[68] On October 14, Menderes, Bayar, their cabinet and some 400 deputies went on trial charged with violating the constitution, treason, misuse of public funds, arbitrary electoral procedures, and various other crimes, including profiteering. Altogether the allegations against the regime boiled down to a cynical corrupt disregard for Ataturk's legacy to the Turkish people, and the parliamentary democracy which his successor Inönü had set before the people. The initial weeks of the trial, however, concerned such apparent trivia as Bayar's sale of an afghan hound, a gift from King Zahir Shah, to the Ankara zoo for $2,200 and Adnan Menderes' love affairs. With some pro-Menderes sentiment still around, Turkey's new leaders felt a need to find a legal basis for their revolution as well as to discredit utterly the former leaders in the eyes of the rural population. Regarding the trend of democracy in Turkey, the cold, hard facts of the country's economy were that it was a mess. When the Committee of

[68] Lewis, "Turkey," points out that Bayar's nickname as a C.U.P. lieutenant before World War I was "Comitadji," a label applied to ruthless guerrilla patriots in the Balkans; further, that he was not a mere figurehead in the regime.

National Unity took stock after the coup, it found that Menderes' last bequest was more than $1 billion in unpaid bills. The C.N.U. made appeals for public aid to replenish the Treasury; women even patriotically turned in their gold wedding rings. What economists would call a thorough (and probably painful) readjustment certainly lay in store for the hard-pressed Turks, if they sincerely wished to avoid the vicious circle of foreign credit, inflation; and over-extension which had plagued the government of the First Republic. In November 1960 the Committee of National Unity announced that fourteen members, including the controversial Col. Turkeş, had been dropped, and were being reassigned, mostly to foreign posts as ambassadors or ministers. The reduction in force was the outcome of a division in the Committee's ranks between the extreme nationalists, led by Turkeş, and the moderate nationalists, led by the highly regarded General Madanoğlu. The two groups divided over the question of the direction of the revolution, with Turkeş ready to break with Kemalism and adopt a more aggressive foreign policy. No one questioned his patriotism but neither Pan-Turan nor Neo-Fascism suited Kemalist Turkey in the mid-twentieth century.

The lock-up of all deputies of the ousted Democrats left that party without a head but with a strong support on the grass-roots level where Menderes was attributed with having diverted an increased share of the national income out of the cities and into the villages and small towns.[69] The sacking of Turkeş was in part a sacrifice to rural opinion, as was the new government's position on Algeria. The Constituent Assembly, appointed to write new election laws and a new Constitution mirroring the true spirit of Kemalism, finished its work in 1961. The Electoral Law of May, which provided for secret ballot and direct, universal suffrage for all citizens over twenty-one, included for the first time military officers on active duty. Equal campaign time and opportunities were guaranteed to all the parties formed after political activity had again been permitted; in this way the government hoped that the flagrant electioneering abuses characteristic of the Menderes epoch would be eliminated.

The first test of the caretaker government's plans for "New Turkey" came in July, when the constitution was submitted to a national referendum. The result was qualified approval; out of 13.5 million eligible voters, 6.35 million voted yes, 3.94 million voted no, and 3.21 million

[69] Robinson, R. D., and Lerner, Daniel, "Swords into Ploughshares: the Turkish Army as a Modernizing Force," *World Politics,* October, 1960, p. 43.

abstained. The charter thus introduced into Turkish national life by the support of 47 per cent of the electorate, had a number of features lacking in its 1924 predecessor. A system of checks and balances excluded any danger of future personal dictatorship such as Menderes had exercised. The Grand National Assembly was expanded to two chambers, a House of Representatives of 450 members for legislation and a Senate of 150 members for legislative review and final approval. The new Assembly would also be responsible jointly for the election of each Turkish president, for a single seven-year term. The most significant new feature was an independent judicial system. All parliamentary legislation would be subject to review by a constitutional court, and could be abrogated if deemed to infringe upon the constitution. Also an Assembly of Judges was established to screen judges in order to prevent political abuses in their appointments.

Several anti-government plots were also uncovered during 1961, whether Communist-inspired (an East European radio station which beamed poems of the exiled Turkish poet-Communist Nazim Hikmet to Turkish villages was so popular among the villagers that Ankara initiated a drive to convince them that "Bizim Radyo" was *not* Turkish) or merely reflecting deep cleavages in Turkish popular opinion was not clear. Nevertheless and despite the lack of majority support for the constitution the government went ahead with the promised elections in October.

Four parties campaigned: the Republican Peoples' Party of Inönü; the Justice Party, comprised of former supporters of Menderes and members of the proscribed Demokrat Partisi; the right-wing New Turkey (Yeni Turkiye) Party; and the rural, conservative Peasant Nation Party. The results gave no one party a clear majority—the R.P.P. won 183 seats in the Assembly to 155 for the Justice Party, with the other two parties bringing up the rear but winning enough seats to provide the balance of power. The situation was reversed in the Senate, where the Justice Party won 70 seats to 48 for the R.P.P. After days of wrangling failed to produce a coalition government, the respective commanders of the armed forces issued an ultimatum to the four parties, threatening to seize power if they did not reach agreement. The military threat provided the desired catalyst; a coalition was formed with General Gursel as the new President (one of the conditions of the ultimatum) and seventy-eight-year-old Ismet Inönü as Prime Minister. The major task of the old war hero and associate of Ataturk remained—lacking the inherited power he had enjoyed in his previous tours of leadership, he had to win the full cooperation of his political rivals in Turkey's struggle toward functioning parliamentary democracy.

The verdict on the Yassiada trials of former government leaders shocked some Western observers. After 220 days of testimony, the special court convened to try them convicted Menderes, ex-President Bayar, ex-Foreign Minister Zorlu, and 450 out of 592 government officials, army officers and Democratic Party deputies of various violations of the Constitution and the laws of the state. Menderes, Zorlu, and Finance Minister Polatkan were promptly hanged; Bayar received a life sentence because of his age (seventy-seven), and the remaining defendants were given prison sentences varying from life to four years. The stiff verdicts reflected the bitter personal hatred between Inönü and his former colleagues, particularly Bayar. They also suggested the new government's need to emphasize the evils of the former regime, by example and harsh action, to the rural population and other sections of public opinion which were still loyal to the previous regime. There was enough vocal criticism for government leaders to make statements that the executions were necessary because the men had violated every principle of Turkish national life since the establishment of the Republic. Turkey's allies in NATO also sent formal protests, and it was remembered significantly that Adnan Menderes had been the architect of her adherence to the Western alliance system.

EXTERNAL RELATIONS SINCE WORLD WAR II

The extensive changes that took place in Turkey's internal politics after World War II were not matched by similar changes in foreign policy. The consistency of Turkey's foreign policy in some areas has been in fact unusual in view of various temptations. At the Potsdam Conference and afterward, the USSR put heavy pressure on Turkey to revise the Montreux Convention, in favor of a sort of Black Sea Pact.[70] The Turks pointed out that Chicherin, the Russian delegate to Lausanne, had complained about the International Commission as a flagrant violation of Turkish sovereignty over her territory (i.e., the Straits). The Soviets also in the flush of post-war aggrandizement, demanded the return of the eastern territories of Kars, Ardahan, Artvin, Giresun, and Trebizond. Along with a parallel Communist threat to Greece, the action aroused great concern among the Western powers,

[70] Kiliç, Altemur, *Turkey and the World*, Washington: Public Affairs Press, 1959, pp. 128 ff.

while Turkey rejected the Soviet demands out of hand. Out of Turkish firmness and America's changing views of the USSR, the policy was conceived which became the Marshall Plan in economic aid and the "Northern Tier" containment program expressed by the Baghdad Pact. Turkey has steadfastly equated communism with Russian Imperialism. The Turkish Brigade in Korea went there not only in answer to the UN request for military units from members, but from a deep national conviction that the USSR with its associated nations alone would benefit by the fall of South Korea. Soviet Premier Khrushchev's message to General Gursel in June, 1960, suggesting that the new regime might seek to improve Turkish-Soviet relations, was answered firmly, yet amicably. Gursel wrote that Turkey's loyalty to its international commitments was perfectly compatible with improved relations. Failing an international system of controlled disarmament, however, Turkey's foreign policies must follow the best method of ensuring her security. The same brand of *realpolitik* has dominated Turkey's relations with her neighbors and fellow-members of NATO, CENTO, and the UN with whom the Turks have contacts. Underlying this realpolitik is a hard determination that the line must be drawn where national identity is endangered. Thus the Turks replied to a United Arab Republic resolution for the return of the Hatay, with the declaration that the Hatay is, was, and forever would be, Turkish.[71] The only real display of emotionalism in Turkish foreign policy involved the explosive Cyprus issue. When guerrilla warfare at Cyprus in 1955 became serious enough that Britain was reported to be considering negotiations with Greece over *Enosis* (the demand of Greek Cypriots for union with the mother country), Turks in Istanbul went on a rampage. On September 5–6, 1955, many Greek churches, most shops, and a great number of other business establishments were looted and sacked by well-organized rioters. There is strong evidence that Menderes organized the riots to prove to Greece and Britain that Turkish public opinion was solidly united in opposition to Enosis, and he was so charged with complicity at the Yassiada trials. Official and unofficial statements regarding Cyprus up to 1959 gave the Turkish position as follows: Turkey had ceded the island to Britain in 1878, in return for British support in an Anglo-Ottoman defensive alliance against Russia. Prior to that, Cyprus had been a part of the Ottoman Empire for over 300 years, its longest continuous occupation by a single power. It had

[71] *News From Turkey,* August 4, 1960.

never belonged to Greece (in the sense of the modern Greek nation). The British occupation had become *de jure* in 1914, and was recognized by Turkey in Article 20 of the Lausanne Treaty. In view of the sizeable Turkish minority (20 per cent) on Cyprus and its proximity to Turkish soil, however, Turkish national interests were definitely involved in any surrender of British sovereignty. Next to Britain, Turkey, far more than remote Greece, had the best right to control the island, and would do so if necessary.

What had become an extremely difficult issue, embittering relations between three members of NATO, was fortunately solved by the Zurich Agreement of 1959. Cyprus was to become an independent island republic, with a Greek Cypriot President, and a Turkish Cypriot Vice-President. Its Assembly was to be based on communal, confessional representation, with Greeks in the majority. Its projected constitution would bar either union with Greece, or partition between Greek and Turk Cypriots. Britain was confirmed in her possession of military bases, and Turkish troops (along with Greeks) stationed in Cyprus were a further guarantee of joint national interests. In this manner face was saved on all sides, and in August, 1960, after settlement of a protracted dispute between Cyprus and Britain over the size of British bases, the island republic entered the family of nations.

As a footnote to Turkey's foreign policy vis-a-vis her political evolution, in the troubled year of 1957, when the Democratic campaign of restriction was at its height, the campaign between the party and its opponents was fought out entirely on domestic issues. There was no mention in the press of a bitter dispute raging between Turkey and Syria over border provocations, a dispute which reached the UN before Syria withdrew her complaints. The dignified bearing of the Turkish delegate was in marked contrast to the shrill Syrian complaints—and to the fierce campaign at home. The Ottoman Turks ruled the Arabs for 400 years, then World War I cut the two peoples apart. Until 1950 the Turkish proverb "Neither all the candy from Damascus, nor the face of the Arab" mirrored Turkey's behavior towards the Arab states of the Middle East, cool, correct, aloof.[72] The Turks recognized Israel promptly in 1949, emphasizing their westernization in line with Ataturk's dicta by their action. Increasing Soviet aggressiveness in the Middle East after Stalin's death in 1953, impelled Turkey to rethink its policy toward its

[72] Kiliç, *op. cit.*, p. 188.

neighbors to the south. The Baghdad Pact, beginning as a Turko-Iraqi alliance in 1955, was designed as a sort of objective, bipartisan panacea for the Middle East. Turkey hoped that its Muslim nature would encourage other Arab states to adhere, and the regional emphasis allow them to participate without losing face through association with the oft-beaten horse of imperialism. The reaction to the pact among these nations is described in subsequent chapters. There exists a considerable body of opinion among informed Turks that the pact had the opposite effect intended; it encouraged Communist-Arab cooperation and whetted Arab-Western nationalism. In the Turkish view, American failure to become a full member of the pact, instead of placating Nasir and company undermined its position in political bargaining. While insisting that Turkey will honor all foreign commitments (the CENTO headquarters was moved to Ankara after Iraq withdrew), General Gursel had stated that Turkey seeks friendlier relations with her neighbors, Communist, Arab, and Muslim, without discrimination. Improved Turkish-Arab relations may well mean that an emerging moderate Arab nationalism, dedicated to self-improvement and nonintervention, can look to Turkey as a model of progress toward Democracy without violent upheavals.

An example of this tutorial attitude of the Turkish government is the recent offer to mediate between France and the Algerian Provisional Government of the F.L.N. The French rejection of this offer out of hand—only De Gaulle is qualified to deal with Algerian rebels—does not mean that this unusual step for an ally to take unilaterally will not bear fruit eventually. The action has pleased the pro-Menderes peasants, thus broadening popular support at home and set the stage for closer ties with the Arabs who have championed the F.L.N. cause. By such steps Turkey is moving toward a normalized Middle Eastern policy relationship.

RECOMMENDED READINGS

1. Allen, Henry E., *The Turkish Transformation,* Chicago: University of Chicago Press, 1935.
2. Armstrong, Harold E., *Grey Wolf, Mustafa Kemal,* London: Barker, 1932.
3. Bisbee, Eleanor, *The New Turks,* Philadelphia: University of Pennsylvania Press, 1951.
4. Djemal Pasha, *Memoirs of a Turkish Statesman,* 1913–1919, New York: Doran, 1922.

5. Ekrem, Selma, *Turkey Old and New*, New York: Charles Scribner's Sons, 1947.

6. Gökalp, Ziya, *Turkish Nationalism and Western Civilization*, Transl. by Niyazi Berkes, New York: Columbia University Press, 1959.

7. Halide Edib (Adivar), *The Turkish Ordeal*, New York: Century, 1928.

8. Heyd, Uriel, *Foundations of Turkish Nationalism: The Life and Teachings of Ziya Gökalp*, London: Luzac, 1950.

9. Hostler, Charles, *Turkism and The Soviets*, New York: Frederick A. Praeger, Inc., 1957.

10. Hurewitz, J. C., *Diplomacy in the Near and Middle East*, 2 vol. Princeton: D. Van Nostrand Co., Inc., 1956.

11. Jaschke, G., *Die Turkei in den Jahren 1942–1951*, Wiesbaden: Harrassowitz, 1955.

12. Karpat, Kemal, *Turkey's Politics*, Princeton: Princeton University Press, 1959.

13. Kiliç, Altemur, *Turkey and The World*, Washington, D. C.: Public Affairs Press, 1959.

14. Lerner, Daniel, *The Passing of Traditional Society*, Glencoe, Ill.: Free Press, 1960.

15. Lewis, Bernard, *The Emergence of Modern Turkey*, London: Oxford (for the Royal Institute of International Affairs), 1961.

16. Lewis, Geoffrey, *Turkey*, New York: Frederick A. Praeger, 1955.

17. Mustapha Kemal Ataturk, *Speech Before The Opening of The Grand National Assembly*, 1927.

18. Papen, Franz von, *Memoirs*, London: Andre Deutsch, 1952.

19. Spencer, William, *The Land and People of Turkey*, Philadelphia: J. B. Lippincott Co., 1958.

20. Thomas, Lewis V., and Frye, R. N., *The United States and Turkey and Iran*, Cambridge: Harvard University Press, 1951.

21. Thornburg, Max, *et al.*, *Turkey: an Economic Appraisal*, New York: The Twentieth Century Fund, 1949.

22. Turkey and the UN (by The Carnegie Endowment for International Peace), New York: Manhattan Publishing Co., 1961.

23. Webster, Donald E., *The Turkey of Ataturk*, Philadelphia: American Academy of Political and Social Science, 1939.

24. Yalman, Ahmed Emin, *Turkey in My Time*, Norman: University of Oklahoma Press, 1956.

See also *News From Turkey*, Published by The Turkish Information Office, New York, N. Y.

CHAPTER 4

TWENTIETH-CENTURY IRAN

Historical Background: Isolation and Medievalism

$\mathcal{T}$he territorial and political barriers erected between Persia and Europe by the formation of Ottoman power effectively isolated the Persian state, which had suffered greatly from Mongol and Tartar invasions, from the reviving European spirit of the Renaissance. Having penetrated deeply into Europe, the Ottomans were in a position to observe the developments which in time revolutionized the West, bringing on modern industrial technology. That they did not keep pace was due to other factors. Persia, centrally located in Asia, but an Asian rather than "bridge" country, was exposed very little to these developments. Consequently the customary pattern of native alternating with foreign dynasties continued well into modern times.

In the sixteenth century a new ruling house, the Safavid, succeeded to the throne of Cyrus. Shah Ismail, founder of the dynasty and restorer of Persian sovereignty, has a special place in Persian history. He was a Sayyid, a descendant of Husayn, the Prophet's grandson, and ultimately of Muhammad himself, and it was he who established the Shi'a doctrine of Islam as the official one for Persia. But the Safavid ruler who did most for the country was Shah Abbas I, "The Great" (1587–1629). Abbas was a contemporary of Queen Elizabeth I, Charles V, and Sulayman the Magnificent, adding a genuine Oriental note to the striking intellectual and political achievements of these rulers. During Shah Abbas's reign two English noblemen, the Sherley brothers, made their way to the Persian court where they secured special privileges for Christian merchants and helped train the Shah's army. Shah Abbas made Isfahan his capital

99

and embellished the center of the city with the magnificent buildings which make it memorable even among Persian cities, for Persians say, *"Isfahan nisf i-jahan"*—"Isfahan is half the world." He strengthened national unity under Shi'ism by making Meshed a pilgrimage center, and on one occasion he walked the entire eight hundred miles to the shrine of Imam Riza there.[1] Shah Abbas, by these forceful and visible methods, brought order to Persia and consolidated the tribes and various peoples into a national state such as had not been achieved since Sassanid times. Nevertheless it was a purely Oriental, Muslim state, ruled by a monarch who did not hesitate to behead his sons on sheer suspicion and who ruled in the autocratic manner of his forebears.

The state of politics in Persia for the next two and one-half centuries supported the notion of Peter the Great that the country's decadence was a golden opportunity for expansion southward.[2] The oft-repeated story of foreign conquest continued. The Safavids were overthrown by Afghan invaders who in turn were expelled by Nadir Kuli, a shepherd from Khurasan who had won some importance as the leader of a robber band and subsequently entered the service of the monarchy. In his capacity as a commander of troops, Nadir restored Persia's fortunes; and on the death of the infant Shah, the nobles elevated him to the vacant throne as Nadir Shah (1736–1747). Nadir is often referred to as the last great Asiatic conqueror, but it is difficult to see what constructive work he did for Persia. Technically Nadir was a usurper; the struggle for power at his death brought Persia a brief respite with the success of the Zands (so-called because Karim Khan, the *de facto* ruler for twenty-nine years, was a member of the Zand section of the Lak tribe). During the Zand period, British and Dutch commercial interests established themselves in Persia, the latter with a factory at Bushire on the Persian Gulf (1763). The Zands were tossed out by the Qajars, under whom Persia came into full view of the West.

The nineteenth century was a critical one for Persia. The Qajars, a Turkish rather than Iranian tribe by origin and one of the seven tribes (the Kizilbash or "Red Heads" from their head gear) that had aided Shah Ismail in establishing the Safavid dynasty, gave the state a leadership of relative peace but increasing moral bankruptcy. Founded in blood —the first Qajar ruler, Agha Muhammad, blinded twenty thousand

[1] Sykes, Sir Percy. *A History of Persia,* Vol. II, London: Macmillan, 1930, p. 3.
[2] *Ibid.,* pp. 244–245. The Will of Peter the Great gives an extraordinary clarification of Russian global aims which applies equally well today.

inhabitants of Kerman—the dynasty ended in utter weakness. Like Ottoman Turkey, Persia fought a number of wars with Russia and lost just as often; but Britain's determination to maintain its links with India deterred the Czars from complete absorption. The Treaty of Gulistan in 1813 confirmed Russian possession of Georgia; the Treaty of Turkomanchai (1828) following the capture of Tabriz, gave Russia the districts of Erivan and Nakhichevan, reserved navigation on the Caspian Sea to her ships, and provided her with capitulatory privileges. The treaty formed the basis of all subsequent intercourse between European powers and Persia up to Reza Shah's time, including capitulations granted to other powers which existed until 1928, and established the present Russo-Persian boundary at the Aras River. Britain opposed the invasion of Afghanistan by Nasr al-din Shah Qajar in 1856 and forced the Shah to withdraw. By the Treaty of Paris (1857) he recognized Afghan independence. The principle of the integrity of Persia was a corollary to the principle of Ottoman territorial integrity in British foreign policy for a century.[3]

Anglo-Russian rivalry in Persia was busiest in the economic sphere. In 1872, Baron Reuter, a British subject and founder of the news agency that bears his name, secured a seventy-year concession from Nasr al-din Shah covering construction of a railway, mineral resources, waterworks, and street-car transportation. In the following year, the Shah made a European tour and was "persuaded" at St. Petersburg to cancel the concession. Later Reuter got another concession to establish the Imperial Bank of Persia, backed by British capital; another British firm got the short-lived tobacco monopoly. The Russians meanwhile set up and trained a Persian Cossack Brigade under their own officers; it was designed to serve Russian strategic interests, of course, but ironically it was to form the nucleus of Persian nationalism later, as the single organized and disciplined unit in the Persian Army. The Russians also secured fishing rights in the Caspian and opened a discount bank.

Nasr al-din's long reign (1834–1896) brought Persia comparative peace, but the Shah's intentions of modernizing the country along Western lines met a fate similar to those of Mahmud II and Abdul Majid in the Ottoman Empire. The Shah believed that the proper adjustment could be achieved by grafting Western institutions and technical knowledge onto traditional Oriental society. He encouraged Western missions,

[3] Lenczowski, George. *The Middle East in World Affairs,* 2nd ed., Ithaca: Cornell University Press, 1956, p. 30.

concessions, and the importation of goods, only to find that profiteers, confidence men, and all sorts of shady schemers were flocking to Persia to take advantage of the naïve Persians. "I wish," he said once, "that never a European had set his foot on my country's soil, for then we would have been spared all these tribulations." [4] The various concessions brought some revenue into Persia, but this was counter-balanced by the loss of political maneuverability so that the Shah was forced to conclude that "reforms do not agree with Persia."

To sum up the machinery of government prior to the constitutional crisis of the twentieth century, the Shah was an absolute monarch, the commander of the army, the judiciary, and the legislature. In accordance with Oriental custom, he held daily court (*Diwan* in Persian) at which officials and even private citizens presented their petitions for redress. The Grand Vizier controlled all departments of the government, and he was in turn controlled by the Shah. The situation recalled the statement of an earlier Shah to an English visitor: "There you see all my ministers; I can cut all their heads off. . . . That is real power." In the manner of the Achaemenians, Persia was divided into provinces, each ruled by a royal governor who was required to pay a certain amount of annual revenue to the court and who would himself sell all subordinate posts in order to meet his own expenses. The Shari'a was the law of the land as interpreted by the *mullas* and *mujtahids,* the latter being learned doctors of law who interpreted Koranic law in a frequently venal fashion.[5] Foreigners enjoyed capitulatory privileges similar to those in the Ottoman Empire, but Persia's distance from trading centers and its status as an undeveloped state, attracted fewer of the international riff-raff than Constantinople did. Corruption, which originated with the sale of provincial governorships, extended down to the lowest rank of civil servant, all offices being sold to the highest bidder. Little trade existed, and the landed aristocracy found their strength not only in tax exactions but also in a firm resistance to any sort of tolerant or democratic behavior toward the peasantry. Outside the towns and villages, in the *dasht* (untilled land) the tribes obeyed no authority save that of their chief, observed a rudimentary democracy in their tribal assemblies, and maintained an independent parallel existence.

[4] Haas, William, *Iran,* New York: Columbia University Press, 1946, p. 35.
[5] According to Sykes, *op. cit.,* p. 385, the mujtahids of Najaf and Kerbela were generally of a higher character and an exception to this rule.

THE STRUGGLE FOR PARLIAMENTARY GOVERNMENT,
1905–1921

The outbreak of popular feeling which resulted in Persia's first constitution had its roots in the events of the late 1800's—events which
proved very clearly to educated Persians how weak and dependent on
European economic interests their nation was. Some of the concessions
given by the Shah have already been mentioned. The one which seems
to have sparked the nationalists was the Tobacco Regie of 1890–1892.
Following the Shah's return from Europe, he gave the Persian Tobacco
Monopoly Company, an English company, a monopoly over the production, export, and sale of tobacco in Persia. The Persian Government
would receive £15,000 rent per annum plus one-fourth of the profits;
however, the Persian *people* had to buy back the tobacco they had previously grown, at inflated prices, from British entrepreneurs. Even more
important, their own tobacco had to pass through Christian hands to
reach their water-pipes and was, hence, defiled. The depth of the popular reaction forced the Shah to repeal the concession in 1892. It was an
expensive lesson in international finance; Persia paid the British con-
cessionaires £500,000 for termination, borrowing the money from the
Imperial Bank at six per cent![6]
The results of cancellation were twofold: England lost her favored
position in Persia, and the Shah became aware of the subtle, yet firmly
cohesive nationalism which has enabled Persia to survive throughout the
centuries. There was no general intellectual ferment; grievances were
specific; the minute educated class had no such ideals or philosophy as
animated the American patriots in 1776. Nevertheless, the specific
grievances of the peasantry and the vague yearnings for a more democratic life of the urban class combined to inaugurate unexpected change
in the medieval Qajar state.
A main source of the parliamentary movement came from Jamal al-
Din al-Afghani, a Persian teacher and thinker who may be compared
with Ziya Gökalp in Ottoman Turkey in his influence on Persian nationalists. Jamal al-Din spent more time outside Persia than inside and
lived for many years in Afghanistan, hence his surname "The Afghan."

[6] *"De Concession en concession la Perse sera bientot toute entiere dans les mains
des etrangers."* Cf. Browne, E. G., *The Persian Revolution*, 1905–1909, Cambridge: Cambridge University Press, 1910, p. 32.

Like Gökalp he was an advocate of Pan-Islam and travelled throughout the Islamic world lecturing on the movement; however, he was not an Islamic nationalist in the traditional sense. "The stream of renovation flows quickly toward the East," he wrote. In 1882 he went to Paris where, with his disciple Muhammad 'Abduh, he founded an Arabic weekly newspaper. Jamal al-Din is associated with Pan-Islam in much the same way as Gökalp is with the Young Turk movement and Muhammad 'Abduh with Pan-Arabism, as a sort of Nestor surrounded by young firebrands. He gave both the Sultan and the Shah a hard time, each handing him off gingerly to the other for long periods. Afghani's chief collaborator in the task of arousing Persian nationalism and resistance to Qajar despotism (which he hated so much that he accepted an appointment as the Shah's confidential advisor only to foment unrest against the monarch) was the Armenian Prince, Malkom Khan, a converted Muslim who had advanced rapidly in the royal service because he was a skilled magician! [7] Together they published a paper called *Qanun* (Law) in Persia, attacking the corrupt state of the government. They called for a fixed code of laws, a parliament representative of the people, and guarantees of individual security. The effect of *Qanun* on the public was that of an electric shock applied to a sleeping patient, arousing him to galvanic motion.

In 1896 Nasr ad-din Shah was assassinated. His successor, Muzaffar al-Din, did nothing to refill Persia's treasury or to rebuild her reputation abroad. The Shah's chief asset seemed to be a pair of sweeping black mustaches; these earned him considerable publicity on his European tours but no money. After the collapse of the Tobacco Regie, the Shah was graciously invited to England to receive the Order of the Garter, but even that was withheld through a misunderstanding. Russia, on the other hand, gave generously in return for concessions plus Persian guarantees not to contract loans with any other nation. Since Persia's total annual revenues did not quite equal the amount of the Russian loans, the result was increased indebtedness.

In 1905 the first *bast* of the constitutional movement took place. [8] The prima facie cause was the beating of some merchants by the bodyguards of the governor of Tehran on charges of cornering the sugar market.

---

[7] He founded the first Masonic Temple in Persia, called Faramush Khana, or "House of Forgetfulness."
[8] *Bast* is a Persian tradition by which officials and even ordinary citizens are immune from arrest if they take refuge in certain public buildings.

Other merchants protested, demanding the dismissal of certain unpopular ministers, and took refuge in the Masjid-i-Shah where they were joined by a number of mullas. Another cause for discontent which was aired was the *'urf* (civil law) which was not truly legal but which nevertheless governed the civil relationships of the population in place of law courts. The number of *bast*-takers increased steadily, and the Shah found the government unable to carry on normal activity. He yielded to the demands of his now-rebellious subjects by dismissing the hated Grand Vizier, Ayn-u-Dola (who was also his son-in-law), and by agreeing to convene a House of Justice to consider political reform. There was no talk at this time of a constitution.

The *dast-khatt,* or autographed fiat according to which the Shah accepted the demands received wide circulation. The government, with that curious ophthalmia which seems to afflict autocratic regimes in the presence of genuine popular movements, did nothing for a year. In April, 1906, the 'ulema of Tehran presented a petition to Muzaffar asking him to fulfil his promises. The extent to which democratic desires had spread may be seen by the fact that the 'ulema supported the constitutional movement although its success would mean curtailment of *their* powers too. Muzaffar was paralyzed in bed; and Ayn-u-Dola, still in office, threw them out and expelled one of the leaders. About fifteen persons were killed during subsequent mob demonstrations, and the bazaars were shut in protest. Ayn-u-Dola ordered them reopened. This set off the Great Bast of August, 1906. The mujtahids of Teheran fled to Qum, where they sent the Shah a note threatening to leave the country unless he fulfilled the terms of the *dast-khatt.* Their threat, if carried out, would have had the effect of stopping all legal transactions, since Persia was a Muslim state and even the Shah's actions needed religious sanction. At the same time the chief merchants and bankers led a movement to the British Legation where they were assured of sanctuary. Before long 12,000 men were camped in orderly fashion in the garden of the Legation, which took on the appearance of a Boy Scout Jamboree. Tehran was paralyzed—all official and commercial activity ceased. The Shah again yielded; Ayn-u-Dola was sacked. But this time the constitutionalists wanted further guarantees. As a result, under extreme pressure from the Western-minded leaders of the movement, the Shah signed the official document which created the first National Assembly (Majlis) and gave Persia its first constitution. It was his last official act; he died a few days later from the after-effects of his stroke and was succeeded by his son, Muhammad Ali. In the Legation the confused dissidents struck their tents and stole away.

The Organic Law of Persia contains fifty-one basic and 107 supplementary laws, the latter adopted in 1907 to cover several important omissions. The basic law set up a bicameral Majlis, a lower house of between 162 and 200 members where legislative activity was centered, and a Senate of sixty members. The lower house, which has become known as the Majlis, was responsible for all foreign concessions, treaties, budget supervision, and legislation. The Senate, composed of landowners, was an advisory body although its approval was necessary for final passage of a bill. The Shah was not given the veto power. The supplementary laws were an attempt to equate democratic processes with Persian culture and tradition. Thus the national religion was written into law as "Islam, according to the orthodox Ja'fari doctrine of the Church of the Twelve Imams (i.e. Shi'ism) which faith the Shah must profess and promote." Other articles provided for the protection of foreign nationals, equality before the law and other individual rights, and for separation of powers. Article 35 conveys the throne as a Divine gift in trust to the Shah, yet he is required to appear before the Majlis prior to investiture and swear to uphold the Constitution.[9] Articles 36 and 37 declare that the powers of government, all derived from the people, are to be divided into legislature, executive, and judiciary, all divided from each other. Article 32 defines conflict of interest: a deputy to the Majlis cannot simultaneously hold a salaried public office. Ministers must be Muslims and of Iranian nationality. In order to ensure that the Majlis did not pass laws at variance with the rules and laws of Islam, Article 2 prescribed the formulation of a committee of mujtahids to test their legality; however, the committee became inoperative under Reza Shah, who wished to control the clergy, so presumably all laws passed in Iran since 1922 are open to challenge.

The relatively swift success of the Persian constitutionalists, in contrast to the century-long struggle of the reformist elements in the Ottoman Empire, may be ascribed to a number of factors. One was the Persian character; Gandhi's tenets of "passive resistance," as developed in India later on, are well illustrated by the spectacle of 12,000 Persians—the bulk of the business community—sitting on the grass in the British

---

[9] Browne, *op. cit.*, pp. 362–384, has the full text. There have been three amendments, in 1925, 1949, and 1951. The Majlis actually had 136 deputies until 1957 when the number was increased to 164.

Legation compound and waiting until the complete stoppage of activity forced the Shah to capitulate. The success of the Japanese against Russia showed educated Persians that a backward oriental nation could defeat an advanced Western one. Nationalist stirrings in Russia itself were transmitted seismographically southward.

The Russians, who had asserted full control over Central Asia by the end of the nineteenth century, moved into a dominant position vis-à-vis North Persia. Britain, concerned over protection for India, took as its "sphere of influence" South Persia up to (but not including) Tehran. The success of the nationalists caused the rival powers to take a second look at their eastern policies; a revitalized Persia might throw both of them out. In 1907 they signed a convention delineating their interests and guaranteeing the integrity of a "friendly" Persia.

Muhammad Ali Shah Qajar came to the throne determined to crush the constitutionalists. A despot not unlike Egypt's ex-King Faruq in appearance and inclinations, he worked along divide-and-rule principles. In December 1907, he suddenly arrested the newly-appointed Premier and tried to dissolve the Majlis. At this time his chief support was his Russian-officered Cossack Brigade. For some peculiar reason, he failed to follow up the advantage of surprise, and the threat of a *jihad* forced him to back down. Under nationalist pressure he swore on a sealed Koran (the most solemn oath in Persia) to defend the Constitution. In 1908, however, the Shah ordered his troops to seize Tehran and again dissolved the Majlis. The constitutionalists held out in Tabriz, however, and joined forces with the traditionally antiroyalist Bakhtiari tribesmen against the Shah, while a Russian force moved into Azerbaijan to "restore order." In 1909 the nationalists defeated the half-hearted opposition of the Cossack Brigade outside Tehran, and entered the capital. Muhammad Ali Shah found it expedient to abdicate and to retire to Moscow, and constitutional government returned to Persia. The new ruler, Ahmad Shah, did not oppose reinstatement of the Majlis, since he was only eleven years old at the time.

Persia's ordeal was not over, however. A financial crisis arose immediately to plague the reconstituted government. Two improvident sovereigns plus the venality of many officials had left nothing in the till. The Russians, meanwhile, insisted that the Anglo-Russian agreement limited Persia to loans from these two powers alone at the customary rates of interest. The only chance to escape this deadlock lay in help from a disinterested nation. In 1911 the Cabinet arranged for the United States to supply financial advisors, and Dr. Morgan Shuster went to Tehran as head of the first American financial mission. It was the first serious contact between the two nations.[10] Shuster recommended stern measures to stabilize the economy and asked for powers tantamount to dictatorship to carry out his program. He had the support of the nationalists, but Russia viewed him with extreme disfavor and followed up an ultimatum for his removal with armed intervention. Shuster went home to write his classic attack on imperialism, *The Strangling of Persia.* Although the mission failed, it left behind a reservoir of good will for the United States which was to bear fruit many years later.

The effect of World War I on Persia was to bring German influence to bear on a situation which had been previously limited to Anglo-Russian interests. The Iranian Democratic Party, the main arm of the constitutionalists, was opposed to both, and welcomed German support. When war broke out, Persia declared its neutrality, while the Premier, Mustaufi al Mamalek, secretly concluded an alliance with the German Ambassador, Prince von Reuss. The treaty guaranteed Persian independence, promised arms and munitions, and assured the Shah of political asylum in Germany if he were compelled to flee his country. German agents also won the allegiance of the Swedish-officered gendarmerie and the tribes. The most successful agent was Wassmuss, former German Consul at Bushire.[11] During his consulship, Wassmuss had spent considerable time among the tribes of southern Iran, learning their language and buttering them up through lavish entertainment and largesse. On his return to Persia he organized an anti-British confederacy which was soon in open rebellion; the British garrison in Shiraz was surrounded and forced to surrender. Since southern Persia was a declared British sphere of influence, astride the lines to India, the British reacted quickly. Sir Percy Sykes recruited a Persian brigade, the South Persia Rifles; and in a series of lightning marches from city to city, he regained control of the area. Wassmuss himself was captured.

The end of the war found Persia in a state of anarchy. The Bolsheviki were active along the northern frontiers, while the south was under direct British military "protection." Fearing further dismember-

[10] In 1900 an American missionary, Chester Labaree, was murdered by tribesmen in northern Iran. The Labaree murder became a cause celebre and because of it a number of Congressmen learned that Persia still existed as a state.

[11] A full and vivid account of Wassmuss's career may be found in Christopher Sykes, *Wassmuss: the German Lawrence,* London: Longmans, 1936.

ment of the country, Curzon negotiated with the Shah the Anglo-Persian Agreement of 1919. "A peaceful Persia, a stable Persia, a friendly Persia, an independent Persia have been the cornerstones of British policy," he declared.[12] The agreement also promised Persia a substantial loan at 7 per cent, payable monthly. Curzon's interest in keeping the Bolsheviki out of the country appears in retrospect the only laudable element in the affair. Public sentiment in Persia ran high against the agreement, which was regarded as an attempt to create a British mandate; the Tehran press denounced Premier Vosuq-ed-Dowleh for his timidity and cowardice. Persian rancor was not alleviated by the experience of the Persian delegation to the Peace Conference. Sparked by British intransigence, the Allied nations rejected Persia's claims to territory in the Caucasus and Central Asia by Czarist Russia in the nineteenth century. Britain insisted that as Persia had not participated in the war it was not entitled to be seated as an Allied nation. Wilson's protest at what he called "usurpation of the rights of Persia" went unanswered as did all humanitarian goals sought at the Conference.

In 1920 Vosuq-ed-Dowleh resigned, a victim of these assorted pressures. His successor, Mushir-ed-Dowleh, pressed the Majlis into suspending the Agreement. After four months, he too resigned. His parting comment—"The eagle should permit the small birds to sing and care not wherefore they sang"[13]—fell on deaf ears although it was particularly prophetic in view of the care with which the "eagles" of the 1960's listen to the claque of their smaller feathered colleagues lest one off-key twitter might presage a revolution. Britain, presented with a gilt-edged opportunity to regain Persian support and crush the Communists in the north, instead withdrew military support from the White armies and forced the resignations of all Czarist officers serving on the Persian payroll. The parliamentary crisis continued to mount through the end of the year as Persians demonstrated that combination of inability to work in concert and personal vindictiveness which has hampered the easy growth of Western democratic procedures there along with the Eastern tendency to rely on arbitrary leaders. In 1921 the crisis was resolved by a coup led by Ziya al-Din Tabatabai, a Sayyid who had joined the reform movement as a writer, and Reza Khan, commander of the Persian Cos-

---

[12] Fatemi, N., *Diplomatic History of Persia, 1917–1923,* New York: R. F. Moore, 1952, p. 10.
[13] *Ibid.,* p. 105.

sack Brigade. The two men denounced the Anglo-Persian Agreement publicly and five days after the coup signed a treaty with the Soviet government.

The treaty was a sharp contrast to the abortive Anglo-Persian agreement concluded earlier, but it suited the duality of Soviet policy—repudiation of Czarist imperialism along with calls for a revolt of "Muhammadan toilers of the East" against Western oppression and local pashas. The Soviet government renounced all Czarist concessions and properties in Persia. Both signatories agreed not to interfere in each other's internal affairs and to crack down on subversive organizations. An important provision allowed Russia the right to send troops into Persian territory in the event of anti-Soviet aggression from there. This presumably was a Soviet safeguard against eventual attack by counter-revolutionary "White" forces. The Persians, though unhappy, accepted the clause in return for the agreed-on withdrawal of Soviet forces from Gilan.[14]

While the Soviets were negotiating the treaty, emphasizing coexistence, their agents worked busily to undermine Persian solidarity and pave the way ultimately for a coup. The best opportunity to "fish in troubled waters" came in Gilan Province just south of the Caspian. The densely forested slopes and marshes of Gilan were ideal for extralegal operations of any kind. After the war Kuchik Khan, a Persian nationalist and Qajar agent, set himself up as a sort of Robin Hood who kidnapped the rich for ransom rather than merely emptying their pockets. Kuchik's band were called *Jangalis* because of the jungle terrain in which they operated (*Jangal* is Persian for "jungle"). Persia's anarchic state and the inhospitable marshes of Gilan favored their regime, and the militia left them alone. But Kuchik was quite a "fisherman" himself. He founded a brotherhood, Ittihad-al-Islam (Union of Islam); they swore not to shave their beards or heads until all foreign aggressors had been driven from "the sacred soil of Persia." Kuchik had the backing of the Germans, the Turks, and the constitutionalists. Had he been cut from the same bolt of cloth as Reza Khan, he could easily have marched on Tehran and assumed the Qajar throne. Instead, he expended his forces in futile assaults on the British and later the White Russians. In 1920 a Soviet expeditionary force entered Gilan on the pretext of rounding up White rebels. It established contact with Kuchik; and in return for a free hand in the province, Russia backed the formation of a provisional govern-

[14] Lenczowski, *op. cit.*, p. 164 n. There is some confusion on this point.

ment of Gilan, the first Soviet-sponsored state outside the confines of territorial Russia. The Communists soon began to bicker among themselves as well as with Kuchik, however, on which group should be the leader and which economic and political methods would be most effective in communizing Gilan. The signing of the Irano-Soviet Treaty removed whatever pretext the Soviet troops had for remaining in Gilan; they were withdrawn in October, 1921, and Kuchik Khan "fished" no more.

The honeymoon between Reza Khan and Ziya al-Din Tabatabai was brief. The first governmental alignment had Reza as Minister of War and Ziya as Premier. Ziya's radical reforms enraged the wealthy conservative landowners, and his disagreements with Reza over reform methods cost him army support. Three months later Reza forced him into exile from which he did not return after World War II. Reza moved slowly. First he reorganized the army and established public security. In 1923 he became Premier. The Majlis, in 1925 formally terminated the Qajar rule and named Reza as the provisional head of state, and shortly thereafter it passed an amendment to the Constitution naming him Shah and replacing the Qajar succession with Reza Shah's new Pahlavi dynasty.[15] This amendment notes that "if the Shah has no male issue, the Crown Prince shall be proposed by him and approved by the Majlis, provided that the said heir shall not belong to the Qajar family." [16] Had the Shah's third wife, Queen Farah, failed to provide the expected male heir, which she did late in 1960, the succession could have passed out of the Pahlavi family, at least the direct line.

REZA SHAH (1925–1941)

With the advent to power of the Pahlavis the wheel came full circle; a genuine native authority again presided over the destinies of Persia and led a national regeneration of the country (officially renamed Iran.) [17] Reza Shah, who almost alone led Iran into the twentieth century, was of pure native stock, born in 1878 in Mazanderan Province south of the Caspian. This region, by tradition, is the aboriginal home of the Iranians. His ancestry was one reason why Reza gained control so

[15] Reza himself chose the name of the old Persian language spoken in Sassanian times for his new dynasty.
[16] Lockhart, Laurence. "The Constitutional Laws of Persia," *Middle East Journal,* Autumn, 1959, p. 379.
[17] The change of name became official in 1925.

easily. The hated Qajars, a Turkish tribe originally, were regarded as a foreign dynasty by most Iranians.

Reza found the ladder of success via service in the Cossack Brigade. A British officer who met him before he had become prominent noted his quick mind, military bearing, and intelligent interest in European weapons.

At the outset of Reza Shah's reign there was considerable agitation in Iran for a republic. He seems to have supported the movement and agreed to become its first president. The sweeping actions of the Turkish Grand National Assembly under Mustafa Kemal in abolishing the Caliphate and separating Islam from the state frightened Iran's religious leaders. They denounced the movement; while Reza swiftly changed course and announced publicly that the Shi'a religion was not consonant with republicanism. It was the wisest course. Not only did it ensure his own position, but republicanism would have meant a return to anarchy.

Reza was determined to reunite Iran under the control of the central government, to establish internal security, to stabilize the economy, and to build a strong modern nation in the land of Cyrus. Like his neighbor, Ataturk, he was an uncompromising nationalist. Iran must be purged of foreign influences. The paradox in Reza's thinking was that the importation of Western reforms and technology was necessary to accomplish modernization. Unlike Ataturk who insisted on a complete break with Ottoman institutions and a volte-face into the twentieth century, Reza worked within the carefully-erected fabric of Persian civilization which had endured longer than any other in the Middle East except Egypt's. It was his deliberate policy to encourage his people to look two ways—back to the ancient glories of the Sassanians and Achaemenians and forward to a revived, modernized Iran. Even Iran's Islamic age was to him a "foreign" period; his most energetic attacks were directed against the Shi'a clergy and their reactionary hold on Iran.

The first step was to restore order and strengthen the army. In a series of campaigns, Reza brought the tribes under direct government control and ended the Republic of Gilan. Shaykh Khazal of Muhammera, who enjoyed a privileged position tantamount to autonomy as head of the Arab tribes of southern Iran and had the support of the Anglo-Iranian Oil Company, was locked up after he demanded that the concessions made to him by the Qajar monarchs be continued. The tribes were more difficult to curb; the Lurs, in particular, rebelled when construction began on a road through their territory and were brought to heel only after severe fighting. A policy combining force with a real attempt to redress tribal grievances (such as the dismissal of corrupt officials) and resettlement on newly-constructed villages was quite successful in bringing the tribes into the larger political framework of the nation, although cases of banditry occur even today.[18]

Internal reform was urgently needed, less in the political than in the economic and cultural spheres. Reza Shah set about his reforms with furious energy—he often arrived at government offices at the opening hour to make sure that the officials in charge were there on time.[19] He did not tamper with the Constitution or the Majlis. Instead he kept the assembly in existence but packed it and gave it no real power. Certain deputies who opposed his methods, notably Muhammad Musaddiq, were pressured into exile or quiet pasturage at their country homes. The greatest problem facing Iran, he knew, was financial; unless the treasury were solvent, the great leap forward would be matched by two steps backward into renewed dependence on foreign loans and subsequent political serfdom. In 1922 he invited Dr. Arthur Millspaugh to head a U.S. mission to reorganize Iranian finances. Millspaugh, then economic advisor to the U.S. State Department, stayed for five years. His mission enjoyed the complete cooperation of the Shah at first and achieved a number of vital reforms. These included tax collections from wealthy landowners and tribal shaykhs (a novelty practically unknown in Iran), the introduction of a civil service merit system, and the establishment of a steady governmental income by means of a new tax on tea and sugar. The added income was used to finance construction of the Trans-Iranian Railway, Reza's pet project, linking Tehran with the Caspian Sea and Persian Gulf.

The major source of opposition to any form of modernization in Iran came from the religious groups; the clergy, as previously noted, were instrumental in blocking the republican movement at the start of Reza's regime. The Shah was not particularly religious himself although not so savage an iconoclast as his neighbor Ataturk. Furthermore, the Shi'a ritual in Iran is essentially mystical. Some basic element in the Iranian

---

[18] Elwell-Sutton, L. P., *Modern Iran,* London: Routledge, 1941, notes that a tribal rebellion broke out in 1937. Also in 1956 two American aid officials plus a jeep driver and the wife of one were ambushed in southeastern Iran by a tribal bandit, Dadshah, and his band of outlaws. Part of the band was subsequently rounded up in Pakistan and returned to Iran to face trial, while Dadshah himself died in a gun battle with Iranian police.

[19] Haas, *op. cit.,* p. 146.

*Reza Shah at the dedication of the Trans-Iranian Railway.
(Courtesy Press Attache of Iranian Embassy)*

national character has added extensive symbols and ceremonies to the simple faith of Muhammad. Without attacking religion itself, Reza moved against those outward forms which he felt militated against progress. The dervishes, men in white with tall conical caps, dressed panther skins over one shoulder, begging bowls, carrying axes (the symbol of religious power) and an antelope horn, were a familiar sight in Iranian towns where they begged for their existence. They would enter a town crying, "Ya Hak!" (O Truth!), some dispensing "pills of gladness," others talismans to ward off the evil eye, and others would tell fortunes. Only a few were genuine religious men sworn to vows of poverty and chastity. Reza put them to work or drove them into the remote countryside. Pilgrimages were discouraged. The *tazzieh* or passion play celebrating the martyrdom of Husayn, the son of Ali, was an event reminiscent of the Middle Ages in Europe; fanatics paraded through the streets flagellating themselves as they cried out, "Ya Ali, Ya

Hasan, Ya Husayn!" in hopes of sharing some of the crumbs of martyr-dom themselves. Reza outlawed this too. Even before these measures were enacted the power of the clergy had been effectively stifled by the sequestration of the *waqf* properties. Henceforth the mullas had to de-pend on the state for their living.

In the field of law, the Shah also introduced far-reaching changes. The Shari'a, formerly the only legal code in Muslim countries, was circum-scribed in Iran by the various Western codes which the Majlis adopted— commercial (1925), criminal (1926), civil (1928). Other new laws conferred divorce and property settlement rights on women, the com-pulsory use of Western clothing (1929), and the abolition of capitulatory privileges for foreigners. Reza Shah did not attempt the drastic social measures of Ataturk, however. Thus the dervish orders were not abol-ished—their lodges and *medersas* (schools) continued to operate—but the dervishes themselves were forbidden to beg or to preach in the towns.

He took a similarly cautious path in relation to women. The women of Iran, except for the tribeswomen, had been in the past excluded from public life. Even the Bakhtiari women who never veiled in their own territory, who managed the settlements when the men were away, and who were consulted by their husbands on every important issue before a decision was taken, wore the chador when they went into town.[20] As late as 1923, for example, it was noted that "royal ladies never go out except in a closed carriage with an eunuch on the box. In passing through a town . . . riders often precede it, crying out: 'Men, turn your eyes away!' . . . Every respectable townswoman and girl, rich or poor, wears a chador. . . . It is a complete disguise, and a man has difficulty in recognizing his own wife on the street."[21] Even in 1928 a speaker was expelled from the pulpit in the Shrine of the Imam Riza in Meshed because he advocated education for girls. He was accused of striking at the very foundations of the faith.[22]

In 1931 the Marriage Act granted them access to the civil courts and the administration and disposal of their property without their hus-band's permission, as well as putting severe restraints on polygamy. In 1935 another law fixed the lowest marriageable age for women at fif-

[20] Ross, E. H. M., *A Lady Doctor in Bakhtiari Land,* London: Dutton, 1923, pp. 102–103, 125 ff.
[21] Rice, Clara, *Persian Women and Their Ways,* New York: J. B. Lippincott Company, 1923, p. 39.
[22] Donaldson, Bess, *The Wild Rue,* London: Luzac, 1938, Preface, p. viii.

teen and men at eighteen. A man could not take a second wife without the full knowledge and consent of both his first wife and the prospective one. The educated upper-class women took the lead in abandoning the veil, never as common in Iran with its independent traditions and strong tribal consciousness as in the Arab countries. In 1935 the Queen appeared unveiled at a public ceremony. The veil was forbidden by law after 1936; no shop could serve a veiled woman; none were admitted into public vehicles or even allowed on the streets, and a fund of £25,-000 was voted to assist poor women to buy clothes to replace their chadors, the traditional shapeless black outdoor costume. In 1938 Reza Shah declared the full emancipation of Iranian women, although how far this has extended in practice is difficult to say.[23] As of 1941 women were equal to men in all respects except five—polygamy, divorce, inheritance rights, legal control of children, and voting or running for the Majlis.

Considerable progress was also made in education. Before Reza, Iranian education was disorganized. The most effective schools were foreign. In the nineteenth century, French, British, and American missions established a number of them and assisted ultimately in the constitutional movement through the inculcation of Western ideas. In 1932, the Shah's increasing obsession with foreign influences led him to ban all foreign schools in Iran, and by 1941 all foreign educational institutions were controlled by the government. In the meantime a single educational system, modeled on the French, had been established. Reza also sent several hundred students a year abroad to study.

Reza was favorably disposed at the start towards foreign assistance; but as Iran grew stronger and as his own devotion to his reform task intensified, he became increasingly hostile. The Millspaugh Mission was dismissed in 1927. Of the Shah, Millspaugh observed perceptively: "He seemed to me unmoral rather than immoral. It is proverbial in Persia that honest men are lazy, and active men are dishonest; and Reza Shah doubtless prized activity too highly. . . . He did not amend the constitution, close the parliament, or abolish the cabinet, . . . but in practice he acted completely contrary to the spirit of the constitution and its provisions."[24] Reza was extremely thin-skinned, also, and had a soldier's

---

[23] Elwell-Sutton, op. cit.
[24] Millspaugh, Arthur, Americans in Persia, Washington: The Brookings Institute, 1946, pp. 36–37.

ignorance of the outside world combined with oriental misunderstanding of a free press. The jokes and cartoons about him in Paris and London newspapers enraged him. In his later years this became a xenophobic obsession with him. He kept more and more to himself. Incapable of delegating authority, he was at the same time morbidly suspicious of those around him. The arrest and subsequent death of the Minister of Court, Timurtash, removed the last sound link between him and his people. The tribes hated him because of his brutal suppression of their autonomy. The dismissal of Millspaugh led to economic maladministration, the Shah's ambition to beautify Tehran and memorialize himself as a builder to extravagance. Yet his main objective, that of restoring national self-confidence, was reached. In 1941, faced with an Anglo-Russian ultimatum, he abdicated, ironically handing authority back to the very powers from whom he had taken it twenty years before. Abdication was totally unlike him; yet the far-sighted move maintained the Pahlavis in power, assured an orderly post-war transfer of control, and maintained Iranian dignity and self-respect in the face of foreign belligerency.

IRAN DURING WORLD WAR II

Iran's foreign relations between the wars were relatively uneventful. In 1927 a quarrel broke out between Iran and Britain over the Bahrein Islands off the Arabian coast, which Iran claimed on the basis of an occupation from 1622 to 1783 and the acceptance from that time of Iranian sovereignty by the ruling Shaykhs. The claim was of approximately the same degree of credibility as those put forward to the Peace Conference after World War I by the Iranian delegation to all Kurdistan and the Caucasus. Britain refused to consider it, and the matter was ostensibly solved by the 1928 Anglo-Iranian Treaty. (It is still revived occasionally to prove the virility of Iranian nationalism.) Traditional enmity between Iran and Turkey, which stemmed from the power struggle of the Safavids and the Ottomans for leadership in western Asia, lost much of its force with the treaty of friendship concluded in 1926. (Afghanistan was also a signatory to that treaty.) The settlement of the Kurdish problem with Turkey relocating many of her Kurdish families away from the border areas further improved relations. The Saadabad Pact of 1937 between Iran, Iraq, Turkey, and Afghanistan prohibited the signatories from interfering in each others internal affairs. It also defined frontiers and provided for mutual consultation (but not mutal action guarantees) in the event of an external threat to any one member. The Russians attacked the Pact as a potential hostile encirclement but without the violence shown to the subsequent Baghdad Pact of 1955.

Tremendous expansion in German activity in Iran before and during the early years of World War II placed Reza Shah in a difficult position. He declared Iran's neutrality at the start of the war, but he could not ignore the tremendous volume of vital trade between Iran and Germany nor the large number of German experts and technicians helping his country. The totalitarian setup in Germany permitted the Nazis to offer attractive economic propositions, while every German in Iran was a potential agent of the Nazis. Reza's uncompromising hostility to Communism—he even arrested a group of intellectuals in 1937 as Communists and instructed the court to find them guilty!—also found him on the side of the Germans at least in sympathy. He tried to cooperate with the British and Soviets in controlling German efforts to subvert Iran and jailed about 700 German nationals. The Shah expected that the Soviets would put pressure on him to declare war after the German invasion of Russia, but he was totally unprepared for the behavior of the British. The B.B.C. sent up a propaganda barrage in the Persian language criticizing his autocracy. Not surprisingly, the Shah preferred Nazi totalitarianism to democracy as a style of government. But the British had aided his accession to the throne; he respected their military skill; and he probably assumed fair play from them. He was doubtless uninformed about the world situation (he left Iran only once, to visit Turkey) and viewed it exclusively in terms of the Communists. The Anglo-Russian demands for a Persian supply corridor and their concern with possible Japanese moves made no impression on him.

On August 26, 1941, Russian forces entered Iran from the Caucasus and British troops landed at the head of the Gulf. The British navy sank the small Persian fleet off Khorramshahr. The two land armies converged on Tehran. The Shah observed: "Our friends, England and Russia, are giving us exactly the same treatment which Hitler gave to Belgium and Mussolini gave to Greece." He thought it over for three days; then he abdicated in favor of his son, Muhammad Reza. Indeed he had little choice. The only concession which the occupying powers granted him was the agreement to transfer $13 million to his son to be used for national development and public welfare. He was taken to Mauritius in

Reza Shah (right) and his son, Prince Muhammad Reza.
(Courtesy Press Attache, Iranian Embassy)

a British gunboat and later transferred to South Africa where he died in 1944. He never saw his native land again.

The young Shah named Foroughi, a venerated elder statesman, as Premier with the responsibility of normalizing relations between Iran and the occupying powers. On January 29, 1942, the three nations signed the Tripartite Alliance. In contrast to the 1907 Anglo-Russian Agreement in which Iran was unilaterally divided into spheres of influence, the two Allied powers included Iran as an equal partner. Britain and Russia also pledged the territorial integrity, sovereignty, and political independence of Iran. Other clauses defined the limits of the Allied occupation and Iran's participation in the war. The five northern provinces became a Russian "zone"; the rest of the country was designated a British zone, while Tehran was "neutral" ground. The language, tenor, purport, and participation of the Tripartite Alliance proved the achievement of Reza Shah better than any government brochure. Iran agreed to provide transit and communications facilities to the Allies. A clause which was to prove highly significant later made withdrawal of all foreign troops from Iran mandatory six months after the cessation of hostilities. Iran had already declared war on Germany, and in 1943 she announced her adherence to the Declaration of the United Nations. In late 1942 the U.S. Persian Gulf Command took over operation of the supply routes northward to the Soviet Union.

Iran was the setting, in November, 1943, for the Roosevelt-Churchill-Stalin conference that resulted in the Tehran Declaration. In this document the Allied leaders recognized Iran's help, agreed to continue economic aid, and re-emphasized the country's territorial integrity. The Declaration came none too soon. The Soviets in their sector were taking advantage of every opportunity to create the cadre of a satellite state which would seize control after the withdrawal of their own troops. They set up the *Tudeh* (Masses) party from a group of leftist politicians jailed under Reza Shah, organized trade unions in Tehran, Meshed, Tabriz, and Isfahan. Meanwhile their troops systematically stripped the zone of machinery, vehicles, armaments, and food. Qajar princes, genuine Communists, disgruntled intellectuals, and landlords all joined forces with the Soviets in hopes of recovering power lost under Reza. Wartime difficulties—a severe food shortage, inflation, the failure to replace Reza's autocracy with stable democratic government—added to Iran's problems. A natural sympathy for Germany, a European nation which was not tainted by the long foreign domination of Iran, died hard. Free of Reza's firm hand, the tribes reverted to their old independence of Tehran. The British tried to counterbalance Soviet pressures with similar tactics in their zone, although they were handicapped by their determination to help the Russians in their efforts to defeat Germany, the common enemy. The British supported the Eredaye Melli (National Will) party formed by Ziya al-Din Tabatabai in opposition to the Tudeh and encouraged anti-Soviet newspapers and magazines, even with actual cash. The Iranian government, under British protection, kept a tight rein on Communists but was powerless to operate in the Soviet zone. Tehran was too close to the Russians to permit any independence of spirit. Eight Tudeh deputies were elected to the fourteenth session of the Majlis (1944–1946); but the election of Ja'far Pishevari, Moscow's man in northern Iran, was contested after his first and only speech from the floor, and Pishevari returned to Tabriz to organize the separatist movement in Azerbaijan.[25]

POSTWAR IRAN: AZERBAIJAN, MAHABAD CRISES

From the collapse of Kuchik Khan's regime in Gilan to the end of World War II, the Soviets made no overt attempt to subvert Iran. Reza Shah did not permit Communism, either native or imported, to gain even a toehold. The wartime occupation and Reza's departure played into the hands of the Russians. In Pishevari they had an old Bolshevik who was also a political and intellectual leader in Iran. Furthermore, Soviet armed forces were on hand to aid any movement of the "downtrodden working classes" against the imperialists. The end of the war found both Pishevari and the Soviets ready to attempt a take-over of the northern provinces in the name of "people's democracy," the prelude to complete absorption of the country. In August 1945, Pishevari's men murdered the landlord of the village of Ligavan outside Tabriz and his family. The "Ligavan massacre" was reported to the Majlis as an action taken by the workers of Tabriz against a reactionary feudal oppressor. The government took no action. Thereafter the by-now familiar pattern developed, to the shocked surprise of a world which had just finished the war to end all wars and was building a new system through the medium of the United Nations. The Russians billeted in a town or village would announce that the Democrats were taking over the administration in the name of order. Any Iranian government forces in the vicinity would be detained in their barracks. A handful of Pishevari's armed followers would seize control of key government buildings at dawn; and the mass of the antigovernment force, a mixed bag of Tudeh members, Communists, and plain opportunists, would enter the "liberated" town singing and waving banners. In Tabriz the Soviets refused to allow the 400-man government garrison to circulate at all until Pishevari's authority was complete. In December, 1945, he announced the formation of the "All Peoples Assembly of Iranian Azerbaijan." He was Prime Minister, naturally; the post of Minister of Interior went to Muhammad Beria, another old Bolshevik, and the other leaders were either Russian Azeris or Iranians

[25] See Van Wagenen, R. W., *The Iranian Case, 1946*, New York: Carnegie Endowment for International Peace, 1952, pp. 23–24. Pishevari was not a Tudeh member and considered the party as "me-tooist" with no objectives and little vision. Cf. Fatemi, *op. cit.*, p. 263.

long resident in Moscow.[26] Beria instituted a reign of terror similar to those of his more famous (but unrelated) namesake. The estates of Azerbaijani landlords who had fled to the British zone were confiscated; jails filled rapidly, and progovernment officers were either purged or went into hiding. Fear settled like the desert dust on the people of Azerbaijan. The manifesto of the Peoples' Republic indicated the direction it would take: a purge of all "traitors and reactionaries," autonomy for Azerbaijan, a provincial militia, Azeri Turkish to become the state language, and adoption of Soviet Army uniforms and training for the new national army.

The government of Iran, unable to move into Azerbaijan because of the presence of Soviet troops, notified the United Nations Security Council of Russian interference in its internal affairs, the first such case to be brought before the Council. Unfortunately, the British and American troops stationed in Iran during the war had been withdrawn in accordance with the terms of the Tripartite Alliance, the Americans first and the British on March 2, 1946. Soviet troops stayed pending "clarification" of the situation, well past the deadline, and were even reinforced. The surviving atmosphere in 1946 of sweetness and light further deterred the Anglo-Americans from forceful action; Soviet intentions were not fully realized until after Churchill's Iron Curtain speech. The relative weakness of the Iranian government in the face of a disciplined, well-intrenched resistance movement backed by Soviet force augured well for an extension of Pishevari's republic to the whole of Iran, especially as the Soviets were operating discreetly behind a band of sincere nationalists apparently working for a better, more democratic Iran.

Within the year, however, an astonishing reversal had occurred. Pishevari's apparently strong government had collapsed, and the veteran Communist was back in Moscow. A number of factors worked in the Iranian government's favor. The existence of the United Nations gave Iran a chance to bring its case before the bar of world opinion. Fifty years earlier equally highhanded treatment by Russia got no public hearing at all. The West, notably the United States, acted with firmness. The Premier, Qavam-as-Sultanah, outsmarted the Soviets at their own poker game. Finally, the Soviet troop withdrawal showed that the Pishevari government lacked both popular and military support.

---

[26] *Ibid.,* pp. 275–276. There was a joke in Tabriz at the time that one or two Iranians had been appointed to the cabinet because none of the members could speak either Persian or the Turkish dialect of Azerbaijan!

The United States was dilatory in recognizing the threat to Iran and the threat to the ultimate peace of the world which was posed by Soviet actions, but then Iran was remote and backward, and few Americans had had any contact with it. The Labaree murder wounded a few missionary souls, and the three American financial missions aroused some Congressional interest; but even during the war when U.S. troops manned the Persian Gulf Command, American political interest was seen through British lenses. Nor were potential relations improved when Millspaugh resigned after a violent campaign against him in the press and returned to Washington in 1945.[27] When the USSR made threatening noises at Greece and Turkey, however, the U.S. government became concerned. James Byrnes, then Secretary of State, asked Stalin at the Moscow Conference to explain how 30,000 Russian soldiers in Azerbaijan could be "endangered" by the presence of 1,500 Iranian gendarmes.[28] The U.S. Ambassador to Iran, George V. Allen, strongly supported the Qavam government's attempts to reestablish its authority over Azerbaijan. Then President Truman sent an ultimatum to Stalin telling him that if Soviet forces were not withdrawn from Iran within six weeks, American forces would go back to their former stations there.

How effective these protests and demands would have been alone under postwar demobilization conditions is problematical since similar actions were taken in Czechoslovakia. The Iranians themselves, however, triumphed in the main event. Premier Qavam, bolstered by U.S. firmness, reached agreement with the USSR on troop withdrawal. As part of the price, he accepted Soviet demands for an Irano-Soviet oil company which would exploit oil resources in the northern provinces. Qavam also accepted the Pishevari government as a *de facto* autonomous provincial authority in Azerbaijan with Pishevari nominally responsible to a royal governor-general. It seemed that the Soviets had got all they wanted and the Iranians had saved face.

But the wily Persian had not put down all his cards. He neutralized the Tudeh by appointing three members to his Cabinet. Since the party had consistently attacked all governments in Tehran as corrupt, the ground was cut from beneath its basic policy. Next, government agents stirred up tribal rebellion in Fars. Qavam dismissed the three ministers and called for elections. Other agents nurtured a revolt in Azerbaijan itself. An army column entered the province "to supervise elections."

[27] See Millspaugh's own book for his side of the controversy.
[28] Quoted in Fatemi, *op. cit.*, p. 280.

Even the youthful Iranian labor movement was affected. The Iranian Federation of Trade Unions, a member of the WFTU, was alleged to be giving support to the Azerbaijan separatist movement, and recognition for bargaining purposes was given instead to the SKI (Sazmani Kargarani Iran). The U.S. representative in the United Nations observed piously that Iran had a perfect right to send troops into any part of its own territory to maintain order; thus all pretext for a Soviet reoccupation was eliminated. The People's Republic collapsed almost upon the appearance of the royal column. Pishevari and Beria escaped, but the leaders who did not were massacred by the irate people of Tabriz. In December, 1946, Azerbaijan reverted to central government control, to vanish from the stage of international conflict. The Fifteenth Majlis, convened the following year, unanimously voted to void the Soviet oil concession.

Adjacent to Azerbaijan is the area of Persian Kurdistan, inhabited by the same Kurdish people who spill over into Turkey and Iraq at the confluence of the three countries. Reza Shah's determination to unify Iran had worked much hardship on the Kurds. Their national dress was outlawed, tribal meetings forbidden, and strict military control exercised over their mountain homeland. The reaction to Reza's abdication plus the example of Azerbaijan led to the formation in 1946 of the Komala, an association of Kurdish nationalists. Saif-i-Qazi Muhammad, a venerated Kurdish mulla, was chosen as leader. Although the Komala was non-Communist, the Soviets saw in it another means of extending their influence over Iran and openly backed its national aspirations. In the same year, the Komala declared they had established the Kurdish Republic of Mahabad; it was immediately recognized by the USSR. A treaty between Pishevari's government and Mahabad complicated matters. But the failure of the Soviet effort in Azerbaijan plus the basic disunity of the Kurds doomed the republic. Iraqi and Turkish Kurds did not respond to Qazi's call for a greater Kurdistan. Mahabad collapsed shortly after Pishevari's departure for Russia. The cancellation of the oil concession provoked loud Soviet reaction and many threats but no positive action, proving the adage that Russia traditionally respects firmness and avoids direct conflict where she is obviously the aggressor.

POSTWAR PROBLEMS: OIL NATIONALIZATION

With the cancellation of the abortive Soviet oil concession, Iran was once again in control of her own destinies. For the first time in six years there were no foreign troops on Iranian soil. Many problems continued to plague the state, however. The general economic instability and domination of the government by intrenched, privileged interests touched off a wave of political extremism. The Democrat Party founded by Qavam himself represented the strongest and most central political element, but the Tudeh on the left and the Shi'a clergy led by Mulla Ayatollah Kashani clashed in many political battles. The young Shah, beginning to take an active part, played the constitutional monarch. In 1948 at his behest, the Majlis activated the Senate, its upper house, which had been provided for in the 1906 constitution but had never existed. It had sixty senators, thirty of them appointed by the Shah and the rest elected. In this way the Shah improved his position in relation to the Majlis since bills he favored had more chance of being adopted. He played an important role in the adoption of several acts designed to improve Iran's economic position, which had deteriorated badly owing to nonpayment of taxes and several bad harvests. In 1949 the Majlis approved a seven-year development program with an outlay of $650 million, to be financed basically from oil royalties. The improvement of U.S.–Iranian relations and in developing American awareness of Iran's value in the Cold War was shown by the development program, based on recommendations by an American consortium, Overseas Consultants, Inc., and in the inclusion of Iran in the technical assistance program. Unfortunately the Shah's trip to Washington produced only $25 million instead of the hoped-for $250 million; the seven year program was delayed, and O.C.I. contracts were not extended.

Iran's oil industry, operated by a foreign company, did not suffer from the general economic malaise. From the start of successful production in 1908 until World War II, there was periodic friction between the company, which operated the oil fields, and the state, which literally "owned" them, but no really serious attempt to take over complete operation. The Iranians recognized that the extraction, refining, and marketing of oil is a highly complex process requiring technical skill of a high order. Such skill was not available in Iran; furthermore, the traditional way of life, agricultural and pastoral with almost no mechanization, created little demand within Iran for its most valuable product. Thus the oil royalties Iran received came with very little effort on her part. It was not until the postwar period, with its challenging concepts of nationhood, that the Iranians became acutely conscious of foreign management.

Petroleum was probably known to the earliest inhabitants of Iran. The nomadic tribesmen used gas fires, seeping up from cracks in the ground over the oil-bearing beds, to warm themselves on cold nights in the desert. Other nomads found they could do rudimentary cooking over the fires; still others used them for signal flares. During the Persian Empire of Cyrus, the predominant religion was Mazdaism, founded by Zoroaster. Fire in general became an object of worship. Because no one could explain the source of the oil-fires, they were especially venerated, and temples were built to house them. One such temple, the Masjid-i-Sulayman, still stands in the middle of a modern oilfield.[29] The poorest villagers in Shah Abbas's time collected the oil from shallow pools and burned it for want of a better fuel. But no systematic use was made of the black viscous substance until modern times.

In 1901 the Qajar Shah granted a special concession "to prospect, obtain, exploit, develop, prepare for commerce, and export and sell natural gas, petroleum, asphalt, and mineral wax throughout the Persian Empire for sixty years" to one William Knox D'Arcy. D'Arcy himself was an Englishman who had made a fortune in the Australian goldfields and was interested in speculative investments, primarily in mining. A French report appearing in *Les Annales Mines* about the presence of extensive oil deposits in the Qasr-i-Shirin region of Iran, near the Turkish border, caught his eye. He made inquiries and learned that the rights of one of the principals in the original Reuter concession of 1872 could be purchased for £50,000. This seemed like a worthwhile investment. D'Arcy formed several companies to pursue his concessions, poured most of his own capital into the venture, and drilled for seven years without any results. London financial and brokerage circles merely raised eyebrows when he tried to peddle a wildcat scheme to develop a dry hole. Then, in 1908, when he was on the point of selling his concession to foreign interests, the company struck oil at Masjid-i-Sulayman, symbolically near the temple of the Magian fire-worshipers. The column of black mud, sand, and gas that spewed forth from the ground on that May day signaled the start of the jet age.

In 1909, the Anglo-Persian Oil Company (renamed Anglo-Iranian Oil Company in 1935) took over the operation of D'Arcy's concession. The British government provided considerable initial financing and gradually became the major stockholder, although the company remained a private organization and was duly registered as such under

---

[29] Wilber, Donald, *Iran Past and Present,* 3rd ed., Princeton: Princeton University Press, 1955, p. 134.

Aerial view of Abadan refinery. (Courtesy Press Attache, Iranian Embassy)

Persian law. D'Arcy disappeared from the oil scene.[30] During World War I the Iranian oilfields were a major fuel supplier, at cheap rates, for the British Navy. The medieval political structure and continued instability of the country made it easy for the APOC to grow rapidly. Abadan, a swampy island in 1901, became the site of a vast refinery and a modern city. The company also provided housing, medical care, education, and relatively high wages to thousands of Iranian workers and their families. It also added a significant element to Iran's finances through royalty payments. Until the advent of Reza Khan, the Persians themselves took little interest and less part in their own industry, while the APOC, snug in its corner, saw no danger in the constitutional struggle and the Persian national renaissance. Lord Strathcona, Board Chairman of APOC, said in 1911: "As our part of Persia is within the Territories of the Sheikh of Mohammerah and the Bakhtiyari chiefs, we are fortu-

[30] Fatemi, *op. cit.*, pp. 12 ff., gives a vivid but perhaps overwrought tale about D'Arcy being tricked by a British secret agent. En route to the United States and disillusioned with his treatment at the hands of people from whom he expected help, D'Arcy fell into conversation with a priest. The priest persuaded him that he could best help the people of Persia, the real goal, by donating his concession to a nonprofit organization which would use oil profits to further the general welfare. The assumed priest was really Sidney Reilly, British intelligence agent, and by this devious means the British government obtained control of the Anglo-Iranian Oil Company. Almost nothing seems to be known about D'Arcy's life or what happened to him after he left Iran.

nately able to view the present political situation with perfect equa-
nimity." [31]

In 1932 the Iranian Government suddenly cancelled the D'Arcy concession. Feeling in Iran had been running high against the APOC for
some years. Among other complaints the Iranians felt that British pressure and duplicity were responsible for the murder of American Vice-
Consul Imbrie, which started a chain of events that led to the termination of the Sinclair concession in northern Iran. Britain, in short, seemed
via APOC to be blocking American aid to Iran. The letter of cancellation from Finance Minster Taq-i-Zadeh merely stated that the company had failed to satisfy the rights and interests of the Iranian nation.
Specifically there were other grievances. Despite the company's growth,
Iran had received no increase in royalties. Reza Shah, on a visit to Khuzistan, was appalled at the backwardness of the one-time granary province
and disturbed to find that Arab and Indian workers were paid three times
as much as Iranian workers. The government also said privately that royalties had not been paid between 1909 and 1920, that income taxes had
never been paid, and generally accused the company of not complying
with the terms of the concession. The Shah also felt that a concession
given by the despised Qajars did not suit a revived Iranian self-respect.

The British rejected the cancellation out of hand, pointedly reminding
the Shah of the fate of his neighbor, King Amanullah of Afghanistan,
and of the presence of fast cruisers in the Persian Gulf. The dispute went
before the League of Nations. The case for Britain, given by Sir John
Simon, was far better presented than the Iranian from either a legal or a
political standpoint. The Iranians knew their cause was right, but they
lacked the political maturity to convince others. In 1933, the Company
negotiated a new concession, covering the following points:

(1) A decrease in the concession area to 100,000 square miles.
(2) Royalty payments to the government of four shillings per ton of
oil exported or sold domestically.
(3) An additional 20 per cent payment of net profits annually after
the first £671,000 had been paid to shareholders.
(4) Payment of taxes.
(5) Progressive Iranization of the labor force.
(6) A concession until 1993.

The political implications of the new agreement were that it delayed for

[31] Elwell-Sutton, L. P., *Persian Oil*, London: Lawrence & Wishart, 1951, pp.
65–66.

another sixty years Iran's enjoyment of the full benefits of her major industry and limited the government's authority to those parts of the country outside the concession area. However, the principle of company indebtedness for income taxes was established and royalties were slightly increased.

Iran's oil entered the realm of political and international diplomacy on two other occasions before the nationalization of 1951. The first was the 1944 oil crises; the second was the Azerbaijan postwar revolt, when, as noted, the price for Soviet troop withdrawal included a new concession covering the five northern provinces. This was not the first Soviet attempt to assert economic hegemony over the area, however. During World War II, the Majlis, at the Shah's request, invited Dr. Millspaugh to head a second economic mission. Although Millspaugh again failed to establish long-term reforms,[32] the groundwork was laid, and negotiations were proceeding smoothly for American capital investment in Iranian oil exploitation. Then the Russians dropped their monkey-wrench. A Soviet mission led by Foreign Affairs Minister Kavtaradze arrived in Tehran. After much socializing at cocktail parties, its real purpose came to light. Kavtaradze formally demanded a seventy-five-year concession for the USSR in Azerbaijan, Gilan, Mazanderan, Astrabad, and Khorasan, the five provinces of traditional Russian interest. The Iranians displayed that combination of gentle elusiveness which has always characterized their modern dealings with bigger powers. Premier Sa'id equivocated, then notified the occupying powers that all concessions would be deferred until the end of the war. A violent attack on the government by Tudeh deputies and pro-Soviet press organs followed. Kavtaradze announced that Iran had broken an earlier pledge. Tudeh deputies monopolized the floor of the Majlis for a solid week filibustering in favor of the concession. Then unexpectedly, Dr. Muhammad Musaddiq, an ardent nationalist with a reputation for scrupulous honesty, introduced a bill prohibiting all negotiations with foreign countries. In a two-day speech, he described the history of oil concessions in Iran; he hammered away at the theme of an Iran free of foreign domination. He demanded a "negative equilibrium," i.e., no favors to any powers. He reminded the Majlis of his long fight against Reza's dictatorship, his patriotism, and the duty of every Muslim to defend his country. During the debate, he told Kashavarz,

---

[32] Fatemi, who worked with him, claims Millspaugh was stubborn, tactless, and interfered needlessly in local politics. Millspaugh says opposition deputies and the Soviets were out to get him. The truth probably lies *in medias res*.

Tudeh deputy from Bandar Pahlavi, that the Soviet demand for a concession to match the British concession reminded him of the man who had lost his right hand and then voluntarily cut off his left to establish a balance of power. Musaddiq's bill was approved, and Premier Sa'id resigned. Since Soviet dislike was aimed directly at him, the Soviets were completely checkmated. The toothless Morteza Qoli Bayat, his successor and their choice as Premier, was himself voted out of office in the following year.[33]

OIL NATIONALIZATION, 1951–1954

The Iranian government in 1949 signed a Supplemental Agreement with the AIOC. Iran would receive a royalty increase to six shillings per ton, a one-shilling per ton payment in lieu of income tax, annual payments of 20 per cent of the company's annual reserve (the first payment immediately), and a 25 per cent cut in world prices on all oil marketed within the country. On paper the agreement looked good, but the company refused even to discuss Iran's two basic desires—for a fifty-fifty split in royalties modeled on the Venezuela and Saudi-Arabian-Aramco arrangements and for national control over company operations. Iranian authority still stopped at the border of Khuzistan. The Gass-Golshayan Agreement, as it was called, was denounced in the Majlis and led to Premier Sa'id's downfall when he failed to get a vote of confidence. Dr. Musaddiq emerged as the leader of a group of deputies called the National Front who were pledged to defeat the agreement and to nationalize the industry. The Shah, who wished to stay impartial on the controversy and yet to encourage the United States to expand its aid program on the basis of the stability of Iran, appointed General Ali Razmara, a career soldier with considerable ability to enforce unpopular decisions, as Premier. Razmara reported to the Majlis that nationalization would be premature since Iran lacked the technicians and the marketing facilities to operate such a complex industry. However, he pressed the Company for a fifty-fifty royalty arrangement. Given time and a less explosive situation, Razmara might have succeeded, but he was opposed to an immovable object (the AIOC) and an irresistible combination of extremists and nationalists. On March 7, 1951, he was assassinated by a

---

[33] Fatemi, *op. cit.*, p. 251; Wilber, *op. cit.*, pp. 114–115. Former Ambassador to Iran, Wallace Murray, cites this and the 1947 rejection of the Soviet concession as the two most notable examples of the part played by the Majlis in blocking Soviet penetration in Iran.

member of the Feda'iyan-i-Islam, or Devotees of Islam, a fanatic movement whose head was Mulla Abu al-Qasim Kashani, an important clerical leader. An indication of the temper of the times was shown when the assassin was only imprisoned; and shortly thereafter the Feda'iyan issued a bulletin threatening to kill the Shah if he were not released.

Iranian nationalism now began to turn cartwheels en route to complete nationalization. The various cross-currents of internal politics—the fanaticism of the Feda'iyan, the histrionics of Musaddiq, the en-bloc formation of the National Front, Tudeh opportunism—plus the Shah's hands-off policy and the arrogance of the company itself flowed together into an unchecked stream. Public support was achieved through the usual channels of Iranian public opinion—the coffeehouses and bazaars. On March 15, a week after the assassination, the Majlis passed a nine-point law, which was confirmed by the Senate on March 20, nationalizing the oil industry. Musaddiq who had spearheaded the drive became Premier on April 28 when the Shah's choice, the veteran statesman Husayn Ala, failed to win a vote of confidence. Since he does not have the veto power, the Shah was forced to sign the nationalization bill. March 20, the date of signing, became an official holiday.

The man who was to become identified throughout the world with the struggle of a weak nation against a strong one to wrest control of a vital international industry was seventy years old and somewhat of an anomaly in Persian politics. He came from a wealthy and prominent family; he himself owned vast lands where he had retired in opposition to Reza's dictatorship. Until he sponsored the 1944 bill prohibiting concessions, he had made no great stir in national affairs but was known for uncompromising patriotism and honesty. It is important to note that he came to power as the advocate of a policy of negative action. The Iranians had little idea of how to manage the industry. This negativism spawned a variety of parties, such as the Persian Toilers' and the National Association for Struggle Against Imperialist Oil Companies, plus the already-established Tudeh, Feda'iyan, and others, all supporting Musaddiq on nationalization but differing on subsequent action. The situation became so complex that on May 13, 1951, Musaddiq took *bast* in the Majlis, claiming the Feda'iyan had threatened his life.[34]

The Iranian oil industry closed down. Iranian guards surrounded the Abadan refinery. British technicians and personnel were evacuated, the

[34] Elwell-Sutton, *op. cit.*, p. 221.

last in October. Britain, in retaliation, slapped a ban on Iran's credits abroad and on her essential imports. In this way, the British apparently reasoned, Iran would be brought economically to heel first, after which political surrender would follow automatically. They discounted a number of factors. Oil royalties had never made up more than 15 per cent of the national budget. Reza Shah's modernization program, while ambitious, had not changed Iran's predominantly agricultural economy and motorless way of life. Few Iranian peasants owned tractors and fewer still had automobiles. Furthermore, a matter of principle was involved, and in the end Allah would provide.

The pattern of subsequent events assumed a near-comic-opera appearance. Musaddiq came to New York to appear personally before the United Nations Security Council and answer the British complaint (that Iranian nationalization was causing a threat to world peace). He said that Iran demanded only the right "to enter the family of nations on terms of freedom and complete equality." These had already been given to India, Pakistan, and Idonesia, he reminded the smaller nations.[35] He observed that after fifty years of AIOC contributions to Iranian welfare, Iran still lacked enough technicians to operate her oilfields. The Security Council in an inconclusive resolution ruled its incompetence to judge the dispute and passed the matter along to the International Court of Justice, which in turn ruled *its* incompetence. Musaddiq, holding court on a hospital bed at Walter Reed Army Medical Center in his pajamas, tried to get additional U.S. aid but was unable to shake Anglo-American solidarity or the oil cartel, and aid was continued on a crash basis. The $120 million that Iran sought was not available. The American attitude stemmed from a variety of sources—the carry-over of Congressional suspicion, based on experience with Chiang Kai-Shek, that aid to Asia was simply money down a rathole; Iran's rejection of the seven-year plan of O.C.I. (although Max Thornburg, head of O.C.I., accused AIOC of responsibility for Iran's difficulties by failing to recognize her legitimate interest in the oil industry); and the powerful influence of the oil companies on Middle Eastern policy. Nevertheless, in retrospect it is difficult to believe that the United States, so heavily committed to encirclement of the Soviet Union, would allow a quarrel between an ally and a small nation with a record of solid resistance to Communism to become a serious international issue.

Negotiations continued inconclusively through 1952–53. The Inter-

[35] *Ibid.,* p. 261. Time named Musaddiq Man of the Year in 1951, but called him "by Western standards an appalling caricature of a statesman."

national Bank offered to operate the oilfields as an independent agent with British technical help and to sell oil at a discount to the AIOC with a fifty-fifty split in royalties. But Iran insisted on sovereign control and refused even to contemplate the return of the British. Iran's long-range oil potentialities suffered because of a rapid buildup of oil production elsewhere, notably in Kuwait. The big oil companies also expanded their refining capacities in an effort to fill the gap. In October, 1952, Iran broke off diplomatic relations with Great Britain.

Meanwhile, the money pinch began to hurt Iran. Alton Jones, president of Cities Service, visited Iran at the Premier's invitation to study the problem. Through his visit, Iranian officials learned for the first time that the world had filled the gap in production caused by the loss of their own oil. Various conflicting interests within the country gradually fermented into a severe internal crisis. The Tudeh had earlier sent an open letter to Musaddiq asking for such things as expulsion of the American military mission, which was training Iran's army; legalization of the party; recognition of Communist China; and recovery of the long-lost Bahein oilfields. Musaddiq's failure to come back from Washington with a check or a bundle of credits weakened his popularity. In order to stay in power and continue his negative program, he had to listen to a coalition of extremists, Tudeh members, sincere patriots, and mere opportunists. Mob action gradually became dominant in public politics as Musaddiq, throughout his whole life an uncompromising enemy of dictatorship, shed his old skin and turned into a dictator. He steadily centralized his own power over the National Front, the party of antigovernment deputies which had joined with him in the earlier fight for nationalization and which had become dominant in the confused political struggle. The Majlis gave him the power to rule by decree for six months; the army and the government were purged of anti-Musaddiq elements. The Premier moved toward a showdown with the Shah, as much out of personal hatred for the Pahlavis as out of nationalism. He even set up his own land reform program in opposition to the Shah's. Using his decree powers, he extended martial law, imposed a strict law against upsetting public security, prohibited strikes, suspended the Senate, and ordered severe restrictions on the press and on movements of foreigners in the oil areas. All these efforts were typical of strong rulers throughout the country's long history but completely atypical of Musaddiq who was, after all, not only an incorruptible patriot but also a member of the oligarchic aristocracy.

In mid-1953, with the Shah ostensibly on vacation and General Fazlollah Zahedi, his chief of staff, in hiding to avoid arrest, Musaddiq called for the dissolution of the Majlis, clearly an unconstitutional move since only the Shah could do this. By this time, many of his former supporters had deserted him, either because he had failed to reward them for their support or because they no longer believed he could deliver American financial aid. A rigged referendum then "proved" that a majority of Iranians desired new elections. The Shah, who had earlier threatened to leave the country, dismissed him by a *firman* and appointed Zahedi Premier. Musaddiq rejected the order, and this time the Shah did leave Iran.[36] Six days later he returned to Tehran where a confused but rapid series of events saved the country from anarchy. When the news of his departure first reached Tehran, nationalists and Tudeh members engaged in an orgy of destruction, smashing windows in shops and pulling down statues of the Shah and his father. The Tudeh called for the end of the monarchy and the establishment of a republic. Husayn Fatemi, Musaddiq's Minister of Foreign Affairs and a prominent newspaper publisher, printed diatribes calling the Shah a snake and a traitor. But the attacks on the Shah's person and the monarchy were too much. Gradually a ground-swell of loyalty to the regime developed. As in 1922, the people of Iran were unwilling to discard the familiar constitutional monarchy for the uncharted seas of republicanism. Rallying around the person of Zahedi, who was still in hiding, the nationalists and the army joined forces to overthrow Musaddiq. The Premier was arrested, the National Front dissolved, and the Shah flew home. A special court, one of those which may be convoked to try officials, Crown ministers and judges tried Musaddiq in 1954 and sentenced him to five years' imprisonment in a trial in which the prosecuting attorneys were made to look like fools by the old Premier's spirited insistence that what he had done was for the country's good. As an example of his "crimes against the state," one may cite a 1952 law giving Iran's more than 40,000 villages the right to have partly-elected councils, their own incomes, and bank accounts.[37] Since it had been the change in his methods, not in his aims, that had led him "in the wrong direction," he was released in 1959 to return to his estates where he resumed the quiet contemplative life he had abandoned after the abdication of Reza Shah.

[36] A variety of *bast* which by Persian tradition would be followed by an uprising in favor of the monarch.

[37] Djamalzadeh, M. A., "An Outline of the Social and Economic Structure of Iran," *International Labor Review*, LXIII, January, 1951, p. 27.

H.I.M., The Shah, opening an exhibit of Persian calligraphy. (Courtesy Press Attache, Iranian Embassy)

The fall of Musaddiq produced a political effect in Iran favorable to the resumption of ties with the West but unalterably opposed to the return of the British oil company. The United States advanced $45 million in aid to supplement the $23,400,000 already earmarked for Iran under the technical assistance program. In 1954 the Iranian government accepted a proposal to allow an international Consortium of eight Western oil companies to operate the oil industry.[38] The National Iranian Oil Company (NIOC), created by the nationalization bill, would manage the over-all operation, while the Consortium would do the actual extraction, marketing, and refining. Strict limits were placed on production at first so as not to set off an oil race. These were increased until in 1957 the Consortium was producing 731,000 barrels a day, more than in pre-nationalization days. The fantastic oil strike in 1956 at Qum indicated an oil potential for Iran greater than any other nation in the world. But the Iranians were coming of age in the modern world; the Majlis confidently passed a law that Qum would be developed by NIOC

[38] The division of the Consortium was as follows:
British Petroleum—40 per cent participation
Royal Dutch Shell—14 per cent participation
Campagnie Francaise des Petroles—6 per cent participation
5 U.S. companies—8 per cent participation each.

Entrance to Parliament House (Majlis), Tehran.
(Courtesy Press Attache, Iranian Embassy)

and displayed strong negotiating powers when approached by other foreign concession-seekers without any of the xenophobia of the Musaddiq period. In 1957 Iran signed an agreement with the Italian State Exploration Company (AGIP) which called for a fifty-fifty split in royalties from future production plus a 25 per cent interest for Iran in a joint producing company. The actual value of the extra twenty-five per cent was dubious, but the psychological value was tremendous. For the first time in their modern history, the Iranians were partners in their own industry.

INTERNAL POLITICS SINCE WORLD WAR II

The present Shah did not seek any changes in the Fundamental Laws until well after World War II although he ascended the throne in 1941. During the postwar period, the extensive use of filibustering tactics and lack of a quorum meant that important legislation was held up, and government leaders began to feel that the Majlis had become too powerful. Accordingly the Senate was convened for the first time under the provisions of the original constitution in 1950 with a membership of sixty, half appointed by the Shah and half elected. In the previous year a Constituent Assembly called by the Shah to revise the Fundamental Laws had set up a procedure for future revisions and had returned to the Shah a portion of the ruler's lost autocracy by giving him power to dissolve either or both of the two Houses provided he gives his reasons for doing so in a *firman* (official rescript) and immediately orders new elections. The latest constitutional revision came in 1957, as follows:

(1) The number of the deputies in the Majlis was raised to two hundred.

(2) the term of office of the Majlis was extended from two years to four.

(3) a majority was to be determined by the votes of more than half of the deputies.

(4) the Shah would be permitted to return any financial bill passed by the Majlis to that body for revision, *but not* to veto it, while a subsequent majority of three-quarters of those present is sufficent for final passage.[39]

With these modifications Iran very nearly became a true constitutional monarchy. But development of democratic participation in government in Iran on all levels has always been hindered by lack of contact between local and national administrators to say nothing of the gulf between the ordinary Iranian citizen and the central government. In 1959 Premier Manuchehr Eghbal undertook the notable experiment of literally bringing Tehran to the people. Cabinet meetings were held in public, usually in the larger towns but even in some villages; villagers and townsmen were encouraged to present their views and to submit grievances to the Ministers. The inevitable extension of this willingness to hear criticism to Iran's students, who are as volatile and eager for change as their Arab colleagues, should be credited with a large assist in producing the political crisis of 1961.

Political Parties. Although political parties as such have existed in Iran since the granting of the Constitution in 1906, they have mostly been loose confederations around some strong personality. As yet, the only party with an organization in the Western sense is the *Tudeh* (Masses) Party. It was founded in the 1930's by one Dr. Arani, a leftist intellectual, and in 1933 began publication of a weekly newspaper,

---

[39] Lockhart, *op. cit.,* p. 388.

Dunya (World). In 1937 Dr. Arani and fifty-two of his followers were arrested and sentenced to long prison terms. Dr. Arani died in prison; the others were released in 1941 in the general amnesty which followed the abdication of Reza Shah. They reformed the Tudeh under the leadership of Sulayman Muhsin Iskandari, a Qajar prince "with a long-standing tradition of liberal politics dating from 1906." [40] The Tudeh absorbed other leftist groups, notably the Anti-Fascist Society founded by a high official in the Anglo-Iranian Oil Company, forming a Freedom Front in 1943. During the wartime Anglo-Russian occupation of Iran, the Tudeh transferred its main effort to Azerbaijan where it joined forces with the Moscow-trained Communist agitator Ja'far Pishevari and his colleagues. The Tudeh also played an active role in the 1951 oil nationalization proceedings when it supported Musaddiq. After his overthrow, it was disbanded and went underground. Traditionally the Tudeh has appealed to young intellectuals, especially those who are educated but lack the family connections still necessary for public advancement, and to industrial workers.

Sayyid Zia al-Din Tabatabai, Reza's co-conspirator in the 1921 coup who left the country after three months because he disagreed with Reza on the method of reform best for Iran, returned from exile in 1943 to organize the National Will Party. His platform stressed neutrality, and the party was organized in "circles" of nine members each under a circle-leader. The party lasted until 1946 when Zia was again forced out of politics; and Premier Qavam as-Sultanah, faced with the Azerbaijan revolt, formed the Iran Democrat Party which absorbed the Tudeh and the National Will only to destroy their power. The general proliferation of parties after the repressive Reza period did not mean the arrival of democracy. Except for the Tudeh, most of them consisted of a few people grouped around some personality. Their platforms were interchangeable and their influence narrowly sectarian. A number of small parties were spawned during the 1951 oil crisis, and eventually Premier Musaddiq formed his own National Front. Political activity was suspended in 1954 after the downfall of Musaddiq; but with the return to economic and political normalcy, Premier Ala in 1957 on the Shah's advice permitted an opposition party, *Mardom,* to form. It was composed of diverse elements—landlords, shopowners, and some workers. In 1958 Premier Eghbal formed his own party, the Nation Party (*Milliyun*), re-

[40] Elwell-Sutton, L. P., "Political Parties in Iran, 1941–1948," *Middle East Journal,* January, 1949.

turning Iran to the two-party system for the first time since 1953. Since this government majority party also was built around one strong personality, there seems to be little tendency for training junior political leaders on the American model within the framework of either party. Only the *Tudeh* of all Iran's past and present political parties, reflects broad-gauged public opinion and cuts across social lines.

As 1960 drew to a close, however, an event took place in Iran which would have been inconceivable forty years earlier. In August the government of Premier Eghbal held national elections for the Majlis. The election was to be the first called under the new two-party system, with Eghbal's Milliyun Party and Asadollah Alam's Mardom Party (the opposition) contesting the seats. The Premier's party won a narrow majority (104 seats) in the Majlis. Criticism of the elections, which ranged from charges of mere ballot stuffing to rigging the polls and transporting voters in trucks to several polling places to leave their ballots, became so intense that a constitutional crisis seemed in the making. Numerous merchants who had joined the opposition, threatened to take *bast,* which would stop all business activity, a serious threat in view of Iran's expanding economy. Early in September Eghbal resigned. The Shah, reportedly annoyed by the uproar, appointed a nonparty man, Ja'far Sharif Aymani, as Premier and ordered new elections to be held as soon as possible. The assumption was that the deputies, who had all resigned too, would be given a chance to win back their seats fairly and squarely. It was a reminder that one of the world's oldest nations in continuous political history was not yet ready to graduate into a higher school of political democracy.

Recent Developments. In general, stability returned to Iran in the wake of the Consortium agreement and the overthrow of Musaddiq. The Shah, moving carefully to avoid the dictatorial role assumed by his late father, has nevertheless exercised more direct influence on government affairs than in the past. General Zahedi stayed on as Premier until 1955. The chief events of his period in office were the uncovering of a large Communist plot in the army, involving some six hundred officers, which was moving to assassinate the Shah. As a result of the discovery the Tudeh was effectively dismantled, but the narrow escape again pointed up Iran's chronic instability and susceptibility to virulent factionalism. General Zahedi also revived the Seven-Year Plan Organization and appointed Abol Hasan Ebtehaj, a leading financier (he resigned in 1958 and wrote a *Washington Post* reporter in 1962 that he was under arrest for misappropriation of Plan funds), as its director with a budget of $650 million.

In foreign affairs, Iran reached a settlement with the USSR on the boundary question; Russia also returned eleven tons of gold owed since 1947. A more significant event was Iran's adherence to the Baghdad Pact. She was the last of the five member nations to join and the most exposed due to the long common frontier with the Soviet Union. Several factors may have aided in making the relatively bold move, with its risks of provocation. Iran's traditional mistrust of Russian motives caused her to look more keenly than she had before for nearby allies when Khrushchev succeeded Stalin. Where the Georgian dictator's policies changed little from year to year, the "new look" in Russia was more irrational and hence more dangerous. There was still a legacy of the Musaddiq period current in the country which might be described as the joy of thumbing one's nose at one's bigger protectors. Realism dictated that Western military aid and economic guarantees stood to gain more for Iran in the long run. Turkish President Celal Bayar's state visit to Tehran in 1955 was the deciding factor since the Turks, equally mistrustful of Russia, had firmly committed themselves to the Pact. Accordingly Iran became a member in October, 1955, and has since taken the lead in a number of intra-Pact or CENTO projects being pushed forward, such as telecommunications improvements and a major pipeline across Turkey from the Qum oilfields to the port of Iskenderun.

There was no broad national support for the Baghdad Pact in Iran and not a great deal in evidence when the Central Treaty Organization was formed from the members remaining after the defection of Iraq in 1958. This was because British adherence and American unwillingness to enter into full participation paint the old picture in nonofficial minds of another British creation imposed on the Iranians from without. When the royalist government of Iraq was toppled on July 14, 1958, the Shah immediately rushed army units to the border and declared a state of emergency although the circumspect behavior of General Qasim quickly allayed his fears.

In accordance with the Shah's desire that constitutional government be restored to Iran, elections were held early in 1961, to select deputies for the new Majlis. Two parties, Mellyoun and Mardom, were allowed to put up candidates and to campaign. Just the faintest touch of irony was discernible in the fact that the former Premier, Dr. Eghbal, who had been dismissed by the Shah in 1960, for his part in "rigged" elections, was re-elected as a deputy from Meshed. Little violence or anti-election protest occurred in an election campaign which was carried on apathetically by any standards—in fact the popular joke was that the elections were "free" because the vote-counter or tally reader who called off the votes to his fellow-workers in each precinct was free to read any names he chose.[41]

The results of the election returned fifty-five Mellyoun deputies to forty-six for Mardom and fourteen independents. Essentially the upper-class landowner and professional makeup of the Majlis did not change. But the calm of February was temporary. Too many of the elements needed for another revolutionary change in Middle Eastern governments were present in combustible form, and, as informed observers had predicted for several years, upheaval in Iran was only a matter of time. The tempo of change in Iran was also highly dependent on the Shah, who had kept his seat in 1953 through popular appeal and army support, but was now faced with a challenge from the new middle class as well as the land-owning aristocracy into which he had been born.

In May the crisis came to a head. As in Turkey the year before, the spark was set off by students and teachers, by the future hope of Iran. At first the teachers went on strike for higher wages. It was a sit-down strike in the old *bast* tradition, and the Tehran police tried to break it up by firing on the teachers. This brought 10,000 students out to roam the streets and shout for other reforms. When the demonstrations reached general strike proportions, the Shah dismissed Premier Aymani and appointed Ali Amini, former Ambassador to the U.S., in his place, with a government pledged to full-scale economic and political reforms. The Majlis was dissolved and Amini given broad powers to carry out his reform program.

Three general areas of crisis confronted Dr. Amini as he took office. These were financial chaos, the determination of the emerging business-professional class to have some say in national policies, and widespread deep-rooted corruption.

The extent of Iran's financial distress is only now becoming apparent, and the intoxicated joy of articulate, urban Iranians at what they called a "white revolution" against corruption and repression, was sobered by the realization that hard times lay ahead. Despite revenues of $275 million from oil royalties and $70 million in American aid, Iran's foreign debt was over $500 million in 1960. One of Amini's problems was where

[41] *The New York Times,* February 4, 1961.

to find $4 million to meet the teachers' salary demands. The basic reason was that Iran was "economically irresponsible," as two of her American advisers pointed out.[42] Unchanged since the days of Fath Ali Shah was the custom of over-borrowing, the use of short-term high-interest loans to meet current obligations. Overspending for luxury goods was another part of the problem. The cost of maintaining the Iranian Army of 200,000 men absorbed 40 per cent of the budget, clearly a disproportionate amount in view of its inability to stop a Soviet attack. (Although the main objective of the army was to control internal disaffection.)

Part and parcel of Iran's financial irresponsibility was the public attitude toward fiscal matters. Financial dishonesty had been assumed to be a part of life, extending downward from the Shah himself to landowners, rich merchants, and army generals who were not above taking bribes (or giving them) on contracts. Premier Amini cracked down hard on corruption. Dozens of officials and five generals were arrested on charges of misusing public funds—as an example, the Mayor of Teheran had gained a corner on the onion market, so that the price of onions grown just outside the city was twenty-three cents a pound. After his arrest the price dropped to six cents a pound for Iran's favorite vegetable![43]

Another aspect of Amini's reform program is land reform. Himself a wealthy landowner, the new Premier warned his colleagues that unless they distributed their holdings they risked losing everything in a "black" revolution of the peasants. Twenty of Iran's "first families," including one who supposedly owns more land than all of Switzerland, agreed to do so. While a 1960 law permitting landowners to return up to 800 acres of land limited the immediate effectiveness of the gesture, it was another bit of evidence that Amini was willing to go to any lengths, backed by the Shah, to keep Iran from utter collapse and a Communist takeover in the name of the people.

For the revolution in Iran has just begun. Premier Amini must tread carefully between two hostile fires—his own class and the reformists. Every action he takes in the name of reform will be fought by the privileged, yet in order to secure their needed cooperation and continue government by trained administrators, he must rely on some of those same persons whose abuse of privilege has led to the present crisis. As one observer noted, "What is needed is a basic change in the value system of society . . . you must have a population which can work together

[42] *The Washington Post,* May 9, 1961.
[43] *The Washington Star,* June 2, 1961.

toward common goals." [44] If Premier Amini can unite these disparate elements, without losing the trust of either the landowners or the middle class, he will be well on the way to recovering Iran's political and financial stability. Forty years after the overthrow of the Qajar Dynasty, the son of Reza Shah finds himself in the position of having to rely on a direct descendant of the Qajars [45] not only to save his throne, but to rebuild monarchical government in modern constitutional terms.

RECOMMENDED READINGS

1. Balfour, James M., *Recent Happenings in Persia,* London: Blackwood, 1922.
2. Browne, E. G., *The Persian Revolution, 1905–1909,* Cambridge: Cambridge University Press, 1910.
3. Elwell-Sutton, L. P., *Modern Iran,* London: Routledge, 1941.
4. ———, *Persian Oil: A Study in Power Politics,* London: Laurence & Wishart, 1955.
5. Fatemi, Nasrollah, *Diplomatic History of Persia,* 1917–1923, New York: R. F. Moore, 1952.
6. Ford, Alan W., *The Anglo-Iranian Oil Dispute of 1951–52,* Berkeley: University of California Press, 1954.
7. Frye, R. N., *Iran,* New York: Henry Holt & Co., 1953.
8. Furon, Raymond, *L'Iran,* Paris: Payot, 1952.
9. Haas, William S., *Iran,* New York: Columbia University Press, 1946.
10. Hamzavi, A. H., *Persia and The Powers,* New York: Hutchinson, 1946.
11. Kemp, Norman, *Abadan: A Firsthand Account of the Persian Oil Crisis,* London: Allan Wingate, 1953.
12. Lenczowski, George, *Russia and The West in Iran 1918–1948,* Ithaca: Cornell University Press, 1949.
13. Millspaugh, Arthur C., *Americans in Persia,* Washington: The Brookings Institution, 1946.
14. Schultze-Holthus, Bernhardt, *Daybreak in Iran: A Story of The German Intelligence Service,* Transl. by M. Savill. London: Staples Press, 1954.
15. Shuster, W. Morgan, *The Strangling of Persia,* New York: Century, 1912.
16. Sykes, Christopher, *Wassmuss, The German Lawrence,* London: Longmans, 1936.
17. Sykes, Sir Percy, *A History of Persia,* 2 vols., London: Macmillan, 1930.
18. Thomas, Lewis, & Frye, R. N., *The United States and Turkey and Iran,* Cambridge: Harvard University Press, 1951.

[44] Woodruff, Richard B., quoted in *The Washington Post,* May 9, 1961.
[45] Khanna, K. C., "A Critical Look at Iran's Regime," *The Times of India,* n. d. Amini is a Qajar by birth and the heir to vast estates.

19. Upton, J. M., *The History of Modern Iran,* Cambridge: Harvard University Press, 1960.
20. Van Wagenen, R. W., *The Iranian Case, 1946,* New York: Carnegie Endowment for International Peace, 1952.
21. Wilber, Donald N., *Iran Past and Present,* 4th ed., Princeton: Princeton University Press, 1958.

CHAPTER 5

THE LAND OF THE HINDU KUSH

𝒜round 1334 A.D. the eminent and peripatetic Muslim philosopher Ibn Batuta traversed a great mountain range in south-central Asia on his way to India. Apparently influenced by the existing local situation, he exercised an explorer's privilege by calling this range Hindu Kush, or "Hindu Killer," because "so many of the slaves, male and female, brought from India die on the passage of this mountain owing to the severe cold and quantity of snow." [1] Almost unwittingly, Ibn Batuta established for the country we now call Afghanistan, "the land of the Hindu Kush," its geographical dominance, its political and social orientation. For Afghanistan is a land of mountains, a high tableland; these mountains foster independence, yet they are grooved with passes that have served traditionally as invasion gateways to India. The Hindu Kush, dividing Afghanistan from west to east, makes the country both the far right wing of the Middle East, and the left flank of India. For a thousand years the dominating religion was Buddhist, up from India; then Muslim armies swept over Afghanistan to convert it to Islam, relegating Buddhism to stone ruins. But the same mountains contained Islam, keeping it aloof from the schismatic development that eventually broke up the Caliphate. This isolation bred a conservative, rigid orthodoxy as strict as any in Islam and long-lasting; even today the power of the clergy in Afghanistan is stronger than in any other Muslim Middle Eastern state.

The Afghans themselves are a complex mixture of cultural traits, grafted on a tribal base. Although Afghan territory is a natural extension

---

[1] Fraser-Tytler, W. K., *Afghanistan,* London: Oxford, 1950, p. 4.

of eastern Iran (it was once called Khurasan, or "land of the rising sun"), the Afghans do not share the subtlety, deviousness, and sophistication of the Persians. "The qualities that are most striking about the Afghan people are their toughness, their poverty, their self-respect, their religious outlook, their conservatism, and their frugality." [2] The passion for freedom of the Afghans is unexcelled among Middle Eastern peoples; even the Turks, in many ways most like the Afghans of their neighbors, tend to accept controls passively. Furthermore Turkish nationalism, even younger than Arab nationalism, is a revival of the twentieth century; the Afghans, even before they were called by this name, were disputing bitterly with invaders for control of their mountain land. Afghan tribalism, fostered by geographic disunity, religion, and foreign invasion, is the main catalytic agent in the above-described series of characteristics—a curious blend of virtues and vices, personal bravery but mass cowardice, energy and laziness.

The Afghan people are a diverse mixture of races, the main groups being the Pushtuns or "true Afghans," the Hazaras, the Tajiks, the Uzbeks, the Turkomans, and the Kafirs. The tribal, ethnic interrelationship is important in political terms because it indicates the Afghan government's difficulty in establishing a stable central organism, and because it affects directly the major foreign policy issue. The Pushtuns, in their various tribes, form the bulk of the population, and their language, Pushtu (related to Persian but more complex grammatically), is the country's second language. While they are probably descended from Aryan tribes who migrated into the Indus Valley from Central Asia, the Pushtuns have a legend to account for their origin that a son of King David, Afghana, led his forty sons to safety in the mountains after the fall of Israel (i.e. the Ten Lost Tribes of Israel). The present ruling family belongs to the Durrani tribe of the Pushtuns. The Hazaras are more Mongoloid than other Afghan peoples; they are also mainly Shi'a Muslims, where the majority is Sunni. In the valleys of the Wakhan and Badakshan, and in all Afghan towns, live the Tajiks, possibly remnants of the aboriginal inhabitants of Afghanistan. Northern Afghanistan has Turkomans and Uzbeks akin to those across the Soviet Russian border. In the high ranges of northeastern Afghanistan live the Kafirs (i.e. infidels) now called Nuris since their forcible conversion to Islam under the Amir Abdur Rahman in the 1890's. The present name of this

---

[2] Wilber, Donald, *Afghanistan,* New Haven: HRAF Press, 1956, p. 3.

group comes from their country, renamed Nuristan (the land of light) now that the "light" of Islam has been introduced there. In former times, Kafir warriors gained status in the community by killing Muslims, taking home an ear or scalp as proof of each killing. From what little is known of their present attitudes, they seem to have been completely Islamized.

While it is outside the province of this chapter, much work needs to be done on Afghan ethnic groupings and social strata, as they affect very seriously progress toward political maturity, before the country can be considered adequately studied. Depending upon the speed with which the world-wide communications revolution reaches Afghanistan, one can hope for a few more years in which to study a national mosaic of peoples whose various cultures have survived nearly intact in the mid-twentieth century.

HISTORICAL BACKGROUND

The modern kingdom of Afghanistan is about the size of Texas. Two centuries ago, when the present ruling dynasty came to power, it was much larger, but for most of its recorded history the land of the Hindu Kush formed a part of other empires. Even so, great military leaders came out of the Afghan hills, so often that India came to regard everything blowing from the northwest as an ill wind bringing no good. Much as the Russians have traditionally sought a warm-water port on the Persian Gulf, the tribesmen of Central Asia have always struggled toward India, the goal of their dreams, a land where all is soft and pleasant, not harsh like the steppes.

Around 540 B.C. the highlands came under Persian rule; they were incorporated into the Achaemenian Empire and divided into provinces or satrapies. The main provinces were Drangiana (north Afghanistan), Arachosia (the northeast), and Paropamisus (the Kabul valley). Lesser satrapies were Aria (Herat), Bactria, Sogdiana, corresponding altogether to the general area of the modern kingdom plus Khurasan in eastern Persia. Ptolemy and other classical geographers called the whole territory from the Persian salt deserts to the Sulayman Mountains Aryana, the land of the Aryans; they believed, not without some truth, that this was the homeland of the migratory peoples who had irrupted the civilized world in perhaps 3000 B.C.[3] Whatever the nature of the pre-Aryan inhabitants of Afghanistan, they were thoroughly absorbed or driven into

[3] Meaning land of the Aryans, as described in the Persian sacred books, the Avesta. Later superseded by Khurasan.

remote mountain pockets, possibly to survive as such minority peoples as the Nuristanis. Before and during this first Persian conquest, Persian cultural influences fastened themselves upon Afghanistan, while migrating peoples came, transited, or settled into clans under a strong leader or family. Even these tended to break up as "the fissiparous tendencies of the Great Divide between Central and South Asia reasserted themselves." [4]

About twelve miles from Mazar-i-Sharif, the most important trading center of northern Afghanistan (Afghan Turkestan), are the ruins of Balkh, called by Arab historians 'Umm al-Balad, "Mother of Cities." [5] While these ruins have deteriorated over the centuries into an unimpressive waste, according to the *Avesta* it was there that the wandering Aryans founded their first city, "Bakhdim Soriram Ordovo Darafsham" (Balkh, the city of lofty banners.) Like Troy, the ruins of Balkh will probably yield layer upon layer of cities dating back thousands of years B.C., for the place was inhabited until the fifteenth century. Even in decay it suggests the glorious past which is so important in Afghan culture. [6]

Some time between 700 B.C. and 1000 B.C.—there is no agreement in sight on his dates—Zoroaster, a great religious teacher, lived in Balkh. He was the first to teach a dualistic religious faith, and in his emphasis on contemplation, good works, and the "right way," he foreshadowed Buddhism, which also reached a high level of growth in the valleys of Afghanistan. Among Zoroaster's converts were King Vishtaspa, the ruler of Bactria, and his queen, who became the paternal grandmother of Darius the Great. In this way Zoroastrianism was introduced into Persia, where it became the state religion and acquired a priesthood called the Magi.

Probably the most important influence in classical history on Afghanistan was Alexander the Great. Driven by a combination of curiosity, egotism, and a sense of his divine mission to rule the world, he crossed the Persian Empire from one end to the other. In 328 B.C. he crossed the Hindu Kush, and marched up the Kabul Valley in a campaign duplicated some 2,200 years later by General Roberts with a British relief army. The British found that Alexander's maps and descriptions of landmarks were still remarkably accurate!

Alexander secured the allegiance of the Aryan tribes throughout the country, with a display of military skill which has never been equalled.

[4] Fraser-Tytler, *op. cit.*, p. 16.
[5] Ali, Muhammad, *A New Guide to Afghanistan*, Kabul, 1955, p. 73.
[6] Pazhwak, A., *Aryana* (Ancient Afghanistan), London: n. d., p. 5.

He also founded cities named (what else?) Alexandria, at strategic locations, garrisoning them with mixed Macedonian and native auxiliary troops. The major modern cities of Afghanistan, Kabul, Herat, Kandahar for example, derive mainly from Alexander in their development. So profound was Alexander's impact that his name in Persian, Sikandar Zulqarnain (Alexander, Lord of Two Horns) is still associated with personal bravery among the Afghans. The Khalif ferry across the Oxus River is revered as the place where Sikandar crossed, and the local guide points out footprints on a rock as those of the Macedonian.[7] Pathan tribes like the Afridis have a tradition of descent from the Greeks, and some young warriors display a striking likeness to Alexander. More significant was the fact that with Alexander Greek civilization and thought, even Greek ideals, were brought to Afghanistan.[8] His empire broke up after his death, but Bactria became the center of an Indo-Greek kingdom which endured through various vicissitudes for 200 years. Its history is known exclusively from its coins, but this itself is indicative of the bond between the Bactrians and the Greeks, since the minting of coins was a Lydian Greek invention, whereas most of Asia used the barter system.

From the first century B.C. until the seventeenth century A.D., Afghan history may be described as a lonely lighthouse, far out at sea, that casts fitful beams of light on the restless sea around it. Dynasty followed dynasty, invasion succeeded invasion, and rarely were rulers of military skill and force of character able to stabilize the country. The Bactrians were destroyed by the Sakas, a Central Asian horde set in motion by the same forces which sent the Huns against the Roman Empire. The Sakas were crushed by the Kushans, or Yueh-chi, another Turanian horde. Under their greatest ruler, Kanishka (c.128 A.D.), Afghan territory was the center of an empire stretching from Benares to the Gobi Desert. The Kushans made the caravan routes secure, maintained trade relations with China, and met the Parthians as equals. They adopted Buddhism, infusing the Greco-Bactrian culture which they found surviving in Aryana with Buddhist and their Central Asian shamanist elements; the Greek language was replaced by various Iranian tongues. Under Kushan

[7] Shah, Ikbal Ali S., *Afghanistan of the Afghans,* London: Diamond Press, 1928, p. 3.

[8] Caroe, Sir Olaf, The *Pathans,* New York: St. Martin's Press, Inc., 1958, Chapter III. Caroe claims that the Greek impact developed out of the later Arab-Muslim conquest, when Arab scholars translated Greek philosophy and recirculated it in Asia, reviving oral traditions. The name for Alexander may come from his alleged descent from Zeus, whose oracle at Siwa had a two-horned bull as its symbol. However, the two-horned god is common in eastern symbolism.

patronage Buddhist art reached a high level of expression. The section of the great India-China pilgrimage road which traverses Afghanistan, from Balkh to the Khyber Pass, was dotted with *stupas* (mounds enclosing relics of the Lord Buddha), monasteries, and rock-carvings. In the valley of Bamiyan, an important halting-place on the road, a vertical cliff of conglomerate attracted Buddhist stone-carvers, who carved there two gigantic Buddhas 170 and 115 feet high. Mutilated but still extant, they are mute testimony to the state of pre-Islamic civilization in the land of the Hindu Kush.

Christianity was unsuccessful in penetrating into Afghanistan, but Islam finally broke the Buddhist hold on the country, weakened by numerous invasions from Central Asia. The Muslim Arab invaders, who overran Iran with such ease, had much greater difficulty in Afghanistan. In 672 A.D. troops of the Caliph Muawiya occupied Kabul, but were driven out; while Herat became one of the principal cities of the Caliphate, the petty kingdoms to the east were not Islamized until the ninth century. In 871 the Arab general Yacub Ibn Layth took Kabul and forcibly converted the inhabitants. Since that time the tribal Afghans have been fanatical, literal adherents to the faith of Muhammad. The most important of the various Muslim rulers of all (or part of) Afghanistan was Sultan Mahmud of Ghazni, who made twelve separate expeditions into India and triumphed in every one. With the profits from these raiding expeditions he built palaces and mosques at Balkh and his capital at Ghazni. He founded a university at Ghazni, and was said to be patron to over 400 resident poets, including the Persian poet laureate Firdausi. Nothing remains of the splendor of Ghazni under Mahmud except two minaret "towers of victory," nearly 100 feet high, and some rubble.

The Afghans were first mentioned as such in 982 A.D. in the *Hudud al-Alam*, a history of the Muslim peoples. To the cultivated people of Iran they were a race of highland robbers, crude, lawless, untrustworthy. Yet many rulers found them valuable. Babur, a descendant of Tamerlane who founded the Moghul Empire in India, mounted his campaign from an Afghan base; when he died his body was brought back to Kabul, his favorite city, for burial. The Moghul Emperors vied with the Persians for control of Afghanistan; like the British who followed them, the Moghuls considered the eastern Afghan tribes essential to protect their territories, and used a combination of military force and subsidies to keep them in line. It often did not work. Babur's son Humayun was driven out of Delhi for a time by the Afghan chieftain Sher Shah, in the eighteenth century.

The Founding of the Durrani Dynasty

As the eighteenth century unrolled there was little to suggest in the Afghan spectacle that the country would ever be united. More than one conqueror found Afghan tribesmen the means to empire, but in their own territory the tribes were unable to compose themselves even into a confederation. The lack of internal unity was an enticement to both the Moghuls and the Persians; thus Kabul was held by the Moghul Emperor Aurangzeb, while Kandahar remained the easternmost outpost of the Safavis of Persia. Neither Safavi nor Moghul writ extended very far into the hills, however. The two major tribal clans of the Afghans, the Ghilzais [9] and the Abdalis, took constant advantage of the increasing weakness of both empires, playing one against the other. The Abdalis around Kandahar won a concession from Shah Abbas the Great to have one of their leaders, Sado, recognized as chief. His descendants, the Saddozais, became the ruling family, and in 1716 they seized Herat, establishing a shaky authority over Khurasan. Because they were the most westerly of Afghan tribes, they had extensive contact with Persia; their leaders adopted Persian manners and dress and spoke a vulgar form of Persian, facts which were to assume much greater importance following the unification of Afghanistan under them. The Ghilzais, nearly equal to them in numbers and lands, despised the Persians and lost no opportunity to intrigue against them, which may prove there is some truth in their "illicit" origin. A Ghilzai chief, Mir Wais, rebelled against the Persian governor of Kandahar province; his son Mahmud captured Isfahan in a campaign against the Safavis, and treacherously butchered all the leading citizens at a banquet, establishing the tradition by which Afghans regard Persians as effeminate and Persians regard Afghans as rude, boorish, and untrustworthy. Fortunately for Afghan unity and Persian sanity, Mahmud, a sort of junior-grade Genghis Khan, and the Ghilzais totally lacked any capacity for statecraft; they overextended

[9] *Ghilzai,* in Pushtu, means "born of a thief," from *ghil* thief, and *zai,* born of or son of. Ghilzai tradition says that a descendant of Noah, who had fled with his people from oppression and settled in the Hari Rud country, had a secret love affair with the daughter of a local chief. (He later married her.) Their offspring was called Ghilzye, for obvious reasons. It is more likely that the tribe is descended from nomadic Turks.

themselves in bloody campaigns against Iran and were crushed after several struggles by Nadir Shah. Nadir also brought the Abdalis under Persian control in 1729, but recognizing their military value he formed an elite corps of Afghan mercenaries from both Ghilzais and Abdalis. This cavalry, between 4,000 and 16,000 in strength, were the new "Immortals" of the Persian army, and Nadir apparently relied on them more than on his own Turkomans, the Qizilbash (Redheads). The jealousy of the Turkomans led to Nadir's assassination in his tent in 1747 by Muhammad Khan Qajar. The Afghan contingent, who had remained fanatically loyal to Nadir and saved his neck in the Khyber Pass, now found itself surrounded by personally hostile troops. Led by Ahmad Khan, the younger son of the Abdali chief, they cut their way through Nadir's army and started home. At the age of twenty-four, jobless, but possessed of the finest small army in Asia, and (so the Afghan chroniclers say) a large slice of Nadir's Indian treasure, Ahmad got to thinking about his future prospects, and realized that before him lay the opportunity to found an empire, or at least a kingdom, in his own country. He may not have been the first Afghan to think politically, rather than tribally, but he was the first to put his thoughts to practical use. The parallel between the ancient Greeks and the Afghans continued.

Ahmad Khan proceeded to Kandahar, where the chiefs of the various tribes all accepted his authority, reportedly after a holy man, placing an ear of wheat on his head, had declared that he alone gave no cause for dissension and was fit to rule. In 1747 he was crowned Ahmad Shah, called Dur-i-Durran because of his penchant for wearing a pearl earring. Although he may justly be called the founder of the present Afghan state and one of the four great leaders in its national history, he was really a tribal adventurer-turned-king, and ruled over a much larger territory than his collateral descendant Zahir Shah does. The Afghan Empire of the eighteenth century included Kashmir, the Indus Basin, and the Punjab. Ahmad Shah ruled for twenty-six years (1747–1773) from his capital at Kandahar. To assist himself with the machinery of government he created a council of nine *sirdars*. He also curbed the tribesmen with a combination of force, grants for service in the army, and outright subsidies, and formed matrimonial alliances with the daughters of many tribal *maliks* (chiefs). His requirement that each tribe give an estimate of its military strength was the first rough census of the population. Although Ahmad Shah has been called "the very ideal of the Afghan genius, hardy and enterprising, fitted for conquest yet incapable of empire," [10] he founded a monarchy which has endured under the same royal house—albeit from a branch of this house—for over 200 years, while the other ruling dynasties of Asia at the time have long since passed from the scene.

Modern Afghan irredentism—what there is of it—may be traced from the reigns of Ahmad Shah and his son and successor Timur Shah (1773–1795). Ahmad's possession of Kashmir gave rise to the rather special attitude of eastern Afghans toward that long-lost province. *"Har cha ta khpal mulk Kashmir day"* (Unto every man his own country is Kashmir), they say. [11] Ahmad Shah had the common touch; he wrote poetry in Pushtu, lived simply (except for the addiction to pearls), and preferred to spend his time among his tribesmen. Timur Shah went in a different direction. He moved the capital to Kabul, with a winter capital at Peshawar, on the Indian side of the Khyber in what is now an integral part of West Pakistan. The importance thus given to Peshawar and to Pathan tribal territory has its modern echo in Afghanistan's agitation for a sovereign state of Pushtunistan in the former North West Frontier Province; in sentimental and emotional terms the issue predates the Durand Line. If Afghanistan cannot have Ahmad's empire back, she at least would like a say in what goes on politically in the missing portions.

Timur had little use for Pushtu and for Pushtuns generally, and preferred the company of Persian courtiers to the crude leaders of the Durranis. He discarded his father's system of tribal levies, and though he retained the Durrani *sirdars* as advisers he trimmed their powers by creating duplicate council posts manned by Persians. He had a large family, twenty-three sons and countless daughters by many different wives, but he set up no law of succession and had no real favorite, and his death was the signal for a scramble among the princes for the Afghan throne. Meanwhile the eastern provinces of the empire were detached by the Sikhs, the Persians reasserted themselves in the west, the tribes of the frontier went back to their customary role of undisciplined robbery. Three Saddozais, Shah Zaman, Shah Mahmud, and Shah Shuja, contended with and succeeded each other; Mahmud blinded his brother Zaman, then twice held the throne and was each time ejected by his brother Shuja. In the end there were none; except for a brief British-sponsored reappearance by Shah Shuja, Afghan rule passed to the

[10] From Cunningham, *History of the Sikhs,* London: John Murray, 1849.
[11] *Caroe, op. cit.,* p. 261.

Barakzai clan of the Durranis. The Durrani Empire shrank to an amirate, the principal Amir being Dost Muhammad Khan. With the Dost, as he was affectionately called by the British, Afghanistan entered the realm of nineteenth-century power politics. British commercial-political interests moved north toward an eventual showdown with Czarist Russian territorial expansionism moving south, and, their logical point of collision was the Hindu Kush.

Great Britain, Russia, and Afghanistan. Dost Muhammad's policy was to regain control of Kandahar and Herat, plus the territories between the Oxus and the Hindu Kush, at an early date. He faced formidable obstacles. The Qajars had consolidated their hold on Persia. The Sikhs under the adroit Ranjit Singh had seized Kashmir, the Punjab, and Peshawar. Between the advancing Russian power and the British in India, there were no stable regimes, only the medieval khanates of Central Asia, the nomadic Kirghiz and Turkmen, and the weak Amirate of Afghanistan. No political situation called more clearly for a buffer status, in order to survive, than Afghanistan's.

The Peace of Tilsit (1807) between Napoleon and the Czar Alexander enabled the two rulers to plan combined measures for the invasion of India via Persia. Britain sent an emissary, Mountstuart Elphinstone, to Peshawar and "the Kingdom of Caubul" to arrange a defensive alliance with Shah Shuja in 1809. Elphinstone did not go beyond Peshawar, where he concluded a mutual defense treaty with the Shah which would have blocked Napoleon's designs on India had he proceeded that far. In 1814 Elphinstone published an official record of his mission, *Caubul,* which describes better than any traveler before or since the life and structure of the Afghan Kingdom. Rather prophetically, he observed that British rule in Asia should end desirably when the peoples themselves "should reach such a standard that retention of the government by foreigners would become impossible." [12]

An old Indian proverb states, "He alone can be Emperor of Hindustan who is first lord of Kabul." [13] The British penetrated deeper and deeper into Afghanistan and became more enmeshed in a political situation of oriental complexity, in their attempts to forestall Russia's southward advance. Three wars and a century of ill-will proved three things—that liberty is a precious commodity to Afghans, that no tactic is despicable

[12] Carve, *op. cit.,* p. 279.
[13] Habberton, W., *Anglo-Russian Relations Concerning Afghanistan,* Urbana: University of Illinois Press, 1937, p. 9.

when they seek to regain liberty taken from them unjustly, and that British intrigues created much of the suspicion which still motivates Afghan attitudes toward foreigners, the remainder being caused by Russian faithlessness. The British and Russian Foreign Ministers, Palmerston and Count Nesselrode, were found "playing the pieces on the dim, distant chessboard of Central Asia with little knowledge of the details but a shrewd understanding of the fundamental principles of the game"; [14] neither side ever displayed any real awareness of the Afghan mentality or of Afghan rulers. The British fought three Afghan Wars (1839–42, 1878–79, 1919) all on the basis of an erroneous concept of Afghan intentions. The First Afghan War resulted from Britain's attempts to restore Shah Shuja, who was unpopular in Afghanistan, to the throne of the amirate in place of the popular Dost Muhammad. A British force under Sir William MacNaughten occupied Kabul in 1839, and settled down to what appeared to the liberty-loving Afghans as a permanent occupation; wives and camp-followers joined the troops, houses were built for them, and furniture was imported from India. The highly moral Afghans soon grew even more indignant at the heavy traffic which went on between the British camp and newly-established houses of prostitution. The proverb "necessity is the mother of invention and the father of the Eurasian" was soon to receive tragic proof in Kabul in 1840.[15]

Dost Muhammad reappeared in the autumn of that year, but was brought to bay near Kabul and surrendered in return for a safe-conduct to exile in India. The total illogicality of Britain's policy in Afghanistan became apparent when the Dost was returned to power as Amir at the end of the First Afghan War. Seldom has a conflict ended so disastrously for the Empire. In 1841 resentment at the continued presence of the British and their puppet, Shah Shuja, took the form of a general insurrection. MacNaughten, the only British leader with a semblance of will-power, was murdered by the Dost's son, Akbar, during a durbar to discuss evacuation, which finally began in January, 1842.[16] Out of 4,500 men, 12,000 wives, children, and camp-followers, and uncounted tons of baggage, one person, Dr. Brydon, lived to see India again. Britain's tarnished military prestige in the Hindu Kush was somewhat brightened

[14] Fraser-Tytler, *op. cit.*, p. 84.
[15] *Ibid.*, p. 114.
[16] MacMunn, *Afghanistan From Darius to Amanullah*, London: Bell, 1929, p. 142.

by the reoccupation of Kabul in autumn and the burning of the Grand Bazaar, but from this period established the two-fold impulses of Afghan foreign policy, positive neutralism (i.e. playing one major power against another), and suspicion of the *feringhi* (foreigner). In 1857 came the final irony—a full rapprochement with Dost Muhammad which confirmed him as Amir and gave him a subsidy to maintain himself against the Persians, who had seized Herat. In return the Dost pledged his word in alliance with Britain.[17] This he kept, all through the Sepoy Mutiny when a tribal invasion of Muslims through the Khyber Pass could have annihilated the hard-pressed British. Like the great Durrani rulers who followed him, the Dost kept his word remarkably well.

While the British were thus crossing mallets with the Afghans, the Russians were imperturbably pressing southward through the political chaos of Central Asia. By 1863 they held the steppes northeast of the Caspian; between 1865 and 1868 the independent khanates of Tashkent and Samarqand were incorporated into the new Russian province of Turkestan. In 1869 the Khanate of Bokhara became a Russian vassal; Russian influence had reached the Oxus. Russian military advances were succeeded by a horde of administrators and colonists. Much of this progress went unnoticed in Britain, until the Russians annexed Khiva in 1873 and served notice that the Indus River was more logically the termination of their sphere of influence than the Oxus. The Second Afghan War (1878–79) was the direct result of added Russian expansion southward, which forced Britain to drop the nonintervention mask she had worn in Afghanistan since 1842. The Russians annexed the Khanate of Khokand to their dominions in 1877, and simultaneously began hostilities with Ottoman Turkey. British determination to keep the territorial status quo in both places nearly led to a general war, but in 1878 the Congress of Berlin temporarily settled the "Eastern Question." Yet the British Government continued to view with concern "the probable influence of that situation (i.e. the Russian army's advance toward India's borders) upon the uncertain character of an Oriental chief whose ill-defined dominions are thus brought within a steadily narrowing circle, between the conflicting pressures of two great military empires, one of which expostulates and remains passive, while the other apologizes and continues to move forward."[18] The British reaction was displayed in a second invasion of Afghanistan, the annihilation of a

---

[17] As he signed the document he said: "I have made an alliance with the British Government and I will keep it till death come what may."

[18] *Memorandum of Instructions to Lord Lytton.*

second military mission in Kabul, and a general occupation under General Roberts. Fortune smiled on the British as it had not in 1842. The Amir Abdur Rahman, grandson of the Dost and the second of the four great leaders of unified Afghanistan, returned from asylum in Russia and began to pick up the pieces of the nearly-shattered kingdom.[19]

The Amir Abdur Rahman, who was to rule Afghanistan "with a rod of iron" for twenty-one years (1880–1901), was described as follows by a British official sent to negotiate with him: "He appeared animated by a sincere desire to be on cordial terms with the British Government, and although his expectations were, as might have been anticipated, larger than Government is prepared to satisfy, yet he did not press them with any discourteous insistence. . . ."[20] Although he had spent twelve years in Russia, one of Abdur Rahman's first acts was to sign a treaty of friendship with Britain. In return for retention of Kandahar and British control over Afghan foreign relations (Afghanistan would not have direct relations with any foreign power), the British vested their "rights" in Afghanistan in Abdur Rahman, assuming that he would restore order and maintain it. In this they were correct, and thenceforth the Afghans became in nineteenth century diplomatic parlance pawns in the great game between empires from the west in Asia. Abdur Rahman said gloomily, "When I look about me, I see to one side a bear, and to the other a lion, and each about to devour this poor goat, Afghanistan." The respect felt by the British toward him did not extend to the Afghan people, and the Russian attitude toward them, characteristically, was that of populating another backward area with progressive-minded Russians. Other than Abdur Rahman's comments, the feelings of the mute mass of Afghans at the new buffer status of their country have not been recorded.

The borders of the Afghan Kingdom were delineated in Abdur Rahman's time as direct results of the Anglo-Russian power play. In 1888 a Joint Border Commission defined the northern border, at mid-channel of the Amu Darya (Oxus) River except for the extreme western and eastern sections. The British, it was noted, had "the much-desired hard granite of a legal compact with their adversary in Central Asia, and the sense of security that accompanied it."[21] The detachment of Central Asia, once ruled by Ahmad Shah, and of Baluchistan was an accom-

[19] Afghanistan's four great rulers have all spent periods out of the country only to return swiftly at the scent of danger and rise to power.
[20] Lepel Griffin to the Government of India (letter) August 4, 1880.
[21] Habberton, *op. cit.,* p. 57.

plished fact. In 1895, a joint Anglo-Russian Technical Commission carried the Afghan frontier with Russia eastward through the narrow Wakhan Valley, less than eight miles wide at some points. The surveying party placed boundary markers as far as they could go, and then projected the border officially into space, across a region of perpetual snow and ice in the high Pamirs. The chief surveyor wrote picturesquely: "Amidst the voiceless waste of a vast white wilderness, absolutely inaccessible to man and within the ken of no living creature but the Pamir eagles—there the three great empires actually meet. It is a fitting trijunction." [22]

Afghanistan's eastern border with British India (now West Pakistan) was settled by the agreement of 1893 between Sir Mortimer Durand and Abdur Rahman. The delimitation has since become known as the Durand Line. Some border demarcation was needed because the internal stability which Abdur Rahman had achieved permitted him to look abroad, with more than a hint that he was interested in reconstructing the Durrani Empire. As the Amir of Afghanistan, his influence was paramount among the Muslim tribes of northwestern India for religious reasons, and in addition he was related to them, at least the leading Pathan tribes. Accordingly, a line was drawn roughly down the middle of this tribal territory, and each party pledged itself not to "exercise interference" in the territories of the other lying beyond the line. The British on their side alternated between a "close border" policy and a "forward" policy, according to whose views were in the ascendancy in Delhi; in the former, they kept outposts to guard the settled districts and left the tribes alone; in the latter, they sent advance contingents into the tribal areas. On their side the Afghan Government sought to maintain Afghan influence by inviting deputations of tribal leaders to Kabul as state guests, and sending agents among the tribes. The illogicality of the Durand Line—it cuts across tribal grazing and territorial lands, and even splits some tribes in two—does not obscure the fact that it worked as a compromise until the departure of the British *raj* from India in 1947.

The establishment of public security was Abdur Rahman's chief contribution to Afghan progress. "You call me a hard man, but I rule a hard people," he said. The Amir was once eating ice cream with a visiting British engineer at his palace when four hundred mutineers from Herat were brought to him. He scowled, and ordered, "Poke their eyes

[22] Actually the three empires—Russia, China, India—were separated by the Wakhan.

out." The order was carried out on the spot, while he finished his ice-cream. On another occasion a British official left his belt on a tree by the roadside during a trip. When he next passed that way a farmer returned the belt. The Englishman was so pleased by this act of honesty that he took the farmer to meet the Amir. Abdur Rahman asked the man which hand had picked up the belt, and the farmer demonstrated. "Cut it off!" roared the Amir. "How often must I tell you Afghans not to touch other people's things!" [23]

Abdur Rahman was a thoroughgoing autocrat, in the oriental manner, but even he gave deference to Afghan tribalism and love for independence by consulting with three political bodies, a royal council drawn from the aristocracy of ministers, *sardars* (hereditary nobility) and tribal khans, an Assembly of Commoners comprised of the leaders of towns and villages, and the *mullahs*. However, consultation with the Assembly of Commoners was purely perfunctory and rare. The Amir also developed a standing army and a strong-arm police to bring rebellious tribes to heel. He strengthened the authority of the ruler by having himself accepted as the head of Islam in Afghanistan, and his name mentioned in the Friday prayers at the larger mosques. He also expropriated certain church properties, although not to the extent of Reza Shah or Ataturk. His last will and testament contains the revealing comment, "unity and unity alone can make Afghanistan a great power." Limited in his imagination, and restrained by the extremely rudimentary state of Afghan political thinking, the Amir none the less brought his country into the twentieth century a strong, stable state. At his death his son Habibullah succeeded him in a smooth transfer of power.

THE TWENTIETH CENTURY

Habibullah (1901–1919) lacked the iron force of his father, but the newly-won stability and sovereignty of Afghanistan was successfully continued. The new Amir was more suspicious of foreign influence than his father had been, so that although he continued to accept the subsidy of £1,800,000 which the British as a matter of policy had bestowed on Abdur Rahman, he lost no time in indicating to both Britain and Russia that Afghanistan would go her own way regardless of external pressures. In 1904 a British mission under Louis Dane visited Kabul intending to regularize Anglo-Afghan relations. The Afghans, much im-

[23] MacMunn, *op. cit.*, p. 246.

pressed by Japanese successes over Russia in the Far East, wanted Britain to join them in an attack on Russia, and to build a railway into southern Afghanistan for the defence of Kandahar. Britain was unprepared to do this, in view of the current attitude of sweet reasonableness toward the Czars, and the negotiating Afghans became uncooperative and resentful. The treaty which was eventually signed in 1905 merely gave Britain control (which they already had) over Afghanistan's foreign relations in return for a subsidy of £160,000 and permission for the Afghans to import munitions through India.[24] In 1907 the Anglo-Russian Convention of St. Petersburg formally recognized Afghanistan as a buffer state whose borders were accepted by both great powers. Habibullah was angry because he had not been consulted and refused to sign the Convention or its protocols; in fact, he would not even answer the British request for concurrence for a year. Nevertheless the Convention went into effect *de facto*. In the same year the Amir made a royal visit to India, where he was received with great cordiality and made to feel considerably more charitable toward Britain; this visit did much to ensure Afghanistan's neutrality during World War I, when the country was courted by Turkish and German agents. During his visit to India, Habibullah was initiated into the Scottish Rite by MacMahon and Kitchener.[25]

Afghan neutrality during World War I was purchased at a price. A pro-war group in the court headed by Habibullah's brother Nasrullah Khan pressed the Amir strongly to accept the call to *jihad* (holy war) of the Ottoman Sultan. Another factor drawing the country closer to a Turkish alliance was the natural sympathy of Sunni Afghans (the vast majority) for Sunni Turks, while the ethnically Turkish tribes of the north (as well as some who merely remembered the fighting qualities of the Ottomans) were fanatical in their pro-Ottomanism. A joint Turkish-German mission, the Niedermayer mission, entered Afghanistan secretly from Iran and tried to bring Habibullah round, but even this did not budge him. The remarkable talent of the Durranis for keeping their pledges was again demonstrated.

The new Asian nationalism which erupted from the ashes of the Russo-Japanese War found expression among the small literate elite

[24] Fraser-Tytler, *op. cit.*, pp. 179 ff., notes the value of conciliating Afghan rulers instead of adopting a high standard of international morality which they cannot comprehend.
[25] MacMunn, *op. cit.*, p. 251. He was criticized by the mullahs for accepting membership in a non-Muslim, secret order!

in Afghanistan with the forming of an Afghan nationalist movement. This was led by Mahmud Tarzi, the editor of the newspaper *Sarraj-al-Akbar* and father-in-law of the royal princes Inayatullah and Amanullah. Tarzi was a bitter antagonist of the British, who had engineered his exile under Abdur Rahman. The nationalists got Habibullah to demand a seat for Afghanistan at the peace conference. In a letter to the Viceroy of India, Habibullah pointed out that Afghanistan had stayed neutral during the war despite considerable temptation; he asked the conference to recognize Afghanistan's "absolute liberty, freedom of action, and perpetual independence." [26] Habibullah never received an answer; he died before one could be sent. On February 20, 1919, he was assassinated by unknown persons at his hunting camp. The murder has never been solved, although a scapegoat was condemned on scanty evidence at the time. Whatever the cause, the motive for the deed probably lies in the tangled relationships of the Afghan court, and the rising tide of nationalism which, even in the remote and isolated kingdom, identified Habibullah with a pro-British tradition. The Amir's brother, Nasrullah, declared himself the successor to the throne, but the third son, Amanullah, rejected the claim, and won the allegiance of the country by the simple expedient of controlling the state treasury and the Kabul garrison. In 1919 he was formally accepted as Amir, and promptly imprisoned his uncle for complicity in Habibullah's murder, an act that enraged the mullahs.

THE MODERN AFGHAN STATE, 1919–1960

The Amir Amanullah (1919–1929) holds a peculiar position in modern Afghan politics. Essentially a weak and vacillating ruler, the last in the line of Dost Muhammad and downgraded by the present Yahya Khel dynasty which has superseded his line,[27] summarily exiled from his homeland in 1929, he nevertheless was the responsible agent for Afghanistan's timid steps into the modern world, and for verification of her independence. Here is how it happened. The early surge of nationalism which brought him to the throne turned sour because of the action of imprisoning his uncle, who was not involved in the assassina-

[26] Quoted in Wilber, *op. cit.*, p. 147.
[27] See Wilber, Fig. 5 (pp. 100–101) for a geneological chart of the Muhammadzai family. Nadir Shah and Amanullah were descended from two sons of Payindah Khan, Sultan Muhammad Khan and Amir Dost Muhammad Khan. Although they do not head the government, descendents of Amanullah are respected and hold positions of prominence at court.

tion of Habibullah, and releasing members of the Musahiban family, who were. The mullahs sided with Nasrullah, the young nationalists and army officers were angry because they believed another autocracy was in the making. In order to solidify his position, Amanullah used the familiar trick of focusing his people's attention abroad. He called a *jihad* on the British in India, in 1919–20. This affair, which is commonly known as the Third Afghan War, is now regarded by Afghans as their War of Independence. Afghan troops led by General Nadir Khan occupied the town of Thal briefly; elsewhere hastily-assembled British levies drove back the untrained Afghans. A rebellion in Peshawar, near the entrance to the Khyber Pass, was planned by Amanullah's agent, the Afghan postmaster Ghulam Haidar, in conjunction with Indian revolutionary elements. The British got wind of it and blocked it merely by closing the walled city's gates and turning off the water supply. But Britain had had enough of war, even in India, and was not anxious to enter into a protracted tribal conflict. In November, 1921, an Anglo-Afghan Treaty of Friendship formally re-established good relations and recognized Afghan sovereignty. Afghanistan signed a treaty with the new Soviet power in the same year which guaranteed the independence of Bokhara (seized by the Soviets two years later) and the return of the Panjdeh district taken by Russia in 1885 (which was not done).

The Reforms of Amanullah. The new ruler was determined to elevate Afghanistan into the select circle of recognized world powers, and to make it a modern state. In this goal he was not alone in the Middle East, for his era was the era of Mustafa Kemal and Reza Shah. Even more than those strong-minded reformers, Amanullah had unformed, malleable human clay to work with, for the Afghans were healthy, vigorous, basically intelligent, undisfigured by war, and the country had excellent opportunities for development. Amanullah himself was a patriotic nationalist, a fact on which he counted, not unreasonably, to secure him the loyalty of the more lawless elements who still regarded the Durranis as *primus inter pares.*

In 1923 Amanullah codified the first Afghan constitution, modeled on Turkish administrative law and the 1906 Persian constitution.[28] The new constitution had seventy-three articles and named Afghanistan an

[28] Previous Afghan rulers had governed as absolute sovereigns, but in consultation with three councils, represented by the aristocracy, commoners, and mullahs.

hereditary monarchy under the family of Amanullah. In 1926 he assumed the title of Pad-i-Shah (commonly abbreviated to Shah). Aside from an abortive attempt to support the Pan-Turanism movement in Muslim Central Asia, his first error was a bill to provide education for women. Reaction among the tribes took the form of a rebellion in Khost province in 1924–25; the Afghan regular forces were badly mauled by the tribesmen, who advanced to within thirty-five miles of Kabul before they were checked, primarily through the use of two British airplanes flown by German pilots! The revolt collapsed after its chief instigator, the Lame Mullah, was executed in Kabul, but Amanullah was forced by a Loe Jirga (Tribal Assembly) to withdraw the constitutional amendment guaranteeing certain rights and status to women and giving them education beyond the twelfth year.[29] His failure to oppose the conservative religious and tribal leaders was to bring serious consequences four years later.

An invitation from the Italian Government in 1927–28 impelled the King to set out on a world tour. He visited all the major capitals of Europe, as well as Turkey and Iran, and the progress achieved by his opposite numbers in Ankara and Tehran inspired him with a fanatical determination to do the same with his own Afghans. Throughout the tour, while the King was winning the respect of Europeans for his dignity and manners and genuine efforts to accommodate himself to Western habits, reports filtered back to Afghanistan of his undignified behavior. The King had performed the prayer ritual at Al-Azhar Mosque in Cairo in a grey top hat, it was whispered. The Queen was seen unveiled in public on numerous occasions. Why, His Majesty had even accepted a foreign decoration from the King of Italy! Upon his return to Afghanistan, however, Amanullah took no notice of this. Instead, he issued a series of regulations designed to force the people to adopt Western dress (after all, Ataturk had done so) and to impose constitutional democracy on them. He convened another Loe Jirga, whose members, wearing ill-assorted black morning coats, white shirts, black ties, and soft hats, heard their ruler propose the formation of a parliament of 150 elected representatives, the total emancipation of women, monogamy, compulsory education for both sexes, separation of church from state, and currency reforms. In 1929 Queen Suraya appeared unveiled at a public function

[29] Pathan (i.e., Afghan) social codes permitted a father to dispose of his wife and daughter as he pleased.

at the King's side, tearing it off amid applause as the king announced himself a revolutionary determined to alter completely Afghan social and political life.

Amanullah's proposals clearly grew out of his conversations with Ataturk and Reza Shah, but in his enthusiasm for the ends he failed to see that the means for accomplishing them did not exist in Afghanistan. The educated elite were pitifully few, and half of them opposed Amanullah for his treatment of his uncle and because of his choice of advisers. The mullahs were reactionary and supreme among the illiterate, naive mass of the people. The tribal leaders felt that the King had gone contrary both to Islam and to the Pushtun code by importing foreign ways. The army, so often the means of change in Eastern countries, was underpaid. Most important of all, the very tribal nature of Afghan social organization defeated him. Some of the most ironic lines ever penned about a national leader were written about him in 1928: ". . . the Henry the Second of Afghanistan . . . he is a constitutional monarch with a tendency to enact the role of beneficent autocrat. Under his masculine regime, Afghanistan cannot but go forward from strength to strength. . . ." [30]

The rebellion against Amanullah began among the Shinwaris in eastern Afghanistan, then spread to Khost. At first there was no opposition leader strong enough to unite the various disaffected elements. Then a bandit chieftain who styled himself Habibullah Khan, but was better known as Bacha-i-Saqqo (Son of the Water-Carrier), appeared on the scene. The Bacha was actually a Tajik, of the ancient Iranian stock which had been ruled by the dominant Afghans (and the Greeks left by Alexander) for some 2,200 years. Of humble birth, he had served in the Afghan army but had deserted, had been a tea-seller in Peshawar and a domestic servant, and had escaped to the hills following a prison sentence for housebreaking. He slowly collected an equally desperate group of bandits around him and followed the life of a Robin Hood for some time. None of these actions particularly qualified him to sit on the Durrani throne; but he did have a gift for leadership, and the timing of his move was excellent. Even the troops who remained loyal to Amanullah fought half-heartedly, fearing that the King would probably restore his reforms if they defeated the rebels. Most of the

[30] Shah, Ikbal, *op. cit.,* p. 249.

people swung over to support the Bacha; even the great Ghilzai tribe preferred the leadership of a member of the Tajik minority (at first) to that of the hated Amanullah. Recognizing the inevitable, the King went into exile in Italy. His last words—"I now leave my country as a rejected monarch . . . but why?" served as a warning to his successors and an indication of his failure to comprehend his people.[31]

Bacha-i-Saqqo now styled himself Habibullah Ghazi; his name was called at the Friday prayers. His writ extended only to Kabul and vicinity; Herat was under the control of another Tajik, and the Pathan tribes now rejected his authority. The Bacha's regime lasted for eight months; Afghanistan was delivered from chaos by General Nadir Khan and his brothers, all cousins of Amanullah but out of favor. Nadir Khan, who had served as Ambassador to France after the Third Afghan War and retired to the Riviera because of ill-health, returned to Afghanistan literally on a stretcher to lead a campaign to deliver Afghanistan from the Bacha, in what might be called the "fourth Afghan war," except that it involved only Afghans. General Nadir had acquired great prestige in his country during the Third Afghan War. At the conclusion of the war he was hailed as the liberator, and the Column of Independence in Kabul was erected in his honor. Amanullah named him Minister of War, and then Commander-in-Chief of the armed forces. But his success and popularity among the martial Pushtun tribes made him many enemies at court, and apparently as the result of sharp differences of opinion between him and Muhammad Wali, the Amir's favorite and Minister of War, caused Amanullah to re-assign him to Paris, where he remained until his resignation. The upheaval of 1929 brought him back to Afghanistan with his brothers, Muhammad Hashim, Shah Wali, and Shah Mahmud, all three destined to play important roles in the "restoration."

The four brothers returned to their country with little more than the clothes on their backs, and less money. At first Nadir's attempts to raise tribal levies, were rather unsuccessful, and it is reported that he had to swear an oath that he was not in sympathy with Amanullah before the tribesmen would follow his cause. The British were also unwilling to let him recruit Wazir and Mohmand tribesmen from their side of the Durand Line. Finally Nadir managed to raise a tribal army and

---

[31] Shah, Ikbal, *Modern Afghanistan,* London: Sampson Low, 1939, p. 170.

marched on Kabul, which was liberated by his brother Shah Wali on October 12, 1929; two days later he was proclaimed Shah of Afghanistan.[32] The only unfortunate aspects of the liberation were the execution of the Bacha and the thorough looting of Kabul (even to the carpet from the staircase of the royal palace), both demanded as the price of support by Nadir's tribal army.

Nadir Shah (1929–1933) is the fourth great ruler in modern Afghan history. Ahmad Shah laid the family foundations and created a purely Afghan national tradition, Abdur Rhaman provided stability and set frontiers, Amanullah won international recognition for the state. Nadir Shah brought together tribal, dynastic, and religious traditions into a functioning modern state, so well-fused that government continued without a hitch when he was assassinated four years later.

Nadir's intentions were to make Afghanistan into a modern state, but at a pace consistent with tradition, experience, and the popular will. His years abroad—he had grown up in India—had exposed him to British parliamentarianism, and he had also lived in France. His leadership of tribal forces gave him considerable insight into the tribal mentality. Amanullah had lacked all these advantages; his knowledge of world politics was confined to one brief tour. Nadir accordingly dissociated himself from Amanullah's reform program. He declared that government would be in accordance with Islamic law of the Hanafi rite, an act which brought smiles to the faces of the mullahs. Without any foreign assistance except 10,000 rifles and a gift of £180,000 from the British government, he restored internal security. Shah Mahmud, now become Commander-in-Chief of the army, defeated one Ibrahim Beg, an adherent of the Bacha who was using Afghan Turkestan as a base for attacks on the Soviets across the border. Ibrahim's actions brought tension between the two countries and even a brief Soviet invasion; fortunately Shah Mahmud drove him across the Oxus in 1931 and the cause for friction was removed. In the same year the Governor of Herat, a prudent fellow, decided that the wind was blowing Nadir's way and presented his province for reincorporation in Afghanistan. The poor communications exposed in the Ibrahim campaign drove Nadir to build a road through the Hindu-Kush, connecting the Oxus and Indus valleys via the Shibar Pass. He was the first in 5,000 years or more

---

[32] The Bacha had taken refuge in the Kabul citadel (the Arg) where Nadir's family was imprisoned, but at the last moment he lost his nerve and surrendered. Fraser-Tytler, *op. cit.,* pp. 220–222, has full details.

of Afghan history to discover that there was an easier way to the plains of Turkestan than the biting summits of the Hindu Kush.[33]

A Loe Jirga of 1930 set up a National Council of 105 members under a president which would sit at regular intervals and advise the ruler on public policy. Nadir Shah also formed an assembly of nobles and a cabinet of ten members under a prime minister. His brother Muhammad Hashim was the first prime minister, and Shah Mahmud became Minister of War. Shah Wali became Ambassador to the Court of St. James and Muhammad Aziz, the fourth brother, Ambassador to Moscow. Thus did Nadir Shah intend to perpetuate the regime and found the unique "family monarchy" which survived his death and continues to the present day. In the long and often bloody history of Afghan rulership, there are few such examples of fraternal loyalty.

The major political achievement of Nadir Shah's brief rule was the Constitution of 1931, which remains with almost no alterations as the law of the land. The Constitution placed legislative power in the hands of a bicameral legislature which was required to consult and cooperate with the ruler. The Senate (Majlis-i-Ayan) is limited to forty members nominated by the Shah, the lower house or National Assembly (Majlis-i-Shura Milli) to 120 elected members. To become law, bills must have the approval of the Assembly and the ruler.

The Constitution not unnaturally reflects Nadir's formative experiences in Western Europe and his preoccupation with the introduction of Western democratic concepts into his country's medieval, conservative, traditional social structure. At his coronation he said: "The inhabitants of Afghanistan shall without distinction of race or creed have equal rights and shall be as brothers. . . . Purdeh shall be observed in accordance with Islamic law."[34] He added that all government employees would have to swear by the Koran that they would not accept bribes or presents from the people. . . . "The sale of liquor, public and private, is prohibited in the whole country, and the inhabitants are not allowed to brew liquors."

The Constitution contains a limited bill of rights (Articles 9–26); slavery is banned and a due process of law clause provided which, at least in theory, forbids arbitrary or wilful interference with personal

---

[33] *Ibid.*, pp. 230–234. The Ak Robat and Nil passes were the traditional routes for caravans, conquerors, pilgrims, and wayfarers, until Nadir Shah found "a better mousetrap."

[34] Shah, Ikbal, *op. cit.*, p. 219.

liberty. Women are not mentioned although legally they can claim the franchise since this is constitutionally available to all Afghan nationals; Nadir was careful not to risk the anger of both the mullahs and Afghan husbands and fathers, as Amanullah had mistakenly done.

The only problem which Nadir Shah could not settle was the question of tribal allegiance to Kabul, and it was to cost him his life. In the early 1930's the Charkhi family, a clan which had held high office under Amanullah and had been dispossessed by Nadir Shah, began plotting seriously to overthrow him. Their efforts were aided by the attitude of the eastern tribes, who were angry with the Shah because of his refusal to give them any more than moral aid against Britain. It will be remembered that this was the period of British expansion into the North West Frontier in order to secure firm control of the territory up to the Durand Line; the Afridis rebelled in 1930–31, the Mohmands in 1933, and Abdul Ghaffar Khan (the "Frontier Gandhi") had organized a nationalist tribal movement called the Redshirts parallel to the general Indian nationalist movement. The pro-Amanullah group seized the advantage brought by this anti-British feeling to spread the rumor that Nadir Shah was a British puppet and that Britain had secretly taken over Afghanistan. The rumor spread wildly in the bazaars and tea houses of the radio-less, telephone-less country, poor in communications but rich in oral transfer of information. Into this potentially dangerous situation stepped General Ghulam Nabi, senior member of the Charkhis. He returned to Kabul from Russia in 1932 under a safe-conduct and began to organize a revolt. But his plans were discovered, and Nadir promptly had him executed for high treason. The political clash between the government and the pro-Amanullah faction now became a Pathan blood-feud between families. In June, 1933, the Shah's brother Muhammad Aziz, Ambassador to Germany, was assassinated by an Afghan student in Berlin. On November 8, the anniversary of Ghulam Nabi's execution, Nadir Shah was shot and killed by a natural son of Ghulam while he was passing out prizes at a school parade in the garden of the palace.

The expected upheaval in Afghan sovereignty did not materialize. The loyalty of his brothers to the dead Shah held firm, and the attitude throughout the country was one of shame and sympathy. Shah Mahmud, the only brother in Kabul at the time, immediately named Nadir's only son, eighteen-year-old Prince Muhammad Zahir, to replace his father; the senior brother, Prime Minister Hashim, became regent for the remainder of Zahir's minority, although the Prince received the crown of the Durranis. The more or less benevolent autocracy based on family rule which Nadir established may well have been his most enduring contribution to Afghan stability. Gradually the older generation of the Yahya Khel family has given way to the younger generation, with the pattern continuing; thus Zahir Shah's cousins, Muhammad Da'ud and Muhammad Naim, are the strongest members of the government outside of the Shah himself—some say, even stronger.

DEVELOPMENTS SINCE 1933

Since Zahir Shah's accession Afghanistan has been relatively quiet and stable internally, and externally has remained outside of the limelight of world concern. This in itself is a tribute to the statesmanship of the Durrani rulers. A policy of caution and circumspection was followed with regard to foreign relations. Nadir Shah had signed treaties of friendship with Japan, Estonia, Saudi Arabia, Iraq, and the USSR. The new government concluded a pact with Russia in 1936 which pledged mutual noninterference in internal affairs; coming as it did on the heels of the Italian aggrandizement in Ethiopia, the pact gave Afghans some relief from the fear that they might be marked by one or the other of their big neighbors for aggression. Relations with Turkey, which had deteriorated in the wake of Amanullah's departure and the failure of his Turkish-inspired reform program, improved. Turkey sent military instructors to train the Afghan army. In 1934 Afghanistan joined the League of Nations, with Turkish (and Soviet) backing, more "because it was the thing to do" than for any sound political reason. The Saadabad Pact of 1937 between Afghanistan, Iran, Iraq and Turkey was the first "Northern Tier" regional grouping, although it was not directed at the USSR but was a concrete expression of Islamic policy and Islamic solidarity among the Muslim peoples directly south of Russia. It bound the signatories to noninterference in each other's internal affairs and to consultation with each other in the event of international conflicts affecting them. When they failed to reach conclusions at the onset of World War II, the Pact became inoperative. The Prime Minister called a Loe Jirga to debate a joint Anglo-Russian request for the expulsion of all German and Italian nationals except those engaged in the diplomatic missions after the German attack on Russia. Although enraged at what they considered an infringement on their independence, the Afghan leaders finally consented to do so, meanwhile affirming a policy of rigid neutrality. Thus while the Afghan government stayed neutral during the worst days of the British Empire, the desperate period after Dunkirk, the Afghan people, through their leaders as well as their officials, stressed their neutrality in the war, and have remained outside of bloc commitments ever since. In the United Nations, Afghanistan generally votes with other Muslim countries; for example, it opposed the partition of Palestine resolution in 1947, and during the Israeli invasion of Sinai in 1956 and the subsequent Anglo-French attack on the Suez Canal, large numbers of Afghans were reported volunteering to fight with Egypt against the invaders.[35]

Afghan foreign policy in the post-war period involves the replacement of the British by the United States as a counterweight to Soviet Russian influence. Diplomatic relations between Kabul and Washington were established during the war, but there was little real contact before 1950. Small amounts of American aid began coming in thereafter, and the emphasis placed by the Afghan government on basic education has resulted in some rather interesting low-cost, long-range projects. The long Afghan habit of living in a hermit country renders political indoctrination (i.e., interchanges leading to a Western alignment in the manner of modern Iran), and even normal conversational intercourse between Afghan officials and Americans, difficult. There is, however, a vaguely expressed but real feeling of friendship between the two peoples, notably since evidence has piled up that the United States is anything but an Asian colonial power.

The extent of Soviet economic control of Afghanistan is well documented but does not justify the conclusion that the country is or will soon become a puppet Soviet state or satellite. The economic backwardness of Afghanistan is a strong theme in the Soviet press, with invidious comparisons between the well-fed Uzbeks north of the Oxus and the poverty-stricken ones south of the river. Even as late as 1954 Soviet writers described Afghanistan as a country unable to keep its population above the starvation level through agriculture. In December, 1955, the Afghan government invited Khrushchev and Bulganin to Kabul. The two Russian leaders supported Pushtunistan and left behind them an agreement to extend Afghanistan $100 million in long-term credits, plus a ten-year extension of the 1951 treaty of neutrality and non-aggression. Soviet efforts since the visit have been concentrated on "impact"

[35] There were comments at the time that the Afghans were volunteering as much to get out of Afghanistan as to help their brothers in Egypt.

projects whose results are immediately (or shortly) visible to the Afghans —grain silos, mills, a hospital in Jalalabad, an oil pipeline from Mazar-i-Sharif to Termez in Soviet territory, and paved roads. When President Eisenhower visited Afghanistan in December, 1959, he rode from the airport to Kabul on a Russian-built asphalt road. Conversely, U.S. economic assistance outside of the Morrison-Knudsen projects in the Helmand Valley, have been of a long-term nature, such as educational missions to train Afghan teachers of English, aid to the educational system in general and the literacy campaign, and expansion of the airport facilities at Kabul and Kandahar. In 1959 a U.S. State Department report showed that 50 per cent of Afghanistan's trade was with the USSR.

Nevertheless its modern history indicates that the landlocked country of the Hindu Kush is unlikely to go the way of Hungary or Czechoslovakia. Aside from the inordinate Afghan love of freedom, the strength of Islam in Afghanistan militates against Communism. There is no native Communist movement, and Communists are regarded as godless "People without a Book." The Afghans were also unique in observing the Bolshevik conquest of Central Asia, and the treatment of Muslims there. Nor is Afghanistan itself of particular value to the Soviets, except as a staging area for India.

PUSHTUNISTAN

The one recent issue which has become a matter of national concern to all Afghans is Pushtunistan. It concerns the status of the Afghan (or Pushtun) tribes on both sides of the Durand Line. When Britain withdrew from the Indian subcontinent in 1947, the Muslim population of India seceded from the state and formed the independent republic of Pakistan. This meant that an Islamic power had inherited the North West Frontier Province, a predominantly Muslim area, up to the Durand Line. As far as the anti-British propaganda carried on by tribal spokesmen abetted by the Afghan government for some thirty years was concerned, the handwriting was on the wall; a Muslim authority was about to replace the former Christian, infidel power. Just before partition took place, a militant tribal group led by Abdul Ghaffar Khan called Khudai Khedmatgar (Servants of God) demanded the right to have an independent Pushtun state to be called Pushtunistan. When a referendum took place in the NWFP, as in all princely and semiautonomous regions after partition, 51 per cent of the eligible voters abstained. The rest voted en bloc to join Pakistan.

Pakistan has consistently held that the 1921 Anglo-Afghan Treaty binds Afghanistan to the Durand Line as its permanent frontier and that Pakistan has inherited British rights and privileges along with British headaches in the area. In the beginning Pakistan continued the system of subsidies to keep the tribes in line, but in 1955 they abolished these and announced incorporation of the tribal area into a single province, an integral part of Pakistan. The Afghan government, claiming to act as the agent of the Pushtuns, called this a hostile move, and a band of rioters sacked the Pakistani embassy in Kabul. It was the second instance of grave disrespect shown by one Muslim state to another.[36] Pakistan in retaliation closed the border to commercial traffic, imposing a serious hardship in Afghanistan, which had to export most of its karakul to Soviet Russia. The Loe Jirga was called into session late in 1955, for the first time since 1940, as a result of the dispute. Prime Minister Daʻud told the assembly that "the balance of power between Pakistan and Afghanistan has been destroyed by Pakistan's military alliance with the United States." [37] He asked the five hundred members if Afghanistan should continue to press for a plebiscite among the "oppressed" Pushtuns, and if Afghanistan should take steps to restore the balance of power. He received a resounding "yes" to both questions, plus a resolution that Pushtunistan should not be considered part of Pakistan. A month later the two gentlemen from Moscow paid their visit.

Much of the sound and fury in the Pushtunistan issue emanates from Afghanistan, and very little from the tribesmen themselves. Pakistan's extension of centralized authority to them, plus resettlement, housing, and a basic education program, is proving very attractive to the once-lawless Pushtuns, who have furthermore the opportunity to participate in an independent Muslim state of their own. In part the Afghan position stems from the lost empire of Ahmad Shah and the desire to regain access to the sea, and no doubt the Afghan rulers have found Irredentism a useful tool in keeping their own people in line. Since an independent Pushtunistan would not be a viable state anyway, in time the issue will probably become similar to the Greek dream of recovering Constantinople.

[36] The first was when the Afghan representative to the UN (Afghanistan was admitted in 1946) voted against Pakistan's admission; he subsequently reversed himself when the unkindness of his act toward another Muslim state was pointed out to him.
[37] *The New York Times,* November 16, 1955.

PROSPECTS

Afghanistan in the 1960's is still one of the least advanced of Middle Eastern countries. Political parties do not exist, the constitution is rudimentary, the government paternalistic, literacy stands at about 10 per cent for males and less for females. Society and social thinking are tribal outside of Kabul, and the regime must tread warily between the mullahs, the arch-enemies of progress, and the tribal leaders who fear loss of freedom. Nevertheless a revolution is clearly under way, the same revolution which began in Turkey in the 1920's and has spread across the Middle East. When Prime Minister Da'ud announced in 1959 that Afghan women would be freed from purdah hereafter, that they must discard the veil and *borqa,* he was actually throwing down the gauntlet thrown down by his uncle Amanullah thirty years earlier. But Amanullah failed; Afghanistan was but two decades removed from the medieval savagery of Abdur Rahman. The present Prime Minister's action brought similar reactions; the mullahs have publicly criticized the ban, and in December there were serious riots in Kandahar, where an American ICA official was beaten. Aside from the joy of Afghan women, at their emancipation, the state of the world in the 1960's, shrunken and interconnected so that whispers in Kabul may be heard in Washington and vice versa, suggests that the land of the Hindu Kush is moving forward, not backward.

RECOMMENDED READINGS

1. Ahmad, Jamal-ud-din, and Muhammad Abdul Aziz, *Afghanistan: A Brief Survey,* New York: Longmans, Green & Co., Inc., 1936.
2. Caspani, E. and Cagnacci, E., *Afghanistan, Crocevia della Asia* (Afghanistan, Crossroads of Asia), Milan: Antonio Vallardi, 1951.
3. Cervin, Vladimir, "Problems in the Integration of the Afghan Nation," *Middle East Journal,* 1952, pp. 400–416.
4. Franck, Dorothea, "Pakhtunistan, Disputed Disposition of a Tribal Land," *Middle East Journal,* Winter, 1952, pp. 49–68.
5. Fraser-Tytler, W. K., *Afghanistan,* 2nd ed., London: Oxford University Press, 1953.
6. Furon, Raymond, *L'Iran, Perse et Afghanistan,* Paris: Payot, 1951.
7. Habberton, William, *Anglo-Russian Relations Concerning Afghanistan, 1837–1907,* Urbana: University of Illinois Press, 1937.
8. MacMunn, *Afghanistan from Darius to Amanullah,* London: Bell, 1929.

9. Pazhwak, Abdur Rahman, *Aryana* (*Ancient Afghanistan*), London: Office of Information, Embassy of Afghanistan, n.d.

10. Ramazani, R. K., "Afghanistan and the USSR," *Middle East Journal,* Spring, 1958, pp. 144–152.

11. Shah, Sardar Ikbal Ali, *Afghanistan of the Afghans,* London: Diamond Press, 1928.

12. ———, *Modern Afghanistan,* London: Sampson Low, 1939.

13. ———, *The Tragedy of Amanullah,* London: Alexander-Ousley, 1933.

14. Wilber, Donald, *Afghanistan,* New Haven: HRAF Press, 1956.

15. ———, "Afghanistan, Independent and Encircled," *Foreign Affairs,* 1953, pp. 486–494.

CHAPTER 6

THE FERTILE CRESCENT I: SYRIA, LEBANON, JORDAN

Between the eastern end of the Mediterranean and the head of the Persian Gulf, the latter a body of water which Arab chauvinists have begun to call the "Arabian Gulf," is an arc-shaped expanse of land often described as the Fertile Crescent. The crescent image is distorted at best, and much of the territory is desert, but the astonishing fertility of parts of it makes the appellation reasonably accurate. The ancient Fertile Crescent bulks large in world history; civilization evolved there, as did political concepts which underlie Western law and patterns of society. But the cyclical tragedies which afflict civilization over the long haul reduced the Fertile Crescent to something less than fertile, agriculturally, politically, perhaps even morally. After the twin devastations of Mongol and Tatar, the glittering accomplishments of the Abbasid Caliphate proved, as had been suspected, to be founded upon political sand. It is only in the present century and due to external impulses that the Crescent shows signs of revival.

There are presently four identifiable political units in the Fertile Crescent—Iraq, Lebanon, Jordan, and Israel. A fifth, Syria, bartered its sovereignty to Egypt in exchange for "Arab unity," resulting in the anomaly of a noncontiguous United Arab Republic.[1] The vagaries of international politics in the twentieth century are forcefully expressed in this region: Britain detached Palestine from other Ottoman possessions; Hitler made a Jewish state there possible; Syria, logically the center or heartland, turned to a non-Asian country for alignment; Jordan

[1] In October, 1961, it resumed its political identity.

175

is still more of a geographical name than a political entity; only Iraq has a legitimate claim to national status, since Lebanon forms the logical coastline of "greater Syria." Yet the cry of nationalism is strong in these separate states.[2] They exist not in vacuum but in conflict; and their political progress during this century is more turbulent, more complex, than in many of their larger neighbors.

SYRIA AND LEBANON

Although there never was an independent *state* exclusively Syrian in the past, Syria as a geographical unit, *"ash-Shams"* to Arab geographers, or "the sun," comprised the greater portion of the Fertile Crescent; while the Lebanon referred to mountain ranges and their hinterland within Syria.

The special status of the Lebanon was established by the Ottomans with much help from France in the late nineteenth century. The status was, ironically, the protection of a minority group within the Empire, although the people of *ash-Shams* had been fully Arabised over a period of twelve centuries and were themselves protected as a minority group under the *millet* system. But Mount Lebanon by tradition was a place of refuge for all sects. Its various communities—Orthodox Christian, Maronite, Druze, etc.—had gone there to escape persecution. (The Byzantine Christians were harsher in their treatment of their co-religionists than the Muslims.) They flourished and worked out a relative inter-community harmony of existence, made simpler by the fact that there was little difference between them except religion. The crumbling of Ottoman authority was one factor contributing to the decay of this edifice. Others were the increased French interest in the Near East after 1800, the Egyptian rule of Muhammad Ali, and Ottoman distrust of suspected foreign interference.[3]

Other French historical associations with the Levant were educational and cultural. The Université de St. Joseph in Beirut was founded by the Jesuit Fathers, as were other institutions of learning in the region. Roman Catholic and other French educational agencies operated schools with enrollment of more than twenty thousand by 1908,[4] plus

[2] Palestine-Israel will be treated in a separate chapter since Britain detached it under mandate and since its history has such a large non-Arab element.

[3] Longrigg, S., *Syria and Lebanon under French Mandate,* London: Oxford, 1958, pp. 21 ff.

[4] Ziadeh, Nicola, *Syria and Lebanon,* New York: Frederick A. Praeger, Inc., 1957, p. 37. Cf. Longrigg, *op. cit.,* p. 43, who claims fifty thousand by 1914.

five hundred at St. Joseph. This was more than three times the number attending American schools. The Alliance Israélite Universelle, in its various institutions, provided French teachers for Syrian-Lebanese Jews. The Maronite church looked to France as its inspiration and protector. French-language books, magazines, and newspapers developed wide circulation as the literacy rate grew. French capital was responsible for nearly all industries, from silk to chemicals to tourism. France's determination to supervise the Levant after the Ottoman defeat, which went counter to Wilsonian principles and even to Britain's attitude of fair play, is justifiable (if at all) when viewed in the light of these French efforts to prepare the region for colonial status.[5]

Independence for Syria and Lebanon. In terms of the nationalist expectations of 1920, the French mandate fell far short. Arab unity was denied fulfillment. More specifically, the Arab kingdom of Syria was submerged under the territorial ambitions of the Western powers. Divisions within the mandates themselves were intensified. In Lebanon the confessional system was perpetuated and constitutionalized. Syria survived as a truncated state with the minority Druzes and 'Alawis assured of self-preservation. Economic development lagged. In some areas, notably Jabal Druze, development projects were carried out before the people were ready for them, in addition to incurring the hostility of the owning and controlling classes, the feudal families. In others, local investment capital was taken out of the country rather than put to work domestically. French control of the currency, which was tied to the franc, was another grievance. Yet the mandate had at least two constructive results: it paved the way for a broad revival of Arab nationalism, and it introduced political activity into the region. The parties that developed—Kutla and Ash-Sha'b (Populist) in Syria, the Constitutional Bloc and the Partie Populaire Syrienne (P.P.S.) in Lebanon—were foci of political action as independence became a fact.

The fall of France in 1940 involved Syria-Lebanon in international affairs after a lapse of twenty years and was to prove of incalculable value in bringing the nationalists within reach of their goals. The French Army in the Levant under General Mittlehauser pulled out of the war in obedience to Vichy, and the uniformly defeatist High Commissioners accepted Vichy's dictates to the extent of freely permitting Ger-

[5] Syria and Lebanon together were often described as "the France of the East" in the nineteenth century, and Lamartine observed that Syria "was an admirable French colony—waiting for France."

man infiltration. German agents became extremely active, encouraging Arab nationalist ambitions to expel the French entirely. The coup of Rashid Ali in neighboring Iraq brought Britain into the situation directly since the British were dead set against conversion of the Levant into a German base. General de Gaulle's Free French, who had been accepted by Britain as allies, agreed on the necessity of rescuing the region from the Germans. De Gaulle's motive, however, was to recover the provinces for France, while Britain insisted on some sort of bold gesture which would win over the population to support an invasion against its Vichy masters. On June 8, 1941, planes dropped leaflets over Syria-Lebanon signed by Free France's General Georges Catroux which stated unequivocally the termination of the French mandate.[6]

After a spirited contest of a little over a month, a joint Anglo-Free French task force succeeded in forcing the Vichy commander, General Dentz, to negotiate for an armistice. The occupation of the Levantine states by Free French forces succeeded and was hailed by the Allies as securing their position in the eastern Mediterranean. All that remained, it seemed, was for France to implement the Catroux pledges, subject only to wartime safeguards. The implementation required five years, a tribute to French tenacity in holding to a privileged position once it had been gained.[7] French strategy in the negotiations (which were based on the 1936 treaties, where no reference was made to Syro-Lebanese sovereignty) was to delay recognition as long as possible, to solidify French privileges, and to offer the least possible guarantees of independence. Other governments, with the notable exception of the remaining Arab states, recognized the independence of the two new states in 1942–1943. The British also pressed France to transfer the machinery of government to the Arabs as quickly as possible. The U.S., feeling that the mandate should be replaced by bilateral treaties between France and the two Levant states before recognition should take place, merely appointed a consul-general and diplomatic agent, George Wadsworth, to both.

The Lebanese were the first to challenge France to carry out her pledged transfer of powers. On November 7, 1943, the newly-elected Prime Minister, Riyadh al-Sulh, announced his government's intention

---

[6] Ziadeh, *op. cit.*, pp. 65–66, contains the full declaration.
[7] De Gaulle himself wrote (*Memoirs*, I, p. 175), *"notre grandeur et notre force consistent uniquement dans l'entransigence pour ce qui concerne les droits de la France."*

to revise the Constitution. Ten articles were to be amended: Art. 1 would eliminate references to the mandate and describe Lebanon as "sovereign"; Article 11 would eliminate French as an official language; Articles 52, 90–94, 95 and 102, all of which limited Lebanon's constitutional and treaty-making powers, would be changed to conform to the nationalists' goal of a truly independent state. The proposed revision was passed by the Chamber with a 48–0 vote. The French reacted with their customary vigor. The new Delegate-General (a term which had replaced that of High Commissioner), M. Helleu, arrested President Bishara al-Khuri and the entire elected cabinet, declared the amendments void, and installed a government of pliable pro-French officials. Scattered riots broke out all over Lebanon, but the reactions of the U.S. and Britain were of more value to the nationalist cause. The U.S. took the position of complete disapproval of the French action, as Cordell Hull reports in his *Memoirs,* and ordered Wadsworth to have no dealings with the new French regime. The British, who commanded the defense forces in Lebanon, informed the Free French National Committee (C.F.L.N.) in Algiers that unless the duly elected Lebanese government were reinstated by November 22, they would declare martial law. Faced with these pressures, the French gave in. The Lebanese nationalists had won. Although final and complete transfer of power was not effected until 1946, the events of November, 1943, constitute for Lebanese the inauguration of national independence.

The suspended constitutions were reinstated in 1943, and elections in that year returned nationalist majorities to parliaments in Damascus and Beirut. Catroux, in common with his chief, displayed a tenacious determination to carry on France's *mission civilisatrice,* wanted or not, and an Anglophobia bordering on the fanatical. In Syria, old leaders of the nationalist *Kutla* bloc returned to power, notably Faris al-Khuri, Sa'dullah al-Jabri, and Jamil Mardam, while its new leader, Shukri al-Quwwatli, was named President. In Lebanon, nationalist Bishara al-Khuri was elected President over the pro-French Maronite, Emile Edde, while Riyadh al-Sulh, a Muslim nationalist, became Premier.

At this time an unwritten agreement between Khuri and al-Sulh was set up which had an important bearing on Lebanon's political development. It came to be called the National Covenant. Khuri, a Maronite Christian, agreed that Lebanon was an Arab state. Al-Sulh, a Sunni Muslim, agreed to accept the independence of Lebanon and to make no effort to incorporate it in a greater Arab state. Thus the doctrine implicit in the Constitution that the Lebanese President should be a Christian and the Premier a Muslim was worked out in terms of practical politics.

Transfer of power from the mandatory government began in earnest in 1944, and most departments had been turned over to Arab administration by the end of the year. Previously the errors in judgment of Helleu had aroused Lebanon to fever pitch. Demonstrations of sympathy also erupted in Syria. The outcry was so great that de Gaulle recalled Helleu and sent General Catroux to smooth things over. But many Frenchmen were still bemused by the mandate; *"leur jugement etait obscurci par cet etat d'esprit passionel qui leur voilait les realités et les necessités."* [8] They were unwilling to transfer the *Troupes Speciales*, local levies recruited chiefly from the minorities and loyal to France. This prevented the two republics from forming their own national armies; it was regarded, obviously, as a bargaining weapon through which France hoped to salvage something of her privileged status in the Levant. The French hoped to hold onto the *Troupes Speciales* until a favorable treaty had been signed. But a favorable treaty (or any agreement) based on the 1936 model was unacceptable to the two republics. Jabal Druze and the ʻAlawi sanjaq passed peacefully by decree into Syrian hands; also separatism continued to be a favorite topic in the coffee-houses. Only the presence of French garrisons and French control over the *Troupes Speciales* intervened between Syrian-Lebanese patriots and full independence.

To their surprise, additional Senegalese troops disembarked in Beirut during May, 1945, ostensibly to keep order during the treaty negotiations. General Beynet, the Commander-in-Chief, informed local representatives that under the proposed treaty the *Troupes Speciales* would remain under French command for the time being; and special conventions would ensure French cultural domination, military bases, and economic relations. These qualifying phrases were of course unacceptable to the Arabs. A general strike was called. Anti-French demonstrations with ugly harassment of French troops by the street mob in Syria broke out almost daily. The French retaliated by bombarding Damascus. Only firm British intervention, with French forces ordered to their barracks, kept relations from breaking down completely.

Two external events now made it possible for the Levant states to

[8] Catroux, Georges, *Dans la Bataille de Mediterranee*, Paris: Plon, 1949, p. 414.

free themselves completely from France. They had declared war on Germany on February 27, 1945, and were therefore invited to San Francisco as sovereign nations. They adhered to the Charter of the United Nations and were recognized by nearly all countries as independent within a short time. They also adhered to the Covenant of the League of Arab States in 1945. While the League had no power for positive action against France, it provided a useful sounding board by which Arab public opinion could express its support. The UN was even more useful. In January, 1946, Syria and Lebanon submitted a joint protest to the General Assembly over the continued presence of French troops. Although no concrete resolution was passed as a result, the members agreed informally that evacuation should take place as soon as feasible. The French and British reacted promptly. During 1946, troops of both powers were pulled out. The *Troupes Speciales* were given over to Arab control. Evacuation Day, the date of final departure of foreign troops, is celebrated as a national holiday in Syria and Lebanon; it marked the beginning of a new, significant, and still-unfinished phase in the long history of the Levant.

The Republic of Lebanon, 1946–1960. With the final grant of independence, the breakup of the Fertile Crescent became a political reality. The two republics of Syria and Lebanon went their separate ways, disagreeing more than they agreed, even to the extent of imposing customs barriers and entrance taxes.[9] More significantly, the Lebanese National Covenant directed Lebanon toward a policy of cooperation with Western Christian nations, while Muslim Syria followed the path of Arab nationalism and Arab unity. The latter path has proved less profitable for the Syrians than Lebanon's shaky neutrality.

Lebanon's ambiguous role in Arab politics was suggested by the first Prime Minister, Riyadh al-Sulh, in 1943 when he was describing the National Covenant to Parliament: "Lebanon is a country of Arab character which nevertheless seeks to profit by the best that Western civilization can give. We do not wish Lebanon to be a foreign exploitation ground, and they (i.e. other Arab countries) do not want it to be a passage for imperialist conquerors. They therefore agree with us in wishing Lebanon to be a dignified, independent, sovereign and free country." [10]

[9] See *Middle East Journal,* Chronology, 1957. Syrians entering Lebanon were assessed LS 15 per motorcar.

[10] Patai, Raphael, ed., *The Republic of Lebanon* (2 vol.), New Haven: HRAF Press, 1956 (subcontractor's Monograph), p. 568.

Syrian pique at Lebanon's consistent refusal to become identified with Arab unity, particularly after 1952, derived from many factors. Not the least of these was Lebanon's tradition as a place of political refuge since Ottoman days. "Victims of coups d'etat and leaders of banned political parties from Syria, Egypt, and elsewhere found a pleasant refuge in Lebanon and were free from the threat of extradition."[11] Thus Fawzi al-Kawukji, a Palestinian revolutionary who had led Arab raiding bands there in the 1936–1939 Arab Revolt, returned to Lebanon from exile in Germany and resumed his activities with the tacit support of the Lebanese.

Even the Alexandria Protocol, which chartered the League of Arab States, affirmed Lebanese independence within the boundaries of the former mandate. Although Lebanon sided with the other members over the growing Palestine crisis, support was of the lip variety rather than activist. The Lebanese sent token forces into Palestine following the Arab League's decision to intervene militarily against the Jews, but these had no real heart for the struggle. In fact, many southern Lebanese farmers had their natural trading outlets in northern Palestine and were quite indifferent to the mode of government there, preferring merely to keep the outlets open.[12]

Independence meant the continuation of familiar practices in Lebanon, in internal politics as well as relations with other states. Being economic realists, the Lebanese tend to seek compromise on political issues. "It is traditional that successful Lebanese politicians never take extreme positions on any political or economic issue. Indeed it has been difficult to pin down Lebanese politicians as to just what they did advocate or oppose."[13] The fact that each religious community was represented in parliament (and its interests protected within the framework of the confessional system) paradoxically divided Lebanon into self-interest factions while encouraging a viable political unity under the prevailing "don't rock the boat" attitude. The Lebanese government at first encouraged foreign investment and the establishment of business offices by exemption from local taxes. Beirut, also a free port, soon de-

[11] K. S., "The Lebanese Crisis in Perspective," *World Today,* September 14, 1958, p. 371.
[12] Cf. Ellis, Harry, *Israel and the Middle East,* New York: The Ronald Press Company, 1957. Israeli Foreign Minister Sharett remarked: "I don't know which Arab state will be the first to make peace with Israel. But Lebanon will be the second."
[13] Harari, Maurice, "The Dynamics of Lebanese Nationalism," *Current History,* February, 1959, p. 99.

veloped into an air depot and trading center for the entire Middle East. In general, the United States replaced France as Lebanon's tutor in international relations, without imposing the direct political-military supervision which had alienated the Lebanese during World War II and, of course, avoiding the role of religious protector.

Internally, political parties revived along much the same lines as in the mandate years. Elections held in 1947 continued Bishara al-Khuri and Riyadh al-Sulh in their respective positions. Antun Sa'ada returned from exile in Germany (where he had been since 1938) and activated the Syrian National Socialist Party. The Phalanges Libanaises and the Communist Party found new life under familiar leaders. A young Druze, Kamal Janbalat, formed the Progressive Socialist Party which aimed at support from Lebanese intellectuals toward a mild form of socialism. The government's supporters were organized as the Constitutionalist Party and enjoyed a majority in Parliament.[14] Janbalat's followers, the fanatically Lebanese Phalanges, and various other groups including some independents led by a rising young lawyer, Camille Chamoun (Sha'-mun) composed the opposition.

The S.N.P. in 1949–1950 crossed swords with the Phalanges over their policy of unity with Syria; their ideal of a unified Syrian nation did not attract popular Lebanese support, however. In 1949 the leader of the Syrian National Socialist Party, Antun Sa'ada, fled to Damascus following an abortive "revolution" on behalf of Syrian-Lebanese unity which the Lebanese government had crushed at a cost of two deaths. Col. Husni al-Zaim, dictator of Syria at the time, was pressured to deny the usual right of political refuge and extradited Sa'ada to Lebanon, where he was executed as a traitor. The members of the S.N.P. have always felt that Egypt was the power behind Zaim's action.[15] The Lebanese government next instituted vigorous measures to curb violent political opposition. The Lebanese press, traditionally the most candid in the Arab world, was placed under stiff controls. President Khuri forced a law through Parliament in 1949 which would permit him, contrary to constitutional procedure, to run for a second four-year term of office.

The Inkilab, 1952. The political coup of 1952 ("Inkilab," or "over-

---

[14] See Longrigg, *op. cit.,* pp. 358–359, for a summary of Lebanese political parties.
[15] Lenczowski, George, *The Middle East in World Affairs,* 2nd ed., Ithaca: Cornell University Press, 1956, p. 287. It was later proved that members of the SNP had shot him in revenge for the execution of Sa'ada. Five days later King Abdullah was also shot.

turn" in Arabic) resulted from the law and its attendant fear of dictatorial government. There were also more general causes of discontent. To the Lebanese in the street, national politics seemed to be an endless game of musical chairs, played always by the same people. Those in power were the heads (or members) of feudal landowning families, wealthy city-lords, or clerical leaders. Opportunity for advancement or a contributive life was so limited that many promising young Lebanese were forced to emigrate. The policies of recurring governments—such reforms as strengthening the army, female suffrage, labor laws, economic agreements with Syria, lowering of taxes and prices, etc.—were repetitious promises with no action. The administration of justice, still hamstrung by partial adherence to Shari'a law and antiquated Ottoman codes, was a particular grievance. Another, from the urbanites' point of view, was Khuri's alliance with the large landowners and the resultant nepotism and corruption in politics. Economic distress also played a role; unemployment was widespread and the cost of living high.

Three opposition parties—Janbalat's Progressives, the National Bloc of Emile Edde (devoted to Lebanese independence), and the National Call Party—joined forces in the National Socialist Front (N.S.F.). Various independent deputies, including Chamoun, also joined the Front. The N.S.F. had a voting strength of only seven deputies in Parliament, but it had popular support. Its leaders were a fresh breeze in antifeudal and antisectarian Lebanon. The successful overthrow of King Faruq by an officers' group in Egypt on July 23 stimulated the antiKhuri forces to a serious effort. On August 17, the N.S.F. held a mass rally at Dayr-al-Kamar. The speakers, including Janbalat and Chamoun, threatened to rebel if their reform demands were not met and if the President did not resign. Premier Sami al-Sulh, who had taken office earlier in the year and had had to contend with several strikes during his brief tenure in office, now accepted the Front's demands for reform. He broke with Khuri and denounced the ruling clique for a variety of irregular actions. He even suggested that it had been responsible for the murder of his cousin, former Premier Riyadh al-Sulh, in Amman in 1951. Then he resigned. Matters began to move too rapidly for the embattled President of Lebanon. On September 15–16, a general strike paralyzed the country.

The deciding factor in the Inkilab, however, was not the N.S.F. but the Lebanese Army. Its attitude was crucial. General Fuad Shihab, Army Chief of Staff, was asked if the army would support the government against civilians, if necessary even firing on them to control hostile demonstrations. Shihab's answer was that the army would keep order, but that it would not shoot civilians. Since the popular will was intensely worked up against Khuri, he had no choice but to resign. Camille Chamoun, independent but the leader of the opposition, was elected President and faced the curious situation of a parliament with a majority loyal to his deposed predecessor. Nothing illustrates better the vagaries of Lebanese politics.

Late in 1952 a new electoral law lessened the grip of the confessional system somewhat by dividing the country into thirty-three electoral constituencies. The Chamber of Deputies was also cut down from seventy-seven to forty-four members. Women were allowed to vote if they met certain educational requirements. The 1953 election, however, brought a turnout of only 60 per cent of the electorate, with most deputies retaining their seats. One leader expressed the feelings of a large number of disappointed N.S.F. patriots when he said: "One could almost say that the State does not exist. Those in authority say that the financial situation is healthy. Well, there are many today who do not satisfy their hunger, industry is wobbly, and most of the taxpayers don't pay their taxes. . . . What matters at this hour is to mete out justice to those who have betrayed the September revolution and the people." [16] The bud of dissension which was to ripen with such explosive force in 1958 was visible five years earlier.

Lebanon's dilemma intensified after Camille Chamoun became President in 1952 and 'Abd al-Nasir began to direct openly the affairs of the military junta in Egypt. Chamoun's policy was to play the role of an "honest broker" in Arab politics, while maintaining Western ties to the advantage of Lebanon's trading structure. Chamoun made official visits to Egypt, Saudi Arabia, Iraq, Syria, and Jordan. The government stressed its neutrality when the announcement of the Turco-Iraqi Pact came in 1955, although it was greatly disturbed. In the May debates on foreign policy in Parliament, it became clear that Lebanon did not wish to see Iraq excluded from the Arab family circle. The deputies felt that Iraq (like any country) should be free to conclude any agreements which would enhance its stability. But on the eve of Turkish President Bayar's state visit to Lebanon, a group of opposition deputies issued a statement saying: "Lebanese public opinion is determined

[16] Ziadeh, *op. cit.*, p. 277.

to stand in the face of any policy which is likely to tamper with the Constitution, national sovereignty, Lebanese interests, or common Arab aims." Malik himself, despite his enormous prestige, felt the pull of this curious siren-song of Lebanese nationalism (for lack of a better description). As Foreign Minister and later President of the General Assembly of the UN, Malik chided the Arabs out of one side of his mouth, and out of the other warned the Western nations that they must find a common Arab policy or see the Arab world look increasingly toward the Communists.

The Lebanese Crisis of 1958. The "civil war" in Lebanon in May–November, 1958, was triggered by a relatively minor incident; but as often happens in the making of historic events, the *casus belli* merely removed the lid from a pot boiling with conflicting pressures. In retrospect, it is astonishing that the delicate balance of forces in Lebanon lasted as long as it did without a major explosion. Lebanon's "open window to the West" was the target of heavy Arab nationalist abuse, particularly as Syrian businessmen in increasing numbers took refuge in Beirut or established branch offices there. President Chamoun was damned by the Arab states for refusing to break diplomatic relations with Britain and France in November, 1956, although Chamoun denounced the invasion. The military reverse suffered by the Egyptians in the Sinai Peninsula was rather a setback for Lebanese Muslims who hoped for an Arab unity early under Nasir's leadership. Elections in the spring of 1957 overwhelmingly endorsed the government's policies, although there were opposition claims that the elections were rigged in some areas. Then Chamoun made two "mistakes." By including Malik in the Cabinet as Minister of Foreign Affairs, he showed that he intended to continue the traditional policy of sympathy for the West and neutrality in intra-Arab disputes. No doubt, swayed more by fear of rising Soviet influence in Syria than by considerations of the internal opposition, Lebanon next endorsed the Eisenhower Doctrine. During the attempted coup against King Husayn in Jordan in early 1957, Chamoun also permitted the U. S. Sixth Fleet to stand by in Beirut while Husayn smashed the opposition. Chamoun's own personality continued to work against him, antagonizing Maronite, Sunni, and even Druze leaders. Only his own "loyalist" coalition and the Christian *Phalanges Libanaises* stood by him. Having lost the elections, many Lebanese leaders found themselves out of Parliament and unable to exercise the traditional patronage. Deprived of con-

stitutional means of expression, they took to the streets with their followers.[17]

The Sunnis of Lebanon took the view that acceptance of the Eisenhower Doctrine was a breach of the National Pact since it seemed to
commit the country to a non-Arab bloc. They made contact with Sunnis
in Syria, and the propaganda war intensified. Some Lebanese even la-
beled Chamoun and Malik traitors to the cause of Lebanese independence and Arab unity. But the allegation that Chamoun was planning to
amend the Constitution by parliamentary action to permit himself to run
for another term of office—which was the action that had initially
brought opposition leaders together in a sort of "National Front"—was
pushed into the background as personal vendettas, anti-Westernism, pro-
Nasserism, religious antagonism, and all the other currents of Lebanese
politics swirled across the little state. The Maronite Patriarch, Paul
Maʿushi, compounded the confusion when he too demanded Chamoun's
resignation and the election of General Fuad Shihab, Army Chief of
Staff, as President. The general lines of battle were laid down early.
Around Tripoli former Premier Rashid Karami controlled the Muslims,
in the Druze area Kamal Janbalat; and in Beirut itself the Basta (Muslim
quarter) was under the control of another ex-Premier, Saʿib Salam.
Salam stated that the best thing Lebanon could do would be to join the
UAR to protect its own independence.

Such was the situation when, in May, 1958, a left-wing Christian
journalist named Nasib Matni, editor of *Al-Talaghraf*, was murdered in
Beirut by unknown persons. His newspaper was pro-Arab nationalist
and had not even supported Chamoun. But as the violence developed
this fact proved immaterial. Anti-government rioting began in Muslim
Tripoli and then spread to Beirut. The small police force did what it
could, but the slightly larger Lebanese army under General Shihab held
its fire. It even held friendly talks with rebel leaders, giving the civil
war a sort of *opera bouffe* air.[18] The government estimated that ten to
twelve thousand persons were in actual revolt.

On May 13 Malik became the first government official to state publicly that the rebellion had been instigated by the UAR; he said that

---

[17] Nolte, Richard, "American Policy in the Middle East," *Journal of International Affairs,* XIII, 2, 1959, p. 121.
[18] Perlmann, Moshe, "Midsummer Madness," *Middle Eastern Affairs,* August–
September, 1958, pp. 246–247.

hundreds of armed agents were entering Lebanon from Syria. The crisis was fully internationalized in June, first in the Arab League and then at the UN. Slightly less than two years after Lebanon had supported Egypt in the Suez Canal invasion, Lebanon accused Egypt of flagrant interference in its internal affairs. The League met at Benghazi, Libya, to hear Lebanon's complaint. Premier Sami al-Sulh told other League representatives that the *aide memoire* circulated by the UAR denying the complaint was full of "falsifications and deplorable allegations." [19] The League tried to adopt a compromise resolution whereby members agreed not to meddle in each other's affairs without naming any aggressors, but the resolution failed, and on June 6, Malik presented Lebanon's complaint to the Security Council.

In Lebanon itself the violence spread over the entire country; various rebel forces controlled large sections in June and July. The army continued to hold its fire; the rumor was that Shihab was playing a waiting game in the expectation that he would be named president as a compromise candidate. Nor were the rebel groups themselves united. There was bitter enmity between Karami and Janbalat, for example.

President Chamoun, anxious to investigate arms smuggling along the Syrian borders, called upon the UN for assistance, and the Secretary-General, Dag Hammarskjöld, plus an observer team from neutral nations, hurried to the scene. Galo Plaza of Colombia, who led the team, said that the struggle in Lebanon was clearly a civil war. The assumption was that the presence of the observer team along the border would prevent further infiltration, which had happened where the UN Expeditionary Force was stationed along the Egyptian-Israeli border. But the team could not even get into some rebel-held areas. Janbalat said he would invite volunteers, even Russians and Chinese, if foreign intervention were attempted. His statement was balanced by gestures of support for Chamoun by the Baghdad Pact powers.

On July 15, Chamoun asked the United States for armed support under the Eisenhower Doctrine and Article 51 of the UN Charter. Secretary Dulles had previously stated that the U.S. might consider intervention as follows: "I don't think there is any analogy between the situation in Lebanon, where the lawful government is calling for assistance, and the Suez case, where the armed intervention was against the will of the government. . . . The presence in Lebanon of foreign

---

[19] *Middle East Journal,* Chronology, Summer, 1958.

The Security Council debates the Lebanese crisis.
(Courtesy The Middle East Institute)

troops, however justifiable, is not as good a solution as for the Lebanese to find a solution themselves."[20] Thirty-six hundred U.S. Marines in combat readiness went ashore in Lebanon. The "intervention" build-up continued until it reached a total of 14,300 men. President Eisenhower sent Under Secretary of State Robert Murphy (as someone quipped, this was the equivalent of another battalion of Marines) to Lebanon to attempt a political reconciliation.

The American action, which may be called "brinkmanship" or "brush-firism" according to one's political convictions, caused some unexpected reactions. In Moscow large Soviet crowds demonstrated before the United States Embassy, protesting the troop landings. Ghana's Prime Minister Kwame Nkrumah urged the creation of a UN force to replace the American troops; while Canada's Secretary of State for External Affairs, Lester Pearson, proposed the neutralization of Lebanon. And so it went, with many nations expressing concern in one way or another over the misfortunes of the little multireligious republic. As if suddenly aware of their importance in international affairs, the members of the Lebanese Parliament met in extraordinary session. In a compromise move, General Shihab was elected president by a 48–7 vote over a Maronite lawyer, Raymond Edde. Foreign Minister Malik was endorsed by both

[20] Perlmann, *op. cit.,* p. 249.

Shihab and Camille Chamoun as Lebanon's candidate for the presidency of the UN General Assembly (which he later became). Shihab, who had apparently been waiting for this opportunity, now named a four-man provisional cabinet under Rashid Karami to restore order. Slowly the various opposition factions began to disband and to turn in their arms, or at least to pack them away (for nearly everyone in Lebanon likes to have a pistol or two available for noise-making during festivals).

Although to a large extent Lebanon has put its own house in order, the really giant step taken in the Middle East to restore order in the wake of the three crises came from the Arab states collectively. In an historic and unusual move, the Foreign Minister of the Sudan presented to the United Nations, on behalf of the Arab League, a resolution asking for withdrawal of foreign troops from Jordan and Lebanon and invoking Article VIII of the Arab League Covenant as the means of restoring stability to the area. Collective League action became possible when the UAR recognized the revolutionary government of Iraq, and the latter in turn reaffirmed the League Charter and the Arab Collective Security Pact. U.S. troops began pulling out of Lebanon in September and all were gone by December. The Lebanese crisis, which had cost Lebanon $100 million in compensation claims alone, had dislocated the economy, seriously impeded tourism, and nearly destroyed the country's independence, was over. But the causes which had produced it remained. These were: the natural gravitation toward the West with its cultural-educational legacy and its large number of Lebanese immigrants; the counter-pull of aggressive Arab nationalism under a new symbol, Nasir; the traditional pride of Lebanese in their own heritage, especially the "asylum" concept; and the necessity for realistic Lebanese to receive economic support, of whatever kind, in order to exist as a nation.

Whether General Shihab could alter the fundamental structure of the Republic without running the risk of recurrent chaos that plagued neighboring Jordan was doubtful. Beyond the limited control which Lebanon could exert over its own affairs was the enigma of 'Abd al-Nasir, who had plainly asserted the necessity for all the Arab states to merge into one state, but on his terms only.

The Republic of Syria, 1946–1958. With the departure of French troops in 1946, Syrian independence was a reality for the first time since 1920. The brave hopes of Faisal's Arab Syrian kingdom were lacking, however, in its 1946 descendant. In Arab eyes the Syrian Republic was a truncated state, deprived by French imperialist tactics of two of its best provinces, Alexandretta and the Lebanon. French reprisal tactics during the 1925 revolt and the 1945 Damascus bombardment had further hardened the Syrian people to a distrust of anything European.[21] Lack of a genuine effort by the mandatory to train responsible political leaders emphasized traditional factionalism. The men who had come to power during the mandate had become accustomed to limited authority; theirs had been essentially a negative program of thwarting the French, and they could not easily shift gears in positive directions. They had grown too old in the rather vague service of Syrian nationalism to provide the fresh, flexible approach needed.

From 1946 to 1949, Syrian politics underwent violent fluctuations without developing any real stability. In the elections of 1947, the first held under the new electoral law permitting direct suffrage, Jamil Mardam continued in office even though the *Kutla* lost its dominant majority to the People's Party, another party of Arab unity, composed mostly of landowners from the Jazira and Aleppo areas, which later came out in favor of union with Iraq. Shukri al-Quwwatli was chosen President of the Republic and in 1948 was re-elected for a second term. Ironically, neither the President nor the Prime Minister was a member of the People's Party.

While dissatisfaction was general, notably over the failure of the Quwwatli-Mardam government to devote its effort to constructive economic reforms and over its obsession with Ottoman-style nationalism,[22] the Arab-Israeli war coalesced the latent discontent into positive action. Syrian forces won one major engagement, at Mishmar Hayarden in east Palestine, but lost several minor ones. The over-all failure of the Arabs to unite or to prosecute the war rankled in Syria, however; and the administration, not unjustly, was blamed for it. Late in 1948 Mardam was forced by strikes and riots to resign. He was succeeded by another member of the oligarchy, Khalid al-'Azm, who took certain measures to improve the bleak economic picture but aroused the anger of the Syrian army, already boiling about the lack of home support which it felt had not permitted it to follow up its early successes. In 1949 the Army in-

[21] Casualty estimates were: 400 civilians killed, 1,500 civilians wounded, 80 gendarmes killed. Ziadeh, *op. cit.,* p. 84.
[22] An observer noted that "the first generation of political leaders . . . had received their nationalist schooling in the days of the Ottoman Empire and the French Mandate. Its bent was toward the removal of a foreign incubus rather than the construction of a state." *Ibid.,* p. 100.

tervened directly in Syrian politics and set the new pattern which was to continue for five years.

On March 30, 1949, Col. Husni al-Zaim, the Chief of Staff, carried out a coup d'etat. Quwwatli, al-'Azm, and others were arrested. Zaim and his fellow-officers, though outside of politics, were disgusted with the ruling oligarchy, and their bold action was initially popular with the people who were themselves worked up over inflation and other economic maladjustments. Zaim reached agreement with Tapline over the construction of the pipeline. He also launched the important Euphrates project to provide Aleppo with a stable water supply and another project to deepen Latakia harbor. A draft constitution was undertaken. Another important contribution during Zaim's brief period in office—he was not officially named President of Syria until the referendum in June—was his reorganization of the legal system. New codes of civil, commercial, and penal law were put into effect. The private *waqfs* were abolished. Zaim concluded a monetary agreement with France, settling outstanding financial issues.

In spite of these measures and of widespread popularity among rank and file Syrians, Zaim's regime lasted four and one-half months. On August 14, he was arrested by a fellow-conspirator, Col. Hinnawi, and shot. Various reasons have been advanced for the fall of Zaim. His extradition of Antun Sa'ada to Lebanon against the rules of political asylum was probably one. Another was his assumption of the presidency without an election, only a referendum and after abolition of political parties. Even more fatal was his vacillating policy. At first he cooperated with Iraq, to the extent of desiring an Iraqi-Syrian unity; then he veered to determined statements that Syria would resist any threat to her borders or independence. His last public statement was that he was prepared to sponsor a NATO-type defensive alliance in the Middle East, provided that the U.S. would give financial aid.[23]

Col. Hinnawi, who replaced Zaim, felt that the latter had abused the Army's original purpose in effecting a coup. He favored both the Fertile Crescent and Greater Syrian unity plans, hence had the support of the People's Party and the Ba'thists. But Hinnawi's colleagues could see little value in the attachment of republican Syria to monarchical Jordan or Iraq. In December Col. Adib Shishakli arrested Hinnawi on charges of high treason.

[23] *Ibid.*, pp. 101–103, suggests that he was a weak person who tried merely to safeguard his own powers. Shishakli, one of his successors, wrote: "He wanted to employ the state's powers for his own ends."

Shishakli's period in power (1949–1954) was the longest of the three military coups and in many ways the most effective government Syria has had since the war. The first two years were conducted behind the facade of constitutional government. For the remainder of his term, Shishakli reverted to open, personal supervision of the state. This was a reversal of the brief Hinnawi regime, which had given over the civil administration of the country to a civilian government under former President Hashim al-Atasi and permitted ratification of a new electoral law. But political conditions in 1950–1951 were extremely unstable and surely warranted a firm centralization of authority. The Constituent Assembly was working on a new constitution, having been given the green light by the electorate. The army worked behind the scenes, while the various cabinets which fronted for it had no confidence in their ability to govern under such pressure. Approval of the Constitution did not help matters. In October, 1951, the Western powers offered Egypt (and other Arab countries by implication) participation in a joint Middle Eastern defensive alliance. The Egyptians rejected the offer out of hand; Syria followed suit, but there was a sharp disagreement among members of the Cabinet over the rejection. Shishakli then deposed it and took over direct control. He appointed Colonel Salu as Prime Minister; but of himself, he said: "I do not want to become a dictator. I am a simple Colonel, and my duty is Chief of Staff. All the country's responsibilities are in the hands of Salu." [24]

As mentioned earlier, the Constitution of 1950 was the major achievement of Shishakli's regime; although it was begun under his predecessor, and he himself drafted an abortive organic law in 1953–54 to replace it.[25] It did not greatly alter the instruments of the 1930 Constitution. Parliament was kept to one chamber; the office of President of the Republic and the Cabinet were unchanged. But other changes reveal the trend of Syrian nationalist thinking over the years after the mandate, as well as a gradual growth in national (and social) consciousness. Article 1 declared Syria to be "a part of the Arab nation." An attempt in the Constituent Assembly to write Islam into the Constitution as the state religion was sharply attacked by the Christians of Syria; accordingly Article 3 of the 1930 Constitution was reiterated, stating that "the religion of the President of the Republic is Islam." The President was given extensive powers; he could veto, dissolve the Chamber, appoint or dismiss Ministers,

[24] Quoted, *ibid.,* p. 114.
[25] Cf. Khadduri, Majid, "Constitutional Development in Syria," *Middle East Journal,* Spring, 1951.

and could be judged for his actions only by the Supreme Court. He was elected by the Chamber (in practice, he was chosen by Shishakli) for a five-year term. The Chamber of Deputies, elected for a four-year term, was chosen by direct universal suffrage; Syrian women, however, were barred from running for office.

Another key feature of the 1950 Constitution was a Bill of Rights of twenty-eight articles. It was a combination of liberal democratic principles and creeping socialism. Both public and private property were defined. Elementary education under state supervision was made compulsory. Military service was also made compulsory; it was the patriotic "right" of the individual to serve his country in uniform. Various articles indicated also the socialist trend of the economy, since this was given over to the state under a Permanent Economic Council in the interests of full employment, a higher standard of living, etc.

Formally, Salu was Prime Minister with Shishakli as his deputy; but in practice Shishakli ran the Syrian state, more thoroughly than any other man until the advent of 'Abd al-Nasir. Having displaced the People's Party, he suspended the Supreme Court, assigned its functions to the Ministry of Justice, and ruled by legislative decree. The Ba'th Party (q.v.) was suppressed, chiefly due to its identification with Arab unity but also because Shishakli, in the manner of dictators, wished to avoid association with parties which had helped him. In April, 1952, all political parties were dissolved. Instead the Arab Liberation Movement, like Mussolini's Black Shirts, was created to carry Shishakli's program forward. Great military parades were held to whip up popular enthusiasm, and the anniversary of Salu's appointment was designated "National Day." Shishakli also decreed a Constitution in 1953 which placed more power in the hands of the President. In July, 1953, elections were held for the presidency, with one candidate on the ballot—Shishakli. Out of 995,417 registered voters, 864,425 went to the polls. The new President and Prime Minister (the two offices were fused) thanked the public profusely for rallying to his support and called upon "all members of the Syrian family to work for the realization of social aims and national principles, and to cooperate in building up the Syrian state." [26]

Although Shishakli's regime appeared soundly established, it collapsed within a year. The disintegration was due largely to the efforts of the Syrians themselves. They felt that Shishakli's opposition to Arab

[26] In a speech, Shishakli referred to Damascus as "the Capital of present-day Arabism and the heart of the Arab nation." *Al-Yawm*, December 5, 1952.

unity was not due to his interest in maintaining Syria's sovereignty but in keeping himself in power. Curtailment of individual liberties was another charge against him. Thus he reduced the number of seats in the Chamber from one hundred eight to eighty-two; and only two parties —his own and the Syrian National Social Party—were allowed to participate in the 1953 elections. Numerous army dismissals following the discovery of a conspiracy against him in 1952 weakened army support. Also three Syrian Socialist Party leaders, Akram Hourani, Michel 'Aflaq, and Salah al-Bitar, broke with Shishakli and left Syria. Even so, only concerted action by the army made Shishakli's removal possible. A "Free Syrian Radio" came on the air unexpectedly to broadcast that the country had risen against Shishakli. Col. Mustafa Hamdun, Commandant in Aleppo, declared himself and all his forces against the regime. Other garrisons followed suit. At the end of February, Shishakli, seeing that every man's hand was against him, took asylum in the Saudi Arabian Embassy at Damascus and then left Syria for good.

Constitutional government returned to Syria after Shishakli's departure, with a Nationalist Prime Minister, Sabri al-'Asali, in office. The impetus aroused by Shishakli and the unified reaction to his policies quickly spent themselves, however. A democratically functioning Syria was no more of a viable political organism than its dictatorial predecessor.

The period from 1954 to 1958 was a crucial one for the Middle East generally as the Baghdad Pact upset "normal" inter-Arab relationships; the Suez crisis darkened Western hopes for a rapprochement; and finally, the Anglo-Franco-Israeli invasions brought about world intervention. Syria, at the vortex of Arab politics by location as well as by history, was greatly affected by these external pressures and events. The initiative for internal political action, with one glaring exception, passed from the hands of the Syrian nationalists—and the parties which they had formed out of their differing views of nationalism—to the possession either of the advocates of Pan-Arabism or of its Western-sponsored counterweights. This same period also witnessed the entrance of Soviet power into the Arab parts of the Middle East. The "articles of faith" of Syrian sovereignty, then, were subject to heavy qualifications from elsewhere.

If any pattern emerged from Syria's foreign relations during its last three years of separate sovereignty, it was one of irregularity. Cooperation among the Arab states had, in 1950, achieved a regional Collective Security Pact. This provided for a joint Defense Council, a permanent military committee, economic cooperation, and unification of military policies. The first of these, and the second, came into existence somewhat tardily. Economic cooperation between Syria and her Arab colleagues, until 1958, consisted of pledges (such as an oft-reiterated customs union with Jordan) alternating with bitter recriminations. Although their economies could be complementary, Syria and Lebanon were unable to reach a definitive agreement on exchange of products, tariff restrictions, transit, etc. Lebanese determination to keep trade windows opened in both directions was matched by Syrian intransigence on the subject of Western trade. In 1955, military unification advanced a step when Egypt and Syria signed a mutual defense pact creating a joint command under the Egyptian General 'Abd al-Hakim Amr. The pact permitted Egyptian troops to be sent to Syria in case of extreme danger; this was done in October, 1955, and again in 1957.

With Iraq, at the other end of the Fertile Crescent and the spectrum of Arab political alignments, relations were equally irregular. The Populist Party (Sha'b) which returned to the government after Shishakli's defeat was more favorably disposed toward the West, as well as toward Iraq and Turkey, than other Syrian parties. Their refusal to take a strong stand against Iraq over the Baghdad Pact enraged Egypt, but it also caused another government crisis. The new Cabinet formed by Sabri al-'Asali was able to secure a functioning majority in the Chamber by allying itself with independents and others whose sole common bond was opposition to the Baghdad Pact. When Israeli forces marched into Sinai, Iraq specifically asked Syria to refrain from acts of sabotage against Western-owned oil facilities. Syrian "patriots" blew up pipelines of the Iraq Pipeline Company anyway, shutting off the flow of oil across Syria. In 1957, forty-seven defendants (including Shishakli and a number of others *in absentia*) went on trial for treason in Damascus. A number of defendants claimed that Iraqi agents had been working with them to undermine the government in favor of a Syro-Iraqi union.

A further weakening of Syria's ancient ties with Iraq was produced by the assassination of Col. Adnan al-Maliki, adjutant to the Chief of Staff. The assassin, an army sergeant, committed suicide on the spot. He was also a member of the Syrian National Socialist Party. A mass purge of the S.N.S.P. got under way immediately, with particular attention paid to army officers who were also party members. The one S.N.S.P. deputy in the Chamber lost his immunity and was brought to trial along with many others on charges of conspiracy and treason. The trial indicated the extent of army influence on national politics, although it had ostensibly withdrawn following the overthrow of Shishakli. The S.N.S.P. and its greatest rival, the Ba'th, were competing vigorously for army loyalty and support.[27]

THE EGYPTIAN-SYRIAN MERGER, 1958

Shukri al-Quwwatli became the last president of Syria in 1955 just prior to the signing of the Egyptian-Syrian Defense Pact. The savage Israeli attack on December 11, 1958, on Syrian positions near Lake Tiberias made a rapprochement with Western-aligned Iraq even less likely. But events in the little country were moving too rapidly for the Iraqis under Nuri's rather ossified leadership to make any flexible countermoves. The signing of a Russian economic aid agreement—$180 million repayable in twelve years at 2.5 per cent giving the Soviets the chance to participate in nearly all facets of Syrian economic development —was an important clue to the direction Syria was taking.

Behind the political façade of constitutional government, a serious contest for power was developing in late 1957 between two organizations, the Ba'th and the Communists. The Ba'th, or Arab Socialist Resurrection Party, had been formed by the merger in 1954 of the Arab Socialist Party, founded in 1940 by Akram Hourani, and the Arab Renaissance (Resurrection) Party of Michel 'Aflaq and Salah al-Din Bitar. The Communists, who had spent much of their time underground but emerged to participate in the 1954 elections, wrangled their leader, the able Khalid Baqdash, into Parliament. A rising group of educated young army officers, notably Gen. Afif Bizri and Lt. Col. 'Abd al-Hamid Sarraj, were courted by one or the other of the two parties. The civilian constitutional element in the government, led by President Quwwatli, was outmaneuvered increasingly in the struggle between the Communists and the Ba'th. Elsewhere in national life, there was little cohesion. Peasants, landowners, religious leaders, students, intellectuals, all voiced their special interests to the exclusion of others. To quote Dickens (*A Tale of Two Cities*), "It was the best of times. It was the worst of times."

Because the Ba'thists supplied the impetus to Syro-Egyptian unity, the principles of Ba'thism must be enumerated briefly. They are:

(1) The Arab people represent one united people. They should be and must be unified. Any Arab who opposes unity is considered a traitor to the Arab cause.

[27] See Lenczowski, *op. cit.*, pp. 308–309, for a detailed analysis of the importance of the Maliki trials.

(2) While the struggle for political unity is carried on, and even after the goal is achieved, the Arab people must strive to raise their economic standards.

(3) The main enemies of political and economic progress are not only foreign imperialists, but also feudal, conservative landlords within the Arab world.[28]

(4) To pursue these twin goals, alliances with any supporting forces, even Communists, are all right on a temporary basis.

Sometime during January, 1958, a delegation of Ba'thists waited on Egypt's President Nasir. They told him that the Communists in Syria were gaining strength so rapidly, with the aid of propaganda about the Soviet loan, that they stood to win the forthcoming spring elections. The only way to forestall a Communist victory, they declared, was to implement Ba'thist principles and forge a union of Egypt and Syria—the first step, of course, toward a larger Arab union. Nasir agreed, and on February 1, 1958, a merger of the two states into the United Arab Republic was proclaimed.[29] Political activity was suspended; Baqdash fled to Czechoslovakia to return to Damascus later and then to depart for Peking, where he assailed Nasserism (and the U.A.R. concept) from the "neutral" platform of the Chinese Communists. The U.A.R. was set up as two regions, each with its council for local affairs, four vice-presidents (two for each region), and a joint assembly as the legislative authority. A constitution of seventeen points was approved in a plebiscite by 99 per cent of the electorate. The same land reform program which had been instituted in Egypt was applied to Syria, as was a common penal code. Political parties, including the Ba'th, were dissolved. The imposition of export controls troubled Syrian businessmen, used to dealing with the free, although slippery, Lebanese market. The Republic of Syria, after twelve troubled years, ceased to exist, linking its destinies, at least in theory, with Egypt's. And the likelihood of a political unity in the Fertile Crescent, Abdullah's dream, vanished.

JORDAN

Trans-Jordan Under the Mandate. Politically and internationally Jordan's development was marked by three distinct changes. First was the creation of the state under British tutelage after World War I, sec-

---

[28] T. R. L., "The Egyptian-Syrian Merger," *World Today.*

[29] The accession of Yemen on a federative basis later in the year added the name, United Arab State. (See Chapter 3 for the Syrian Revolt of 1961 and dissolution of the federation.)

ond its transition to independence after World War II, and third its full participation in world affairs with the annexation of the west bank of the Jordan in 1950. The last is the most significant. Carried out by the state's first ruler, King Abdullah, it brought into play a dual relationship which was inherited by his son Talal and then his grandson, King Husayn, and still plagues national unity. The formal announcement of the Hashimite Kingdom of Jordan, with the incorporation of both banks of the Jordan in one state, was made April 24, 1950, by a Council of Representatives equally divided between Palestinians and Transjordanians. The vast difference between the two populations is suggested by the statement that "it is impossible for Jordan to have a foreign policy supported by a general consensus of the politically articulate sections of the population." [30]

Before Great Britain set up the emirate of Transjordan, the region had no separate political history. It was by very nature a part of something else, and for most of the time was an extension of Syria (the region, not the republic). The Ottoman Turks administered Transjordan loosely from Damascus and made agreements with the local sheikhs similar to those made in inner Arabia. Turkish expansion into the Hejaz and the construction of the Damascus-Medina Railway increased the Ottoman interest in Transjordan. An attempt in 1908 to take a census of Karak district resulted in a rebellion which was crushed with great severity, and Ottoman garrisons were placed in the towns. The Transjordanians themselves took little part in the Arab revolt, although many of them joined Faisal's forces for the march on Damascus.

As Peake noted: "In March, 1921, Winston Churchill held a conference in Cairo which was attended by representatives from all the countries in the Middle East in which we had interests. Word came to this meeting that Abdullah was moving north toward Syria to try to restore his brother to the throne. Subsequently Churchill and the Emir Abdullah met in Jerusalem, and Churchill proposed that Transjordan be made an emirate under him. The only condition was that the Emir should restore law and order and stop armed bands from raiding into Syria. The Emir accepted." [31] In this after-breakfast manner Abdullah was somewhat compensated for his brother Faisal's expulsion from Syria by the French. Since Abdullah had gathered a large number of enthu-

---

[30] Harris, George, ed., *Jordan,* New Haven: HRAF Press, 1958, p. 107.
[31] Peake, F. G., *A History of Jordan,* Coral Gables: University of Miami Press, 1958, p. 105.

siastic supporters on his way north, anyway, it must have seemed natural to create a new province where none existed and give it to a Hashimite. The new emirate involved Abdullah in a protracted conflict with the Mufti of Jerusalem, Haj al-Amin al-Husayni. During the Arab Revolt, the Mufti had recruited Arab levies in Palestine for Faisal's army. The mandates enraged him. Because Britain had sponsored Hashimite kings in Iraq and Transjordan, his resentment veered toward the family. His agents worked ceaselessly from then on to undermine Anglo-Hashimite positions in the Arab world, and in 1951 their plotting was to cost Abdullah his life.

Transjordan's foreign relations were carried on almost exclusively through Great Britain before 1946. Independence was promised in 1923 by Sir Herbert Samuel, the High Commissioner for Palestine, but formal transfer did not take place until 1928. The dispute between the Hashimite family and Ibn Saʿud, initiated by a boorish letter from Husayn to "Bin Saʿud," omitting the customary honorific titles, and sparked by Husayn's assumption of the Caliphate, reached Transjordan in 1924. Saʿud's warriors overran the Hejaz, and Husayn took refuge in the port of Aqaba. An international problem arose as to whether the Maʿan-Aqaba district was part of Transjordan or of the Hejaz. The fact that a large raiding party of Wahhabis (apparently without Ibn Saʿud's knowledge) had penetrated to within fifteen miles of Amman before being driven off by British armor and planes, made a decision of some importance. The British said that as the district had been included in the Vilayet of Damascus under the Turks, it should be included in Transjordan. Abdullah was instructed to annex it, which he did "on the authority of His Hashimite Majesty King Ali, King of the Holy Hejaz." [32] (Ali had previously abandoned the Hejaz to Ibn Saʿud thus cleaning the Hashimite family out of Arabia.) Ibn Saʿud was very angry at losing the district. In 1926 he signed the Jidda Agreement with British representative Sir Gilbert Clayton defining the Najd-Transjordan and Najd-Iraq boundaries. But as regards Maʿan-Aqaba he merely agreed to accept the status quo and not to interfere in its administration "until favorable circumstances should permit a final settlement of this question." [33] An Islamic Congress held in Mecca the same year passed a resolution that the

---

[32] *Memoirs of King Abdullah,* New York: Philosophical Library, Inc., 1950, p. 217.

[33] Shwadran, Benjamin, *Jordan: A State of Tension,* New York: Council for Middle Eastern Affairs, 1959, p. 159 and note.

annexation was a violation of Muhammad's last injunction that no non-Muslim power should rule part of the Holy Hejaz; presumably the Saudi reservation is still in effect.

Transjordan was run as a Crown Colony (not as a Mandate) until 1928. According to a resident, the desert emirate of Transjordan, covering thirty-seven thousand square miles of territory on the eastern side of the Jordan River between Saudi Arabia and Palestine, was for sixteen years "one of the happiest little countries in the world." He adds, "In spite of troubles and upheavals in neighboring countries, Transjordan seemed to lead a charmed life. The people acquired an almost superstitious confidence in their country's happiness." [34] It is probably true that under the benevolent British Raj, the pastoralists of Transjordan were happy; they certainly had only the barest minimum of contact with international affairs. If any real Jordanian national consciousness existed before World War II, it was the typical one of a patriarchal society with some elements of resentment at the Emir Abdullah's failure to shuck his British supervisors.

The country was divided for administrative purposes into three districts—Ajlun, Balqa, and Karak—later expanded into six with the addition of Amman, Ma'an and the desert. The population was estimated at 250,000 in 1926, 95 per cent Muslim Arabs and primarily pastoralists. Neglect under the Ottoman Turks, who had regarded Transjordan as little more than a border region, seriously hampered the efforts of the Emir and his British tutors to establish a stable land administration in the predominantly agricultural emirate. Following extensive surveys, the Department of Lands and Surveys undertook a land program which aimed at unification of scattered tribal holdings, clarification of ownership as far as possible in a Muslim area where inheritance was rarely documented in writing, and began organized taxation. Given its meager resources, Transjordan could not hope to develop without outside help. The table on page 202 shows the extent of British aid in the first seven years of the emirate.

The mandatory also adopted the policy of seconding officers from Palestine for service in Transjordan. Sir Alec Kirkbride was appointed financial and political advisor to the Emir in 1926; and Palestine officers served as Chief Secretary, Postmaster General, Director of Public Health, Director of Public Works. By 1929 the majority of government

[34] Glubb, John Bagot, *A Soldier with the Arabs,* London: Hodder & Stroughton, 1957, pp. 26–27.

Government Finances, 1924–1931
(in pounds sterling)

Year	Total Revenue	Expenditure	British Grant-in-aid
1924–1925	280,673	274,868	77,572
1925–1926	282,459	274,573	103,957
1926–1927	302,520	274,920	66,000
1927–1928	282,073	318,260	45,000
1928–1929	307,555	318,950	40,000
1929–1930	316,147	338,461	40,000
1930–1931	367,516	350,332	84,000 [1]

[1] Great Britain. Colonial Office Report . . . 1935, Col. #112,328. The total of grants made during the first three years of the emirate were £420,000. In addition, Britain advanced to Transjordan for its share in maintenance of the Transjordan Frontier Force the following sums: 1928/29—£27,644, 1929/30—£36,975, 1930/31—£33,452. *Ibid.*, Report . . . 1932, Col. #82,208.

posts were occupied by British, not counting the Resident (who acted under the final jurisdiction of the High Commissioner for Palestine) and his staff.

Nevertheless Abdullah remained reasonable. He said once: "Nations only achieve their aims by reason, and reason demands order. Those who resort to terrorism are nothing but a danger to their country. . . . It is true that we hoped after the world war to be masters of our own country, but who says we should oppose other people in order to achieve our object?" [35]

Agitation for a change in the political structure increased, and in 1928 the British signed the first Anglo-Transjordan Treaty with the Emir. This confirmed him in office and announced that Transjordan was independent. Responsibility for finance and foreign affairs remained in British hands, and the British also agreed to provide a subsidy to meet budgetary deficits and maintain the armed forces. Britain also undertook the defense of Transjordan's frontiers, due to the increase in raids from Saudi Arabia and the fear that the Palestine gendarmerie, a British-officered force, would become a cause of friction between Arabs and Jews in Palestine.

Transjordan accepted the presence of the British Resident as the channel of communication between its government and all other powers. Although extremist elements in Transjordan were distressed over Abdullah's complete acquiescence to the agreement, in fact, the Emir could do little else. He owed his throne to the British.

[35] Shwadran, *op. cit.*, p. 215.

Hasan Khalid Abul Huda became the first Prime Minister of Jordan (1928–1931). Abdullah, and his Jordanian and British advisors, drew up an Organic Law in 1928 which had seven sections and set up *limited* constitutional government. Personal freedom and civil equality was guaranteed by law. The Emir Abdullah was designated head of state with the succession passing to his male heirs and descendants. He was to sanction and execute all laws with limited veto power; he could appoint and dismiss the Prime Minister and all public officials. An Executive Council of five members and the Prime Minister carried out the affairs of Transjordan and all the *Irades* (decrees) of the Emir. The Organic Law also created a Legislative Council of elected representatives sitting for three year terms. Subject to Transjordan's treaty obligations, it could pass laws by majority vote. Proportional representation in the Council was given to religious and racial minorities, such as the Christians and Circassians, and to the Bedouin. Civil, religious, and special courts were also established, always acting in the name of the Emir. Article 69 also gave him emergency powers to declare martial law and rule by decree.

There developed in the emirate three different levels of government. At the top was the mandatory government, represented by the British Resident in Amman and his staff of advisors attached to various departments. Next, or perhaps a little off to one side, stood the Emir, theoretically a sovereign ruler, but circumscribed by his treaty obligations, yet ruling an Arab kingdom in the patriarchal manner of a desert *shaykh*. Below the Emir was a native Arab government, composed of a mixture of the heads of prominent families and former civil servants from the collapsed Syrian Arab kingdom of Faisal. This part of the government was the seat of the minuscule agitation for self-government that went on before 1948. The native program consisted of: modification of the Anglo-Transjordanian Treaty, free elections, social reforms, Arab unity.

The sole internal feature which differentiated pre-war Transjordan from other mandated areas in the Middle East and which gave it some sense of nationality was the Arab Legion. It was formed in 1921 as a private army for the Emir; and Captain Frederick G. Peake, a British officer who had previously commanded the Egyptian land corps, built the Legion into an efficient force, threw its ranks open to volunteers from any Arab country, and encouraged bedouin tribesmen to join. When the Wahhabis began raiding across the frontier again, a Desert Patrol of the Legion was organized under Major John Bagot Glubb.[36]

---

[36] See Peake, F. G., *A History of Jordan*, Coral Gables: University of Miami Press, 1958, for his account.

"Glubb's Girls" [37] were so effective in policing their own deserts that raiding ended in 1932, and Ibn Sa'ud signed a treaty of friendship with Abdullah.

Abdullah remained neutral between Jews and Arabs during the entire period of the British mandate over Palestine, but it was not easy. In his original talks with Churchill, Abdullah had said: "As for the people of Palestine, they refuse the Balfour Declaration and insist on the retention of the Arab character of Palestine. We shall not agree to the annihilation of the Arabs for the sake of the Jews. The Arabs are not like trees, which, when cut, grow again." [38] Subsequently, Britain issued a White Paper excluding Transjordan from the area of Jewish settlement. Abdullah wanted a unified Arab state with Palestine as an integral part, but he was also a realist. When Arab resistance to the mandate and to continued Jewish settlement intensified during 1936–1939, he kept Transjordan aloof, although aid and comfort were freely given to the guerrillas. He was greatly concerned about Zionism in the Holy Land. In a communication to the Prime Minister of Egypt, Nahhas Pasha, he wrote: "Palestine is still suffering from the ambitions of its Arab parties. The Arabs are in a backward state of development, while the Jews are constantly increasing their hold on the country. . . . I was astonished to see the progress the Jewish colonies had made." [39]

In private the Emir corresponded frequently with the British High Commissioner for Palestine, Sir Arthur Wauchope. He proposed a kingdom of Transjordan and Palestine with himself as ruler, the Jewish community to enjoy the same rights as other Palestinian citizens. When the Peel Commission issued its report in 1937 recommending the partition of Palestine into Arab and Jewish states, with a permanent British mandate between them, this enraged the Arab Higher Committee which theoretically represented the Arabs of Palestine. Abdullah, motivated by the desire to have stability along his borders, guardedly accepted the proposal. He said: "Since the people of Palestine have confined themselves to making protests, I have considered it my duty under my religion . . . to strive to ward off the calamity by bringing about the union of Palestine and Transjordan. The inhabitants of Palestine are one hundred thousand more than those of Transjordan and would ably

[37] So called because their uniform consisted of a brown *aba* (cloak), braided, under it a white calico shirt with long sleeves, leather sandals, and on their heads a red and white *kaffiyah* (shawl) held in place by an *iqal* (braided cord).
[38] *Memoirs of King Abdullah, op. cit.*, p. 253.
[39] *Ibid.*, p. 204.

take over the leadership of such a state."[40] The Emir's words were prophetic; after 1948, the Palestinians did take over leadership of Jordan.

Internal politics in Transjordan from the adoption of the Organic Law to World War II were uneventful. The first elections for the Legislative Council were held in 1929, and Abdullah Sarraj was named Prime Minister. Elections were held again in 1931, but the second Legislative Council ran into difficulties. The Emir, exercising his prerogatives, dismissed Sarraj and named Ibrahim Hashim Prime Minister. A 1934 decree strengthened the Executive Council by requiring it to give permission for all public meetings. Grumbling for more freedom continued, however. Abdullah was none too popular in Transjordan, and the British tried a series of concessions to build him up in the popular image. At the 1939 Palestine Conference, held in London, the British agreed to relax their tight controls over finance and administration; the Executive Council was raised to a Council of Ministers; Transjordanization of ministries began in earnest, and the Emir was allowed to raise forces in Transjordan without express British consent. In the same year, Sir Percy Cox, a fine Arabist but stiff-necked as far as the Transjordanians were concerned, was replaced as Resident by Alec Kirkbride, also an Arabist but a better friend to the Arabs according to Abdullah.

As the shadow of war grew longer over the world during 1938–1939, Britain became concerned over centers of support and strategic arrangements in the Middle East as elsewhere. Completion of the Baghdad-Haifa road, one-third of which passed through Transjordan, focused British attention on the Emirate. Glubb succeeded Peake as commander of the Arab Legion in 1939. Technically he was a British subject in the pay of the Transjordanian government. Since the money to maintain the Legion came from his native land, there was an understandable interest on Britain's part in preparing this small efficient force for possible combat use. Numbering 1,642 men in all categories in 1939, the Legion was used as an auxiliary force with British columns to retake Baghdad after the coup of Rashid Ali in 1941 (q.v.); it also won a small engagement at Sukhna during the Anglo-Free French reconquest of the Levant. Thereafter it saw only guard duty, but it did hold the distinction of having been the only organized Arab force to participate in the war with the Allies, and the Legionaries at least received a taste of war. This fact was to prove of crucial importance to Jordan after the war.

[40] Shwadran, *op. cit.*, p. 230.

Internal Politics in Jordan. Jordan's independent history really begins with the postwar settlement. The Emir Abdullah and Prime Minister Ibrahim Hashim signed a Treaty of Alliance with Great Britain in 1946 which recognized Transjordan as a fully independent state. The only limitations on Transjordanian sovereignty in the treaty were that both powers should have "full and frank consultation on all matters of foreign policy which might affect their common interests," and that Britain could station forces at Mafraq and Amman air bases and train Jordan's armed forces. The two countries agreed to exchange diplomatic representatives. Britain promised to continue its subsidy to the Arab Legion and to defend the state against foreign aggression. Abdullah then assumed the title of King. The new name, the Hashimite Kingdom of Jordan, was designed to eliminate the stigma attached to the mandate and to attract those Arabs whose loyalties still lay with the Hashimite house. The treaty also gave Jordan a new Constitution, replacing the one drawn up in 1928 under the mandate. The Constitution declared Jordan to be a hereditary constitutional monarchy, with King Abdullah the first head of state and the succession passing by primogeniture. Because at the time Jordan was still limited to the pastoral east bank of the Jordan River, there were few limitations on the ruler's power other than those supplied by his patriarchal good sense. The prime ministers he appointed were cut from the same cloth—only four, Tawfiq Abul Huda; Samir al-Rifai; Ibrahim Hashim; and Said al-Mufti, a Circassian, alternated in office until Abdullah's assassination in 1951. The Constitution also established a bicameral legislature but made it responsible to the king. Legislation was initiated by the Cabinet, also responsible to the king, and the upper chamber (House of Notables) was filled entirely by royal appointment. Furthermore, the king's signature was necessary for all bills, and his veto power was absolute. While Jordan remained in a pastoralist, undeveloped, somnolent state of existence, this constitutional arrangement with a strong executive worked well enough. In the 1947 elections 40 per cent of male citizens over eighteen elected 20 members of the House of Deputies—sixteen Muslims and four Christians. Only one party, *Al-Nahda* (Revival) took part in the campaign, and it was government-sponsored.[41] Otherwise the affairs of Jordan continued on a relatively even keel until 1948.

---

[41] Shwadran, *op. cit.*, p. 241, refers to the outlawed Arabic Transjordan Party whose platform was repudiation of the 1946 treaty, expulsion of British troops, etc.

The pressures caused by the approaching withdrawal of Britain from Palestine and the UN partition resolutions of 1947 placed Jordan in an awkward position. Jordan seemed too Anglophilic for Arab nationalist purposes. Even Jordanians felt that the 1946 treaty had made Jordan a junior partner in the firm as evidenced by Russia's veto of Jordan's application to the UN in 1947 and several times thereafter. In March, 1948, this treaty was superseded by the Anglo-Jordanian Treaty of Alliance (which regulated relations between the two partners until 1957 when it was abrogated by King Husayn). Britain renounced all military prerogatives in Jordan except the two air bases and agreed to continue the maintenance of the Arab Legion. A joint defense board was set up to deal with Jordan's external security. The treaty was set to run for twenty years but could be revised in fifteen. An incredible piece of irony was supplied at the time by an American magazine article which said: "The new treaty provides Britain with the one certain base of military operations which she still can maintain in the Near East. It is unlikely that 'those opposing the King' can become so vocal as to force its abandonment." [42]

As the mandate over Palestine drew to a close in 1948, King Abdullah became worried about the collapse of authority. An educated Arab element led by Sulayman Tuqan in Nablus appealed to Jordan to interpose a responsible government under Abdullah between Arabs and Jews. Abdullah urged Britain to allow his forces to occupy the area as soon as the mandate ended. Unfortunately a Labor government had come to power in England. Foreign Secretary Bevin listened politely but gave the proposal no encouragement. The Zionists had swung world opinion to their side.

As Britain prepared to relinquish the mandate over Palestine, British interests dictated a preference for King Abdullah as ruler over the proposed Arab state there. Although the Hashimite leader was not popular with the Arab rank and file or with the extremists who swung behind the Mufti of Jerusalem, his obligations to Great Britain made him at least amenable to her purposes. Abdullah's ambition to dominate Arab Palestine was all right too—what if it did run counter to secretly nursed Egyptian-Syrian ambitions? Realist as he was about Arab chances in a war with the Jews over Palestine, Abdullah weakened the Arab cause still more by his counsels to avoid war, although he was certainly right.

[42] *American Perspective,* June, 1948, pp. 136–137.

In terms of Jordan's future foreign policy, its international relations, and its very existence as a tenable state, the annexation in 1948 of the territory on the west bank of the Jordan River must rank as a landmark. On the map, West Jordan is a huge bulge thrusting deep into the state of Israel. The bulk of it was included in the UN partition resolutions and was occupied by the Arab Legion during the Arab-Jewish war and annexed unilaterally with some additional territory to Jordan following the armistice. King Abdullah did not believe that war with the Jews was inevitable; he felt that partition would go through and would be accepted without actual fighting. As Glubb notes: "When the Arab Legion originally planned to enter Palestine on the termination of the Mandate, no war with the Jews had been visualized. It was only to occupy the central and largest area of Palestine allotted to the Arabs in the 1947 Palestine partition." [43] Having lived closest to the Jews and having more knowledge than the majority of the Arab leaders of them, their capabilities, and of warfare, Abdullah was anxious to avoid conflict. He met secretly with Golda Myerson (later Meir) of the Political Department of the Jewish Agency, in an effort to avoid war. The failure of their negotiations has been attributed to Jewish intransigence, but quite possibly it was caused by the increasing reluctance of Britain to back Abdullah in his efforts. He himself said: "My conclusion from all this is that the Arabs must give up day-dreaming and apply themselves to realities." [44] The Arab Legion fought bravely, although short of ammunition and spread over a broad front. It succeeded in capturing and holding the Old City of Jerusalem plus the major section of the Arab section of Palestine. These were officially added to Jordan in early 1949, with Abdullah acting in response to requests by congresses of Palestinian Arab notables.

Meanwhile, the General Armistice Agreement of Rhodes (April 3, 1949) temporarily brought an armistice in the Palestine war and laid down an equally temporary frontier between Jordan and Israel. The frontier was never intended to be permanent, but after a dozen years it is still there. Jordan's refusal to recognize Israel meant that all dealings between the two were conducted via the UN, on the primary level through the Mixed Armistice Commission (MAC) and thereafter the UN Truce Supervision Organization (UNTSO). Ultimately a dis-

---

[43] Glubb, *op. cit.*, p. 96. U. S. recognition was delayed until 1949 due to pressure from Zionists who felt that Jordan belonged to the reconstituted Jewish state.
[44] *Memoirs of King Abdullah, op. cit.*, p. 30.

agreement would go to the General Assembly. In addition to the general armistice, agreements were reached through UN mediation in 1948 on Mount Scopus, the Jewish enclave entirely within the Arab part of Jerusalem. These agreements provided for demilitarization of the enclave (which contains Hadassah Hospital, the Hebrew University, and the Arab village of Issawiya) and for the periodic relief and provisioning of Israeli personnel there. In practice, Israel has used the agreement to stockpile military equipment on Mt. Scopus and Jordan to harass its convoys. Since the Rhodes Agreement, the Jordan-Israel frontier has remained the most active one of the four Arab-Israeli borders. Because the last military actions of Israel's forces had deprived many Arab villages in central Palestine of their farmlands and orchards, there was much bitterness. Refugees began sneaking across the armistice line at night to find food or water or to visit relatives. Isolated reprisals followed beginning in 1948 against Israeli settlers, and in retaliation Israel adopted a "hard" policy of organized military raids against Jordanian towns. On October 14, 1953, the village of Qibya was destroyed by an Israeli force of half a battalion, and forty-two inhabitants were killed. The UN Security Council censured Israel for the attack, as it was to do on numerous other occasions, but could take no direct action. Jordan, on its side, undertook seriously to control the infiltrators whose actions, carried out in defiance of their own government, were causing such violent Israeli counterattacks, organized against towns in areas where frequent infiltration had been the rule. It too boycotted sessions of the MAC when decisions went against it.

Not only did the annexation split the Arab world, but even the United States piously called Abdullah an aggressor against Israel and accused Britain of collusion by means of the Arab Legion. Jordan was almost drummed out of the Arab League. Cooler heads prevailed in 1950, however; the United States, Britain, and France signed a Tripartite Agreement promising to take joint action in the event of any violation of the Jordan-Israel borders and by implication confirming Abdullah's annexation.

Relations between Britain and Jordan began to deteriorate after the annexation had taken place. The subsidy to the Arab Legion was tripled, but the Palestine Arabs discounted this as well as the educational, social, and administrative progress gained under three decades of British governance, because they associated Britain with the creation of Israel. They believed that Israel was even more the handiwork of Britain than of

America. Many of them were, or had been, adherents of the Mufti. Whether or not "the sterile character of the British Mandate in Palestine had conditioned its Arab people as an irrepressible opposition,"[45] by comparison with the Transjordanians, the people of the west bank were far advanced. The patriarchal rule of King Abdullah galled them. Sulayman Nabulsi, a former Cabinet Minister who had broken with the ruling clique, became head of a "National Front" which quickly came to dominate Parliament and attacked all aspects of Abdullah's policy, including foreign affairs.

The year 1951 was a bleak one anyway for Jordan; three-fourths of the wheat crop failed, the public debt reached two million dinars ($5.6 million), and Parliamentary rejection of the budget forced Abdullah into the unpopular position of dissolving the legislature. His assassination was planned during the interval of royal autocracy, but the conspirators' task was made simpler by Abdullah's penchant for abrupt dismissals of criticism, his indifference to personal danger, and his willingness to take moderate, reasonable stands on unpopular issues. As a devout Muslim and a descendant of the luckless Sharif Husayn, Abdullah would have anticipated death, sudden and violent, but in God's time. Abdullah in death won his greatest triumph for Jordan. Instead of revolution, the two ill-joined halves of the country clung together firmly around the Hashimite house. (It would be a mistake to compare Abdullah with other strong leaders of the Middle East—Ataturk, Reza Shah, etc. He was backed by no such resources in his barren country, either human or economic. Abdullah also had to weave his way through the mazes of Arab tribal politics, transported to the urban Arab world.)

King Abdullah was assassinated in July, 1951, by a member of the Mufti's activist group *Jihad Muqaddas* (Holy Struggle) while entering the Aqsa Mosque in Jerusalem for prayers. The feelings of the people of Jordan, to a man, expressed deep sorrow and loyalty. Within a month, a ten-day trial resulted in death sentences for six men plus the dead assassin. The chief conspirator in Jordan proved to be Dr. Musa al-Husayni, a relative of the Mufti who had led the movement uniting West Palestine to Transjordan in 1949–50. The murder removed another "old-style Arab nationalist" whose major "crime" was loyalty and cooperation with Britain. But his annexation of Palestine had mortally offended his old enemy the Mufti who was well supplied with Egyptian gold. His death deprived Jordan of its only unifying factor at a critical

[45] Dearden, Ann, *Jordan,* London: Robert Hale, 1958, pp. 93–94.

time. Of all the Hashimites, Abdullah was the only one who adapted the codes and upbringing of the desert bedouin to modern politics. Realism and moderation, it would seem, are the two qualities which are anathema to the Arabs in a leader.

Abdullah was succeeded by his son, Prince Talal, who was under treatment for an illness, after a brief contest for the throne with his brother Amir Naif. King Talal first announced that he would continue friendly relations with Britain. He also made state visits to Riyadh and Cairo, and in 1952 Jordan joined the Arab League Collective Security Pact. Talal was not close to his father, and as he grew older he set himself against Abdullah in politics. The latter in turn regretted late in life what he considered his failure to provide a proper upbringing for his son.[46] But he did not follow the anti-British policy which some Palestinians expected of him. Late in 1952 his doctors ruled out any recovery as long as he was burdened with affairs of state, and he was deposed by Parliament in favor of his son, Prince Husayn, who had already been named Crown Prince to forestall Naif. A council of three elder Transjordanian statesmen ruled Jordan until 1953 when the Prince reached his majority at eighteen and was crowned King, the same day as his cousin, King Faisal II of Iraq.

In his short reign, young King Husayn has in some ways recalled his grandfather. Abdullah was irrevocably pro-British and was a product of a time when the Middle East wore a British look, albeit resentfully. With Husayn the break with Britain, while not complete, has been much more extensive, and the United States has become at least the economic father confessor. In 1954, the U.S. concluded an economic aid agreement with Jordan for $8 million, the beginning of an endless bailing act that could be averted if Fertile Crescent unity would ever materialize.

Internally, great changes came to Jordan after the annexation of Arab Palestine. The population increased three-fold, from 400,000 to 1,372,-000, the increase coming from residents of the west bank, from 100,-000 self-supporting refugees from Israel, and from 472,000 destitute Palestinians dependent on international charity. The establishment of Israel blocked off Jordan's normal access routes to the Mediterranean, for although the emirate was inland, British control of Palestine provided free access for such goods as were exported. Now Jordan was reduced to the undeveloped port of Aqaba on the Red Sea.

---

[46] *Ibid.,* pp. 91–93, for an estimate of Talal's character.

H.M., King Husayn I of Jordan. (Courtesy The
Middle East Institute)

The Palestinian refugees added a permanently discontented element to Jordan's population. The large bloc of politically mature Palestinians introduced a permanent opposition. It became impossible for the government to function without including Palestinian leaders. An example of the trend was the inclusion of Anwar Nuseibeh, a member of a prominent Jerusalem family and a lawyer trained in Britain, in the Cabinet in several ministerial posts. Mr. Nuseibeh's house was cut off from his garden by the fighting between the Israelis and the Arab Legion in the Old City and was permanently separated by the armistice line.

Well before Husayn's time this political opposition had begun to dictate to the government. By 1950 it held twenty seats out of forty in the Chamber of Deputies. In 1951 it rejected Abdullah's budget and had to be dissolved with new elections to be held before the government could gain a slim majority. A revision of the Constitution gave the Chamber power to dismiss the Cabinet by a two-thirds vote of no confidence. Parliamentary pressure in 1953 forced King Husayn to dismiss Tawfiq Abul Huda, one of "Abdullah's boys" and a dominant figure in Transjordanian politics. He was replaced by Fawzi al-Mulki, a Circassian but thought to be more progressive. Not until 1955 was the government able to reassert control over the Chamber, mainly by *force majeure:* first it was dissolved, then political parties were suspended, special powers were given to the Cabinet, and the elections when they were held were so tightly controlled as to bring charges of rigging by the opposition. The Ba'th Party head in Jordan, Sulayman al-Hadidi, and Sulayman Nabulsi, head of the National Front, both spent election week in jail.

Economic difficulties kept pace with political. Jordan was even less viable as a double state than it had been as Transjordan. The British subsidy, £8.5 million in 1954, barely covered military and security expenditures. Additional amounts were allocated to help economic development. Also in 1954, the U.S. came into the picture with an $8 million economic aid agreement. Even so, Jordan's economic prospects were not bright.

The combination of militant anti-Westernism and Arab nationalism was almost too much for King Husayn. His training at Victoria College, Harrow, and Sandhurst hardly qualified him to compete in the rough seas of inter-Arab politics, let alone the world. Husayn's first crisis came in 1955. The Turco-Iraqi Pact had become a regional defense agreement; and in December, the British Chief of Staff, Sir Gerald Templer, visited Amman. The British had stalled on earlier requests that the 1948 treaty be readjusted to allow direct payment of the military subsidy (now £7.5 million) to the Jordan government in order to give Jordan full control over the army. The timing of Templer's visit was poor since Egypt had just completed an arms agreement with the Communist bloc. The Arab world itself was breaking into two blocs—one Iraqi-led and the other Egyptian-led. The first council meeting of the Baghdad Pact had failed to make any strong statements on the Palestine problem. Templer talked with the Jordanian government in secret. He emphasized that Jordan's adherence to the Pact would not affect its Arab commitments. Economic and military aid on a vast scale were also offered. Hazza' al-Majali, the new prime minister,[47] then foolishly announced that the government had "approved in principle Jordan's adherence to the Pact but that there were still differences between Britain and Jordan." [48]

The announcement touched off a national explosion. Crowds attacked the American, British, and Turkish consulates in Jerusalem, the U.S. technical aid center in Amman, and UNRWA headquarters. They were protesting "foreign pacts," Western imperialism, Israel, and British control over the Arab Legion. The government imposed martial law but was forced to reject the offer of membership in the Pact. But the mob was not satisfied. British influence still remained in Jordan. King Husayn next moved to dismiss the commander of the Legion, General Glubb. Publicly the reason given was that Glubb had refused to prepare the Legion to meet an expected Israeli attack. He was also criticized for tactics of defensive action against the frontier provocations of Israel although the extremists who shouted for Israeli blood were not Legionnaires and did not appreciate the dangers of an open war. Also "it is said that the prick that goaded the King into action was an article in a British weekly newspaper describing Glubb as the real ruler in Jordan." [49] At any rate a normally internal matter (Glubb was a British subject in the employ of the Jordanian government) became an international affair, as Husayn became tremendously popular overnight with the Palestine Arabs and with Arab leaders everywhere. As Glubb sadly packed his bags and left for "retirement" in an England he barely knew, the break with Britain seemed complete. In fact, relations continued much as they had, teetering along. The British subsidy was raised to £12.5 million for 1956–57. But the Anglo-French intervention in Egypt completed the wreck of the hopes raised thirty-five years earlier for a stable Arab state fully committed to Britain in the Middle East. As early as October, 1956, the British Government had warned Israel that an attack on Jordan would mean British assistance under the 1948 treaty. Jordan's Arabness rushed to the surface, in November, 1956, how-

---

[47] Al-Majali was assassinated in August, 1960, in the explosion of two time bombs which wrecked the Foreign Ministry building in Amman.
[48] *The New York Times,* December 18, 1955.
[49] *Middle East Journal,* Chronology, Spring, 1956. "Glubb rules the Legion with an iron hand, and the Legion rules Jordan."

ever, when British paratroopers landed in Port Said. The Chamber of Deputies unanimously recommended abrogation of the treaty, and much to everyone's relief Britain agreed. She returned the air bases and agreed to pull her troops out within six months. Jordan agreed to pay £4,250,-000 in six yearly installments for British property. With the break went not only the British subsidies but also Britain's guarantee of Jordanian frontiers against aggression.

Abrogation of the treaty did not automatically solve Jordan's economic problems any more than it stabilized Jordan's politics. The nationalist government veered away from Hashimite Iraq, toward the "new Arab front" of Egypt, Saudi Arabia, and Syria. Premier Nabulsi's government, which had won a majority in the November elections, began a frenzied search for aid to replace the British subsidies. The United States, previously an onlooker in Jordan's affairs, assumed the economic role vacated by Britain, partly in line with its general policy of blocking Soviet advances into Middle Eastern dominance and partly to appease Arab nationalism which too often associated the U.S. with European imperialism.

The Egyptian-Syrian-Saudi axis of Arab politics reacted favorably at first to the new anti-Western look in Jordan. There was a matter of pride involved as well since these countries had based their propaganda blasts at King Husayn on the financial apron strings that kept Jordan leashed to Britain. They had also reiterated, in the grand Arab manner, their readiness to replace British-tainted funds in Jordan with pure Arab ones. Now they were to be called to the test. In January 19, 1957, the three formally agreed to supply Jordan with an annual subsidy of £12,500,-000, equal to the 1956–57 one from Britain for ten years, apportioned as follows: Egypt, £5 million; Saudi Arabia, £5 million; Syria, £2.5 million. With the Egyptian, Jordanian, and Syrian armies already linked into a unified command under the Egyptian General Amr, it seemed almost as if the millennium had arrived for Arab unity.

Unhappily the reverse developed, illustrating once more the gulf between Arabic speech and Arab thought and the difficulties involved in Arab cooperation. The Israeli invasion of Sinai proved the ineffectiveness of the Arab military command. On the economic side, Saudi Arabia alone paid part of its portion of the pledged subsidy; nothing came from Syria or Egypt. Some British funds kept coming, in accordance with a 1953 five-year development program. But the U.S. performed the major bailing act. Between 1949 and 1957, U.S. Point Four aid was $34 million. In 1957 we sent $40 million in military equipment to help Husayn stave off the most serious coups against his regime. Jordan's membership in the sterling bloc also made it possible for the British to meet the country's deficits without recourse to treaties or formal negotiations.

The Maturity of King Husayn. The experience in politics of the eighteen-year-old boy who was crowned King of Jordan in 1953 had been limited to the British regimental sergeant-major at Sandhurst who bellowed, "Mr. King of Jordan, Sir," [50] when he got out of step. It was a long and shadow-haunted step from a military academy to an Arab throne; and Husayn carried with him the remembrance of his grandfather's murder. He himself was in the line of fire, but Abdullah's body shielded him. Something of the political maneuverability of the man who had taken Palestine from five other Arab states survived in the grandson; and Husayn probably matured more quickly, of necessity, than his teen-aged contemporaries.

Husayn's expulsion of Glubb and his willingness to align Jordan with Egypt and Syria in 1956 seem, in retrospect, less of a surrender to anti-Western elements than clever parliamentary maneuvers. A large section of the Arab Legion remained loyal to the Hashimite house, distrusting the rise of an urban Arab officer group, typified by General Nuwar, to power. These dissidents were afraid that Husayn had sold out to the opposition, which could mean only the end of the Hashimites in Jordan.

The 1956 elections, held honestly by secret ballot, also disturbed the "monarchists." Jordan's loose nationality law, which allowed any Palestine Arab to vote without residence or property requirements, also favored the anti-Western forces. Of the three legal and four illegal political parties which participated in the elections, the National Socialist Party of Nabulsi, with a program of mild social reform, neutrality, and better ties with Egypt–Syria–Saudi-Arabia, dominated the Chamber with eleven seats. The Ba'th (Arab Resurrection Party, which has or had branches in other Arab states), also anti-Western and strongly pro-Arab unity, won two seats; while the Arab Constitutional Party, a right-wing conservative landlord group, dropped to eight seats. The four illegal parties—the Muslim Brotherhood, the Islamic Liberation Movement, the Arab Nationalists, and the National Front (Communist)—also elected representatives, which accounted for the shift in parliamentary and cabinet makeup. Even with popular cheers ringing in his ears

[50] See Morris, James, *The Hashimite Kings,* New York: Pantheon Books, Inc., 1959.

for his actions, Husayn was unable to find a means of cooperating with the Nabulsi government. The contest became in a real sense one between labor and management over who would rule Jordan.

Early in 1957 Husayn attempted to encourage the formation of a pro-Jordanian policy which could receive aid from all sources—even Britain. Nabulsi's reaction was the formal termination of the Anglo-Jordan Treaty. A series of resignations and counter-resignations followed. The King and his Cabinet grew further apart. With the end of the British subsidy at hand and no replacements visible from the three pledged Arab sources, the King turned to the United States which provided $10 million without strings. Meanwhile, another contest was building up between the Bedouin army units—officially reorganized into the Jordanian National Army but personally loyal to the Arab Legion concept—and the xenophobic, pro-Egyptian mobs of the towns. A clash took place on April 14 at Zarqa base between loyal officers and a group of "Free Officers," who were secretly in Egyptian pay. When Husayn rushed to Zarqa, taking Nuwar with him, not only officers but common soldiers of the army swore loyalty to him. He then dismissed Nuwar (who fled to Damascus, leaving unmasked the details of a well-organized plot to set up a republic in Jordan). A National Steering Committee of political leaders demanded that Jordan reject the Eisenhower Doctrine and form a new government with all the anti-Western parties represented. Husayn, backed now by the loyalty of the army, rejected the demands. Moving swiftly, he established control by stiff police methods over the country. The U.S. Sixth Fleet steamed to the eastern Mediterranean, while President Eisenhower declared that the Doctrine applied to the independence and territorial integrity of Jordan, which the King had said publicly was threatened by international Communism.

Jordan's federation with Iraq in February, 1958, is described in the next chapter. During its brief political life, Jordan received some $24,-500,000 in aid from Iraq. When the revolution took place in Iraq in July, 1958, King Husayn at first refused to recognize the republic and called on Iraqis to obey him as ruler of the federation. The Iraqis did not answer the call, and Husayn did not attempt to send his own troops into what was obviously a popular reaction against the Hashimites. On August 2, 1958, he officially buried the bones of the Federation. In 1959 Jordan resumed diplomatic relations with the United Arab Republic, and the incessant propaganda war between the two states stopped temporarily. But in 1960 it was started and stopped several times, indicating once again that nothing may endure for long except change, which is permanent.

The odds against King Husayn have diminished somewhat in the years since Zarqa, but they are still heavy. The necessity of maintaining martial law and repressive methods, such as the abolition of political parties, make the King a prime target for Arab propagandists elsewhere; while in neighboring Arab states (most obviously in one) it is claimed that government is progressing rapidly in the direction of democracy. Nor as yet are there signs of an economic breakthrough or any resource in quantity except potash. The bombing of August, 1960, has unquestionably reinforced the government's caution, besides depriving the King of another of his grandfather's conservative advisors. In truth, whatever unity of purpose, whatever sense of nationality, Jordan possesses revolves around its ruler. Errors in judgment, such as the attempt of a Syrian plane in 1958 to shoot down his plane over Syria, enhance his popularity among Jordanians. But as the last Hashimite ruler of a nation, Husayn represents an outdated approach via tribal, Bedouin loyalties which appeals to a vanishing fraction of the Fertile Crescent.

RECOMMENDED READINGS

1. Abdullah ibn Husayn, *Memoirs of King Abdullah of Transjordan,* transl. by G. Khuri, New York: Philosophical Library, Inc., 1950.
2. ——, *My Memoirs Completed,* transl. by Harold Glidden, Washington: ACLS, 1954.
3. Abouchdid, E. E., *Thirty Years of Syria and Lebanon* (1917–1947), Beirut: Rihani Printers, 1948.
4. Dearden, Ann, *Jordan,* London: Robert Hale, 1957.
5. Glubb, John B., *A Soldier with The Arabs,* London: Hodder & Stoughton, 1957.
6. ——, *The Story of The Arab Legion,* London: Hodder & Stoughton, 1948.
7. Haddad, George, *Fifty Years of Modern Syria and Lebanon,* Beirut: Khayat's Bookshop, 1950.
8. Harris, George, ed., *Jordan,* New Haven: HRAF Press, 1958.
9. Hitti, Philip K., *History of Syria,* New York: The Macmillan Co., 1951.
10. ——, *Lebanon in History,* New York: The Macmillan Co., 1956.
11. Hourani, Albert H., *Syria and Lebanon: A Political Essay,* London: Oxford University Press, 1946.
12. International Bank for Reconstruction and Development, *The Economic Development of Jordan,* Baltimore: The Johns Hopkins Press, 1957.

13. ———, *The Economic Development of Syria*, Baltimore: The Johns Hopkins Press, 1955.
14. Lias, Godfrey, *Glubb's Legion*, London: Evans, 1956.
15. Longrigg, S. H., *Syria and Lebanon Under French Mandate*, London: Oxford, 1958.
16. Luke, H. C., *Handbook of Palestine and Transjordan*, London: Macmillan, 1930.
17. MacCallum, Elizabeth, *The Nationalist Crusade in Syria*, New York: Foreign Policy Association, 1928.
18. Peake, F. G., *A History of Jordan*, Coral Gables: University of Miami Press, 1958.
19. Qubain, Fahim, *Crisis in Lebanon*, Washington: Middle East Institute, 1961.
20. Shwadran, Benjamin, *Jordan: A State of Tension*, New York: Council for Middle Eastern Affairs, 1959.
21. Young, Peter, *Bedouin Command: With The Arab Legion 1953–1956*, London: William Kimber, 1956.
22. Ziadeh, Nicola, *Syria and Lebanon*, New York: Frederick A. Praeger Inc., 1957.

CHAPTER 7

THE FERTILE CRESCENT II: IRAQ

𝕮𝖍𝖊 modern republic of Iraq is a youngster in international relations. As a republic, in fact, it is scarcely two years old, and in political viability it is a child of the twentieth century. The area occupied by modern Iraq, however, has a special significance in Arab history. In its palmiest days, nearly a thousand years ago, Baghdad was the capital, not of a small impoverished province, but of a world-empire. The Abbasid Caliphate stretched from Spain to India; the light of learning shone in Baghdad while the lamps were out in Europe. Politically (and militarily) there were rivals who could match the Abbasid Caliph at times and even declare their rights to leadership of Islam; but none could match the opulence, the artistic and literary productiveness of the Abbasid capital. And it was merely the first among many cities of rank in the region; nearby Karbala was a shrine of the Shi'a sect of Islam, for example.

Then in the year 1258 A.D., the Mongols under Genghis Khan's son, Hulagu, captured and sacked Baghdad. In 1405 the Tatar chief, Timur-i-Leng (Tamerlane) sacked the city again. In addition to destroying Baghdad, the two conquerors destroyed the irrigation system which was based on tunnels and canals dug to carry water from the Tigris and Euphrates Rivers. It was said that prior to these invasions Iraq had nearly 15 million people compared with 6.5 million today. After the Mongol and Tatar invasions had spent their force, various northern tribal confederations became dominant, then the Persians, and finally the Ottoman Turks. Iraq was under Turkish rule until World War I and seems to have been thoroughly downgraded. It was designated as a *vilayet* (province), and governors sent there were usually those out of favor at the Ottoman Court; they used the assignment as a means of recovering their fortunes. The governorship of Midhat Pasha (1869–1872) was a notable exception

220

when some effort was made to improve conditions and to tap the province's potential of natural resources.

THE BRITISH MANDATE

Iraq was the first Arab country, and perhaps the first in the world, to receive its independence under due processes of international law and through the efforts of international organizations. Two decades before the young Arab nationalists of Nasir's entourage made "British (i.e., Western) imperialism" a term of infamy in the Middle East, British imperialism came to terms with the old Arab nationalists and ended the League of Nations mandate over Iraq. Admittedly certain British privileges were continued, and admittedly the Iraqi government weathered certain crises only through British help. But the term *freedom* has many shades of meaning and is strongly affected by local conditions. Outside of the social sphere, the British record as mandatory power in Iraq will stand comparison with any other period of external control; and Soviet Russia, the presumed champion of self-determination for small nations, has yet to release a single one of its "mandated" territories, Muslim or other. Here international politics clearly become relative.

Although it was largely forgotten by its Ottoman overlords, Iraq in the nineteenth century attracted considerable interest on the part of foreign powers. The French and even some Americans carried out educational and missionary work which in the former case helped to spread *la mission civilisatrice de France*. Russian agents were at work among the Kurds as part of the grand design on Persia. The Germans had completed the Iraqi sections of the Berlin-Baghdad Railway. British interests were the most extensive, however. A British trading post had been established at Basra in the eighteenth century. Britons ran the post offices, the Persian-Gulf and the river steamship lines, and a British Resident was installed with due ceremony in Baghdad. It was British fear of the loss of her favored position in the Gulf plus determination to protect communication with India and the nascent oil industry in southern Persia that led to the British invasion of Iraq in World War I. Between 1915 and 1917, British forces dislodged the Turks from all of Iraq without serious loss except for the capture of General Townsend's army after a 140-day siege at Kut.[1] The two vilayets of Mosul and southern Iraq were in British hands by the end of 1918.

[1] Longrigg, Stephen, and Stoakes, Frank, *Iraq*, London: Ernest Benn, 1959, pp. 78–79.

On November 7, 1918, France and Britain had declared their joint intention of installing in Syria and Iraq "national governments . . . which shall derive their authority from the free exercise of the initiative and choice of the indigenous population."[2] But due to the exigencies of international statesmanship, this was not to be the case. Led by Woodrow Wilson and General Jan Christian Smuts, statesmen of the various powers were devising a system of mandates for the Arab regions of the former Ottoman Empire. Article 22 of the League Charter set forth the terms of the mandatory system. When France imposed its mandate over Syria, the Emir Faisal, who had been widely acclaimed by the Arabs as king of an independent Arab state there in accordance with the wartime commitments of the Allies, was forced to leave Damascus. After some hesitation he made his way to Baghdad, where in 1921 he was chosen king of Iraq by a hastily-organized referendum. Although British advisers dominated the government, the executive, at least, was in Arab hands.[3]

Iraq had few external contacts during the mandate (1922–32); British supervision and training for self-government were spelled out in the 1922 treaty which set up the mandate. There was considerable internal opposition to the treaty, notably from the large Shi'a minority; in fact, elections for a constituent assembly to ratify the treaty were possible only when all the Shi'a *mujtahids* (theologians), who were Persians, retired to Persia following an alleged insult to their order and did not return in time. There is a curious parallel between this action, which made it possible to restore order in Iraq, and the United Nations in 1950, when a Soviet walkout made intervention in Korea possible.

The mandate period was marked by only one problem of international significance—the Mosul question. Mosul in northern Iraq, with a population mainly of Sunni Kurds, had been awarded to Iraq as a part of the mandate by the League of Nations. Under the Treaty of Lausanne, it was specifically excluded from Turkey. The Turks in their mood of revived nationalism began pressing their claims to Mosul. They took the position that since the population was predominantly Turkish (actually Kurdish), ethnically akin to their own Turkish people (i.e., Kurds) in eastern Turkey, the region should be part of Turkey on ethnic grounds. The Turks adopted a very truculent attitude and several times occupied

[2] *Ibid.*, p. 80.
[3] Birdwood, Lord, *Nuri as-Said*, London: Cassell, 1959, p. 126, notes that Faisal's father, Sharif Husayn of Mecca, was not keen on having his son occupy the throne of a place where his ancestor Husayn bin Ali had been murdered twelve centuries earlier (at Karbala).

villages on the Iraqi side of the provisional border laid down by the League (the so-called Brussels Line). The League sent a three-man committee headed by Estonian General Laidoner to make an inquiry and on the strength of its report (which noted that the Turks had inflated population statistics to give a rather misleading picture of the area's "Turkishness") awarded Mosul to Iraq with the clear understanding that "in administering the Kurdish areas, due regard should be paid to their language, racial distinctness, and susceptibilities." [4] Turkey at first refused to accept the League's verdict, and there was even talk of war with Britain; but in July, 1926, the Turks gave in, and the decision was stabilized by an Anglo-Turco-Iraqi Treaty which lengthened the mandate period to twenty-five years and guaranteed Turkey 10 per cent of future royalties on Mosul oil (which had not yet been developed in commercial quantity). Britain also agreed to press for Iraq's admission to the League, though the lengthened mandate period reflected international doubts of Iraq's readiness for self-government.

Another treaty with Britain was signed in 1927, but Britain postponed Iraq's League candidacy for another five years. Nuri al-Said, the dean of Arab nationalists because of his long service and key leadership in the Arab Revolt, now became Minister of Foreign Affairs; and in 1930 Prime Minister, for the first of thirteen times. On June 30, 1930, Nuri signed a third Anglo-Iraq treaty with Sir Francis Humphreys, the British High Commissioner. The mandate was replaced by a "close alliance," although Iraqi membership in the League had to wait another two years. The new treaty ignored the proviso in the Mosul Agreement which had pledged Britain to continue the mandate for twenty-five years and declared the "unfettered sovereignty of Iraq." [5] However, British forces were continued in possession of the R.A.F. bases at Shu'aiba and Habbaniya. After making guarantees to protect its Assyrian Christian minority, Iraq entered the League of Nations.[6]

A boundary pact between Iraq and Iran in the same year settled the troublesome dispute over the Shatt-al-Arab. This waterway, actually the point of confluence of the Tigris and Euphrates and the flow south-

---

[4] Longrigg and Stoakes, *op. cit.*, p. 86.

[5] Vesey-Fitzgerald, S. G., "The Iraq Treaty, 1930," transactions of the Grotius Society, Vol. XVII, 1932, pp. 55–67. This essay takes Britain to task for having failed to protect the Assyrian Christians and for having given in too easily to Iraqi nationalists without requiring safeguards for the minorities.

[6] The Assyrians were absorbed into the Iraqi population, but the British found them valuable as fighters and gave them a sort of separate identity as garrison troops around the air bases.

ward to the Persian Gulf, had been a bone of contention between the Persian and Ottoman Empires from the time of Sultan Selim II, with Iraq being claimed by both powers. After World War I, Iraq inherited the controversy as part of her Ottoman legacy along with Mosul. The Iraqi position, as placed before the League of Nations, was that the Shatt-al-Arab was her only outlet to the sea and that she could not countenance foreign command of the channel from one bank and, further, that Iran was not dependent on the channel, having a sea frontage already. The Persians based their claim on the 1847 Treaty of Erzurum and claimed riparian rights to the *thalweg* or mid-channel. The darkening world situation of 1936–1937, with Mussolini defying the League and the principle of collective security, brought the two nations closer together, and League mediation brought a settlement. Iraq accepted the boundary as running along the left bank of the Shatt, except for the Abadan section of eight kilometers where it was set at mid-channel. The fact that external forces in part caused the two countries to agree left a true settlement based on mutual interest unconcluded. In 1959, the dispute was revived, mainly over the Abadan sector with the aggressively nationalist government of Iraq claiming provocation and armed threats from the Persian side.

At the same time Iraq joined the Saadabad Pact with Turkey, Iran, and Afghanistan; this was designed for mutual defense primarily against possible Italian threats, and it bound the signatories to consult in the event of external aggression against any one member. It was the first regional pact among these states and, at a time of relative Russian weakness, might have served as the fount of their mutual cooperation if their common interests had been stronger. As things turned out, the signatories failed to act in concert when World War II broke out.

Iraq in World War II

Rashid Ali succeeded Nuri Pasha as Prime Minister in 1940. Axis agents had been active among the extreme nationalists in Iraq for some time, and it was no secret that the latter wished to speed the British on their merry way. King Ghazi's death in a motor-accident in 1939 left a further gap in the ranks of the pro-British leadership. He was succeeded by his son, the six-year-old Faisal II, whose uncle, Prince 'Abd al-Ilah, became regent. Rashid himself was no friend of Britain. He refused to break off relations with Italy (Nuri had broken with Germany the year before), imposed restrictions on British troop passage across Iraq, and made contact with von Papen in Turkey with the idea of opening discussions on a possible alliance. In 1941 Rashid and a group of generals, called the "Golden Square," staged a coup, asked the Axis for aid, and tried to expel the British. Parliament was convened and forced to depose the Regent, who had fled to Transjordan along with Nuri. The Rashidis were in power for about a month and even received some German airplanes before the Arab Legion entered Iraq from Transjordan and smashed them. Rashid Ali went into exile and did not return to Iraq until 1958. Iraq cooperated fully with Britain for the rest of the war, declared war on Germany in 1943, and established diplomatic relations.

Nuri Sa'id took the lead in creating (under British patronage) the League of Arab States in 1945. Ever since the 1930's Iraq had been concerned about the status of the Arabs of Palestine and had tried to mediate with Britain to improve their position under the mandate. In 1943, Nuri sent a letter to Richard Casey, British Minister of State for Middle East Affairs in Cairo, describing his views on Arab unity. His letter became the basis of the "Blue Book" which had wide circulation as his concept of a Fertile Crescent scheme.[7] Nuri was concerned about aggressive Zionism, particularly the American variety which had just put forth the Biltmore program giving *its* view of a Jewish National Home in Palestine. To Nuri this was a transparent grab for power in the guise of a religious mystique. He was also worried about the deterioration of Arab-Jewish relations in the Arab lands. Third, he felt that the essential natural unity of the Fertile Crescent should be restored. The Ottomans, although they had misgoverned, had at least kept this unity.

Nuri proposed a greater Syrian state made up of Iraq, Syria, Lebanon, Transjordan, and Palestine, with recognition of the special status of the Jews in Palestine. Just as the Maronites of the Lebanon had had their own millet under Turkish rule, the Jews, about one-third of the population of Palestine, would form a permanent minority, self-administered within the Arab state but incapable of aggressive Zionist expansion. Jerusalem would be part of the Syrian state, but special commissions from the three monotheistic religions would ensure freedom of worship and pilgrimage. Nuri did not choose between total unification or federation; but he said that when the new Arab state had been formed, other Arab states could join it in an Arab League if they so desired. Nuri wrote, "Many of

[7] *Arab Independence and Unity,* Baghdad: Government Press, 1943. The "Blue Book" is also referred to as the Memorandum to Richard Casey. See Birdwood, *op. cit.,* for details.

our problems are the same; we are all part of one civilization; we generally think along the same lines; and we are all animated by the same ideals of freedom of conscience, liberty of speech, equality before the law, and the basic brotherhood of mankind." [8]

Nothing came of Nuri's counsels. Ironically, the same leader was to be denounced a decade later as a traitor to the Arab cause, a "lackey" of British imperialism. When the Arab League did emerge, the Egyptians, not the Iraqis, were the dominant force. Arab leaders like Nuri, who had made common cause with Britain in the war with the expectation of establishing Arab unity, were shunted aside as the Egyptian leaders, backed by Egypt's wealth, cultural and journalistic leadership, and pivotal location, quickly established the Egyptian brand of Arab nationalism in the League's councils. Also, barely three years after its inception the League received another blow. The alien, non-Muslim state of Israel arose in the heart of Nuri's Fertile Crescent, and ironically the "friends" of the Arabs of World War II backed it to the hilt.

IRAQ AND THE WEST

Both during the mandate and for most of its independent existence, Iraq has dealt more with Great Britain than any other foreign power. The 1930 treaty required both countries to consult on foreign policy matters of mutual interest and to avoid acts of foreign policy which might embarrass each other. Britain agreed to supply military training missions to the Iraqi armed forces, while Iraq agreed to furnish communications and service facilities and to allow British troops to cross its territory in the event of war. As was noted previously, it was the refusal to meet this part of the treaty in 1940–1941 that led to British re-occupation of Iraq and the expulsion of Rashid Ali, who immediately assumed near-heroic proportions as a fighter against imperialism among many Iraqi nationalists.

After the war, Iraqi leaders, including Nuri, pressed Britain to revise the 1930 treaty. They pointed out that aggressive Zionism and the Cold War had altered the status quo in the Middle East and implied at least that British prestige was on the decline. Salih Jabr, who later became head of the National Socialist Party, became Prime Minister in 1947, the first Shi'a to hold that office. Nuri became president of the senate. The new Prime Minister signed the Treaty of Portsmouth with Britain

---

[8] *Ibid.,* pp. 205–206.

in 1948. The latter was determined to retain her special position in Iraq and to block Soviet advances in the direction of the Persian Gulf. Accordingly the air bases were returned to Iraq, but British personnel stayed, and Anglo-Iraqi defense was coordinated by a Joint Defense Board, which was also to standardize British and Iraqi equipment and training methods.

The terms of the revised treaty were not to the nationalists' liking and set off a political detonation of Baghdad. Politicking was on again, with six political parties representing various degrees of Arab nationalism in opposition to the government and only the Communists banned.[9] The opposition groups were angry about the treaty which seemed to have been imposed on Iraq; they were distressed by the deteriorating Palestine situation and the inability of the squabbling Arab governments to improve it, and they were enraged by British troop landings at Basra.[10] Between January 1948 and December 1949 (except for the period of martial law which coincided with the Palestine War) strikes and rioting laid several cabinets low. Nuri al-Said at the time, noted, speaking of the Portsmouth Treaty: "If you take all the money in the Bank of England to Baghdad, they (i.e., the Iraqi people) will refuse it unless they can feel that they have shared in its negotiation." Western statesmen might well have profited by his insight in their own negotiations with the Arabs. He became Prime Minister, for the tenth time, in 1949. By then the treaty had been repudiated, and the 1930 treaty remained the basis of Anglo-Iraqi relations until 1955.

A definite alignment with non-Arab Muslim and Western sovereignties took place when Iraq and Turkey formed the Baghdad Pact, as it was called from 1955 until the end of 1958. Soviet aggressive expansionism demonstrated the need for some sort of formula by which Britain and Iraq could contribute to Middle Eastern defense, and Secretary of State John Foster Dulles worked actively to forge an encirclement to contain the USSR. Iraq had been favorably disposed toward a Middle East Defense Organization (MEDO) which was torpedoed by Egypt in 1951. Not wishing to break its Arab ties, Iraq began to look for allies who would be more dependable and would yet permit her to retain those ties. Turkey and Iran were the most logical. The Turco-Iraqi treaty of friendship of 1946 was a natural starting point. In 1954 Nuri visited Istanbul and stated that Iraq would consider joining the Turco-Pakistani pact. He

[9] Longrigg and Stoakes, *op. cit.*, p. 103.
[10] Due to riots at Abadan, Iran.

said that "an alignment of northern Muslim states offers a better assurance against aggression than anything the Arab League has to offer."[11] Shortly before Turkey's Prime Minister Adnan Menderes was to arrive in Baghdad for a return state visit, Iraq abruptly suspended diplomatic relations with Soviet Russia and ordered the staff of the Soviet embassy to leave. The USSR accused Iraq of "taking this step in accordance with its present policy of waging an open fight against Communists in the country,"[12] but Iraq did not budge. In due course, Menderes arrived and was the first foreigner to address the Iraqi parliament. In February, 1955, the two nations signed a mutual defense agreement which brought howls of "treachery" from Egypt. The Egyptian government was apparently most angered by Iraq's failure to consult either it or the Arab League first.

The treaty set up mutual exchanges in internal security matters and technical progress. Both Arab and friendly non-Arab states in the Middle East were invited to join. Israel was specifically excluded; Article 5 stated that both Turkey and Iraq would have to recognize any state intending to adhere to the treaty. The time limit was set at five years, with provisions for renewal. There was never a point at which the Turco-Iraqi Pact became formally known as the Baghdad Pact, but the name came to be applied after the other three members joined. Britain signed a new defense treaty with Iraq in April, 1955, and simultaneously acceded to the Pact. The new treaty did not commit Iraq to action beyond its own frontiers, a feature designed to placate other Arab states. The Shu'aiba and Habbaniya bases reverted to Iraqi control; all British units left except for a small training cadre. Then Pakistan and Iran joined and signed separate bilateral agreements with Iraq. At the first meeting of the Pact secretariat in November, Nuri al-Said stated that there was no inconsistency in Iraqi membership in both the Pact and the Arab League Collective Security Pact.[13] The Pact was also justified under Article 51 of the United Nations Charter, which permits member nations the right of collective self-defense. The United States sent an observer delegation but refused to join officially although we had first advanced the concept of the "Northern Tier" defense plan. Eagerness to be liked by all became timidity at the conference table. The United States after 1952 nurtured a Middle East policy of support for the Pact members (but not too

[11] "The Baghdad Pact," *The Round Table,* XLVII, 187, June 1957, p. 217.
[12] *Ibid.,* p. 218.
[13] Harris, George, ed., *Iraq,* New Haven: HRAF Press, 1958, p. 154.

much), cultivation of the "new" Arab nationalism (but not too much), friendship for Israel, and avoidance of provocation of the USSR. In the case of Iraq, the half-hearted guarantees given Nuri al-Saʿid were to bring tragedy to him and chaos to the government.

The door to membership was left open to any member of the Arab League or any nation in the region fully recognized by the members. The Turco-Iraqi Pact also stipulated that the two parties would work for a solution of the Arab-Israeli conflict on the basis of the 1947 UN resolutions. Thus Iraq became the first Arab country to concern itself with matters of policy not directly concerned with Israel.

The cards were stacked against the Pact from the beginning. Britain joined at the height of a newspaper strike so that there was no publicity at home and no chance for editors to point out to Arab nationalists that the United Kingdom was an ally on equal terms of a former mandate.[14] The failure of the United States to join or to do more than make pious noises about the Pact's value was an even heavier blow. The most painful hour for Iraq as a Pact member came in November, 1956, when Britain invaded Egypt. The British said (along with the French) that they had gone in to separate the combatants, but Iraqis saw collusion with Israel and an act of petty spite toward Nasir by Anthony Eden. Serious anti-British and anti-Pact riots broke out at Najaf and Karbala, while Syrian saboteurs blew up the main Iraq Petroleum Company pipeline to Sidon, Lebanon. Iraq agreed to attend special Pact meetings provided that Britain did not and went along with resolutions that urged a permanent international force be established between Egypt and Israel, separation of the Suez Canal issue from national politics, and continued resistance to Soviet attempts at subversion. Iraq broke relations with France and refused to attend Pact meetings with Britain until 1957.

For all practical purposes the Baghdad Pact died there in July, 1958. The men who overthrew the Hashimite monarchy, placed over Iraq with British help three decades earlier, said at first that Iraq would "honor existing political and economic commitments."[15] The other members of the Pact promptly recognized the revolutionary government. So did the Soviet Union, Communist China, and several weeks later the United States. Iraq veered sharply toward the East, however, at least as

[14] The Daily Worker commented in 1956, "His (Nuri's) police state is dubbed progressive because it is the stanchion around which the rope of the Baghdad Pact is lashed." (Birdwood, *op. cit.,* p. 242).
[15] Longrigg and Stoakes, *op. cit.,* p. 247.

indicated by the number of trade and cultural agreements signed with Communist countries. The most important of these was with the USSR for an eventual total of $237 million in military and economic aid. Early in 1959, Iraq's new Prime Minister, Brigadier General Abd al-Karim Qasim, announced formal withdrawal from the Baghdad Pact.

Iraq has been so preoccupied with internal difficulties since the July, 1958, revolution that guidelines for its future foreign policy are not easy to come by. Adding to the complexities of the domestic conflict is the personality of al-Qasim himself, a military man with no experience whatsoever in inter-Arab politics, who has said that it is far easier to come to power than to rule. Certainly the regime of his predecessor, an oligarchy backed by feudal landowners with a self-perpetuating structure, permitted the masses little opportunity for education in foreign policy.[16] By eliminating its enemies as well as all representatives of the "British period," the government defeats its own purposes by depriving itself of those who alone have had experience representing Iraq in international affairs. If the revolution in Iraq runs according to the pattern of the earlier Arab revolution in Egypt, it may, in time, seek the best from both East and West, compromising with neither. It may be wholly absorbed in the social revolution of the present Middle East. In the past, unfortunately, army officers have frequently intervened in Iraqi politics for personal gain and thus merely replaced one oligarchy with another.

IRAQ AND ISRAEL

Iraq was the only Arab state actively engaged in the Palestine War which did not conclude an armistice with Israel and has not yet done so. Numbers of volunteers from Iraq joined the Arab Liberation Army under Fawzi Kawukji which carried on guerrilla war against Jewish forces before the armies of the Arab states entered Palestine. Some eight to ten thousand Iraqi troops held the Nablus-Tulkarm-Jenin salient until they were recalled in 1949. During 1950–1951, more than one hundred thousand Iraqi Jews left for Israel in chartered aircraft. The few Jews who remain, perhaps five thousand, have forsworn Zionism and are completely loyal to the Iraqi state. Iraqi forces have been sent to Jordan on several occasions to help repel a threatened Israeli invasion; one of these troop transfers permitted the revolutionaries to take control of Baghdad. Otherwise Iraq is fully Arab as far as having no dealings with Israel.

[16] Newman, K. J., "The New Monarchies of the Middle East," *Journal of International Affairs*, 2, 1959, pp. 164–165.

IRAQ AND THE ARAB STATES

The well-advertised contest between Iraq and Egypt for Arab leadership is partly one of personality. While he was alive, Nuri al-Sa'id felt that he was rightfully entitled to a leading role in Arab politics. After all, he had fought for unity and Arab independence before Nasir had outgrown knee pants. Nuri and the older generation of Arab nationalists also believed in a policy of gradualism. Since the great powers were unable or unwilling to live up to their commitments, the best solution was to work with them, learning the mechanics of self-government, and eventually to kick them out. The younger generation which has made Nasir its symbol is too impatient for gradualism. It favors action, the bold stroke, the defiant red flag in the face of the bull. Also it has learned the value of propaganda (which the older generation could not). Iraq's former leaders believed that Britain and the Western powers really wanted to live and trade in peace and that Arab aspirations could be promoted in amity with the West.[17] Because the reins of government in Iraq were retained for so long by a group of men who had fought in the Arab Revolt and by a man personally convinced that "Iraq's future lay in cooperation with Britain, profoundly distrusted Soviet Russia and Nasserite Egypt, and was bitterly opposed to revolutionary social ideals,"[18] Iraq became associated in the younger Arab mind with entrenched, reactionary conservatism.

The creation of Israel posed a problem for Iraq's foreign policy which Nuri al-Sa'id could never solve. Egypt, because she was one hundred per cent anti-British, began a new quest for Arab unity unhampered by ties with the "colonialist" powers. Nuri's program, which included closer ties with Turkey and Iran, did not bring him the broad-gauge Western support which he needed to convince his new Arab rivals of the wisdom of gradualism. The West itself, having encouraged the establishment of Israel, found itself on the horns of a dilemma. The United States in Arab eyes was the protector of Israel (as well as its nourisher through the hundreds of bond drives and private contributions). Any approach made to the Arab states was regarded with some suspicion since it stopped short of abandoning this position. Iraq was also regarded as being in the British sphere; hence recommendations for more aid and comfort to the Iraqi

[17] "Revolution in Iraq," *World Today,* 14, August 1958, p. 323.
[18] Troutbeck, Sir John, "The Revolution in Iraq," *Current History,* February, 1959, p. 84.

leaders were channeled to Whitehall. Nor did Nuri's aim of a Fertile Crescent unity win much backing there either.

The error of the Iraqi monarchy in its dealings with other Arab states was one of inflexibility. The ruling oligarchy detested and distrusted Communism; after 1954, convicted Communists were deprived of Iraqi nationality. Nuri's most ruthless political actions were directed against them; and driven underground, the hard-core party members could only wait until some unforeseen coalition should unseat him. But the oligarchy created no large popular support which could substitute national solidarity for the Communist appeal. The Iraqi intellectuals and the growing middle class derived economic benefits but were allowed no moral leadership. Across the Suez Canal, 'Abd al-Nasir had found the West a convenient device for stirring up *his* brand of Arab unity. The Iraqis had no answer for the Czech arms deal and the propaganda victory at Suez. They had relied on Britain, and Britain had failed them.

Iraqi-Egyptian rivalry thus dates from the post-war period and is an outgrowth of the altered complexion of the Arab League. Egypt denounced Iraq's adherence to the Baghdad Pact because Iraq had taken an independent position without consulting other League members (particularly Egypt).

The Iraq-Jordan Federation took place in 1958, but efforts toward some form of integration between the two states had been going on for a dozen years. In 1947, the two Hashimite monarchies signed a treaty of brotherhood which contained a military assistance clause. Nuri al-Sa'id envisaged a "Fertile Crescent Plan" embracing Iraq, Syria, Palestine, and Transjordan. This unity would form the nucleus of a larger Arab League into which other Arab states, like Egypt, would be invited. In Jordan, King Abdullah wanted a union of Transjordan, Syria, Palestine, and Lebanon, with possible Iraqi adherence in a sort of federal state. Both goals fell afoul of international politics; and for a few months in 1958, the world saw two competing Arab unions. The two Hashimite cousins, King Faisal II of Iraq and King Husayn of Jordan, reached their majority on the same day in 1953. Iraq's entry into the Baghdad Pact strained relations for a time, while the neutralist pro-Egyptian cabinet which took office in Jordan after Glubb Pasha had been expelled leaned toward the Egyptian-Syrian axis. When Syria abruptly joined Egypt in a unitary state, the old-style Arab nationalists realized that rapid action was necessary. On February 14, 1958, Iraq and Jordan agreed to federate. The two kingdoms kept their independence and their existing governments in the

Arab Federation, while a federal government supervised over-all affairs. King Faisal became the head of the federation, and Nuri al-Sa'id was named Prime Minister. The federal agreement noted that "existing international agreements would be binding only on the states which had already contracted them; this represented a compromise on Iraq's membership in the Baghdad Pact." [19] Membership was left open to any Arab country, and both Saudi Arabia and Kuwait made noises in that direction. Iraq's relations with Saudi Arabia were bad until 1956, and the Saudis were even accused of fomenting the riots in Jordan in 1955 when that country was considering membership in the Baghdad Pact. After 1956, things improved; state visits were exchanged, trade and cultural agreements concluded, and Iraq was invited to send a military mission to Saudi Arabia. But King Sa'ud took no action, nor did Kuwait. Kuwait had had a long-standing border dispute with Iraq which was not resolved until 1932. And Iraq was suspicious of periodic smuggling across the desert boundary; while on their side, the Kuwaitis distrusted periodic Iraqi claims to all of Kuwait. Lebanon, which had friendly relations with Iraq but which was concerned about her Christian population, said she would cooperate with both blocs but join neither. In Iraq itself the Federation enjoyed only limited support. In July, 1958, public apathy greeted the announcement that the union did not apply to the independent republic. Not long thereafter Jordan's King Husayn dissolved the federation by royal decree.

INTERNAL POLITICS SINCE THE MANDATE

Throughout its modern history Iraq has struggled with the problem of reconciling diverse ethnic, cultural, and religious groups. The revolution of 1958 and its subsequent upheavals have merely re-emphasized these divisions. One found Turkoman fighting Turkoman and Kurds at each other's throats in the Mosul and Kirkuk uprisings. The monarchy, whatever its faults, was at least a rallying point for these disparate elements. The new republican regime, while closer to the Iraqi people, reflects only too clearly the differences of opinion among Communists, leftists, Arab nationalists, conservatives and various other factions as to the legitimate direction of the revolution.

Although Iraqi national life was outwardly simpler during the twelve-year British mandate (1921–1932) and the ensuing decade of Anglo-

[19] Longrigg and Stoakes, *op. cit.,* p. 218.

philic native leadership, the same instability existed. Throughout her long history, in fact, the land between the Twin Rivers has been pushed about by forces over which she had little control. Once the area ceased to be a center of civilization and its diverse peoples became docile, the pattern developed irrevocably—external pressures from every direction so that even the glittering Abbasid period could not claim to be politically just or stable. When Faisal ibn Husayn, second son of the Sharif of Mecca, arrived in Basra in 1921 to cement his candidacy to the throne of the "new" state, he received a warm welcome, not too difficult to understand in view of the presence of the British officials of the mandate who were backing him. Faisal had been led to believe that the Iraqis were unanimously behind him; and it was a bitter shock to find that many segments were not, especially after his misfortunes in Syria. Yet the situation which faced Faisal in 1921 was duplicated with a sort of reverse irony, since he was regarded as a willing tool for British imperialism, in 1958 with the advent to power of General Qasim whose purpose was to rid Iraq of this same British-tainted monarchy. It would seem that shrimps can whistle and bears sing in the marketplace.

Through a succession of skillful maneuvers, Faisal won the various factions to his side, even the Naqib of Baghdad, Abd al-Rahman al-Gailani, who had declared in no uncertain terms in 1919 that, "I would rather a thousand times have the Turks back in Iraq than see the Sharif or his sons installed here." [20] On July 11, 1921, the Provisional Council of State, with the Naqib acting as president, proclaimed Faisal King of Iraq, "with the requirement that the government be constitutional, representative, democratic, and limited by law." On August 23, Faisal was enthroned, to the tune of "God Save the King" and a twenty-one gun salute.

The next step in the political evolution of Iraq from Ottoman *vilayet* to sovereign state was the Anglo-Iraqi Treaty of 1922 referred to elsewhere in this chapter. A difference in views prevailed, however, between British and Iraqi conceptions of their treaty relationship. The country had been governed by a provisional government under High Commissioner Sir Percy Cox since the insurrection of 1920, in accordance with the provisions of the mandate entrusted to Britain by the League of Nations. The insurrection was put down but at a higher human and material cost than was anticipated. It also indicated an inchoate Iraqi

[20] Quoted in Ireland, Philip, *Iraq: A Study in Political Development*, New York: The Macmillan Co., 1938, p. 320.

national consciousness as well as the generalized resentment among Fertile Crescent Arab peoples over the entire mandate system. The British may have been stimulated to press ahead with a policy of replacing direct mandatory rule, but the difference was more in method of procedure than in spirit. As Churchill observed, "We are not entitled to disclaim the mandate, we are acknowledging an Arab state—we are creating an independent state and making a treaty with that state." [21] This sort of masterly equivocation was in the course of time to lead Britain into trap after trap elsewhere in the Middle East; but forty years ago British power linked three continents; and force was available to support the view that the Persian Gulf, as well as the land between the rivers, was a strategic area on the imperial way to India.

To the Iraqis, the treaty really meant the end of the mandate. It meant sovereignty and independence and full assistance in developing the economy. The more extreme nationalists saw the end of occupation by Indian detachments and uncultured troops from the Midlands, the end of mandate, which was synonymous with colonialism. The British announcement that the mandate would end as soon as Iraq could be admitted to the League mollified the opposition, and Faisal joyously reported to the people that elections could be held and a constitution framed now that Britain firmly supported Iraq's right to self-determination.

Article 3 of the treaty specified the terms of the future constitution and the fundamental principles of government. The Organic Law, finally promulgated in 1925 after the elections for a constituent assembly to approve it were held up by the Shi'a clergy (*ulema*) for two years, set up a limited constitutional monarchy operating a unitary state. Arab tradition and British interest in working through and with the Hashimite family made a monarchical system inevitable.[22]

The basic Organic Law of Iraq, with but two amendments, remained the law of the land until 1958 when it was suspended by the revolutionary government. Article III of the 1922 treaty set down the conditions of it in part as follows:

His Majesty, the King of Iraq, agrees to frame an Organic Law for presentation to the Constituent Assembly of Iraq and to give effect to the said Law, which . . . shall take account of the rights, wishes, and interests of all the population inhabiting Iraq. This Organic Law shall ensure to all complete

---

[21] Quoted in Foster, Henry, *"The Making of Modern Iraq,"* Norman: University of Oklahoma Press, 1935, p. 114.
[22] Cf. Khadduri, Majid, *Independent Iraq,* London: Oxford, 1958, pp. 19–21.

freedom of conscience and free exercise of all forms of worship. . . . It shall provide that no discrimination of any kind shall be made between the inhabitants of Iraq on the grounds of race, religion, or language, and shall secure the right of each community to maintain its own schools . . . in its own language, while conforming to such educational requirements of a general nature as the Government of Iraq may impose. . . . It shall prescribe the constitutional procedure, whether legislative or executive . . . involving questions of fiscal, financial, and military policy.[23]

In this manner and pursuant to the terms of the Article, the framers, the British working in English and the Iraqis in Arabic, somehow managed to forge a document designed to protect the infant's toddling steps toward constitutional government. Britain was anxious to provide for a strong kingly executive, the Iraqis to limit royal prerogatives since they were afraid that these would further entrench British interests. Many Constitutions served as models, among them the Australian, Persian, the Republic of Turkey's, and Japan's. Unlike the British Constitution, the Iraqi was rather inflexible. The amending process was difficult; and furthermore, internal laws were grouped into "ordinary" and "constitutional," which meant that even a minor regulation might require a constitutional precedent. Amendents to the Constitution were governed by Articles 118 and 119; Parliament had the right to amend secondary matters by a two-thirds vote; otherwise, amendment was possible only by a two-thirds majority of both houses after which the lower chamber would be dissolved and the amendment presented to the new chamber for reconfirmation and then transmitted to the King for final confirmation after which it became law.

The Organic Law was amended only twice before its demise in 1958. The first amendment, in 1925, set up a representative for the King in the event of his absence abroad. In 1942, the problem, not covered in the law, of how to control or eliminate cabinets whose actions were endangering the nation, became a paramount one because of Rashid Ali Gailani's attempt to align Iraq with the Axis. A special constitutional committee presented a number of proposals to Parliament. These included: (a) the King's right to dismiss the Prime Minister; (b) clarification of the succession—an important question since King Faisal II was under-age —by providing an heir presumptive from the family of Regent Abd'al-Ilah, the eldest Iraqi male heir of Sharif Husayn; (c) payment of members' salaries if the chamber were dissolved; (d) limitation of the number

[23] Harris, George, ed., *Iraq*, New Haven: HRAF Press, 1958, pp. 107–108.

of senators to one-fourth the number of deputies and provision for Parliament to meet outside Baghdad in case of an emergency; (e) a general provision enabling the government to adopt constitutional procedures from other countries by a joint resolution of both houses. These provisions were added as a second amendment to the Organic Law; but several others (the most significant, and progressive, being the replacement of the shariʿa courts of personal status with civil courts) were not adopted. Iraq was still not ready in 1942 to break with her traditional Islamic sociolegal past. Outside of the still-small educated community, the general public paid no more attention to the amendment than it had to the Constitution twenty years earlier. The provision allowing the King to dismiss the Prime Minister aroused the most debate since it appeared to infringe upon constitutional protection; but little could be done under wartime controls, and the power was not used anyway.

The Organic Law set up Iraq's governmental structure. Transfer of power from mandate to independent administration was primarily a change of venue. One of its features, quite reasonably, was a strong executive. Faisal I enjoyed greater powers than his counterparts in either the United States or Britain. His royal powers were: commander-in-chief of the armed forces, with the power to declare martial law and take personal command in national crises; confirmation and promulgation of laws; and issuance of special ordinances covering nearly all governmental actions in the absence of parliament; appointment of the Prime Minister, his cabinet, and members of the senate. Royal powers were executed by decrees (*iradas*) which, because of the concurrence and countersignature of the ministers, had the effect of delegating the royal responsibility to them without surrendering any real authority.

Although in theory the King, with his extensive powers, was dominant over the legislature, in practice, particularly after the termination of the mandate, the cabinet, or Council of Ministers, became the real governing power. Because cabinet posts tended to shift among a small select group of strong leaders, the legislature had little opportunity to oppose executive policy. Article 28 of the constitution which vested legislative power in the parliament and king jointly was thus a dead letter.

The Iraqi Parliament (before 1958) consisted of two chambers, a Senate and a Chamber of Deputies. Under the limited legislative power indicated above, the upper house fared better than the lower. The Senators appointed by the King for an eight-year term (half retiring every four years) and eligible for reappointment, able to criticize the government but lacking the power to call for a vote of confidence, acquired the status of colleagues of the executive. The Chamber of Deputies, elected for a four-session period of six months each, on the basis of one deputy per 20,000 male inhabitants, corresponded more to the House of Commons. Because it was empowered to initiate legislation, to criticize policies, and to call for a vote of confidence, the Chamber often shared the fate of similar bodies in all countries with authoritarian traditions. Between 1925 and 1956 only two of the fifteen chambers elected completed their terms.

The principle of separation of powers was also applied to Iraq by the framers of the Organic Law, with an independent judiciary, theoretically nonpartisan, and civil, tribal, religious, and mixed or special courts. The diversity of court systems re-emphasizes the varied social motifs of the country. The civil courts, a development of the mandate based on Articles 68 and 74 of the Constitution, were modeled on the French system. Their jurisdiction extends to all matters of civil, commercial, and religious law, and nonreligious actions involving the government. The Muslim religious courts, dealing with matters of a personal nature—marriage, divorce, dowry, control of *waqfs* (pious foundations), etc.—have been retained although they are disappearing elsewhere in the Muslim world. Christian and Jewish communities have their own religious courts. The tribes, the third largest segment of the population, are supervised by tribal courts which are either tribal councils (*majalis*) or individual tribal leaders appointed by the government to arbitrate disputes. These tribal courts attempt to interpret tribal customary law so as to bring it into the framework of constitutional government. The High Court and the Special Courts (*Diwan-i-Khas*) could be convened at any time to try public officials or to interpret laws, making them equal in constitutional power to the U.S. Supreme Court, except that they do not sit regularly. It should be noted that although the constitution provided for it, the special Supreme Military Court set up by the revolutionary government in 1958 to try officials of the old regime derived its power from a special law.[24]

The unusual fact about Iraq's constitutional and governmental structure was not the existence of the familiar Western political institutions but their presence in a backward, impoverished Oriental state. Few nations possessed so many obstacles to self-government—large racial and

[24] See Shwadran, B., *The Power Struggle in Iraq*, New York: Council for Middle Eastern Affairs Press, 1960, Chapter V.

religious minorities, widespread illiteracy, many centuries of economic neglect with its corrosive effect upon the spirit. The handful of leaders capable of governing had almost no experience in statecraft; most of them had fought the Turks and campaigned for a national state with little administrative training other than military. The cleavage was sharp, also, between them and the conservative clergy whom the mass of the population followed blindly still—as if it were hiding behind their robes from the Ottoman tax collectors.

INDEPENDENCE ON TRIAL

The granting of "full" independence in 1932 and Iraq's entry into the League of Nations after a stiff oral examination of Nuri al-Sa'id developed less favorably at home than abroad where the British lion kept close watch on its cub. The strains present in Iraqi politics under the mandate, notably the pro- and anti-British factions, now came into the open. At this juncture occurred the untimely death of King Faisal I, the only real unifying bond in the country. He had been on a state visit to England since June, having previously appointed Rashid Ali al-Gailani as Prime Minister of a new Cabinet dominated by the *Ikha al-Watani* (National Brotherhood) Party, the major focus of opposition to Nuri al-Sa'id. The Ikha, dedicated to the principle of freedom from British ties, had refused to accept the Anglo-Iraq Treaty of 1930 which initiated the process of the transfer of power. Faisal exerted great pressure on them, even suggesting that he would abdicate if they failed to appreciate his gradualist policy. The Ikha finally agreed to accept the treaty; when Rashid Ali published the new government's program, he alluded to Iraq's respect for international obligations and promised sweeping reforms throughout the government.[25]

The tragic "Assyrian incident"[26] seems to have hastened Faisal's death. In his absence, tension developed between the Muslim Iraqis and the Assyrian Christian minority. The Ikha leaders, who were anti-British, saw in the still-unexplained exodus of hundreds of armed Assyrians across the Syrian border a British plot to restore the mandate. The French authorities in Syria turned back the Assyrians who then ran into

---

[25] Ambitious programs and vast promises impossible of fulfillment seem to characterize Iraq's internal policies. Cf. Khadduri, *op. cit.*, pp. 36–39.
[26] The fullest accounts are Stafford, R. S., *Tragedy of the Assyrians,* London: Allen & Unwin, 1935; and Longrigg, S. H., *Iraq 1900–1950,* London: Oxford, 1953.

Iraqi army roadblocks. Clashes developed as the Assyrians refused to surrender their arms; and General Bakr Sidqi, divisional commander at Mosul, ordered a general slaughter of them in northern Iraq. Hundreds were massacred before the government (which appears to have been in sympathy with Sidqi's policies) stepped in. Faisal returned hurriedly to Baghdad but had little effect. Even his son, Amir Ghazi, professed sympathy with the Ikha and the need to eliminate the traitorous Assyrians. The King headed for Switzerland and medical treatment and died there of a heart attack suddenly on September 7, 1933. He was brought home for a state funeral and succeeded by Ghazi (1933–1939).

It has become lately fashionable in the Arab world to denigrate the Hashimite family. The violent ends which have come to several of them, the misfortunes that have dogged their efforts to create enduring castles, the stigma attached to them because of British backing, have collectively instilled in the Arab mind, particularly of the younger generation, the impression that the Hashimites represented a divisive, not a unifying trend. Their contributions and their role in whatever progress the Arabs have shown in the direction of their goals of unity and self-determination make little stir. Hashimite influence has been reduced to the lonely slight figure of King Husayn, whose role is to pass as the leader of Jordan and not as the great-grandson of the Sharif of Mecca.

Nevertheless, the Hashimites bulked large in the early twentieth century. Without question no other leaders existed in the Arab provinces of the Ottoman Empire who could rally dissident elements and work with the British under the realities of international politics. No Hashimite was more skilled at this than Faisal. He understood the tribal, Bedouin mentality. In the Meccan custom, he had been wet-nursed by Bedouin tribeswomen in the Hejaz. The tribes of Iraq were the first to swear allegiance to him.[27] Many years of public experience had given him the diplomacy and tact needed to reconcile conflicting loyalties; this was to prove vital in Iraq. Being a descendant of the Prophet, he was entitled to great respect from all ranks of Islam. He was especially good at dealing with his British overlords, extracting a concession here, accepting a pledge there. On each side of Faisal's Iraq lay old states that were being transformed by single-minded strong nationalists—Kemal Ataturk in Turkey to the west and Reza Shah in Iran to the

[27] Morris, James, *The Hashemite Kings,* New York: Pantheon Books, Inc., 1959, 78. He once said that "the happiest moment of my life is when I am riding with a friend silently across the desert on our camels in the moonlight."

east. Faisal's contributions to Middle East political stability could not be measured in Ataturk's or Reza's terms, but his job in a way was more difficult—guiding a conquered territory, without a sense of nationhood, through a transitional period to independence. Significantly, the decade after Faisal's death was infinitely more dangerous to Iraqi unity than his decade of orderly progress toward it.

King Ghazi lacked nearly all of his father's abilities and found his chief outlets in fast sports cars and horse racing. The role of the executive under him slipped well below its ultra-constitutional pinnacle of Faisal's time. Iraqi politics between 1933 and 1936 were rudderless. The Ikha Party, which had split with the Watani, stayed in power through the excitement whipped up by the Assyrian affair and through frequent use of martial law and house arrest. Factionalism was rife. Nuri al-Sa'id, gradually emerging as the strong man, did not hold the Prime Ministership; but as Foreign Minister and leader of one (non-Ikha) faction, he consistently opposed the Ikha leaders—Rashid Ali, Hikmat Sulayman, and others. Seven cabinets were formed and toppled.[28] The last, and longest (eighteen months), of Yasin al-Hashimi, formerly the chief of staff of the Arab army in Damascus during the war, fell by a military coup d'etat.

The Coup of 1936, first in the modern Arab world, was carried out by the army under Bakr Sidqi and a civilian nationalist group called the Ahali. The Ahali, formed in 1931, was socialist without being Marxist, although it began as a group of liberal young men whose only common concern was the political domination of the country by a small clique of old men.[29] One of the members of the Ahali was Abd al-Fattah who had become interested in the Soviet system as a graduate student at Columbia University. Because of the religious and conservative influences which were highly significant in Iraqi society, the Ahali preferred to call the system they designed, *Sha'biyah* (Populism), rather than socialism. The aim of Sha'biyah was "the welfare of the people" without regard for class distinctions. The Ahali advocated the principles of the French Revolution—at least liberty and equality—and harnessed these in a muzzy way to state socialism. They did not recognize the class struggle or the inevitability of revolutionary social change. But they repudiated nationalism since it led to the domination by one class of the

---

[28] See Khadduri, *op. cit.*, Chapter III for details.
[29] Nuri al-Sa'id observed of this: "When you have a small pack of cards, you must shuffle them often."

others. The parliamentary system of government was also maintained.
Sha'biyah smelled too much like Communism in a different suit for
the government; furthermore, it was too vague for the public to understand and did not consider the realities of Iraq's social needs. The Ahali
decided to put the doctrine in cold storage temporarily and to make common cause with disaffected army officers, the other main opposition
group. These latter felt little but contempt for the politicians bickering
in Baghdad while the army was only used to crush tribal uprisings.
The military regimes in Turkey and Iran with their ruthless efficiency
appealed to the Iraqi officers as the most sensible method of achieving
the national ideal. Bakr Sidqi, a national hero because of his role in the
Assyrian affair, was the strongest of these.

On October 29, 1936, Bakr Sidqi, in cooperation with Hikmat Sulayman, a former Ikha member and leader of the Ahali, carried out his coup.
The army marched on Baghdad; and Sidqi, as leader of the "National
Reform Force," issued a proclamation ordering Prime Minister Yasin
al-Hashimi to resign in favor of Hikmat. The King had little choice but
to agree. While the coup was relatively bloodless—the only important
casualty being Defense Minister Ja'far al-Askari, who had tried to assert
his authority over Sidqi—the portents were ominous. In less than a year,
Sidqi was dead, the victim of the same soldiers he had led in triumph
to Baghdad. Typically, his ambitions of restoring the army led to authoritarian excesses, which, it was whispered, were thwarting the purposes of the National Reform Force.[30]

Bakr Sidqi's assassination did not curb the influence of the military
on Iraqi politics; but it put an end to the Ahali group, which had ridden
his coat-tails to the post of Prime Minister. Between 1937 and 1941 there
were seven military coups, the last carried out by Rashid Ali in 1941.

The instability that had plagued Iraq ever since King Faisal's death
was lifted, at least temporarily, by the British war-time occupation.[31]
Nuri al-Sa'id picked up the reins of office in 1941 and did not lay them
down until 1944, a three-year record for Iraqi cabinets. From 1944 until
1946 the elder statesman, Hamdi al-Pachachi, held the post, while Nuri
reverted to the less arduous role of Senator. The Regency arrangement
under Prince 'Abd al-Ilah (who was King Ghazi's cousin and the brother

[30] Khadduri, *op. cit.*, Chapter III, *passim.*
[31] Nuri observed in 1941: "Since the untimely death of King Faisal, Iraq has
not had a chance of having a strong head of state who could firmly control the
country." Birdwood, *op. cit.*, p. 186.

of the dead king's wife, Queen Aliyah) further complicated Iraq's internal politics since what loyalty to the House of Faisal that was left did not extend to his elder brother's family.[32] 'Abd al-Ilah, cold and suave where Ghazi had been reckless and colorful, played at kingship with a mournful seriousness. He directed the work of Parliament; supported Nuri al-Sa'id, thus tarring him with the pro-English brush; and ordered the execution of the four Golden Square generals. The last action damned him forever in the eyes of those Iraqis who considered the 1941 coup a legitimate nationalist uprising against foreign pressures.

The years after World War II were crowded and difficult ones for Iraq. The pack of cards was shuffled and dealt so often that the faces of the leaders blurred and their spots began to wear off so that they looked much alike. From 1920 to 1950 there were forty-five different cabinets, and less than 120 politicians served in them. Nuri himself was Prime Minister fourteen times, plus the fifteenth tour as Prime Minister of the federation, which ended with his death in 1958. From 1950 to 1958, he was out of office for a total of only twenty months; yet Nuri did not provide stability, only repression. The lifting of wartime controls brought back political parties. The Liberal (Al-Ahram) Party, quiescent since 1939, was revived with a modest social reform program. The Ahali reappeared for a time, but its program consisted of negativist hostility to Nuri and the "Palace Guard." Other parties formed[33] were: The Independence Party (Al-Hizb al-Istiqlal), of right-wing nationalists sympathetic to Rashid Ali, anti-foreign rather than anti-West, whose leaders were Faik as-Samarra'i' and Siddiq Shanshal; the National Democratic Party (Al-Hizb al-Watani al-Dimuqrati) led by Kamil Chadurchi, popular with young intellectuals and "positively neutralist"; the National Union Party (Ittihad al-Watani), which was a reconstitution of the Ahali; and the Sha'b (People's) Party of Aziz Sharif which strongly supported the Soviet Union and attacked the West.

The new Electoral Law of 1946 for a time encouraged party activity. It increased the number of constituencies, with one or two seats in the

---

[32] Khadduri, *op. cit.*, p. 138, states that his death was regarded as a national calamity because of his outspoken anti-Westernism. Rumors that his death was a British plot spread; and the British consul at Mosul was killed with a pick-ax when he attempted to tell a crowd the truth.

[33] The first decade of independence had not had political parties in the formal Western sense but rather groupings around one leader or coalitions of politicians. Cf. Harris, *op cit.*, Chapter VII.

Chamber of Deputies instead of as many as fifteen seats per provincial constituency. Elections and candidacies were also required to be announced in advance. But the government was no more interested than any other shaky authoritarian regime in permitting democratic evolution through constructive criticism and wider participation of the electorate. Universal male suffrage for mentally competent Iraqis over twenty was quite enough, thank you! Party newspapers were interfered with and then suppressed—the Sha'b and National Union newspapers went as early as 1946. Party activity was curtailed by martial law during the Palestine War, and the two afore-mentioned parties were forced to disband because of their pro-Communist, antigovernment tactics. In 1950 martial law and press censorship were lifted. Nuri then formed his own party, the Constitutional Unionists, intended to appeal to all ranks of society and to strike a balance between right and left. Decidedly pro-Western, it nevertheless advocated social reforms. Salih Jabr formed a rival party, the National Socialist, drawn mainly from the Shi'ite community (of which he himself was a member), from tribal chiefs, and from landowners. The Party favored continued cooperation with the West, but paradoxically closer ties with the Arab world. Two lesser parties of pronounced neutralist views were also permitted to form. A 1953 amendment to the Electoral Law set up single-stage elections for the Chamber of Deputies. Nuri and his colleagues, however, had grown up in the party-less Ottoman Empire. He had no faith in the system. When the parties began to bicker as the individual politicians had in earlier years, he simply suspended all political activity, including his own party's.

From 1954 to 1958 political rule in Iraq can best be described as one of increasing inflexibility. The ruling oligarchy detested and distrusted Communism. After 1954, convicted Communists were deprived of Iraqi nationality. Nuri's most ruthless political actions were directed against them; and driven underground, the hard-core party members could only wait until some unforeseen coalition could unseat him. But the oligarchy created no large unit of popular support which could substitute national solidarity for the Communist appeal. The Iraqi intellectuals and the growing middle class derived economic benefits but were allowed no moral leadership. Nuri al-Said was no Ataturk; advancing years and bitterness over Israel blinded him to the trend of events in his own country; and he did not know (or care perhaps) that the respect, which had never been affection, of the people diminished with each passing year. According to one writer, his methods and views had not changed since his Ottoman days; "True to the old tradition of the Turks, he knew only two ways of dealing with opponents, gifts and force." [34] Again, unlike Ataturk (although he came to wield the same batons of power), Nuri did not publicize the things he did for his country, the really constructive achievements. The Iraq Development Board, created in 1950 to develop the country's productive resources and to raise living standards, was given 70 per cent of the oil royalties for its job. The projects undertaken were vast in scope and truly beneficial in the long run. The destructive Tigris floods were stopped by the great Wadi Tharthar dam; paved roads radiated from Baghdad, and a beginning was made in public housing. But the Board paid little attention to Iraq's human and social needs. It was apparently obsessed with its own vision of the future. Little was done of an "impact" nature. A few hundred *fellahin* were given land at Al Musaiyib, south of Baghdad, but land distribution was not accompanied by education in its use. The large factories were well subsidized, but the small businessmen received little help. Thus the Iraqi people came to believe that they had no part in the growth of their country and were receiving none of the benefits of modernization, which went instead straight into the hands of those who had always sat at the apex of the social pyramid. The well-advertised "Development Week" in early 1958 was a belated effort to get the mass of the people behind the program (and, incidentally, behind the government). Workers' housing was dedicated in Baghdad; and the first tenants moved into the completely new city of Erbil, a suburb for lower-income families, built on the plain below ancient Arbela where Alexander of Macedon demolished a Persian autocracy twenty-two centuries earlier.

THE REVOLUTION OF 1958

The events of July, 1958, now may be seen in clearer perspective, although the direction of the new regime and internal agreement on its principles are still shadowed in confusion. The July affair should be termed a revolution, in contradistinction to Iraq's long series of pre-war coups, because it had popular support. Nearly all elements of Iraqi society welcomed it. Those who subscribed to Nasir's Egyptian call for Arab unity felt that Iraq could come to terms with the United Arab Republic since both Nasir and General Qasim had the same general

[34] "Caractacus," *Revolution in Iraq*, London: Victor Gollancz, 1959, p. 46.

views (at least Qasim's associates did). The largest of Iraq's non-Arab minorities, the Kurds, disliked the Baghdad Pact, because it seemed to revive the Saadabad Pact and thus suppress what remained of separate Kurdish nationalist aims. They objected even more to Nuri's Iraq-Jordan Federation as a step toward Pan-Arabism with no guarantee that their Kurdish communal separateness would be maintained. The thousands of people in the jails, often on mere pretexts, could see no benefits in a state which deprived them of personal liberty in return for promises of future riches. The greatest grievances of the have-nots, however, were directed not at Nuri, whom they respected even if they did hate his lizard eyes, cold stare, unanswerable logic, and harsh conviction that he alone knew the right way for Iraq. They were bitter for moral and psychological reasons—because they were deprived of participation in the national "operation bootstrap" and because the regime had failed to recast the traditional form of society into modern, socially productive forms.

This revolution, which was to unleash all the contradictory forces of Iraqi society and send them tumbling toward some unglimpsed goal, became possible through a series of coincidences. Civil crisis was tearing at Lebanon; and Nuri al-Sa'id, afraid that the contagion would spread to Jordan, ordered units of the Armored Division to reinforce the Jordan-Syria frontier. The 19th and 20th Brigades of this division, respectively commanded by Brigadier 'Abd al-Karim Qasim and Colonel 'Abd as-Salam Muhammad Arif, were designated. To reach the frontier they had to pass through Baghdad at night. Both King Faisal and Nuri were scheduled to leave for a meeting of the Baghdad Pact powers the next day in Ankara, and 'Abd al-Ilah had just returned from London to act in his nephew's absence. Thus for a few brief hours the normally tight grip of the government would be relaxed.

Instead of continuing to the frontier, the two brigades deployed in Baghdad and by dawn had seized the key points of control—the railway, the radio stations, and police headquarters. The military efficiency of the planners (Qasim and Arif are said to have schemed for three years) was abetted by these coincidences. In a still undetermined manner, the King, the Crown Prince, and the royal family were shot down.[35] Nuri remained in hiding for a day and a half but also met his death in an

[35] Accounts differ widely on the actual killings. The violence of the Iraqi crowds, however, seemed to be directed at 'Abd al-Ilah more than at the King. Birdwood, *op. cit.*, Chapter XIX; Morris, *op. cit.*, pp. 177–178; "Caractacus," *op. cit.*, pp. 126–129.

unknown way; according to some, when a child saw his pajamas hanging down below the black *aba* (the standard costume of elderly Iraqi
women) which he was wearing as a disguise, it cried out as a joke,
"There goes Nuri al-Sa'id." What is certain is that by nightfall on
July 15, 1958, the cast of characters that had held the stage in Iraq's national drama for nearly forty years had all been replaced.

The initial actions of the revolutionary government harmonized with
the popular desires. Qasim declared Iraq to be a republic. At first a Council of Sovereignty, with three members—Lieutenant General Najib al-
Rubai, a Sunni Arab; Khalid Naqshabandi, a Kurd; and Mahmud Mahdi
Kubbah, a Shi'a and former leader of the Independence Party—ruled.
Then Qasim became Prime Minister and formed the first republican
cabinet, which contained a number of generals and political enemies of
Nuri who had been jailed under the old regime. On July 20 a special
military tribunal under Qasim's cousin, Colonel Fadhil Abbas al-Mah-
dawi, was set up to try ministers of the royalist regime for conspiring
against the state. On the twenty-seventh a temporary republican constitutional law was announced. According to Article 2, "Iraq is part of the
Arab Union," although which Arab Union was meant was not specified.
Article 7 declares that "the people are the source of all powers," and Article 17 that the armed forces "are the property of the people." Personal
and religious freedom, the sanctity of the home and the independence of
the courts are similarly "guaranteed" to the people. Executive power is in
the hands of a Council of Ministers headed by the Prime Minister. But
its actions are subject to approval by the Council of Sovereignty. Iraq is
an independent Islamic republic, with Kurds and Arabs treated as equal
partners. The constitutional law is binding until a plebiscite takes place.[36]

On September 30 an agrarian law was put into effect limiting land
ownership to one thousand *dunums* (two hundred fifty acres) of irri-
gated land and two thousand *dunums* of unirrigated land. Since a vital
impulse for the coup d'etat sprang from Iraq's antiquated feudal agrarian
system and since Qasim himself had stated that land reform was the
crux of social problems, the law was not unexpected. Little actual redis-
tribution has taken place in two years, however, and only in selected
areas.

Constitutional and land reform were in line with the broad objectives
of the revolutionary government as outlined in a series of public pronouncements and press conferences of Qasim. He declared: "We will

[36] *Middle East Journal,* Chronology, Autumn 1958.

bring civilization into . . . every part of this homeland. . . . We will not lower the standard of the rich, but we will raise the standard of the poor. . . . We must raise the . . . standards of the people so that they can decide what is good for them. . . . Democracy means noble nationalism characterized by benevolence—and it does not entail aggression but respects individual freedom." [37]

With the interim Constitution and the agrarian reform law, Qasim declared a transitional period of two years or less after which the Iraqi people would freely choose their (unspecified) form of government. The transitional period came to an end January 6, 1960, after which date political parties were permitted to form and to function under government licenses. During the transitional period, however, newspapers were permitted to be published although criticism of the government was prohibited. The Iraq Development Board was abolished, and economic development was continued on a stop-gap, short-range basis with projects allocated among various ministries. As of mid-1960 there was still no sign of the 400 million dinar building program often mentioned by Qasim in his press conferences. Dr. Ibrahim Kubbah, Minister of Agrarian Reform and the only trained economic thinker among the revolutionary leaders, recognized the limitations of Iraqi society and the necessity for agrarian reform as the prerequisite to social reform, democratic development, and internal stability. Kubbah emphasized the transformation and leveling of Iraqi society into four classes: farmers, workers, petit bourgeoisie, national bourgeoisie. It is significant that the great split between elements in Iraq which has occurred since 1958 has been widened by the ineffectual nature of agrarian reform. The landlords opposed it, of course, but so did the peasants, suspicious, after years of bitter experience, of the enlightenment of *any* government.

Agrarian reform and social progress have had to take a back seat, from the beginning of the republic, to political maneuvering and factionalism. Qasim, who has described himself as one who has dedicated himself for twenty years to the cause of the Iraqi people, was threatened from all sides by factions which sought to pervert the revolution to their own ends. His strategy has been to balance the conflicting forces against each other while remaining detached, *above* the struggle. Four different series of events have been noted as challenging his right to speak for Iraq, or his conception of the direction of the revolutionary government. The first was the Arif-Rashid Ali affair. Just as Egypt's Nasir had his Naguib,

[37] Shwadran, *op. cit.,* pp. 28–30.

Qasim's co-conspirator, Col. Arif, developed too much popularity in the public eye, for his leading role in the coup. More important, Arif was a disciple of Nasir, a believer in Arab unity in Nasir's terms, and an advocate of nationalizing the oil industry—all ideas which Qasim opposed. In September, 1958, Arif was relieved of his post and assigned as Ambassador to Bonn. He later returned secretly to Baghdad in October and was arrested and sentenced to death (later commuted) by the same people's court which was trying his old enemies. Rashid Ali Gailani, the old leader of the 1941 coup, had returned to Iraq after seventeen years of exile to receive a hero's welcome. In December, 1958, he and a number of high military officers were arrested and accused of plotting "with imperialism, Zionism, and certain Arab statesmen" to undermine the agrarian reform program and unite Iraq with the U.A.R.

Premier Qasim also weathered two counter-revolutions and an assassination attempt during his two years in office. A rebellion of army units at Mosul broke out in March, 1959, but was crushed when calls for help from the Mosul radio brought no volunteers racing across the Syrian border. The leader of the revolt, Col. Shawwaf, apparently died resisting the government's loyal army units. The second revolt took place in Kirkuk, also in northern Iraq, and was notable for its racial aspects. The Kurds split into pro-Communist and anti-Communist factions, battling each other, and also battling with Turkomans near the oilfields. The attempt on Qasim's life took place in October, 1959, and resulted in a roundup of real (or suspected) Ba'thists, the party responsible for Syria's merger with Egypt and a militant Arab unity group.

While the future of the harassed Iraqi Republic is decidedly unclear, the sequence of events described above indicates that one man, of the many who took part in the 1958 coup, has the skill and dedication to a mission to save Iraq, if this is possible, from political disintegration. Qasim has managed to meet each crisis with a flexibility worthy of his Egyptian rival. By demoting Colonel Arif and then arresting him on conspiracy charges, he blocked the nationalists most eager to make common cause with 'Abd al-Nasir. The Mosul uprising was used to purge Nasirist army units and to take advantage of Communist support without recognizing the party. The Kirkuk affair saw the Communists overplaying their hand.[38] Qasim capitalized on this notoriety to remove them

[38] Chiefly through the violence of their purges of known anti-Communist nationalists; hundreds were killed and many dragged through the streets and torn to pieces by Communist mobs.

from cabinet and police positions which might have endangered him. Finally the assassination attempt placed the martyr's halo around the Premier's lean, ascetic face, and his dramatic "Kill me!" won him full popular support. The permission to form political parties was accompanied by a licensing requirement; withholding a license from the Communist Party, yet granting one to a dissident Communist splinter group, had the effect of dividing the Communists with their own methods.

But survival in Iraq is only half the loaf. For the revolution to benefit the country and to stabilize the state as a viable *social* unit, much more is needed. With all her mineral wealth, Iraq suffers from minority troubles, a feudal social structure, an over-representation of tribal units, and few traditions or common bonds. Although Egypt lacks wealth, the Egyptians are a solid national unit. No Arab unity is possible without a fusion of some sort of Iraq and Egypt. But this, under present circumstances, is no more likely than an Arab recognition of Israel.

The third anniversary of the Iraqi Revolution, in 1961, found the country at its familiar stand, battling British imperialism, Pan-Arabism (the Egyptian variety) and Communism as exported from Moscow. Nor was Premier Qasim above a little hanky-panky in the name of Iraqi nationalism. No doubt with complete sincerity in his eyes, but equally out of deep-rooted suspicion of all British motives, Qasim announced shortly after the British grant of full independence to Kuwait, that the principality was really an integral part of Iraq. The statement brought British paratroopers rushing back to Kuwait, and promises of aid and comfort, even troops, from the other big Arab countries, Saudi Arabia and the U.A.R. Qasim stuck to his guns, although he made no overt attempt to annex Kuwait. Having stated his position, he turned his attention to internal matters, as Iraq began a week-long celebration of independence. Dedication of a new National Assembly building in Baghdad showed that the resumption of normal political life might not be too far away. Significantly, as the celebration began, Qasim released the four former premiers jailed since 1958—Rashid Ali Gailani, Fadhil Jamali, Ahmad Mukhtar Baban, and Tawfiq al'-Suwaydi.

RECOMMENDED READINGS

1. Bell, Gertrude L., *Letters,* ed. Lady Florence Bell, 2 vols., New York: Boni & Liveright, 1927.
2. Birdwood, Lord, *Nuri as-Said,* London: Cassell, 1959.
3. Caractacus (pseud.), *Revolution in Iraq,* London: Victor Gollancz, 1959.

4. Crutiansky, Leon, *La Question de Mossoul,* Paris: Presses Modernes, 1927.

5. Foster, Henry, *The Making of Modern Iraq,* Norman: University of Oklahoma Press, 1935.

6. Harris, George, ed., *Iraq,* New Haven: HRAF Press, 1958.

7. International Bank for Reconstruction and Development, *The Economic Development of Iraq,* Baltimore: The Johns Hopkins Press, 1952.

8. Ireland, Philip W., *Iraq: A Study in Political Development,* London: Jonathan Cape, 1937.

9. Khadduri, Majid, *Independent Iraq: A Study in Iraqi Politics Since 1932,* rev. ed., London: Oxford, 1958.

10. Longrigg, S. H., *Iraq 1900–1950,* New York: Oxford, 1953 (Pub. for The Royal Institute of International Affairs).

11. ———, & Stoakes, Frank, *Iraq,* London: Benn, 1959.

12. Main, Ernest, *Iraq from Mandate to Independence,* London: Allen & Unwin, 1935.

13. Al-Marayati, Abid A., *A Diplomatic History of Modern Iraq,* New York: Robert Speller & Sons, 1961.

14. Morris, James, *The Hashemite Kings,* New York: Pantheon Books, Inc., 1959.

15. Qubain, Fahim, *The Reconstruction of Iraq, 1950–1957,* New York: Frederick A. Praeger, Inc., 1958.

16. Shwadran, Benjamin, *The Power Struggle in Iraq,* New York: Council for Middle Eastern Affairs, 1960.

17. Stewart, Desmond & Haylock, John, *New Babylon: A Portrait of Iraq,* London: Collins, 1956.

CHAPTER 8

PALESTINE AND ISRAEL

One of the supreme ironies of twentieth-century politics in the Middle East is the necessity for separate treatment in political terms of Palestine, with its successor state, Israel. In geographical arrangement, and under the laws of economics, Palestine is an integral part of the Fertile Crescent. Until 1948, its demography also linked this land with the greater Arab World, even to the extent of being the Arab "heartland," as demonstrated by the vital roles of leadership filled by Palestinian refugees in other Arab states. The history of Palestine re-emphasizes its lack of a separate identity. Except for two periods, thirty centuries apart, it has not enjoyed a recognized sovereign existence. Being a natural way station on the route between Africa and Asia, it was visited by conquerors as well as traders in the ancient past; minor tribes settled there and took part in the struggles of the great powers of the time. Briefly, in David's time (1000 b.c.) the Semitic Israelite tribes took advantage of the temporary weakness of Egypt and Assyria and expanded their control over the bulk of Palestine. After Solomon's death Israel's authority disintegrated quickly. The rest of Palestine's history is a dreary round of foreign invasions, short bloody revolts against occupying powers, and the role of outpost of empires, Persian, Roman, Ottoman, finally British.

This small, undistinguished land,[1] largely barren and desolate, and crowned by an equally insignificant capital has nevertheless exerted an olympian importance in the affairs not only of the Middle East, but of

[1] "The cultivable area can be crossed in a car from west to east in two hours and from north to south in five hours." Barbour, Nevill, *Palestine: Star or Crescent?*, New York: Odyssey Press, Inc., 1947, p. v.

all men. Three major religions converge in Palestine, and so far as is now known, Palestine alone is associated with the Man who lived among men but was of God Himself. The Muslim, partaking of many elements of Christianity, has elevated Jerusalem to a status just below Mecca and Medina, making it the legendary site of Muhammad's journey to the Most High God. But it remained for the Jew to fasten upon Palestine with an intensity and devotion which, over two thousand years, provided the cement for survival of the traditions of his people.

Thus Palestine must be considered from two viewpoints: the attitude of the Jewish people towards it, and the conflicting pressures of modern international politics. The Jewish accomplishment was to keep alive a feeling of Jewish national identification among a people scattered over all the continents and absorbed into diverse cultures. This sense of identity may loosely be called Zionism. When Europe began to expand technologically in the nineteenth century and to seek sources of raw materials for the looms of Lancashire and Lyon, it became possible for at least a segment of the Jews to translate their Zionism into a political formula. Meanwhile, the European powers cultivated the Arab peoples living under the Ottoman Empire, in part out of a genuine interest in providing the benefits of modern civilization to "benighted Asiatics," in part for selfish economic reasons. World War I lifted the lid on this Pandora's box of assorted ambitions and interests. Stemming directly from this struggle, an agonizing conflict was fought on this "dark and bloody ground" between cousins and neighbors.

THE RISE OF ZIONISM

Biblical tradition ascribes the origin of the Jewish people to Abraham, a Mesopotamian who owned flocks of sheep in the vicinity of Ur. Abraham received several revelations from God, promising Palestine to him and his descendants, in perpetuity,[2] in return for leading his family and followers there, and living in accordance with the laws of God. These promises were repeated, according to the Bible, to Abraham's son Isaac and to his grandson Jacob. Abraham, as one would expect from a seminomadic herdsman, made no real effort to establish a permanent home for his people in Palestine. Before his emigration to Egypt, however, Abraham's grandson Jacob was assured that God would make a great nation of his descendents. Thus, the real association of the Hebrews, or

---

[2] "And I will give unto thee, and to thy seed after thee . . . all the land of Canaan, for an everlasting possession." *Genesis XVII: 8.*

Israelites, with Palestine, and its identity with their permanent home, begins with Jacob.[3]

This story is important because it is one of the bases of Zionism. Whether ethnologically true or false, the fact remains that for more than two millennia Jewish children have been inculcated with this belief in their origin and their historic right to their Palestine homeland. Zionism reaches back deep into the roots of Jewish history for its sustenance and derives much of its strength from an emotionalism unique in political movements (one of which it has become).

A second element in the Zionist creed is the historical role played by the Jews in Palestine. Jewish nationalism in a sense harks back to the David-Solomon period during which the united kingdom of Israel held sway over Palestine. The Philistines who gave the land its name were driven back to the coast; Solomon's kingdom, while nominally owing allegiance to Egypt, exercised practical political control from Dan to Beersheba, over all the tribes of the land of Canaan.

Of more significance to Zionism, however, was the development of a monotheistic religion within a social framework predominantly pastoralist in function, animist in belief. This movement was led by priests and enunciated by prophets such as Naboth, Isaiah, and Elisha, who held great power in the Israelite community. Living around, and sometimes within this community, were many tribes of diverse stocks, who outnumbered the Israelites but lacked the social cohesion, the overriding religious drive which has marked the Jewish people even to today.

The third element in Zionism, and the one which finally geared this emotional force into an organized political movement, modern Zionism, is the *Diaspora* ("Dispersion"—*Galut* in Hebrew). There have been three periods of Diaspora in all, and they correspond to successive stages in the dispersal of the Jewish race from its "ancestral," God-ordained homeland in Palestine. The first Diaspora was 722 B.C., when the Northern Kingdom, with its capital at Samaria, was overrun by Sargon II of Assyria, and its ten tribes which constituted its population were deported.[4] In 586 B.C. Nebuchadnezzar, the King of Babylonia, captured Jerusalem, ending the independence of the Southern Kingdom of Judah. The ma-

---

[3] The word "Israel" was apparently an attribute of Jacob (lit. "contender with God").

[4] These tribes were never again identified as an ethnic unit, and their destination lost to history. While the Afghans (see Chapter 5) have a legend of descent from the Ten Lost Tribes, more probably the bulk of these Jews were assimilated into the Mesopotamian population over a period of years.

jority of the remaining Jews in Palestine were taken to Babylon, where they were allowed to settle in colonies, to cultivate whole districts, and even to maintain their own form of religion. Some rose to high office in the Babylonian conquest of the Near East; the emperor Artaxerxes "authorised all who are minded of their own free will to go up to Jerusalem and restore it. And the builders, everyone, had his sword girded by his side, and so builded." [5] A number did so, but many more remained, and from their descendants sprang the modern Jewish colony of Iraq, with perhaps a longer continuous tenure (2,500 years) there than any other identifiable ethnic group. Yet even these largely assimilated Jews continued to look toward Jerusalem with vague aspirations as the spiritual center of their Palestinian Homeland.

The third and final Diaspora occurred under the Roman Empire. Palestine, as a strategically important border province, experienced an economic-cultural revival during the rule of Herod the Great (40–4 B.C.) who was appointed Tetrarch of Galilee by the Romans pending the firm establishment of imperial government. Previously, in the confused years that succeeded the death of Alexander the Great and the division of his empire among his generals, a family of high priests, the Maccabees, formed an independent kingdom in Judea. Their descendants, Alexander Jannaeus and John Hyrcanus, added most of Palestine and northern Transjordan to the Maccabeean state. The ancient concept of a Jewish national home in Palestine was revived, and continued despite the loss of political sovereignty under the Romans. As Jewish wealth increased in Palestine, Jewish nationalism intensified. The Jews, living under relatively strict monotheism with their lives governed by the socio-legalistic concepts of the Torah, resented Roman polytheism and moral laxity. They also believed that Rome regarded them as second-class citizens, because of its limitations on their political freedom and their practice of Judaism. Roman concessions to them in the form of internal autonomy were not enough. Hence they rebelled.[6] After three years of furious resistance (67–70 A.D.) Emperor Titus captured Jerusalem and leveled the city; even so, rebellions against Roman rule broke out sporadically for the next sixty years. The last one (132–135 A.D.) led by Bar Kochba,

---

[5] Quoted in Sacher, Harry, *Israel: The Establishment of a State*, New York: British Book Centre, Inc., 1952, p. 1, cf. Ezra I, 3–4.

[6] It should be noted that Pontius Pilate refused to save Jesus from crucifixion on the grounds that His fate was an internal matter for the Jewish community, and justified his action by classifying Jesus as the potential leader of a nationalist uprising. Cf. Barbour, *op. cit.,* p. 13.

was crushed by Hadrian. Jerusalem was destroyed, the Temple burned, a new city (New Rome) dedicated on the site. About 600,000 Jews were killed, the rest scattered throughout the Roman Empire. Henceforth, with Jewish nationalism eliminated, Judaism became the single bond of unity for the dispersed Jewish people. And thus was born the contrapuntal impulse of Zionism, the ingathering of the exiles or the return to the Promised Land, as foretold by the prophets from the revelations of God. Nearly nineteen centuries were to pass before Zionism could put on a political complexion again. Only a handful of Jews persisted in Palestine. They became largely farmers, as indeed did most Jews scattered over the Roman empire. They were no longer capable of collective independent action. The Byzantines, who inherited Rome's authority over Palestine and the eastern Mediterranean, discriminated against its Jews more than Rome had, owing to the special, official role of Christianity in the Empire. When the Persians overran Palestine in 611–614 A.D., local Jewry turned violently against the Christian peasantry. In his turn, the Byzantine Emperor Heraclius, after recovering Palestine, in 634 "established the empire's policy as extermination by forcible conversion and the exclusion for all time of Jews from Jerusalem." [7]

Barely two steps behind Heraclius came the Muslim invaders from Arabia. Christian Syria and Palestine, resentful of Byzantine discrimination, simplified the problem of conquering Palestine. When the Caliph Umar rode into Jerusalem on his camel and alighted to pray at the site of the temple, the final aspect of Palestine's tri-dimensional politics began to take shape. The Pact of Umar, under whose terms the surrender of Jerusalem to the Muslims was arranged, governed relations between them and their Christian (and Jewish) subjects. Both were regarded as "People of the Book"; their lives, churches, and property were inviolate, and their freedom of worship guaranteed. In lieu of military service, both groups paid a capitation tax. They were not supposed to hold office in the government, but many did, if only for lack of trained administrators among the Arabs. The substitution of Islamic for Christian rule in the Holy Land removed the Jewish stake in its affairs a degree farther even from the minor efforts of Bar Kochba. The general tolerance of Islam for the "People of the Book" permitted Christians to make the pilgrimage in increasing numbers. The Crusades were a Muslim-Christian show. Meanwhile the Jews living under Christian domination, far from

[7] Polk, W. R.; Asfour, E. Y.; Stamler, D., *Backdrop to Tragedy: the Struggle for Palestine,* Boston: Beacon Press, 1957, p. 8.

Zion, fared somewhat worse than their compatriots in the Muslim world. In both areas they were required to wear a distinctive costume and to reside in a certain quarter of town; in the case of European Jewry this grew into the walled ghetto system.[8] Persecutions of Jews under Christianity during the Middle Ages were more violent and frequent than those under Islam; the latter were usually carried out for military reasons. The restrictions on usury of medieval Christian churches and Islam forced the Jews into undesirable commercial and financial occupations. The innate centrifugality of Judaism was given added appeal by this socioeconomic ostracism, so that Jewish communities were reorganized under both religions, in a way that emphasized their racial separateness.

Nevertheless, at least until the eighteenth century Judaism provided the only link between the Jewish people and Palestine. Through Judaism "the eyes of the Jew rested . . . on the walls of Jerusalem. His thrice daily prayers were directed there; when he built a house he left a portion unpainted to remind him that Jerusalem was as yet unbuilt. At the circumcision mention was made of God's promise to Abraham to give him the land of Israel—and in death a bag of earth from the Holy Land was placed on the grave so that the final resting place might be on sacred soil." [9]

This deep emotional longing for a lost homeland was fostered by the Talmudical priesthood, and by the "Chalukah" system, which was an organized fund drive among Diaspora Jews for the support of Talmudical schools in Palestine. But the depth of the messianic appeal of the Promised Land to Jews everywhere may be seen in the meteoric career of Shabbetai Zevi (b. 1626) who proclaimed himself the Messiah in 1665 in Central Europe. He called for a mass migration of Jews to Palestine. But falling into the hands of the Ottoman Sultan (the Turks, who had held Palestine since 1517 had never permitted immigration by non-Muslims), he was given the choice between Islam and death. Shabbetai became an apostate, the "False Messiah"; even so, many years passed before the hopes he had raised were fully abandoned.

Events far removed from Palestine began in the eighteenth and nine-

[8] Although seemingly discriminatory, the ghetto served to insulate the Jew from constant contact with the Gentile and to give him a degree of personal freedom. It also fulfilled the Jewish penchant for settlement in compact masses. See Barbour, *op. cit.,* pp. 18–20.
[9] Polk *et al., op. cit.,* p. 134.

teenth centuries to redirect the energies of scattered Jewish communities towards the ingathering. Most significant of these was the industrial revolution, which offered enterprising Jews an opportunity for vast capitalist expansion, which could be turned through the age-old Talmudic message into humanitarian support of Palestine immigrants. The Rothschilds were the key instrumentalities in this aspect of Zionism (which was still apolitical). Moses Montefiore, one of twelve licensed Jewish brokers in London was another millionaire who became devoted to the cause of Jewish colonization in Palestine. The other "face" of industrialization, however, was blacker. The majority of European Jews, who were small shopkeepers, artisans, and the like, suffered severely from the changeover; this pressed home the need for emigration, encouraged the belief that Jewish life could be reinvigorated by agricultural labor in Palestine, and caused a tightening of the already compact Jewish communities everywhere.

A second and more direct channeling of Zionist urges came via the *Haskalah* ("Enlightenment"). After the third partition of Poland, Jews in Galicia, Germany, and western Russia were exposed increasingly to European liberal ideas; they also began to feel the keen edge of persecution. As a result the more progressive ones pulled away from the tight circle of traditions represented by the rabbis. The members of Haskalah believed that intellectual and social progress within the Jewish community would earn them a happier existence in the various countries where they lived. Their chief spokesman was Moses Mendelssohn, a Polish Jew whose interest lay in secularizing Jewish life, and in breaking down the medievalism which characterized Jewish thought. Others in the movement, however, foresaw the rebirth of Jewry and the Hebrew language and culture in Palestine. The severe pogroms of the 1880's shattered the hopes of the Enlighteners, but produced for a time a general desire for migration, rather than a specific concentration on Palestine.[10]

A third event, the pogroms mentioned above, was probably the catalytic agent in politicizing Zionism. The emancipative views of Czar Alexander II of Russia, from whom Jews had expected a happier place in the Russian social sun, were abruptly terminated by his assassination in 1881. Jews were connected, rightly or wrongly, with the assassination, and the two decades of persecution that followed surpassed anything endured by the race until the arrival of Hitler, in large part because the

[10] *Ibid.*, pp. 141–142.

terror seemed to be organized by the Russian government iself.[11] Deprived of even the basic rights of Russian serfs, the Jews of Russia fled, where possible, or followed the advice of Dr. Leon Pinsker, of Odessa, who urged the reconstitution of his people as a nation, self-emancipated, but not necessarily required to return to Palestine, rather to locate a land of its own.[12] Other Jews did not fully accept Pinsker's views, and they formed a number of groups called *Hoveve Zion* to advance the cause of Palestine settlement. A prominent Jewish journalist, Asher Ginsberg (Ahad Ha'am) took issue with both Pinsker and the Palestine Zionists, and attracted numerous followers. In an article published in 1889, *"Lo zeh ha-derech"* ("This is not the way") he wrote that Palestine's sole value to the Jewish cause was as a center of Judaism; it was not and could never be a political entity. By establishing in Palestine nothing more than a living Hebrew tradition and a Jewish national culture molded by Judaism, the Jews could achieve best the goals held throughout the Diaspora.

HERZL AND POLITICAL ZIONISM

These conflicting pressures within Zionism and the Jewish people themselves were resolved in the 1890's largely, if impermanently, by the work of another Jewish writer, and one who more than any other person converted emotional, idealistic Zionism into a political movement. This man was Theodor Herzl. Even those Jews who had gone to Palestine to found agricultural colonies were motivated by the idealistic dreams urged by Pinsker and Ha'am. Herzl mined a different clay. A nonpracticing, assimilated Jew himself, he became seriously concerned over the misfortunes of other, more serious Jews, and because of his profession undertook a polemical search for a way to rid them of the shame of belonging to a homeless race.[13] Herzl was a Hungarian Jew who spent most of his life in Vienna, where he wrote for the *Neue Freie Presse*. As a correspondent in Paris during the Dreyfus case, he was shocked by the evidence of anti-Semitism in a supposedly liberal state. In 1896 he published a pamphlet, *Der Judenstaat* (*The Jewish State*), in which he set out his theories. He believed that the only solution to anti-Semitism and the Jewish problem was the establishment of a territory of their own,

---

[11] See Greenberg, L., *The Jews in Russia*, New Haven, Yale University Press, 1951, Vol. II, pp. 21 ff.
[12] Pinsker, Leon, *Auto-Emancipation*, p. 35; quoted in Barbour, *op. cit.*, p. 37.
[13] His first solution, ironically, was the conversion of all Jews to Christianity!

a sovereign Jewish national state. He advocated either Argentina or Palestine as the site of this state and proposed that it be large enough to handle large-scale immigration of Jews under a Colonization Agency created with British help for that purpose. It should be noted that Herzl's approach to Zionism was purely secular, being an interest in eliminating anti-Semitism rather than restoring the Jews to their Promised Land in Palestine.[14] In 1897 Herzl and others convened the first Zionist Congress in Basle, Switzerland. Having realized the force of Jewish sentiment towards Palestine as the center of national aspirations, he set out "to lay the foundation stone which is to shelter the Jewish nation."[15] The Basle Congress enunciated six basic principles, which with certain modifications became the foundation stones of political Zionism. They were:

(1) The Jews have an historic right to Palestine.
(2) Palestine is the only suitable land for them.
(3) Jews must remain loyal everywhere to the goal of the return to Palestine.
(4) The homelessness of the Jews denies them a fundamental human right.
(5) Large-scale Jewish immigration into Palestine is perfectly possible on economic grounds.
(6) The previous work of Jewish colonies already established in Palestine proves the Jewish national right to a home there.

The congress ended with the announcement that Zionism's goal henceforth would be to work for a Jewish home (*Heimstatte*, "homestead") in Palestine secured by public law.[16] Herzl believed this could be done by promoting the establishment of colonies of agricultural and industrial workers in Palestine backed by the organized consciousness of the Jewish people. He also hoped that government consent could be obtained to sanction the undertaking. In this he was to be disappointed. He approached Sultan Abdul-Hamid II, proposing that Jews could help the Ottoman Empire with financial reforms in return for having an autonomous republic within the Ottoman dominions in Palestine. More

[14] Taylor, Alan, *Prelude to Israel,* New York: Philosophical Library, Inc., 1959, pp. 3–4.
[15] Esco Foundation for Palestine, *Palestine, a Study of Jewish, Arab, and British Policies,* New Haven: Yale University Press, 1947, Vol. I, p. 39.
[16] For the text see Hurewitz, J. C., *Diplomacy in the Near and Middle East,* Princeton; D. Van Nostrand Co., Inc., 1956, Vol. I, p. 209.

specifically, he asked for unrestricted Jewish immigration. The Sultan would not agree to this, although he foresaw certain advantages to him in Jewish colonization. These negotiations dragged on for a number of years, but were finally dropped. Thus, political Zionism proceeded toward its goal without legal or official sanction, just as the modern state of Israel was established in its present form, without the formal, legal consent of the controlling government.

Herzl died in 1904, and after his death the "practical Zionists," those influenced by the Hoveve Zion societies, and insistent on Palestine or nothing as a national home, won control of the movement over those who desired merely a solution to the homelessness of the Jews by settlement in any agreed-on place under some form of international sanction.[17] The practicalists, abandoning the Sultan as a lost cause, found their most effective supporters in Britain, where a small group of Jews had become influential all out of proportion to their numbers, and where the British sense of fair play, the strong Judeo-Christian heritage, operated in favor of such minority groups with special emotional issues to promote. At the seventh Zionist Congress (1905), a resolution was passed associating the movement exclusively with Palestine.

In Palestine itself, those various maneuvers within Zionism, and the shift from idealism to politics, caused relatively little stir. Small numbers of Jews had drifted back to the Holy Land throughout Diaspora history, to retire or die in peaceful contemplation of their spiritual achievements. But generally speaking, the prospects for a comfortable life there were bleak and discouraging. Furthermore, the population was almost entirely Muslim or Christian, with the former dominant for eleven centuries. The basis of the small Jewish colony was agricultural; by concentrating on farming and setting up compact living units, the Jews were able to avoid trouble with the Muslim authorities. The favored treatment afforded Jews under the Ottoman Empire (chiefly in preference to Greek and Armenian Christians) helped keep alive these Jewish ties with Palestine.

To a large extent, the gradual expansion of Jewish colonization of Palestine in the nineteenth century created a national entity there, or at least the nucleus of one, where none had existed before. As mentioned, Palestine proper is merely an extension of Syria; the regular imposition of external controls—Roman, Persian, Byzantine, Islamic—in its his-

---

[17] The practicalists had shown their strength in 1903 when they forced Herzl to turn down a British offer, through Colonial Secretary Joseph Chamberlain, of an autonomous Jewish state in Uganda, East Africa.

tory prohibited the growth of a national consciousness among the Muslim and Christian Arab peasants who lived there. Their emotional attachment was to family, village, and district, in that order; their administrative commitments were to the Ottoman Empire and its instruments.[18]

Only the Jews came with a ready-made concept of nationhood. Partly due to this national disinterest, in part from the indifference of the Ottoman rulers, small Jewish colonies took root from the 1830's on. By 1880 there were about 25,000 Jews in Palestine, mostly Sephardim (Spanish Jews expelled after the Christian reconquest of Spain). The contributions of wealthy Jews such as Baron Rothschild helped keep these alive.[19] Between 1880 and 1914, forty to sixty additional agricultural colonies were established comprising 12,000 farmers. By 1914, of a total population of roughly 700,000, there were 80–90,000 Jews in Palestine.[20]

Zionist leaders struck a responsive chord when they turned to England for support. In the nineteenth century (perhaps under Victoria's influence) British officialdom became obsessed with the notion of the return of the Jews to their Palestine homeland under British patronage. It was almost a mystical idea, that God had ordained Britain as the chosen instrument for the ingathering of the exiled Jews. Even George Eliot, in *Daniel Deronda,* described her vision of "a new Judea, poised between East and West, to be a covenant of reconciliation." [21] Admittedly, Palestine had certain strategic advantages for Britain's imperial policy, but the success of Zionist leaders in Britain was expedited by the curious obsession to be protector of Jewry.

The First World War handed Zionism a new opportunity for political action. Chaim Weizmann, a Jewish chemist who had moved to England from Russia, took the lead in establishing rapport with British leaders. A number of influential non-Jews were converted to Weizmann's Zionist viewpoint while the British government itself, owing to his services in developing a cheap method of explosives production, worked on its al-

---

[18] Polk *et al., op. cit.,* p. 232.

[19] Cf. Sacher, *op. cit.,* p. 2, who states that . . . "the service he rendered was beyond price but his system of control was dictatorial and bureaucratic. Philanthropy, however generous, was not the formula for a democratic Jewish state."

[20] These figures are approximate since no census was taken until 1922, and estimates vary according to the source consulted.

[21] Bentwich, Norman, *England In Palestine,* London; Kegan, Paul, 1932, pp. 8–11. For another example of the impact of the Judeo-Zionist appeal on Englishmen, see Sykes, Christopher, *Orde Wingate,* Cleveland: World Publishing Co., 1959.

lies towards obtaining a major commitment to the cause of a Jewish homeland. Weizmann won the sympathy of Lloyd George and Herbert Samuel. C. P. Scott, editor of the *Manchester Guardian,* and his chief editorial writer, Herbert Sidebotham, became attached to the cause; they used the *Guardian* to popularize the erroneous notion that a Jewish state in Palestine would be of strategic value to Britain. As early as 1914, Weizmann was assuming that Palestine would become a British dependency (i.e., mandate) after the war; he took the line that the mandate would, after sufficient immigration, end in a free Jewish state which would continue to serve British interests in the Middle East.[22]

The key convert to Zionism made by Dr. Weizmann was Arthur James Balfour. Balfour had met, and been conquered by, the goateed Jewish scientist some ten years before the war. When Balfour became foreign secretary (December, 1916) the Zionists became extremely optimistic. With both Balfour and Lloyd George in the Cabinet, recognition of their goals was only a matter of time. Furthermore, the support of American Jewry had become more definite with America's entry into the war. Not only President Wilson, but many national leaders were convinced either by such prominent Jews as Justice Brandeis, or by active Zionist agents, of the value of a Jewish home in Palestine.[23]

Mark Sykes, Assistant Secretary to the War Cabinet for Near Eastern Affairs, and co-author of the Sykes-Picot Agreement, was chosen to carry on negotiations with the Zionists; the idea was to win a commitment from world Jewry to the Allied cause, in return for some generalized recognition of Jewish national aspirations. The Zionists sought an unequivocal statement of British recognition of the Jewish right to a national home (which was now grown to the dimensions of a national state) in Palestine. This they were not to receive, although it has become *de rigueur* for them to allude to an ambiguous document of 1917 as carte blanche for a Jewish state in Palestine.

On November 2, 1917, the British Cabinet finally released the document referred to above, the culmination of months of private discussions and a schism between Jews in England, many of whom, including Montefiore, felt strongly that a Jewish state in Palestine would inject politics into the divinely ordained system of holding fast to Judaism while be-

---

[22] See Taylor, *op. cit.,* pp. 12–15, for the diplomatic background.
[23] Cf. Lenczowski, George, *The Middle East in World Affairs,* 2nd Edition, Ithaca: Cornell University Press, 1956, pp. 78–82. These men included William Jennings Bryan, Josephus Daniels, Newton Baker, Col. Edwin House, and others.

coming assimilated into the surrounding culture. The Balfour Declaration suggests this split; it also hints at the British desire not to frighten the Arabs, British determination to please all sides, and a pious hope that such a statement would attract additional support from allies but never be taken literally by its recipients. It was couched in the form of a letter from Balfour to Lord Rothschild as "an expression of sympathy with Jewish Zionist aspirations," and read as follows:

". . . His Majesty's Government view with favor the establishment in Palestine of a national home for the Jewish people, and will use their best endeavors to facilitate the achievement of this object, it being clearly understood that nothing shall be done which may prejudice the civil and religious rights of existing non-Jewish communities in Palestine, or the rights and political status enjoyed by Jews in any other country."

Obviously the Balfour Declaration commits no one, least of all Britain, to a firm course of action towards Palestine, as far as its text is concerned. Generally speaking it recognizes no more than an historic Jewish right, a permanent Arab right, and the need for an improvement in the economic situation of the Palestine peasantry. But the Zionist Organization, with the skill at drawing firm conclusions out of generalized assumptions which has become a hallmark of its operations, publicized the Declaration widely to assure Jews that after two thousand years their prayers had been answered. No such publicity was given it in Palestine, where the people were kept unaware of it by military censorship until 1919, when it was read publicly in Nablus. But then, it was not directed at them anyway; rather it was part of Britain's war strategy, being not even aimed at English Jews, but through them.[24]

The interests of Weizmann and his cohorts coincided neatly with Britain's plans for a Middle-Eastern settlement after the war; thus the Zionist voice resounded louder in the war councils than the voice of those (Jews included) who said there was not, and should not be, any connection between the ideal commonwealth of Israel and a Jewish political state in Palestine. These were the Cassandras; with what seems in retrospect unbridled optimism, the various Allied governments endorsed the Balfour Declaration, and it was written into the Palestine Mandate.[25]

[24] Polk *et al., op. cit.,* p. 63.
[25] The Declaration was approved by France, Italy, the U.S., the Vatican, and Japan. Andrews, Fannie Fern, *The Holy Land Under Mandate,* 2 vols., Boston: Houghton-Mifflin Company, 1931, I, pp. 341–342.

WORLD WAR I AND THE BRITISH MANDATE

The fact that Palestine's future was settled without consulting its people was nothing new. The new element injected into its national history, however, was the organized attempt of an outside group, represented only as a minority, to dislodge the permanent population. The Zionists either failed to see the problem of Palestine in this light or simply dismissed it. The historic right of Jews to a Palestine homeland, they felt, would exercise a sort of automatic readjustment when colonization began in earnest.[26]

A joint Anglo-Arab army under General Allenby, which had a Zion Mule Corps composed of Jewish refugees and some European and American Zionists as one of its auxiliary units, prosecuted the war against the Turks successfully in Palestine. Six centuries of Ottoman rule had more or less insulated the territory from war or foreign invasion, but not from the economic distress caused by Ottoman maladministration and the system of control exercised through local officials. These were at least known and familiar figures; the Palestine farmer had learned, over the centuries, how to cope with them. The attitude of the Ottoman central government was less understood; it found expression mainly in conscription and increased (or unexpected) tax levies. In consequence, the people of Palestine, largely Arabic-speaking Muslims with a large Christian minority and a few non-Zionist Jewish colonies, clung tenaciously to their land. The war brought much tighter Turkish control. Djemal Pasha's arrival in Syria and the Arab Revolt impelled the Turks to act against the Arab populations of both Syria and Palestine, since these were suspected of sympathy if not outright collaboration. The British capture of Jerusalem seemed to herald a new era for Palestine, particularly as Britain appeared to encourage awakening Arab ambitions for a national state, including Palestine.

In 1917–1918 Palestine was placed under a British military government called OETA (Occupied Enemy Territory Administration). OETA felt itself obliged to clarify its own position vis-a-vis the conflicting claims on the territory. Accordingly Allenby issued a proclamation delegating authority to Amir Faisal, as the Arab leader, and notifying him that no changes would be made in Palestine's status or socioeconomic structure pending the peace settlement.[27] During OETA's tenure, how-

---

[26] Weizmann, for example, contradicted his own statements toward the Arabs when he thought of them, which was not often. Taylor, *op. cit.*, p. 117, n. 3.
[27] The text is in Luke, Harry, *Handbook of Palestine and Transjordan,* London: Macmillan, 1930, p. 28.

ever, about 5,000 Jewish immigrants were allowed in, and Hebrew was adopted as one of the official languages. Both Zionists and Arabs sent delegations to the Peace Conference; the Zionists concentrated more narrowly, seeking a formula under which the "promise" of the Balfour Declaration could be carried out, while the Arab delegation sought recognition of an independent Arab state in Syria (including Palestine). The Zionists were more realistic, and their program was better understood abroad than the inchoate, mystical yearning of the Arabs for independence. Although the Peace Settlement did not give Zionism carte blanche, it was clearly established as a stage in the evolution of Herzl's principles of twenty years before.

The British Mandate was instituted formally in 1922, although OETA had installed Sir Herbert Samuel as first High Commissioner, without particular regard for legality, some years earlier. Still earlier, in 1919, Faisal agreed to sign a joint statement with Weizmann accepting the principle of increased Jewish immigration into Palestine in return for full protection of existing Arab rights and mutual cooperation for economic development, and an understanding that Arab aspirations for independence would be recognized.

This was not to be, of course, and Faisal shortly found himself heaved out of Damascus by rough French hands. Lacking an effective leader or central organization, the "existing non-Jewish communities of Palestine" could not act, only react, in response to events.[28] The Arabs of Palestine rioted in 1920, and again in 1921, against the transparency of Zionist ambitions and British support for them. The terms of the mandate whittled down the area of Palestine as defined in the Balfour Declaration by excluding Transjordan and confirmed Arab civil and religious rights. The King-Crane Report, which had recommended, on the basis of field observations, that the Palestine population preferred to be part of a unitary Syrian State and greatly distrusted Zionism, was ignored.

The British Mandate in Palestine (1922–1948) remains a melancholy story, regardless of the material improvements made there. The first six years, however, were a period of relative calm. The so-called Churchill White Paper (1922), modifying the Balfour Declaration, did not set

---

[28] See Polk *et al., op. cit.,* pp. 109–110, for reproduction of the report of Sir Louis Bols, Allenby's successor, vividly displaying the problems imposed on the people of Palestine by the Balfour Declaration and British acceptance of Zionist aims. Bols points out that the OETA pledge to maintain the status quo in Palestine was consistently violated from 1919 on by Zionist activities. Like the later King-Crane report, Bols' report was buried in the files.

Arab fears that Palestine would become "as Jewish as England is English" entirely at rest, but at least it defined Zionist aims in terms of economic absorptive capacity. The White Paper also enabled supporters of the Mandate to push it through Parliament, while Weizmann realistically took what he could get.[29] While Sir Herbert Samuel was High Commissioner (1922–1925) both Arabs and Jews were given opportunity to participate in governmental reforms and to have a say in regulating the local affairs of their separate communities. A Jewish agency, thus, was established to implement Jewish immigration into the *Heimstatte*. Samuel attempted to set up an Advisory Council, composed of Arabs and Jews elected by proportional representation, but this foundered on Arab anti-Zionist intransigence. Nevertheless, Samuel, like his successors, employed some pro-Arab advisers in his administration and inaugurated the program of parallel, bi-racial, social progress which, though it did not solve the problems of Palestine in political terms, at least bequeathed a comparatively high standard of living to the Arabs under the Mandate.

The Palestine Mandate, after formal notification by the League of Nations in 1923, was managed in the style of a British Crown Colony. The High Commissioner was also commander-in-chief of defense forces and enjoyed extensive powers both legislative and executive. British officialdom formed the mandatory government down to the district commissioner level. Because of this absence of indigenous representation, the mandatory government "was at its best benevolent and at its worst autocratic."[30] The terms of the Mandate[31] were largely slanted in favor of recognition of a Jewish national home and the means required to achieve this. In addition to specific reference to a Jewish Agency, and the Jewish National Home, Jewish immigration and close settlement on the land were to be facilitated, subject to the rights and position of the non-Jewish population (Article VI). This meager protection of the Arabs was negated by the Churchill White Paper with its principle of the economic absorption capacity of Palestine. Through the 1920's the two communities developed side by side under the Mandate, with underlying frictions but no serious outbreaks of communal violence. Over-all

[29] Hanna, Paul L., *British Policy in Palestine,* Washington: American Council on Public Affairs, 1942, p. 82. The text is in Hurewitz, *op. cit.,* II, pp. 103–106.
[30] Hurewitz, J. C., *The Struggle for Palestine,* New York: W. W. Norton & Company, 1950, p. 24.
[31] The full text may be found in the Royal Institute of International Affairs, *Great Britain and Palestine,* London, RIIA, 1946, p. 151; significant articles in Sacher, *op. cit.,* pp. 7, 8, and Barbour, *op. cit.,* pp. 116–118.

there was considerable progress under the Mandate. The fiscal system was stabilized; roads, schools, and hospitals were built. The legal system was modernized. The complex system of land tenure inherited from the Ottoman period was simplified and an effort made to ensure proper registry as well as some control over the land purchases.[32] But the political clouds created by Balfour and the Zionists were not easily dispelled. In the shaping of communal strife the Jews held most of the advantages. The Jewish Agency, led by Weizmann, had a standing executive committee in Palestine; its chief was none other than David Ben Gurion. The Agency could select candidates for immigration; the Jewish National Fund, which is controlled, bought land in Palestine, largely from absentee owners, for Jewish settlers. Of more specific value in promoting Jewish interests was the *Yishuv* (Palestine community). The arriving immigrants were rapidly absorbed into a national community, dedicated to management of its own affairs. The strong communalism of spirit and organization, which has become a feature of Diaspora Jewry over the centuries, was now wedded to Zionist aspirations, although the community itself remained an entity distinct from the National Home until 1948. In 1927 formal regulations for the Community were set up by the Mandate. Persons over twenty, with three months residence were allowed to vote for an Elected Assembly. This Assembly in turn nominated a Council (*Vaad Leumi*) which administered the social and religious affairs of the Community. The initial emphasis of Palestine Jewry on religious fundamentalism and selfless labor for Zion gave way slowly to political education towards eventual self-government with over-all planning in the hands of the Zionist Organization. The Arab community in Palestine was organized differently; it had little basic unity. On the one side were the large land-owning families, some having an ancient lineage; on the other was an inarticulate, exploited peasantry. In between these classes, as an aftermath of the war, was an expanding mercantile and professional class. Religious differences also divided the Arabs; a large minority were Christians or Druzes, for example. The Mandate permitted the formation of a Supreme Muslim Council to administer the affairs of that *Millet,* and this Council became by default the spokesman for all the "existing non-Jewish communities," although

[32] From the nineteenth-century ban on foreigners owning land in Palestine, to the departure of the Turkish forces after the war with all the land-records, the land ownership system became a complete maze. Polk *et al., op. cit.,* pp. 232–237, discuss the land question and the semi-mystical feeling of the Arabs for their land, in some detail.

in practice its representation aided only the Muslims. Haj Muhammad Amin al-Husayni, previously named Mufti of Jerusalem under the Mandate, was named President of this Council, and the limited extent of organized Arab action was due in large measure to his efforts. The Mufti was a politician rather than a statesman, however, and he lacked the means to compete with the Zionist Organization for world opinion. Also the most powerful families among the gentry class (called *effendis*), the Husaynis, the Nashashibis, the Dajanis, the Khalidis, and the Abd al-Hadis, were bitterly jealous of each others' positions in internal Palestine politics. Friction between the Husaynis and the Nashashibis, for example, made them oppose each other with such bitterness during the 1925–1929 period that animosity towards the Jews was practically forgotten.[33]

The flood of Jewish immigration dreaded by the Arabs when the contents of the Balfour Declaration were known did not materialize immediately, and this helped stabilize Palestinian attitudes during the first decade of the Mandate. Immigration increased gradually from 5,500 in 1920 to 34,000 in 1925; then it dropped to 13,000 in 1926 and to 2,713 in 1927, an indication of declining economic conditions in Europe and the deliberate policy of Lord Plumer, who succeeded Samuel as High Commissioner. The Arab birth rate also exceeded the Jewish rate, so that although the Arab absolute majority declined slightly with continued Jewish immigration, Arab numbers rose steadily.

The net gain of some 60,000 Jews by 1929 seriously disturbed the Arab leaders, although they could develop no unified means of meeting this expanding threat. Typically, the first serious reaction of the Arabs in nearly a decade to Jewish pushing into Palestine came spontaneously through religion in the Wailing Wall incident. The Wailing Wall in Jerusalem is the holiest shrine of Judaism, being part of the outer wall enclosing the site of the Temple. It is also the western wall of the Aqsa Mosque in the *Haram ash-Sharif* (Dome of the Rock), sacrosanct to Muslims as the spot whence Muhammad ascended into heaven and held converse with God. Always fearful of their rights under unremitting pressure, the Arabs were incensed by reports that the Zionist Organization intended to buy the shrine from the government. In August, 1929, Jews organized a demonstration at the Wailing Wall, where the Zionist

[33] Hurewitz, J. C., ESCO Foundation, *Palestine, a Study of Jewish, Arab, and British Policies,* New Haven: Yale University Press, 1947, pp. 500–516, discusses the social distinctions in the Arab community in some detail.

flag was raised and the Zionist anthem sung. This act, climaxing a series of communal disagreements over repairs and ritual procedure, enraged the Arabs. Riots broke out all over Palestine; when British troops finally restored order, the casualties numbered nearly 500 Jews and half as many Arabs. The Shaw Commission was appointed by the Crown to investigate the Palestine troubles. It concluded, like its predecessor in 1921, that "the Arabs have come to see in the Jewish immigrant not only a menace to their livelihood, but a possible overlord of the future . . . and the results of Jewish enterprise and penetration have been such as to confirm that they will be excluded from the Soil." [34]

From Conflict to Partition, 1930–1947

The irreconcilable interests of Zionists and Arabs, and the inability of the mandatory government to take any effective measures toward a lasting solution, became apparent in the 1930's. When Jewish immigration was stopped, to placate the Arabs and further the creation of a biracial Palestine legislature, the Zionist Organization marshalled the effective guns of international opinion and accused Britain of reneging on the Balfour "commitment." When immigration was resumed, the Arabs boycotted government programs, went on strike, and engaged increasingly in anti-Jewish violence. Unwilling (or unable) to abandon fully its position with respect to either community, Britain was forced steadily into a dilemma without a solution by holding onto the Mandate.

From 1931 to 1936 the Zionist program in Palestine achieved success beyond its expectations. A White Paper issued in 1930 placing a ban on immigration was subsequently revoked due to an effective Zionist propaganda campaign in Britain. Prime Minister MacDonald appointed Sir Arthur Wauchope High Commissioner after Weizmann signified that he would be acceptable to the Jews. Anti-Semitism in Europe after 1933 assured the Jewish Agency of a steady supply of immigrants, and Levantine shipowners were not averse to smuggling Jews into Palestine, as long as they had the price. Immigration rose sharply in 1931–36 to a total of 175,000, slightly more than double the total Jewish population in 1931. In 1933–34 72,500 arrived, and in 1935 alone 61,854 plus 25,000 illegal immigrants entered. The total population of Palestine was estimated at 1,336,518 in 1936; 370,483 or 27.7 per cent were Jews. It

---

[34] Cmd 3530, *Commission on the Palestine Disturbances of August, 1929,* London, HMSO, 1930, p. 150.

became apparent to the Arabs that this rate of entry, if maintained, would mean a Jewish majority in the 1940's.

The relatively streamlined organizational structure of the National Home, through the WZO, the Jewish National Fund (Keren Kaye-meth), and the Palestine Executive Committee, has already been com-mented on. The Jews of Palestine took advantage of the Mandate to progress in other ways as well. The original Zionist goal had been a re-generation of the Jewish nation through agricultural labor, with the de-velopment of Palestine following as a natural consequence. Jews were encouraged to settle in cooperative agrarian communities. There were three types of these collective settlements, the *kibbutz,* the *kvutza,* and the *moshav ovdim.* The *kvutza,* the oldest type, was organized along communistic lines, with exclusive membership; its highest purpose was "to create the possibility of becoming masters of our own life and estab-lish a form of life based on economic and social equality between the Members." [35] The *moshav ovdim* (worker's settlement), run along looser lines, permitted private ownership of property and even some ac-cumulation of private capital. The *kibbutz* were almost identical to the *kvutza.*[36] All the collective settlements were dedicated to the concept of labor (*Hapoel Hatzair*); their land was leased from the Jewish National Fund, with the consequent advantages of group action, while their com-munal nature gave them the basic unity which was to prepare them for frontier defense in self-contained units when war returned to Pales-tine. Due to the hardships of life there, the immigrants who came were almost entirely young and vigorous men and women; release from Eu-rope's ghettos meant a chance for bold, aggressive behavior, which would free the Jews from tradition as well as alien bondage. Lastly, political action developed rather quickly through economic as well as semipoliti-cal organizations. Most prominent under the Mandate was the *Histadrut* (General Federation of Jewish Labor), founded in 1920 by some 4,400 farmer-workers. By 1936 this had grown to 87,000 members, with an-other 16,000 enrolled in associated confederations. Histadrut thus em-braced 90 per cent of the Jewish labor force, operated some 770 coopera-tive settlements, and was the largest single employer in Palestine.[37] The

[35] Quoted in ESCO, *op. cit.,* I, p. 355.
[36] See Spiro, Melford, *Kibbutz: Venture in Utopia,* Cambridge: Harvard University Press, 1956.
[37] Hurewitz, *op. cit.,* p. 31. Histadrut also ran schools, newspapers, and the Jewish National Health Service (Kupat Halim). Membership was restricted to male and female workers over eighteen.

Palestine Jews were of course very limited in the scope of political action they could undertake by one operation of the Mandate. Nevertheless, the *Yishuv* went ahead with political parties. Three major political groups were formed; the Zionists and affiliates, the Revisionists, and *Agudath Israel*, a purely religious body. The Zionists were further divided into seven parties (after 1942): *Mapai* (Socialist Labor), the largest; *Hashomer Hatzair*, a leftwing group favoring a bi-national state; *Poale Zion* (leftwing), the General Zionists, representing professional and middle-class people; *Aliya Hadasha* (1942: New Immigrants Party) of settlers from central Europe; and the *Ihud* (Union), a university and intellectual party led by Dr. Judah Magnes, which aimed for a bi-national state with the Arabs dominant. In 1935, Vladimir Jabotinsky, a former member of the Zionist Executive who had previously (in 1925) formed the World Union of Revisionist Zionists to carry on militant Zionism, formed the New Zionist Organization. The Palestine branch of the NZO took the name "Revisionists"; they accused the Zionists of timidity and urged the population of Greater Palestine (Eretz Israel, which includes Transjordan, the Hauran in Syria, and southern Lebanon) with up to 18 million Jews, half of whom would be young pioneers transported free in return for national service.

The problem of land ownership, which disturbed the Arabs even more than the tide of immigration, became acute in the 1930's. In fairness to the immigrants, it should be noted that much of the land sold by Arabs to individual Jews or to the Jewish National Fund was submarginal, or waste land; the collective energy and intelligence of the new settlers, however, turned it into productive land in the same manner as the French pioneers in Algeria in the nineteenth century.

Between 1919 and 1936 the Jews invested over $400 million in the Palestinian economy. This represented, then as today in Israel, the pump-priming of Diaspora Jews. About $75 million of it was taken up in land purchases, while payments for services and produce by Jews to Arabs reached a peak of $13,750,000 in 1935. The extensively practiced Arab system of absentee landholding worked in favor of the Jews; Arab landowners sold large tracts of land to the Jewish National Fund at inflated prices, while the Arab tenant families, unwilling to accept a Jewish landlord, moved away, usually to the towns to create a minor urban problem.[38] Palestine's relative scarcity of natural resources compounded

[38] Sakran, Frank, *Palestine Dilemma,* Washington: Public Affairs Press, 1948, p. 118.

the sensitivity of Arab farmers to the contemplated loss of their land through Jewish immigration and purchase. As one author writes: "the implication of a Jewish National Home in Palestine is a thorough-going reorganization of the internal relations of a semifeudal Arab society. . . . The Jew brings with him Western ideas, often Western socialist ideas, which cut right across a traditionally historical pattern, the beneficiaries of which seek at any cost to defend their claims." [39] The relative fragmentation of Arab landholding in 1936—only 27 per cent of holdings were more than 250 acres—increased the almost mystical concern of the average Arab farmer for his plot of ground.

These accumulated pressures reached the saturation point in 1936. For the next three years the Arabs of Palestine were in a state varying from open rebellion against the mandatory government to sporadic attacks on the Jews. The five major semipolitical Arab groupings of the leading families, in 1936, formed the Arab Higher Committee, led by the Mufti but with the influence of Raghid Bey Nashashibi, Mayor of Jerusalem, clearly discernible. The committee called a strike of all Palestine Arabs to protest Britain's policy of continued immigration and land sales to Jews. The Arabs boycotted Jewish goods, while bands of Arab guerrillas including volunteers from Syria and Lebanon made attacks on Jewish settlements and factories, with considerable success. Eventually, Britain moved a division of troops into Palestine; the withdrawal of support from neighboring Arab rulers (who were not then anxious to stir up too much anti-Semitism in their countries) forced the Higher Committee to call off the strike.

The next dreary round of commission hearings in Palestine was followed by a report which never attacked the problem of Arab-Jewish relations from the heart, but instead admitted the irreconcilability of their views and recommended that the same half-hearted measures be continued. The Royal Commission (1936), headed by Lord Peel, was the first to propose a partition plan. The Higher Arab Committee at first refused to cooperate with the commission, but later agreed to at the request of other Arab rulers.[40] The Commission concluded in its report that the Mandate was unworkable in its present form. The conflict was inherent in the situation from the outset. The terms of the Mandate tend to con-

---

[39] Quoted in Polk *et al.*, *op. cit.*, p. 326, n. 8.
[40] The British Government not only refused to suspend Jewish immigration temporarily, during the commission's investigation, but published an expanded list of permits.

firm it. . . . In the earlier period, hostility to the Jews was not widespread among the *fellahin*. It is now general. . . ."[41]

The commission recommended division of Palestine into a small Jewish state, a large Arab state, and an international enclave around Jerusalem. Self-rule was to be recognized in each state (but not the Jerusalem enclave). Recognizing Arab fears and grievances toward the externally imposed Jewish National Home which haunted them, the report recommended a limit to Jewish immigration of 12,000 a year for five years, to be fixed thereafter by the economic capacity of their state (whatever that meant). The Commission hoped that Arab independence plus the removal of the unrestricted Jewish immigration threat and the National Home would bring about Arab acceptance, while moderate Zionists would be satisfied with a guaranteed, if shrunken, country of their own.

Leadership in both the Zionist movement and the Arab community split initially over the proposal, with some members willing to accept it guardedly, others rejecting it out of hand. Realization that partition would block Arab hopes of uniting Palestine with other Arab states, and require wholesale transfers of population if 250,000 Arabs were not to find permanent subjection in the Jewish state, caused the Arab Higher Committee to reject it finally. The Zionist Congress tabled the proposal by authorizing its Executive to negotiate with the mandatory government for a definite Jewish state.

Another British Commission, the Woodhead, arrived in Palestine in 1938 to study the possibilities of partition. The atmosphere was gloomy. Previously, Arab terrorists had murdered a British official in Galilee, and the Government had outlawed the Arab Higher Committee, ordering its leaders arrested and deported. The Mufti himself escaped to Syria. Although its leaders were scattered or under detention, the Arab community had finally become united, and the Woodhead Commission found no one willing to listen. The Arab position, as outlined by the Higher Committee before its dissolution, did not deviate from the following points:

(1) The recognition of the right of the Arabs to complete independence in their own land.

(2) The end of the Jewish National Home.

(3) The end of the Mandate and its replacement by a treaty of

---

[41] Cmd 5479, Palestine: *Royal Commission's Report*, 1937.

close alliance similar to the one with Iraq, making Palestine a sovereign state.

(4) Pending such a treaty, the complete stoppage of Jewish immigration and land sales.[42]

The Woodhead Commission recommended three possible partition plans, which differed from each other mainly in the extent of territory retained by the mandatory government and the compactness of the Arab state.[43] Having authorized the partition proposals, the British government then dropped them as quickly as possible and instead called a conference in London in 1939 for Arab and Zionist representatives. Delegates from the existing Arab states also attended.[44] The Palestine Arabs were represented by Raghib Bey Nashashibi, by other moderates, and by certain ex-members of the Higher Committee, but not the Mufti. The Jewish delegation was headed by Weizmann. The inclusion of delegates from the then independent Arab states—Egypt, Iraq, Saudi Arabia, Yemen—impelled the Palestine problem into international politics, where it has remained ever since. Because of the transparent danger of Italo-German militarism and the surge of anti-Semitism in Germany, the British were anxious to achieve an agreement. If nothing else, this would forestall German backing of the Arab cause and consequent penetration into the Middle East.

Agreement on anything was doomed to fail, however; Jews and Arabs refused to budge from their separate positions. When the conference disbanded, the British published a White Paper which laid down new principles. It proposed that Palestine become an independent state within ten years, with its own constitution and legislature. Arabs and Jews would cooperate and would participate in the government in the proper proportions. Jewish immigration would be limited to 75,000 for the next five years after which it would cease unless allowed to continue by Arab consent. Land transfers (i.e., sales) were to be strictly controlled by the High Commissioner, and in a third of Palestine they were to be prohibited.

The White Paper had the effect, among others, of turning the Jewish community in Palestine against the mandatory government; previously its retaliatory efforts had been directed at Arab terrorism. During the

[42] Hurewitz, *op. cit.*, pp. 79–80.
[43] The three plans are reproduced in Polk *et al.*, *op. cit.*, pp. 101–103.
[44] At the Bludan Conference (1937) of Arab leaders, a resolution was unanimously passed naming Palestine as an inseparable part of the Arab homeland.

1930's Arab guerrillas had struck at Jewish settlements and government facilities impartially; in 1938 alone, 5,708 incidents of violence were reported, 2,500 persons were interned and more than a thousand Arab rebels killed by British troops. But the Arab rebellion, although conducted with some skill by guerrilla tacticians such as Fawzi Kawakji, and valuable to the Arab cause by its arousal of public opinion in Britain, never approached in magnitude the Jewish terrorism of 1943–1947. The campaign of Jewish extermination carried on in Europe by the Nazis added a note of desperation to the efforts of the Zionists to provide a haven for immigrants in Palestine. This campaign also gave Zionism an invaluable propaganda weapon, to be used effectively against Britain, for ensuring the deaths of hundreds of thousands of Jews in Europe by its ban on immigration, and to inflame world opinion against the Arabs, whose leaders (notably the Mufti) had opted for Germany. The original sources of the Palestine problem were systematically discounted.

Illegal Jewish immigration put the British to a supreme test during the war years. Prior to the Second World War, the Nazis even collaborated with the Jewish underground at a price, in aiding German Jews to enter Palestine.[45] The desperate methods used by the underground and British measures to seal off Palestine caused many tragedies. The steamer *Patria* was sunk in Haifa harbor with the loss of 202 illegal immigrants in 1940. In 1942 the *Struma,* a converted yacht which was barely seaworthy, sank just outside Istanbul in the Bosphorus, with the loss of 769 Jews. The Zionists made this vessel a *cause célèbre* in their campaign to coerce Britain into lifting the ban on immigration, denigrating the vessel's condition and the prompt action of British rescuers in other cases. Indeed the *Struma* episode provided major fuel for Zionists in America, where the brunt of the campaign shifted in the middle years of the war. American Zionism had always taken a back seat to its British cousin; aside from a 1922 Congressional resolution favoring Palestine as a Jewish National Home, little had been done this side of the Atlantic to implement Herzl's scheme. British intransigence and the sufferings of the Jews in occupied Europe accelerated Zionism in this country. In May, 1942, the American branch of the WZO, meeting at the Hotel Biltmore in New York, adopted the so-called "Biltmore Program" offered to it by David Ben Gurion (who was now head of the Jewish

[45] See Jon Kimche, *The Secret Roads,* London: Secker and Warfield, 1954, Chapter II, *passim.* The Gestapo Central Bureau was designed for this very purpose; its head was Adolf Eichmann.

Agency's executive committee).[46] In brief, the program called for an independent Jewish state, with:

(1) Its own army, flag, and administration.
(2) Cancellation of the 1939 White Paper.
(3) Transfer of immigration control to the Jewish Agency.
(4) Definitive labeling of the Balfour Declaration as a British statement of intent to help form a Jewish commonwealth in Palestine.

The Biltmore Program precipitated a split in Jewish ranks which has not healed to this day. The American Council for Judaism,[47] openly anti-Zionist, was founded to combat the political claims of the WZO to speak for all Jews. Dr. Judah Magnes' *Ihud* also broke with the movement, declaring that Arab-Jewish co-existence was not only possible but also necessary. The Zionists were more supple and aggressive than their rivals, however; in the person of Ben Gurion they had an eloquent Palestinian spokesman for the National Home. American Jewish leaders like Bernard Baruch and Felix Frankfurter lent their names to the cause. President Roosevelt, though refusing to commit himself to public support of the Zionist cause, was privately favorable, while attempts to obtain a joint congressional resolution backing the Biltmore program nearly succeeded. By 1944 then, the Zionists were confident that they had the organization and the support in America sufficient to bring very strong pressure to bear for the establishment of their state, once the war was over.

The terrorist tactics of Jewish groups in Palestine in the latter stages of the war were intensified. The extremist wing of Zionism (the Revisionists), had seceded in 1938 from Haganah, the *sub rosa* Jewish Defense Force, and formed a group known as *Irgun Zvai Leumi* (National Military Organization). It advocated active military operations against both Arab and British. A splinter group from the Irgun, the Stern Gang, under Abraham Stern's leadership, were even more violent. In 1944 terrorists almost assassinated the High Commissioner, Sir Harold MacMichel, while two Stern Gang members killed Lord Moyne, British Minister of State for the Middle East in Cairo. The Moyne murder shocked the Zionists nearly as much as it enraged the British. Haganah

[46] Weizmann and Nahum Goldmann, head of the Administrative Committee of the World Jewish Congress, also addressed the meeting.
[47] For a statement of its origin, growth, and position, see Lenczowski, *op. cit.,* p. 366, n. 79.

disavowed any connection with terrorism, as did Jewish Agency leaders. Yet this act of violence plus innumerable others in 1944–45 focused world attention on Palestine.

It was clear to both Britain and the United States that *something* had to replace the Mandate. But what? In 1946 an Anglo-American committee of inquiry went to Palestine at Britain's request to study the situation. On the previous year President Truman, who as a devout Christian held the commonly accepted American view that the Jews somehow belonged rightfully in Palestine, had injected the issue into American domestic politics, during the New York State election campaign, when he called for immediate admission of 100,000 Jewish refugees. The committee's report, when published, included this 100,000 figure; it also recommended a continuation of the existing Mandate. When the report got no response (except increased Jewish terrorism: the Jewish Agency itself was now implicated in terrorism, as was Haganah, and terrorists blew up the King David Hotel in Jerusalem, in reprisal for mass arrests of Agency personnel), the British offered a compromise plan—two separate provinces with local autonomy, with direct British rule in the Negev and Jerusalem. This plan foundered, as before, on twin shoals; the Arab, that Palestine should be a sovereign Arab state; the Jewish, that it should be a Jewish Commonwealth.

In February, 1947, Britain turned the Palestine problem over to the United Nations. She really had no choice. Official American pronouncements by both party leaders, Truman and Dewey, urging wholesale Jewish immigration, the support for Zionism of many American leaders, the ever-increasing cost of maintaining order in the Mandate, had placed the British in an untenable position. And as Foreign Secretary Ernest Bevin said, "(we) are faced with an irreconcilable conflict of principles. . . . The discussions of the past month have shown that there is no prospect of resolving this conflict by any settlement negotiable between the parties."[48]

PARTITION AND THE CREATION OF ISRAEL

On May 15, 1947, the UN approved a special committee on Palestine (UNSCOP) which was empowered to study the problem and submit proposals for a solution. Eleven disinterested nations[49] were repre-

[48] Quoted in Polk *et al., op. cit.,* pp. 115–116.
[49] Australia, Canada, Czechoslovakia, Guatemala, India, Iran, Netherlands, Peru, Sweden, Uruguay, and Yugoslavia.

sented on the committee. UNSCOP members spent the summer and early autumn in the Middle East, where they learned for themselves the incredible difficulties which had beset the mandate administration.[50] UNSCOP received full cooperation from the Jews, including the Irgun; but the Arab Higher Committee refused even to attend meetings. In November UNSCOP submitted its report, which illustrated in a most forceful way the hazards of agreement on Palestine. While there was general agreement on the speedy termination of the Mandate, two separate proposals were offered as solutions. The plan favored by a majority of members would have partitioned Palestine into two separate states. Under such an arrangement, the Arab state would have 725,000 Arabs and 8,000 to 10,000 Jews; the Jewish state 498,000 Jews and 407,000 Arabs, while the population of Jerusalem would be equally divided between Arabs and Jews.

Three members of the committee, Iran, India, and Yugoslavia, proposed a federal state, with local Arab-Jewish autonomy and a three-year limit on Jewish immigration. They pointed out realistically that partition would accelerate separatism, perhaps breaking up the natural unity of Palestine forever. When the UNSCOP proposals came up for debate, however, there were several surprises, and evidence of excellent Zionist homework. The Jewish Agency accepted the principle of partition as better than nothing; the Arabs rejected it out of hand. Egyptian newspapers predicted that "the Palestine Arabs will launch a relentless war to repel this attack on their country, especially as they know that all the Arab countries will back them, with men, money, and ammunition." [51] The delegate of the USSR, Andrei Gromyko, declared that Russia supported the minority plan. Zionist pressure was brought to bear heavily on the "uncommitted nations," such as Haiti, to support the majority plan. Britain announced that she would not provide forces to impose decisions favorable to either side. On November 29, the UNSCOP majority plan for partition was approved by a vote of 33–13 in the General Assembly, with ten abstentions. All Asian and Middle Eastern nations abstained. No machinery for the enforcement of the resolution was provided. The British government announced that the Mandate would end on May 1, 1948 (later revised to May 15) and that all British forces would be

[50] Graves, R. M., *Experiment in Anarchy*, London: Gollancz, 1949, Chapter IV, *et passim*, is the diary of the chairman of the Jerusalem municipal commission for 1947–48. It contains some lucid observations on the UNSCOP reception.
[51] Kirk, G. E., *The Middle East, 1949–1950*, London, RIIA, 1954, p. 247.

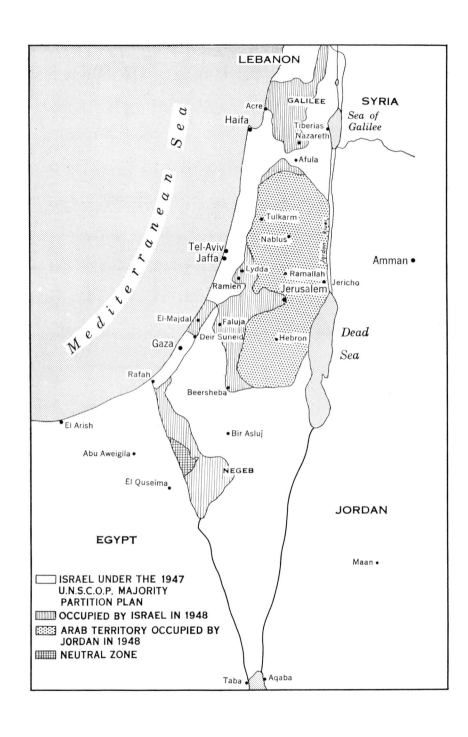

LEBANON

SYRIA

Acre
Haifa
GALILEE
Tiberias
Nazareth
Sea of
Galilee

•Afula

•Tulkarm

Tel-Aviv
Jaffa
Nablus•

Amman •

Lydda
•Ramallah
Ramien
Jericho
Jerusalem

Dead

Sea

El-Majdal
Faluja
Deir Suneid
Gaza •
•Hebron

Rafah

Beersheba

• El Arish
•Bir Asluj

Abu Aweigila •

NEGEB

El Quseima •

JORDAN

EGYPT

Maan •

☐ ISRAEL UNDER THE 1947
U.N.S.C.O.P. MAJORITY
PARTITION PLAN

▨ OCCUPIED BY ISRAEL IN 1948

▨ ARAB TERRITORY OCCUPIED BY
JORDAN IN 1948

▨ NEUTRAL ZONE

Taba • Aqaba

out of Palestine by August. This timetable was never carried out; in fact, the announcement was Britain's last official exercise of mandatory authority. The people of Palestine, the Arabs who had lived there so long, the Jews whose messianic longing had brought them there, at last took the country's fate into their hands, and hammered out, for better or worse, a decision.

The Mandate ended on May 14, 1948. Earlier on the same day, David Ben Gurion announced in Tel Aviv the establishment of the state of Israel. The 1939 White Paper was annulled, and all laws restricting Jewish land purchase or immigration were invalidated. The new state was to be based on liberty, justice and peace, with social and political equality and freedom of conscience. The new state would cooperate with the UN and respect the holy places of other faiths.[52] The United States recognized Israel eleven minutes after Ben Gurion's proclamation; it was, naturally, the first state to do so.[53]

Having declared their independence, the Jews of Palestine fought a short, brutal, and generally successful war to secure it. As British forces withdrew from the various garrison points, evidence of systematic Zionist planning and organization for the great day mounted. The various Jewish military organizations were not unified, but they had a common objective. The Arabs of Palestine, in contrast, were still divided along the traditional family-clan lines which had impeded them in past dealings; their most effective leader, the Mufti, was out of the country, and they had developed little in the way of a military structure. The surrounding Arab states, despite their talk of brotherhood, were equally divided by petty personal jealousies and conflicting aims.

The Arab Higher Committee initially organized more than 200 local committees in a sort of home-guard defense. But the brunt of Arab retaliation was carried by the Arab Liberation Army, an irregular force led by Kawukji, who now re-entered Palestine from Lebanon. The Arab Liberation Army had some success at first in isolating Jewish settlements. For tactical and psychological reasons the Arabs did not take well to sustained battles or sieges, preferring quick hit-and-run raids, which suited

---

[52] St. John, Robert, *Ben Gurion*, New York: Doubleday & Company, Inc., 1959, p. 148.

[53] Even more so than other aspects of the Palestine problem, the United States recognition and the methods used in bringing it about are bitterly controversial. The writer can attest from personal knowledge to the fact that the Department of State was *ordered* by the White House to extend recognition, indeed against the judgment of many high-ranking officers.

better their temperament and resembled the famous *ghazus* (raids) over the deserts of Arabia in times past.

The Arab Liberation Army was followed by the regular armies of some of the Arab states, namely, Iraq, Egypt, Syria, Transjordan, and a token force from Lebanon. There was no unified command; indeed, the leaders of the Arab governments concerned disagreed violently among themselves, even withholding vital supplies from each other.[54] Even so, with over 170,000 men pitted against a maximum of 75,000, the Arabs were supremely confident that they would drive the Jews into the Mediterranean.[55] Not only were Arab regular armies marching into Palestine, but the Liberation Army was already there, and the Palestine Arabs themselves had formed the "Army of Judea," under Abd al-Qadir al-Husayni, nephew of the Mufti.

The actual military operations of the Arab-Israeli War of 1948–49 have been described exhaustively elsewhere.[56] Generally speaking the war followed a pattern of activity phases followed by armistices arranged by the UN. Israel gradually passed from the defensive to the offensive through these phases, as Arab morale deteriorated and Arab military weaknesses became apparent. The most effective Arab force was the Arab Legion of Transjordan, commanded by General Glubb and largely British-officered. The Legion, though it had only 5,000 men of all ranks and was too short of ammunition at times to mount a sustained offensive, held the Old City of Jerusalem and eastern Palestine. The Lebanese contributed little to the action, while the Iraqis, who had to cross the Syrian Desert to reach Palestine, showed up well in one or two clashes but failed to follow up their advantages. The Syrian and Egyptian forces were badly mauled in the latter stages of the war. A large body of Egyptian troops was surrounded at Faluja, in southern Galilee, but it managed to hold out until an armistice was arranged. One of its officers was Gamal 'Abd al-Nasir, already dreaming of greater battles to be fought on Egyptian soil.

Israeli success during the brief war may be measured in terms of land,

[54] Cf. Glubb, John B., *A Soldier with the Arabs*, London: Hodder & Stoughton, 1957, for anecdotes about the singular unpreparedness of Syrian and Jordanian leaders.

[55] The Government of Israel has claimed that the Arab leaders were so confident of victory they ordered the Palestine Arabs to leave their villages and clear the way for the advance of the Arab armies. Peretz, Don, *Israel and the Palestine Arabs*, Washington: Middle East Institute, 1958, pp. 6 *ff.*

[56] See O'Ballance, Edgar, *The Arab-Israeli War, 1948*, New York: Frederick A. Praeger, 1957.

men, and organization. Military action gave them much more territory than they had been allotted even under the UN resolution. Three fourths of Palestine was theirs, 2,380 square miles plus the 5,670 square miles previously assigned to them. The Negev was theirs all the way to the port of Eilat on the Gulf of Aquaba; Haifa on the Mediterranean, New Jerusalem, all of Galilee, were incorporated into the new Jewish state.[57] (See map.) The war also coalesced Israeli energies and united the various groups which had been battling the British (and sometimes their compatriots). Haganah, the old semisecret Jewish force, became the core of the new Israeli Army; it was composed of the elite Palmach, backed by the Mapam (Socialist Labor Party), Hish, a field force, and Mishmar, the home guard. The two clandestine terrorist organizations, Irgun and the Stern Gang, operated independently of the Haganah, but such excesses as the Dayr Yasin massacre (q.v.) and the murder of Count Folke Bernadotte produced such a stir abroad against Israel that the two groups had to be merged with Haganah. Finally, the successful prosecution of the war gave credence to the belief, assiduously sponsored by the WZO, that the Jews were a people fighting for their lives to establish their rightful homeland and established the massive aid precedent which still continues.

UN mediation, as mentioned, achieved two truces between the belligerents. In January, 1949, Dr. Ralph Bunche, successor as mediator to Bernadotte, began armistice discussions on the island of Rhodes. Between January and July separate armistice agreements were signed between Israel and Egypt, Syria, Lebanon, and Jordan (Iraq refused to sign an armistice, and theoretically a state of war still exists between the two countries). The armistices were based on the assumption that peace treaties would be worked out following the necessary "cooling off" period; as of 1961 these agreements have hardened into what might be described as the peace which is peaceless.

Aside from alteration of boundaries in the Middle East caused by Israel's success, the major result of the Arab-Israeli War was the refugee problem. In terms of military casualties the war was not costly, but in terms of human suffering and civilian dislocation it ranks high in international annals. The roots of the problem lay in the intensification of communal struggle in the postwar years. As the Mandate neared its end, the Jews, afraid of being submerged in an Arab sea, took desperate and

[57] Ellis, Harry, *Israel and the Middle East,* New York: The Ronald Press Company, 1957, p. 120.

bold measures. About 30,000 Arabs left Palestine early in 1948; they were mostly well-to-do people who fully expected to return when things calmed down. On April 9–10, Irgun terrorists slaughtered the entire population of Dayr Yasin, a village near Jerusalem, for unknown reasons.[58] The Irgun then called a press conference to announce that this was the beginning of the Jewish conquest of Palestine and Transjordan.[59] The massacre seems to have introduced a mass fear psychosis into the Arab population; this was intensified by Arab radio exhortations to stay out of the way of the armies, the breakdown in administration caused by the British departure, the lack of Arab community leaders, the absence of communications, and the word-of-mouth prevalence of atrocity stories. By the time the armistice was signed, nearly all the Arab community of Palestine had fled to nearby countries, to be classed as refugees ever since. The United Nations, which inherited the problem by default, estimated in November, 1949, that 940,000 destitute Arabs were eligible for aid, having fled from their homes. These were divided as follows: Lebanon, 127,800; Syria, 78,200; Transjordan, 94,000; Arab Palestine (annexed by King Abdullah), 357,400; Gaza Strip, 245,000; and Israel proper, 37,600.[60]

THE STATE OF ISRAEL

Four effects stemmed from Israel's declaration of independence and successful prosecution of her war with the Arabs. Statehood for Israel at the epicenter of Arab-populated lands shifted the balance of political power in the Middle East. In another sense, it completed the fragmentation of the area since the Arab states were presented with a problem which defied solution under the existing circumstances. Third, world political recognition of Israel wrote another chapter in the long history of external intervention in area affairs. Fourth, the extent of support provided the new state from Western gentile sources, financial, material, and moral, profoundly undermined the Western position in the area. The emerging Arab states, themselves unused to statehood, began to look to Soviet Russia, with the consequent transfer of the East-West struggle directly to the heart of the Middle East.

From the Zionist viewpoint, as from Israel's, the period from 1949 to

[58] The village was apparently nonpartisan and had even refused to permit Arab guerrillas to use it as a base of anti-Jewish operations. Graves, *op. cit.*, p. 260, n. 5.
[59] Polk *et al.*, *op. cit.*, p. 291.
[60] Lenczowski, *op. cit.*, p. 340, n. 43.

the present is the greatest in the history of the Jewish people since Solomon's time. The Zionists must inevitably make some reservations, however, for the total aims of Zionism have not been achieved. The majority of Jews still live in the Diaspora, and Israel does not comprise the historic borders of ancient Palestine (Eretz Israel); also, the identification of most Diaspora Jews stops short of emigration to Israel. The recent statement of Mr. Ben Gurion to a Jerusalem press conference that every Jew's first loyalty is to Israel, although somewhat distorted, was in line with previous statements and other Zionist spokesmen, and the furor it aroused suggests their difficulties in continuing to impose the Zionist ideal on assimilated Jewry elsewhere.[61]

The success of the people of Israel in molding an independent, stable, progressive national state against tremendous odds is little short of remarkable. If one applies total objectivity to the creation of the state and considers only its political evolution within the boundaries imposed by a neutral tribunal, Israel stands almost alone in human history. It is a state developed by mass immigration with an organized social transformation applied directly to the immigrants from their arrival. The efficient administration of the Jewish community in Mandatory Palestine, which was built up under the assumption of eventual Jewish independence, was the framework out of which Israeli nationhood and Israeli Jewish social identification were fashioned.[62] Though immigration has declined steadily since 1949–52 when 100,000 immigrants entered Israel, the present population of two million reflects graphically its impact. Israel's political structure and political outlook differ sharply from those of the Arab states surrounding her, with their clan-orientation family loyalties, and cult of strong, dictatorial political leadership, the hero image of President Nasir (Ironically, the growth of democratic institutions in these countries brings them slowly into closer alignment almost by default, with Israel). Israel began with a Western style parliamentary democracy, and political evolution has continued in this direction. The first elections were held in

---

[61] Cf. the General Zionist Creed: "The State of Israel does not exist for its own sake but as an instrument for the implantation of the Zionist ideal." Taylor, *op. cit.*, p. 111, n. 14. See also Lazaron, Morris, *Olive Trees in Storm*, New York: American Friends of the Middle East, 1955, Chapter IX, for an eloquent statement of the dilemma of the non-Zionist Jew.

[62] Crossman, Richard, *A Nation Reborn*, New York: Atheneum Publishers, 1960, pp. 131 *et seq.* This interesting book emphasizes the split between Israelis and Diaspora Jews, "The ones who refused to live in the Bronx or Whitechapel," in Ben Gurion's words. Thus Zionism tends to accentuate the Israeliness of Israelis.

January 1949, for a unicameral legislature of one hundred and twenty members, the Knesset. Ben Gurion was chosen Prime Minister and Minister of Defense. For the man born David Green in Plonsk, Russia, who migrated to Palestine as a young man, labored with pick and shovel in Jewish agricultural settlements, helped found Haganah and Histadrut, the Jewish Labor Federation, formed the Mapai (Moderate Socialist) Party in the 1930's, and spoke the words of independence, it was his hour. For Chaim Weizmann, elected as Israel's first president, it was the end of a road marked out thirty-two years earlier when he had convinced Balfour to express publicly Britain's support for a Palestine Jewish State. The office of President in Israel is largely an honorary one as in France; there is some evidence that Weizmann favored a strong executive in the American manner, but Ben Gurion, who preferred the legislature to be dominant, saw this policy adopted.[63] In 1952 Weizmann died; he was succeeded by Itzhak Ben-Zvi, a veteran Zionist with a background similar to that of Ben Gurion's. He was re-elected in 1957 to a second five-year term.[64]

The dominant political party in Israel from the beginning has been Mapai, Ben Gurion's party. Its program and policies are somewhat similar to those of the British Labour Party; it is dedicated to "the unifying mission of the working class in Israel"; its long experience as a component of the Jewish Agency and Vaad Leumi, and its control of Histadrut, prepared it better than any other party for leadership.[65] A much weaker but still important labor party is *Mapam,* a leftwing socialist party formed in 1948 from a merger of Hashomer Hatzair, the general confederation of kibbutzim of the Mandate period and Ahdut Avoda, strong advocates of Zionism. Mapam follows a general Marxist and pro-Soviet line, as a result of its kibbutz orientation; it favors complete equality for Arabs in Israel. Ahdut Avoda seceded from Mapam in 1954, following increasing anti-Zionism in Russia and the Soviet-Israeli break in diplomatic relations in 1953.

There are three other groups in Israel's political spectrum, the General Zionists, the religious parties, and the Herut. The General Zionists,

[63] Williams, L. F. Rushbrook, *The State of Israel,* London: Faber, 1957, pp. 154–155, discusses the viewpoints of the two men, concluding that lack of precedent or constitutional training made Ben Gurion's view more desirable.

[64] His wife was equally prominent; once when an Israeli child was asked the name of Israel's President, he answered, "Ben-Zvi and his wife." Bentwich, Norman, *Israel Resurgent,* New York: Frederick A. Praeger, Inc., 1960, p. 110.

[65] Bernstein, Marver, *The Politics of Israel,* Princeton: Princeton University Press, 1957, p. 60 ff.

strongly nationalistic, were the second largest party in the Knesset in the early 1950's but lack of a constructive, specific policy hurt them and their percentage of popular support has declined since then. The various religious parties, four in number, united in 1949 in the United Religious Front but split up after the second General Elections in 1951. They are *Mizrahi* and *Hapoel Mizrahi*, who seek the transformation of Israel into a state based directly on the ethical, social, and ritual principles of Judaism. The *Agudat Israel* and its labor wing, *Poale Agudat*, stand for strict observance of Judaic Law, and many of Israel's internal political problems are caused by the intransigence of this group. They have particularly attracted converts among the immigrants from North Africa and Asia, in areas where a stricter observance of the Judaic code prevails. The government has had difficulties with these people ranging from boycotting and interference with public transportation on Sundays, to agitation over sales of pork, conscription of women, and religious education in schools. Recently an ultra-conservative grandparent from one of these parties kidnapped his grandson, hiding him from the authorities as well as from his own parents, on grounds the boy was not being reared properly in the precepts of Judaism. The Herut, the party of the extreme right, was kept out of the coalition government in 1949–1950 because of its extreme views. It is anti-British and seeks to expand Israeli control over all Palestine. The Knesset in 1949 passed a Transition Law (the small constitution) which provides the legal, constitutional law on which the government has functioned.[66] No written constitution has been promulgated, the intent being to let one develop out of experience. The first Knesset sat from 1951 to 1955, the second from 1951 to 1955, and the third from 1955 to 1959.[67] The term of the Knesset as fixed by the Transition Law is four years. The Law also created a cabinet under a Prime Minister responsible to the Knesset, and a formal Presidency without legislative powers. Elections to the Knesset are by direct, universal suffrage and secret ballot. The Transition Law also guarantees equal voting rights, freedom of conscience, a separate judiciary with theoretical powers of review, and proportional representation in the Knesset. Despite the range of parties, stable government has been possible through a coalition of parties, usually Mapai, the General Zionists, and the religious parties.

[66] Also called a Draft Revisional Law, and an Interim Organic Law.
[67] From 1948 to 1957 Israel had eight cabinets under two Prime Ministers, Ben Gurion (6), and Moshe Sharett (2). Only one cabinet resignation was due to lack of a parliamentary majority. Bernstein, *op. cit.,* p. 125.

The Transition Law has been supplemented by several Organic Laws. One of these is the Law of Return (1950) which gives every Jew the right to immigrate to Israel, to be received on the basis of a visa, and to remain if he (or she) so desires. A second law provided for the trial and punishment of persons who have committed crimes against Israel and the Jewish people; this law has been cited by Ben Gurion as the legal basis of its case against Adolf Eichmann, who was tried and convicted as the result of extra-legal methods, but who has clearly violated this law. After thirteen years of statehood, Israel still exists in an anomalous situation, a country neither integrated into nor accepted by the countries which surround her, yet too well-intrenched to be removed from the area.

Israel's relations with these neighbors in the broader context of international relations will be considered in the final chapter of this book. Internally the periodic political crises which blow up in (and outside) the Knesset concern either personality differences or religious questions. The long-established, well-knit social organization of the Israeli people, the genuine dedication to Israel aroused by Zionism, and the unremitting hostility of the Arabs, re-emphasize this extraordinary solidarity, the present manifestation of two thousand years of cellular growth and cherished longing.

RECOMMENDED READINGS*

1. Abcarius, M. F., *Palestine Through The Fog of Propaganda,* London: Hutchinson, 1946 (a).
2. Barbour, Nevill, *Palestine: Star or Crescent?* (Pub. in Britain as *Nisi Dominus*), New York: The Odyssey Press, Inc., 1947 (a).
3. Begin, Menachem, *The Revolt: The Story of the Irgun,* New York: Schuman, 1951 (b).
4. Bentwich, Norman, *Israel,* New York: McGraw-Hill Book Co., Inc., 1953 (b).
5. ———, *Israel Resurgent,* New York: Frederick A. Praeger, Inc., 1960 (b).
6. Ben Gurion, David, *The Rebirth and Destiny of Israel,* New York: Philosophical Library, Inc., 1953.
7. Bernstein, Marver, *The Politics of Israel,* Princeton: Princeton University Press, 1957.
8. Crossman, Richard, *Palestine Mission,* New York: Harper & Brothers, 1947 (b).

* Books which show a generally clear pro-Arab bias are marked (a); those generally pro-Israeli or Jewish are marked (b).

9. Ellis, Harry B., *Israel and The Middle East,* New York: The Ronald Press Company, 1957.
10. ESCO Foundation for Palestine, *Palestine, A Study of Jewish, Arab, and British Policies,* 2 vols., New Haven: Yale University Press, 1947 (b).
11. Graves, R. M., *Experiment in Anarchy,* London: Victor Gollancz, 1949.
12. Hanna, Paul L., *British Policy in Palestine,* Washington: Public Affairs Press, 1952.
13. Hurewitz, J. C., *The Struggle For Palestine,* New York: W. W. Norton & Company, Inc., 1950.
14. Jeffries, J. M., *Palestine: The Reality,* New York: Longmans, 1939 (a).
15. Kimche, Jon & David, *The Secret Roads,* London: Suker & Warburg, 1955 (b).
16. Kirk, George, *The Middle East 1945–1950,* London: RIIA, 1954.
17. Lilienthal, Alfred M., *What Price Israel?* Chicago: Henry Regnery Co., 1953.
18. McDonald, James G., *My Mission in Israel,* New York: Simon & Schuster, Inc., 1951.
19. Peretz, Don, *Israel and the Palestine Arabs,* Washington: Middle East Institute, 1959.
20. Polk, W. R., Stamler, D. M., Asfour, E. Y., *Backdrop To Tragedy: The Struggle for Palestine,* Boston: Beacon Press, 1957.
21. Rackman, Emanuel, *Israel's Emerging Constitution, 1948–51,* New York: Columbia University Press, 1955.
22. Sacher, Harry, *Israel: The Establishment of a State,* New York: British Book Centre, Inc., 1952 (b).
23. St. John, Robert, *Ben-Gurion,* New York: Doubleday & Company, Inc., 1959.
24. Schechtman, Joseph, *Rebel and Statesman: The Story of Vladimir Jabotinsky,* Vol. I, New York: Thomas Yoseloff, Inc., 1956.
25. Spiro, Milford, *Kibbutz: Venture into Utopia,* Cambridge: Harvard University Press, 1956.
26. Stein, Leonard, *The Balfour Declaration,* New York: Simon & Schuster, 1961.
27. Taylor, Alan, *Prelude to Israel,* New York: Philosophical Library, Inc., 1959.
28. Weizmann, Chaim, *Trial and Error: The Autobiography of Chaim Weizmann,* New York: Harper & Brothers, 1949.

CHAPTER 9

THE ARABIAN PENINSULA I: SAUDI
ARABIA—THE WAHHABI STATE

$\mathcal{The}$ heartland of Islam is the Arabian Peninsula. Wherever devout Muslims are on the globe when they pray, they look toward Mecca in the Arabian Hejaz; and when they die, they are buried so as to be facing that city. Mecca and Medina, its neighbor some two hundred and sixty miles to the northeast, are the two most sacred cities of Islam. The Prophet Muhammad lived and preached in Mecca; and when opposition from the Meccans threatened him, he went to Yathrib where he was welcomed by the people as an arbitrator and the leader of a community, and Yathrib was renamed Medina. The aim of the devout Muslim is to make the *Hajj,* the pilgrimage to Mecca, at least once in his life; this is one of the five pillars of his religious faith. Hence Arabia, at least that part of it which is linked with Islamic origins, has a very special significance for the world of Islam, and the Arabian ruler or leader whose position gives him the guardianship of its Holy Places is an extremely important personage.

Although it is the heartland, the peninsula has been less touched by the external world than the "fringe" areas of the Arab-Muslim world. There seems almost to be a conspiracy on the part of more secular Islamic states to keep Arabia pure and undefiled. The warriors who spread the green banner of Islam across Asia and Africa and even into Europe did not return to their homeland, as later world travelers were to do, laden with rich treasures and tales of wondrous foreign civilizations. They had rather a mission to send their Muslim beliefs *into* these civilizations. In the end, there was a sort of dual absorption—of Islam into the existing world, altering it for all time, and of Muslims into the peoples they overcame. Thus in a country like Tunisia, for example, it is practically impossible to separate Berbers from Arabs although Berbers were the root-stock. Only in Arabia can a relatively pure Arab stock be distinguished, and even this stock was not Muslim once.[1]

The Arabian Peninsula, then, is the last Arab area to feel the impact of modern twentieth-century politics. Of its three politically definable sections—Saudi Arabia, Yemen, and the small British-sponsored states—the first has received the rudest awakening, an even larger irony since it has the fewest natural resources. The oil underlying Saudi Arabia's lands (and seas) had no takers until the twentieth century; it aroused no interest on the part of the population. In the places where it was visible on the surface, this oil was regarded more as an object of superstitious veneration than as something with vast practical uses. Deep in the desert, the Bedouin lived as their forebears had in Abraham's time, and the rare traveler could see all the details of Old Testament life almost unchanged. As for the desert Arab's personality, "his thoughts, too (were) much the same as in the days of Job, his arrogance, independence, pride and self-sufficiency . . . intensified by Islam . . . his religious life . . . moulded into a rigid system of creed and formality." [2] Even the peninsular townsmen were unprepared for the riches which accrued to them out of the production and marketing of Arabian oil. The Saudi Arabian state, created upon a bedrock of religion, upon a recrudescence of pure Islam, met the arrival of the oil-seeking foreigners with something of the shock of the *sail,* the water-flood that sweeps down the wadis of Arabia when the rains come. Mercilessly this *sail* was to tear at Wahhabi doctrine; at the proud self-satisfied life of the desert; and at the composed, if not tranquil, life of the country, with consequences which are still in evolution.[3]

THE RISE OF WAHHABISM

The modern political unity of Saudi Arabia is derived from two generating factors—an eighteenth-century religious covenant and the ability of a great leader to channel revived religious puritanism into organized effort. In one sense the state is the lineal heir of the theocratic

[1] See Chapter 1 for the historical background of Islam relating to Wahhabism.
[2] Dickson, H. R. P., *Kuwait and Her Neighbors,* London: Allen & Unwin, 1956, p. 570.
[3] Van der Meulen, D., *The Wells of Ibn Saud,* New York: Frederick A. Praeger, Inc., 1957, p. 148.

state established by Muhammad in Mecca. Muhammad wielded both spiritual and temporal authority in his lifetime; after his death, his followers ranged far and wide to create an earthly kingdom in his name. The founder of Saudi Arabia acquired the same sort of leadership over the puritanical Wahhabi sect, using Wahhabism to dominate the bulk of the peninsula in time. His ancestors had made a pact with Wahhabism two centuries earlier as a means to territorial expansion. He applied the pact to the founding and stabilization of an Arabian nation.

In the eighteenth century, Arabia was nominally controlled by the Ottoman Turks. But beyond the regions bordering the Red Sea, in Najd and eastward, self-government existed in the form of independent districts ruled by a tribal chief under Bedouin protection. The greatest penetration of Turkish control had come when Sultan Selim I annexed Mecca and Medina and Yemen to his territories in 1524. As Ottoman power declined, it became simpler to govern by remote control, merely requiring allegiance to the Sultan as the Caliph of Islam. Only the pilgrim roads from Damascus and Cairo to the Hejaz were definitely under Ottoman guardianship. The lack of political unity, the absorption of the tribes in raiding, counter-raiding, personal disputes, the absence of leadership, all contributed toward keeping Arabia as a remote rimland of the empire, rarely visited, as forgotten as it was before Muhammad's time. Life went on, of course, and the townsmen of the Hejaz maintained contact with the external Muslim world, but inland Islam lost its dynamism and was corrupted with strange rites and superstitions. Sufism and the Persian cast of mind had altered Islam's outlook everywhere else, but the Najdis fell back on the customs of pre-Islamic Arabia. "Laxity in the observance of the prescribed rites, in sexual relationships, and in other ways was ignored rather than approved by folks of decent standing. Superstitious belief in the efficacy of charms, offerings, and sacrifices and in the powers of trees, rocks, and certain tombs to effect or hasten the gratification of normal human desires was but the measure of ignorance in the masses."[4] Ancient Sabean rites, such as the worship of the sun, moon, and stars, again became popular, while circumcision and the marriage ceremonies nearly disappeared. To the righteous, Arabia seemed to need a spiritual rebirth; and early in the eighteenth century, their prayers were answered.

Sometime between 1691 and 1703, a certain Muhammad ibn 'Abd

[4] Philby, H. St. J. B., *Saudi Arabia*, London: Ernest Benn, 1955, pp. 34–35.

al-Wahhab was born at 'Ayaina in the Najd. He was of the Bani Tamim tribe, which dominated Jabal Shammar in southern Najd at the time, and his father was a *qadi* (religious judge). He was also the grandson of a well-known Muslim theologian, Shaykh Sulayman.[5] Wahhab was thus exposed to Muslim theology and Hanbali jurisprudence from an early age, and he showed considerable precocity; by the age of ten he had memorized the Koran.[6] He was married at twelve; and presumably to support his bride as much as to enter man's estate, he became a merchant. Commercial journeys took him to Basra, Baghdad, and Damascus, where he met some of the learned shaykhs of the town and completed studies in religious law. In these respects his career paralleled Muhammad's; but Wahhab was no inspired prophet, merely a reformist preacher with great physical and intellectual vigor. (He died in 1787 having lived for move than eighty-four years.) His experiences and discussions had taught him that the correct "Way" in Islam was that taught by the Prophet and followed by his *Ansari* (companions) some twelve centuries earlier. All else in the religion was superfluous accretion. His chief teachings were:

(1) The re-establishment of Muslim beliefs as taught by the Koran.

(2) The denial of all spiritual authority to the Sultan-Caliph and of any special respect paid to any persons (such as the Sharifs of Mecca).

(3) The restoration of discipline in the matter of prayer, fasting, and the pilgrimage to Mecca.

(4) A strict prohibition of wine, tobacco, games of chance, magic, silk and gold dress, and tombstones for the dead.[7]

Wahhab's views got him into trouble in Basra, where he had journeyed; and he was expelled from the city, nearly dying of thirst in the desert before he got back to Najd. Back in 'Ayaina he came under the patronage of the local ruler, 'Uthman. He began to carry out acts in support of his doctrine of purification. First he cut down a sacred tree; nothing happened to him. Next he demolished the tomb of a holy man, Zaid ibn al-Khattab, in the face of warnings from the superstitious Najdis of divine retribution. These successful defiances of custom enhanced his fame too much to please 'Uthman, and again he was expelled. In 1745,

---

[5] Philby gives this grandfather's pedigree as follows: Shaykh Sulaiman ibn 'Ali ibn Muhammad ibn Ahmad ibn Rashid ibn Barid ibn Mushrif ibn 'Umar ibn Ma'dhar ibn Idris ibn Zakhir ibn Muhammad ibn 'Alawi ibn Wuhib, or sixteen generations to greatness.

[6] Lipsky, George, ed., *Saudi Arabia*, New Haven: HRAF Press, 1958, p. 10.

[7] Dickson, *op. cit.*, p. 112.

the wandering iconoclast came to Dar'iya, a settlement in the Wadi Hanifa under the control of the Sa'ud family. The wife of Muhammad ibn Sa'ud, who was the head of the family at the time, became interested in the movement and was converted. Imposing the traditional harem influence over her husband's thinking, she got *him* interested in the movement. It is reported that she said to him: "This man is sent to thee by Allah." [8] The prince made an alliance with the preacher, to cover both their lifetimes but destined to endure into modern times and to provide the cement for an earthly kingdom. The bond also stipulated that the daughters of Muhammad 'Abd al-Wahhab were to marry the sons of the Amir Sa'ud, and vice versa; Sa'ud himself married the Shaykh's first daughter.[9]

The alliance gave 'Abd al-Wahhab a political arm for this theological program and assured Muhammad ibn Sa'ud of sanction from a recognized theologian as well as a fanatical body of believers to do battle for him. Although they considered themselves the purifiers of Islam, the Wahhabis did not use the term; they merely described themselves as *muwahhidin* ("unitarians"). Their predecessors in reforming Islam, the Kharijites, used the same term, and the two groups shared a deep-rooted belief that they alone were following the straight path of Islam. All other groups, including the Sunnis, were considered deviates. Although the Kharijites were never numerous and had died out completely before Wahhabism developed, their creed and purpose undoubtedly inspired many elements of the later sect.

Wahhabism offered a single message: return to the ways of primeval Islam. It rejected all the accretions of the faith—Sufi mysticism, theological interpretation according to the four schools, all forms of iconography, the worship of holy men or saints, the rituals, even all dissentions. The faith is the Law, said 'Abd al-Wahhab—the classical Law in its original, rigid Hanbali version, unchanged, laid down for all time. The Wahhabi goal was to make a society which would dedicate its earthly life entirely to the classical purposes of God and live in accordance with strict Hanbali law. The working out of Wahhabism deep in the desert of Arabia has produced the modern state of Saudi Arabia.[10]

[8] Van der Meulen, *op. cit.*, p. 32.
[9] Smith, Wilfred C., *Islam in Modern History*, Princeton: Princeton University Press, 1957, p. 41.
[10] Hitti, Philip K., *History of the Arabs*, 6th ed., New York: St Martin's Press, Inc., 1957, p. 41.

In the late eighteenth and early nineteenth centuries, the first Wahhabi state expanded far beyond the confines of Najd. The rulers of Dar'iya learned quickly that their Bedouin warriors, fortified by religious approval, were only too glad to extend their most popular sport—*ghazu* (raiding) into settled areas. The Wahhabis were not always successful. In 1764, Muhammad ibn Sa'ud's son, 'Abd al-Aziz, was soundly beaten by the Lord of Najran. When the survivors came before 'Abd al-Wahhab, he quoted a sura from the Koran: "Rejoice not nor mourn, for ye shall overcome if ye be faithful." [11] In the same year, 'Abd al-Aziz succeeded his father; and in 1773, he seized Riyadh, the city henceforth to be identified with the rise and fall and the ultimate glory of the House of Sa'ud. 'Abd al-Wahhab lived on until 1787. As districts came under Saudi control, he visited them and ordered them to acknowledge the Amir as their lord and his son as their future ruler, both temporal and spiritual. Meanwhile, 'Abd al-Aziz I (so numbered to distinguish him from his descendant, the founder of modern Saudi Arabia) made it his practice to build moated forts, manned by mercenary Wahhabis, outside of captured towns and to install a cadi and a mufti, both responsible to him, in each town. In this way, religion was used to substructure the state and to ensure a stable succession.

In 1801–1802, the Wahhabis took Karbala and Najaf in Iraq, both centers of Shi'a pilgrimage, and slaughtered the population and desecrated the tomb of Husayn ibn Ali, Muhammad's grandson. This was "the first doughty blow struck in the service of the true faith against a dispensation which was regarded in Wahhabi eyes as the incarnation of infidelity." [12] In 1803 and 1804, Mecca and Medina were taken. The conquest coincided with the pilgrimage season, so the Wahhabis put on their pilgrim garments and made their ablutions, and the Amir declared an amnesty. Then everything that smacked of the glorification of man was destroyed, even the *qubbas* built over the graves of the Prophet's Ansari (Companions). The Wahhabis now assumed the guardianship of the Holy Places. By 1814, under Sa'ud II (Sa'ud the Great), the Wahhabi state stretched from Syria to Oman, from the Red Sea to the Persian Gulf. This progress brought the Saudis under the eyes of the Ottoman Turks. The pilgrims who visited Mecca during this period of the "new look" were repelled rather than inspired by Wahhabi puritanism. The Wahhabis seemed more like wild men from the desert than the saviors of

[11] Philby, *op. cit.*, p. 58.
[12] *Ibid.*, p. 93.

Islam. Wahhabism had to be stopped, but the Sublime Porte in Constantinople was too weak to do the job. However, the viceroy of Egypt, Muhammad Ali, had territorial ambitions of his own, and the Porte ordered him to drive them from the Hejaz. The viceroy's son, Ibrahim Pasha, invaded Arabia with a large expeditionary force and, after a series of savage battles and sieges lasting six months, utterly broke Wahhabi power. The Saudi Amir, Abdullah, was marched off to Constantinople and executed publicly there in front of Ayasofya Mosque. Dar'iya was burned to the ground. The remaining members of the family retired to Riyadh, where they became engrossed in inter-tribal feuds. But Wahhabism itself, forced back to its deserts, was kept alive by *mutawwas* (missionaries) who continued to spread reading and writing among the tribes so that they could study the Koran and the *hadith* of Muhammad. Like an underground mine-fire, the movement smouldered on, waiting for someone to give it life.

Establishment of Saudi Arabia

A member of the family, Turki, re-established a truncated version of the Wahhabi state around Riyadh in 1820. Rather than attempt to rule Najd, the Ottomans played the tribes against each other, using subsidy and blackmail. Later in the century, the Saudis themselves began fighting over the succession. The youngest son, 'Abd al-Rahman, came into conflict with ibn-Rashid, the powerful ruler of the Shammar tribes and the nominal overlord of the degenerate Saudis. He was defeated several times and finally forced to leave Riyadh. Whatever elements of Arabian nationalism remained in Najd now centered around the Rashids, with the discredited Saudis taking refuge first in Hail, then among the Murra tribes along the great Empty Quarter (Rub al-Khali) of Arabia, and finally in Kuwait. Although he was an outcast, 'Abd al-Rahman was determined to restore Saudi power and extend the Wahhabi creed to all Arabia, perhaps throughout Islam. He instilled these ambitions in his fourth child and third son, 'Abd al-Aziz ibn 'Abd al-Rahman al-Faisal al-Sa'ud, more familiarly known in the West as ibn Sa'ud.[13] Perhaps because of the harshness of his boyhood, for from the age of ten he knew little security, ibn Sa'ud learned more quickly and thoroughly than his

---

[13] Because of the confusion of names, the practice of calling the former King (ibn Sa'ud) by his familiar name, King 'Abd al-Aziz, is increasing. See Harrington, Charles W., "The Saudi Arabian Council of Ministers," *Middle East Journal*, Winter 1958, n. 1.

brothers the lessons he needed in order to achieve that ambition. Living with the Murra, the poorest, most backward, and most feared of the tribes of southern Arabia for their sudden *ghazus,* he learned how to survive in the desert, how to travel great distances with only a handful of dates and camels' milk for food, how to read the signs and footmarks in the sands, and the value of mobility. The Murra were true nomads, traveling continuously. His father despised them as unclean, worse than infidels, and could never adjust to the life of a refugee among them.[14] What his son learned from them led the Saudis, in time, back to Riyadh.

In 1891 the Turks, wishing to set up a counterweight to the Rashids, sent an invitation to 'Abd al-Rahman to visit their ally the Shaykh of Kuwait. In Kuwait ibn Sa'ud met an intellectual life no less stimulating than his physical life in the Murra camps. His best friend was young Mubarak, a half-brother of Muhammad, the ruler of Kuwait. The ruler was supposed to keep the Sa'ud family supplied with a subsidy, actually supplied by the Turks, but he was a penny-pincher; and when the Turks did not pay, he did not pay. Mubarak hated both the Shaykh and the Turks and in 1896 killed him and seized control of the town. Ibn Sa'ud's fortunes now began to rocket upwards. His friend introduced him to the niceties of international politics. To forestall the drive of Germany toward the east, the *Drang nach Osten,* which was being fronted by the Turks, Mubarak arranged for Kuwait to come under British protection. He also attempted a surprise attack on the Rashids but was defeated. As a diversionary move, ibn Sa'ud moved with a small group of followers into Najd to attack Riyadh. In a campaign which today reads like a fairy tale, he and twenty-three men hid in the house of the wife of the Rashidi governor after scaling the outer wall of the town by means of a palm tree trunk. The wife and her women were locked in her bedroom. When the governor came to visit his wife after prayers as was his morning custom, he was overpowered, and ibn Sa'ud decapitated him. Then he announced to the startled townspeople: "Who is on my side—who? Your own Amir is back again among you!"[15] The Rashidi garrison panicked, and those who did not escape were taken prisoner. In this Arabian Nights manner, in January, 1902, ibn Sa'ud, acting as both Amir and Imam of his people, restored the Saudi-Wahhabi power in the peninsula.

By the onset of World War I, ibn Sa'ud had recovered much of the

[14] Armstrong, H. C., *Lord of Arabia,* London: Barker, 1934, pp. 33–34.
[15] Dickson, *op. cit.,* p. 138; see also van der Meulen, Armstrong, *op. cit.,* for the story.

territory of his Saudi forefathers. All of Najd yielded to him between 1903 and 1906; between 1907 and 1913, he added al-Hasa and part of the Hejaz. The Rashids and their Turkish allies were beaten; and through the mediation of Mubarak, the Sultan agreed to recognize ibn Sa'ud as the lawful ruler of Najd, in return for the stationing of a small Turkish garrison there (which was soon withdrawn because of the difficulties of supplying it and because of the hostility of the population). But the Najdi state was still loosely organized, politically tribal. Ibn Sa'ud, whose own Wahhabi faith was the bedrock of his religious convictions, determined to use Wahhabism as the basis of his state, linking his followers into a political unity. He had the nucleus of a theocratic state in the *ulema,* many of them descended from the great Wahhab, and in the *mutawwas* who still carried on their preaching among the tribes. He himself was their Imam, the lineal descendant of the great Sa'ud and the spiritual successor of Muhammad 'Abd al-Wahhab. But all these strengths were of little avail against the self-generating nomadism of the Bedouin, however fanatical. So ibn Sa'ud invented a new technique for Arabia. Those who embraced Wahhabism were pressured into settling in colonies of *Ikhwan* (Brethren) to become agriculturalists. No longer lords of the desert, they would become servants of the land and in the process bend their faith to political uses. The first Ikhwan was a colony of fifty families established at al-Artawiya between Kuwait and the Qasim. By 1916 it had grown to ten thousand, and other Ikhwan colonies were springing up all over Najd. The Ikhwan had their own levies in ibn Sa'ud's armies. Their fanatical zeal for the destruction of the infidel (a term liberally interpreted by them to include not only non-Muslims but also all Muslims who did not share their fundamentalist conception of the true faith) required their leader to watch them with care and to provide them with certain services.[16] The Ikhwan were given seed and agricultural implements; an amir was appointed to oversee justice in each community, Ikhwan shaykhs were sent to ulema school at the great mosque in Riyadh; and other ulema were assigned to the communities. Ibn Sa'ud directed that the Ikhwan obey him as their leader and pay him a *zakat* or tax in that capacity and ordered all Bedouin to join the movement (although this last was not enforced). His tax-collectors played a dual role. As they collected the *zakat,* they spread the gospel of Wahhabism. Tribes were mixed up in the various colonies to break the

[16] Philby, *op. cit.,* p. 262.

hold of tribalism. The Ikhwan were taught that they alone were the true Muslims. They were allowed to wear a white strip of cloth around their headcloths instead of the usual black wool head cord. Certain Ikhwan shaykhs were invited to remain in attendance on ibn Sa'ud in Riyadh after they had completed their religious training. It is said that within ninety-six hours the ruler could put a fanatical force of twenty-five thousand Ikhwan in the field.[17]

One author reported that during an audience with ibn Sa'ud, the king had said: "Today, old Wahhabism, with the new impetus of Ikhwanism, is the purest of all religions in the world. . . . Don't worry, I am the Ikhwan—no one else." Undoubtedly the movement was defensive in character; but in the main it was a distrust of foreigners with a deep-felt determination to retain at all costs Arabia and Najd in particular for the Arabs. Having created this institution and harnessed it to his own chariot, ibn Sa'ud found himself forced to go along with it, and control increasingly became a problem. He explained that the monthly subsidy of Rs. 75,000 from the British government was really a *jizya* (the poll tax paid by Christians to the early Muslim state of Muhammad's successors as an exemption from military service) and not a cash revenue provided by foreign infidels. This explanation satisfied the Ikhwan chiefs for the time being. Whenever the Ikhwan gathered for audiences with their ruler, he was forced to express antiforeign sentiments which he did not necessarily believe in. Thus one British official from the Persian Gulf who visited him reported:

He also warned me in *majlis* (assembly) that the use of tobacco was forbidden and that anyone indulging in it in Najd was breaking the law. . . . Then he sent round to me after dark a couple of tins of excellent Egyptian cigarettes, with the request that I should only smoke them in the privacy of my room.[18]

During the First World War, ibn Sa'ud made his first serious foreign contacts, first with Ottoman Turkey and later with Britain. His British contacts involved him in the first serious quarrel within the Arab world—between himself and the Grand Sharif of Mecca, Husayn. In 1915, Britain sent Captain W. Shakespear, the Political Resident Agent of the Crown in Kuwait, to treat with the Wahhabi Imam and to induce him to give aid to General Townshend's hard-pressed army in Arabia. But Shakespear, who had refused to wear Arab dress, was accidentally killed

---

[17] Lipsky, *op. cit.,* pp. 12–13.
[18] Dickson, *op. cit.,* p. 12.

while participating in a battle between the Ikhwan and the Rashids, and the negotiations were never completed. Britain gave him a thousand rifles and £20,000 as a subsidy from the India Office; but the Foreign Office, via the Arab Bureau in Cairo, supported Sharif Husayn as the most suitable leader of an Arab revolt against the Turks. Ibn Sa'ud remained neutral, using his British aid and friendship to advance his position in central Arabia, while Husayn with his sons Abdullah and Faisal became active allies of the British, as they saw it, buying Arab independence under Hashimite leadership. In the light of subsequent events, it is interesting to compare the views of the Wahhabi leader of the two eminent English Arabists, T. E. Lawrence and H. St. J. B. Philby. Lawrence, the Hashimite champion, said of ibn Sa'ud: "What is he? A great Bedouin chief of outstanding ability, like others who have passed across the Arabian stage leaving nothing like a permanent organization. The Sharifian family alone has the political and religious prestige needed for building something permanent in Arabia, to fit the country into the picture of the modern world." Philby, ibn Sa'ud's champion and the recipient of his bounty, replied that "with the Ikhwan cantonments he is building up a powerful territorial army . . . and breaking down the old tribal jealousies which led to Bedouin raiding and intertribal wars. The Arabia he leaves behind will be so different from the country we now know that his successor will have no serious difficulty in taking it on as a running show." [19]

After the war, open conflict broke out between the House of Sa'ud and the House of Hashim. Ibn Sa'ud had expanded his territory to include the amirate of Hail, al-Hasa, and Asir Province between the Hejaz and Yemen; he was styled "Sultan of Najd and its dependencies." Meanwhile Husayn had sought from the Allies the tribute due him as *the* Arab leader. He called himself King of the Hejaz. When the leader of the new Turkish Republic, Mustafa Kemal, abolished the Caliphate in 1924 (he had abolished the Ottoman Sultanate previously), Husayn declared that he was the rightful Caliph. He could point to many qualifications for the job—he was a descendant of Muhammad and he was the protector of the *Haramain*, the Holy Places of Mecca and Medina. He went to Amman, on the pretext of visiting his son, the Amir Abdullah of Transjordan, and was there proclaimed Caliph. But reaction in the Muslim world was not generally favorable. Many people who had made

[19] Philby, *Arabian Days*, London: Robert Hale, 1948, pp. 158–160.

the pilgrimage, notably Indian Muslims, were unhappy with the extortions of Husayn's tax collectors and the general lack of protection for pilgrims. Other Muslims felt that Husayn had attained his new position through Christian powers who had gotten him to rebel against his lawful Muslim overlord, the Sultan.[20] Angriest of all were the Wahhabis who felt that their lawful leadership of the true religion had been usurped. Ibn Sa'ud called his Ikhwan, and the Saudi army entered the Hejaz to expel the Hashimites and to recover the Holy Places. The Grand Sharif abdicated in favor of his eldest son, Ali, and went to Aqaba, later to Cyprus, and finally to Amman where he ended his days forgotten and unmourned by the Arabs who had once called him monarch. Ali kept up the struggle until December, 1925, from Jidda; then, he too abdicated and was taken on a British warship to Iraq where his brother Faisal had acquired a kingdom.

Ibn Sa'ud and his Wahhabis entered Mecca as pilgrims though in reality they were conquerors. Ibn Sa'ud himself, like any other pilgrim, entered the town bareheaded, wearing seamless white garments. He entered the Holy Mosque and seven times performed the circumambulation of the Ka'ba to complete the ritual. The Wahhabis "purified" the Holy City. They leveled the tombs of holy men, destroyed all ornaments and decoration on the mosques, banished musical instruments and pictures of human beings from public places, and even eliminated a row of images beside the Ka'ba. The capture of Mecca and the annexation of the Hejaz brought the Saudi state to its present size and area. In 1926–27, Great Britain recognized Ibn Sa'ud as King of the Hejaz, Najd and dependencies in the Treaty of Jidda. In 1932 a royal decree proclaimed the existence of the kingdom of Saudi Arabia, a state firmly founded upon religious principles.

IDEOLOGICAL PROBLEMS

Having almost single-handedly established his Wahhabi state against great obstacles and having been recognized by the Muslim states as the proper trustee for the Holy Cities of Islam, ibn Sa'ud's main problem became one of utilizing a rigid puritan creed in the building of a modern enduring state in Arabia. The clearest expression of his purposes in this respect came from his own lips in the course of a long interview with the Dutch Consul-General at Jidda. Ibn Sa'ud spoke as follows:

[20] Van der Meulen, *op. cit.,* pp. 92–93.

We want you to know who we are, what we are doing, and how and why. You, like all the others from the West, think of us as wild, rough fanatics, backward and narrow-minded people. . . . We have often acted severely, even mercilessly, and with Allah's help we have beaten a wicked enemy. This country shall now at last have security, peace, and order and shall know justice. . . . Bedouin have to be treated in a very hard way for only then do they learn their lesson; and if Allah wills, once they have learned their lesson, they will never forget it. We teach them the hard way, not to be cruel but out of mercy. And once we have punished them we shall not in the mercy of Allah have to do it again as long as we live.

The distances in our country are great. We can often only make justice effective in the remoteness of our deserts by the reports of the justice we dealt out. . . . We know the bedouin and we know how he has to be ruled. Is it not safe now in this country where the robbing of pilgrims flourished for centuries? By Allah, people have only begun to know us here. . . .

You have doubtless also heard many stories about the fanaticism of the Wahhabis. It is good that you should know the truth about our creed. . . . We believe that Allah the Exalted One uses us as His instrument. As long as we serve Him we will succeed. . . . Should we become a useless weapon in His hands then He will throw us aside, *wa sanahmiduhu,*—and we shall praise Him.[21]

As ibn Sa'ud embarked on his cautious program of unifying Arabia and modernizing his state while giving due deference to Wahhabism, his greatest difficulties developed among his own Ikhwan. Schooled with the fanatical notion that they alone were the "true believers" and that rigid Wahhabism was the only true path for Muslims to follow, they became bitterly hostile to the King. In their eyes all foreign instruments and contact were evil and sinful. Like the Roundheads of Cromwell in an earlier England, they marched with the sword and the Book. Their war-cry, *"sami'in, lami'in"* ["hearing and (our swords) gleaming, we come!"], was a warning not only to backsliders but also to their own Imam, should he betray the sacred trust of Wahhabism.[22] Complaints from the Ikhwan mounted, and in 1927 ibn Sa'ud called a conference of tribal and religious leaders. The Ikhwan boycotted the conference and continued raiding settlements across the border in Iraq, indifferent to the King's agreements with Great Britain. Ibn Sa'ud was criticized for dealing with infidels and adopting such "instruments of the devil" as the radio, the automobile, and the telephone. The opposition leaders particularly noted that communication by radio was an act not specifically authorized

[21] Van der Meulen, D., *The Wells of Ibn Saud,* New York: Frederick A. Praeger, Inc., 1957, pp. 99–100.
[22] Rihani, Ameen, *Maker of Modern Arabia,* Boston: Houghton Mifflin, 1928, Chapter XVIII.

by the Prophet. Ibn Saʿud replied that neither the Koran nor the *hadith* said anything against the use of radio. Then he had a selection of Koranic readings repeated over the radio. "Can anything be bad," he said, "which transmits the Word of God?" [23] In this curious way modern communications facilities, without which a state cannot function in the twentieth century, were made acceptable to the Wahhabis.

Another example of the effect of Wahhabi literalism on the growth of Saudi Arabia was the *"mahmal* incident." Egyptian pilgrims to Mecca were accustomed to bringing a litter (*mahmal*) with them, by tradition the same one in which the Fatimid queen, Shajar-al-Durr, rode in her pilgrimage in the thirteenth century. The Wahhabis viewed the ornately decorated mahmal as an idol, particularly as it was brought into Mecca with an armed escort and a drum and bugle corps. They refused to permit the procession to have a place in the pilgrimage rites. A riot broke out, and twenty-five persons were killed and hundreds injured. The Egyptian government refused to apologize for allowing the mahmal to be sent to Mecca, and Ibn Saʿud angrily suspended the entire ceremony until 1936. The repercussions of this disagreement hampered relations between Egypt and Saudi Arabia as late as World War II.

By 1928 it had become apparent that the Ikhwan would have to be brought to heel. They were raiding extensively into Iraq and had nearly involved ibn Saʿud in war with Britain. Also they were seriously hindering the modernization of the state. They demanded that all modern "infidel" inventions in use in Saudi Arabia be destroyed; ibn Saʿud countered by agreeing to do so if the Ikhwan in turn would destroy their infidel-manufactured arms and ammunition. By such tactics he won over the majority of the brethren; but there remained one large section against him, composed of the Mutair, Ajman, and ʿUtaiba tribes. In 1929 Shaykh Faisal al-Duwish of the Mutair raised the standard of revolt. He had been one of ibn Saʿud's ablest strategists in his rise to power; but he was too stern a visionary to see things, as the King could, from a politician's and statesman's point of view. He criticized the King for his laxity in using modern communications, taxing pilgrims (though it was the state's only source of revenue to speak of), and holding intercourse with infidels (in Iraq). The King, forced to move quickly and helped by Britain's ability to keep Iraq and Kuwait neutral, collected a motorized force, raced across the desert, and defeated the rebels. Shaykh al-Duwish was par-

[23] Sanger, Richard, *The Arabian Peninsula,* Ithaca: Cornell University Press, 1954, p. 33.

H.M., King 'Abd al-Aziz, with Crown Prince Sa'ud.
(Courtesy Arabian-American Oil Company)

doned because he had acted out of principle rather than personal en-mity, but other Ikhwan leaders were imprisoned in Riyadh and later in Hofuf where they still are presumably.[24] The surrender terms and the punishment meted out to the Ikhwan rebels illustrate better than any other actions of Ibn Sa'ud the difference in his thinking. They were deprived of their camels and livestock but not their rifles!

WAHHABISM AND THE MODERN AGE

With the defeat of the Ikhwan rebellion, internal resistance to the regime of ibn Sa'ud ended. Not until 1958 did internal dissatisfaction develop to the point of endangering Saudi family leadership. From 1930

[24] See Dickson, *op. cit.*, Chapter XIII, for a firsthand account of the revolt.

until his death in 1953, ibn Saʿud was the undisputed ruler of the country; and as Philby had predicted, the succession passed smoothly to his eldest surviving son, Saʿud ibn ʿAbd al-Aziz al-Saʿud. (Turki, the eldest and Ibn Saʿud's favorite, had died in the influenza epidemic of 1916.) But the bedrock of the Saudi state was its Wahhabi faith, and the still-unsolved problem which ibn Saʿud bequeathed his heirs was that of reconciling Wahhabism with the great and unexpected wealth brought by oil revenues.

There is an element of evangelism in the Wahhabi creed. As Smith notes:

The Wahhabi reform named as the source of inspiration . . . the Koran and pure Sunna. . . . The interpretation of Islam against which they were fighting was that which had become dominant, that Islam is the purpose of God for mankind as expressed in the Koran and as at work in the on-going community. . . . Their summons was to obedience and to a society that would embody His decrees.[25]

Once the Holy Places were secured for Wahhabism, establishing ibn Saʿud as the new (and better) Grand Sharif, the religion became respectable. In fact the King took the lead in promoting improved relations between Muslim nations. Following the annexation of Asir in 1934, he concluded a treaty of Islamic brotherhood and friendship with the Imam Yahya of Yemen. Another such treaty was concluded in 1937, and Yemen adhered to the Iraq-Saudi Arabian treaty of amity signed in 1936. The mahmal incident was officially closed and the Egyptians again permitted to bring their litter with its ceremonial covering, the *kiswa,* albeit without the former musical escort.

The tenets of Wahhabism and the very laudable dream of a purified, revived society contained inadequate preparation for the impact that oil was to have on Saudi Arabia. In a sense its survival as a theocratic state depends on the adjustment of the people not only to the industry itself but also to the infidel breed of men that accompanies it. In 1930 a group of Bedouin landed at Hofuf in al-Hasa; though they wore the proper dress and beards, it was soon discovered that they did not pray and spoke no Arabic. They were arrested and taken before the governor; but when ibn Saʿud learned that they were American oil prospectors, not secret agents of a foreign power, he instructed the governor to let them go

[25] Smith, *op. cit.,* pp. 43–44.

about their business. In 1933 he granted a concession to the Standard Oil Company of California; in 1936 the first strike was made; and in 1938 oil was brought in in quantity in the Dammam oilfield.[26] Favorably disposed toward the Americans from the beginning because of the help given by Charles R. Crane, the engineer Karl S. Twitchell, Kenneth Edwards (supervisor of the al-Kharj model agricultural scheme) and others, Ibn Sa'ud said, upon granting the concession, "American companies enjoy great independence in relation to their government; moreover, the United States are the farthest from Arabia and unlike the European powers have no political designs on it." [27] In strict Wahhabi terms, this was an unholy alliance, nevertheless.

Yet the King held to it, not only because it made him one of the world's richest men—royalties paid to him by Aramco amounted to $440,000 per day during 1948–1953, or $160 million per year—but also because he believed in the ultimate value of the oil company in regenerating and modernizing his people. "Believe me I know the worth of Aramco and shall defend it against anyone who tries to harm it," he once said. The royalties were used for electrification, for a communications network, for public education, for "acts of prestige" toward other Arab states, for imports of equipment and certain foodstuffs. Regrettably perhaps, they came increasingly to be used, even in the King's lifetime, for other, less productive purposes. While little change was seen in the King's own habits—he preferred a plain piece of matting to the beds in his modern palaces—the royal family, notably the younger generation, took more rapidly to the new comforts.

While adaptation to modern ways took place among the Saudi Arabians, the Americans themselves found certain adjustments useful. They adopted the *iqal*, the Arab headcloth, instead of caps while working in the oilfields, for the iqal gave better protection against the sun. Although Dhahran, the oil capital, was a purely imported bit of America—"The laurel bushes arrived in crates and the lawns in rolls," wrote one author [28]—where American families enjoyed the creature comforts they were supposed to have left behind, Wahhabi law based on the literal Koran governed even their actions. After 1952 the importation of alcohol was banned in Saudi Arabia; church bells were not to be rung; and

[26] Benoist-Mechin, Jacques, *Arabian Destiny,* translated by Denis Weaver. London: Elek Books, 1956, pp. 206–210 *passim.*
[27] *Ibid.,* p. 207.
[28] Coquet, James de, "Petrole 1951," *Le Figaro,* March 24–25, 1951.

Aramco personnel managers were asked not to employ Jews.[29] Yet in the oilfields Wahhabi psalms and Lutheran chants mingled in reasonably good harmony.[30] American urgings were also able to mitigate somewhat the rigorous penal code of Wahhabism; thus the swords used by the executioner to sever the right hands of men accused of theft came to be sterilized, and doctors were permitted to treat the stumps with chromate of mercury. A recent decree is said to have limited this punishment to the left hand only.

Officially Saudi Arabia remains a theocratic state operated under the principles of Wahhabism. The death of ibn Sa'ud on November 9, 1953, was in one sense the departure of an irreplaceable leader who *was* the state. In another sense it meant the end of a patriarchy and a way of life ill-suited to the mid-twentieth century. Unquestionably Arabia had skipped many stages of evolution to leap into the modern world under his leadership. Unquestionably the winning of three-quarters of Arabia and an income of half a million dollars a day by a penniless, property-less scion of a degraded house was a remarkable achievement. But the King had somehow failed to instill in his sons his own rigid faith, his respect for law and right. And as he grew older he fell prey to the common vice of well-to-do grandfathers, indulgence of the young. The swift changes around him may have bewildered him; particularly, after the creation of Israel he was beset with intelligent, embittered Palestinian advisors who kept whispering to him that the United States was really no better than imperialistic Britain and France. Doubtless the confusion in ibn Sa'ud's mind communicated itself to his people. As Gerald de Gaury writes: "Islam has a rigid code and it may not be easy for its devotees to adhere to it closely and to pursue the fully industrialized life offered by the West. There go with industrial life new ambitions and new taboos, a new philosophy of living and a conception of security on fixed wages; and with the change may go boredom or disgust, for many men . . . sigh for the olden days, when . . . there was adventure of the soul, of the body, of the mind. Those who were successful in the old life can hardly be successful in the new; inevitably men of

---

[29] In a recent court case in New York State, the Court of Appeals issued a decision enjoining Aramco from discriminating against Jewish personnel and stated that religion could not be considered grounds for rejecting an employee or prospective candidate for service in Saudi Arabia. See my article in *The World Book Encyclopedia, Annual Supplement 1959,* on Saudi Arabia.

[30] Benoist-Mechin, *op. cit.,* p. 213.

another stamp will rise to set an example to the race." [31] The new Saudi princes are of this stamp. Their seniors, King Saʿud and his brothers, are men half-way between the emerging world and the world of custom prescribed by Ibn Saʿud.

Between 1953 and 1958 King Saʿud, in the pattern of his father, played three roles of office. The first was the Shaykh of Shaykhs. Ibn Saʿud often said of himself, *"Ana badawiyy."* (I am a Bedouin.) [32] According to tribal custom he was sent to live with a Bedouin family as a boy, and Prince Saʿud received the same treatment. The Saudi lineage, descended from a noble Bedouin tribe, is considered important by the family as well as the tribesmen. As Shaykh of Shaykhs, King Saʿud keeps a royal bodyguard and holds public council near Riyadh in the springtime when he distributes money and gifts to key tribal leaders in return for their allegiance. This is the famous "visiting custom"; during this period the late ibn Saʿud used to cement matrimonial alliances with daughters of chieftains who struck his fancy, politically as well as physically. However confused King Saʿud may be by the twists of international (and Arab) politics, he is very much at home among the Saudi Bedouin. Indeed his chief value to the realm has been considered his ability to retain the loyalty of the tribes.

King Saʿud is also Imam of Islam according to Wahhabi doctrine. His mission is to spread the doctrine of the true faith throughout Islam, and he is also the spiritual leader of the Saudi people. Thirdly, the King plays the role of *malik* (king), responsible for the kingdom's internal security and external defense. Since Saudi Arabia has no written constitution—the nearest approach is a set of Organic Instructions codified for the Hejaz in 1926 and the 1953 and 1958 decrees setting up a Council of Ministers—authority is highly centralized and theocratic. Legal interpretations are by learned judges. Higher education was until recently available only in Islamic law or theology though the secular University of Riyadh will surely provide a breakthrough in education. The government still has such offices as the Collector of Zakat (alms) and the Chief of the Committee for the Encouragement of Good and the Suppression of Evil,[33] reminders of the not-too-distant days when the puritans of Najd entered the Holy City and cleaned it up. The *ʿulema,* still headed by descendents of Muhammad ʿAbd al-Wahhab, is consulted on

[31] De Gaury, Gerald, *Arabia Phoenix,* London: Harrap, 1946, p. 133.
[32] Lipsky, *op. cit.,* p. 108.
[33] *Ibid.,* p. 45.

matters of both domestic and foreign policy and is either subsidized by the government or paid by *waqf* funds. The muftis do not enjoy the same high status as the ulema but are also consulted on most matters and give legal opinions based almost entirely on Hanbali jurisprudence. The chief mufti of Riyadh is related to the royal family by marriage and is a descendent of Wahhab. The public laws prevailing in Saudi Arabia derive from the Koran; and as was noted above, the penal system is harsh.

A hint of the future direction of the Saudi theocracy and its adjustment to modern problems was supplied early in 1958 when the kingdom was faced with financial chaos and had acquired a bad reputation abroad due to an alleged plot against Egypt's President Nasir. Fearing for the very continuance of the monarchy, the family of Sa'ud met in conclave and issued what amounted to an ultimatum to the King. As a result, Prince Faisal, the second eldest son, took over full control of finances and foreign policy, leaving King Sa'ud as the titular ruler but functioning as Shaykh of Shaykhs rather than as Malik. Faisal, strict and realistic in financial matters, sharply reduced free government spending and conspicuous waste and introduced an orderly government for the first time in Saudi Arabia's history in the two years since he ac-

*Twentieth-century Arabia—a shopping center. (Courtesy
Arabian-American Oil Company)*

quired these powers. King Saʻud went on the equivalent of a nation-wide political tour; and using the methods of his father—tribal subsidies, political marriages, dedication of new facilities—he won the Bedouin tribes, the backbone of Wahhabism, to renewed support of the monarchy. In the towns and small cities of Saudi Arabia, loyalty to the House of Saʻud has been diluted, if not completely altered, by Arab nationalism emanating from more sophisticated parts of the Arab world. At present there appears to be no alternative to the royal family, however. The middle class is still nascent; all forms of labor organization are banned; Communists are invisible; the armed forces of thirteen thousand men are spread thinly over the country, and their ammunition is rationed. The Wahhabi tribesman, thanks to such maneuvers as King Saʻud's tour, are solidly behind the monarchy thus far. Nonetheless, monarchies in the Saudi pattern are becoming outdated in the Arab world as elsewhere. A recent report stated that in 1958, 557,801 pilgrims made the *hajj* to Mecca, 350,630 of these from Saudi Arabia, and that Iraq's Premier Qasim would make the *hajj* in 1960.[34] If his constitutional powers are lessening, Saʻud's spiritual authority seems to be on the increase.

OIL IN SAUDI ARABIA

It has become a cliché to say that the modern world has been built on oil. This basic fuel that drives modern economies is found many places under the earth's surface but nowhere as extensively as in the Middle East. Proven reserves in the four major oil-producing states there—Saudi Arabia, Iran, Iraq, and Kuwait—in 1958 alone were 165 billion barrels! If all this oil were tapped at once, we would be virtually floating on the sea of oil which has been gloomily predicted by oil men if Soviet Russia engages in full-scale competition (which would also involve dumping) with Free World oil companies.

It should be noted from the tables[35] that the two largest oil producers in the Middle East are Kuwait and Saudi Arabia, both on the Arabian Peninsula. The significance of this should not be overlooked. The production of oil in commercial quantities has given Arabia an acceleration of development not seen since the appearance of Islam. The existence of Saudi Arabia derives primarily from the strength and foresight of an untutored leader, but the forward progress of the kingdom was possible only because of "black gold." Oil production in Saudi Arabia has a com-

[34] *The Muslim World*, January, 1960.
[35] See Appendix.

paratively short history. The first oil concession granted by ibn Sa'ud was given to the Standard Oil Company of California (SOCAL) in 1933; it followed by a year the discoveries in Bahrain. There was a lively competition among the American oil men (Twitchell was one) and representatives of the Iraq Petroleum Company. Ibn Sa'ud decided in favor of the U.S. because he believed Americans to be practical, efficient, disinterested politically, anti-imperialist—and because they had offered immediate payment in gold.[36] The original concession covered 281,000 square miles, roughly half of the country, and was to expire in sixty years. In 1939 the concession area was increased to 440,000 square miles and the concession period extended to the year 2000. Since the war, the area has been reduced to about 365,000 square miles plus the off-shore areas of the eastern province.

Drilling began in 1933 under the California Arabian Standard Oil Company, a SOCAL subsidiary. In 1936 the Texas Company took a half-interest and the company's name was changed to the Arabian American Oil Company (ARAMCO). Drilling results were negative until 1938 when the first geyser of sand, stones, and dirt was flung into the air over Dammam Field. This was followed by the exploding gas forced up by the oil pressure below the sand. The twentieth century thus arrived in Saudi Arabia.

Further discoveries followed at Abu Hadriya, Abqaiq, and Abawar fields. The first oil was shipped to Bahrain for refining by the world's longest undersea pipeline. Aramco completed a three-thousand-barrel-a-day refinery in 1939; and in 1945, with military and industrial demands expanding, the company competed with the International Bechtel Construction Firm, a fifty-thousand-barrel-a-day refinery at Ras Tanura. This capacity has since been expanded to more than one hundred thirty thousand barrels a day. This refinery handled seventy-two million barrels of crude in 1956.[37] Additional fields have been discovered from time to time, most recently at Khursanujah and Fadhli; the extremely productive undersea field of As-Saffaniyah was brought in in 1957, marking a reversal of the trend of Aramco's explorations north and westward across the sands. With these various fields expanding, the value of Aramco's investment is over a billion dollars, making it a high prize for

---

[36] As the deal was about to be closed the U.S. went off the gold standard. Matters were finally settled to the King's satisfaction by agreeing to pay him 4 sh. gold per ton or the equivalent in dollars or pounds sterling. See Sanger, *op. cit.*, p. 101.
[37] Lipsky, *op. cit.*, p. 227 and map.

ambitious Arab leaders and a stake of American prestige in the Middle East worth defending.

The complicating pressures of inter-Arab politics were imposed on Saudi-Aramco relations after World War II, initially for economic reasons. The cost of shipping oil by tanker around the peninsula from Ras Tanura on the Persian Gulf to the Red Sea proved expensive, and the high toll rates in the Suez Canal—twenty-two cents a barrel—meant that Aramco's product could not compete with cheap Venezuelan oil for the European market. Therefore, a pipeline to the Mediterranean became a practical necessity. In 1945 the Trans-Arabian Pipeline Company was formed. After two years of difficult construction, which was complicated by the problem of shipping eleven hundred miles of thirty-inch pipe across the Atlantic since there was no mill available for fabricating the sections in the Middle East, Tapline, the shortened name of the big pipeline, opened for business in 1950. This permitted oil transshipment across the desert from Abqaiq to Sidon, Lebanon, where another refinery processes it.[38] More than half of Aramco's oil in 1960 went via Tapline, the rest by tanker.

Because the pipeline crosses Syria, Jordan, and Lebanon, these three "transit" countries had to be consulted as well as compensated. Jordan's permission was easily obtained in 1946 in return for a $250,000 annual payment for its section. Lebanon signed for $180,000 since the refinery meant employment as well as revenue for its citizens. Syria was the holdout; not until 1949, following the Arab-Israeli armistice, did Syria come to terms with the company and then on a higher basis than the other two—annual payments of £20,000, a toll of £.0015 per ton, a guarantee to supply Syria with two hundred thousand tons of crude at world prices, and a minimum payment of £40,000 to cover costs of government protection of property and employees.[39]

Also in 1950 Aramco and Saudi Arabia concluded a fifty-fifty profit-sharing agreement, first in the industry and a landmark in relations between the Middle East and the oil companies. This agreement, in fact, had repercussions in Iran which did not stop until the Anglo-Iranian Oil Company had been nationalized.

Saudi Arabia, for a variety of reasons, was not particularly affected

---

[38] Lipsky, *op. cit.*, pp. 247 ff. Tapline built only a portion of the pipeline east from Sidon. The greater part was built westward from the Persian Gulf by Aramco. See Sanger, *op. cit.*, pp. 120–121, for an excellent brief description of construction methods.

[39] Lipsky, *op. cit.*, p. 248.

by the nationalist fever which swept the Arab Middle East after Gamal Abd al-Nasir's rise to power in Egypt. The fifty-fifty agreement was an important factor in maintaining good relations between the company and the government. The American nature of Aramco—representative of and identified with political disinterestedness—was another. The rudimentary nature of Saudi political and social consciousness and the autocratic rule of the Sauds deterred over-penetration of the new Arab slogans—although prosperity turned Saudi middle-class ears increasingly to Radio Cairo. Finally, the company itself engaged in a variety of activities not normally the functions of an alien concern to maintain the necessary good relations with the Saudi government. It has set up a Government Relations Department under a vice-president to maintain liaison with Saudi officials at both national and local levels. While much of this liaison concerns details of the concession agreement, the department through its local representatives has handled problems ranging from deportation of a contract employee to technical assistance of great variety.[40] The Arabian Affairs Division produces basic research studies on Saudi life. So extensive, in fact, is the work of the Government Relations Department and so close the relationship with the royal government that Aramco is often accused of handling U.S. foreign relations with Saudi Arabia.

Other "nonproductive" services of Aramco include an Arab Industrial Development Department which makes capital and know-how available to would-be Saudi entrepreneurs; extensive press and public relations campaigns with newspaper advertising in Arabic publications which emphasize the benefits to the countries of their work; and perhaps most important, the creation of a trained, literate labor force.[41] A five-year training program was undertaken in 1949 in line with the stipulation in the concession agreement that the company fill as many positions as possible with Saudis. In 1954–55 program emphasis was shifted to career development for Saudis and training of *mushrifs* (supervisors), both aspects reinforcing the notion that Aramco's Saudi employees had generally reached a sufficient level of basic skills with some ready to realize their leadership potentialities. Sixty Saudis were selected for personal development and in 1957 one hundred forty-two more. In addition

[40] See Lenczowski, George, *Oil and State in the Middle East,* Ithaca: Cornell University Press, 1960, Chapter V, pp. 113–117.

[41] *Ibid.,* Chapter XII, p. 243. One of these ads pointing to a new employee dining hall at Dhahran was headed "Good Food at Low Cost."

American and Saudi employees of ARAMCO check hydrant
pressure at Ras Tanura. (Courtesy Arabian-American
Oil Company)

the number sent abroad for study tripled, from fifteen in 1954 to fifty in 1957.

Prerequisites or fringe benefits were another key aspect of Aramco's determination to avoid the "exploitation" label. Minimum daily wages rose from SR 1.5 in 1945 to SR 7.5 in 1957 (U.S.$.40 to $2.02). In September, 1958, the work week was reduced to forty-two hours. There is a system of cash awards and a retirement plan which avoids the Wahhabi strictures against usury by paying no interest to employees who left sums on deposit with the company. Saudis may buy food and clothing at subsidized prices. Extensive free medical services are also provided including a full year's wages to employees who become totally incapacitated either on or off the job.

In providing these and other services, Aramco not only improves upon American company practice but also is well in advance of Saudi Arabian labor legislation. The first Saudi labor decree was promulgated in 1947;

it does little more than establish an eight-hour day and six-day week (interrupted at intervals for prayers), arbitration procedures for grievances (to be settled by a committee of two representing the employer and the government), requirement of work permits, and provision for trial in shari'a courts for foreign workers accused of personal offenses against a Saudi subject.[42] A supplementary decree of 1956, inspired no doubt by a strike on October 17, 1953, of 13,000 Saudi employees of Aramco which became a challenge to the government's authority—they defied a back-to-work order—forbids strikes and disturbances.

Whether these various non-profit making activities will delay the inevitable transfer from Aramco to Saudi ownership is a moot point. Oil men realize that their product is both perishable and exhaustible; once out of the ground, it is gone forever. Having invested millions to get it out, they follow the principle of "make as much as you can as fast as you can." On the other hand, Aramco owners, more realistic than the men of AIOC, believe that long-term good relations and an orderly transfer of power are more likely through such an enlightened program. Because Aramco has consistently stressed the purely commercial character of its enterprise, it is less associated in Saudi eyes with the erratic course of American foreign policy or its periodic involvement with France and Britain. During the Suez crisis of 1956, Aramco employees donated SR 178,000 to the Egyptian Red Crescent Society for Egyptian relief; and the company's American character ensured the orderly flow of oil through the pipeline to the Mediterranean although Saudi Arabia broke diplomatic relations with France and Britain and banned oil shipments to the two aggressors.

INTERNAL CRISIS

In 1955 oil production in Saudi Arabia was 951,000 barrels per day; in 1956 it reached the coveted goal of a million barrels per day. It dropped to 893,000 in 1957 after the Suez crisis, rose to 991,300 in 1958, and 1,095,399 in 1959. Royalties of more than forty cents per barrel mean that King Sa'ud's annual income is over $300 million.[43] It must be remembered that the ruler and the government are the same. Therefore, King Sa'ud's revenues must go for the upkeep of the royal

[42] *Ibid.*, pp. 258–259.
[43] The Getty Oil Company, which has a half-share of the concession in the Kuwait-Saudi Arabia neutral zone, pays royalties of $.55 per barrel and other fees to the Saudi government. Lipsky, *op. cit.*, p. 190.

house as well as for governmental operations. Nevertheless it has become clear to observers that the enormous revenues continue to become deficits; in short, the Kingdom of Saudi Arabia is in a parlous financial state.

Ibn Sa'ud had no interest in budgets as such; and while the royal finances consisted largely of disbursements to tribes in return for their allegiance, accountings were neither made nor necessary. After the King began to receive revenues in bulk from oil royalties, his generosity, extraordinary even for an Arab, became incredible. The royal family's extravagances abroad are well-known—such as the prince who asked for $15,000 at breakfast because "we're going to be in New York for three days." [44] At home, waste was equally conspicuous—for example, to each prince his own air-conditioned castle and Cadillac. Unscrupulous speculators from the Levant frequently bilked the government of large sums for evanescent projects. The pleasures of credit were clearly understood but not the final obligation; future royalties were pledged against current expenses.

The steadily increasing cost of government itself compounded Saudi Arabia's budgetary problems. Unlike Kuwait and Bahrain which, by their compactness, are able to set aside oil revenues for future reserves, Saudi Arabia has had to devote all revenues not siphoned off by royal largesse to modernization in every sector of national life. No capital formation is yet possible, and the strictures of Wahhabism discourage individual saving. King Sa'ud must also pay for the upkeep of the Holy Cities. The Wahhabi influence has kept Saudi Arabia less prone to the "great leap forward" of Nasir's United Arab Republic and has upheld the traditional Arab virtues—a cardinal one is the prestige of a ruler which is best demonstrated by his generosity. What Westerners may consider needless overspending, therefore, is in Saudi Arabia the accepted custom.

In 1954 the Council of Ministers, until then chiefly an advisory body, was given constitutional powers to approve the annual budget, including any new appropriations. Crown Prince Faisal, King Sa'ud's younger brother, was the President of the Council but owing to his health was out of the country during much of 1955–1957. In 1957 an International Monetary Fund mission exposed the financial deterioration and made numerous recommendations. Alarmed by foreign criticisms of mismanagement and fearing a coup d'etat, several princes, including the

[44] Sanger, op. cit., p. 51.

repatriate Faisal, had a showdown which apparently brought the ultimatum: Reform or resign. As a result, Prince Faisal became Saudi Arabia's Prime Minister with complete authority over fiscal matters in early 1958. The Saudi Arabian Monetary Agency, founded in 1952 to stabilize the *riyal,* was given the function of a central bank. A strict austerity program went into effect. (For example, air conditioning in the King's new palace at Riyadh was not completed.) Cabinet ministers were forbidden to hold private jobs at the same time. King Sa'ud, turning over the reins to his brother, concentrated on restoring the loyalty of the tribes, where he was most effective. The absence of any relaxation of the control of the royal family, the lack of participation in government by most educated Saudis, and the continued reliance on one major source of income do not suggest an early solution for Saudi Arabia's financial instability.

In December, 1960, Prince Faisal again resigned and withdrew from active participation in the government. Although apparently the result of a combination of factors—his own poor health, his feeling that he had laid the groundwork for Saudi Arabia's development and could surrender its implementation safely to others, and the maneuverings of factions within the royal family—the move really opened the way for the country to progress further from personal to bureaucratic, impersonal administration. Younger members of the House of Sa'ud, substituting efficiency and education for personal magnetism, were speaking up in government councils; more significantly, their views were being accepted. The most articulate was King Sa'ud's younger brother Talal ibn 'Abd al-Aziz, who became Finance Minister in the 1961 Cabinet. Acting upon the recommendations of the World Bank, Talal and his more articulate brothers and cousins, with the King's blessing, inaugurated Saudi Arabia's first development program of a long-range nature. To set it up, the Saudis reversed their customary pattern of reserving all final judgments and began actively recruiting a nucleus of about forty foreign advisers. Prince Talal admitted that previous government spending had been frequently unwise, perhaps the understatement of the year. With the Saudis ready, apparently, to accept foreign advice, the way was clear for organized planning in the desert kingdom. Whether the House of Sa'ud and its strict Koranic laws would long survive a successful modernization program depended on what centers of power and leadership might arise in the country, as education and military training received wider application; and the success of these centers, if any, depended in turn on the behavior of the royal family. In any case, political democracy was clearly a long way off for Saudi Arabia.

INTERNATIONAL RELATIONS

Since most of Saudi Arabia's boundary agreements with its neighbors have been solved or put in abeyance, the only issue which has complicated its foreign relations is the Buraimi dispute. The Buraimi oasis, a string of villages at the confluence of important caravan tracks in eastern Arabia, north of the Empty Quarter, is claimed equally by Saudi Arabia, the Shaykhdom of Abu Dhabi, and the Sultanate of Muscat-Oman. The latter two have treaty relations with Great Britain, which represents them in external affairs. The discovery of oil in the Arabian Peninsula made Buraimi important, not for its oil but as the hub of a communications network. In 1952 Saudi forces occupied the northern part of the oasis but reached an agreement with the British, who had objected to the occupation, that both sides would remain where they were pending arbitration. A five-man tribunal of one Briton, one Saudi, and three neutrals met in Geneva in 1955 to arbitrate the dispute. But after five days the British arbiter, Sir Reader Bullard, resigned, saying that the Saudi representative, Deputy Foreign Affairs Minister Yusuf Yasin, was not impartial. Later the Foreign Office accused Saudi Arabia of trying to bribe the Buraimis into accepting their authority. Dark imprecations also came from Whitehall that Aramco was engaged in a sinister plot to drive oil interests from Arabia, using Buraimi as a lever. British-trained Trucial Oman Levies then drove the Saudi forces from the oasis and reclaimed it for the Shaykh of Abu Dhabi.

The Saudi government protested to the UN and published several thick volumes of a "Memorial" of its case for Buraimi, but it took no other action. In 1958 Prince Faisal said that diplomatic relations with Britain (broken off in 1956) could be resumed if the British either accepted arbitration again or withdrew from Buraimi. The latest development in the dispute came in 1960 when UN Secretary Hammarskjold asked the Swedish Ambassador to Spain to arbitrate, with a view to possible placement of a UN force in the oasis. The irony of the situation for Britain remains—it could profitably build a friendship with the House of Sa'ud and incidentally protect its small Arabian protectorates, enabling them to get a better start on the road to self-government, yet it finds itself bound by moral and political commitments to support autocratic patriarchs who are in the way of Arab progress. An equal sort of irony was visited upon the United States, which by implication and through

Aramco had supported the Saudi position. King Saʿud, having announced that his foreign policy consisted of neutralism and cooperation with other Arab countries, notified the U.S. that its lease on the big Dhahran air base would not be renewed after its expiration in 1962. Although the Saudis graciously granted permission to the U.S. Air Force to complete a new air terminal now under construction at Dhahran, it was made clear that we would have no military rights to the base after April, 1962. The descendants of Ibn Saʿud, who had accepted oil technicians from America because he believed they were politically disinterested, had no such illusions about the leading power of the Free World.

GENEALOGY OF THE HOUSE OF SAʿUD [45]

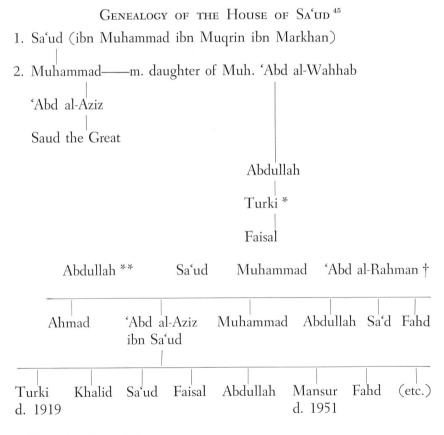

1. Saʿud (ibn Muhammad ibn Muqrin ibn Markhan)

2. Muhammad——m. daughter of Muh. ʿAbd al-Wahhab

ʿAbd al-Aziz

Saud the Great

Abdullah

Turki *

Faisal

Abdullah **   Saʿud   Muhammad   ʿAbd al-Rahman †

Ahmad   ʿAbd al-Aziz   Muhammad   Abdullah   Saʿd   Fahd
                  ibn Saʿud

Turki   Khalid   Saʿud   Faisal   Abdullah   Mansur   Fahd   (etc.)
d. 1919   d. 1951

* Founder of second Saudi state
** Deposed 1818–1819 by Ibrahim and executed in Constantinople
† His brothers, Abdullah and Saʿud, contested, leaving him in partial control for a while.
[45] Twitchell, K. S., *Saudi Arabia*, 2nd ed., Princeton: Princeton University Press, 1958, p. 149. See also Benoist-Mechin, *op. cit.*, p. 288.

RECOMMENDED READINGS

1. Aldington, Richard, *Lawrence of Arabia,* London: Collins, 1955.
2. Armstrong, H. C., *Lord of Arabia: Ibn Saud,* London: Barker, 1934.
3. Benoist-Mechin, J., *Le Loup et le Leopard: Ibn Seoud,* Paris: Albin Michel, 1955.
4. ———, *Arabian Destiny,* transl. by Denis Weaver, London: Elek Books, 1956.
5. de Gaury, Gerald, *Arabia Phoenix,* London: Harrap, 1946.
6. Hitti, Philip, *History of The Arabs,* 6th ed., New York: St Martin's Press, Inc., 1957.
7. Lenczowski, George, *Oil and State in the Middle East,* Ithaca: Cornell University Press, 1960.
8. Lipsky, George, ed., *Saudi Arabia,* New Haven: HRAF Press, 1958.
9. Philby, H. St. J. B., *Arabian Days,* London: Robert Hale, 1948.
10. ———, *Arabian Jubilee,* New York: The John Day Company, Inc., 1953.
11. ———, *Saudi Arabia,* New York: Frederick A. Praeger, Inc., 1955.
12. Rihani, Ameen, *Makers of Modern Arabia,* Boston: Houghton Mifflin Company, 1928.
13. Sanger, Richard, *The Arabian Peninsula,* Ithaca: Cornell University Press, 1954.
14. Thomas, Bertram, *The Arabs,* London: Butterworth, 1937.
15. Twitchell, K. S., *Saudi Arabia,* 3rd ed., Princeton: Princeton University Press, 1958.
16. Van der Meulen, Daniel, *The Wells of Ibn Saud,* New York: Frederick A. Praeger, Inc., 1957.
17. Vidal, F. S., *The Oasis of al-Hasa,* New York: Aramco, 1955.

CHAPTER 10

THE ARABIAN PENINSULA II: YEMEN AND THE PROTECTORATES

Yemen—The Theocratic Kingdom

$\mathcal{O}$t is said in a *hadith* (a saying of the Prophet Muhammad) that "Wisdom is of the Yemen." In the southwestern corner of Arabia, stretching inland from the Red Sea across unnamed broken mountain ranges, is the Mutawakilite Kingdom of Yemen, a theocratic state little different today from what it was when the present Zaidi dynasty took command in the eighteenth century. In classical days, the region was called "Arabia Felix"; several distinguished pre-Islamic civilizations flourished there, and religious concepts took deep root among the inhabitants. Each of the three great monotheistic religions held sway in Yemen for a time; but where Christianity disappeared almost without a trace and Judaism survived (until 1948) only among the Jewish community of San'a, Islam was accepted en masse by the Yemenis. Having done so, they became fierce guardians of the true faith, not in the Wahhabi sense of following the sole "right path," but in the familiar sense of war against the unbelievers. When the Syrian writer, Ameen Rihani, set out to visit Yemen in the 1920's, he was warned of what would happen once he set foot in the country. Because he was a Christian, the Yemenis would cut off his head, he was told.[1] In fact, Rihani, who made a point of traveling with a number of Arab friends *who could speak no English,* had no such difficulties in Yemen and came out with his head intact. In 1933 the American anthropologist, Carleton Coon, had an audience with the

---

[1] Rihani, Ameen, *Arabian Peak and Desert,* Boston: Houghton Mifflin Company, 1930, pp. 1–3.

Imam Yahya, father of the present ruler of Yemen. He noted that "in deference to our Christian lack of squatting facets, two Sunday-school chairs were placed in front of the Imam for our use. This was an act of great courtesy, since it placed our heads higher than his. . . . On another occasion I had the privilege of acting as his confidential secretary in helping him pay a premium for his life insurance." [2] Nonetheless, Yemen remains a closed country for most Christians (and Americans), requiring a personal invitation from the Imam for admittance. Another of history's ironies is shown by the fact that the bulk of foreigners presently in Yemen is composed of the atheistic Marxist Russians and Chinese!

During the first five centuries of the Christian era, a number of kings in Yemen expanded their control along the Hadhramaut and the Red Sea. This brought them into friction with the Ethiopians. Previously, a Christian mission from the Roman Emperor Constantius II had converted many pagans in north Yemen, and the influence of the Christian Ethiopians helped to spread Christianity further in the Happy Kingdom. The Himyarites, the generic name for these Christian rulers, evolved an important civilization. They were tolerant to the point of encouraging Judaism along with Christianity. The last Himyarite king, in fact, was a Jew. When he massacred the Christians of Najran, the remaining ones called on Ethiopia to help. The Ethiopians sent an army of seventy thousand men across the Red Sea and not only drove this ruler out but also destroyed his kingdom, rendering it subservient to Ethiopia. Christianity vanished from south Arabia, but Judaism survived in the small Jewish colony of San'a, which numbered about fifty thousand in 1947. Many of the Jews of San'a traced their lineage back to the Second Diaspora (70 A.D.). (The men always wore long gray robes and skullcaps; their hair was long, black, and curled in ringlets. The women were unveiled and wore headdresses with elaborate silver decorations.) Yemenite Jews were excused from military service, veiling, and the prohibition on wine; but they were required to remain in their own quarter of San'a after dark, could not own land, and were forbidden to ride on a horse or in an automobile or carry a weapon. Their houses were also limited to two stories in height. They were judged by their own chief rabbi; and only when disputes arose between Jew and Muslim did

---

[2] Coon, Carleton, *Caravan*, rev. ed., New York: Henry Holt & Co., Inc., 1958, p. 291.

they go before the Imam's court.[3] The Jews of San'a were the silver-smiths as well as the wine-makers. When all of them (except one) emigrated to Israel in 1948, their departure left an occupational as well as an architectural gap in the community.[4]

Yemen was the first area outside of Muhammad's own region of the Hejaz to accept Islam. Muhammad had sent Mu'adh to Yemen to spread the gospel of his new faith. The messenger arrived in Al Janad, now a cluster of hovels but then an important provincial center ruled by a Persian governor. At first the governor said he could not accept Islam unless authorized to do so by the Persian Great King, his superior. (The Persians ruled Yemen at this time.) Fortuitously for the messen-ger, the Great King had just died. When he informed the governor of this seemingly miraculous fact, he and all his subjects are said to have been converted on the spot. They built a mosque which according to tradition was the first built outside of Hejaz during Muhammad's life-time.

The "Great Schism" which divided Islam into two major groups—the Sunnis and the Shi'as, with their various offshoots—affected Yemen in a manner reversed from the pattern current in other Arab countries. There are both Sunnis and Shi'as in Yemen, with the Sunnis living mainly in the Tihama, the hot coastal Red Sea littoral, and the lower plateau and the Shi'as in the High Yemen. No census is available of the population of Yemen, and the relative size of each group is unknown. The ruling family, and in fact the dominant force in the country, is Shi'a, however. The Shi'as of Yemen are Zaidis; their beliefs differ in a few respects from the two main branches of Shi'ism, the Twelvers and the Seveners. Thus they reject the belief in a Twelfth or "Hidden" Imam, and the Ismaili belief in a sequence of seven imams, the last also hidden. Instead they maintain that the Imamate must remain in the direct line of Muhammad but that it does not require the succession of the first born—the ablest, mentally, physically, and spiritually, may be chosen for the job. The Zaidis trace their lineage back to Zaid ibn Ali Zain al-'Abidin, the son of Husayn, who was the son of Ali and Fatima, Mu-hammad's daughter. The present dynasty goes back to al-Hadi ila'l Haqq Yahya, a grandson of Ali Qasim al-Rassi, descended in the sixth

---

[3] *Ibid.*, p. 101.
[4] Fayein, Claudie, *A French Doctor in the Yemen*, London: Robert Hale, 1957, p. 70.

generation from Ali and Fatima. Genealogically they are qualified for the job.

Other elements of Zaidi belief are as follows: They are Mu'tazilites (rationalists), claiming that beyond direct revelation reason determines man's acts, which are carried out under free will. They reject predestination. The only eternity is God; such attributes as knowledge, power, goodness, etc., are only eternal in God. Hence they maintain that the Koran was created in time, not in eternity. This sets them off from the fundamentalist Wahhabis of Yemen's northern neighbor, if for no other reason. The modern Zaidis also believe that reason is the determining factor in religious thought; they say they are the "Protestants" of Islam.

The Zaidis follow the Hanafi ritual. They state, for example, that it is permissible to combine two prayers when circumstances do not permit offering a prayer at the proper time. The Sunni Yemenis of the Tihama and the Middle Yemen follow the Shafi'i ritual; both Taiz, the present capital, and the key port of Hodeida are predominantly Sunni. However, the younger generation of Yemenis is less concerned over these differences than their elders; they speak of the Yemeni nation as a part of the future Arab nation in which such differences will be conveniently forgotten.[5]

Political Developments.   Until 1918 Yemen was a part of the Ottoman Empire. The Imam Yahya, who had succeeded to Zaidi leadership according to the prescribed ritual, was confirmed in his local sovereignty by the Turks who carried on Yemen's external representation from Constantinople. The Imam supported Turkey during the First World War, but this had little effect since British control of Aden neutralized Yemen's Turkish garrison. When Ottoman Turkey collapsed, the Imam asserted *de facto* authority over Yemen as an independent ruler although no official proclamation was issued. The British evacuated the Turkish garrison. The Zaidi ruler laid claim not only to the highlands but to the coast as well, even parts of Britain's Aden Protectorate. In 1925, the previously independent principality of Asir was partitioned between ibn Sa'ud's rising Wahhabi power and the Imamate, bringing Yemen up to its present boundaries.

Under the iron-fisted leadership of the Imam Yahya, Yemen continued its medieval ways up to and through World War II. Foreign contacts were rare, and the kingdom's only significance in international

⁵ Bethmann, Eric, *Yemen on the Threshold,* Washington: American Friends of the Middle East, 1960, pp. 43–45.

affairs was as a focal point in Anglo-Italian rivalry following the rise of Mussolini. Britain found it far more difficult to extend direct control into Yemen, particularly over the hardy mountaineers of the Zaidi highlands, than to rule the petty sheikhdoms elsewhere in Arabia. Yet the position of Yemen astride the Bab al-Mandeb at the southern end of the Red Sea was a serious concern to British strategic and economic thinking. Yemenite power in the wrong hands could threaten the water routes to India. Sir Gilbert Clayton, early in 1925, tried for nearly a month to get the Imam's signature on an agreement but without success. The next year, the Zaidi monarch initialed a ten-year treaty of friendship and commerce with Italy. Italy also recognized Yemen's full independence, which Britain had not done. A Yemenite state visit to Italy in 1927 and an arms agreement were further evidence of Il Duce's fishing in troubled waters. Since Italy already had Eritrea, across the Red Sea, domination of Yemen even through economic means would place her in a position for a squeeze play on Britain's vital lifeline.

The Imam signed a treaty with the USSR in 1928 which allowed the Soviets to establish a commercial mission in San'a, the capital—an early example of the flood-tide of Soviet penetration through "peaceful" economic means that has swept the Middle East since the early 1950's. Yemeni tribesmen also attacked villages in the Western Aden Protectorate; Britain retaliated with the use of Royal Air Force planes. The Imam agreed to enter into negotiations in 1931; but it was not until 1934, on February 11, that the Anglo-Yemeni Treaty of San'a was concluded. The treaty provided for friendship and mutual cooperation plus stabilization of the Yemen-Aden boundary for forty years. Britain also recognized Yemen's full independence. The power of religion in the Arabian theocracy was shown by the Imam's refusal to abandon specifically his claims to Aden because he said the boundaries of the Mutawakilite Kingdom were ordained by God alone!

Shortly thereafter Yemen clashed with Saudi Arabia. Ibn Saud's forces invaded the Yemen portion of Asir province and charged that Yemen was abetting the former ruler of Asir in his raids on the Saudi half of Asir. The Yemenis were defeated and forced to sue for peace, but Ibn Sa'ud did not impose territorial claims. The treaty, which was followed by a tripartite pact among Yemen, Saudi Arabia, and Iraq, indicated Yemen's gradual approach to participation with others as an Arab state. The Imam continued to hold Britain at arms-length (though this could be said of all his foreign contacts in truth). Treaties were concluded with the Netherlands and France. The 1926 treaty with Italy was renewed for a year in 1936 and then replaced by a grandiose twenty-five-year alliance with the unprecedented permission for Italian doctors to take up permanent residence in San'a and for engineers to assist in its development.[6]

Although Britain and Italy more or less settled their differences regarding the Middle East in 1938, Imam Yahya remained suspicious of Anglo-Saxon intentions through much of World War II. Officially Yemen was neutral. In 1943 the Imam broke diplomatic relations with the Axis powers, arrested forty Italians and two Germans, and closed down the two radio stations they had been operating. Yemen was a charter member of the League of Arab States but did not declare war on Germany and Japan; this made it necessary for her to enter the United Nations by a separate application in 1947.

Internal Crises of 1948 and 1955.   The anomaly of Yemen's medieval existence and hierarchical politics in the twentieth century was paraded before the world in 1948 and again in 1955. The effect of the internal revolutions of these years on modern public opinion was perhaps the reaction of a man who enters a hotel to find men in armor sitting in the lobby! It seemed unbelievable to find a country in which currency was the Maria Theresa thaler carried around in sacks, a country where men with the mutilated stumps of right hands severed for some crime were not uncommon, where the death of a ruler evoked the same fratricide practiced by the Ottoman Turks in the fifteenth century.

On February 17, 1948, Sayyid Abdullah ibn-al-Wazir, a former minister of state and a member of the most powerful family in Yemen, carried out a coup d'etat. Imam Yahya, who had been taken for a ride in the country as a ruse, was assassinated, along with Prime Minister Qadi Abdullah al'Umair, two sons of the Imam, and various other persons.[7] Abdullah named himself Imam and appointed Yahya's sixth son, Amir Saif al-Haqq Ibrahim,[8] Prime Minister. Ibrahim was a leader in the Free Yemenis, or Greater Yemeni Society, a group composed of Yemenis, mostly in Aden, or Yemenis who had been outside their country and

---

[6] Fayein, *op. cit.*, notes that in 1948 there were four practicing Italian doctors in Yemen, and one Frenchman.

[7] Macro, Eric, "Yemen: a Brief Survey," *Royal Central Asian Journal,* January, 1949.

[8] Seif al-Haqq means "Sword of Truth." Although rivals, the Wazir and Yahya families are both Zaidis and have a common interest in perpetuating their rule in Yemen over the lowlanders.

seen the progress in other nations. The Free Yemenis made common cause with the al-Wazir family which resented the Imam's preference for Prince Ahmad as his successor.

Since Yemen has no constitutional authority, the murdered Imam's eldest son and heir apparent, Ahmad, defied the Waziri and announced that *he* was the Imam. Zaidi tribesmen supported Ahmad; he attacked San'a, which had accepted the rule of the usurper, and in March the city surrendered. Abdullah was executed; and Ibrahim died in prison, either of a heart attack or a badly-digested meal. San'a was given over to looting for a day or two. The Arab League, under pressure from Ibn Sa'ud, who criticized the assassination, recognized the new government. Raghib Bey, who had sided with Ahmad, was renamed Foreign Minister. Peace returned to Arabia Felix with the only change being that Imam Ahmad transferred the government to Taiz.[9]

Matters continued more or less serenely in Yemen until 1955, when a conspiracy to remove Imam Ahmad in favor of a modernist, reform government developed. None of the causes of the 1948 insurrection had been removed. The more prosperous Sanahanis resented the elevation of the backward tribesmen and remembered the looting of 1948. Yemen's participation in the Arab League and the UN brought more and more Yemenis into contact with foreign influences; students sent to Cairo, in particular, received a full dosage of Arab nationalism with its parallel reformist concepts. The Imam's failure to introduce any development or technical projects widened the gulf between his administration and the progressives.

The conspirators made common cause with army units and attacked the royal guards in Taiz. Ahmad fled to the al-Udi fortress, while Yemenite religious leaders, who had tried to mediate at first, agreed with the rebel leaders on March 31 to depose Ahmad in favor of his more liberal brother, Abdullah. However, the 1948 situation repeated itself. Ahmad's son, Crown Prince Badr, escaped to High Yemen where he appealed to the same Hashid and Bakin tribes that had aided his father's cause after his grandfather's murder.[10] The tribesmen rallied to Badr and in a fierce battle defeated the Yemenite army which was handicapped by the fact

[9] Partly out of bitterness and in part because the modernization slowly coming to Yemen will come through Taiz, the natural gateway.

[10] It was said that Badr won the support of these tribes by the dramatic gesture of throwing his turban and *jambiya* (ceremonial dagger) on the ground. Lenczowski, George, *Oil and the State in the Middle East,* Ithaca: Cornell University Press, 1960, Chapter V, pp. 113–117.

328 The Arabian Peninsula II: Yemen and the Protectorates

that its ammunition was inside al-Udi fortress. Another round of executions followed. But Imam Ahmad, back on his throne, felt that some reforms were in order. He named Badr Prime Minister with orders to modernize the administration and opened the treasury of his late father (estimated at between $56 million and $280 million) for development purposes. Prince Badr, who has visited Cairo and the Soviet Union, stated during a visit to the former that his father wished to establish a democratic government for his people.

Five years have passed since this pronouncement and since the restoration of Imam Ahmad. Have the Yemenis received their promised democratic government? Probably not. In 1950 the administration of the country was by the *divan*, or council—the Imam presiding over his ministers, about fifteen of them, squatting in a circle around him. Council sessions were held at night usually; any citizen could address a petition to the Imam, frequently by telegram with pre-paid reply to get direct action. The Imam would read each request, toss it on the floor if the reply was negative or write an answer if favorable and toss it to the appropriate minister for execution under the royal red seal. In this fashion, everything from an expenditure for inkwells to a million-dollar project came under the royal eye.[11]

Yemen in International Relations. The observation that Yemen is rushing headlong into the fourteenth century applies equally to Yemen's foreign and internal affairs. The Imam Yahya's deliberate policy was one of isolation and remoteness; his was the only Arab country which did not permit the residence of British representatives. Yemen does not permit the coinage of money; the only currency is the heavy, eighteenth-century Maria Theresa thaler, negotiable only in Aden. There is no bank; government disbursements are made in sacks of the heavy thalers. Even today the would-be visitor to Yemen must obtain an official invitation from the Iman before entering. Despite this near-hermetic isolation, the conflict of East and West has not by-passed Yemen. Although an early treaty had been signed with the Soviet Union, the United States held an early advantage. In 1926–1927, Charles R. Crane went to Yemen and won the Imam's friendship. Crane, equally well-known in the Middle East for his part in the King-Crane Commission, agreed to supply *gratis* the services of an American engineer to help develop Yemen's mineral resources and transport if the Imam would accept one. The

---

[11] Fayein, *op. cit.*, pp. 47–48. Reportedly the Imam could act on two hundred telegrams at a sitting.

Imam agreed to accept his new friend's recommendation. Karl S. Twitchell, an American engineer visiting Aden at the time, heard about the opening and applied for it. In this casual manner one of the great partnerships of the twentieth century arose in the Middle East. Twitchell laid out roads, made mineral surveys, even built the only steel truss bridge in Arabia over the Wadi La'a in Yemen—and Crane paid the bills. Twitchell went on to greater accomplishments in Saudi Arabia, but the residue of good will engendered by the Crane-Twitchell tandem lasted a long time. The first official U.S. mission to Yemen, headed by the distinguished Arabist, Colonel W. R. Eddy, Minister to Saudi Arabia, arrived in 1946. After protracted discussions in the Oriental manner, which broke down once because Prince Husayn, third son of the Imam, was determined to sabotage them, the mission concluded a treaty of friendship and commerce with Yemen.[12] In the following year, Yemen received credits of $1 million to buy American surplus machinery and trucks, and Prince Abdullah visited the U.S. where he met President Truman. In 1955, Yemen granted the Yemen Development Corporation, an American firm, a thirty-year concession for exploration and development of oil and mineral resources.

In view of these overtures, it seems almost incredible that since 1956 Yemen has become the Arab state most heavily penetrated by Soviet bloc technicians. A recent visitor to Yemen estimated that there were several hundred Russian and Chinese technical experts there, the Russians working on the airfields and the Chinese Communists on the roads. The Yemen Development Company's concession was terminated; the U.S. is represented (other than by an American free-lance geologist) by the Minister to Saudi Arabia.

One might well ask, why this complete turnabout? There appear to be a number of reasons why Yemen has chosen Soviet bloc over Western assistance—without as yet sacrificing the Imam's absolute authority. One is the behavior of the 1950–1951 expedition of Wendell Phillips, archaeological in intent, but which apparently enraged the Imam for reasons as yet unclear. Another was the lack of concrete results from the Y.D.C. explorations. A third may be the vagaries of international politics; as Yemen has drawn closer to the other Arab states, the Imam subscribes increasingly to the Arab policy of "positive neutralism" and

---

[12] Sanger, Richard, *The Arabian Peninsula*, Ithaca: Cornell University Press, 1954, pp. 266–271, has a first-hand account of these curious negotiations and the incredible performance of the Turkish-born Yemeni Foreign Minister, Raghib Bey.

along with it distrust of the United States for its support of Israel. The U.S. is also identified with Britain, still Yemen's *bête noire*, and American disinterest in Yemen's dispute with Britain over Aden rankles.[13]

The Yemen-Aden dispute is at present the only significant external problem. Yemen's border with the Aden Protectorate has never been defined. After they seized Aden Colony in 1839, the British built up a system of interlocking alliances with various petty shaykhs and sultans. Some of these were quite powerful; others ruled little more than an oasis of palm-trees. The familiar British pattern of protecting key colonial areas through support of native rulers emerged. Since World War II, these protectorate states have been encouraged to expand economic and social reforms for their subjects with British help. The British have also promoted a federation scheme for the Protectorate, and in January, 1959, seven states formed the West Aden Federation with a federal council. Three more sultanates joined in 1960. Yemen regards this as a violation of the 1934 treaty and has supported raiding into the Protectorate by irregular forces, the British countering with RAF sorties. It is a strange little war that kills very few people, but affords the Yemenis an excuse for complaining to the Arab League and the UN. Also, as Yemen joined the United Arab Republic in a loose federation (with no loss of sovereignty), its dispute with Britain gives President Nasir another weapon in his anticolonial arsenal. What the Imam fears most, apparently, is that a successful Aden Federation will cause disaffection among his lowland Sunni-Shafi'i subjects. This may account, also, for the increased pace of development in Arabia Felix.

Unlike other Arab countries, where the challenge to traditional Islam comes from Western modernizing and liberalizing influences, the major threat in Yemen to the old religious ways comes from materialistic societies. The majority of foreigners entering Yemen (presumably by personal invitation of the Imam) are Russians and Chinese Communists. Since they are technicians rather than missionaries, it is highly unlikely that they would endanger the Communist foothold on the Red Sea by active promotion of Marxist ideology. Nevertheless their acceptance poses problems both for Yemen's monolithic feudalism and for the survival of religion there. The incompatibility of true Islam and Communism seems

---

[13] According to *Arab News and Views*, published by the Arab Information Center, New York, N.Y., the first participants in the Yemen–U.S. technical aid program arrived in this country in June, 1961, to begin a ninety-day training program at Greer Technical Institute, Braidwood, Ill., in heavy equipment maintenance.

Crowds converging on the Royal Palace in San'a to congratulate Imam Ahmad on Yemen-Egypt Federation. (Courtesy The Middle East Institute)

obvious to a Western-educated person, living under capitalistic free enterprise. But Arab nationalists in other parts of the Middle East have found it convenient to overlook the attitude of the Soviet government toward its Muslims and the ruthless suppression of the Muslim Kazakhs in Sinkiang by the Chinese Communists, and the younger generation of Yemenis may reach the same conclusions as Yemen progresses. In this connection, the statements of two Yemeni officials are of value. According to one (possibly Prince Badr), "Yemen and Saudi Arabia are the only two countries in the world without Communists, because their peoples are ignorant. If they were educated, they would become Communist up to 95 per cent." [14] In contrast, the Qadi of Ibb, a Yemeni equivalent of an elder stateman, said recently, "Communism is a reversal of all we stand for. It is not a power which can be fought with weapons, because it sets son against father and daughter against daughter-in-law. It can be overcome only by a greater spiritual force." [15] Aside from the obvious value of this statement as a text for Western man, it represents a call for Yemeni unity transcending Sunni-Shi'a factionalism. The hope for Yemen is that the strong force of Islam there, which bolstered Muslims

[14] *Ibid.*, p. 224.
[15] Bethmann, *op. cit.*, p. 24.

in the Middle East for many centuries under foreign domination, will blunt the new materialism, while still shaping it for the best national purposes.

In 1961 and approximately on schedule another attempt was made to assassinate the Imam. Again he survived, although wounded, encouraging the widespread superstition among Yemenis that he bears a charmed life and cannot die. Details of this newest conspiracy were lacking as this book went to press, but reportedly two of the conspirators were hanged in public in Taiz. Other rumors had the Imam voluntarily abdicating in favor of Prince Badr. By the end of the year, however, the Imam was well enough to fire off a broadside, in the form of a poem, criticizing President Nasir for his methods of achieving Arab unity. Nasir retaliated by announcing the dissolution of the U.A.R.–Yemen Federation.

BRITAIN'S ARABIAN PROTECTORATES

Outside of the independent Arab states of Saudi Arabia and Yemen, the Arabian Peninsula is divided into a number of petty states of various sizes which share a common association with the British Crown. The states may also be categorized into two groups—those facing or adjoining the Persian Gulf and those along the Indian Ocean and Arabian Sea. In the former group are Kuwait, the Bahrain Islands, Qatar, the so-called Trucial Shaykhdoms, and Muscat-Oman. The latter includes Aden Colony, Aden Protectorate, and the Wadi Hadhramaut. Muscat-Oman occupies a sort of keystone position in this geographical grouping, for while Muscat itself faces the Persian Gulf, "the cork in the bottle," Oman extends to the southwest along the coast of southern Arabia and inland to the Jabal Akhadar, the "Green Mountain," one of the least explored places on earth.

The two groups of states acquired British patronage in somewhat different ways. Those in south Arabia did so under "Ingrams's Peace"— Harold Ingrams, a British official, convinced the tribes of Aden Protectorate and the Hadhramaut to suspend intertribal warfare in 1937. Slavery and feuds were halted by the truce, and Ingrams became Political Adviser to the Sultans of Mukalla and Saiyun. Ingrams's Peace did not extend to Aden Colony, because it had been occupied in 1839 by an armed expedition from British India, ostensibly in retaliation for the mistreatment of English sailors shipwrecked nearby but more probably due to Britain's interest in controlling the only good harbor between India and Egypt.[16] Along the Persian Gulf, the problem was one of piracy at first and later of slavery. As British commercial interests expanded and trading stations were established on the routes to India, Britain's trading men came into direct contact with these age-old practices of the coastal Arabs. Piracy and the slave trade were not only a livelihood, but a very lucrative one at that. The pirates operated both in conjunction with and in defiance of the local rulers. Wahhabism added a religious dimension to these customs in the early nineteenth century when it reached the Gulf; "the right of conquest over infidels, the promulgation of the faith by fire and sword, and the right to dispose of the lives and properties of prisoners became not merely admissible but indispensable duties." [17] The East India Company had established a Residency at Bushire, Iran, in 1763; and forty years later the piratical attacks on its merchantmen had become so numerous that an expedition was sent to Ras al-Khaimah, the pirate headquarters on the "Trucial Coast," to burn the town. A second attack on the town in 1819, after the first had not deterred the pirates, was more successful, and in 1820 a treaty was signed between Great Britain and the Shaykhs of the Trucial Coast and Bahrain under which these rulers agreed to abstain from plunder and piracy on land and sea except in a state of declared war. This did not work too well either, and in 1835 they were induced to sign a Maritime Truce with the British and to agree not to engage in hostilities by sea. In 1853 this was superseded by a Perpetual Maritime Truce containing a clause that the British would ensure peace in the area. These two truces are the basis of the British "protectorate" over seven Trucial Shaykhdoms —Abu Dhabi, Dubai, Sharjah, Ajman, Umm al-Qaiwain, Ras al-Khaimah, Fujairah.[18]

The basis of British hegemony over Kuwait (now a relic of the past), Qatar, and Muscat-Oman is slightly different although the result and the binding agreements are the same. Kuwait, which means "little fort," was founded in 1716 by Bedouin of the Bani Utub, a subsection of the Anaiza tribal confederation. Their leaders were the al-Sabah family; and as the settlement grew, the family retained its leadership. In the nineteenth century, Kuwait was nominally under Ottoman Turkish control based

---

[16] Hickinbotham, Sir Tom, *Aden*, London: Constable, 1958, p. 12.

[17] Wilson, Arnold, *The Persian Gulf*, 2nd ed., London: Allen & Unwin, 1954, p. 197.

[18] Hay, Rupert, *The Persian Gulf States*, Washington: Middle East Institute, 1959, Chapter II, *passim.*

at Basra. In 1871 the Turks invested the Al-Sabah ruler at the time, Abdullah ibn Sabah, with the title of Qaimmaqam (district ruler); his successor, Muhammad, permitted the Turks to establish a firmer basis of authority, but his half-brother Mubarak killed him and seized the throne. As was mentioned earlier, it was Mubarak who encouraged ibn Saʿud to recover his ancestral fief in Najd. In 1899 Mubarak turned to the British to avoid becoming subordinate to the Turks and signed a comprehensive treaty with provisions similar to those in the Bahrain and Trucial Coast agreements. The Qatar Peninsula was occupied by the Turks from 1871 to 1914. When they withdrew at the outset of World War I, the British recognized their local Deputy Governor, Abdullah ibn-Jasim of the al-Thani family, as the ruler and in 1916 entered into treaty relations with him on the same basis. In general, the agreements with these Persian Gulf states are "exclusive" agreements. The local rulers undertook not to have direct relations with any other foreign power or to sell, lease, or cede land to any such power. The Shaykh of Kuwait in 1904 also agreed to ban all post offices other than those appointed from India to operate in his territory. Britain undertook in turn to maintain the rulers on their often-shaky thrones, to defend them against foreign aggression, and to represent them abroad. It should be noted that the setup created by these treaties went into effect long before the discovery of oil; and what is now regarded as an outdated imperial patriarchy by Arab nationalism certainly stabilized areas which were anarchic at best. Curzon's words in 1903—"We saved you from extinction at the hands of your neighbors. We opened these seas to the ships of all nations. . . . We have not destroyed your independence but have preserved it. . . . The peace of these waters must still be maintained, your independence will continue to be upheld. . . ." [19]—had the ring of truth.

BAHRAIN ISLANDS

The Bahrain archipelago is a group of islands lying about twenty miles off the coast of Saudi Arabia and eighteen from the Qatar Peninsula at the entrance to the Gulf of Salwa. There are five principal islands —Bahrain itself which is about thirty miles long and eight to ten miles wide; Sitra, Nabi Salih, a date-growing center; Jiddah, used as a penal colony; and ʿUmm al-Naʿsan, private property of the ruler of Bahrain and used as a breeding ground for gazelle and black buck. The name

[19] Freeth, Zahra, *Kuwait Was My Home*, London: Allen & Unwin, 1956, p. 24.

*The Suq, Manama, decorated for the Ruler of Bahrain's
return from Queen Elizabeth's coronation. (Courtesy
The Middle East Institute)*

Bahr-ayn ("Two Seas") is derived from the existence of two strata of
water around the islands; the upper one is extremely salty, while the
deeper consists of "sweet water with a very pleasant taste." [20]
Iran ruled Bahrain through its tributaries, the kings of Hormuz, for
two hundred sixty years (1335–1595 A.D.) except for a brief Portuguese
interregnum. The Imam of Oman took the islands in 1700, and the
Persians took them back in 1718. After the death of Nadir Shah in
1747, Iran was shattered by internal dissension and could not exercise
direct control over Bahrain. The local Arab tribes, particularly the Utub,
who had migrated there from central Arabia, asserted their independence. Until Great Britain, through the East India Company, came to
intervene directly in Persian Gulf affairs, the Shaykhs of Bahrain

[20] Faroughy, Abbas, *The Bahrein Islands,* New York: Very Fisher, 1951, p. 13.
Hay, *op. cit.,* pp. 88–89, says it is brackish and not very palatable. The explanation
for this subterranean fresh water is in dispute.

played the role of double agent. When the Persians showed firmness, they paid their taxes and the annual tribute. When the Muscatis were strong and threatened to invade Bahrain, the shaykhs called on Iran for protection. At other times they defied everybody. On one occasion they asked the Wahhabis of Najd for help against Muscat. The Wahhabis defeated Muscat and having occupied Bahrain tried to convert the inhabitants to Wahhabism by force. Several members of the ruling family were carried off to Najd as hostages. But the men of Bahrain are not easily intimidated. When the Wahhabis threatened to execute the hostages, the ruling shaykh told their messengers, "Go back and tell the Amir that we have forgotten our relatives; and if our sails could carry us to Dar'iya we would raze it to the ground." [21] The prisoners were subsequently released through Persian intervention. The incident illustrates in a way the unique nature of Bahrain in peninsular affairs—an Arab island within sight of the harsh deserts of Wahhabism, yet turning away from Arabia to look toward Iran for inspiration, in politics as well as religion.

The Saudi Amir later made more claims to authority over Bahrain. To forestall this and to strengthen Britain's position in the Gulf in view of Russian expansion and Persian weakness, the British in 1861 signed a treaty with Shaykh Muhammad as "the independent ruler of Bahrain." He agreed to refrain from piracy and acts of war in return for British protection and support. However, he continued to regard himself as a vassal of Persia, until his stubbornness forced the British to expel him. In Curzon's words, "No form of words or signature could bind the crafty old fox." [22] In 1880 Britain and her intractable vassal signed an "exclusive" agreement in which Bahrain agreed to abstain from entering relations of any sort with any government without British consent. A British Resident stationed in Manama, the capital, advised the paramount ruler on all foreign problems. The Resident, who is subordinate to the Secretary of State for Foreign Affairs in London, supervises the activities of all the protectorates on the Gulf; he holds the rank of Ambassador and is entitled to a salute of fifteen guns.[23] From 1927 to 1956 the Resident was Sir Charles Belgrave, who had answered an advertisement for the job in a London newspaper and who came to be a sort of "Warwick-the-Kingmaker" on Bahrain. The only international agree-

[21] Faroughy, *op. cit.*, p. 74.
[22] *Ibid.*, p. 85.
[23] Hay, *op. cit.*, p. 19.

ment which Bahrain has signed is the International Postal Union (1949).

Bahrain's racial structure is considerably mixed; but the aboriginal inhabitants, the Baharinah, though considerably diluted, act as a solid bloc. They are said to be descended from Arabs taken by Nebuchadnezzar into Mesopotamia during his campaigns in the Fertile Crescent; later they fled to Bahrain. The ruling family, the al-Khalifa, are Sunnis; and the Sunnis form the majority although many of the Utub are Wahhabi, indicating some success on the part of the Wahhabi *mutawwas*. The hostility between Sunnis and Shi'a on Bahrain is far stronger than that between either Muslim group and the foreigners there. Riots broke out during Muharram (the festival celebrated by Shi'as honoring the martyrdom of Ali's sons) in September, 1953, and it took the entire police force plus a curfew to restore order. In July, 1954, all Shi'a workers went on strike after several of their number had been convicted for fighting with Sunnis; and in December, 1954, they called another general strike. The Sunnis form the majority and include the ruling family; but the Shi'as who live by themselves in their own villages as in al-Hasa are a solid bloc. Lately the Sunnis have emphasized the unity and brotherhood of all Muslims and Arabs, and their announced goals of expelling the foreigner and achieving pan-Arabism find a response among the Shi'as. Furthermore, the oil industry has brought new economic opportunity to the Shi'as. No longer are they restricted to agriculture; now both groups can collaborate as members of an economic group. And with economic solidarity increasing among Muslim Bahrainis, while the industry continues to produce and the present reinvestment of revenues in development projects continues, the assumption is that confessional friction will steadily be reduced.

KUWAIT AND QATAR

Until mid-1961 the two small principalities of Kuwait and Qatar (pronounced "Gut-er") formed collectively a sort of pleasant father-and-son team on the Persian Gulf. Although Kuwait could easily absorb all of Qatar (area 4,000 square miles; population 40,000), it too is an extremely small dot on the Arabian Peninsula with its 20,000 square miles and 250,000 population, nearly all of them found in Kuwait Town. Both are relatively new principalities and are almost exclusively the offspring of an economic ancestor, petroleum. Kuwaiti *dhows* (a type of schooner peculiar to the Persian Gulf) still work the oyster beds in the ocean for pearls, but the pearl industry has always been too uncertain and hazardous to provide a major source of wealth to Kuwait. Oil, however, proved not only easy to produce but enjoyed ready and nearly universal markets. Qatar, a barren, sandy peninsula, started with even less than Kuwait; its capital, Doha, was little more than a double row of mud huts and a small palace where the ruling shaykh lived.

The Qatar Petroleum Company, a subsidiary of IPC, began producing oil in Qatar in 1950, and the state's annual income climbed swiftly to its present average of $50 million a year. Being Wahhabis, the people of Qatar regarded this windfall as provided by Allah, since their uncomplicated faith could not conceive of modern capitalism; they also believed that their rulers were entitled to the largest share. The ruling family, taking the logical path blazed by the family of Sa'ud, began spending their money as fast as it came in, although in deference to their British advisers they put about $80 million into roads, schools, a 120-bed hospital, and public works. Soon the plot became familiar and the action predictable, even to the ending in bankruptcy, as Qataris spent their cash outside the country and bought their imports on credit. The paramount ruler, Shaykh Ali bin Abdullah al-Thani, a contemporary of ibn Sa'ud, was equally ill at ease in the presence of great wealth. Finally late in 1960 he abdicated. His eldest son, Shaykh Ahmad bin Ali al-Thani, became paramount shaykh, and a nephew, Khalifa bin Ali al-Thani, was appointed Crown Prince as well as Finance Minister. Khalifa immediately undertook an austerity, no-credit program, the idea being that Qataris should live within the national income, which at approximately $1,100.00 per capita was extremely good for the Middle East.[24] Britain hoped that Qatar would emulate the social welfare program of Kuwait, so that when the Qataris were ready for full independence they would not be quite so eager to discard their British bonds for the handcuffs of Nasir and his Arab nationalism.

The growth of Kuwait has been paternalistic in the broadest sense. Well-advised by the British, and endowed with intelligence and foresight rare in an Arab leader, Shaykh Abdullah al-Salim al-Sabah, its ruler, has consistently dedicated one-third of his income to current expenses, one-third to development, and placed one-third on deposit in London banks. This income was $415 million in 1958 and is currently estimated to be running around $450 million. Kuwait's rapid growth, its homogeneous population, stable government, the presence of a British Resident, and the extraordinary social welfare program made possible by oil

[24] *The New York Times,* March 6, 1961.

revenues, discouraged the development of rabid Arab nationalism even during the worst periods of anti-Western activity in the Middle East.

In 1961 Britain decided to give up her role entirely as protector of Kuwait and turn full control over to the principality of its international relations, the only rights reserved under the 1899 treaty. The ruler and British Resident Sir William Luce signed an exchange of notes replacing the treaty with one of friendship and close alliance. Shaykh Abdullah was knighted, the Kuwait Finance Department announced formation of the Kuwait Petrochemical Company, with 40 per cent Italian ownership, to encourage foreign investment. Apparently all was well. But Kuwait's venture into the international affairs of the Middle East set off a time bomb. Premier Abd al-Karim Qasim of Iraq promptly claimed the entire principality. He said that the 1899 treaty was a forgery through which Kuwait was "stolen" from the Iraqi motherland.[25] Qasim evidently felt that with the British out of Kuwait, it would be simple to annex the little state in the name of Arab unity and Iraqi progress (to say nothing of Kuwait's oil reserves of 62 billion barrels and daily production of 1,700,000 barrels, making it the world's fourth largest oil producer). He expected, by some inscrutable exercise of logic, that the Shaykh of Kuwait would happily accept his new position as a mere Iraqi provincial governor. However, reactions to the Iraqi move in various quarters revived once more the Middle East's title to paramountcy among regions as the home of perpetual crisis. Shaykh Abdullah rejected Qasim's claim and said that Kuwait would reject any attempt at Iraqi annexation. The British supported his position; crack British troops moved into position along the sunbaked Kuwait border. Britain's move was to be expected, but the support which Iraq apparently expected from the other Arab states did not materialize. Instead, both the United Arab Republic and Saudi Arabia came out against the move, while other Arab states avoided comment.

Iraq's move, while it won no support, confronted both Kuwait and the Arabs in general with the dilemma of returning troops of a former colonial power. The Kuwaiti army of 2,400 men was obviously no match for Iraq, so British forces were necessary to defend the principality's newly won independence against external attack, and indeed the ruler had requested them. But their presence meant that independence was no more genuine than it had been. If Iraq really meant to invade Kuwait, the spectre was raised of Arab soldiers fighting side by side with British forces against other Arab soldiers!

[25] *The Washington Post,* June 25, 1961.

In July, Kuwait, although not a member of the United Nations, asked the world body to meet in emergency session to investigate Iraqi aggression.[26] Subsequently the UAR and Russia both asked the Security Council to press for withdrawal from Kuwait of British forces. However, the UAR delegate, Omar Loutfi, admitted that logically the crisis should be handled by the Arab League. Having considered the matter, the Security Council then referred it to the League. On July 20, Kuwait was admitted as the eleventh member of the League by "unanimous" vote, the Iraqi delegate having walked out while the vote was being tallied. Membership now made it possible for Kuwait to dispense with British protection, eliminating the problem of the invited but unwelcome guest. According to a formal defense agreement drawn up between the League and its newest member, forces drawn collectively from other members would replace the already-withdrawing British troops as soon as feasible.

It is of course premature to judge what policies newly-independent Kuwait will take. The extensive program of welfare socialism which the ruler has been carrying out ever since oil royalties made it possible has not been duplicated elsewhere in the Arab World, but the increased trend of state-controlled development in other Arab countries, notably the UAR and Iraq, suggest that Kuwait's internal policies will find favor in Arab eyes. At the same time, the very fact that the Arab League has agreed to defend the shaykhdom from possible external aggression puts Kuwait in a dependent and highly vulnerable position. At the very least, Kuwait will probably be expected to share its wealth with have-not Arab nations; and it is not unlikely that Kuwait will find herself trading her dependence on Britain to dependence on her fellow-Arabs. Membership in the UN might help, except that Syria was once a UN member too. Kuwait's own nationalism is the unknown factor in the equation, and the degree to which Shaykh Abdullah, who represents patriarchal, traditionalist Arab leadership, is able to retain the loyalty of his subjects in the face of their first real opportunity to taste, unhindered, the joys of Nasir's brand will determine whether the state keeps its national identity or disappears quickly into some larger Arab union.

MUSCAT-OMAN

The ruling family of Muscat, the al-Bu Saids, and a large portion of the tribes of Oman are Ibadhi Muslims, a sect said to be derived from the fanatical Kharijites who broke with orthodox Islam in the time of Ali

[26] *The New York Times,* July 1, 1961.

and who murdered him at Najaf in 661 A.D. Nominally the Sultan of Muscat-Oman rules the entire territory; but he has only recently been able to assert his authority in Oman proper, which consists of the interior and the southern coast as far as Dhufar. The conflict between spiritual and temporal rulers of the same territory, which was a feature of the Middle Ages, is found in very few places today—one is Oman. The Ibadhis of the interior believe that the Imam should be elected as Sultan also. The founder of the present dynasty, Saiyid Ahmad, was elected Imam of the Omanis in 1744 after he had driven the Persians out of Oman. His successors ignored the elective principle of Ibadhi leadership and established a hereditary line. From its base at Muscat Town, Omani seapower grew strong and, as was mentioned earlier, became a force to be reckoned with in the affairs of the Persian Gulf. In addition to their periodic control of Bahrain, the Omani sea-lords held Gwadar, an enclave on the Makran coast of what is now Pakistan, until 1958. Meanwhile, the tribes of the interior, naturally inbred and hostile to strangers, came to resent the dynasty's treaties with foreign powers and its arbitrary assumption of the imamate. In 1913 the Ghafari and Hanawi tribes rebelled and named Salim ibn Rashid al-Kharusi as their proper Imam, with headquarters at Nizwa. The British defeated him outside Muscat in 1915; and in 1920 he was murdered, much after the pattern of his presumed predecessor Ali. Abdullah ibn Muhammad al-Khalili was elected his successor and held the allegiance of the tribes until he died in 1954 and was succeeded by the present Imam, Ghalib ibn Ali al-Hinawi. Previously, in 1920, Sultan Taimur, father of the present ruler, made an agreement usually called the Treaty of Sib with the Omani shaykhs. This curious document defines the relationship between the government at Muscat and the people of Oman, limits the tax on merchandise brought out from the interior to 5 per cent, permits free visiting between Muscat and Oman, guarantees mutual freedom of extradition, and commits the Sultan not to interfere in the "internal affairs" of the Omanis. In return, the tribes and their shaykhs promise not to interfere with the government or to attack the coastal towns and to accept shari'a justice in the event of claims against them by merchants or travelers.[27] Both the present Sultan, Sa'id ibn Taimur, and his father took the position that the agreement did not involve any abrogation of their sovereignty over Oman or their control over its external affairs. During his lifetime, the Imam Khalili accepted their position, did not communicate with any

[27] *Middle East Journal,* Summer 1957, pp. 282–283.

foreign power, and in fact wrote a letter to the Sultan at the time of the Saudi penetration of Buraimi in 1952, calling on him to lead the tribes against the "aggressor."[28]

The election of the new Imam, Ghalib, coincided with a number of events which were to undermine this rather peaceful division of authority. One of these events occurring in 1954 was the signing of the Anglo-Egyptian Suez Agreement, under which the British began to withdraw from the canal zone. Arab nationalism was advancing aggressively on all fronts against the "imperialists." From Cairo and Riyadh the Imam was seen as the freely elected leader of his Arab people striving to win freedom for them from the unjust usurpation of the Sultan who was in power only because of the backing of British bayonets. The Imam began negotiations with the Saudis which the Sultan regarded as a breach of the Treaty of Sib. In 1955 he traversed the interior of Oman with an armed escort (and one British journalist), everywhere receiving the allegiance of the tribes. He was the first Sultan of Muscat to sit in majlis at Nizwa, where he dispensed justice in place of the escaped Imam. In the summer of 1957, the Imam, with the help of some arms and much propaganda from the Arab League, raised another revolt which was put down by the British-trained-and-officered Trucial Oman Levies. Again the Imam escaped and took refuge in the Jabal Akhadar with his brother Talib and the paramount shaykh of that area, Sulaiman ibn Hamyar.[29] In February, 1959, he fled to Saudi Arabia. An American reporter who interviewed him and Talib at Dammam wrote that the Imam wanted to establish diplomatic relations with the United States and to have foreign oil companies develop his country. He said that the chief quarrel of the Omanis was with the British forces which had established positions in the interior and with the British oil companies who were working unlawfully in Oman because their concession had been granted by the Sultan. Bands of Omanis, he declared, were carrying on a *jihad* against the British. The Imam refused to allow himself to be photographed because of his Ibadhi restrictions.[30]

[28] Hay, *op. cit.*, p. 131.
[29] Thesiger, Wilfred, *Arabian Sands,* New York: E. P. Dutton & Co., Inc., 1959. He says that in 1949 he met this shaykh in the course of trying to get permission from the Imam to explore the Oman mountains. At the time Hamyar hinted that he could get it in return for British recognition of his sovereign status on the same basis as the Trucial Coast shaykhs.
[30] *The New York Herald Tribune,* November 18, 1959.

ADEN AND THE HADHRAMAUT

South of the kingdom of Yemen at the heel of the Arabian "boot," and eastward along the coast to the Muscat-Oman border at Ras Darbat Ali are the twenty-five British-protected states of Aden Protectorate and the Hadhramaut. The former is a political term, the latter a geographical one. In addition to the Protectorate, which is administered under an arrangement similar to that existing in the Persian Gulf, the port city and hinterland of Aden are a British Crown Colony. In Aden Colony the British element has been dominant since the early nineteenth century; but like the other seaports of Arabia, Aden has faced the world for centuries, and the population is greatly mixed. When the British fleet first arrived in 1839, they brought with them Indian clerks and some Indian artisans, the assumption being that the local Arabs were incapable due to lack of education and ambition. India continued to be the recruiting ground for skilled and semiskilled labor well after World War I, and a tradition developed that the Arabs would never become skilled craftsmen or useful clerks. When education was made available to them, they proved that the reverse was true. One of Aden's major problems in the social (and religious) sphere in the twentieth century has been the resentment of an expanding Arab middle and artisan class at the presence of large numbers of Indians occupying positions which the former group feel are rightfully Arab.[31] The Arab nationalist movement, as might be expected, played this sort of discrimination up as part of its anti-imperialist theme. As the success of the Arab call to unity made Aden increasingly vulnerable, the Indian community there adopted the dual policies of avoiding politics like the plague and of giving generously to charities such as assistance to Yemeni refugees.

Long before Arabs and Jews went to war in Palestine, communal riots had occurred in 1931 in Aden, when Arab worshippers at a mosque on the edge of the Jewish quarter became excited for some unknown reason and invaded the quarter. More serious interracial tension came in 1947 as a sequel to events in Palestine. Order had to be restored by the Royal Navy and Air Force; many people were killed and the Jewish quarter was reduced to blackened ruin. After this the Jews of Aden began to emigrate to Israel, and within a few years there were only seven hundred left. When one considers that the British have governed Aden and

[31] Hickinbotham, *op. cit.*, pp. 182–183.

deliberately kept it out of touch with inter-Arab politics for over a century, the power of Arab unity as an appeal is evident.

The various states of the Aden Protectorate, which are in the process of forming a federation, range in size from the Qu'aiti Sultanate of Shihr and Mukalla (40,000 square miles) to the few unproductive acres of the Sultan of Bir Ali, little more than a palm-tree toll station. The senior state and the first one to enter into treaty relations with the British is the Sultanate of Lahej. Due to *Sulh Ingrams* (Ingrams's Peace) and their own efforts, the various rulers in the Protectorate, be they sultans, shaykhs, amirs, naqibs (there is no connection between the importance of a state and the title of its ruler), have acquired internal independence limited only by tradition and the degree of independence of the tribes themselves. This varies according to geographical location; thus the rule in the remote Yafa Highlands is "every man a law unto himself," while the lowland states rely on their rulers (and British backing) against Yemeni raids. The Protectorate probably came into existence as much for religious as for political reasons. Its population is Shafi'i; in neighboring Yemen, the Shafi'is are also a majority, but the Zaidi Imam with his Zaidi tribesmen has consistently maintained political control. The fear and distrust of the Shafi'is of Yemen for the Zaidis and the sympathy of the Protectorate Shafi'is for their co-religionists unquestionably motivated the rulers toward settlement of their feuds under British supervision.

The functioning of one of these Protectorate states may be seen in the organization of the Kathiri Sultanate of the Hadhramaut, which has an area of six thousand square miles and a population of sixty thousand, one-third of which is in Saiyun, the capital. Administrative machinery is patterned after the previous system of Malaya. The Sultan is the executive authority; he is assisted by a Council of State of which he is president, and of which the British Political Resident is an ex-officio member. The Sultan has his own postage stamps, coat of arms, national flag, and he is entitled to a nine-gun salute. But he cannot enter into correspondence with any foreign government without the consent of the British government. In addition to the political structure, there are other Malay influences. The Kathiri economy depends on remittances from branches of leading Kathiri families, like the al-Kaf who live in Singapore and Jakarta. They send over $2.5 million each year to the little state. Malay is the court language at Saiyun and among the educated Kathiris. Even the common dress worn by well-to-do Kathiris, a high-collared tunic, is

Malay-inspired. Thus the wandering tendencies of the people of the Hadhramaut—the travelers and seafarers of southern Arabia—create in the homeland glimpses of the cultures of far-off places without losing the essential Muslim Arab culture and religion which must remain strong if Arabia is to remain the heartland of Islam.[32]

Political Development in the Protectorate. As they have in other parts of the world when confronted with rigidly traditional societies and political anarchy (one is tempted to say "arrested development"), the British in Arabia pursued a well-defined course of righteous duty in their dealings with these societies. Colonel Hamilton, who was posted to the Aden Levies in 1931 as commander of a camel troop, spoke for the entire corps of imperial outriders when he wrote:

We, the British, had a clear duty to perform. . . . It was clearly our duty to pacify the country which chance had opened to us, so freely. To open the roads, to assist in agriculture and water conservancy, to establish federal courts of law and bodies of police. Until life was safe, . . . nothing could come of our labour. . . . If we did not make peace among this people sunk in hopeless anarchy, the only peace in the land would be the peace of death.[33]

This concept of the *duty* of the English toward politically immature peoples is balanced by considerable respect for their native culture and traditions—and *this* is balanced by an unquestioning importation of the British way of life along with its political institutions. The result is that the British protectorates have been allowed to mature in only one political direction. Their rulers have maintained their arbitrary exercise of power with the advice and consent of British political advisors. Their finances are carefully administered; the ruler of Kuwait thus deposits one-third of his revenue in London banks, uses one-third for his domestic expenditures, and holds one-third in reserve. What is viewed by other Arabs as intractable arrogance has become in the Arabian Peninsula a British cushion against too-rapid immersion in the waters of modern international politics. And if the political evolution of the rest of the Arab states were used as an example, this measured progress of a small but homogenous Arab grouping may be the best method in the long run.

Political development in Aden Colony has proceeded at a faster pace than in the other protectorates, not unnaturally since it is a Crown Col-

[32] Smith, R. W., "Notes on the Kathiri State of Hadhramaut," *Middle East Journal,* Autumn, 1953.
[33] The Master of Beltraven, *The Kingdom of Melchior,* London: John Murray, 1949, p. 157.

ony and has had a longer association with Britain. The Colony is ruled by a Legislative Council which was extensively changed, according to the Gazette Extraordinary of 1957, to give the "unofficial elected" members (i.e., those elected from the constituencies) a majority over the ex-officio members. Another constitutional change provides that the Executive Council, the supreme governing body, be changed to represent local opinion as well as ex-officio decisions. Though ultimate executive-legislative powers are reserved to the Governor and the franchise limited to persons of Aden birth or British subjects, at least opportunities for participation in the governing process do exist. Aden Colony also has three political parties—the Aden Association, composed of moderates who seek internal self-government; the South Arabian League, which seeks self-determination and union with Aden Protectorate; and the National Front, advocating a South Arabian state of Yemen, Muscat-Oman, the Colony, and the Protectorate. Arab nationalism has made the strongest inroads among the two latter groups. Since Arab unity and Arab independence are appeals which are interpreted emotionally by the Arabs, the practical, methodical approach of the British in Arabia has no answer for them. In the Protectorates the British have encouraged federation; but the question of how this federative impulse can be sold to the people as compensation for nonadherence to Yemen and hence to the mainspring of Arab unity emanating from Cairo, remains unanswered.

RECOMMENDED READINGS

1. Bethmann, Erich, *Yemen on the Threshold,* Washington: American Friends of the Middle East, 1960.
2. Dickson, R. P., *Kuwait and Her Neighbors,* London: Allen & Unwin, 1956.
3. Faroughy, Abbas, *The Bahrein Islands* (*750–1951*), New York: Very Fisher, 1951.
4. ———, *Introducing Yemen,* New York: Orientalia, 1947.
5. Fayein, Claudie, *A French Doctor in The Yemen,* transl. by Douglas McKee, London: Robert Hale, 1957.
6. Freeth, Zahra, *Kuwait Was My Home,* London: Allen & Unwin, 1956.
7. Hay, Rupert, *The Persian Gulf States,* Washington: Middle East Institute, 1959.
8. Hickinbotham, Tom, *Aden,* London: Constable, 1958.
9. Ingrams, W. I., *Arabia and The Isles,* London: John Murray, 1942.
10. Morris, James, *Sultan in Oman,* New York: Pantheon Books, Inc., 1957.

11. Sanger, Richard, *The Arabian Peninsula,* Ithaca: Cornell University Press, 1954.
12. Thesiger, Wilfred, *Arabian Sands,* New York: E. P. Dutton & Co., Inc., 1959.
13. Tritton, Arthur S., *Rise of the Imans of Sanaa,* London: Oxford, 1925.
14. Wilson, Arnold, *The Persian Gulf,* 2nd ed., London: Allen & Unwin, 1954.

CHAPTER 11

EGYPT: THE PATH TO INDEPENDENCE

Like one of the familiar palm trees along its banks, the Nile sprouts upward, flowing north from desert to sea. Its two main root-systems, the White and Blue Niles, meet at Khartoum (Arabic "elephant's trunk," in the Sudan). The combined river gouges a green trough through the gray desert for 1,400 miles; then flows northward to the Delta, shaped like a palm crown, where myriad streams carry what is left of the water to the sea. Its total length, 4,145 miles, makes it the longest river in the world. Long before this, the hardworking cotton farmers of Sudan's Jazira and the equally industrious *fellahin* of Egypt have drawn off much of the water (though much is wasted). When the new high dam at Aswan, now under construction, is completed (possibly in 1975), reportedly not a drop of Nile water will reach the sea, all of it being channeled into agricultural uses. This picture in microcosm reveals the importance of geography to politics in the Nile Valley. Without the Nile, northeast Africa would swiftly become a desert waste, like southern Libya; yet the struggle of Egypt to evolve into a healthy, modern nation depends basically on this single natural resource.

Northeast Africa, from the Mediterranean coast south to Ethiopia and the "horn" of Somalia, and westward from the Red Sea to the Libyan desert, is a corridor between the Muslim, Arab Middle East and tropical Africa. Modern Egypt and Sudan, the two northeast African states with which we are concerned, have thrown in their lot with the course of Arab unity. Meanwhile Egyptian teachers and officials and Muslim evangelists tramp the tropical jungles of Africa carrying out the declared goals

348

of African leadership for President Gamal 'Abd al-Nasir.[1] The Sudan, "whose boundaries extend far into the depths of Africa, bringing into contiguity the politically sensitive regions in that area,"[2] is even more sharply split between northern Arabic-speaking Muslims and pagan Nilotic tribes. Largely dependent on a single resource, and passed between ancient, long civilized peoples and those barely conscious of larger than tribal loyalties, the Egyptians, and to a lesser extent the Sudanese, have adopted a rather special attitude toward all peoples, but particularly toward their Middle Eastern neighbors (exclusive of Israel). It is an attitude of loftiness mixed with fatalism, a somewhat patronizing tone, and considerable suspicion.

THE WEIGHT OF THE PAST

In Egypt the past is omnipresent, and the political change of name from Egypt to United Arab Republic (Egypt) has not yet reduced to any visible degree the resistance of the Egyptians to any form of absorption. It is a truism that Egyptian *fellahin* refuse to emigrate, however crowded and dirty their villages. This appears to be due to a profound attachment to the soil of the valley, in a historical as well as an agricultural sense. The past is present not only through such visual means as the Pyramids, Sphinx, Valley of the Kings, etc., but through the continued preference of the Egyptian people for oligarchic rule, and their racial homogeneity, apart from the differences in physical stamina that exist between the people of Upper and Lower Egypt. Memories of ancient grandeur have haunted the rulers of Egypt through the centuries, and it is noteworthy that the Egyptian rulers most ambitious for power—Sultan Baybars, Muhammad Ali, Khedive Ismail, in our day Zaghlul Pasha and Gamal 'Abd al-Nasir—have had a sort of Pharaonic complex in their makeup.[3]

Ancient Egypt, up and down the Nile as far as the cataracts, was "the

[1] "The peoples of Africa will continue to look to us who guard their northern gate, and who constitute their link with the outside world." Gamal Abdel Nasser, *The Philosophy of the Revolution,* Washington: Public Affairs Press, 1955, pp. 109–110.

[2] *Ibid.*

[3] Nasir, *op. cit.*, writes that at Faluja (the battle in which Egyptian troops in Palestine were surrounded by the Israelis, but gave a good account of themselves despite defective ammunition) his mind focused on Egypt and her lost greatness. See also Naguib, Mohammed, *Egypt's Destiny,* Garden City: Doubleday & Company, Inc., 1955.

other" of the Middle East "antique lands," and the Pharaohs who ruled it may be compared in pomp and splendor with the Ozymandias of Shelley's vision. Unlike their Mesopotamian counterparts, the Pharaohs built in social as well as architectural terms; their legacy to the modern Egyptians was a compact, cohesive society, highly civilized though not always dynamic. Pharaonic Egypt attracted other peoples as the barbarian Goths were later attracted to Rome; an obscure tribe, the Israelites, improved their material position sufficiently by their sojourn in Egypt so that after their exodus they were able to establish firm control over their sector of Palestine.

The Pharaonic factor, then, gives the Egyptian a certain loftiness in dealing with his Middle Eastern neighbors. The name "Egypt," a Greek corruption of the hieroglyphics *Ka,* "the life principle," plus *Ptah,* "god," confirms this loftiness. The power of the Pharaohs waxed and waned according to the ability of individuals to project themselves into the affairs of the ancient world; however, during the Eighteenth Dynasty, for example, Thutmose III and Queen Hatshepsut (ca. 1504–1450 B.C.) and Amenhotep III built the first real world-empire. Amenhotep IV, who followed them, changed his name to Akhenaton, and dissipated this power in an introspective pursuit of a new religious philosophy, the worship of the Sun-Disc as the One God.[4] His successor, Tutankhamen, restored the power, but the cycle of rise and decline took permanent shape. The dichotomy of Egypt was also established in these ancient times, by the pattern of foreign and native rulers beginning with the irruption of the Hyksos (Horse-Kings) around 1700 B.C. Of obscure stock, probably Semitic, horsemen and pastoralists, they were the first of many such invaders of the fair (and overcrowded) land of Egypt. Romans, Byzantines, Arabs, Turks, finally the French and British, acquired power in Egypt; but once there, they found Egypt as slippery as the asp which Cleopatra carried in her basket; thus all but one of these successive conquerors failed to comprehend, or grasp, anything other than temporal political power.

The Arab conquest of the seventh century, however, brought a profound alteration in the civilization of the Nile Valley. The dictum that Islam operates in the name of both religion and society was nowhere better illustrated. Between 639 and 641 A.D., the Caliph 'Umar sent his

[4] See Finegan, Jack, *Light From the Ancient Past,* Princeton: Princeton University Press, Rev. ed., 1955; Glanville, S. K., *The Legacy of Egypt,* London: Oxford University Press, 1942, and many others.

best general, Amr ibn al-As, to Egypt, then a province of the Byzantine Empire. Despite the great age of the Christian (Coptic) Church in Egypt, by repute founded by St. Mark, and the crucial role of Alexandria in Christian theological activity,[5] the Christian population of Egypt readily accepted their change of masters. The Byzantines, who insisted that their Eastern Orthodoxy was the true Christianity, treated the rival Copts roughly; however, the Muslims displayed that tolerance of organized creeds which marked their early conquests. The Byzantine system of government was retained, and relatively little interference made in the lives of the ordinary Egyptians in the beginning. As time went on, however, the inclusive nature of Islam and the deterioration of stable authority, plus the extortions of the Baghdad caliphs, drove a great majority of the Egyptians to accept Islam.[6] The Coptic Church was reduced to a hard-bitten core, its language reverted to the liturgy, and Egypt for all practical purposes became an Islamic country. Large-scale Arab immigrations from neighboring lands in the eighth and ninth centuries added credence to the present insistence that Egypt has always been an integral part of the Arab world.

The long twilight of the caliphate reserved some of its most tragic phases for Egypt. The Fatimids (969–1171 A.D.) who challenged, successfully, the orthodox Abbasid Caliphate, founded Cairo in 969 as the new capital of their Shi'a Caliphate. They named their new capital according to the astrologers—Mars (*Al-Kahira*) happened to be in the ascendant, and the Fatimids believed that their descent from Mohammad's daughter Fatima, Ali's wife, would turn this bad omen into a good one. The war god's city prospered under them, rivaling Baghdad in the Middle Ages. It also contributed its share to the general sectarian confusion. One of the oddest Fatimid Caliphs was al-Hakim, nicknamed "the lizard" from his habit of sneaking incognito through crowded streets. He had an obsession with night and proscribed all daytime business activities. With bland impartiality, he executed his officials, Muslims as well as Christians and Jews, for the most trivial reasons. It was his custom to ride through the countryside at odd hours, mounted on a gray ass and howling at the stars like a wolf. During one of these rides he was mur-

---

[5] The Arian and Athanasian heresies were both nourished in Alexandria by the bishops having these names.

[6] The Egyptians still managed to keep an individuality and adaptability to changes of fortune, under Islam, which marks them off from other Middle Eastern "Arab" peoples. In fact, the word "Arab" was customarily applied until the present era by *fellahin* as a term of contempt, meaning "thief" or "vagabond."

dered by unknown assassins; later his clothes were found but never his body. A minor Persian mystic named al-Darazi ("the tailor") later announced that al-Hakim was in hiding and would return in due time as the Mahdi. There were many in Egypt who believed this, and a group settled in Lebanon and Syria called the Druzez (after al-Darazi) who still believe in al-Hakim and worship him as part of their esoteric, neo-Islamic rites. Such was the stuff of dreams in Medieval Egypt.

Worse was to come. In the twelfth century Saladin, a Kurdish officer in the army of the local potentate of Syria, aided the Fatimid Caliph in eliminating Christian power from the Holy Land, and in turn founded the Aghlabid dynasty (1193–1250). Saladin had employed companies of *Mamluks* (lit. "slaves") in his wars against the "infidel" Franks. Mamluks were war captives or slaves purchased in Asian markets and trained, like the Janissaries, for total perfection in the arts of war. This policy was continued by his successors. A Mamluk general, Baybars, administered a stunning defeat to the Mongols in 1260 in Syria, saving Egypt from this Asian scourge. Baybars, who had ideas of his own, then murdered his Sultan and replaced him as Sultan of Mamluk Egypt.[7] The Mamluk dynasty, which Baybars founded, was probably a worse visitation than the Mongols would have been, if nothing else because it lasted so much longer. For the better part of six centuries (1260–1811), during which time Europe moved from medievalism through its renaissance and into the early stages of industrialism, an incredibly archaic misrule fell upon the land of the Pharaohs. The discoveries of European explorers cut off the few remaining vestiges of trans-Mediterranean trade, and Egypt's normally strategic position was of small consequence to the expanding maritime powers—Holland, Spain, Britain, and France. Left to themselves, the Mamluks fed on each other like starved rats in an empty barn. No law of succession was ever established; with the exception of Baybars, Qalaun, and his successor al-Nasir, the various rulers governed as long as they could control a stronger military machine than their rivals. Nominally the sultans were advised by amirs or beys (noblemen); in practice this advice was given by the sword or bowstring. The average length of a Sultan's reign was about a year; fourteen out of twenty-five in one series averaged less than eight months.

[7] Saladin had earlier accepted the authority of the Caliph of Baghdad over Egypt. See S. F. Sadeque, *Baybars I of Egypt,* London: Oxford, 1956; William Popper, *Egypt and Syria Under the Circassian Sultans,* Berkeley: University of California Press, 1955; also David Ayalon, *Gunpowder & Firearms in the Mamluk Kingdom,* London: Valentine Mitchell, 1956.

The conquest of Egypt by the Ottoman Sultan Selim in 1517 changed this structure very little. An Ottoman governor (pasha) represented the Sublime Porte in Cairo, but the Mamluks retained much authority. So much, in fact, that the cry *"Inzil, ya Pasha!"* ("Descend, O Pasha!") echoed regularly through Cairo's streets as a Mamluk herald waited on the Ottoman representative to tell him his services were no longer needed. The departure rate of pashas was nearly as high as that of Mamluk beys, or modern football coaches.[8] This state of archaic despotism endured for another two centuries. While Europe was eagerly testing new ideas and sending out long fingers of exploration, Egypt, once the purveyor of civilization, retreated within its medieval shell. Christian European traders, chiefly Venetian or Genoese, either left or adopted Muslim costume—kaftans of silk, slippers, sashes—to disguise themselves. By the end of the eighteenth century East-West trade through Egypt had dwindled to nothing owing to the exactions of the Mamluks and the uncertain state of political health of the country. Perhaps the sole alleviating factor in this misery was that the Egyptians, isolated from foreign contact, knew no other way of life and had made their adjustment, within limits, to their governors.

MUHAMMAD ALI AND THE ARRIVAL OF EUROPE

In June, 1798, the contest between France and England for empire, itself a part of the struggle between Revolutionary France and the old regimes of Europe, spilled over into Egypt. The Directory which governed France sent Napoleon Bonaparte, already its chief military support, with a huge army to seize Egypt as the first step in an ultimate campaign against British India. *"L'expedition assure la destruction de la Puissance Britannique dans l'Inde,"* wrote Talleyrand to the Directory.[9]

Evidence points strongly to Napoleon himself as the moving spirit behind the expedition. The ambitious consul visualized a French Empire of the East surpassing (and replacing) Britain's. The more conventional reasons for an Egyptian invasion—desire to restore French overland trade with the Orient and to cripple British trade by bringing the Mamluks under control and to maintain French military prestige on a relatively safe front—were shared by Bonaparte with the Directory. The

[8] The custom was for the Mamluk faction in control at the time, if opposed to the Pasha, to send a single herald, wearing black and riding on a donkey, to make the announcement. Withdrawal of Ottoman troops took away the Pasha's main method of enforcing his decrees.

[9] Young, George, *Egypt,* New York: Charles Scribner's Sons, 1927, p. 28.

French armada which debarked off Alexandria carried with it Egyptologists, Jesuit priests, educators, and civilian experts in various classifications, mute evidence that France intended to remain in those regions indefinitely.

The French conquest was made ridiculously easy by the fantastic ignorance of the Mamluks of modern firepower, or of European politics. In the Battle of the Pyramids,[10] Bonaparte's army of 40,000 seasoned veterans confronted a Mamluk host whose center consisted of the Mamluk beys themselves, numbering about 10,000. The beys, wearing chain mail over embroidered robes, mounted on Arab horses, and equipped individually with every kind of side arm from a carbine to a scimitar, were no match for the French squares. Those who were not shot down in their cavalry charge drowned in the Nile from the weight of their armor. Napoleon entered Cairo amid pomp and opulence reminiscent of the early Fatimid Caliphs, and in fact the notion of a Franco-Egyptian Empire, under his authority, haunted him to the end of his days. Unfortunately this was not to be. Nelson, the British admiral, caught the French fleet at anchor in Abukir Bay and destroyed it with the exception of three ships which escaped. Marooned on Egyptian soil, Napoleon attempted to consolidate France's authority and to expand it into the Levant as a sort of Latin restoration. He was thwarted in these designs by Britain and Ottoman Turkey, in a new coalition. The French army won a number of battles against numerically superior Turkish forces, but like a football team which loses by its own errors, they fumbled away their best opportunities. The fortress seaport of Acre was crucial, as it dominated the eastern Mediterranean and barred the way to Syria, but the French failed to take it in fourteen assaults.[11] In 1799 Bonaparte left Egypt for France, where he became First Consul and then Emperor of France. The attitude of the Egyptians toward the French occupation changed drastically after Bonaparte's departure. His successor, General Kléber, lacked the flair for propaganda and the bargaining skill of the First Consul. Initially the Egyptian people were favorably disposed toward the French even though the latter were infidels, since any new government promised a change from the arbitrary Mamluks. The French troops, however, committed their share of excesses, like armies everywhere; furthermore they favored the Christian Copts over the Mus-

---

[10] Before this battle, Napoleon coined the familiar phrase "Forty centuries look down upon you!" in a speech to his army.

[11] Napoleon said at St. Helena, "Had I taken Acre I should have reached Constantinople and there founded a dynasty." Young, *op. cit.,* pp. 34–35.

lims. French reorganization of the fiscal system brought order out of chaos but its efficiency deprived local officials of their customary slices of the prevailing graft. A rebellion broke out in Cairo when the French attempted to impose a house tax. Communications were constantly being cut between Upper and Lower Egypt by Bedouin raids, and guerrilla warfare soon became widespread. The French learned, the hard way, as the British were to learn a century later, that Egypt is easy to conquer but difficult to govern. In 1800 Kléber was assassinated. His successor, Menou, proved no more capable of winning the support of the Mamluks or the population. This indigenous support might have enabled the French to prevail against the British sea-blockade and joint Anglo-Turkish expeditionary forces, but it was not forthcoming. Finally in 1801 an armistice was arranged, and all French forces departed after an occupation of about three years.

The French left two legacies of a sort behind them. One was French culture, diffused in various directions by the experts who had accompanied Napoleon. Egyptologists founded an Institut d'Egypte modeled after the Institut de France, and set to work refurbishing the Pharaonic past. Jesuit educators set up schools. French was introduced as a competitor to Arabic. Scientific teams began investigation into the problems of the imbalanced and antiquated Egyptian economy. Without altering the basic Islamic structure and attitudes of society, the *Civilization Française* was thus subtly introduced into Egyptian culture.

The second "legacy" was fresh recognition of Egypt's historical strategic position in world politics. The defeat of Mamluk chivalry removed forever the remoteness of Egypt from power centers. Napoleon realized that Egypt was the key to success, in a broader sense, against Britain. The British developed their imperial lifeline concept based on control over the Nile Valley and Red Sea, with Egypt an irreducible part of the equation.

The brief British occupation of 1801–1803 also provided Egypt with a legacy in the person of one Muhammad Ali. This obscure individual turned a most unpromising initial exposure to the Nile Valley into a personal triumph and the start of a dynasty which lasted more than a century. His individual talents were considerable, but the prevailing anarchy in Egypt was tailored for them.

British forces had been evacuated from Egypt in 1803, two years after the French; they had done little more than continue the administration quasi-organized by their rivals. Britain then returned Egypt to its pre-Bonaparte arrangement of a Turkish governorship assisted by Mamluk officials who more often than not intrigued against their nominal superior. The garrison consisted of a mixed force of Turks and Albanians under the Ottoman standard. The second in command of the Albanian contingent was Muhammad Ali. Of obscure parentage, probably Albanian, he grew up in the service of the local governor of Kavalla, on the north Aegean coast of what is now Greek Thrace, made a small living as a tobacco factor, and then was recruited into the Ottoman army during its first abortive effort to recapture Alexandria in 1799. He was nearly drowned in the evacuation and was rescued by a British ship. He returned with the Ottomans in 1801, and presumably better acquainted with topography, made his way to Cairo with his fellow Albanians. Because of their cohesion and military effectiveness, the Albanians became a balance wheel in the internal wrestling match which developed in the wake of the British departure. The nominal commander of the Albanians, Tahir Pasha, was murdered and his head thrown out of a Cairo window. Muhammad Ali succeeded him. Two groups of Mamluks were contending in the customary fashion, one backed by the Ottoman governor, the other opposing him. British officers who had remained in Egypt to oversee the transition of government even found themselves opposing each other. In 1804–1805 the Egyptian people rebelled against a Mamluk attempt to levy new taxes (to pay Muhammad Ali's Albanians, ironically), and the wily Albanian put his forces at the head of the rebellion. He then declared himself Pasha of Egypt; the Sultan confirmed his *fait accompli* when it became apparent that no Mamluk plot (backed by the Ottomans, naturally) could supersede him. Then in 1806 Muhammad Ali became *de facto* as well as *de jure* ruler of Egypt.

Muhammad Ali ushered Egypt into the anteroom of modern technological civilization, although to a large degree he ruled as oppressively as any Fatimid or Mamluk. His ambition was to make Egypt into a vigorous modern state capable of dealing equally with the European powers and the Sultan of Turkey, in other words, restoring Egypt's traditional role as the pivot of world affairs, courted by many, subordinate to none.[12] In 1807 the British, still underestimating Muhammad Ali, sent an army under General Fraser to reoccupy Egypt, in order to keep the country from again falling into French hands. This army was beaten by the

[12] President Nasir has essayed a similar role for Egypt in the present century. *Vide,* his speech to Parliament in 1958: "A great state has arisen in the east . . . a state whose well being shall have its effect on those around us and on the entire human race." St. John, Robert, *The Boss,* New York: McGraw-Hill, Book Co., Inc., 1960, p. 281.

Egyptians and driven into Alexandria, while "some 450 heads of British soldiers were exposed in the Uzbekieh to the derisive gaze of the Cairo populace."[13] This success gave Muhammad Ali a means of identification with the Egyptian people, whose nascent nationalism and self-respect surged around the stocky figure of a man who was lineally just another foreign usurper.

The second act which endeared the Pasha to his subjects was the elimination of the Mamluks. Having lulled these miscreants into a false sense of security, he arranged a reception in the great hall of the Cairo citadel; all the Mamluk chiefs were invited to observe the ceremony of investing one of his sons to lead a force to Arabia and recover the Holy Cities from the Wahhabis. On their way down from the citadel after this performance, the Mamluks were trapped in a narrow passage and slaughtered to the last man, some 480 of them. Subsequently a nation-wide manhunt killed or dispersed their followers.[14]

Thus established, Muhammad Ali proceeded to govern Egypt like any Oriental autocrat, except that his driving, autocratic ambition was to remake his adopted country into a powerful, efficient state. He made few changes in the political structure except that a single voice of authority, his own, superseded the babel of the Mamluks. He introduced a constitution in 1826, but this bore little resemblance to twentieth century democratic examples. It merely reorganized the customary *divan,* or public audience held by Oriental rulers, into a Council of State and Cabinet of Ministers, with the ruler having the final word on all matters brought before the Council. Muhammad Ali also formed the nucleus of a modern Egyptian army. When his Albanians kicked over their cooking pots over suggestions that they obey the Pasha's discipline, he had them replaced by Sudanese recruited forcibly from the Sudan. The expeditionary force which he sent to the Sudan for this purpose added the southern Nile Valley territory to his dominions. He founded a military academy to train officers for the new army, and to fill its classrooms turned to the *fellahin,* who "volunteered" in droves. In this fashion the long-suffering common people of Egypt found themselves, for almost the first time in history, taking part in a nineteenth-century great leap forward.[15]

[13] Chirol, Valentine, *The Egyptian Problem,* London: Macmillan, 1920, p. 4.
[14] See Jarvis, H. Wood, *Pharaoh To Farouk,* London: John Murray, 1955, pp. 123–126.
[15] Col. Sève, a French officer, was invited to train the new officers; later he turned Muslim and changed his name to Soliman Pasha. Soliman Pasha Street in Cairo is named after him.

Muhammad Ali's greatest progress was made in economic reforms. King Cotton, the long-staple variety, was introduced into Egypt; it flourished under a benign sun and through a perennial irrigation system (another innovation) drawn from the Nile in a series of canals. The Mahmoudiya Canal, connecting Alexandria with Cairo, concentrated export-import traffic in that port city. The restoration of the basin system of irrigation was improved to the point where cultivation of two-season crops became possible. Land reform was begun. Muhammad Ali initially abolished the system of *Multazimin* (tax-gatherers, later provincial governors) and declared all land to be the property of the state. Then he broke up the Mamluk estates, giving most of their land to his courtiers and family. The remaining land was leased for cultivation to tenants who became in time *de facto* owners—to collect taxes, maintain public security and control irrigation. Egypt was redistricted into *mudiriyas* (provinces) under a *mudir* (governor); the *mudiriyas* were subdivided into *markazes* (districts), whose head (*mamur*) was the superior of the village headmen (*umdas*).

Muhammad Ali was less fortunate in foreign affairs. His primary concern was to cajole or intimidate the Ottoman Sultan into recognizing the autonomy of Egypt. The corollary was to restore Egyptian dominance in the Middle East. Much of his period in office coincided with Sultan Mahmud II, the reformer who blew up the Janissaries in their barracks; Mahmud's concentration on internal problems eased Muhammad Ali's task. He sent his son Ibrahim against the Wahhabis in Arabia, defeating them in a bitter campaign which was generally applauded by the Islamic world as the conquest of a schismatic sect. The Sudan followed. In return for support against the Greek rebels, the Sultan promised Muhammad Ali the Pashaliks of Crete, Damascus, Tripoli, and Syria. Ibrahim's newly-organized army of *fellahin* temporarily checked the Greeks and reoccupied the Peloponnesus; but the European powers were not prepared to let a Christian population be transported en masse as slaves to Cairo, and Ibrahim was forced to withdraw. Balked, Muhammad Ali turned his son's army against the Porte itself. The army invaded Syria in 1831 and cleaned out the Sultan's troops. In 1838 the Pasha, picturing in his dreams a revived Pharaonic Empire of the east, declared his independence of the Sultan. The Ottoman Army was beaten decisively by Ibrahim at the Battle of Nisib, near Aleppo, in 1839. Ibrahim then marched northward into Anatolia; only a disorganized rabble barred his way to Constantinople.

But the prize which Muhammad Ali had earned from the Ottomans was taken from him by the Western powers, themselves determined to maintain the empire's integrity. His hope that France would support him against Britain (he was not too concerned about Russia although that power harbored in no uncertain terms a similar ambition for Constantinople) was not justified; the French took part in European naval maneuvers with the Turks, defeating Egyptian naval squadrons. An Anglo-Turkish force landed in Lebanon and defeated Ibrahim. Much as the British were to do a century later with King Faruq, Commodore Napier went to Muhammad Ali's palace and gave him an ultimatum to wit: "If Your Highness will not listen to my unofficial appeal, by God, I will bombard you and put a bomb right where you are sitting." [16] The Pasha yielded; the European stick was considerably bigger then than it is now. The imperial idea was lost, but by the Treaty of London (1841) Muhammad Ali gained the hereditary right to the government of Egypt, for himself and the eldest male in his line thereafter. In 1849 the founder of Modern Egypt died, leaving as his appropriate epitaph the words: "I will pursue the well-being of this land even at the cost of my life and the lives of my kindred." [17]

ANGLO-FRENCH RIVALRY, 1820–1880

The limited gains which Muhammad Ali had achieved for Egypt were largely dissipated by his successors in the dynasty which he had created. He was succeeded by his grandson Abbas; on the latter's death his uncle, Said, became hereditary Pasha, and in 1863 Ismail, the son of Ibrahim, became Khedive of Egypt.[18] Said Pasha had made friends with Ferdinand de Lesseps, the son of the French Consul-General, as a youth in Cairo. When he was named ruler of Egypt he set out to reverse his father's policy of avoiding Western encroachment on Egyptian sovereignty. He also remembered his old friend. De Lesseps returned to Cairo, and was granted in 1854 a concession to build a canal from the Red Sea to the Mediterranean. In 1856 this concession was replaced by a more detailed one given to the Compagnie Universelle du Canal Maritime de Suez, formed by de Lesseps. Work began in earnest on a canal in 1859, and ten years later the Suez Canal opened for business.

[16] Young, *op. cit.*, p. 58.
[17] Jarvis, *op. cit.*, p. 135.
[18] "Khedive" means lord or viceroy; Ismail purchased the title from the Sultan in 1866, along with the right of primogeniture. See Marlowe, John, *Anglo-Egyptian Relations 1800–1953*, London: Cresset Press, 1954, p. 84 n.

Ferdinand de Lesseps. (Courtesy The   Khedive Ismail. (Courtesy The
Middle East Institute)   Middle East Institute)

We will consider in a subsequent chapter the complex role played by this "shortcut to the East" in international affairs, and its effect on Europe's relations with the Middle East. As far as Egypt is concerned, the Canal was the largest link in a chain forged by the Khedives to lead the country into economic bankruptcy, followed by political loss of Muhammad Ali's gains. The attraction of Egypt is such, however, that even nations whose power ambitions lie elsewhere have been unable to disregard her. In the nineteenth century the mere fact of her growing insolvency set off a spate of maneuvers in the capitals of Europe.

Said's giveaway program was peanuts compared to the ambition of his successor. Said merely pledged a strip of cultivable land in the heart of the Nile Valley to a foreign company, for the ultimate benefit of outside interests, in return for 15 per cent of future profits. Ismail inherited the dreams of his grandfather, but while Muhammad Ali had thirsted for power, Ismail was obsessed by opulence.[19] The public "unveiling" of the canal in 1869 provided a sample of the Khedive's generosity. When

[19] Cromer notes that "roughly speaking, Ismail added on an average of £7 million a year for thirteen years to the debt of Egypt." Cromer, Lord (Sir Evelyn Barring), *Modern Egypt*, 2 vols., London: Macmillan, 1908, vol. 1, p. 5.

the Empress Eugénie expressed a desire to see the Pyramids by dawn, but feared the long journey, he built a road for her. Verdi was commissioned to compose *Aida* for the occasion, and it had its first public performance in Cairo, in a brand new opera house. The town of Ismailia, named after him, appeared as if by magic on the empty sands halfway down the canal, and there the climactic entertainment was held. It was one of the most elaborate public gatherings ever given—and an important reason for Ismail's bankruptcy. Six years later he sold his last asset, his shares in the Suez Canal Company, to Britain for £4 million. This 44 per cent block gave the British a controlling interest and a stake in Egypt's territorial politics dictated by this financial interest. The financial indebtedness to foreign powers was merely a step away from deposition, for Ismail. In a desperate effort to save his throne, he laid debt consolidation proposals before his creditors. In 1876 a mission headed by M. Joubert (France) and Mr. Goschen (Britain) attempted to make a settlement with the Khedive on behalf of foreign landholders. A number of these, taking advantage of the capitulatory privilege afforded them in Egypt under Ottoman statutes, sued for recovery of their debts. The unsuccessful Goschen-Joubert mission gave way to an international Committee of Inquiry. Unexpectedly, Ismail dismissed his Prime Minister (who had been sitting on the committee) and appointed a tripartite international government consisting of an Armenian Christian, Nubar Pasha, an Englishman, Rivers Wilson, and a Frenchman, de Blignieres, to supervise Egypt's finances. The idea was to transfer the onus of debt collection to the foreigners; secondarily to inspirit the debilitated people of Egypt behind him. In 1879 the German Chancellor, Bismarck, intervened, accusing Ismail of not honoring an international agreement. Britain and France called for him to abdicate. When no volunteers responded to his call for a *jihad* against the infidels, the Sultan deposed him in favor of his son Tawfiq. The Khedive left Egypt in a royal manner, on a yacht loaded with jewels, as his descendant Faruq was to do in the present century.[20]

There are two sharply contradictory shades of opinion regarding the Khedive Ismail. British administrators like Cromer and Lord Milner, horrified by Ismail's evident financial disorganization, contrasted their Sunday-School ethics with his Oriental viewpoint, with extremely unfavorable results. As Lord Salisbury wrote, ". . . the English Government

[20] For a good account see Little, Tom, *Egypt*, New York: Frederick A. Praeger, Inc., 1958, p. 76.

Port Taufiq in 1869—from a water color by Riou. (Courtesy
The Middle East Institute)

. . . are bound, both by duty and interest to do all that lies in their
power to arrest misgovernment, before it results in the material ruin
and almost incurable disorder evident by other Oriental examples. . . ." [21] Other authors found him much "maligned," the victim of
an unfavorable press in Europe, Anglo-French cupidity, and his own
high hopes for Egypt.[22] An American observer was harsher—Anglo-
French rivalry made Ismail's abdication a certainty. "Nothing less than
the blood of the Khedive could satisfy a Frenchman. 'Une revanche
éclantante' was what they publicly demanded in Paris." [23]

The true role of the Khedive of Ismail was probably a combination of
Horatio Alger and an Oriental "Rake's Progress." Certainly he was thoroughly exploited by those around him, his own officials and the foreigners he dealt with. The appellation of "the land of baksheesh" received
full play in nineteenth-century Egypt. At the same time Ismail's contribution to material progress was considerable. The public education system instituted by Muhammad Ali was greatly expanded. By 1878 there
were 5,800 schools in Egypt against 185 in 1805. Foreign educational
missions were cheerfully accepted, and young Egyptians began going to
Europe to study in military academies. The army was reorganized, and a
number of American officers, including some from the armies of the
South, were brought in on contract to train the fellahin. The Khedive also

[21] Quoted in Cromer, op. cit., Vol. I, page 137.
[22] See, for example, Pierre Crabites, Ismail, The Maligned Khedive, London:
Routledge, 1933, Chapter XVII et passim.
[23] Farman, Elbert, Egypt and its Betrayal, New York: Grafton Press, 1908,
p. 251.

Port Said on opening day, 1869—from a water color by Beraud. (Courtesy The Middle East Institute)

contracted for an extensive public works program of railroads, highways, canals, telegraph and postal services, port improvements, even gas and fresh water for Cairo and Alexandria. Whether by choice or design, Egypt remained politically stable, with internal safety for Christians as for Muslims during Ismail's sixteen-year reign. The foundations of an administrative system which the British developed so well were laid. In sum, Ismail's failure may be ascribed to a supreme effort "to create new and vigorous states by engrafting modern civilization on the stocks of old ones . . . the possible success of which remained to be demonstrated." [24]

THE ARABI REVOLT, 1881

An Anglo-French Dual Control Administration was placed in Egypt to assist the government and supervise finances in 1879, although Tawfiq held office as Khedive. Cromer was named Comptroller by Lord Salisbury. The two powers indirectly had contributed to Egypt's bankruptcy by encouraging expeditions into the Sudan and Equatorial Africa to suppress the slave trade, and by the building of the Suez Canal. Now they faced the same problem of financial chaos which had toppled Ismail. The Dual Control was destined not to work, however; in the wake of Ismail's deposition, Egyptian nationalism went berserk, plaguing the new-found cooperation between the two European powers.

[24] Crabites, *op. cit.*, p. 295.

This hitherto unexpressed nationalism of the people of Egypt was compounded of many ingredients. But three stood out. One was the Islamic reformism of Jamal al-din-al-Afghani, interpreted in Egypt by the Rector of Al-Azhar University and liberal thinker, Mohammad 'Abduh. This school of thought, which held that material progress in the Western pattern could be reconciled with Islam, attracted many younger *'ulema* and educated intellectual laymen; distilled down to village level, it acquired for the Muslim *fellahin* the aura of a Muslim revival which would sweep Egypt clean of alien growths, including the khedivial family, the Turkish official class, ultimately the Christians. Consciousness of their past, notably the Islamic period, was fostered through the introduction of the Arabic printing press; by the 1880's Cairo had become the Middle East's publishing center. (Significantly, the Egyptian nationalist movement did not think of itself as Arab, nor preach the ideal of a unified Arab state, until much later.)

The second element of the movement was "constitutionalism." Vaguely similar to the constitutionalist wing of the Young Turk movement, the Egyptian constitutionalists, mostly men of means and position, deplored the arrangement of a non-Egyptian, medieval Khedive ruling arbitrarily but subject to the decrees of a European board of control. They cooperated closely with the Chamber of Notables set up by Ismail in 1866 to govern the provinces. The third, and perhaps most interesting, element was the "native Egyptian" movement, centered among the young army officers. The native-born Egyptians found advancement nearly impossible, owing to the presence of Turkish Circassian or Albanian officers in the higher positions, under the Ottoman policy of seconding officers to posts throughout the Empire. This barrier —even the language used by the army was officially Turkish—intensified their "Egyptianist" feelings.

The actions of the Dual Control helped to bring these disparate elements together. Taxation fell heavier on the population than in Ismail's day, owing to the enforcement of the law of liquidation to pay off his foreign debts. The number of European officials paid out of the Egyptian treasury reached 1,325. The capitulatory privileges became especially attractive because they were available under a regime which was itself a captive, and speculators descended on Cairo like the wild ducks which winter near there. Also, the army was reduced from nearly 60,000 men under Ismail to 18,000 under Tawfiq (by the imperial *firman* which authorized his accession). This froze about one half of the officers out of their careers, with the Egyptians the first to be reduced in force.

Egyptian nationalism found the necessary leader in Colonel Ahmad Arabi. Arabi, the son of a village shaykh, educated at Al-Azhar, was nevertheless a man of the people, with roots deep in Nilotic ground. He was a big man, slow of speech, deeply patriotic, capable of the passionate religious oratory which his counterpart of the 1950's has employed with such telling effect on the Egyptian masses.

In 1881 Arabi, and a group of army colonels, succeeded in forcing the Khedive to appoint their own choices to the Ministry and to dismiss the Circassian–Turkish appointees. Their success made Arabi and his colleagues bolder. He became Minister of War; the army was Egyptianized and expanded. But Arabi was in the position of having defied duly constituted authority, yet of being forced to justify his own authority. In June, 1882, violent anti-Christian riots broke out in Alexandria, sparked by a fight between a Maltese and an Egyptian but expressive of the deep-lying discontent with the Dual Control and aggressive nationalism. The city was looted and nearly all the Europeans fled, before Arabi's troops could restore order. Nationalist ambitions for constitutional reform ran counter to Anglo-French interests as well as to Tawfiq's policy, and the Western powers found themselves squeezed into the position of having to intervene against a militant Muslim crusade.

At this point France withdrew from the Dual Control, being opposed to what had become in effect a conquest, and left Britain to uphold the Khedive. The British completely misjudged the popular support, and the intentions of Arabi's revolt. Gladstone, the Prime Minister, saw the Egyptian leader in much the same light as Eden saw Gamal 'Abd al-Nasir, as a nuisance and a hindrance to normal relationships. On the flimsy pretext of restoring the legal Khedivial government, the British first bombarded Alexandria and next landed an expeditionary force of 20,000 under Sir Garnet Wolseley. On September 12, 1882, Wolseley's forces made a night surprise attack on the main Egyptian positions at Tal-al-Kabir between the undefended Suez Canal and Cairo. Arabi, when thus put to the test, was in bed, and fled without his boots,[25] but the core of his army, the trained artillerymen and the guards, made a *succes d'estime* by their gallantry in a losing cause. More than 10,000 of

---

[25] The night march and subsequent battle are vividly described in Gen-Sir Edward Hutton's diary. See Jarvis, *op. cit.,* pp. 163–166, for excerpts.

them died on the field. The British, on the next day, sent a small party into Cairo and deceived the 6,000 man garrison of the Citadel into surrendering.[26] The Khedive issued a decree, "the Army is dissolved," and Arabi was exiled; he later returned to Cairo to live in retirement on his restored pension but to remain out of politics. With this whimper, the Egyptian nationalists' effort to break away from foreign control foundered on the rocks of European economic imperialism. If Arabi's military skills had equalled his spell-binding ability over the Cairo masses, the result might have been different.

THE BRITISH OCCUPATION, 1882–1922

The Khedive remained titular sovereign in Egypt after the defeat of Arabi but in practice the British were occupiers, with full authorities. As Lord Lloyd pointed out, "the position of the British Consul-General was anomalous, the highest authority in Egypt yet possessing no more legal authority than any other Consul-General . . . the presence of British officials was utterly anomalous—legally servants of the Khedive, in practice taking their orders from the Consul-General." [27]

This state of ill-defined sovereignty endured until World War I. One observer concluded at the start of the occupation, that "England has now a magnificent opportunity (toward Egypt). It will be her own fault if she has no noble fruit to show of which she may be proud." [28] From the viewpoint of the French, this harvest was far from having been reached by 1922. France, secretly bitter over the Napoleonic defeats in the eastern Mediterranean, and perhaps annoyed at having withdrawn from the Dual Control only to see the British take advantage of a free hand in Egypt, saw little good in the British occupation. At least one French author could find no evidence "that any area of human activity—education, communications, public health, business—had benefited during the occupation by the reforming genius of the West." [29] What the individual Egyptian thought of the latest *foreign* accession has not been recorded, but collectively they resisted. The tide of nationalism rose slowly, and after 1894, when Abbas Hilmi II succeeded his father Tawfiq as Khedive, cooperation became minimal between the Egyptians and the British.

[26] Cf. the proverb: "He who holds the Citadel holds Cairo; he who holds Cairo holds Egypt."
[27] Quoted in Little, *op. cit.*, p. 91.
[28] Stuart, Villiers, *Egypt After the War,* London: John Murray, 1883, p. VIII.
[29] Cf. Lacouture, Jean and Simone, *L'Egypte en Mouvement,* Paris: Editions du Seuil, 1936, Chapter VIII *passim.*

Lord Cromer returned to Egypt in 1883 as British agent and Consul-General; whatever "noble fruit" Britain may have produced in the Nile Valley was the result of his careful horticulture. Mention has been made of the piousness with which British officials approached the task of redeeming an Oriental anarchy, but their efforts at least provided representative government of a sort and financial stabilization, plus a start toward adequate land use. "It was this radical reversal of the distribution of Nile water that gave the British presence in Egypt its revolutionary value."[30]

Cromer's achievements lay in the fields of administration and finances. The extravagances of the previous Khedives were not repeated, and during his twenty-four-year term (1883–1907) Egypt's finances were completely reorganized. Authority over them devolved completely to Britain after the signing of an Anglo-French Agreement in 1904. Public expenditures were kept to a minimum, with the stress laid on irrigation schemes and reduction of taxation. Cromer believed that the function of government was to act as a policeman, not a nursemaid; in regulating Egypt's finances he hoped that the consequent relief would encourage the Egyptians to develop their own resources. Therefore, the *corvée,* the ancient system of recruiting forced labor to clear the Nile silt from irrigation canals and perform other public services, was abolished and paid labor introduced. The crack of the *courbash* echoed no more across the valley.[31] The new dignity of the fellah worker eased the task of British engineers improving the irrigation system. The Delta Barrage was reconstructed; in 1903, after seven years of preparation, the Aswan Dam was completed, bringing perennial irrigation to upper Egypt at a cost of £2 million.

Reforms were also carried out in the judiciary system, in medicine and public health and to a lesser extent in education. The nucleus of a volunteer Egyptian army was laid, and the downtrodden fellah soldier acquitted himself very well under British officers in the Sudan. Judicial reform was less successful, owing to the continuation of the capitulations and the diversity of courts. Cromer operated as a dictator or sorts, but he was genuinely dedicated to Egyptian progress, and the Egyptians themselves came to regard him with real devotion.[32] Even so, the weakness of Cromer was his essential paternalistic decency. It did not occur

[30] *Ibid.,* p. 75.
[31] The *courbash* was the rawhide whip used by overseers to stimulate the corvée workers. Marlowe, *op. cit.,* p. 175.
[32] See, for example, Amine, Youssef, *Independent Egypt,* London: John Murray, 1940, pp. 8–12.

to him to train Egyptian officials *con spirito* for the eventual transfer of power into their hands, since Egypt lacked utterly a democratic tradition and culture. The assumption of Cromer and his successors Gorst and Kitchener was: first, that the *fellahin* were content with British rule, the alternative being misrule; second, that parliamentary institutions in the European style would be anachronistic still in Egypt. Such an appraisal, accurate in the short run, ignored the long-run accumulated evidence of history and dissociated Egypt from the gathering swell of Arabism. Where Britain has been able to build mirrored parliamentarianism, in a raw clan culture, she has succeeded relatively well in leaving a residence of good relations; but in Egypt the British engendered only resentment, finding no means of accommodation with Egyptian cultural bedrock and therefore seeking merely to bolster it with good English stone. This has been the disaster of Anglo-Egyptian relations from Cromer to Churchill and Eden.

The First World War brought the inexorable march of events to a climax with a formal British protectorate over Egypt. Egyptian nationalism had begun to call for "Egypt for the Egyptians"—but the cry was irresolute, confined to scattered groups. The declaration of the protectorate, however, placed Egypt's predominantly Muslim population in the position of supporting a Christian power against their Turkish co-religionists.[33]

Egypt was a major military base during World War I; the British had nearly a million men under arms and the campaigns against Gallipoli, Mesopotamia, and Palestine, were mounted largely from Cairo. The British raised a labor corps of 117,000 in Egypt of whom 10,000 went to France as volunteers behind the Allied lines. About 135,000 took part in the Syrian campaign. The presence of the military brought wealth into the country, but it encouraged profiteering and accentuated social divisions. The *fellahin* grew poorer while the distinctions between the ruling class of Turko-Circassians, the Copto-Syrian middle class, and the Arab-Nubian peasantry now gave way to a reclassification of the Western type—wealthy, well-to-do, and workers. The war also ended the life of the Constitution of 1913 which set up a parliament of eighty-one members, fifteen appointed by the Khedive and sixty-six indirectly elected; while powerless to enact legislation, it was at least a step in the direction desired by nationalist leaders.

[33] "Himaya," the Arabic word used in the proclamation of the protectorate, implied protectionism for foreigners . . . , "therefore related . . . to all the worse abuses of the capitulatory system." Little, *op. cit.,* p. 125.

In 1917 Prince Fuad succeeded his brother on the throne of the Khe-dives.[34] His arrival coincided with a spate of activity on the part of the National Party, which had been moribund since the early part of the century. One of its leaders who now came to the fore was Sa'd Zaghlul, a man of peasant stock who had been trained as a lawyer and advanced himself into the alien ruling class through his friendship with one of the royal princesses. Although of *fellah* stock, Zaghlul had served under Cromer as Minister of Education, and was not exactly free of the col-laborationist taint. But his native Egyptian sentiments impelled him to-ward the nationalist movement, as it developed. After the Armistice had ended the war, Zaghlul called on the then British Resident Agent, Sir Reginald Wingate, as the head of a nationalist delegation. They re-quested the immediate and complete independence of Egypt. Wingate, referred the delegation to London and notified the Foreign Office that the Egyptians should be received. For his boldness, he was recalled and not permitted to return to Egypt.

The British piled blunder upon blunder. Seeking to block the national-ist movement by removing the head, they deported Zaghlul and other leaders to Malta in 1919. The Egyptian populace rioted, forcing the re-imposition of martial law. Allenby, the deliverer of Jerusalem, was next sent to replace Wingate as High Commissioner; he ordered the national-ist leaders released from Malta to go to Paris, where they could present their case to the Peace Conference. The group of men who went to Paris were called the *Wafd* "delegation" or *Al-Wafd Al-Misri* ("The delegation of Egypt"). The cards were stacked against them even before their arrival; Britain had determined that Egypt was "unready" for inde-pendence—Article 147 of the Versailles Treaty confirmed the British protectorate over the Nile Valley.

In November, 1919, the British Government sent a mission under Lord Milner to study the deteriorating situation in Egypt and to begin work on a constitution. The terms of reference of the commission were indistinguishable from those of any League of Nations, Mandatory ap-pointment. The Wafdist leaders, still in exile and unable to press their case successfully in Paris, opposed it bitterly. Zaghlul, in Paris, ordered a boycott of the mission, and in subsequent negotiations put forward

---

[34] Abbas Hilmi II, while visiting Constantinople in 1914, was deposed coinci-dent with the outbreak of war; the British named his son Husayn as his successor, with the title of Sultan. Fuad inherited this title. See Sir Valentine Chirol, *The Egyptian Problem,* London: Macmillan, 1920, Chapter VII. For an opposing view see Arden Beaman, *Development of the Khedive,* London: Allen & Unwin, 1929, pp. 66–70.

amendments to its memorandum which would have practically eliminated the British "presence" in Egypt. Lord Milner refused to accept this; he then published the memorandum as it stood. In essence, its recommendations were:

(1) Recognition of Egypt's sovereignty as a constitutional monarchy.
(2) An Anglo-Egyptian "Close Alliance" to replace the Protectorate, with Britain responsible for Egypt's defense.
(3) Egyptianization of the civil service.
(4) British judicial and financial advisers.
(5) Transfer to Britain of the capitulatory rights of the foreign powers.

The memorandum was the starting point for all subsequent treaty negotiations between England and Egypt.[35] The British had admittedly made concessions from the point at which Prime Minister Balfour had told the House of Commons: "British supremacy exists in Egypt. British supremacy is going to be maintained." Allenby went to England, where he pointed out the extreme instability of the Egyptian situation and the relative weakness of the British position. Zaghlul was deported again, this time to the Seychelles Islands. The deportation stirred fresh violence among the Egyptian people; Britain, like a man sleepwalking who awakes to find himself leaning from a second-story open window, rushed into another concessionary period. In 1922 a declaration officially and unilaterally terminated the Protectorate. Egypt became a "sovereign" independent state," with Fuad's title modulated from Sultan to King. This sovereignty was limited in four areas which were "absolutely reserved to the discretion of His Majesty's Government" for an indefinite period. These were communications, external defense, protection of foreign interests and minorities in Egypt, and the Sudan.

King Fuad next formed a government under Sarwat Pasha, and a commission began to work out the details of a constitution, which was promulgated in 1923. It vested power in the King, ruling with a bicameral legislature, partly elected and partly appointed by him. Terrorism ceased. The Wafd came into the open as a political party. In elections held in 1924 it received 90 per cent of the popular vote and 188 seats out of 215 available in the legislature. Zaghlul became Prime Minister, with at least the possibility that the conciliatory attitude of the British would be matched by this Egyptian official who stood alone as the nationalist symbol in his country.

[35] See Marlowe, *op. cit.,* pp. 242–243, for text.

TREATY NEGOTIATIONS, 1924–36

Relations between Great Britain and her unruly ward followed a pattern as tortuous as that blazed by the Mamluks in their centuries of intrigue, for the next dozen years. Initially a forecast of relative Anglo-Egyptian amity was clouded by the murder of Sir Lee Stack, Sirdar (C-in-C) of the Egyptian Army and Governor-General of the Sudan. In November, 1924, as he started from the War Office for his home in Cairo, seven men dressed as students ambushed him on the sidewalk and pumped bullets into his body at close range. The murder prompted an ultimatum from Allenby, a close friend of Stack's, to Zaghlul. It demanded an apology, reparations, prosecution of the murderers (who were later executed when one turned state's evidence) and removal of Egyptian forces from the Sudan, which remained until 1953 a purely British province. The Wafd was not found to have been connected with the murder, which was another instance of random Egyptian anti-foreign violence, but it was temporarily discredited.

Zaghlul died in 1927, and with him went any real possibility that moderate nationalism might work with the British or that the Wafd would spearhead parliamentary development, or even introduce a Kemalist note of stability. Zaghlul had alienated a number of able political leaders, such as Ismail Sidqi, Adly Yeghen, Sarwat Pasha, and Muhammad Mahmud, who formed other political parties or simply went into political opposition. But there was no question of his patriotism, nor the affection he inspired among the *fellahin* from whom he had sprung. Nahhas Pasha, his chief lieutenant, assumed the mantle of Wafd leadership, but the Wafd slowly lost under him its universal representativeness for Egypt. He never acquired the popularity of his predecessor, nor could he control *fellahin* excesses or direct their energies. Where the Wafd had been in the truest sense the expression of all Egyptians, their delegate and the source of political activity, the tide of events turned it into a bastion of reaction. Yet it could not be ignored, whether in or out of power, since it spoke for so many Egyptians and retained an aura imposed by its prosecution of the 1922 Declaration of Independence.[36] Other parties opposed it—Ismail Sidqi's Liberal Constitutionalists, Mustafa

---

[36] "The Wafd seemed to bring all possible Egypts together . . . it contained all the generosity, intellectual muddle, good nature, contradictions . . . of its millions of supporters. It united unlimited poverty . . . and bloated fortunes, the demand for change and the demand for conservation, reaction and movement. . . ." Lacouture, *op. cit.*, p. 91.

Kamil's extreme nationalists, the *Ittihad* (Union) party formed with royal backing from a palace clique—but none managed to do more than snip away at the big Wafdist majorities in Parliament.

Egyptian politics thus developed a triangular appearance. King Fuad, who exerted increasing influence either through the minority parties or through national leaders, was at one point; the Wafd occupied another; and the British, protecting their interest, held the third. The balance of internal power shifted between the King, the Wafd, and the other parties, while the British Resident played *divide et impera* with all three. Cabinets shuffled in and out with monotonous rapidity during the early thirties. Needed reforms were postponed. The 1923 Constitution was abrogated in 1930; a royal decree instituted a new draft constitution and electoral law which strengthened the executive and insured the defeat of the Wafd in the 1931 elections. For the next five years, governments headed by Ismail Sidqi and his successors maintained the triangular relationship in a fairly steady keel.

Meanwhile negotiations went on (and on) between Britain and Egypt for a treaty revising the 1922 agreement. The British held fast to their strategic commitments—Suez, Sudan, authority to speak for Egypt in external matters—while Nahhas Pasha first, and later all governments, insisted on rejection of these reserved points. Nahhas told Lord Lloyd, the Resident, that he would not agree to a single British soldier remaining in Egypt. Sessions at the conference table in 1927, 1929, and 1930 broke down over these points, plus the personal jealousies of the Egyptian leaders. Italy's imperial adventures proved the catalyst. A settlement became important to Britain, who feared interference with the Suez—the economic lifeline to India—and also a loss of dominance in the Middle East, and to Egypt to whom the authority of Italy was nearly as reprehensible as Britain's. Early in 1936 King Fuad, who was pro-Italian anyway,[37] died, leaving Nahhas a free hand, and control over two legs of the political triangle. In May, agreement was reached on a treaty.

The Anglo-Egyptian Treaty of 1936, which governed relations between the two states until the Revolution of 1952, granted Egypt no genuinely new concessions, but it did bring the Nile Valley a little closer to sovereign world recognition. Britain agreed to sponsor Egypt's membership in the League of Nations, and did so in 1937. The British agreed to press other foreign powers for an early end to the Capitula-

[37] He had been educated in Italy, and at the start of his reign spoke Italian better than Arabic.

tions (which were still applied in Egypt, sixteen years after the Ottoman demise, thirteen after Lausanne).[38] The convention of 1899 setting up an Anglo-Egyptian Dual Control over the Sudan was reaffirmed, with troop units from both states to be stationed there and Egyptian immigration permitted. The British military occupation was replaced by an alliance of twenty years. British troops up to a peacetime limit of 10,000 were allowed in the Suez Canal Zone, while the Royal Navy and Air Force received similar but broader privileges. In return Britain undertook to defend Egypt from invasion and to train Egyptian troops.

The Anglo-Egyptian Treaty gained little for Egypt except recognition of her internal sovereignty, while it legalized Britain's position in Suez and the Sudan. The Wafd leaders accepted it, however, figuring that with a new king on the throne, and the deterioration of the world situation, they would be able to maneuver Britain into a corner, where she would need allies, and bargain for the removal of its offending clauses.

Events worked against them, however. In the first place, when Faruq reached his majority in 1937, he undertook a more effective program than they had expected. He was determined to raise the national standard of living, and he instituted a number of irrigation schemes which endeared him momentarily to the *fellahin*. (He was much thinner, then, ascetic and not unhandsome.) Secondly, the Muslim Brotherhood, founded in 1928 by Shaykh Hasan al Banna as a purifying movement in Islam, turned definitely into politics. Its new purpose was the achievement of power, which would be used for social reform, liberation of the Nile Valley from foreign usurpation, and Arab unity. The wave of disillusionment that swept Egypt when the terms of the treaty were fully aired aided the Brotherhood and downgraded the Wafd. In the 1938 election the Wafd was defeated; Nahhas Pasha was replaced as Prime Minister by the independent liberal politician Muhammad Mahmud and then by Ali Mahir, Chief of the Royal Cabinet. A group of Wafdists led by his brother Ahmad formed a new party, the Saʻd Wafd, claiming they were the true successors to Saʻd Zaghlul.

The outbreak of war cancelled the few remaining advantages Egypt held under the Treaty. When British reverses in North Africa began to suggest to Egyptian leaders that they might do well to join the Axis, the British served up an ultimatum to Faruq; obey your previous commit-

[38] The Montreux Convention (1937) governing settlement of the Turkish Straits contained a section abolishing all capitulatory privileges in Egypt except for the Mixed Courts (q.v.) which were to surrender their jurisdiction over foreigners to Egypt's National Courts in 1949.

ments to support us, or we will form a government of our choice. The King bowed to the inevitable, and it is said that his corpulence (and political indifference) dates from this failure to assert Egypt's self-determination. Throughout the remainder of World War II, Egypt was the major British (or Allied) base in the Middle East, politically loyal, nationalistically docile, under British re-occupation.

PRELUDE TO REVOLUTION, 1946–1952

In February, 1945, Egypt declared war on Germany and Japan and signed the Charter of the United Nations. The declaration of war had one specific adverse effect; Prime Minister Ahmad Mahir was assassinated by a fanatic, a member of the extremist group *Misr al-Fatat.* The murder was the first in a campaign, which combined violence and intimidation, against those persons believed responsible for the continued subjection of Egypt. Ultimately it broadened under the aegis of the Muslim Brotherhood to match those whose aims of secular progress were deemed contrary to Islam's; Nasir himself was nearly made a victim of this extremism before it could be fully eliminated.

In the immediate postwar years the Wafd, the Muslim Brotherhood, and various secret organizations worked, above as well as below ground, to revise or to abrogate the Anglo-Egyptian Treaty.[39] Egypt tried to bring her case for self-determination before the UN, but her insistence on recovering the Sudan was received unfavorably by the General Assembly, which felt that the Nile Valley was really composed of diverse peoples whose wishes should be taken into consideration. The establishment in 1947 of a Legislative Assembly and an Executive Council in the Sudan and a program of constitutional reforms promulgated in 1948 further divorced the latter country from Egypt; though the adherents of Nile Valley unity used both physical and persuasive efforts to hold the Sudan within the Egyptian orbit, *"ces actes . . . ne purent detourner la Grande-Bretagne de sa politique . . . les anciennes provinces soudanaises, jadis conquises par Muhammad 'Ali, s'engageaient dans la voie d'autonomie."* [40]

The war's end found Egypt essentially leaderless. Faruq, whose meta-

---

[39] Anwar al-Sadat, one of the conspirators who carried out the 1952 revolution, says that he functioned as liaison between the RCC and Hasan al-Banna, in the early years of the war. See his *Revolt on the Nile,* London: Allan Wingate, 1957, p. 30.

[40] Colombe, Marcel, *L'Evolution de l'Egypte 1924–1950,* Paris: Maisson-Neune, 1951, p. 241.

morphosis from an idealistic young man to a playboy ruler roughly paralleled that of the country, had become unstable, given to unpredictable displays. Because of the relative prestige of his office, there was grouped around him a court society which was a mixture of genuine patriots and opportunists. The Wafd, no longer a revolutionary organization, refused to consider any treaty revision or change of government which they could not dominate. The Muslim Brotherhood, whose daily newspaper *Ikhwan al-Muslimin* was for a while the leading publication in Egypt, had many supporters in the universities and among dark conspiratorial groups. But no leader in this recurrent political triangle possessed the magic aura of Zaghlul or had the dynamism necessary to unite this sorely divided nation.

Two mediocre politicians, Ismail Sidqi Pasha and Nuqrashi Pasha, alternated as Prime Ministers in 1947–48 and negotiated with some sincerity with Britain for a revision of the 1936 Treaty. Sidqi in particular cracked down hard on strikes, leftist agitation, and extremist activity of any kind except for the shadowy army conspirators. Sidqi went to London and early in 1947 initialed with Foreign Minister Ernest Bevin the Sidqi–Bevin agreement, or draft treaty. Britain agreed to evacuate Egypt entirely by 1949. A joint defense board would coordinate Anglo-Egyptian military postures and defense in the event of an attack on Egypt. The Sudan question was left in abeyance by a protocol which stated that the Condominium would continue. But the negotiations broke down over this very point, with Egypt insisting on unification with the Sudan.

Any further progress toward a revision of the treaty was nullified by the UN Partition Plan for Palestine and the consequent Arab-Israeli War. "Egypt, being by temperament insular, was not pro-Arab, but history and Islam had made it Pan-Arab." [41] Having become affiliated with Pan-Arabism through membership in the Arab League, Egypt set out to dominate through size, population, political, economic and intellectual maturity. The exiled Mufti of Jerusalem, Hajj al-Amin al Husayni, masterminded public opinion in Egypt toward the Jews in Palestine from his office in Cairo. The Mufti's shrill propaganda certainly had much to do with Egypt's decision to send troops against Israel, but there were many other factors. The King and his advisers certainly welcomed the chance to regain popularity through a military success. The government headed by Nuqrashi saw a means of out-maneuvering the Muslim Brotherhood,

[41] Little, *op. cit.*, p. 176.

who were calling for a *jihad*. Egyptian industrialists may have wished to neutralize growing Jewish competition for Middle-Eastern markets. The average Egyptian, fed a diet of Anglo-Jewish atrocities and the glories of the Arab cause, eagerly anticipated the annihilation of the Israelis.[42]

It did not happen. Only the Army had known what would happen; some army officers, including Brigadier Muhammad Najib, told the King firmly that Egypt's armed forces were not ready to fight.[43] The report was suppressed. The army received a number of humiliating defeats. Its supplies were late in arriving, and much of its equipment proved defective. Except for a small defensive pocket of Faluja, where a young officer named Gamal 'abd-al Nasir held out bravely with his men, the Egyptians were driven back everywhere until in February, 1949, they signed an armistice agreement. The idea for the revolution of 1952 certainly predated Faluja, but the determination to act was crystallized there.

The last three years of the monarchy were marked by an increasing vacillation in government policy. Bursts of energy alternated with near paralysis. The choice between a formal, Oriental, Islamic way of life, with traditional institutions, and the vigorous economic, social, political concepts of Europe—a choice hanging over Egypt since the appearance of Napoleon—had to be made, by leaders who were either unwilling or unable to decide.[44] Financial difficulties became acute; government manipulation of cotton prices for the benefit of certain firms in which it had an interest left the 1951–52 crop unsold. Salary increases for middle-income personnel, part of a broad scheme for social security spearheaded by an independent Minister of Social Welfare, Ahmad Husayn, were more than balanced by cost of living increases. Ahmad Husayn resigned when it became apparent that the scheme was being misused to benefit Wafdist leaders. The traditional imbalance of Egypt's social structure— a small clique of "vested interests" (wealthy landowner pashas) at the

---

[42] Nasir himself writes, *op. cit.*, p. 44 "whenever I saw an airplane . . . I used to shout '*Ya 'aziz, Dahiyatakhud al-Ingliz*' (O Lord, Disaster Take the English) . . . just as our forefathers the Mamelukes used to say '*ya Rabb ya Mutajelli, ahlik al uthmenli*' (O Lord, O self-revealed, annihilate the Ottomans)".

[43] Wheelock, Keith, *Nasser's New Egypt,* New York: Frederick A. Praeger, Inc., 1960, p. 7.

[44] Cf. Marcel Colombe's conclusion (*op. cit.*, pp. 272 ff) that Egypt sought to make a compromise between formal Islam and representative Western institutions without realizing how long these had taken to evolve, or how deep-rooted they were in society.

top, an educated professional class, growing but helpless, in the middle, and a mute mass of peasantry carrying both on their broad backs—had reached the stage of utter futility.

Meanwhile the trading game with Britain continued on its nervous course, given a slight twist by the presence of Israel but at bottom unchanged. Britain still dominated an Egypt whose military frailty was only too apparent. Diplomatic exchanges were confined to Egyptian protest notes and non-committal British replies. In January, 1950, Nahhas Pasha, speaking for the Throne, declared that the 1936 Treaty ought to be abrogated. The climate of world affairs was as unfavorable as the snows of North Korea, and Britain refused to negotiate. In the following year a proposal for a joint Middle East Defense Organization (MEDO), prepared by Britain, France, Turkey, and the United States, was presented to Egypt, in the pious hope that such a multilateral grouping would encourage the Egyptian government to cooperate in achieving Middle East stability. The proposal was not only ill-timed and imprudent; it reckoned without Egypt's long obsession with anti-foreignism. Reaction was two-fold. The proposal was turned down flatly, on October 16, 1951, when the Chamber of Deputies approved Nahhas' decrees for the unilateral abrogation of both the 1936 Treaty and the proclamation of Faruq as King of Egypt and the Sudan. The Chamber also approved the outlines of a Sudanese constitution, giving Egypt the dominant role in a Nile Valley partnership; the Sudanese were not consulted.

These unilateral acts made an increase in sabotage and terrorism against British forces in the canal zone justifiable, from the Egyptian viewpoint, but they did nothing to expedite a British withdrawal or a settlement on terms of mutual advantage. The British began to fight back, with or without orders. However, their freedom of action was limited by having to operate within their treaty zone. Even minimal defensive action was frowned upon by the British government, which sought (in some vague way) an ultimate understanding with Egypt. Finally the incessant anti-British propaganda, the partial boycott of the Suez Base by Egyptian labor, the interference with supplies, and the guerrilla attacks, forced decisive British action. On January 25, 1952, a battalion of armed Egyptian auxiliary police was surrounded in its barracks at Ismailia and ordered to surrender its arms and ammunition. The ultimatum had a one-hour time limit; the Minister of Interior, Fuad Sarag al-Din, was barely apprised of it before it expired. He ordered the battalion to resist. It did so, and fought with pathetic courage until forty-three had been killed and many wounded; then it capitulated.[45]

When information of the Ismailia action reached Cairo, it set off an orgy of self-destruction. This was the notorious "Black Saturday," January 26, 1952, in which the Cairo familiar to wartime transit visitors and those assigned to Middle East commands was almost obliterated.

Black Saturday had four stages.[46] At first there were demonstrations; the always excitable Cairo rabble, augmented by unemployed laborers from the canal zone, was stirred to frenzy by professional agitators. A policeman drinking whiskey with a cabaret dancer ("Why aren't you fighting the English with your comrades?") became a cause célèbre; cabarets, famous landmarks like Shepheard's Hotel, the Opera House, Robert's Department Store, and Groppi's, were gutted by incendiaries. Yet except for twelve Englishmen trapped in the Turf Club, little violence was done to foreigners. Somewhat in the fashion of *fellahin,* who without warning smash their own agricultural implements in protest against their lot, the Cairo mob on Black Saturday looted and destroyed at random.

The Cairo police did not interfere at all with the rioters, and the army remained in its barracks. Fuad Sarag al-Din, who was responsible for order, stated in defense of the government later that he had been unable to reach the King for instructions.[47] Faruq, out of touch with events, was holding a reception for the officer corps at Abdin Palace at the time. Not until late in the evening of January 26 did the army finally intervene to take charge of the smoking city.

Many allegations of direct responsibility for Black Saturday have been advanced: collusion between the King and certain army officers to discredit the Wafd, action by Wafdists to discredit the King, the extreme right-wing Green Shirts, the Communists, the Cairo mob itself, skillfully manipulated by one or more of these. The truth probably lies between, in a coalition of anti-foreignism, pressure groups, and dissatisfaction with the regime. Neither can the influence of the Muslim Brotherhood be overlooked. The events of January 26, however, provided an aperture through which forces seldom seen before in Egyptian politics began to pour—forces like middle-class decency and morality

[45] *The London Times,* January 26, 1952.

[46] Lacouture, *op. cit.,* Chapter XII pp. 105 ff., presents the most detailed account.

[47] Published in *Al-Misr,* the Wafd newspaper, February 10, 1952.

and even technical skill. The result has been a genuine revolution from within and not the traditional one imposed from without.

THE EGYPTIAN REVOLUTION, 1952

On the night of July 22, 1952, a small group of military officers, who called themselves the Free Officers Society, carried out a bold and all-but-bloodless coup in Cairo.[48] King Faruq was ordered to abdicate, obviously in the best interests of Egypt, and he left the country in a style reminiscent of his predecessor, grandly but with equal futility, on July 26. A Regency Council was set up by the Free Officers to govern in the name of his infant son, King Fuad II, to whom Faruq had entrusted the throne in his statement of abdication.[49] The next step in this nicely logical transition was to abolish the monarchy in favor of a republic. This was done on June 18, 1953; General Muhammad Naguib was named its first president. Government remained in the hands of the same small group of Free Officers which had plotted the revolution, although they now called themselves the Revolutionary Command Committee. Not only were they unknown outside of Egypt; they were practically unknown *inside* the country. Although the recurrent pattern of Middle Eastern political evolution shows again and again the swift rise to power of unknown, unheralded leaders, the advent of the Free Officers is somewhat unusual in view of the obstacles set in their path and the fact that they set out to remake Egyptian society.

The majority of the Free Officers were middle-class young men, with army training and discipline as well as education (which alone set them apart from most of their fellow-citizens). In the 1930's, as schoolboys, they became imbued with the general desire of their generation of urban Egyptians for liberation from the British yoke. Most of them concentrated on acts of specific violence, but one had grander dreams. His name was Gamal 'Abd al-Nasir ("Slave of the servant of God"), and he was a postmaster's son in Beni Mir, Province of Assiut. He says that from his school days there grew in his mind a picture of "a revolution springing from the heart of the people, expressing their hopes, following the same path they had already envisioned as the great highway to Freedom." [50]

[48] According to eyewitness reports two soldiers killed outside of Army Headquarters were the only casualties.
[49] The texts of this statement and the notice of deposition are to be found in Sadat, *op. cit.*, pp. 125–127.
[50] Nasser, *op. cit.*, p. 58.

During the twenty years of his apprenticeship, his ultimate purpose never changed. He tried, and discarded, positive action, group pressure, and even assassination. At length, after his enrollment in the Military Academy at Abbasia in 1937, he evolved the concept of the Free Officers. He observed of the army that, "We have been used by Tyranny to give the people nightmares; it is therefore up to us to turn against Tyranny and scatter his dreams of glory." [51] After graduation he was assigned to garrison duty at Mankabad, in Upper Egypt. There, early in 1939, he formed with a group of fellow officers a secret revolutionary society dedicated to Egypt's liberation. It had (after 1942) branches throughout the armed services, controlled by a central committee of 12 members. Anwar al-Sadat, one of the original conspirators, writes of it, "The aim of the Committee was to establish by force a democratic and republican government, which implied the expulsion of the British from Egyptian soil and the destruction of the feudalist oligarchy which ruled our country. . . . It was a long-term plan, and Gamal Abdul Nasser (sic) was to be the architect and strategist. . . . Gamal's wisdom preserved us from premature action and from many dangerous adventures." [52]

From that time until July 23, 1952, Nasir worked silently, steadily, in the best manner of the professional spy or Florentine conspirator. [53] Although not well versed in Western (or Communist) political theory, and ideologically naive, he was steeped in the lore of plotting. While the armistice negotiations were going on in Palestine, he engaged in earnest conversations with Israeli officers. Not surprisingly, he was learning the methods and tactics used by the Jews in their struggle with the British under the Mandate, and their techniques of swinging world opinion behind their cause.

Egypt's political history since the coup may be divided into three phases: the consolidation of revolutionary power (1952–54), the emergence of the country as a focus of international tension (1955–57) and the merger with Syria (1958–61). In 1953 a period of transition from military authoritarianism to republican democracy was decreed; although slated to end in three years, it is still going on, indicating a degree of disillusionment with the Egyptian populace on the part of its leaders. The

[51] *Ibid.,* p. 19.
[52] Sadat, *op. cit.,* pp. 14–15.
[53] Indeed, the atmosphere in Egypt just prior to the coup was reminiscent of a fifteenth century Florentine chronicle. There was "an abundance of condottiere, courtesans, hired assassins, comings and goings of various sinister kinds." Lacouture, *op. cit.,* p. 142.

aim of the Committee, nothing less than a transmutation of the political, social, economic, even cultural structure of Egypt, has been distorted into channels of Pan-Arabism, if only to survive. Thus far no antidote to the easygoing, disorganized Egyptian character, capable of immense but usually temporary bursts of energy, has presented itself in adequate amounts to the rulers of Egypt.

Popular support, also, did not maintain the same enthusiasm which it displayed initially with the expulsion of Faruq. Nasir soon learned that the *fellahin,* and even the urban lower-class population, were far behind his "commando vanguard." He writes, "We needed order, but we found nothing behind us but chaos. We needed unity, but we found nothing behind us but dissention (sic). We needed work, but we found behind us only baseness and sloth." [54] An equal vacuum had existed in the land of the Pharaohs at the advent of Muhammad Ali, but at that time European imperial power stood ready to cover any serious international mistakes he might have made. Nasir and his cohorts, on the other hand, were venturing into the muddy and uncharted waters of mid-twentieth century international politics, in which domestic mistakes could be expected to have equally serious repercussions. Their sole rock of support was their belief in Nasir (and his in himself). "There is in Egypt a role in search of a hero to give it life," he said, "a role of interaction . . . which involves making use of the tremendous latent strength in the region surrounding us, to create a great power in this area. . . ." [55] This was to be his guideline: to destroy all vested interests and outgrown political organisms; to reform Egypt and rebuild her self-respect; and to make her once again the acknowledged leader of a Third World Power.[56]

The first stage was largely accomplished by 1953. The stress on the restoration of native Egyptian rule after two thousand years bought popular support. In the beginning this centered around the convivial, informal, utterly honest Muhammad Naguib rather than the conspiratorial Gamal 'Abd-al Nasir, and the popular *"Yaish!"* (Long Life) followed the former in the streets. Naguib, who had never been a member of the Free Officers but was their candidate in the Officer's Club elections which were voided by Faruq, now began to appear as its symbol.

[54] Nasser, *op. cit.,* p. 21.
[55] *Ibid.,* pp. 60–61.
[56] A concept which has obsessed Nasir's thinking at various stages in his career is the centrality of Egyptian influence, spreading outward from Egypt's location at the junction of three continents, and involving, under Egypt's dominance, three concentric circles of power, Pan-Arabism, Pan-Africanism, and Pan-Islam.

The Wafd, no longer a "popular" delegation, was easily associated in the public mind with the corruption of Faruq's regime. In January, 1953, it was linked with a military plot against the RCC and thus completely discredited. The next stage was the abolition of all political parties. Naguib announced that it would be necessary for Egypt to undergo a transitional period of three years before representative government could be introduced. A "Liberation Front" replaced partisan political activity, for Nasir, who was manipulating the strings of power although Naguib was the center of public interest, believed that democracy could not be established by parliaments and slogans alone, but by a fundamental change in the life of the people. Within the Liberation Front, the Revolutionary Command Committee had full charge of national administration.

With gradual inevitability, leadership for Egypt narrowed to a contest between Naguib and 'Abd al-Nasir. Enjoying his unexpected popularity, enhanced by baby-kissing national tours in the best political tradition, Naguib set out to increase his executive responsibilities. He felt that he was too often not consulted on important decisions, and he demanded a presidential veto. When the RCC refused to give him this he resigned. The Committee, which went along with Nasir, placed him under house arrest. But this act ricocheted. The Frontier Corps, made up predominantly of Sudanese (Naguib is part Sudanese himself), threatened to mutiny. The Egyptian Army remained loyal to its Commander-in-Chief and broke with the RCC. Nasir gave in; Naguib, who by this time had become the rallying point for all the discontented and the real enemies of the Free Officers, was reinstated as President. It was the zenith of his power.

Two months later Naguib had been discredited and was a virtual prisoner of the military junta. Nasir was too clever a conspirator for him. Naguib was pressed into declaring himself in favor of a return to parliamentary freedom, and in March, 1954, the RCC announced that political activity was permitted to resume. As if on cue, the old hopeless political divisions of the country reappeared, with Naguib helpless to stop the increasing disorder. Even the Liberation Front took part in unruly demonstrations. Eventually the RCC, acting "in response to the popular will," intervened, and Naguib was interned for an indefinite period, not to be seen again in public.

Next to be eliminated as a potential rival to the RCC was the Muslim Brotherhood, which was basically opposed in aim although it had sided with the Committee against Naguib. On October 26, 1954, a Cairo workman fired eight badly-aimed shots at Nasir while he was addressing a crowd. By reports the gunman was linked to both Naguib and the Brotherhood. After elaborately staged show trials, two members of the Inner Council were hanged in public, and the Supreme Guide, al-Hudaybi, sentenced to life imprisonment. Other lesser convictions effectively smashed the Brotherhood.

Having thus consolidated his position as leader of Egypt's sole remaining political force, Nasir inaugurated a socioeconomic revolution which he hoped would lead Egypt toward the standard of living necessary for true parliamentary government. This revolution shows no signs of abating or ending, and considering the obstacles—meager natural resources, a debilitating climate, a population largely illiterate and fiercely conservative, sharply-drawn class lines, and mass xenophobia—he has done well. The Egyptianization of commercial and industrial establishments is largely complete. After the re-intervention of Belgium in the Congo in mid-1960 all Belgian financial institutions in Egypt were nationalized. Some progress has been made in land reform under a law limiting holdings to 200 *feddans*, although this program affects only one-eighth of the total arable land.

Nasir's most conspicuous success between 1954 and 1960 was the elimination of British influence. On July 27, 1954, he initialed an agreement with Minister of State Anthony Nutting, to set up the gradual withdrawal of British troops from the Suez Canal Zone over a twenty-month period, the time limit being June, 1956. The only guarantee which the British salvaged was the right to reoccupy the zone in the event of an attack on Turkey or the Arab states, and this was limited to seven years. Nasir wrote at the time, "After the Suez settlement there is nothing standing in the way of our good relations with the West. But this hammering for pacts will only keep alive the old suspicions in the minds of the people." [57] Without a doubt, Nasir was sincere in his views; without a doubt he expressed the mood of the Egyptian people, since he was one of them, in his desire to avoid foreign entanglements except those (not really foreign in his eyes) which would contribute to the strengthening of Pan-Arabism. But it was no more possible for him to comprehend the coiled frustration of the British, deprived now of their lifeline, than it was for Britain to understand the national ambitions of a postmaster's son from Assiut. The harmony of 1954 was followed by the recriminations

[57] *The New York Times,* August 20, 1954.

of 1956 as Egypt nationalized the Suez Canal; the military landings of Anglo-French paratroopers in the canal zone, lamely managed as they were, represented an attempt by the two Western powers to re-establish some sort of pact relationship in which they believed their interests would somehow be secured.[58]

Although dominated by the occasionally reckless, but essentially negative, foreign policy activities of the Egyptian government during its first six years, domestic policy received some attention. In 1956 the *shari'a* and *milliyah* (the latter being Christian and Jewish) courts were abolished, and their functions transferred to Egyptian national courts. This move was designed partly to weaken the traditional influence of the shaykhs of Al-Azhar University over the population and partly to assimilate the non-Muslim communities further into society, removing their special status and privileges. Next a new constitution was announced, and in June, 1956, it was approved by 99.8 per cent of the electorate. The government of Gamal 'Abd al-Nasir stands to succeed or fail on the basis of what it can do for Egypt within the borders of that state. And it is on precisely this level the fewest assets are available. Egypt's population, which is approximately 26 million at the present time, must exist and create agricultural productivity for itself within an arable land space representing one-twentieth of the total available land. The population density of 26 per square mile is misleading, therefore. Furthermore the net population increase (excess of births over deaths) of between 11.5 and 19.4 per thousand in the past three decades brings annually more mouths to feed into the crowded Nile Valley than the net increase in production. When to this is added the attachment of the *fellahin* to their land, mentioned earlier in this chapter, the result comes closer to visual illustration of the term "population explosion" than perhaps anywhere else in the world.[59]

The government's efforts to meet this challenge have moved along economic as well as political lines. The initial economic effort was land reform. The land reform laws fixed the maximum for holdings at 200 *feddans* (a *feddan* is approximately one acre), with holdings greater than this to be expropriated and their owners compensated in government bonds up to the amount of seventy times the annual tax assessment

[58] It should be noted that Nutting resigned his portfolio at the time of the Suez invasion in protest against his own government's policies, which he considered a violation of the 1954 agreement. See his book for a statement of his views; he also wrote a series of articles for *The New York Herald-Tribune*.

[59] See Table I, Appendix (insert from UN Demographic Yearbook, 1955).

of the expropriated land. This land was distributed to landless *fellahin* in parcels of 3–5 *feddans,* and such publications as the *Egyptian Review* (distributed abroad) frequently feature pictures of smiling *fellahin* receiving deeds to the first acreage they have ever owned from an equally smiling President Nasir. The government recognized, however, that such a distribution program would assist no more than 10 per cent of Egypt's landless peasantry and that land reform itself could not raise the standard of living without a complementary increase in the arable area and expanded industrialization.[60] The first large-scale project undertaken was the "Liberation Province" (*Mudiriyat al-Tahrir*), which was planned to reclaim land and provide model communities for resettlement of *fellahin* in a desert area west of the delta. The Liberation Province was supposed to receive its water for irrigation from the new high dam at Aswan, but when this latter effort became involved in international politics the planners went ahead anyway, with less than spectacular results. The government decided in 1957 that it was to be merely an instrument "of the second phase of a transitional period toward real democracy . . . not an ultimate end," [61] after investigation by the National Assembly formed as a step toward parliamentary restoration had shown it to be an over-priced and badly administered piece of real estate. One observer struck close to the heart of the problem when he wrote: "In the name of progress these people are being torn out of the context of everything that has made their life . . . they are moved and transplanted into the desert for a planned, better future, with the results we have seen. Reforms, yes, but obviously these ought to be introduced gradually, with the start being made at the roots; that is, with life as it is in the villages now existing." [62]

As the Liberation Province assumed the status of a small thrust into the desert (which is itself a major achievement), the Egyptian government finally undertook with Russian financing to build the long-delayed new high dam (Sa'd al-A'li) at Aswan. The first spadeful of earth was turned in January, 1960, and at this writing work is well in progress on the first stage of the dam. Other projects "in the works" are recovery of the vast saline Qattara Depression by means of a canal to the Mediterranean, and the raising of subterranean water along the Kharga-Bahariya

[60] This topic is treated at length in Wheelock, *op. cit.,* p. x; see also Kirk, G. E., *Contemporary Arab Politics,* New York: Frederick A. Praeger, Inc., 1960, Appendix, pp. 177–180.
[61] *Cairo Press Review,* September 3, 1957.
[62] Hottinger, Arnold, "Egypt's Liberation Province—Another Planning Failure," *Swiss Review of World Affairs,* VIII, 9 (1958), p. 15.

line of oases in the western Desert. These measures have a grandness about them which is somehow typical of Egyptian thinking, along with the airy assumption that they will be completed in God's own time whatever the degree of planning, and will collectively solve all of Egypt's problems. As with projects, so with proclamations; we find Nasir declaring in 1959 that the new planning would double the per capita national income in ten years and continue to do so every decade thereafter. If indeed this can be achieved, the world will be the better for it, and Egypt will replace India in the international cynosure as the prime example of a country which has developed an adequate standard of living for its people, with considerable external aid but essentially by its own efforts and without sacrificing one iota of its sovereignty. But time, rather than foreign ideological or military conquest, is Egypt's real enemy in this undertaking.

Egypt's merger with Syria into the United Arab Republic in 1958, although instigated by Ba'thists in Syria fearful of a Communist takeover (see Chapter VI), proved more advantageous to the senior than the junior partner in this first multinational Arab state. The advantages turned out to be more political than economic. Underpopulated Syria was not the magnet to the crowded *fellahin* that Nasir hoped it would be; the land reform in Syria tended to fragment large but efficient estates into uneconomical plots where it was applied. Syrian businessmen accustomed to sharp Levantine trading and free competition chafed under economic controls which served to protect inexperienced Egyptian firms as they entered the international trading arena. Bad harvests in 1958 and 1959 forced the "Syrian Region," normally a grainexporter, to import food, although such an act of divine will cannot be attributed to Nasserism. But the inter-Arab prestige accorded Nasir by the merger more than compensated for the failure to achieve a "Nile Valley Unity" of Egypt and the Sudan, and it gave him a powerful lever in his contest with Iraq and Saudi Arabia to attain Pan-Arabism on Egypt's terms. This leverage was amply demonstrated during the brief squabble over Kuwait in June–July 1961. Britain's conclusion of a treaty with the Shaykh of Kuwait granting full independence to his oil-based desert territory was greeted by Premier Abd al-Karim Qasim of Iraq (not surprising in view of this leader's opportunism and Iraq's traditional relationship toward Kuwait) with a quick announcement that Iraq intended to repossess the shaykhdom. The Shaykh of Kuwait looked for help in two directions: to his former protector Britain, which airlifted troops, and to the Arab League. While deploring the British return to sacred Arab soil, the United Arab Republic took the lead in Arab League Council debate on Iraq's action and assured Kuwait of arms and volunteer support if requested to repel any Iraqi invasion. The UAR was able to isolate Iraq so completely that when the question of Kuwait's membership in the League came up, the Iraqi representative walked out, whereupon Kuwait was offered a seat by "unanimous" vote.

In this its tenth year of operation, the military regime which installed Gamal 'Abd al-Nasir in the seat of the Pharaohs has achieved significant progress toward the goals which animated the Free Officers. The urge to Arab unity was proved by the temporary Egypt-Syria merger and Yemen's prudent adhesion. The concerted attack on socioeconomic backwardness has produced results in a number of sectors—education, industrialization, improvement of agricultural productivity. Even the old self-abasement of the Egyptian lower classes, like the *tarbush* of Faruq and his entourage, is disappearing; privilege in its various forms is no longer self-perpetuating and the possession of the few. In international relations a new term, called indiscriminately "Nasserism" or "positive neutrality," has been given vogue by the Egyptian performance. In the sphere of representative government, however, the regime has yet to prove itself, to prove that the military can be the spearhead of basic democracy in the Middle East.[63] Too often the ease of acquiring power in this region is followed by the unease of distributing it. This will be the test of Nasir in the decades to come.

Recommended Readings

1. Barawy, Rashid el-, *The Military Coup in Egypt,* Cairo: Renaissance Bookshop, 1952.
2. Cleland, W. W., *The Population Problem in Egypt,* Lancaster, Pa.: Science Press, 1936.
3. Colombe, Marcel, *L'Evolution de l'Egypte, 1924–1950,* Paris: Maissoneuve, 1951.
4. Connell, John, *The Most Important Country,* London: Cassell, 1959.
5. Cromer, Evelyn B., Earl of, *Modern Egypt,* 2 vols., New York: The Macmillan Co., 1916.
6. Harris, George, ed., *Egypt,* New Haven: HRAF Press, 1957.
7. Husaini, Ishak Musa, *The Moslem Brethren,* Beirut: Khayat's Bookshop, 1956.

[63] Wheelock, *op. cit.,* p. 285, points out that Nasir is the first native-born Egyptian leader who has undertaken a positive program of national development without first assuring the continuance of a small privileged class.

8. Issawi, Charles, *Egypt at Mid-Century,* New York: Oxford, 1954.

9. Lacouture, Jean & Simone, *Egypt in Transition,* London: Methuen, 1958.

10. Little, Tom, *Egypt,* New York: Frederick A. Praeger, Inc., 1958.

11. Lloyd, Lord, *Egypt Since Cromer,* 2 vols. New York: The Macmillan Co., 1934.

12. Marlowe, John, *Anglo-Egyptian Relations 1800–1953,* London: Cresset Press, 1954.

13. Naguib, Mohammed, *Egypt's Destiny,* New York: Doubleday & Company, Inc., 1955.

14. Nasser, Gamal Abdel, *The Philosophy of the Revolution,* Cairo: Dar el-Maref, 1954 (published in the U. S. as *Egypt's Liberation*).

15. Royal Institute of International Affairs, *Great Britain and Egypt, 1914–1951,* London: R11A, 1952.

16. El Sadat, Anwar, *Revolt on The Nile,* London: Allan Wingate, 1957.

17. St. John, Robert, *The Boss,* New York: McGraw-Hill Book Co., Inc., 1960.

18. Vatikiotis, P. J., *The Egyptian Army in Politics,* Bloomington: Indiana University Press, 1961.

19. Wheelock, Keith, *Nasser's New Egypt,* New York: Frederick A. Praeger, Inc., 1960.

20. Wynn, Wilton, *Nasser of Egypt,* Cambridge: Arlington Books, 1959.

21. Young, George, *Egypt,* New York: Charles Scribner's Sons, 1927.

22. Youssef, Amine, *Independent Egypt,* London: John Murray, 1940.

CHAPTER **12**

INTERNATIONAL PROBLEMS: SUEZ,
SYRIA, AND THE NORTHERN TIER

$\mathcal{I}$n considering the fourteen centuries or so of Middle Eastern political
history with which we have been concerned, the present decade calls to
mind the earlier period of the 'Umayyad Caliphate of Damascus. The
adherents of Islam had not completed the sweeping conquests which
would spread their green banners across lands from the Pyrenees to India
and Central Asia, but they had made a name for themselves in world
affairs. Persia was theirs, and Byzantium recognized a new enemy; Christian kingdoms in North Africa and Spain were in the process of being
Islamized. Just as this process altered forever the social and political (to
say nothing of the religious) faces of the Middle East, so today the direction taken by the majority of nations there points to another fundamental alteration. This may well prove to be the total replacement of a
rigid, stratified, traditionally patterned system by a modern one stressing
social mobility and technical progress—in short, the advancement of these
nations to equal status in their development with Western nations.

The parallel between the 'Umayyad and modern Middle East situa-
tions is illustrated also by the type of leader present and the internal
stability. Muawiya, 'Amr ibn al-As, Musa ibn Nusayr, and their descendants were primarily military men, who took charge of the movement by
the express authority of the civilian caliphs, and the Arab caliphate
evolved rather quickly into a politico-military unit. In the present day
'Abd al-Nasir, Qasim, Gursel of Turkey, Da'ud of Afghanistan, Shihab
of Lebanon, even King Husayn of Jordan, are fundamentally military
leaders whose success in organizing their countries has far outpaced the
efforts of civilian leaders. (Although beyond the scope of this textbook,

the expressed views of two present military dictators, General Ayub of Pakistan and Gen. Ibrahim 'Abbud of Sudan, when they seized power, echoed loudly in the halls of government in the Middle East. Both felt that civilian leadership had failed and that it was necessary for the military to take over and run things.) Military efficiency, military cleanliness, and discipline are visible throughout the Middle East. The military hand is evident in the lack of internal unrest; although there is opposition to each government it has been effectively muzzled, so that the chief threat to each leader comes from his fellow-leaders. Having army support gives these military leaders considerable leverage in their balancing act between the Communist and anti-Communist blocs; for the former they can point to their independence from Western colonial domination and their socialist progress, while for the latter they can emphasize their freedom from Communist domination, their basic democracy, and their stable internal position.

It is unlikely, however, that the Middle East will long remain a spectator rather than a participator in international affairs. Too many bitter issues remain unsolved. The ambitions of these various leaders overlap national boundaries and often run counter to each other. The Soviet Union has a built-in, permanent opportunity to stir up trouble in this region whenever opportunity dictates a shift in its flexible tactics, and lately the Chinese Communists have begun to move in. Furthermore oil, while it remains the world's major fuel, represents to the governments of the Middle East a great attraction, in the form of a basic resource over which they do not have full control.[1]

Oil, for the Arab nationalist, is symptomatic of the things which are his, yet which he does not have. Palestine is another symptom. The Suez Canal was a third—but that's all over now, and it remains an international issue only because of the refusal of the Egyptians to permit Israeli shipping to transit the Canal. But the construction, control, and disposition of the Suez Canal afford a useful object lesson in the Middle East's international relations. The canal is also intimately bound up with the Arab League and, of course, with Arab-Israeli relations; these three constitute the major aspects of the Middle East's external relations.

THE SUEZ CANAL

The Suez Canal created a large headache for the future leaders of the Middle East even before it opened for business in 1869. Unlike other

---

[1] See, for example, Finnie, David H., *Desert Enterprise: The Middle East Oil Industry in its Local Environment,* Cambridge: Harvard University Press, 1958.

international waterways, it was built and managed until 1956 by a private company, officially subject to Egyptian law, which nevertheless possessed many of the attributes of a government. It flowed through the territory of a single state, yet it was not operated to the direct financial benefit of that state, although it must be admitted that the indirect financial benefits were considerable. Aside from the Canal's economic value to both Britain and France, the chief users, both these countries had taken a personal patriarchal interest in it from their initial involvement. Their angry reactions to the nationalization of the Canal in 1956 were emotional, not logical or practical, while the Egyptians and their fellow Arabs regarded it as another return blow at the West for years of humiliation.[2] Basically the Egyptians were right, but it was another of history's ironies that their action cancelled a legal concession negotiated a century earlier by another Egyptian government, with an organization composed of private citizens from abroad.

Located entirely within the geographical and political limits of modern Egypt, the Suez Canal was nevertheless conceived, built, and operated until lately by foreign interests. The original relationship, as mentioned, was between a nominally sovereign state and a private company. As time went on, various powers of Europe, and notably Britain, displayed increasing interest in the Canal. The Constantinople Convention of 1888, as we shall see, was an effort by the international community to regulate it. Britain, initially hostile to the whole idea, soon found she could not "disinterest herself either from the security of her Empire communications through the Suez Canal . . . or permit any other power to gain a foothold there."[3] Therefore she adopted a protectionist and exclusivist position in the Canal Zone which was legalized by treaty with Egypt in 1936.[4] Left to themselves, the government of Egypt and the company might well have worked out a compatible arrangement, but international relations, at least in the nineteenth century, made this impossible.

Although Britain came to assume a greater role than any other foreign power in the management of the Suez Canal, the scheme was initially French and owed its accomplishment to a single Frenchman, de Lesseps. Ferdinand de Lesseps (1805–1894) was a member of a prominent French family from Bayonne. His father, Mathieu, was a diplomat who

---

[2] Marlowe, John, *Arab Nationalism and British Imperialism,* New York: Frederick A. Praeger, Inc., 1961, p. 130 *et seq.*

[3] Siegfried, Andre, *Suez and Panama,* New York: Harcourt, Brace, & Co., 1940, p. 94.

[4] Marlowe, John, *Anglo-Egyptian Relations 1800–1953,* London: Cresset, 1954, Annex III, p. 417, contains the text of the treaty.

held important posts under the Directory and was named Consul-General in Egypt by Napoleon. Trained as a diplomat from his youth, with an engineering education and first-hand experience of Middle Eastern life, de Lesseps was convinced early that his destiny lay in the area and that he could bring glory to France there. During a tour of duty in Alexandria, he became interested in the project of a French engineer, Le Père, to link the Red and Mediterranean Seas. He tried to interest French as well as other financial interests in backing such a project, but without much success. A British official, in what must rank as a classic example of shortsightedness, said of the proposal that a railway parallel to the Red Sea would serve Britain's needs far better than "a long channel deep enough for the largest vessels, without any current flowing through it . . . it would be a stagnant ditch between tideless seas, enormously costly, wholly unprofitable." [5] De Lesseps got even less sympathy from Egypt, who stood to gain most. Abbas Pasha, the Khedive (Viceroy) was under the proverbial British thumb, and associated France with the West's refusal to allow his grandfather Muhammad Ali to dismember the Ottoman Empire. [6] Besides, he had no use for modernization where it involved capital expenditures.

In 1854, however, the situation changed drastically in de Lesseps' favor. Abbas Pasha was murdered and was succeeded by Said Pasha, Muhammad Ali's youngest son. De Lesseps had known the new Viceroy in his childhood, and during his assignment in Alexandria had taught the boy to ride. The Frenchman hurried to Egypt, and for the first time a ruler listened to him. Even the phenomena of nature were on de Lesseps' side, and after listening to him propound his plan for a canal, Said commented: "I am convinced; I accept your plan; we shall concern ourselves with the means for its execution; you can count on me." [7] Shortly thereafter the Viceroy issued a concession authorizing de Lesseps to organize an international company for the construction of a canal, on a 99-year lease from the date of opening. The new company, which was to be called the Compagnie Universelle du Canal Maritime de Suez, would have full

---

[5] Wilson, Arnold, *The Suez Canal: Its Past, Present, Future*, 2nd ed., London: Oxford, 1939, p. 10.

[6] "To the Consuls of Europe he was no more than a shoe. If I too must submit to someone, let me be the servant of the Caliph, and not of the Christian whom I hate." Quoted in Beatty, Charles, *De Lesseps of Suez*, New York: Harper & Brothers, 1956, pp. 86–87.

[7] Quoted in Hallberg, C. W., *The Suez Canal*, New York: Columbia University Press, 1931, p. 117. De Lesseps himself noted that on the morning of the fateful day he saw a brilliant rainbow stretching across the heavens.

authority for the construction and operation of the canal, except that the Egyptian Government retained the privilege of naming its director. Profits would be distributed on the basis of 75 per cent to the company, 10 per cent to the founders and 15 per cent to the Egyptian Government.[8] Finally, the concession was to be ratified by the Ottoman Sultan, the Viceroy's nominal superior since Egypt was still a part of the Empire, before work could actually begin.

The statute also required that the principal nationalities interested in the proposed canal be represented on the Company's Board of Directors. International reaction varied. The British were strongly opposed; they did not like de Lesseps and felt Egypt's sovereignty would be compromised. The French could not fully endorse the idea since they were allied with Britain in the Crimean War, but as might be expected they supported it privately. Italy was very much in favor; two leading Italian engineers, Negrelli and Paleocapa, even joined the company. Due to the recalcitrance of Britain, the Board when finally formed was composed equally of French and Austro-Italian groups.[9] The Ottoman Sultan, although pressed hard, managed to avoid committing himself either for or against the concession, but de Lesseps was determined to go ahead without his approval, and did.

The project's international importance was stressed again when an international commission of engineers and maritime experts, headed by Negrelli, made a survey of various routes. On the basis of their report, Said gave de Lesseps a new and more detailed concession in 1856. The company agreed among other things to pay the entire cost of construction, to build freshwater canals along the main canal, and to employ a labor force which would be four-fifths Egyptian. In return it was granted all necessary lands and exempted from taxes. With a handshake and a signature the builder of the Suez Canal was in business.

The Company was organized as an Egyptian corporation, but its legal and administrative headquarters were in Paris. The original capital was fixed at 200 million francs, divided into 400,000 shares of 500 francs each, and offered for worldwide public sale in 1858. The table on page 394 shows the scheduled distribution and the actual division of shares.

As the table indicates, French stockholders and the Egyptian government (i.e., the Viceroy) emerged as the controlling forces in the com-

[8] Founders were those whose "works, studies, or capital" had previously contributed materially to the enterprise (Art. XI).

[9] See *Italy and the Suez Canal*, New York: Italian Ministry of Information 1939, p. 13.

Table of Share Distribution

Country	Shares Reserved	Shares Purchased
Egyptian Government	64,000	177,642
Egyptian People	42,000	998
France	80,000	207,160
Great Britain	80,000	——
Austria	42,000	163
Russia-Wallachia	24,000	174
Denmark	30,000	7
Portugal	20,000	5
United States	20,000	——
Spain	——	4,161
Italy	——	2,719
Holland	——	2,615
Tunis	——	1,714
All others	——	2,649
	400,000	400,000 [10]

[10] Schonfield, Hugh, *The Suez Canal in World Affairs,* London: Constellation Books, 1952, p. 35.

pany. Purchases by individual Frenchmen reflected widespread resentment with Britain's tactics. Lord Palmerston, the British Prime Minister, denounced the entire project as "an undertaking deemed to rank among the many bubble schemes that from time to time have been palmed upon gullible capitalists . . . a scheme founded in hostility to the interests of this country . . . in regard to the connection of Egypt with Turkey." [11] British opposition in Constantinople, relayed through the Ambassador, Lord Stratford Canning,[12] was so forceful that the Sultan did not dare to ratify the concession until 1866.

Nevertheless work began on the Canal in 1859, and ten years later it was opened to navigation with a ceremony so extravagant that it nearly bankrupted the Khedive, who paid all the expenses. Confronted with a *fait accompli,* Britain became considerably more interested. Constantly aware of her imperial role in world affairs, and somewhat afraid of loss of her commercial supremacy, her leaders began casting about for ways to exercise some influence in the affairs of the new waterway. Here she was aided by the fact that British popular opinion suspected all French motives—and was not de Lesseps a Frenchman? What Briton could be absolutely sure that his proclamation, that the canal would be open to all nations, would not be more honored in the breach than in the observance? That it would not become a French-owned barrier to Britain's eastern trade? Furthermore, the Canal could threaten Britain's Oriental policy

[11] Hallberg, *op. cit.,* p. 147.
[12] Wilson, *op. cit.,* pp. 17–18. He was called "Sultan Stratford" and "Abdul Canning."

by its very location, cutting through the heart of the Ottoman Empire, and British policy was to keep this empire patched together until the last possible moment.[13]

The vagaries of international finance supplied an unexpected opportunity. Ismail Pasha, who had succeeded the corpulent Said as Khedive, harbored ambitions for Egypt similar to his grandfather's, but he lacked Muhammad Ali's iron-willed restraint and, more important, his absolute authority. Ismail initiated a program of development of Egypt's resources which brought the country in short order to the edge of bankruptcy. By 1875, through constant borrowing, he had increased the public debt from 3,293,000 pounds sterling (in 1863) to 98 million, of which 16 million pounds was spent on Suez Canal improvements and the rest squandered.[14]

Prior to 1875 the Ottoman Sultan had answered all Ismail's requests for loans, but in that year he too was broke. Unfortunately for the Khedive, "the word *moratorium* had scarcely found its way into the English language, and international debts were not viewed differently from private obligations." [15] In desperation, Ismail turned to the infidels. French and British banking interests were approached to see if they would purchase his Suez Canal shares, his sole remaining resource. The French failed to exercise their option, and Prime Minister D'Israeli, without consulting his government but acting on its behalf like a man who cannot resist a hot tip, bought Ismail's 177,642 shares for just over 4 million pounds.[16] This purchase did not give Britain majority control of the company, but it was the largest single bloc of stock and enabled the British to exercise a controlling voice in its affairs. The fact that British ships were the Canal's best customers also helped.

THE CONSTANTINOPLE CONVENTION OF 1888

Under Articles 14–15 of the 1856 Concession, the Suez Canal Company was obliged to keep the Canal open as a neutral passage for merchant shipping of all nations, without distinction. Since this obligation was binding on the company only insofar as Egypt was concerned,

---

[13] Marlowe, *op. cit.*, pp. 72–73, observes that the Canal made it impossible for Britain to leave Egypt alone.

[14] Cromer, Earl of, *Modern Egypt,* New York: The Macmillan Co., 1916, I, p. 11.

[15] Wilson, *op. cit.*, p. 48.

[16] The story (perhaps apochryphal) is that D'Israeli went directly to his friend Baron Rothschild for funds, since Parliament was not in session and could not obligate money. The Baron said: "And what is your security?" "The British Government." "You shall have it."

there was a very real question as to sovereignty. Thus, during the Russo-Turkish War of 1877, England warned Russia not to interfere with the operation of the Canal, although legally the waterway was subject to Ottoman authority, being a part of Egypt. The Russians replied that they considered the Canal an international waterway. A further complication ensued when Britain and France assumed a Dual Control over Egypt's administration for the purpose of reorganizing her finances. Colonel Ahmad Arabi, an Egyptian officer with a flair for politics and wide popular support, led a rebellion against the Khedive for permitting a foreign, Christian occupation, and at the same time against all foreigners. This first expression of modern xenophobic Egyptian nationalism was crushed at the battle of Tal-al-Kabir in 1881 by a British force under Sir Garnet Wolseley. The British occupied the Canal for three days and used it as a base of operations, acting on a Khedivial decree authorizing their military occupation for the purpose of establishing order. The occupation secured the victory, while making two obvious points even more so: one, that any threat to the Canal threatened British interests; two, that some form of international control was necessary. Italy called for an international police force for the Canal in 1885. Nine states—Great Britain, Austria-Hungary, France, Germany, Holland, Italy, Russia, Spain, and Turkey—met at Constantinople in 1887–88 and hammered out the details of an international agreement which has come to be called the 1888 Convention.

Essentially the 1888 Convention represented a compromise between British and French points of view. The British were determined to keep other European powers out of Egypt, and accordingly attached the reservation that they be recognized, at least tacitly, as custodians of the Canal. This meant that Britain had the right to defend the Canal in case of aggression against Egypt. Added to the proviso that the Convention would not become effective until the end of the British occupation (which was assumed to be temporary), the reservation meant that the Canal was under *de facto* British control for sixteen more years, until the Entente Cordiale of 1904 brought the Convention into effect with Britain responsible to the signatories for defense and freedom of navigation. Nevertheless the Convention was the basis for an "international neutralism" which continued until the Egyptian nationalization of 1956.[18]

[17] Buell, Raymond, *The Suez Canal and League Sanctions,* in Geneva Special Studies, Vol. VI, no. 3, Geneva, Switzerland, 1935.

[18] Since Egypt has agreed to observe the Convention, presumably it is still in effect.

The Preamble of the Convention defined the intent of the signatory powers to establish "a final regime for the Suez Maritime Canal which would guarantee to all Powers and at all times, free passage through the Suez waterway." [19] It also emphasized that the Convention *completed* (*completer*) the international regime designated for the Canal by the Firmans granted to the Suez Canal Company. Thus the establishment of the company and its privileges relative to the Canal were sanctioned by international fiat.

Article I, in amplifying the Preamble, stated the general principle underscored in the Convention—the right of free and open passage, in time of war as in time of peace, to every vessel of commerce or war, without distinction of flag. The article also imposed an obligation on the high contracting parties not to interfere with this right of free usage and prohibited the exercise of the right of blockade *within* the Canal. Also, no act of hostility was to be allowed within a radius of three miles from the ports of access. Other articles in the Convention elaborated upon or upheld these basic tenets; thus Article IV stipulated that warships could not carry out acts of war against enemy ships in Canal waters. And finally, the Egyptian government was responsible for the defense of the Canal—but if Egypt were unable to discharge this obligation, it could devolve to the Ottoman government.

Articles VIII and IX set up a nominal system of supervision. A committee of representatives in Egypt of the signatories, though without executive powers, had the right to investigate the Canal's security and to recommend protective measures to the Khedive if necessary. In practice, as often happens in international relations, the agreed-on measures worked only where the powers most directly concerned wanted them to work. The Entente Cordiale came about because France agreed not to press for an end to the British occupation of Egypt in return for Britain's pledge to adhere to the provisions of the Convention. Because Britain was in physical possession of the Canal, it remained open not only as a highway for commerce, but also as a corridor for belligerency.[20]

Problems of implementing the Convention have always been difficult owing to the complex nature of international relationships where they affect, or are affected by, the Suez Canal. In 1898, Spain, at war with the United States, sent a fleet through the Canal destined for the Philippines.

[19] Avram, Benno, *The Evolution of the Suez Canal Status, 1869–1956,* Geneva: E. Droz, 1958.

[20] Wilson, *op. cit.,* p. 92, discusses the violation of the rules by Russian warships transiting the Canal en route to fight Japan, Britain's ally.

The fleet wanted to take on coal at Port Said. The Canal's rules of neutrality were that belligerent warships could purchase only enough coal in a neutral port to carry them to the nearest national port. Egyptian authorities, pressured by Britain, refused to allow the fleet to refuel on the grounds that it had enough coal to return to Barcelona, the nearest national port. In this case Britain interpreted the Convention in favor of the United States, towards whom it was benevolently neutral. In 1911, during the Italo-Turkish War, Italian warships transited the Canal although Britain again was neutral and Egypt still a part of the Ottoman Empire.

The knottiest problem posed by the Suez Canal came at the start of World War I. Ottoman Turkey declared war with Germany against Britain, which still occupied Egypt. An Egyptian proclamation authorizing British forces to take war measures as necessary against the Central Powers in Egyptian ports and territories did not help matters. Finally in December, 1914, Britain unilaterally declared a protectorate over Egypt, and put a formal ending to Ottoman sovereignty. During the war the British treated the Canal like any other part of their territory; they seized enemy ships as war prizes and restricted the movement of neutral shipping. At the end of the war the peace treaties confirmed the 1888 Convention and transferred the powers formerly "exercised" by the Ottoman Sultan to the British government. Britain's protectorate over Egypt was also recognized. In the Treaty of Lausanne (1923) Turkey agreed to renounce all title to territories situated outside of present Turkish frontiers (Article 16).

The interwar period saw little change in the international status of the Canal. The protracted struggle between Britain and the Egyptian nationalists, led by the Wafd (Delegation) Party of Sa'd Zaghlul and Nahhas Pasha, did not affect its operations. Article 8 of the 1936 Anglo-Egyptian Treaty recognized the Canal as "an integral part of Egypt," while Britain agreed to "cooperate with Egypt for the defense of the Canal and in safeguarding its free navigation" until the Egyptian Army could do this by its own resources.[21] In 1924, a two-for-one stock split of shares in the Suez Canal Company increased the total to 800,000, with Britain holding 353,204, still the largest minority bloc. The 15 per cent of profits originally reserved for the Egyptian government was sold to a French syndicate. Otherwise the distribution of profits (which were immense) was 71 per cent to ordinary shareholders (mostly French), 10 per cent to the

[21] Marlowe, *op. cit.*, p. 81.

founders, 2 per cent to the Board of Directors, and 2 per cent to the employees. Net profits from 1870 to 1932, to give an illustration, totalled 137.8 million pounds, practically none of which reached Egyptian pocket-books.

The Canal After World War II

Egyptian foreign policy after World War II had been directed toward three objectives: expulsion of the British, incorporation of the Sudan, and prevention of a Jewish national state in Palestine.[22] The last objective was the first to fail of achievement, and the frustrated leaders of Egypt began to equate it with the first, as equally impossible to attain. Britain's withdrawal of all troops from Lower Egypt to station them in the Canal Zone not only did not satisfy the terms of "Egypt for the Egyptians"; it also imposed a *de facto* foreign military occupation on the zone. The 80,000 U. K. troops stationed there represented the heart of Britain's Middle East defense posture; while Britain was willing to negotiate for eventual evacuation, she refused to surrender all re-entry and control rights. Since this was the vital element as far as Egypt was concerned, by 1952, negotiations had bogged down.

Between 1950 and 1952, Egypt put on a campaign of both passive and active resistance against the 80,000-man garrison of the zone.[23] British civilian officials working for Egypt were summarily dismissed. Their Egyptian employees were intimidated into resigning or merely left. Sabotage was widespread although not particularly effective because serious damage either to the Canal, the Sweetwater Canal, or the various pipelines and communication lines in the zone would have been more damaging to Egypt than the company or Great Britain. In a style later copied by the *fida'iyan* raiders in the Gaza Strip, bands of Egyptian volunteers calling themselves Phalanxes of the Liberation, along with locally formed auxiliary police writs, engaged in nuisance raids against the British garrisons. After one of their raids a British force surrounded a battalion of the auxiliaries in their barracks at Ismailia and ordered it to surrender its arms. The auxiliaries rejected the order and fighting broke out. More than fifty of them were killed before the rest surrendered. When word of the clash reached Cairo, January 25, 1952, the population reacted by burning the center of the city. This was "Black Saturday"; six months later a military junta seized power in Egypt.

[22] Schonfield, *op. cit.,* p. 122.
[23] Avram, *op. cit.,* p. 99.

The internal stability of the new Egyptian regime having been achieved by 1954, it was imperative that some comparable action in external affairs be brought to a successful conclusion. The British garrisons in the Suez Canal Zone were the obvious first choice. Negotiations were resumed under circumstances quite different. Large segments of British public opinion felt that Britain should remain in the Middle East,[24] but this attitude was *sotto voce* rather than a call to arms. The RCC, on the other hand, regarded the struggle to reach agreement as a continuation of the century-old effort to make Egypt free and sovereign.

In October, 1954, Britain and Egypt signed the Suez Agreement providing for the total evacuation of the base. The British saved one toehold —in the event of an armed attack by any foreign power on Egypt (or Turkey), they would be able to reoccupy the base. Otherwise Gamal 'Abd al-Nasir had attained the unattainable—Egypt would shortly be free of foreign supervision, the goal sought unsuccessfully by Zaghlul, by Nahhas Pasha, even by Faruq. The provisions of the Suez Agreement were:

1. All British forces would be withdrawn from the Canal Zone within twenty months (i.e., by June 18, 1956).

2. British civilian technicians were allowed to continue servicing the Suez bases.

3. Britain was granted military access to these bases in the event of an armed attack on any member of the Arab League or Turkey, in the ensuing seven years.

4. The Anglo-Egyptian Treaty of 1936 was abrogated.

5. Each party pledged to uphold the 1888 Constantinople Convention guaranteeing freedom of navigation in the Canal.

Much hard bargaining went into the 1954 agreement, and in the end it was probably a major Egyptian concession—the right to re-entry in the event of an attack—that made evacuation at all palatable to British public opinion, and in particular to British military leaders. There were real advantages on both sides to normalizing trade relations, however, and in Britain itself the government realized (as its opponents did not) the necessity of some sort of rapprochement with Egypt in view of the evolution to Commonwealth status of former imperial possessions and the strategic role of Suez in terms of Commonwealth relations. Within the Conservative Party there developed a loose body of members with similar views, known as the Suez Group, however, which was opposed to

[24] Lawyers' Committee on Blockades, *The UN and the Egyptian Blockade of the Suez Canal*, New York, 1953, pp. 14–15. (Published by the same committee.)

a Suez settlement chiefly because the members felt that British evacuation would be the signal for an Egyptian attack on Israel. The arguments of the Suez Group were rejected at the time, but two years later they were to reap better fruit.

The last British soldiers were out of the Canal Zone by June 12, 1956, a week ahead of schedule. There still remained the Suez Canal Company, however, and the feeling grew stronger that Egypt should at least receive a much greater share of Canal revenues, if not exercise direct supervision over the company. In 1949, the government had concluded a new pact with the company, with some significant changes. These were:

1. An increase in the number of Egyptian directors from two to seven.

2. An annual payment to Egypt of 7 per cent of gross profits for the previous year, with a minimum payment of £E350,000.

3. Egyptianization of company staff working in Egypt on the scale of four out of five technical and nine out of ten administrative vacancies.

4. Priority given to twenty Egyptian pilots to fill forthcoming vacancies (an important gain to Egyptian industry in view of the high salaries paid to pilots).

5. Return to the government of Egypt of the Ismailia-Port Said Freshwater Canal.

In view of the fact that the concession was due to expire in 1968, the company's willingness to enter into an Egyptianization program reflected considerable foresight on the part of the its management. As Board Chairman Charles-Roux observed in 1951, "We use our utmost endeavors to be for Egypt, first the most useful screen between that country and the great world interest which the Suez Canal has to satisfy, and secondly, an active instrument of the economic and social development of the province which the Canal has restored to life." [25]

NATIONALIZATION AND WAR, 1956

Between 1954 and 1956 there were occasional rumblings from Egypt, notably in the controlled press, about nationalizing the Canal, and occasional references to the "injustices" committed by the company toward Egyptian sovereignty.[26] But nothing concrete came of it. In any event the concession was scheduled to run only until 1968, at which

[25] Schonfield, *op. cit.*, pp. 131–133.
[26] Wheelock, *Nasser's New Egypt,* New York: Frederick A. Praeger, Inc., 1960, p. 206.

time it would be terminated anyway, unless the Egyptian government chose to renew it.

The year 1956 was a watershed in the affairs of the Middle East. To a degree never achieved before—not even during Muhammad Ali's brief joust with the Ottoman Empire—the area was the cynosure of all eyes. A war was fought there, and very little more would have been required to make this war universal. A strange alliance was forged with the United States against its major Western partners, and these cooperating with the Middle East's most intrusive nation. At the center of the trouble was Suez.

Native rulers of Egypt, from the Pharaohs to Nasir, have been obsessed with a sense of the country's grandeur and its central place in world politics. Nasir's successes in various international ventures encouraged him to seize a dominant role in the Arab movement, but to Western leaders these ventures smacked of opportunism. The highly moral John Foster Dulles was perhaps the most offended of all Western statesmen, and this made it difficult for even reasonable Egyptian requests to get a hearing. Improvement of United States–Egyptian relations also ran counter to American support of Israel. In 1955, a savage Israeli raid into the Gaza Strip prompted Nasir to make a serious effort to buy arms from the United States to put his army on a more equal footing with Israel. He had been trying to buy United States arms for several years, without much success, although in 1954, Egypt did conclude a $40 million agreement with the United States for economic assistance, American officialdom continued to suspect the Egyptian leader's motives.[27] In what seems in retrospect either an incredible error of judgment or a deliberate disregard of the altered political situation in the Middle East, the Eisenhower administration dragged its feet for months over procedural questions, never really intending to supply the items on Egypt's military shopping list. It was inconceivable to both British and American leaders that Nasir (or any Arab politician) would ever turn to atheistic Russia for aid.

Nasir himself supplied the key to Arab thinking when he told a reporter: "From that moment [the Israeli raid on Gaza, February 28, 1955], I had to take the Palestine problem seriously and be prepared to return blow for blow. I pleaded with [the West] but to no avail. So I turned to Soviet Russia and told [them] frankly that I wanted to arm

[27] As Wilton Wynn observes (*Nasser of Egypt*, Cambridge: Arlington Books, 1959, p. 118) the American insistence on "conditions, conditions, conditions" which accompanied the Mutual Security Agreement was an added affront to Egyptian pride, suggesting that we did not trust Egypt.

quickly and could afford no hard currency. I got the answer I wanted in four days." [28] On September 27, 1955, the Egyptian leader summarily announced that Egypt had concluded a barter agreement with Czechoslovakia (later amended to the USSR) of military equipment in unspecified amounts for Egyptian cotton and rice. It was a major blow to Western interests in the Middle East, as well as Russia's first serious opportunity to exert influence there.

While Egyptian patriots counted and recounted the number of MIG's, jet bombers, and Soviet tanks they would shortly receive, and refugees in the Gaza Strip began thinking in terms of "back to Haifa by Christmas," Nasir put on the hero's mantle in the Arab world, and simultaneously received top billing as a villain in the West. The Arabs felt they had a new Saladin, the symbol of Arab unity and the strength of Arab nationalism. To the Western powers, he was the man who had given the Middle East to the Russians on a platter. Nasir's policies were morally reprehensible to the United States, but to Britain (and later France) they were anathema. President Eisenhower sent George V. Allen, then Assistant Secretary of State, on a hasty mission to Cairo, armed with a warning to Nasir of the dangerous consequences of his two-step with Russia; but Allen was kept cooling his heels for many hours before he got to see the Egyptian leader, and his ultimatum was never delivered. Already the Middle East's international relations were narrowing to a matter of personalities and personal revenges—hence the delight of the Egyptians at having kept waiting the emissary of the mighty West.[29]

Meanwhile the proposal for a new high dam at Aswan, which would vastly expand Egypt's industrial output as well as its agricultural capacity, became equally involved in the game of thrust and counterthrust between the three adversaries, the West, Russia, and the Arabs. President Nasir had staked his prestige in Egypt on the scheme, since it appeared to be the only solution to Egypt's impossible land-population ratio. Unfortunately there was little likelihood that Egypt could provide more than a fraction of the necessary cost, and major foreign financing had to be found. Neither Britain nor the United States were particularly anxious

[28] *Jewish Observer and Middle East Review,* January 27, 1956.

[29] As he described it in his speech at Alexandria telling of the nationalization of the Suez Canal, Nasir said that he had been warned by an intermediary of Allen's purpose and his message, and was ready to dismiss him if he came to disparage Egypt. But "Mr. Allen came and did not open his mouth at all." See Kirk, G. E., *Contemporary Arab Politics,* New York: Frederick A. Praeger, Inc., 1960, pp. 39–40.

to sink more funds in a dubious Egyptian venture, but the International Bank for Reconstruction and Development (IBRD), which had already carried out surveys of the project and was considered a sound, conservative banking institution, offered a means by which the dam could be constructed without involving political considerations. The Soviet-Egyptian arms deal, however, spurred the West into action. If the Egyptians would buy weapons from Russia, Western leaders reasoned, they would probably accept Russian funds to build the dam, and in June, 1956, the Western press was told that the USSR was ready to lend Egypt £E4 million ($1.2 billion) repayable in sixty years at 2 per cent.

Although the report was premature, it served to hamper rather than improve relations. The United States had already offered to lend Egypt $56 million, and Britain $14 million, to make surveys and start construction, with the International Bank for Reconstruction and Development picking up an additional tab of $200 million for the initial stages. But in various American circles there was growing opposition to our participation in the project. Secretary Dulles was annoyed at Nasir for his game of "economic neutralism," playing East against West to get the most favorable economic terms. Congress was skeptical of putting American funds into a project whose long-term value was questionable and objected to the blatant anti-Baghdad Pact, anti-Western propaganda emanating from Cairo. The strong Zionist lobby was opposed to any strengthening of militant anti-Israeli leaders. There was also a very real question as to whether Egypt could meet the long-term financing costs involved in the high dam.

In mid-1956, then, Ambassador Ahmad Husayn returned to Washington to discuss final arrangements for Western support of the project. Instead he received a public rebuff. Secretary of State Dulles informed him that the United States had decided to withdraw its previous offer of $56 million toward the high dam. The British then withdrew their offer, as did the IBRD. When Nasir's widely advertised pledge of aid from the Soviet Union for the dam did not materialize,[30] the project seemed doomed, and with it the Egyptian leader's prestige.

The IBRD clearly had sound reasons for the withdrawal of its offer, since Egypt's economy had not been judged sound enough by Bank ex-

---

[30] There is some doubt that Russia ever intended to finance the dam at this stage, and certainly Shepilov's denial (*The New York Times,* June 22, 1956) indicates this. See John Campbell, *Defense of the Middle East,* New York: Harper & Brothers, 1958, pp. 74–76, for additional comments.

perts to carry the burden of the high dam. Furthermore Egypt's unwillingness to meet the Bank's minimum guarantees would have violated its banking principles. The United States and Britain also had good economic and political reasons for their withdrawals—as President Eisenhower noted, "The conditions that had prevailed at the time the offer was made no longer prevailed." [31]

The manner of rejection, however, the public rebuff, enraged Nasir. He was already stirred by Russia's action in signing an agreement to supply oil to Israel, and at his meeting on Brioni Island, Yugoslavia, with neutralist leaders Nehru and Tito, he had been unable to win their support on the Algerian and Palestine questions. These defeats, combined with the imminent collapse of his pet project, were enough to spur him on to some desperate action, and always in the history of Egypt action has been directed at the nearest visible symbol of wrong or oppression, regardless of all other factors.

Thus it was that on July 26, 1956, the Egyptian President made a long speech before 100,000 Egyptians in Alexandria. Much of the two and one-half hour speech was a rather tedious repetition of Egypt's foreign policy since the revolution. Then Nasir came to the point. The Suez Canal had been nationalized. The properties of the Compagnie Universelle Maritime du Canal de Suez had been taken over by the Egyptian government, and henceforth the Canal would be operated as an Egyptian enterprise.[32] Canal company employees were free to leave their jobs or to continue working—on the Egyptian payroll. As Nasir reached the climax of his speech a whole generation of frustrated Egyptian nationalists seemed to be screaming with him: "We shall build the high dam as we desire! The Canal company shall be nationalized! And it will be run by Egyptians! Egyptians! Egyptians!" [33]

Leaving aside political and emotional implications for the moment, the fact remains that Egypt possessed an excellent case for nationalization. The Canal was clearly part of her territory. Provided adequate compensation were made to the shareholders of the company—and the decree of nationalization stipulated that they would be compensated at the rate of the closing price of shares on the Paris Bourse (Exchange) July 25, 1956—its rights had not been violated. International law recog-

[31] *The New York Times,* August 22, 1957.
[32] The Company's operations outside Egypt were not affected by the nationalization decree, and it has continued to function as a holding company managing various enterprises.
[33] Quoted in Paul Johnson, *The Suez War,* New York: Greenberg, 1957, p. 9.

nized the legality of the Egyptian action. Egypt moved to implement nationalization with scrupulous care; strict orders were given not to molest members of the foreign communities, notably the British and French, and Nasir avoided getting into any direct controversy with these two countries. Three factors militated against a normal settlement, however. They were: the Anglo-French attitude toward Suez and Egypt in general, the personal animosity felt by Anglo-French leaders toward Nasir,[34] and the genuine international importance of the Suez Canal.

Although they reserved the right to military action as a final resort, Britain and France agreed with the United States on the importance of some form of international system of control and management for the Canal. Nasir agreed in principle, provided it would not interfere with Egypt's full sovereignty. Traffic continued to transit the Canal without hindrance, and the Egyptians even allowed ships carrying Israeli cargoes bound for Haifa to pass, although the waterway had been closed to Israeli ships since the Palestine War. None of this pleased either Britain or France. The British saw their status as a world power reduced to that of economic dependence on a former colony; the French related Egypt with their troubles in Algeria. Both viewed Nasir as an irresponsible troublemaker and demagogue, determined to injure their interests in the Middle East, and operating from impulse rather than statesmanship.

In the hot, unusually damp weather of August, 1956, twenty-two maritime and/or "interested" nations assembled in London and hammered out a proposal to open discussions with Egypt towards international supervision of the Canal.[35] A committee of representatives of five nations, led by Australia's Prime Minister Menzies, went to Cairo to present the proposal to Nasir. A week of talks ended in deadlock, however, over Nasir's insistence that any attempt to impose international control over Suez would be an infringement on Egyptian sovereignty and would bring chaos to the Middle East. Nasir called it "collective colonialism." John Foster Dulles now took the lead in negotiating and persuaded Britain and France to join in an international association of users of the Canal, which would collect tolls, use its own pilots, and pay Egypt for the facilities provided. At the same time the users began their conference, the last foreign employers left their jobs in the Canal

---

[34] Eden said: "Why, therefore, don't we trust him? The answer is simple. Look at his record. Our quarrel is not with Egypt, still less with the Arab World. It is with Colonel Nasser." Connell, *op. cit.*, p. 117.

[35] Eighteen nations signed the agreement, with the USSR, India, Indonesia, and Ceylon refusing to do so. *Middle East Journal*, Chronology, Autumn 1956.

Zone, and Egypt began operating the canal unaided. This in itself could have meant war, since both Britain and France warned that they would regard any interference with shipping or failure to maintain normal transit schedules as provocations. But the Egyptian Suez Canal Authority, whose director, Colonel Mahmud Yunis, spent twenty-four hours a day on the job during September and October, 1956, kept the Canal open and running smoothly. (They have done so ever since, with the exception of the period during and after the Anglo-French invasion, when the entire Canal was blocked.) In October a Suez Canal Users Association (SCUA) was formally organized. It had fifteen members but only two of them, Iran and Turkey, were from the Middle East. In principle the idea of international collective regulation was fine, but it ran counter to Egypt's shining new sovereignty. Since the United States had expressly opposed the use of force in the dispute, both publicly and in private discussions, there was apparently little the two most aggrieved states could do to impose any sort of solution on Nasir.

Eden and Mollet and their Foreign Ministers, however, had privately begun to make plans for the attack on Suez which both felt must take place. For Britain it was a case of recovering world prestige and domination of the Middle East. France saw a way to remove a major source of material and propaganda support for her Algerian rebels. Both were determined to stop at nothing to rid themselves of this gadfly Nasir. While the political discussions went on, so did the military buildup, and communications between Washington and the other two Western capitals broke down almost completely. In October the UN Security Council produced a six-point memorandum of general principles which could serve as the basis for a negotiated solution between the Users and Egypt. While the U.S. began planning to implement these principles, a different sort of planning was going on in London, Paris,—and Tel Aviv.

THE SINAI WAR AND ANGLO-FRENCH INTERVENTION

In the years that followed the Rhodes Armistice agreements between the Arab states and Israel, their opposing positions had steadily hardened until the "temporary" cease-fire lines in Palestine became *de facto* national borders. The role of the United Nations in these years was somewhere between that of a referee and an auxiliary policeman— it could separate the contestants but not stop them from fighting, and issue warnings but could not arrest. The various Arab-Israeli borders supervised by the UN Truce Supervision Organization (UNTSO) and its subordinate Mixed Armistice Commissions (MAC) were not uniformly the source of trouble, but the Israel-Jordan and Israel-Egypt borders were more frequently violated than the others.

The unlikelihood of a permanent Arab-Israeli settlement, and the need to reduce war tensions, led the United States, Britain, and France to issue a tripartite declaration in May, 1950. The declaration made two major points: first, no armed attacks across existing armistice lines in Palestine would be permitted, with punitive action to be taken both in and out of the UN against any aggressor; second, the signatories would try to maintain a balance between arms deliveries to Israel and the Arab states, so as to eliminate any imbalance that might endanger the peace.[36] The Arab "reply" to this was the Arab League Collective Security Pact, which pledged all members to military support in case of an attack against any one of them.

One of King Faruq's few positive gestures toward Pan-Arab hostility to Israel had been to close the Suez Canal to Israeli shipping. In 1951, the UN Security Council, acting on Israel's complaint, issued a resolution calling on Egypt to adhere to the 1888 Convention, which had specified freedom of navigation for all nations in the Canal and the right of free and innocent passage. Egypt took the position that a "state of war" still existed between the Arabs and Israel and that in denying the use of the Canal to Israeli ships she was merely exercising the rights of a belligerent. Having never recognized Israel as a state, the Egyptians also claimed that no infringement of Israel's rights in the Canal had taken place, since Israel did not exist! Although the Egyptian behavior was clearly a contravention of international law, a resolution of censure was about as far as the UN could go.[37] In 1954, Israel sent a freighter, the *Bat Galim*, through the Canal as a test case; the ship was detained for some months and eventually added to the Egyptian Navy, although the crew was released.[38]

After Nasir had come to power he avoided serious conflict with Israel for the first three years of his regime. Egypt was too weak militarily to fight Israel, and internal reform and the expulsion of the British were the major targets. The bulk of the border incidents during this period

---

[36] *Department of State Bulletin*, June 5, 1950.

[37] For the legal aspects see Bloomfield, Lincoln, *Egypt, Israel, and the Gulf of Aqaba in International Law*, Toronto: Carswell, 1957.

[38] However, about sixty ships bound to or from Israel transited the Canal between 1951 and 1954. Wheelock, *op. cit.*, p. 222.

involved Jordan and Syria.[39] Egypt was even accused of being too moderate towards Israel. Then in early 1955, Egypt convicted thirteen persons of spying and acts of sabotage on behalf of Israel and hanged two of them. The Israeli citizenry was incensed over the verdict, and at this juncture Ben Gurion, whose resignation coincided with an improvement in Arab-Israeli relations, returned from meditation in the desert to rejoin the Cabinet as Minister of Defense. An exponent of the biblical "eye for eye, tooth for tooth" policy for modern Israel, he revived the massive reprisal raids which were designed to shock or terrify the Arabs into negotiation, or at least to deter them from further aggression.

On February 28, 1955, Israel mounted a massive attack on Egyptian positions in the Gaza Strip, causing sixty-nine Egyptian casualties (thirty-eight killed, thirty-one wounded). The attack was justified by Israel on grounds of extreme provocation by Arab *fedayeen* (Ar. *fida'iyan*, "self-sacrificers") raiders, which claim was never substantiated. The raid illustrated Egypt's military weakness with terrible clarity, but it drove Nasir into significant responses. He sought, and got, arms from the Soviet bloc. Secondly, the sporadic acts of violence and sabotage, which had been going on since the Palestine armistice, were organized and patterned. Previously these had involved Palestinian refugees sneaking back across the borders at night to recover possessions, meet relatives, or try to take revenge on some unknown Israeli. The *fida'iyan* were recruited from these same refugees, or came as volunteers from elsewhere in the Arab World. They were formed into squads, taught commando tactics, and sent out on regular missions. But their increasing effectiveness provoked ever stronger Israeli retaliation. Late in 1955, the Israelis destroyed the main *fida'iyan* base at Khan Yunis. Other major raids on al Sabha and Kisufim resulted in far more Egyptian casualties than the number inflicted in Israel by the *fida'iyan*.[40]

Meanwhile Egypt was steadily increasing her military stockpile in the Sinai Peninsula, as armaments poured in from the East (and from Britain, France, and other European powers)—which did little to ensure the workability of the Tripartite Declaration. The armies of Egypt, Jordan,

---

[39] The most serious of these occurred at Qibya in 1953, when fifty-three Arabs were killed.

[40] Nasir said privately that for every Arab life taken, there would be one Israeli life, and for every Arab wounded there would be a wounded Israeli. That was the purpose of the *fida'iyan*. Wynn, *op. cit.*, pp. 124–125. See also Connell, *op. cit.*, pp. 168–169.

and Syria were brought under a nominally unified command, and Iraq, despite its membership in the Baghdad Pact, made preparations to send troops into Jordan to maintain security. Since Iraq alone of the Arab countries involved had never shaken hands with Israel, there was a real possibility that Iraqi troops might lead a re-invasion of Palestine.

These various moves alarmed Israel, despite the continuing superiority of its army. Israel was more aroused by Arab interference with shipping in the Gulf of Aqaba, because the future development of the Negev depended on free access to the port of Elath via the Gulf.[41] Therefore on October 29, 1956, Israeli paratroopers dropped into Egyptian territory; later Israeli army units raced into the Sinai Peninsula and headed for the Suez Canal. The Israeli invasion had as its specific aim the destruction of *fida'iyan* bases and capture of as much Egyptian military equipment as possible; a secondary aim was to force a political settlement which would open the Gulf of Aqaba and possibly Suez itself to their shipping. The military aim had even greater success than in 1948. Egyptian forces fought bravely in isolated engagements, but they had no air support, despite their new Soviet bombers and MIG fighters. Many of their planes were destroyed on the ground, while Nasir hesitated to risk his few trained pilots against the odds, and held them out. Within a hundred hours Israeli forces had killed nearly 3,000 Egyptians and captured 5,600, as against their own casualties of 177 dead and one prisoner.

The United States had asked the Security Council to take up the Israeli invasion almost immediately; but before it could do so an event occurred which had not been foreseen by American planners. This was the intervention of Britain and France. The charge of collusion between these two and Israel, often raised since 1956, will doubtless not be proved (or disproved) until the governments publish their secret archives. But if there was no collusion, there was certainly advance coordination of planning.[42] Furthermore there was a common objective—to eliminate the dangerous Nasir—and community of interest. On October 30, the British and French governments sent a joint note to Egypt and Israel,

---

[41] "The future of the Negev depends on this free outlet. Its existence, safe and free, will turn Elath into a port of international importance and transform Israel's geopolitical position." Ben Gurion before the Knesset, March, 1957, (*Jewish Observer and Middle East Review*).

[42] Cf. Bromberger, Merry and Serge, *Secrets of Suez*, London: Pan Books, 1957; Foot, Michael, and Jones, Merwyn, *Guilty Men 1957: Suez and Cyprus*, New York: Rinehart & Co., 1957, and others.

a note later described by the State Department as "the most brutal ultimatum in modern history." [43] Both nations were ordered to cease and desist from all warlike action and to withdraw their forces to a distance of no less than ten miles from the Canal. Egypt was also ordered to accept a temporary Anglo-French reoccupation of the Suez Canal Zone to ensure freedom of transit. In view of the fact that the only forces within ten miles of the Canal were Egyptian, the intention of the ultimatum was plainly marked, being to intervene regardless of Egypt's reactions in order to bring down the government of Gamal 'Abd al-Nasir. When Egypt rejected the ultimatum as was expected, America's two chief allies intervened.

Compared with the speed and efficiency of Israel's invasion of Sinai, the Anglo-French intervention was a model of ineptitude. In four days the Israeli Army of Gen. Moshe Dayan overran a territory three times the size of Israel, captured intact the Egyptian freighter *Ibrahim al Awal* (off Haifa) destroyed the major *fida'iyan* bases, and acquired the vast stockpile of armaments the Soviet bloc had been supplying Nasir for more than a year. British and French planes bombed Egyptian targets systematically for five days beginning October 31, but not until November 5 was a land action mounted, and it ended in a cease-fire after one day without achieving its declared objectives. British and French paratroopers dropped into Port Said on the fifth, followed by the main seaborne assault force, and the town was secured after a sharp engagement in which Egyptian volunteer resistance groups fought as bravely, against enormous odds, as their predecessors of Tal-al-Kabir. The invasion force then moved south on the road to Ismailia, only to stop short of their final objective with the cease-fire of the sixth.

Placed in the context of modern international relations, the last imperialistic venture of Europe's chief colonial powers was doomed from the start. A century earlier, such aggressions could be accomplished before they were hauled to the conference table for dissection; within the definitive limits of national self-interest bargaining could be carried on with some territorial end in view. But Suez, in 1956, was a topic unsuited to such power relationships, and the timorousness of the invaders lost them the advantage they had gained by surprise. The subtle force of world public opinion worked against them, through the United Nations as well as conventional diplomacy. In a strange duet, the moralistic United States found itself in unholy alliance with the pragmatic Soviet

[43] Connell, *op. cit.*, p. 190.

Union. The customary Soviet objectives in world politics came under severe attack when Soviet tanks crushed the Hungarian revolution, but the world did not notice much—it was too bemused by the spectacle of its leading free state in bitter disagreement with its chief allies.

British public opinion was itself sharply divided over the intervention, so that the French, who were ready to seize the full length of the Canal with nationwide support, could not do so. The attitude of the Soviet government was typically ambiguous, blending threats of armed volunteers for Egypt's defense with support for UN intervention. The U.S. government relied entirely on moral suasion through the UN, where for the first time a British veto was cast. Without attempting to single out any cause for the Anglo-French acceptance of UN resolutions for an end to hostilities, it will suffice to say that on November 6 the two invaders did so.

The results of the two-stage invasion of Egypt in 1956 are difficult to assess. On the practical side, the Canal remained blocked by sunken Egyptian ships for six months; however, in the four years since its reopening, tonnage has increased steadily, and operation by Egypt has proved even more effective than operation by the former Suez Canal Company (which was eventually compensated for its property), with no interference except with Israeli shipping. Israel in 1957 accepted UN guarantees and withdrew from all captured Egyptian territory in Sinai, plus the Gaza Strip and Sharm al-Shaykh in the Gulf of Aqaba. Though a UN Expeditionary Force (UNEF) occupied frontier positions between Egyptian and Israeli forces, administration of the Strip was returned to Egypt. In January, 1957, Prime Minister Eden resigned; the French government reverted to Charles de Gaulle; and Secretary of State Dulles died in 1959, removing from the scenes the major proponents of "personal" international relations, and leaving Nasir to cope with the Middle East.

THE NORTHERN TIER

The portions of the Middle East which the architects of the containment policy designated as the Northern Tier, and where they anticipated a ring of bases girdling the vulnerable southern flank of the Soviet Union, have been no freer from crisis than the Arab states of the region since World War II. The Middle East's baptism in the baths of postwar international politics began with Azerbaijan; Soviet pressure on Turkey brought forth the Marshall Plan; and oil nationalization in Iran pro-

Troops of UNEF set up camp in the Gaza Strip.
(Courtesy The United Nations)

vided a focus of interest for the entire world community. It might have been expected that the successful conclusion of these crises would have produced a modicum of stability in the Northern Tier; and this stability should have been enhanced by the creation of a multilateral regional alliance, the Baghdad Pact (succeeded by the Central Treaty Organization). But the ring of steel envisaged along the Northern Tier has never materialized. Instead, four states exist side by side, with so little in common that even now there is no land link between Turkey and Iran, and Afghanistan receives three times as much aid from Russia as it does from the United States, despite its trumpeted neutrality. Although they have been political entities for considerably longer than their Arab neighbors, the Northern Tier states exhibit less of the political growth necessary for regional stability.

Turkey, for example, was assumed by American strategists, up to 1960, to be a dependable friend and member of the West. The Menderes government, although displaying certain autocratic tendencies and unusually sensitive to external criticism, appeared to have full popular support and to be moving the country ahead in compliance with the principles of

Ataturk. The revolution of May, 1960, illustrated the folly of these easy assumptions. The energy and administrative skill with which the Ottomans built an empire in the name of Islam has long since spent itself, and the magnificent performance of the Turkish Brigade in Korea in the name of the United Nations merely underscored the depth of Turkey's Western-oriented foreign policy. Admittedly it would be profitless to reincarnate for republican Turkey the political institutions of the Ottoman Empire, and yet vestiges of Ottomanism remained after three decades of Ataturk's dynamism. Outside of tampering with the constitution, Prime Minister Menderes' most heinous crime in terms of Turkish political evolution lay in reviving the religious dogmatism of the sultans. Having cast out its devils, so to speak, the Turks of 1961 have returned to the familiar military hero-father figure as their head of state. But the message of General Gursel does not have the ring of truth and force that Ataturk's had, and Ataturk's simple imperatives—"Work! Strive! Fight!"—seem all too puerile in the nuclear world. By logic and experience, Turkey should be the leader of the Northern Tier states, with Ankara the headquarters of a vigorous CENTO; but old wounds ache when the wind howls along the Anatolian steppe, and Turkey has yet to develop a leader with domestic political wisdom and international stature, whose dreams are reasonable.

Even more puzzling is the political evolution of Iran. This ancient land has enormous resources, an intelligent and talented population, a long and brilliant cultural history, and a community of interest centered around the Shah. Yet its feudal social structure, economic inequalities, and political factionalism make it a shining target for Communist subversion, and its stubborn alliance with the United States has not helped to solve its internal problems. The total overturn of the monarchy which many thought would occur after the riots of early 1961 has been staved off thus far. But the Shah and Prime Minister Amini are both working on borrowed time in their furious effort to overhaul the social and economic system and to evolve toward representative government and definable political parties based on popular interests rather than personal loyalties.

Afghanistan, fervently neutral but blessed with two-handed pragmatism where national development with foreign support is concerned, offers another example of how internal disputes between nations of the Middle East invariably involve the international community. The long-simmering "Pushtunistan" dispute recently came to another head when

Pakistan closed all its diplomatic offices in Afghanistan. Pakistan officials returning from Afghanistan said that it had become impossible for them to carry on normal diplomatic business because of constant harassments. (Anyone who has lived in an Asian country for any length of time knows the difficulties encountered merely in the normal course of daily life; when these are made into an official policy they soon become intolerable.) Afghanistan retaliated by closing its diplomatic offices in Pakistan, by breaking off diplomatic relations, and by moving army units up to the border. There were a number of clashes, in which the Pushtun tribesmen fought with Pakistani troops against the cousins who were supposedly trying to liberate them! Afghan exports of fresh fruit and skins piled up in warehouses along the border and began to spoil, while American aid shipments to Afghanistan were unable to transit the normally free port of Karachi.

The logical solution, if international relations were conducted logically, would be effective mediation by the other members of CENTO, backed by regional military force if necessary. Afghanistan's non-membership in CENTO, actually, was less significant than the non-membership of the United States. President Kennedy designated Ambassador Livingston Merchant as a mediator to present our "good offices" in the dispute. The move was diplomatically sound, but in terms of strengthening CENTO as a truly regional alliance, capable of imparting stability to the area and settling purely inter-regional problems, it meant a further downgrading of an organization already dangerously weak.

With Afghanistan's natural trade outlet, the port of Karachi, closed, the easy assumption is that the country will become a reluctant, but real, Soviet satellite. This assumption ignores the traditional bases of Afghan politics, the historic drive for independence. But once again, the dilemma of American policy in the Middle East is apparent. We emphasize education (hence long-range development) in a conservative, family-run feudal monarchy as our foreign aid touchstone, and counter this with military hardware to Pakistan, without taking any position regarding the border dispute between the two neighbors. The Soviets, however, understand only too well that an issue lightly dismissed by Americans, as remote, unimportant, or temporal, often has visceral significance for those involved. While their support (or opposition), given or withheld, always stems from some pragmatic view of world politics, it produces an enormous reaction in the receiver nation. The extent of Afghanistan's "Communization" is likely to be this.

POSTLUDE: THE SYRIAN REVOLT OF 1961

Syria's reversion in September–October 1961 to the independent status she occupied before the merger with Egypt three years earlier prompts a general reassessment of relations between the Arab states and the probable role of the Middle East in the power struggles of the major international blocs. Until this break from the United Arab Republic took place, it was possible to suggest that the Arab peoples had reached a degree of maturity in their political thinking, which would permit adherence to a common goal as well as the means necessary to attain it. The goal remains, but the fact that Syria's new government felt constrained to issue a fourteen-point proposal for a voluntary Pan-Arab union is additional evidence that "Nasserism" is merely one of many ways to reach this goal, and not even the most popular at this writing.

Until late September, the union of Egypt and Syria, which had dropped so neatly into Nasir's lap three years before, seemed destined for a reasonably long life—at least long in Arab terms. In view of their disparity in size and population, the logical course was for Egypt to assume the role of senior partner in the firm, and this Egypt did. Retention of Syria's national identity on a regional basis kept the Syrians happy, while Egypt's preponderance of power provided a more solid backing than they had been accustomed to in dealing with other powers. The elimination of party factionalism from Syrian politics probably had a salutary effect similar to the 1954 cleanup of the Wafd and Muslim Brotherhood in Egypt, while Egypt stood to profit greatly by the addition of a major wheat producer and the possessor of a stable economy.

Forces were at work from the onset of the merger to break it up, however, and the September revolt was less a surprise coup than the coalescence of a number of these forces. The first three years of the UAR were years of drought, in Syria, which cancelled out the grain surplus Nasir had counted on. Syrian businessmen accustomed to free-wheeling deals chafed under the increasing restrictions of Nasir's socialist cooperative state. How keenly Syrian intellectuals and professional men felt the disappearance of political activity is open to conjecture, but they certainly did not care for the increased authority handed to the police and counter-intelligence services. This seeming return to the Shishakli days lacked one essential ingredient, however. This was a leader popular enough, and strong enough, to cleave across factional loyalties and command support in the name of Nasserism (which was supposed to replace Syrian nationalism). Instead of the handsome Shishakli, what the Syrians got was the brooding, bull-necked, venomous Lieutenant Colonel 'Abd'al-Hamid al-Sarraj, Chief of the Army's Deuxieme Bureau.[44]

Throughout the United Arab Republic's brief history Nasir attempted to ride two ill-yoked horses bareback. Pairing the docile Egyptian peasantry with the sturdy, independent farmers of Syria was hardly calculated to win friends. Syrian businessmen were far less malleable, or amenable to centralized controls, than their Egyptian counterparts; furthermore the expectations of graft, on which Egyptians had been nourished for so long, existed only in the form of sharp business practices in Syria. Third, the Syrian army, toughened by its admixture of Kurdish, Turkish, Circassian and other types of northern blood, did not take kindly to being placed under rotund Egyptian officers.

Perhaps sniffing out these obstacles, Nasir moved slowly in his "Egyptianization" of Syria. By the summer of 1961, however, he felt strong enough to put into effect the "democratic, cooperative, socialist" program which he had planned to fuse his two regional entities into one unit and to show the Arab world that he was a statesman with a clear political philosophy. This philosophy he attempted to implement with a series of decrees. The regional cabinet sitting at Damascus was abolished, and its members were absorbed into the national cabinet at the ratio of more than two to one, Egyptians for Syrians. Nationalization of banks, industries, and commercial establishments was almost completed in Egypt, and incomes limited to £E10,000. These actions caused "a panic among Syrian businessmen, a massive flight of capital, and a drop of nearly twenty per cent in the Syrian pound."[45] More significant, the removal of all political authority from Syria, with the government centralized in Cairo, provided a cementing force for quarreling factions within the Syrian military establishment.

Whether from overconfidence or from lack of information, Nasir took

---

[44] In the fall of 1957, a Syrian exchange student registered for the author's course at George Washington University and claimed he was the brother-in-law of Col. Sarraj. He later approached the author with the fantastic story that "they" had been investigating the author, and that the student was to arrange contacts with Arab officials at which "they" would provide the author with financial retainer fees for support of his public relations work informing Americans about the true status of Middle Eastern affairs. Nothing ever came of it. (Personal comment.)

[45] Sterling, Claire, "Syria Secedes from Nasser's Empire," *The Reporter,* October 26, 1961.

little stock of possible disaffection in Syria. Marshal Amr, his personal representative there, returned to Syria late in September. He had been feuding with Sarraj, but with the latter's sudden resignation as Vice President and Minister of Interior, he felt more confident. (Sarraj's departure, ironically, removed the last of the Syrian patriots and right-wingers who had conspired with Nasir to bring the union into existence in the first place.)

During the nights of September 27–28 a group of Syrian officers, newly united and calling themselves the "Supreme Arab Revolutionary Command" carried out a coup d'etat which was unique in that it was directed against fellow-Arabs who were accused of being foreign imperialists. The coup was carried out with a swift efficiency reminiscent of the 1952 revolution in Egypt. Amr, representing Egypt, was surrounded at his Damascus residence by troops of the Syrian Desert Brigade who forced the Egyptian troops guarding it to surrender. Elsewhere army units supported by tanks seized control of the telegraph offices, Damascus Radio, and all ministry buildings, with little or no resistance. Latakia and Aleppo, Syria's other major cities, went over to the "rebels," who from the start signalized a popular movement rather than a rebellion against their lawfully constituted government.[46]

The Syrian coup confronted Nasir with an awkward situation, militarily as well as politically. He lacked the military strength inside Syria to crush the coup. Since the two regions of the UAR were not contiguous, the only military recourse left to Egypt's leader was a seaborne landing. Naval units carrying two battalions of freshly-trained paratroopers headed for Latakia, Syria's chief seaport. But far from requesting reinforcements to help "patriotic elements" against the forces of reaction, as was first reported,[47] the commander of Latakia's garrison had gone over to the revolutionaries. About 120 paratroopers dropped into the port city, and were promptly captured, before Nasir called off his "invasion" and recognized the Supreme Arab Revolutionary Command for what it was, a genuine popular movement determined to restore national identity to Syria.

A new civilian government took office on September 30 and promptly set about "de-Egyptianizing" Syria. All Egyptians, military as well as civil servants and advisers, were ordered to return to Egypt. The new

[46] See the report by Dana Adams Schmidt, in *The New York Times,* October 11, 1961.

[47] *The Washington Post,* September 30, 1961 (UPI dispatch from Cairo).

Prime Minister, Mam'un Kuzbari, declared that the aims of the new regime were to eliminate Egyptian influences, stabilize the economy, and restore constitutional democratic government to the country; he set a timetable of four months. Syrian capital began to flow back. A committee began to look into the problems of restoring Syria's favorable trade balance of pre-merger days, while another laid plans for national elections to be held the end of 1961. A third, judicial committee was named to try Colonel Sarraj, who proved not to have been behind the coup but rather one of its chief causes when he was flushed from hiding and arrested in Damascus.

The international reaction to Syria's new status affords a useful object lesson in the policies which nations are forced to adopt in the twentieth century. Not surprisingly, Russia was the first major power to recognize the new regime and to establish diplomatic relations. She was followed by Bulgaria and Czechoslovakia. This was done despite Kuzbari's statement that his government would continue its ban on the Syrian Communist Party and would not countenance the return of Khalid Baqdash from exile. When Jordan, Turkey, and Iran recognized Syria's independence, Nasir broke relations with both. After delaying for twelve days ostensibly to consult with Nasir, and to continue our traditional post-war policy of taking no sides in the Middle East (other than the permanent honeymoon relationship with Israel), the United States recognized the Kuzbari government. Syria took her old seat at the United Nations, but this time as the 101st member, and subsequently was readmitted to the Arab League.

A major question remains to be answered. Does independence for Syria mean a return to the status quo for the Arab states—and for the Middle East generally? Or having tasted the cup of unity, the wine of success, will Nasir be content with leadership in Egypt and the prominent, but not dominant, role in Arab affairs that comes with it? Regarding Nasir's direct relations with Syria, the answer seems reasonably clear —Egyptian military strength could no more be relied on against a virile, united Syrian army than it could against Israel, and the army made the coup possible.[48] Discretion was the better part of valor, and the grand

[48] According to D. A. Schmidt (*The New York Times*, October 16, 1961), the force behind Kuzbari's government was a group of officers referred to as the Supreme Arab Revolutionary Command, consisting of Major Haidar Kuzbari, Col. Dahman, Lt. Col. Muaffac 'Assafa, Maj. 'Abd al-Karim Mahlawi, Maj. Nassib Hindi, Maj. Hisham 'Abd al-Rabbu'. All are members of prominent Damascus families. Major Mahlawi, the leader of the group, is supposed to have begun plans for the coup in January.

gesture of withdrawal to avoid shedding Arab blood is certain to please the Arab masses. It is worth noting, however, that the new Syrian government promptly put out a fourteen-point proposal for a new, voluntary constitutional union of all Arab states, with a central legislature empowered to determine broad economic, cultural, military and foreign policies, but individual national sovereignties guaranteed. Although it differed little from the original proposals for the League of Arab States (that is, unless the proposed central legislature were given teeth), the Syrian platform was a visible rejection of the cult of personality which Nasir symbolized in inter-Arab affairs. As of 1961, then, there remained many roads to Arab unity, with the distinct possibility that Syria, the *al-Shams* of Arab geographers, might yet become the middle way between Nasir's Arab socialism and the feudal aristocracy personified by Sa'ud and Imam Ahmad.

CONCLUSIONS

In concluding this broad fourteen-hundred-year survey of the Middle East's evolution from a caliphate to a collection of nations, several facts may be deduced from the area's present international position. The first is that the presently inflexible antagonists, Arab and Israeli, are gradually drifting towards a settlement of differences; such a settlement will probably come by default rather than formal negotiation. A second is that while the Arabs do not "unify" easily in political, social, even economic terms, and the Arab League is far from achieving a regional political status, they have at last acquired a charismatic leader in Gamal 'Abd al-Nasir. Not only has Nasir become identified with the aspirations of most Arabs; he has also emerged in the 1960's as a spokesman for the uncommitted nations. When the General Assembly began its famous 1960 meetings, Khrushchev stole the show with his shoe-pounding act —but Nasir made one of the most widely quoted speeches. Again at Belgrade in August, 1961, Nasir's denunciation of nuclear warfare, his plea for disarmament and East-West negotiations, were those of a leader conscious of his new world stature. Although Nasir has taken the path to welfare socialism in his own country, and has not yet developed any real political philosophy or original policies, he has the aura of the successful statesman and to a very large degree has become synonymous with the Middle East.

At this writing, and with the exception of the Suez Canal, the same irritants which have unsettled the Middle East since World War II remain, and there are no better prospects for a *settlement* (in the American sense of the word) than before. President Kennedy stated shortly after his inauguration that he believed the good offices of the United States might effect an Arab-Israeli settlement, with partial compensation and/or limited repatriation for the displaced Palestine refugees. But Israel's continued refusal to consider these concessions except by implication negates any neutral approach, and Ben Gurion's aim is still to have Israel stand for all Jewry. The UN seems destined to go on indefinitely footing the bill for the refugees and for UNEF, although the difficulties of collecting even pledged funds from members seem to increase yearly.

Yet if any guidelines seem to be emerging for the Middle East of future generations, they are of progress by default. Notwithstanding the trial of Adolf Eichmann, the new generation of Israel-born Jews lacks the mighty identification with Jewish historical tradition that has made their elders *different,* hence special or God's elite. Surrounding the Israelis are Arab peoples whose own traditions are melting into a pool of modernization, who stand to become members of the international community, not Arabs with a special set of grievances. The same may well happen in time to the specifically anti-Communist countries, Turkey and Iran. For time, which has so long passed the area by, has now become its solace and its signpost.

Recommended Readings

1. Beatty, Charles, *de Lesseps of Suez,* New York: Harper & Brothers, 1956.
2. Bromberger, Merry and Serge, *Secrets of Suez,* London: Pan Books, 1957.
3. Connell, John, *The Most Important Country,* London: Cassell, 1957.
4. Finnie, David, *Desert Enterprise: The Middle East Oil Industry in its Local Environment,* Cambridge: Harvard University Press, 1958.
5. Foot, Michael, & Mervyn Jones, *Guilty Men 1957: Suez and Cyprus,* New York: Rinehart & Co., 1957.
6. Hallberg, C. W., *The Suez Canal,* New York: Columbia University Press, 1931.
7. Johnson, Paul, *The Suez War,* New York: Greenberg, 1957.
8. Marlowe, John, *Arab Nationalism and British Imperialism,* New York: Frederick A. Praeger, Inc., 1961.
9. Marshall, S. L. A., *Sinai Victory,* New York: William Morrow & Co., Inc., 1958.
10. Schonfield, Hugh, *The Suez Canal in World Affairs,* London: Constellation Books, 1952.

11. Wheelock, Keith, *Nasser's New Egypt,* New York: Frederick A. Praeger, Inc., 1960. No. 8, Foreign Policy Research Institute series, University of Pennsylvania.

12. Wilson, Arnold, *The Suez Canal: Its Past, Present, and Future,* 2nd ed., London: Oxford, 1939.

13. Wint, Guy, & Peter Calvocoressi, *Middle East Crisis,* London: Penguin Books, 1957.

14. Wynn, Wilton, *Nasser of Egypt,* Cambridge: Arlington Books, 1959.

APPENDIX

Proven Oil Reserves, Middle East, 1958

Country	Reserves (000's bbls)	Refining Capacity (000's bbls)
Aden	—	120.0
Bahrain	230,000	186.5
Egypt	400,000	74.7
Iran	33,000,000	493.0
Iraq	25,000,000	55.8
Israel	50,000	87.0
Kuwait	60,000,000	220.0
Lebanon	—	24.0
Neutral Zone	6,000,000	50.0
Qatar	2,500,000	0.6
Saudi Arabia	47,000,000	189.0
Turkey	70,000	6.9

Crude Oil Production in the Middle East
(000's bbls per day, 000's tons per year)

Country	1955		1956		1957		1958	
	BPD	Tons	BPD	Tons	BPD	Tons	BPD	Tons
Bahrain	30.1	1505	30.0	1500	32.5	1625	40.6	2030
Egypt	35.1	1750	32.0	1600	52.3	2615	65.2	3260
Iran	320.0	16,000	530	26,500	689	34,450	808.2	40,410
Iraq	690	34,500	633	31,650	438.6	21,930	756.2	37,810
Israel	—	—	0.6	30	1.2	60	2.0	100
Kuwait	1100	55,000	978	49,350	1250	62,500	1376	68,800
Neutral Zone	24.6	1230	41	2050	78	3900	84.1	4205
Qatar	114	5,700	127	6,850	147	7,350	162	8,100
Saudi Arabia	951	47,550	1000	50,000	893.9	44,695	991.3	49,565
Totals	3,269.2	163,460	3,387	169,850	3,588.8	179,440	4292.1	214,605

Crude Oil Production of Major World Areas, 1958

	BBls per Day	Annual Total
U. S.	6,459,300	322,965,000
Western Hemisphere	10,138,300	506,965,000
Middle East	4,292,100	214,605,000
Free World	15,187,340	759,367,000
Soviet Bloc	2,522,000	126,100,000
Totals	17,709,340	888,467,000

INDEX

POLITICAL EVOLUTION
IN THE
MIDDLE EAST

BY WILLIAM SPENCER

Vivid and readable, POLITICAL EVOLUTION IN THE MIDDLE EAST presents an objective study of the political development of an area that has become of vital importance to the rest of the world. The tracing of this process, against the backdrop of 5,000 years of turbulence, shows that although the *bast* and the *majalis* have survived from the past, the political entities and institutions of the area are largely a product of the twentieth century.

Commencing with the beginning of recorded civilization in the pre-Islamic epoch, the author moves on to an examination of the Muslim era and covers the rise and fall of the Ottoman Empire, with a full assessment of its impact on more recent events. Studies of individual countries interrelate external relations and internal political development. A separate chapter describes the area's international relations.

Inclusion of the British Protectorates of Arabia and Yemen—often overlooked by other writers—is an unusual feature. On the other hand the devoting of an entire chapter to Islam, essential to any study of Middle-Eastern culture and politics, greatly helps the student to grasp the subtle aspects of Middle-Eastern affairs.

This book is admirably suited for courses in Middle East politics and history, non-Western studies, and international affairs as they affect and are affected by developments in this area which has been aptly termed the Crossroads of Civilization.

Jacket design by John Goetz